Lecture Notes in Computer Science   8530

Commenced Publication in 1973
Founding and Former Series Editors:
Gerhard Goos, Juris Hartmanis, and Jan van Leeuwen

Norbert Streitz   Panos Markopoulos (Eds.)

Distributed, Ambient, and Pervasive Interactions

Second International Conference, DAPI 2014
Held as Part of HCI International 2014
Heraklion, Crete, Greece, June 22-27, 2014
Proceedings

Springer

Volume Editors

Norbert Streitz
Smart Future Initiative
Frankfurt am Main, Germany
E-mail: norbert.streitz@smart-future.net

Panos Markopoulos
Eindhoven University of Technology
Department of Industrial Design
Eindhoven, The Netherlands
E-mail: p.markopoulos@tue.nl

ISSN 0302-9743   e-ISSN 1611-3349
ISBN 978-3-319-07787-1   e-ISBN 978-3-319-07788-8
DOI 10.1007/978-3-319-07788-8
Springer Cham Heidelberg New York Dordrecht London

Library of Congress Control Number: 2014940302

LNCS Sublibrary: SL 3 – Information Systems and Application, incl. Internet/Web
and HCI

Typesetting: Camera-ready by author, data conversion by Scientific Publishing Services, Chennai, India

Printed on acid-free paper

Springer is part of Springer Science+Business Media (www.springer.com)

Foreword

The 16th International Conference on Human–Computer Interaction, HCI International 2014, was held in Heraklion, Crete, Greece, during June 22–27, 2014, incorporating 14 conferences/thematic areas:

Thematic areas:

- Human–Computer Interaction
- Human Interface and the Management of Information

Affiliated conferences:

- 11th International Conference on Engineering Psychology and Cognitive Ergonomics
- 8th International Conference on Universal Access in Human–Computer Interaction
- 6th International Conference on Virtual, Augmented and Mixed Reality
- 6th International Conference on Cross-Cultural Design
- 6th International Conference on Social Computing and Social Media
- 8th International Conference on Augmented Cognition
- 5th International Conference on Digital Human Modeling and Applications in Health, Safety, Ergonomics and Risk Management
- Third International Conference on Design, User Experience and Usability
- Second International Conference on Distributed, Ambient and Pervasive Interactions
- Second International Conference on Human Aspects of Information Security, Privacy and Trust
- First International Conference on HCI in Business
- First International Conference on Learning and Collaboration Technologies

A total of 4,766 individuals from academia, research institutes, industry, and governmental agencies from 78 countries submitted contributions, and 1,476 papers and 225 posters were included in the proceedings. These papers address the latest research and development efforts and highlight the human aspects of design and use of computing systems. The papers thoroughly cover the entire field of human–computer interaction, addressing major advances in knowledge and effective use of computers in a variety of application areas.

This volume, edited by Norbert Streitz and Panos Markopoulos, contains papers focusing on the thematic area of distributed, ambient and pervasive interactions, addressing the following major topics:

- Design frameworks, methods and models for intelligent interactive environments

- Natural interaction
- Cognitive, perceptual and emotional issues in Ambient Intelligence
- User experience in intelligent environments
- Developing distributed, pervasive and intelligent environments
- Smart cities

The remaining volumes of the HCI International 2014 proceedings are:

- Volume 1, LNCS 8510, Human–Computer Interaction: HCI Theories, Methods and Tools (Part I), edited by Masaaki Kurosu
- Volume 2, LNCS 8511, Human–Computer Interaction: Advanced Interaction Modalities and Techniques (Part II), edited by Masaaki Kurosu
- Volume 3, LNCS 8512, Human–Computer Interaction: Applications and Services (Part III), edited by Masaaki Kurosu
- Volume 4, LNCS 8513, Universal Access in Human-Computer Interaction: Design and Development Methods for Universal Access (Part I), edited by Constantine Stephanidis and Margherita Antona
- Volume 5, LNCS 8514, Universal Access in Human–Computer Interaction: Universal Access to Information and Knowledge (Part II), edited by Constantine Stephanidis and Margherita Antona
- Volume 6, LNCS 8515, Universal Access in Human–Computer Interaction: Aging and Assistive Environments (Part III), edited by Constantine Stephanidis and Margherita Antona
- Volume 7, LNCS 8516, Universal Access in Human–Computer Interaction: Design for All and Accessibility Practice (Part IV), edited by Constantine Stephanidis and Margherita Antona
- Volume 8, LNCS 8517, Design, User Experience, and Usability: Theories, Methods and Tools for Designing the User Experience (Part I), edited by Aaron Marcus
- Volume 9, LNCS 8518, Design, User Experience, and Usability: User Experience Design for Diverse Interaction Platforms and Environments (Part II), edited by Aaron Marcus
- Volume 10, LNCS 8519, Design, User Experience, and Usability: User Experience Design for Everyday Life Applications and Services (Part III), edited by Aaron Marcus
- Volume 11, LNCS 8520, Design, User Experience, and Usability: User Experience Design Practice (Part IV), edited by Aaron Marcus
- Volume 12, LNCS 8521, Human Interface and the Management of Information: Information and Knowledge Design and Evaluation (Part I), edited by Sakae Yamamoto
- Volume 13, LNCS 8522, Human Interface and the Management of Information: Information and Knowledge in Applications and Services (Part II), edited by Sakae Yamamoto
- Volume 14, LNCS 8523, Learning and Collaboration Technologies: Designing and Developing Novel Learning Experiences (Part I), edited by Panayiotis Zaphiris and Andri Ioannou

- Volume 15, LNCS 8524, Learning and Collaboration Technologies: Technology-rich Environments for Learning and Collaboration (Part II), edited by Panayiotis Zaphiris and Andri Ioannou
- Volume 16, LNCS 8525, Virtual, Augmented and Mixed Reality: Designing and Developing Virtual and Augmented Environments (Part I), edited by Randall Shumaker and Stephanie Lackey
- Volume 17, LNCS 8526, Virtual, Augmented and Mixed Reality: Applications of Virtual and Augmented Reality (Part II), edited by Randall Shumaker and Stephanie Lackey
- Volume 18, LNCS 8527, HCI in Business, edited by Fiona Fui-Hoon Nah
- Volume 19, LNCS 8528, Cross-Cultural Design, edited by P.L. Patrick Rau
- Volume 20, LNCS 8529, Digital Human Modeling and Applications in Health, Safety, Ergonomics and Risk Management, edited by Vincent G. Duffy
- Volume 22, LNCS 8531, Social Computing and Social Media, edited by Gabriele Meiselwitz
- Volume 23, LNAI 8532, Engineering Psychology and Cognitive Ergonomics, edited by Don Harris
- Volume 24, LNCS 8533, Human Aspects of Information Security, Privacy and Trust, edited by Theo Tryfonas and Ioannis Askoxylakis
- Volume 25, LNAI 8534, Foundations of Augmented Cognition, edited by Dylan D. Schmorrow and Cali M. Fidopiastis
- Volume 26, CCIS 434, HCI International 2014 Posters Proceedings (Part I), edited by Constantine Stephanidis
- Volume 27, CCIS 435, HCI International 2014 Posters Proceedings (Part II), edited by Constantine Stephanidis

I would like to thank the Program Chairs and the members of the Program Boards of all affiliated conferences and thematic areas, listed below, for their contribution to the highest scientific quality and the overall success of the HCI International 2014 Conference.

This conference could not have been possible without the continuous support and advice of the founding chair and conference scientific advisor, Prof. Gavriel Salvendy, as well as the dedicated work and outstanding efforts of the communications chair and editor of *HCI International News*, Dr. Abbas Moallem.

I would also like to thank for their contribution towards the smooth organization of the HCI International 2014 Conference the members of the Human–Computer Interaction Laboratory of ICS-FORTH, and in particular George Paparoulis, Maria Pitsoulaki, Maria Bouhli, and George Kapnas.

April 2014   Constantine Stephanidis
                                                 General Chair, HCI International 2014

Organization

Human–Computer Interaction

Program Chair: Masaaki Kurosu, Japan

Jose Abdelnour-Nocera, UK
Sebastiano Bagnara, Italy
Simone Barbosa, Brazil
Adriana Betiol, Brazil
Simone Borsci, UK
Henry Duh, Australia
Xiaowen Fang, USA
Vicki Hanson, UK
Wonil Hwang, Korea
Minna Isomursu, Finland
Yong Gu Ji, Korea
Anirudha Joshi, India
Esther Jun, USA
Kyungdoh Kim, Korea

Heidi Krömker, Germany
Chen Ling, USA
Chang S. Nam, USA
Naoko Okuizumi, Japan
Philippe Palanque, France
Ling Rothrock, USA
Naoki Sakakibara, Japan
Dominique Scapin, France
Guangfeng Song, USA
Sanjay Tripathi, India
Chui Yin Wong, Malaysia
Toshiki Yamaoka, Japan
Kazuhiko Yamazaki, Japan
Ryoji Yoshitake, Japan

Human Interface and the Management of Information

Program Chair: Sakae Yamamoto, Japan

Alan Chan, Hong Kong
Denis A. Coelho, Portugal
Linda Elliott, USA
Shin'ichi Fukuzumi, Japan
Michitaka Hirose, Japan
Makoto Itoh, Japan
Yen-Yu Kang, Taiwan
Koji Kimita, Japan
Daiji Kobayashi, Japan

Hiroyuki Miki, Japan
Hirohiko Mori, Japan
Shogo Nishida, Japan
Robert Proctor, USA
Youngho Rhee, Korea
Ryosuke Saga, Japan
Katsunori Shimohara, Japan
Kim-Phuong Vu, USA
Tomio Watanabe, Japan

Engineering Psychology and Cognitive Ergonomics

Program Chair: Don Harris, UK

Guy Andre Boy, USA
Shan Fu, P.R. China
Hung-Sying Jing, Taiwan
Wen-Chin Li, Taiwan
Mark Neerincx, The Netherlands
Jan Noyes, UK
Paul Salmon, Australia

Axel Schulte, Germany
Siraj Shaikh, UK
Sarah Sharples, UK
Anthony Smoker, UK
Neville Stanton, UK
Alex Stedmon, UK
Andrew Thatcher, South Africa

Universal Access in Human–Computer Interaction

Program Chairs: Constantine Stephanidis, Greece, and Margherita Antona, Greece

Julio Abascal, Spain
Gisela Susanne Bahr, USA
João Barroso, Portugal
Margrit Betke, USA
Anthony Brooks, Denmark
Christian Bühler, Germany
Stefan Carmien, Spain
Hua Dong, P.R. China
Carlos Duarte, Portugal
Pier Luigi Emiliani, Italy
Qin Gao, P.R. China
Andrina Granić, Croatia
Andreas Holzinger, Austria
Josette Jones, USA
Simeon Keates, UK

Georgios Kouroupetroglou, Greece
Patrick Langdon, UK
Barbara Leporini, Italy
Eugene Loos, The Netherlands
Ana Isabel Paraguay, Brazil
Helen Petrie, UK
Michael Pieper, Germany
Enrico Pontelli, USA
Jaime Sanchez, Chile
Alberto Sanna, Italy
Anthony Savidis, Greece
Christian Stary, Austria
Hirotada Ueda, Japan
Gerhard Weber, Germany
Harald Weber, Germany

Virtual, Augmented and Mixed Reality

Program Chairs: Randall Shumaker, USA, and Stephanie Lackey, USA

Roland Blach, Germany
Sheryl Brahnam, USA
Juan Cendan, USA
Jessie Chen, USA
Panagiotis D. Kaklis, UK

Hirokazu Kato, Japan
Denis Laurendeau, Canada
Fotis Liarokapis, UK
Michael Macedonia, USA
Gordon Mair, UK

Jose San Martin, Spain
Tabitha Peck, USA
Christian Sandor, Australia

Christopher Stapleton, USA
Gregory Welch, USA

Cross-Cultural Design

Program Chair: P.L. Patrick Rau, P.R. China

Yee-Yin Choong, USA
Paul Fu, USA
Zhiyong Fu, P.R. China
Pin-Chao Liao, P.R. China
Dyi-Yih Michael Lin, Taiwan
Rungtai Lin, Taiwan
Ta-Ping (Robert) Lu, Taiwan
Liang Ma, P.R. China
Alexander Mädche, Germany

Sheau-Farn Max Liang, Taiwan
Katsuhiko Ogawa, Japan
Tom Plocher, USA
Huatong Sun, USA
Emil Tso, P.R. China
Hsiu-Ping Yueh, Taiwan
Liang (Leon) Zeng, USA
Jia Zhou, P.R. China

Online Communities and Social Media

Program Chair: Gabriele Meiselwitz, USA

Leonelo Almeida, Brazil
Chee Siang Ang, UK
Aneesha Bakharia, Australia
Ania Bobrowicz, UK
James Braman, USA
Farzin Deravi, UK
Carsten Kleiner, Germany
Niki Lambropoulos, Greece
Soo Ling Lim, UK

Anthony Norcio, USA
Portia Pusey, USA
Panote Siriaraya, UK
Stefan Stieglitz, Germany
Giovanni Vincenti, USA
Yuanqiong (Kathy) Wang, USA
June Wei, USA
Brian Wentz, USA

Augmented Cognition

**Program Chairs: Dylan D. Schmorrow, USA,
and Cali M. Fidopiastis, USA**

Ahmed Abdelkhalek, USA
Robert Atkinson, USA
Monique Beaudoin, USA
John Blitch, USA
Alenka Brown, USA

Rosario Cannavò, Italy
Joseph Cohn, USA
Andrew J. Cowell, USA
Martha Crosby, USA
Wai-Tat Fu, USA

Rodolphe Gentili, USA
Frederick Gregory, USA
Michael W. Hail, USA
Monte Hancock, USA
Fei Hu, USA
Ion Juvina, USA
Joe Keebler, USA
Philip Mangos, USA
Rao Mannepalli, USA
David Martinez, USA
Yvonne R. Masakowski, USA
Santosh Mathan, USA
Ranjeev Mittu, USA

Keith Niall, USA
Tatana Olson, USA
Debra Patton, USA
June Pilcher, USA
Robinson Pino, USA
Tiffany Poeppelman, USA
Victoria Romero, USA
Amela Sadagic, USA
Anna Skinner, USA
Ann Speed, USA
Robert Sottilare, USA
Peter Walker, USA

Digital Human Modeling and Applications in Health, Safety, Ergonomics and Risk Management

Program Chair: Vincent G. Duffy, USA

Giuseppe Andreoni, Italy
Daniel Carruth, USA
Elsbeth De Korte, The Netherlands
Afzal A. Godil, USA
Ravindra Goonetilleke, Hong Kong
Noriaki Kuwahara, Japan
Kang Li, USA
Zhizhong Li, P.R. China

Tim Marler, USA
Jianwei Niu, P.R. China
Michelle Robertson, USA
Matthias Rötting, Germany
Mao-Jiun Wang, Taiwan
Xuguang Wang, France
James Yang, USA

Design, User Experience, and Usability

Program Chair: Aaron Marcus, USA

Sisira Adikari, Australia
Claire Ancient, USA
Arne Berger, Germany
Jamie Blustein, Canada
Ana Boa-Ventura, USA
Jan Brejcha, Czech Republic
Lorenzo Cantoni, Switzerland
Marc Fabri, UK
Luciane Maria Fadel, Brazil
Tricia Flanagan, Hong Kong
Jorge Frascara, Mexico

Federico Gobbo, Italy
Emilie Gould, USA
Rüdiger Heimgärtner, Germany
Brigitte Herrmann, Germany
Steffen Hess, Germany
Nouf Khashman, Canada
Fabiola Guillermina Noël, Mexico
Francisco Rebelo, Portugal
Kerem Rızvanoğlu, Turkey
Marcelo Soares, Brazil
Carla Spinillo, Brazil

Distributed, Ambient and Pervasive Interactions

Program Chairs: Norbert Streitz, Germany, and Panos Markopoulos, The Netherlands

Juan Carlos Augusto, UK
Jose Bravo, Spain
Adrian Cheok, UK
Boris de Ruyter, The Netherlands
Anind Dey, USA
Dimitris Grammenos, Greece
Nuno Guimaraes, Portugal
Achilles Kameas, Greece
Javed Vassilis Khan, The Netherlands
Shin'ichi Konomi, Japan
Carsten Magerkurth, Switzerland

Ingrid Mulder, The Netherlands
Anton Nijholt, The Netherlands
Fabio Paternó, Italy
Carsten Röcker, Germany
Teresa Romao, Portugal
Albert Ali Salah, Turkey
Manfred Tscheligi, Austria
Reiner Wichert, Germany
Woontack Woo, Korea
Xenophon Zabulis, Greece

Human Aspects of Information Security, Privacy and Trust

Program Chairs: Theo Tryfonas, UK, and Ioannis Askoxylakis, Greece

Claudio Agostino Ardagna, Italy
Zinaida Benenson, Germany
Daniele Catteddu, Italy
Raoul Chiesa, Italy
Bryan Cline, USA
Sadie Creese, UK
Jorge Cuellar, Germany
Marc Dacier, USA
Dieter Gollmann, Germany
Kirstie Hawkey, Canada
Jaap-Henk Hoepman, The Netherlands
Cagatay Karabat, Turkey
Angelos Keromytis, USA
Ayako Komatsu, Japan
Ronald Leenes, The Netherlands
Javier Lopez, Spain
Steve Marsh, Canada

Gregorio Martinez, Spain
Emilio Mordini, Italy
Yuko Murayama, Japan
Masakatsu Nishigaki, Japan
Aljosa Pasic, Spain
Milan Petković, The Netherlands
Joachim Posegga, Germany
Jean-Jacques Quisquater, Belgium
Damien Sauveron, France
George Spanoudakis, UK
Kerry-Lynn Thomson, South Africa
Julien Touzeau, France
Theo Tryfonas, UK
João Vilela, Portugal
Claire Vishik, UK
Melanie Volkamer, Germany

HCI in Business

Program Chair: Fiona Fui-Hoon Nah, USA

Andreas Auinger, Austria
Michel Avital, Denmark
Traci Carte, USA
Hock Chuan Chan, Singapore
Constantinos Coursaris, USA
Soussan Djamasbi, USA
Brenda Eschenbrenner, USA
Nobuyuki Fukawa, USA
Khaled Hassanein, Canada
Milena Head, Canada
Susanna (Shuk Ying) Ho, Australia
Jack Zhenhui Jiang, Singapore
Jinwoo Kim, Korea
Zoonky Lee, Korea
Honglei Li, UK
Nicholas Lockwood, USA
Eleanor T. Loiacono, USA
Mei Lu, USA

Scott McCoy, USA
Brian Mennecke, USA
Robin Poston, USA
Lingyun Qiu, P.R. China
Rene Riedl, Austria
Matti Rossi, Finland
April Savoy, USA
Shu Schiller, USA
Hong Sheng, USA
Choon Ling Sia, Hong Kong
Chee-Wee Tan, Denmark
Chuan Hoo Tan, Hong Kong
Noam Tractinsky, Israel
Horst Treiblmaier, Austria
Virpi Tuunainen, Finland
Dezhi Wu, USA
I-Chin Wu, Taiwan

Learning and Collaboration Technologies

**Program Chairs: Panayiotis Zaphiris, Cyprus,
and Andri Ioannou, Cyprus**

Ruthi Aladjem, Israel
Abdulaziz Aldaej, UK
John M. Carroll, USA
Maka Eradze, Estonia
Mikhail Fominykh, Norway
Denis Gillet, Switzerland
Mustafa Murat Inceoglu, Turkey
Pernilla Josefsson, Sweden
Marie Joubert, UK
Sauli Kiviranta, Finland
Tomaž Klobučar, Slovenia
Elena Kyza, Cyprus
Maarten de Laat, The Netherlands
David Lamas, Estonia

Edmund Laugasson, Estonia
Ana Loureiro, Portugal
Katherine Maillet, France
Nadia Pantidi, UK
Antigoni Parmaxi, Cyprus
Borzoo Pourabdollahian, Italy
Janet C. Read, UK
Christophe Reffay, France
Nicos Souleles, Cyprus
Ana Luísa Torres, Portugal
Stefan Trausan-Matu, Romania
Aimilia Tzanavari, Cyprus
Johnny Yuen, Hong Kong
Carmen Zahn, Switzerland

External Reviewers

Ilia Adami, Greece
Iosif Klironomos, Greece
Maria Korozi, Greece
Vassilis Kouroumalis, Greece

Asterios Leonidis, Greece
George Margetis, Greece
Stavroula Ntoa, Greece
Nikolaos Partarakis, Greece

HCI International 2015

The 15th International Conference on Human–Computer Interaction, HCI International 2015, will be held jointly with the affiliated conferences in Los Angeles, CA, USA, in the Westin Bonaventure Hotel, August 2–7, 2015. It will cover a broad spectrum of themes related to HCI, including theoretical issues, methods, tools, processes, and case studies in HCI design, as well as novel interaction techniques, interfaces, and applications. The proceedings will be published by Springer. More information will be available on the conference website: http://www.hcii2015.org/

General Chair
Professor Constantine Stephanidis
University of Crete and ICS-FORTH
Heraklion, Crete, Greece
E-mail: cs@ics.forth.gr

Table of Contents

Cognitive, Perceptual and Emotional Issues in Ambient Intelligence

User Experience in Intelligent Environments

Developing Distributed, Pervasive and Intelligent Environments

Smart Cities

Design Frameworks, Methods and Models for Intelligent Interactive Environments

Designing an Ambient Interaction Model
for Mobile Computing

Jonas Elslander and Katsumi Tanaka

Department of Social Informatics
Graduate School of Informatics, Kyoto University, Japan
{jonas,tanaka}@dl.kuis.kyoto-u.ac.jp

Abstract. In this paper, we advocate and propose a new interaction model for mobile computing by positioning ambient notifications central to both the user experience and the operating system interface design process. We suggest a model that visually replaces applications as current first digital citizens in mobile operating systems by a modular stream based notification center. In order to do so, we define the general layers that make up the dynamics of the current as well as the proposed mobile computing experience. We conclude and demonstrate the benefits and areas of improvement of our newly proposed paradigm: an ambient mobile interaction model.

Keywords: Methodology, design, HCI, big data, application, interface, interaction, notification, ambient, push, pull, social, context, discovery.

1 Introduction

1.1 User needs

Present-day mobile operating systems make use of a centralized notification structure in an archaic way by heavily relying on push notifications for nearly all communication [1]. When analyzing the findings of previous research and related works supporting this claim, we realized the potential of significantly improving the whole mobile computing experience by using notifications as a central entity to the interaction model. This had led us to research, design and propose a multi-layered ambient interaction model based on five distinguishable user needs, explicated below. It is important to note that we define the term *notification* as any form of informative on-way communication initiated by the system and directed towards the user.

Context. The contextual environment of the user should allow the operating system's interface to more effectively focus on what's most relevant to the user at any given moment. Notifications imply relevance and are a naturally adequate vehicle therefore.

Social. The social graph of a user greatly influences the perception of consumed mobile information [1], but has yet to be implemented on a system-wide level. The distinction

N. Streitz and P. Markopoulos (Eds.): DAPI 2014, LNCS 8530, pp. 3–14, 2014.

of three social classes[1] and usage of sensorial data can be incorporated in order to achieve this goal.

Visual. The human mind is wired to effortlessly distinguish colors and details and to read emotions and situations. Subsequently, mobile operating systems' interfaces are suggested to use photographic pictures – rather than icons or text – whenever possible as their primary visualization technique for notifications.

Ambient. Currently push notifications are used by the system when information is considered important to the user. Widgets are being offered as an alternative to manually retrieving information from within applications for less urgent communication. As we learned, these opposite styles leave a lot of ground uncovered. An ambient approach can solve the gap between both extremes by presenting information in the peripheral attention of the user, creating a non-invasive way to stay informed.

Time. Introducing the concept of time as a system-wide visual dimension to structure information fosters an improved discovery compared to present-day rigid grid-based interfaces.

1.2   Trends

In addition to the above-mentioned user needs, there are several relevant trends changing the mobile computing landscape. We find ourselves at the advent of wearable computing, with smart watches and smart glasses being the first emerging device categories. These require a significantly different interface and interaction approach, as failed attempts to implement the current model have shown to hamper adoption break-trough. Screen independence is another long-term trend that has recently begun to change mobile computing by allowing data to be stored in 'the cloud'. However, screen independence can be taken much further than the ability to access he same data from various devices based on user identification. Our proposed model provides the opportunity to develop mobile operating systems founded on these broadened trends, as covered further in this publication.

1.3   Paper Structure

The remainder of this paper is structured as follows. Section 2 explicates our conclusive interaction model for current mobile operating systems. All layers and their joint relations are discussed. In section 3, we propose an ambient mobile interaction paradigm by highlighting the differences with the present-day interaction model and elucidating new concepts. In section 4, we conclude our findings and summarize the opportunities supported by the proposed ambient interaction model.

---

[1] 'Favorites', 'friends' and 'others' each account for a different user perception. [1].

2   Current Interaction Model for Mobile Computing

In order to design an interaction model both solving the user needs and facilitating the trend development discussed in section 1, we first synthesized the specifics of the current interaction model for mobile computing on smartphones and tablets. The results are visualized in Figure 1 and will be clarified in this section.

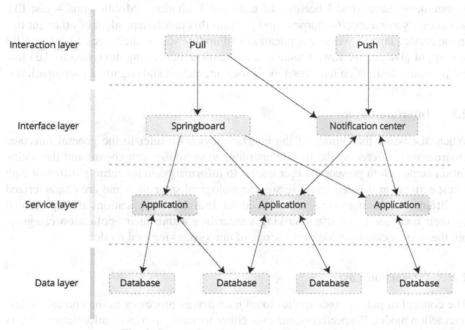

Fig. 1. Current four-layered interaction model

In the model we define four distinct layers: data, service, interface and interaction. The entities in the lower two layers are application-specific while the objects in the upper two layers are regarded as system-specific. This figure represents the information flow towards the user, with the visual endpoints being highlighted in yellow. Subsequently, we clarify the interpretation and scope of each individual layer, as well as their joint edges.

2.1   Data Layer

The data layer encompasses all means of data storage, both locally (i.e. on the mobile device) and externally as a connected database. The data layer bidirectionally communicates with the service layer (see next subsection) by offering and receiving information in the shape of structured data. It is the changing nature of the joint relationship between these two layers that has in great part shaped the interaction model evolution for desktop computing over the past decades.

2.2   Service Layer

We define the service layer as the tier concerned with selecting what information to present to the user as a consistent whole. Presently, an application-centric interaction model characterizes mobile computing. Data sources serve connected applications – or apps – that form the primary haven for users to retrieve information. The desktop computing environment, once recognized by a similar paradigm, has since evolved to a document-centric model because of technical limitations. Mobile apps – just like websites – serve a specific purpose and perform this task independent of other entities in the service layer: a weather application will update you on the forecast while a GPS app might give you the fastest route to a destination, but getting navigated to the closest-by sunny destination requires a lot of user interaction and cognitive participation.

2.3   Interface Layer

When discussing the entities of the interface layer, we refer to the general interface environments offered by the mobile operating system: the springboard and the notification center. Both present the user access to information in an entirely different way – respectively grid-based icons versus chronological snippets – and are characterized by different interactions (see next subsection). Individual applications are represented by their own interfaces, often striking similarities within their application category, but these are located outside of the scope of our system-focused model.

2.4   Interaction Layer

The concept of pull or push applies to all user-driven processes in the current mobile interaction model. Respectively, the user either manually retrieves information or gets interrupted by it while performing any other activity. We specifically define both concepts as follows:

$$F_{pull} = A \land B$$

$$F_{push} = \neg A \land \neg B$$

With A symbolizing the intent of information access[2] and B the presence of human-computer interaction, represented by a set of physical actions. Following this definition, pull-style communication requires both the user's intent of accessing certain information, as well a set of as bodily behavior towards this goal. Push-style communication on the other hand is not directly triggered by intent or by the user's actions. There exists a relation between the interface and interaction layer entities of the present-day interaction model. The springboard is designed to mainly serve as a pull-style navigational structure – with widgets and badges being the only exceptions to the rule – while the notification center has a mixed use. It provides both push-style notifications as well as a pull-style accessible chronological summary of missed information deemed relevant by the system.

---

[2]   The choice of selecting, consuming, evaluating... specific information.

2.5 Edge Values

The application-specific interfaces and notification center interface serve as the endpoints for information flow in our model. Upwards the data is filtered and presented while downwards it is accessed by the user. The uni or bidirectional arrows between the layers represent the edges and their flow orientation. Within every interlayer – the area between two adjacent layers in the model – the weight or value of all edges can be analyzed and compared. These are the topic of related and future work; the interaction-interface interlayer has already been partly covered by our previously referenced research into the use and perception of mobile notifications.

3 Ambient Interaction Model for Mobile Computing

With the user needs and trends – cited in the introductory section of this paper – in mind, we analyzed the current interaction model for mobile computing and allotted its shortcomings. In this section, we clarify those while suggesting improvements that make up the proposed ambient interaction model. A visualized overview is presented in Figure 2.

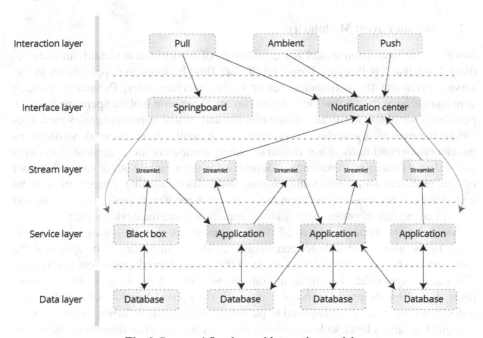

Fig. 2. Proposed five-layered interaction model

We define five distinct layers: data, service, stream, interface and interaction. The entities in the lower two layers are application-specific while those in the upper three layers are regarded as system-specific. As before, the figure represents the information flow towards the user, with the visual endpoints being highlighted. Below, we clarify the interpretation and scope of each individual layer, while focusing on the iconic distinctions with the present-day interaction model: modularity, notification-centricity and ambience.

3.1   Data and Service Layers

Whereas the changing dynamic between the data and service layer primarily fueled the structural changes in the desktop environment user experience (made up by the interaction and interface layers) over the past decades, we propose a different evolutionary approach for the mobile setting. Both application-specific layers and their mutual relationships remain chiefly unchanged, with the prime proposed hypotheses being linked to the three system-specific layers. Concerning the data layer, we envision local and connected information storage to support system services and applications in a similar way. As access to the right (amount of) data is of paramount importance as an asset to developing effective and successful mobile applications, the service layer remains an important pillar to the devised ambient interaction model. However, in subsection 3.4 we will introduce a new interface environment supporting our proposal to replace the application-centric paradigm with notification-centricity.

3.2   Stream Layer: Modularity

Novel to our interaction model is the inclusion of a notification stream, an intermediary layer that handles the chronological data flow between the applications in the service layer and the notification center in the interface layer. Preceding research conclusions have shown that the users of current-generation mobile operating systems perceive smartphone notifications as too many and of low importance/relevance. Providing the user with granular control over which applications can send notifications under certain conditions is not desirable either; computers are complicated systems and a *deus ex machina* experience is desirable for most mobile usage cases. The root of the problems surrounding the current notification-handling framework can be traced back to two concepts inherent to its design: same weight push notifications and a direct connection between every allowed application and the device's user.

Assigning the same weight to all notifications infers them being of same importance to the user while a direct connection, as shown in Figure 1, implies that the applications ultimately control what for (and thus how often) the user gets interrupted. The stream layer offers a solution to both issues while adding an array of new prospects. Based on the portlet concept, entities in the service layer – both applications and system processes – are required to publish their outgoing information into a chronological stream, a layer without a visual component, instead of directly to the notification center. This not only assures that the user doesn't get directly notified for every single event, as not all data will be relayed upwards in the model, but also changes the currently difficult balance in favor of (much) more shared data as the user experience trade-off obstacle has been eliminated. Further reaching are the following possibilities offered by the inclusion of the stream layer.

When the operating system is given access to the entirety of the stream layer data, mobile analytics and search take on new dimensions. Across applications, it becomes for example possible to compute the value of social connections or to determine usage patterns. Removing the barrier of user interruption simply allows for a bigger stream of data. This can be beneficial both as a means towards system personalization and to the user in a more direct way. Moreover, the general definition of search states that something has to be found. Far more often than the unknown, present-day mobile operating system-wide search focuses on retrieving known locally stored information and thus acts as a shortcut rather than as a true searching process. When certain information isn't ruled as immediately relevant to the user but still retained by the system, it can be retrieved later on by a search algorithm calculating the relevance to the changed user environment and/or search query.

Besides making each data package or *streamlet* accessible to the operating system, it can also be made available to other applications (with privacy and safety rules in place). This access renders the entire stream layer modular. Applications can not only learn from information shared by others, but also attach their own information and thus communicate and ameliorate data. The specifics of the stream layer format are the topic of future research.

An overhead algorithmical system process determines the multidimensional weight of every streamlet and pulls those scoring over a certain threshold up to the notification center in the interface layer. The aforementioned scoring dimensions are being determined by the *contextual, social* and *time relevance* of the data. This makes that the notifications are not shown to the user based solely on a timestamp match[3]. Instead, all streamlets are characterized by a *time to live* or TTL for reuse and notification purposes – beyond that point, they are archived for search and analytical purposes. At any moment within the TTL timeframe, notifications can be displayed in the interface layer when deemed contextually, socially or timely relevant. Examples of contextual relevance are the geographical location of the user[4], the time of day[5] or the environment as determined by local or connected sensors[6], while the social relevance is determined by the psychological and/or physical proximity of a connection referenced in the streamlet data. The time relevance is defined by sequence and pattern detection: when certain activities appear in relation to each other (relative) or to time (absolute), the streamlets of linked activities become important once one activity or moment is detected. The study and explicit definition of the scoring dimensions and the selection process comprises the topic of our future research.

As shown in Figure 2, certain streamlets can be deemed not important or content-rich enough for transfer to the notification center, but will be after data is added by another service layer entity. This creates opportunities for *black boxes* or applications without a proper interface. These upload selected data to the stream layer without

---

[3] Example of a timestamp match: if person A sends you a text message at 12:18PM, you will
     be notified of it by the operating system at 12:18PM.
[4] E.g. The position of the user or the change in position (static/dynamic).
[5] E.g. The precise time (07:33AM), morning/evening or holiday/day at work.
[6] E.g. Surrounding sound volume, light intensity, temperature or indoor/outdoor detection.

providing a front-end for the device user. As mobile applications can easily be bought from virtual stores, this could establish a mobile market for direct data monetization.

3.3   Interface Layer: Notification-Centricity

Structurally, the interface layers of the current and proposed interaction models – as presented in Figures 1 and 2 – look alike, sporting both a springboard and a notification center as entities. We advocate two major changes however: a redistribution of the interaction balance between both entities and a redesign of the visual embodiment of the notification center. It is not our vision to fundamentally change the representation of the springboard, but rather to replace it as the primary visual environment on mobile devices. With a notification-centric approach we want to place relevant information front and center, instead of a navigational structure guiding the user through a myriad of application icons. When the screen is activated, information accessed from the stream layer – as described in the previous subsection – is first off visualized in a graphic-rich style, as displayed by the mock-ups[7] in Figure 3.

Fig. 3. Mock-ups of a notification-centric interface

As indicated by the exclusion of any notifications in the first iterations of popular mobile operating systems iOS and Android, the current dedicated notification centers were more of an afterthought to an already established interaction model. We support our claim for placing a redesigned notification center paramount to the springboard by affirming that currently one in three smartphone users checks their phone for missed notifications at least once an hour [1], on top of attending to found ones and given the limited breadth of present notification centers and their contents, making it a critical interaction environment. In our prototypes, we incorporate solutions to all user needs explicated in the introductory section of this paper. As mock-ups, these are prevailingly interpretations for exemplary and research purpose. Photographic pictures of social connections and concepts known to the user (such as places or products) are used when available to create an interface environment suitable for ambient interaction (see next subsection) and small screens (see the subsection 3.5), but also to add

---

[7]   More high-resolution interface mock-ups can be downloaded at
http://bit.ly/AIMinterfaces.

emotions and agility to the communicated information. The contextual surroundings
are the dominant prerequisite for inclusion of information into the notification center,
a dynamic structure – in contrast to the underlying static springboard – that primarily
changes based on the user's situation. All retained information is visually organized
based on the social graph of the user, rather than on the timestamp of the notification
or the category of the application it originated from. Research teaches us that mobile
devices are primarily communication tools – hence the proposed social focus – and a
logging[8] and discovery[9] tool second. The latter is supported by visually dividing the
notification center into three time sections: the past, the present and the future. The
past addresses all alerts, the present handles the user's contextual surroundings and
the future relates to offered suggestions. By navigating between these, the user can
change the balance between briefing and discovery on a three-point scale.

3.4   Interaction layer: ambience

In section 2.4 we explicated the concepts of push and pull in relation to mobile notifications. In our proposed model we introduce an intermediate option, ambient notifications, we define as follows:

$$F_{ambient} = A \wedge \neg B$$

Here, A symbolizes the intent of information access and B the presence of human-
computer interaction, represented by a set of physical actions. Ambient notifications
thus encompass the action of looking for information, but without the component of
action taking. When information discreetly lives in the peripheral field of attention, it
doesn't require a summoning action - differentiating it from pull-style access – nor the
obtrusiveness of a push notification. In the table below, the interrelation between
push, pull and ambient interaction is visualized.

Table 1. Truth table for interaction styles

	User action (B)	No user action (¬B)
User intent (A)	**Pull-style interaction**	**Ambient interaction**
No user intent (¬A)	*Unintentional interaction*	**Pull-style interaction**

For clarification, we use the analogical example of the communicated information
regarding a political election. Searching or browsing the Internet for retrieving the
views and stances of a certain party is considered pull-style interaction, while over-
hearing an outdoor speech on your way to work is labeled as push-style interaction.
Changing focus to the radio news when the poll results are being discussed is an ambient interaction, while being called up on the night before by swing vote influencers
is an unintentional interaction.

---

[8]   E.g. Note taking, picture taking.
[9]   E.g. Internet browsing, social networks, weather forecast.

As the stream layer establishes the groundwork for the reimagined interface layer, so is the latter designed to support ambient interaction. This theoretical concept translates well to communication by gaze. Only important (stream layer) pieces of visually rich (interface layer) information are displayed in the tangential ocular field of the user (interaction layer), culminating in a relevant and immediate information transfer at the user's convenience. For a select minority of notifications, such as incoming phone calls, alarms or calendar reminders, push-style communication is still preferred and supported by the ambient interaction model. As is pull-style access to information displayed by application-specific interfaces, accessible either through navigating the springboard or through interaction with an element in the notification center.

3.5   Trend Inclusion

Besides offering a solution for the shortcomings of current mobile operating systems, represented by the earlier established user needs, our proposed interaction model was devised with the wearable computing and screen independence trends in mind. We are at the advent of integrated and small-footprint mobile device adoption, such as smart watches and smart glasses, which require a new interaction model. Scaling down (a part of) the current interface to fit significantly smaller screens doesn't suffice as current attempts that failed to gain traction have proven. At the same time, the different usage scenarios require a new interaction approach. Smart watches and smart glasses are suitable for displaying information to the user as described in the previous subsections. Both device categories resonate with the ambient interaction concept: they are always on (unlike smartphones and tablets we like to put away when not in use), they're part of the peripheral vision sphere and comprise of a small display surface that requires select relevant information with a high communication transfer rate. In certain related works, wearable devices are referred to as ambient due to their characteristic of physically blending into the surroundings by merging technology with wearable goods, thus labeling their interfaces as ambient. In this paper however, we describe and propose methods for ambient interaction – rather than an ambient interface – between the user and a mobile device, either wearable or portable.

Users carrying numerous mobile devices also raise questions about the optimal usage of screen independent information. When considering this trend, we distinguish the independence of both data collection and display, by suggesting the stream layer of the ambient interaction model to be made internet-accessible (thus, by placing them in 'the cloud'). The systems and applications of multiple mobile devices can feed a common stream layer, from which all service layer entities across devices can access and remix data. The interface and interaction layers of each device are defined by the same interaction model, but can individually focus on content that best fits their usage and aspired user experience by adjusting the threshold parameters for notification center inclusion.

4   Conclusions and Future Work

In this research, we synthesized the information flow within current mobile operating systems and combined it with collected user needs and trends to determine its weaknesses and to define opportunities. Consequently, we proposed an adapted interaction model that introduces:

- A stream layer, enabling mobile data growth and monetization, reducing displeasure and managing all notifications in a modular, analyzable and searchable way;
- A notification-centric interface concept, transforming the notification center into a contextual, social and visual framework structured around time and with ambient usage in mind, while placing it chief to the system's static navigational interface;
- An ambient interaction paradigm that challenges the stasis between push and pull-style communication by heralding a new dynamic between the intent of information retrieval and performed user actions, offering possibilities for both existing and new mobile device categories.

All three topics require further research in order to refine their impact and define their contribution to the shift towards the next interaction model for mobile computing. Future work includes qualitative user studies of situational mock-ups based on the ambient interaction model, as well as a technical evaluation of the processes that construe the communication between the stream layer and its surrounding layers.

References

1. Elslander, J., Tanaka, K.: A Notification-Centric Mobile Interaction Survey and Framework. In: Jatowt, A., et al. (eds.) SocInfo 2013. LNCS, vol. 8238, pp. 443–456. Springer, Heidelberg (2013)
2. Scott McCrickard, D., Chewar, C.M.: Attuning notification design to user goals and attention costs. Commun. ACM 46(3), 67–72 (2003)
3. Maglio, P.P., Campbell, C.S.: Tradeoffs in displaying peripheral information. In: Proceedings of the SIGCHI Conference on Human Factors in Computing Systems (CHI 2000), pp. 241–248. ACM, New York (2000)
4. Maglio, P.P., Barrett, R., Campbell, C.S., Selker, T.: SUITOR: An attentive information system. In: Proceedings of the 5th International Conference on Intelligent User Interfaces, IUI 2000 (2000)
5. Booker, J.E., Chewar, C.M., McCrickard, D.S.: Usability testing of notification interfaces: Are we focused on the best metrics? In: Proceedings of the 42nd Annual Southeast Regional Conference (ACM-SE 42), pp. 128–133. ACM, New York (2004)
6. Grudin, J.: Partitioning digital worlds: Focal and peripheral awareness in multiple monitor use. In: Proceedings of the SIGCHI Conference on Human Factors in Computing Systems (CHI 2001), pp. 458–465. ACM, New York (2001)
7. Erickson, T., Kellogg, W.A.: Social translucence: An approach to designing systems that support social processes. ACM Trans. Comput.-Hum. Interact. 7(1), 59–83 (2000)
8. Saket, B., Prasojo, C., Huang, Y., Zhao, S.: Designing an effective vibration-based notification interface for mobile phones. In: Proceedings of the 2013 Conference on Computer Supported Cooperative Work (CSCW 2013), pp. 149–1504. ACM, New York (2013)
9. Hazlewood, W.R., Stolterman, E., Connelly, K.: Issues in evaluating ambient displays in the wild: two case studies. In: Proceedings of the SIGCHI Conference on Human Factors in Computing Systems (CHI 2011), pp. 877–886. ACM, New York (2011)

10. Messeter, J., Molenaar, D.: Evaluating ambient displays in the wild: Highlighting social aspects of use in public settings. In: Proceedings of the Designing Interactive Systems Conference (DIS 2012), pp. 478–481. ACM, New York (2012)
11. Mankoff, J., Dey, A.K., Hsieh, G., Kientz, J., Lederer, S., Ames, M.: Heuristic evaluation of ambient displays. In: Proceedings of the SIGCHI Conference on Human Factors in Computing Systems (CHI 2003), pp. 169–176. ACM, New York (2003)
12. Kim, T., Hong, H., Magerko, B.: Design requirements for ambient display that supports sustainable lifestyle. In: Proceedings of the 8th ACM Conference on Designing Interactive Systems (DIS 2010), pp. 103–112. ACM, New York (2010)
13. Ryu, H.-S., Yoon, Y.-J., Lim, M.-E., Park, C.-Y., Park, S.-J., Choi, S.-M.: Picture navigation using an ambient display and implicit interactions. In: Proceedings of the 19th Australasian Conference on Computer-Human Interaction: Entertaining User Interfaces (OZCHI 2007), pp. 223–226. ACM, New York (2007)

Models as a Starting Point of Software Development for Smart Environments

Peter Forbrig, Michael Zaki, and Gregor Buchholz

University of Rostock, Department of Computer Science,
Albert Einstein Str. 21,
18055 Rostock, Germany
{peter.forbrig,gregor.buchholz,michael.zaki}@uni-rostock.de

Abstract. Creating a smart environment is a challenging task because of the excessive software development and adaptation required. Additionally, hardware in form of stationary as well as dynamic devices has to be installed. Similar to traditional software development, evaluating only the end product is often very costly in terms of time and effort needed. This is due to the fact that usually a lot of changes have to take place since the system fails to deliver the expected behaviour. Therefore, modelling is of great benefit. Models help to get a shared and thorough understanding of a specific domain. Making the animation of those models feasible allows getting a first impression of the system under development. Such prototypes of a system can be created on different levels of abstraction. The paper aims to demonstrate how modelling the human behaviour from the perspective of the activities performed in the environment can lead to first abstract prototypes. Those prototypes can be further extended and fostered by device models as well as models for the whole environment. In the paper, we also strive to discuss the costs and benefits of offering an abstract environmental model in 2D or 3D.

Keywords: Smart Environment, model-based design, evaluation, prototyping.

1 Introduction

Model-based development of interactive systems is already quite a long tradition (see e.g. [11]). It is based on the idea of analyzing the tasks users currently perform and designing a task model of their envisaged activities. Based on this designed task model the user interface of the system under development is created.

Additionally, usability evaluation of the developed system can be supported by task models. This can even be done remotely (see e.g. [14]). However, it is important to find ways to elaborate in a very early development stage whether the ideas for a new system really fit to the requirements of the users. Prototyping seems to be a good solution for that. This statement is supported by [15]. Regarding evaluation techniques, the authors claim: "Discount methods work well with low fidelity prototypes, which allows evaluations to take place during early development when there is no operational prototype for users to test in a real work setting. These discount methods

N. Streitz and P. Markopoulos (Eds.): DAPI 2014, LNCS 8530, pp. 15–24, 2014.

require some means of understanding and representing the tasks ...". The statement was made in conjunction with traditional systems from the domain of CSCW (Computer Supported Cooperative Work). It seems to be true for Smart Environments as well which are specific CSCW systems.

Different teams have accomplished research aiming to study prototypes of environments for assistive systems in smart environments. Often, elderly people or children are in the focus of such research (see e.g. [3], [23]). Like in our graduate school MuSAMA (Multimodal Smart Appliance Ensembles for Mobile Applications), meeting rooms are also sometimes the embracing environments for such applications. Occasionally the meeting scenario is also used for learning aspects.

Fig. 1. Smart meeting room at our university

The paper is structured in such a way that we provide a discussion of models for smart environments.

2   Models for Smart Environments

There are sometimes controversial discussions about the roles of models in smart environments. Some approaches follow the idea of artificial intelligence, where certain basic ideas are specified as rules, neuronal nets or Bayesian Networks (see e.g. 3]). Support is provided based on training data or a combination of rules during runtime.

We follow a different approach that is founded on experiences in software engineering [7]. According to these experiences design of interactive systems is often helpful [6]. In this way we strive to build design models for smart environments as well [9]. We do not state that this approach is the only gateway for designing models which are compatible with smart environments. However, we believe that this approach is promising and should be followed. That was the reason for designing a language that allows to specify applications in smart meeting rooms. The language is called CTML (collaborative task modelling language). It consists of task models for all stakeholders, a task model for the team, a special model for the environment and models for devices. The following figure provides a visual representation of these models.

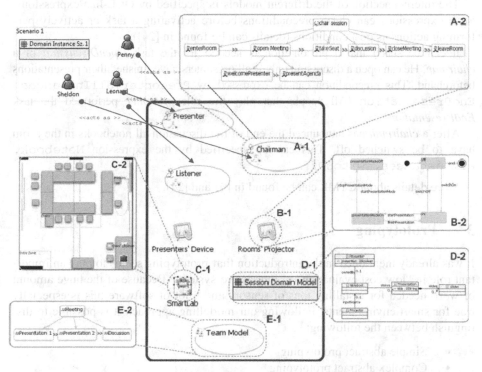

Fig. 2. Schematic representation of models for smart meeting rooms

Most important elements for providing support are task models. They specify tasks for different roles like *presenter*, *listener* or *chairman*. However, there is also a task model for the whole team. It describes the coordination of tasks among the different stakeholders. It is very much related to the sequence in which the meeting has to proceed. Additionally, there is a model for the smart lab that represents the special characteristics of the room and particular zones like the "presentation area".

These modelling entities are shown in the inner circle of Fig. 2 and post fixed with "-1". Models outside of the inner circle are specifications of the corresponding entities and post fixed width "-2".

At the upper left corner of Fig. 2 one can see a scenario specification. Users are assigned to roles. A given role determines the actions a user can perform. In CTML task models are specified in a CTT [13]-like notation where a tree structure represents hierarchically arranged tasks. The leafs of the tree (non refined tasks) are called atomic tasks or actions. Tasks on the same level of abstraction are connected by temporal operators defining the temporal order of task execution.

In the lab different zones are specified. They allow the triggering of specific tasks. If a potential presenter enters the presentation area it can e.g. be assumed that he/she will now have the role of a presenter and the corresponding task model is assigned.

In addition to the general domain model in form of a class diagram there are state chart models for all devices.

The interconnection of the different models is specified by OCL-like expressions. Such expressions can check preconditions before activating a task or actively performing actions as post conditions (details can be found in [24]).

It can be stated that a precondition is needed for the task *OpenDiscussion* of a *chairman*. He can open a discussion only if all presenters have finished their presentations beforehand. This precondition can be expressed by `Presenter.allInstances.EndPresentation` (All people that play the role *presenter* performed the task *EndPresentation.*).

After a *chairman* has announced the end of the discussion all notebooks in the room have to be switched off. This can be specified by the expression `Notebook.allInstances.switchOff`.

More details about CTML can be found in [9] and [24].

3   Prototyping

It was already mentioned in the introduction that prototyping seems to play an important role in "low cost evaluation" of interactive systems. Because of the huge amount of work needed for installing tons of sensors and a lot of software this is especially true for smart environments. Following our modelling approach it is possible to distinguish between the following:

- Simple abstract prototyping
- Complex abstract prototyping
- Prototyping in a virtual environment

Details will be discussed within the following paragraphs.

3.1   Simple Abstract Prototyping

Prototyping in this very abstract sense consists of animating the models for roles, team and devices independently. This might be especially important for task models. Fig. 3 presents an animated task model for the role presenter. The corresponding person entered the presentation area ("move to the front" is already finished). At this state slides can be loaded, discussion can be performed or the presenter can take a seat without presenting anything.

During evaluation of the model it can be discussed whether it is really necessary to load slides before giving a talk or whether discussion is possible without a given talk. Additionally, there might be other activities of interest that were not specified.

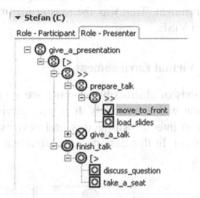

Fig. 3. Animated task model for role presenter

3.2   Complex Abstract Prototyping

Animating models separately gives a first impression of the behaviour of stakeholders and devices. However, dependencies between different models remain unconsidered. Therefore, animation of all models has to be done in parallel. Additionally, preconditions and post-conditions (in our case the OCL-like expressions) have to be executed. An appropriate interpreter is needed for that.

In the discussed way it can be checked whether a certain task can be executed if a specific device is in the state "off". Additionally, the consequences of performing a task can be checked by looking at changes in other models. Fig. 4 gives an overview of different users' respective task models which are animated at the same time.

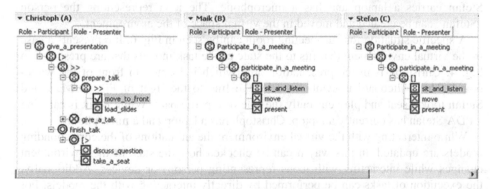

Fig. 4. Different animated models

One can see in Fig. 4 the animated task models for three persons. They all can play the role of a participant and a presenter. Currently Christoph is the presenter. He just moved to the front and the other persons are sitting and listening. At this stage it can e.g. be checked how the models interact and whether it is possible to have two or three presenters.

This kind of evaluation is still abstract. It would be good to have an impression of the situation in the environment. That was the reason for implementing a 2D virtual environment that is called ViSE.

3.3   Prototyping in a Virtual Environment

The already discussed kinds of abstract prototyping are very helpful. However, they require a direct interaction with the models. It is very obvious that having a virtual environment that allows to interact with actors and devices would significantly improve the evaluation process. In this case the later situation in the real world can already be simulated.

Fig. 5. Representation of persons in the virtual environment

Fig. 5 illustrates the way persons are represented in the virtual environment. It is possible to interactively assign roles to such persons. However, this can also be done automatically using post-conditions. Currently Stefan plays the role of a presenter. Additionally, it is possible to assign devices to such persons. In the given example, Stefan carries a laptop and has a microphone. The icon representing the person "Stefan" can be created and moved in the virtual space of the environment.

A specific situation for our meeting room can be seen in Fig. 6. It represents a case in the virtual environment that fits to the state of the task models that are presented in Fig. 4. Christoph is in the presentation area which is located in front of the whiteboard. The whiteboard is symbolised by the line to the right of Fig. 6. Maik and Stefan took a seat and play currently the role of a participant. While Maik is carrying a PDA Stefan has currently a laptop. Christoph has a laptop and a microphone.

While interacting with the virtual environment the animations of the corresponding models are updated. In this way it can be checked how the state of the environment changes while interacting with icons representing persons or devices. Additionally, the execution of tasks can be performed by directly interacting with the models. For moving to the front the corresponding icon has only to be moved to the respective position. However, to load slides the execution of the corresponding task has to be explicitly triggered.

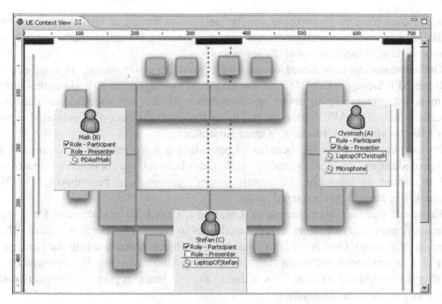

Fig. 6. Virtual meeting room with three persons

This kind of evaluation is not only helpful as long as the real system does not exist. Indeed it supports evaluation very well. For classical interactive systems it is common sense that expert evaluation should be performed before user tests are executed. However, how can expert evaluation be performed in a smart meeting room with three acting people? This requires involving three people who have to follow the existing scripts and play the exact role assigned. This is very costly and time consuming.

In its traditional sense, expert evaluation is only possible with virtual environments. In such environments an expert can control several persons and thus check the behaviour of a specified system. This is a significant advantage guaranteed by means of expert evaluation giving it preference over tests that have to be performed by several people in the real world environment.

4   Discussion and Related Work

In the previous paragraphs we argued for a model-based approach for smart environments based on examples for smart meeting rooms. From our point of view, a detailed analysis of tasks that are performed by potential users helps to understand the domain. Design models for activities in form of task models are beneficial. They are a good representation to think about supporting users. They allow explicit design for the support offered in smart environments.

Using the discussed models allows prototyping at different development stages. Singular models can be animated first. Later they and their dependencies can be evaluated by animation. Other authors argue in a similar way. Some use task models even as a control mechanism for runtime (see e.g. [2] or [19]).

More user friendly prototyping can be performed having a virtual environment available. Such an environment allows expert evaluation because experts are able to control several virtual persons at the same time.

Our experiments were based on an own virtual 2D environment. In conjunction with the APEX-project [20, 21] open simulator [12] is suggested as a 3D virtual environment for prototyping of smart environments. Models are specified as Petri-net specifications. The APEX-framework allows the synchronisation of animated Petri-nets with the virtual environment of open simulator.

Prototyping in 3D has the benefits of providing a more realistic environment. It also provides more realistic interaction techniques between agents in the environment and the smart environment. To certain extent, gestures can be supported in 3D whereas they have to be abstracted in 2D.

However, there are also drawbacks. Creating a virtual 3D environment for a specific application is much more complicated than to provide a 2D environment. That depends of course on the number of available 3D objects. After a while the construction of new environments might decrease a lot. Additionally, the 3D representation asks for more detailed models. This is due to the existence of post-conditions requiring more precise state information.

It seems to be interesting to have both options available. For some cases it might be enough to have a 2D representation available whereas for others prototyping in 3D might be the only way to provide the right experience. There seems to be a need for metrics that help to estimate the necessary effort for both approaches. Additionally, it would be helpful that environments provide features which allow testers to specify parallel activities of agents in a script form. It is even very hard to do this interactively.

For our virtual environment ViSE as well as the real environment, there exists a language for a special kind of middleware. All devices can be controlled via this feature. It is not only a communication channel between all devices but also between the real world and the virtual world. Real meetings can thus be visualised through meetings in the virtual environment. In contrast to videos, this kind of replay allows the analysis of meetings in an anonymous way. Additionally, events from the virtual environment and the real environment can be mixed. A costly new sensor can only be installed in the virtual environment but can give feedback to events from the real world environment. In this way it can be checked whether it makes sense to y the sensor. It will be a challenge for the future to combine a virtual environment with several real world environments. Two real meeting rooms (like two video conference rooms) could be supported by one virtual room.

Finally, more research has to be conducted in order to make it feasible to present the system state by animated models in a convenient human understandable way. A potential solution is actually providing information with different levels of detail that can be interactively changed.

5   Summary and Outlook

A model-based approach seems not only to be a good idea for general interactive systems but also for smart environments. It allows a precise requirements specification and an appropriate design. Models provide the opportunity for evaluations at early stages of software development with relatively low costs. Animations provide excellent chances for communicating ideas of envisaged behaviour for assistive systems with users. Users can already interact with the system under development in an abstract way. This can be done through animated models, virtual 2D environments or virtual 3D systems. Within the paper advantages and disadvantages related to usability evaluation were discussed. Some challenges were identified that raise questions seeking answers in the near future. These challenges are

- Providing metrics for costs of modelling 2D versus 3D.
- Presentation of the system state using animated models in a suitable human understandable way.
- Providing a feature for precise specification for the performance of parallel activities of various agents in the virtual environment.
- Combination of a virtual environment with several real environments.

References

1. APEX: http://twiki.di.uminho.pt/twiki/bin/view/Research/APEX/ WebHome (last accessed January 3, 2014)
2. Blumendorf, M.: Multimodal Interaction in Smart Environments A Model-based Runtime System for Ubiquitous User Interfaces. Dissertation, TU Berlin (2009)
3. Bobick, A.F., Intille, S.S., Davis, J.W., Baird, F., Pinhanez, C.S., Campbell, L.W., Ivanov, Y.A., Schtte, A., Wilson, A.: The kidsroom: Perceptually based interactive and immersive story environment. In: PRESENCE, pp. 367–391 (1999)
4. Coutaz, J.: Meta-User Interfaces for Ambient Spaces. In: Coninx, K., Luyten, K., Schneider, K.A. (eds.) TAMODIA 2006. LNCS, vol. 4385, pp. 1–15. Springer, Heidelberg (2007)
5. Demeure, A., Lehmann, G., Petit, M., Calvary, G.(eds.): Proceedings of the 1st International Workshop on Supportive User Interfaces: SUI 2011, Pisa, Italy, June 13 (2011), http://ceur-ws.org/Vol-828/
6. Dittmar, A., Forbrig, P.: Selective modeling to support task migratability of interactive artifacts. In: Campos, P., Graham, N., Jorge, J., Nunes, N., Palanque, P., Winckler, M. (eds.) INTERACT 2011, Part III. LNCS, vol. 6948, pp. 571–588. Springer, Heidelberg (2011)
7. Forbrig, P., Dittmar, A., Brüning, J., Wurdel, M.: Making Task Modeling Suitable for Stakeholder Driven Workflow specifications. In: Stephanidis, C. (ed.) Universal Access in HCI, Part I, HCII 2011. LNCS, vol. 6765, pp. 51–60. Springer, Heidelberg (2011)
8. Forbrig, P., Wurdel, M., Zaki, M.: 2012: The roles of models and patterns in smart environments. In: EICS Workshop, Copenhagen (2012)
9. Forbrig, P.: 2012: Interactions in Smart Environments and the Importance of Modelling. Romanian Journal of Human - Computer Interaction 5, 1–12 (2012); Special issue: Human Computer Interaction (2012) ISSN 1843-4460, http://rochi.utcluj.ro/rrioc/ en/rochi2012.html
10. Ishii, H., Ulmer, B.: Tangible bits: Towards seamless interfaces between people, bits, and atoms. In: Proceedings of the CHI 1997 Conference on Human Factors in Computing Systems, Atlanta, Georgia, pp. 234–241 (March 1997)

11. Johnson, P., Wilson, S., Markopoulos, P., Pycock, J.: ADEPT: Advanced Design Environment for Prototyping with Task Models. In: Proceedings of the INTERACT 1993 and CHI 1993 Conference on Human Factors in Computing Systems (CHI 1993), p. 56. ACM, New York (1993)
12. OpenSimulator: http://opensimulator.org/wiki/Main_Page (last accessed January 3, 2014)
13. Paterno, F., Meniconi, C.: ConcurTaskTrees: A diagrammatic Notation for Specifying Task Models. In: INTERACT 1997, IFIP TC13, pp. 362–369 (1997)
14. Paterno, F., Ballardin, G.: Model-aided remote usability evaluation. In: Sasse, A., Johnson, C. (eds.) Proceedings of the IFIP TC13 Seventh International Conference on Human-Computer Interaction, pp. 434–442. IOS Press, Amsterdam (1999)
15. Pinelle, D., Gutwin, C., Greenberg, S.: Task Analysis for Groupware Usability Evaluation: Modeling Shared-Workspace Tasks with the Mechanics of Collaboration. ACM TOCHI 10(4) (2003)
16. Propp, S., Forbrig, P.: ViSE – A Virtual Smart Environment for Usability Evaluation. In: Bernhaupt, R., Forbrig, P., Gulliksen, J., Lárusdótti, M. (eds.) HCSE 2010. LNCS, vol. 6409, pp. 38–45. Springer, Heidelberg (2010)
17. Propp, S., Buchholz, G., Forbrig, P.: Integration of usability evaluation and model-based software development. Advances in Engineering Software 40(12), 1223–1230 (2009)
18. Roscher, G., Blumendorf, M., Albayrak, S.: Using Meta User Interfaces to Control Multimodal Interaction in Smart Environments. In: Proceedings of the IUI 2009 Workshop on Model Driven Development of Advanced User Interfaces (2009), http://ceur-ws.org/Vol-439/paper4.pd
19. Roscher, D., Lehmann, G., Blumendorf, M., Albayrak, S.: Design and Implementation of Meta User Interfaces for Interaction in Smart Environments. In: [5]
20. Silva, J.L., Campos, J., Harrison, M.: Formal analysis of ubiquitous computing environments through the APEX framework. In: Proceedings of the 4th ACM SIGCHI Symposium on Engineering Interactive Computing Systems (EICS 2012), pp. 131–140 (2012)
21. Silva, J.L., Ribeiro, O., Fernandes, J.M., Campos, J.C., Harrison, M.D.: (2010)
22. Silva, J.L., Ribeiro, Ó.R., Fernandes, J.M., Campos, J.C., Harrison, M.D.: The APEX framework: prototyping of ubiquitous environments based on Petrinets. In: Bernhaupt, R., Forbrig, P., Gulliksen, J., Lárusdótti, M. (eds.) HCSE 2010. LNCS, vol. 6409, pp. 6–21. Springer, Heidelberg (2010)
23. Srivastava, M., Muntz, R., Potkonjak, M.: Smart kindergarten: Sensor-based wireless networks for smart developmental problem-solving environments. In: Proceedings of the 7th Annual International Conference on Mobile Computing and Networking, MobiCom 2001, pp. 132–138. ACM, New York (2001)
24. Wurdel, M., Sinnig, D., Forbrig, P.: CTML: Domain and Task Modeling for Collaborative Environments. Journal of Universal Computer Science 14 (2008); Special Issue on Human-Computer Interaction
25. Zaki, M., Forbrig, P.: Making task models and dialog graphs suitable for generating assistive and adaptable user interfaces for smart environments. In: PECCS 2013, Barcelona, Spain, Feburary 19-21 (2013)
26. Zaki, M., Wurdel, M., Forbrig, P.: Pattern Driven Task Model Refinement. In: Abraham, A., Corchado, J.M., Rodriguez-Gonzalez, S., De Paz Santana, J.F. (eds.) International Symposium on Distributed Computing and Artificial Intelligence, DCAI 2011, Salamanca, Spain, April 6-8. Advances in Soft Computing, vol. 91, pp. 249–256 (2011) ISBN = 978-3-642-19933-2

Mapping Interactions in a Pervasive Home Environment

Konstantinos Grivas[1,*], Stelios Zerefos[2], and Irene Mavrommati[2]

[1] Department of Architecture, School of Engineering,
University of Patras, Rio, 26500, Greece
kgrivas@upatras.gr
[2] Hellenic Open University, Department of Applied Arts, Greece
{zerefos,mavrommati}@eap.gr

Abstract. This work focuses on the visualisation of interactions in a pervasive home environment. Home as a space and as an activity container is traditionally linked to the habitual acts of the inhabitants. However, the infiltration of wireless connectivity, throughout the home and external to it, suggests that, in contrast to the traditional notion of hominess, we as inhabitants do not have the means to perceive significant data connections that take place throughout our home. These connections may range from simple data transfer to sensing and decision making, all taking place around our home and unseen. To this end we have tried to find the means to represent these connections in a visual way, in order to provide a tool that will help to reveal the structure, form and perplexity of digital connections to the inhabitants of a pervasive home environment. The study concludes that in order to visualise all this data, maps have to be formed that include both the material and immaterial infrastructure of home, as well as the connection between them and the rest of the world. These maps are bound to have the characteristics of centralised, distributed and decentralised networks, rendering them as hybrid maps, depending on the type of information they deal with.

Keywords: pervasive home, cartography, visual representation, spatial concept.

1 From the Shrinking of Physical Space to the Digital Expansion of Home Space

We are witnessing a drastic change in the organization and the characteristics of domestic space. The international trend for less physical home space, that follows the need to minimise energy consumption, brings out lighter forms of housing [1]. Many current examples and initiatives such as *pocketliving* or *micro-homes* point to the same direction. During the last decade, architectural publications and design trends thrive with titles dedicated to small/minimum/tiny/portable/flexible homesetc., which shows that architects and designers have been incorporating and advocating the idea of shrinking living quarters, reflecting a wider social anxiety for a sustainable future. The situation is reminiscent of the conditions that led to the design ethics and construction of the modernist housing schemes in post-war Europe [2].

---

* Corresponding author.

N. Streitz and P. Markopoulos (Eds.): DAPI 2014, LNCS 8530, pp. 25–36, 2014.
© Springer International Publishing Switzerland 2014

Since recorded time, affluent societies considered that the inventory and collections of objects in the home played a central role in the definition and cultivation of the family's identity, however, 20th century consumerism culture has rendered it as a massive phenomenon. In The Meaning of Things [3], the authors explain how certain categories of household possessions were more valued for the symbolic and emotional meanings they embodied and that those possessions changed with age and gender. The excessive materialism of that period led to an increasing need for domestic space that could house collections of personally valued objects. Research has shown that while families in developed countries tend to be smaller, the average size of homes had been increasing up to the year 2000 [4]. In recent years, however, we are witnessing a reverse trend as research shows that in most developed countries the changes in family structure have led to a decrease in the size of the average household [5]. The physical contraction of the domestic envelope means that households can afford less material possessions, so in many cases possessions with limited function or functionality are left out.

Domestic space also becomes, less physically significant perhaps because daily life increasingly focuses around a series of digital habits and objects. Recent research shows that the new class of global nomads forms "situational attachments to objects, appreciate objects primarily for their instrumental use-value, and value immaterial or 'light' possessions as well as practices."[6] They clink to portable and replaceable possessions, especially portable electronics that enable them to stay connected to networks, as they tend to value accessibility more than the object's value per se. As consumerism shifts more to the purchase and storage of digital artefacts, and as we increasingly base our daily activities on digital media, our dependence towards the physical space of home and its objects possibly weakens. The condition of *existenzminimum* (minimum existence), apart from being a necessity and the product of planning strategies, appears as a desirable choice for contemporary city dwellers [7]. According to Aaron Betsky's view, contemporary home can be thought of "as a storage device containing all the domestic products by which we extend our body into the world". For him, we no longer inhabit homes, but they are primarily "places where such objects are collected"[8, p.43]. However, today the number of physical artefacts in a home decreases, as the number of digital artefacts increases,

In contrast to the physical shrinking of home and the diminishing of its possessions and material substance, we experience an infinite expansion of the its operational and sensorial reach, which is more than ever connected to the global thoroughfare. The digitisation of daily life signifies a huge expansion of the domestic realm, far beyond the physical territory defined by the enclosure of the building envelope. At the same time, the division of work and public life from home, and the concepts of free time and privacy, products themselves of the industrial revolution and modernity, are transforming into very thin permeable layers in our daily routine, as we return to a pre-industrial condition where home space becomes, under certain circumstances, inclusive and less private.

In a sense, the evolution of domestic space is analogous to the evolution of many technological products that moved from cumbersome and materially saturated objects with limited functionality to minimised ultra-thin devices with far infinitely complex functionality and connectivity. However, home is not a gadget. This antithetical transformation (physical contraction and operational expansion) of contemporary domestic space augmented with communication and ambient technologies is at once destabilising and de-territorializing the nature of home. If the loss of stability, the augmentation of capacities, or the effort to internalise the effects of the acquisition of new skills is a cause of de-territorialisation of personal identity [9, p.50], then the same might apply to home, the "mirror of self" [10]. The aforementioned transformations have a profound impact on the way domestic space itself is ordered, rendering whatever order there seems to exist obscure and hermetic. Dwelling, unlike the Heideggerian definition of gathering and preserving the fourfold in a place– is being gradually replaced by a kind of multiple, fragmented and provisional inhabitation.

Home becomes a hybrid place. As it becomes increasingly open to other activities (work, education, leisure, healthcare, commerce, etc.), and connects to disparate places, times and cultures, these different cycles and routines get mixed. This multiplication of functions in the home delivers interior spaces supporting daily routines as obscurely and chaotic ordered as the urban sprawl of our cities. For example, the modernist purely functional classification, and ordering of rooms [11] according to their use (e.g. bed-room, bath-room, living-room, dining-room, etc.) seems irrelevant as spaces may support varied and multiple activities other than the basic daily ones.

In addition to its programmatic multiplication, home faces another challenge: the fragmentation of its place and the distribution of inhabitation to disparate places simultaneously or periodically. The destabilising of the traditional family structure, extremely mobile and flexible working patternsand other social phenomena lead more people to adopt nomadic lifestyles. Christos Papoulias' project "Dispersed House" proposed a house whose functions have been dispersed into the fabric of the metropolis, as a reflection on fragmented metropolitan living, and "a search for the end of the unified house" [12]. Actually, the fragmentation of the domestic space is nothing but a by-effect of the individualisation of society, where communities are fragile, short-lived, scattered and erratic, "desperately in need for networking", sharing intimacies as the "only remaining method of 'community building'"[13, p.37]. Ambient communication between disparate intimate spaces is the technological boon that ensures the maximum possible of remote togetherness/intimacy in an otherwise lonesome and fragmented living.

2   "Reading" The Home

Aaron Betsky suggested that architecture may tackle sprawl's elusive order by constructing icons, interfaces and narratives. Icons function as the gathering places or objects, the centres of activities that stand still in a continuously changing world, yet, they remain enigmatic. Interfaces are the structures of coherence that help us understand the interrelations of the objects we accrete for our use, while narratives bridge time and space creating dynamic and changing images of objects or places [8, §2.5]. As Pavlos Lefas points out interpreting Betsky, both the form-giving of physical objects (built environment) as well as the representation of these objects are equally important architectural tasks [14, p.162].

It becomes evident that what Betsky refers to as interfaces and narratives, are actually the artefacts, representations, mappings, communication systems, perceptual and sensorial augmentation, or any other means that enable the reading and linking of the various fragments of home. Moreover, these artefacts excrete their peripheral nature and become integral aspects of home, at least as important as its physical and immaterial form, creating an "archipelago" of discrete islands connected by complex dynamic network connections [15]. Objects communicate among themselves and with networks outside the physical boundaries of home in a fashion that is constantly changing and difficult to trace down all the time. They interact with each other and with points globally dispersed by imperceptible data transfer and background tasks. However, while their main job is not to demand attention, they create a veil of uncertainty that inhabitants might find confusing or discomforting, mainly because home as sanctuary is desecrated by "secret" communications and decisions not directly conferred by the inhabitants.

The fact that immaterial connections between householdobjects become equally important to physical space, presents the need to elaborate on meaningful representations of home that escape the confinements of the traditional plan drawing and become dynamic and multi-layered to reflect their daily use by the inhabitants. In order to understand what is happening inside our home, we have to be able to know - and ultimately see - what communications and decisions take place and when they are active. These personal geographic studies can help create the new home-places by constructing and retaining identity, relationships and memories. Most of us would directly consider an augmented building plan as the means to quickly visualise all this information. However, this cannot be the case, since home is growing into an entity whose range is disproportionately larger than its diminishing physical boundaries. We chose cartography as a means to visualize all this information taking place through contemporary home environments, which constitute unexplored territory in our fully documented world. The next section attempts to address this issue through assessing several network mapping practices and their principles, and reflecting on the visual forms of augmented-home maps.

3   Determining the Map Characteristics

The early representations of hybrid domestic spaces, which incorporated some sort of ubiquitous technology or intelligent monitoring and managing systems, were created by the scientists and researchers who created the first ubiquitous computing experimental homes (Figs. 1 & 2). These static or dynamic representations depict the spatial configuration of connected devices, their links, and their mode of operation. Usually, they are followed by list of the mapped devices. The location of each device is not precise but topologically related to its location within the actual space. Furthermore, some of these representations showed real-time information about the status and activity of each connected device. Although, those depictions of networked home environments were still based on the configuration of the plan of the physical space, one can find similarities with the representations and schematic diagrams for electronic circuits.

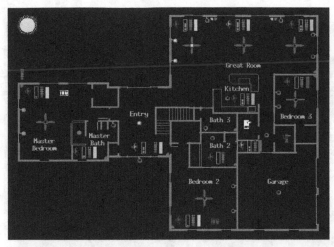

Fig. 1. plan and depiction of devices in the "Adaptive House" Colorado, source: http://www.cs.colorado.edu/~mozer/Research/Projects/Adaptive%20h ouse/java%20interface/ji.html

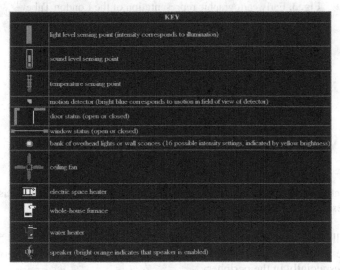

Fig. 2. list of devices in the "Adaptive House" Colorado, source: http://www.cs. colorado.edu/~mozer/Research/Projects/Adaptive%20house/java%20in terface/ji.html

In such representational examples the accuracy of location information is compromised in order to render the patterns of connectivity more comprehensible. An example of a similar process, employed at a much larger scale, is the evolution of the London tube map. Starting as a geographically precise cartographic representation (Fig. 3), it gradually evolved through schematic abstraction to a kind of topological diagram improving on the legibility of lines, stations and connections (Fig. 4). Comparing, the present familiar version of the tube map, with a contemporary

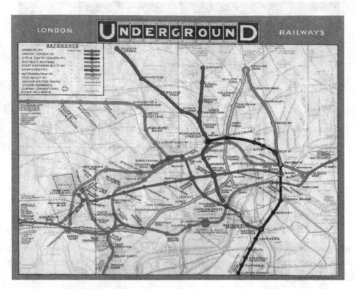

Fig. 3. Early cartographic representation of the London Tube

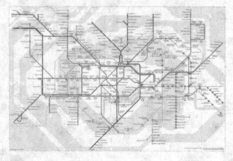

Fig. 4. Current London Tube Map. Notice the abstraction on detail and the precision in node (station) representation.

geographically precise depiction of the same underground network (Fig. 5), one can easily notice the large discrepancies of the former concerning accuracy of distances and shapes, especially in the periphery.

This resembles today's popular visualizations of smart-home networks, which employ a similar semi-decentralized diagram model. In this model connection nodes are grouped into several areas (entertainment, security, energy), then connected to the home controller. The segmentation of networks into areas creates a tree network diagram, where most connections of the same type have a bus structure, thus creating a hybrid map.However, contemporary home devices have the ability to create individual networks where other devices can connect to. In this way a connection diagram could include multiple networks that exchange information through a rhizomatic, or lattice structure, or a distributed network pattern, which is also the main type for visually representing highly complex networks such as ARPANET (1977) (Fig.6), or its later descendent the World-Wide-Web (Fig 7).

ARPANET LOGICAL MAP, MARCH 1977

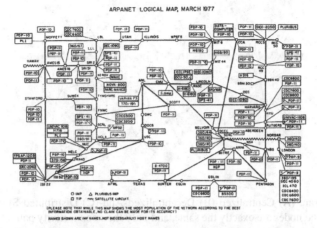

Fig. 6. ARPANET Logical Map, 1977, (http://commons.wikimedia.org/wiki/
File:Arpanet_logical_map,_march_1977.png)

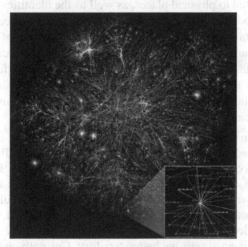

Fig. 7. Partial map (30%) of the Internet based on the January 15, 2005 data found on opte.org.
Nodes are IP addresses. Length of lines indicate delay. Lines are colour-coded according to
their corresponding RFC 1918 allocation. (http://en.wikipedia.org/wiki/File:
Internet_map_1024.jpg).

Complex visualizations of knowledge and networks, specifically, gradually
evolved together with our more intricate understanding of our world, from attempting
to depict "problems of simplicity", with a centralized model (A), to portraying "problems of disorganized complexity" with decentralized diagram models (B), and finally
today to explain "problems of organized complexity" employing distributed models
(C) [16, p.45] (Fig.8).

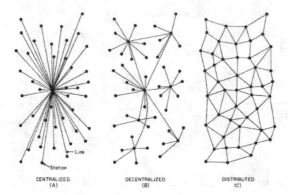

Fig. 8. Paul Baran, (A) Centralized-(B) Decentralized-And-(C) Distributed System, 1964. In those diagrams, the nodes are exactly the same, and only their connectivity pattern changes.

However, it seems that when referring specifically to the structure of home-network, which is closely related to physical places, as well as the identities of people, different types of network models may operate at different scales, or according to where the emphasis is at a certain time. We also anticipate that patterns of connectivity (from centralized to distributed) may differ according to time and occasion resulting in a hybrid network form. According to Lima [16, pp.80-81] the key functions of network visualizations are: a) to document, b) to clarify, c) to reveal, d) to expand, and e) to abstract. Projecting these functions to the environment of home and the visualizations of its networks, one can establish the following:

1. Documenting the trivialities of everyday or personal life is not a new thing. Art and the social sciences have attempted in the past to provide detailed accounts of everyday life of individuals, families and small social groups. However, the more widespread use of embedded or mobile sensing devices with the ability to be located, combined with personal data from social networks results in the accumulation of a vast amount of detailed information (big data), that some of them have never been recorded before. The documentation of this data, which refers to domestic behaviour is an almost uncharted territory. Currently available technologies do not support an accurate (<50cm) tracking of the location of a person or object in interior spaces. This should be improved in order to have accurately situated data of home-life.

2. Documentation of domestic-based big data, through visualizations of home-networks and other interrelations are an indispensable instrumental aid in order to make the complex structure of home intelligible and transparent to everyday people, whose lives are being depicted. Making the complexity of contemporary home visible is one step further to making home once again a core of order.

3. Home-network visualizations will eventually help us identify latent or subconsciously felt patterns concerning the developing of our identities and behaviours, as well as comparing them to similar patterns of other individuals, broader social groups, or globally. They can give us new insights on our everyday interactions,

making it possible for us to take informed decisions and adaptations to our life-styles, social relationships and living goals.

4. The more the complex picture of our home-life is brought to light and new intricate details and patterns emerge, the more we would be encouraged to delve into further exploration. At the same time, the ability of network visualizations to provide abstracted representations of casual life, help promote a reflective mode, and are a vehicle for imaginary exploration.

Lima further identifies fifteen different types of network representations, although new types might emerge[1]. Among those, the ones that appear to afford a more refined topological structure, therefore possibly more appropriate for home-networks visualizations, may be the Area Grouping, The Centralized Burst and Ring, Circular Ties, Organic Rhizome, Ramifications, Scaling Circles.

Independently from the graphic typology of the network representation, it is important to note that, depending on the scale and size of the representation, the depicted information should adjust, and the representation, itself, affords different methods of analysis. Therefore it is important to consider three fundamental views in line with a specific method of analysis: *macro view, relationship view* and *micro view* [16]. Macro view, offers an overview, where one can discern general patterns. Relationships view, offers a representation in an intermediate scale, where one can elaborate on the connectivity patterns and interrelations between individual nodes. Micro view, finally, offers a detailed view of specific entities.

Although the above typologies and guidelines seem logical for any kind of network visualization, we need to consider whether they apply to the visual representation of home-networks, specifically due to their highly individual nature, and the extreme personal engagement with the depicted content. It is possible, for example, that the emotional significance of certain elements of home may dictate their detailed depiction even in macro view modes. In any case, we think that a certain degree of personal engagement and informality is necessary in order to domesticate network representations for home-use.

Cartography gives us some basic clues on how to organize and design the visualization of complex networks. The projection, orientation, scale and graphic language are basic parameters. The appropriate use of each one may result in an effective layout out of the intended information.

Projection describes the method of mapping three-dimensional measurements onto a two-dimensional medium, in relation to the viewing position of the cartographer, which is mainly from above. This is very effective for providing an overview, and appears to match with the cognitive maps of people for their surroundings, matching with the macro view described by Lima. Even in representations of homes and interiors, the plan view is the most common and effective projection for explaining topographical interrelations between objects, that occupy floor space.

---

[1] These 15 types are: Arc Diagram, Area Grouping, Centralized Burst, Centralized Ring, Circled Globe, Circular Ties, Elliptical Implosion, Flow Chart, Organic Rhizome, Radian Convergence, Radial Implosion, Ramification, Scaling Circles, Segmented Radial Convergence, Sphere.

However, we found[2] that a commonly used projection for graphically providing an overview of simple home networks is the perspective or axonometric projection of the interior spaces, where the observer is still out of the depicted territory. Such, projections resolve problems of interrelating devices and nodes that are deployed three-dimensionally[3]. This type of representation does not solve all problems since overlapping and obscured parts, or densely packed three-dimensional information appearing as flattened could occur. Therefore, certain ways to convey "depth" in two or three-dimensional visual representations of home networks, would help the intuitive reading of complex and multi-layered spatial relationships. Such graphic tools might be decreasing focus, detail, and intensity.

Another issue concerning the projection of the map is **orientation**. Geographical maps are usually oriented towards magnetic north. In memory maps, the orientation is highly varied and seldom compass oriented. One hypothesis made by researchers studying home-range mapping by schoolchildren is that orientation tends, either in the direction of the most important element(s) in an individual's home range, or in the direction of the primary path leading away from home. It is also found that sketches of home plans usually place main entrance to the bottom or left of the page following the sequence of rooms from the entrance to the back of the house. From these two examples one can suggest that there is a certain natural directionality of home maps; the point of physical exit (from) or entry to the house is usually depicted closer to the map viewer's body or left hand. Instead, most network visualizations are indifferent to the observer's standpoint. Nevertheless, it is common practice to place the origin of graphs at the bottom-left corner. Other than that complex diagrams favor placing the origin point in a central position, and are usually unidirectional.

The **scale** of the map dictates largely the level of abstraction by which the territory or network structure and the information linked to it are represented. Smaller scale representations of places usually go hand in hand with greater abstraction of features and more general information, while larger representational scales allow greater detail and more information. Yet, in numerous cases, the scale and abstraction varies significantly in the same map, so as to give focus to a specific area. Usually this variation in scale and detail signifies a differentiation in perceived distance, familiarity and emotional significance. Thus, features and areas that are perceived or felt physically closer, or more familiar, or more significant to the author of the map, appear larger and with greater detail. In the opposite, large distances or features devoid of specific meaning are shortened, abstractly represented or omitted.

4   Conclusion

It is quite difficult to create a mental image of a pervasive home environment. Its complex structure, hidden data transfer and dynamic change over time makes it

---

[2] We arrived at this conclusion by examining many such representations, available online, which aim at being easily understood by a broad, non-expert audience (e.g.popular sites about home networks and smart homes, etc.).

[3] For instance, a surveillance camera at the ceiling would be falsely spatially related with a pressure sensor under the floor in a top view.

impossible for anyone to grasp all decisions and traffic throughout the home without a tool to visualize it. Contemporary network visualizations provide us with a set of possibilities for viewing specific parts and activities of the home, without the ability to integrate them into a single knowledge base. Nevertheless, experience from older and established mapping practices can give us valuable insights on how to deal with territorially related information, and cognitive mapping. This work has identified three parameters, referencing the level of detail that could be incorporated into mapping. These in conjunction with properties such as the projection, the orientation and the scaling of the map and its individual elements create a promising formula for identifying basic characteristics used to visualize a pervasive home environment. The hypothesis studied in this paper, needs to be supported by relevant field research and experimentation in the design and construction of such maps, engaging inhabitants and examining real scenarios. The scarce availability of domestic settings with a profound technological augmentation, such as the one envisioned by the ICT community for the near future, is a serious obstacle that needs to be considered, but should, push for imaginative methods to elicit useful findings making use of today's real situations.

References

1. Thackara, J.: In the Bubble: Designing in a complex world. MIT Press, Cambridge (2006)
2. Teige, K.: The Minimum Dwelling. MIT Press, Cambridge (2002)
3. Csikszentmihalyi, M., Rochberg-Halton, E.: The Meaning of Things: Domestic symbols and the self. Cambridge University Press, Cambridge (1981)
4. Susanka, S., Obolensky, K.: The Not So Big House: A blueprint for the way we really live. Taunton Press, Newtown (1998)
5. OECD, Families are Changing, Doing Better for Families (2011), http://www.oecd.org/els/soc/47701118.pdf (accessed January 31, 2014)
6. Fleura, B., Giana, E.M., Eric, A.J.: Liquid Relationship to Possessions. Journal of Consumer Research (October 2012)
7. Ioannidou, E.: The (Existenz-)Minimum Dwelling, PhD in Architecture, The Bartlett School of Architecture, London: UCL (2006)
8. Betsky, A., Adigard, E.: Architecture Must Burn: A manifesto for an architecture beyond building. Thames & Hudson, London (2000)
9. De Landa, M.: A New Philosophy of Society. Bloomsbury, London (2006)
10. Cooper Marcus, C.: House as a Mirror of Self: Exploring the deeper meaning of home. Conari Press (1995)
11. Brooker, G.: Modernity and Domesticity: Appliance House – A Machine for Living In? Manchester Metropolitan University (2006), http://www.ub.edu/gracmon/capapers/Brooker,%20Graeme.pdf
12. Papoulias, C.: "The Dispersed House", inside the exhibition catalogue "Big Big Brother: Architecture and Surveillance". In: Memos, F. (ed.), pp. 63–69. National Museum of Contemporary Art, Athens (2002)
13. Bauman, Z.: Liquid Modernity. Polity, Oxford (2000)

14. Lefas, P.: Dwelling and Architecture: From Heidegger to Koolhaas. Jovis, Berlin (2009)
15. Grivas, K.: Home as Archipelago: Charting the 'new domestic landscape'. In: Proceedings of Hybrid City II, Athens, Greece (2013)
16. Lima, M.: Visual Complexity: Mapping patterns of information. Princeton Architectural Press, New York (2011)

A Personalized Smart Living Room

The New Inter-relationship of Smart Space

Yu-Chun Huang[1] and Scottie Chih-Chieh Huang[2]

[1] College of Design, Tatung University, No.40, Sec. 3, Jhongshan N. Rd. Taipei 104, Taiwan
ych@ttu.edu.tw
[2] College of Architecture, Chung Hua University, 707 Sec.2, WuFu Rd., Hsinchu 300, Taiwan
scottie.c.c.huang@gmail.com

Abstract. Culture, society, and technology heavily influence architectural form, and basic architectural elements and functions evolve to suit users' needs. In the 20th century, with the development of computational technology, architecture underwent dramatic transformation. Human-computer interaction (HCI) has changed architectural space into a smart space, which provides new ways for humans to interact with their living spaces. However, most smart space cases limit their focus to computational technology such as system efficiency and underuse architectural elements of spaces to improve interfaces. Thus this research intends to integrate both architecture and HCI to create a "new inter-relationship system framework" of smart space. An applied scenario called the "Personalized Smart Living Room" showcases the new smart space system. Compared to preexisting smart spaces, which usually focused on a single user, this new system recognizes several different users and gives appropriate personal feedback (such as a personal message or photos) and environmental atmosphere adjustment (interactive wallpaper and personalized music), by monitoring the specific user's posture and personal smartphone.

Keywords: architecture element and function, human-computer interaction, smart space, inter-relationship.

1   Introduction

Human-computer interaction (HCI) has greatly influenced the interface between people and their living spaces. For instance, a device called "Lumitouch" uses sensors and wireless technology to enhance the basic picture frame into an emotional communication channel for long distance families or couples [1]. Another system called the "Smart Floor System" has transformed a traditional, non-interactive floor into a multi-functional floor that modulates the ambient environment by sensing a user's steps [2][3][4]. "AmbientROOM" used augmented reality technology to transform the traditional office into a smart office. In an example that incorporates electronic data, Ishii et al. [5] represented digital information (e.g. the amount of email, internet speed and new information on a note board) onto the physical environment. These cases illustrate that HCI-embedded smart spaces can increase the functionality of the

N. Streitz and P. Markopoulos (Eds.): DAPI 2014, LNCS 8530, pp. 37–47, 2014.

objects and physical features in a room. Architecture uses structural elements such as ceilings, walls, and doors to provide a space for functions like relaxation, work, and entertaiment. Thus, in the digital age, the relationship between structural elements and a space's functionality must be very different from that of traditional, static architecture. With the influence of HCI technology, what is the new inter-relationship between structural elements and their functions in smart spaces?

Researchers have largely approached developing smart spaces by focusing on the direct link between human and computer (such as an intuitive interface). In HCI, the computer directly monitors a user's physical gestures, voice, or brainwaves and uses this information to automate previously analog interfaces such as using a remote controller or turning on a light switch [1][6][7][8][9]. They then work to improve a system's computational efficiency and alternative interactions such as creating a more adaptive ambient environment for users [10][7][8][11][12][13]. However studying smart space through this limited view is not enough, and adding new design features to products without caring about the impact of the peripheral environment or even the related space layout does not optimize the functionality and ease of use of a smart space.

2   Problem and Objective

As computers have become more common and powerful, technology and "ubiquitous computing" [14] have incorporated into people's lives, showing up in such places as offices, homes, and restaurants. Mitchell [15] mentioned as our bodies morph into cyborgs, the buildings are also transforming. Increasingly, telecommunication systems replace physical environment, and the solvent of digital information (invisible elements) decomposes traditional building types. Architecturally, these digital elements can be transferred, grabbed or represented onto different physical features of a room. Smart space consists of physical elements (structures such as walls and ceilings and furniture) and virtual elements (digital information that can be used to create an interactive space). However, few researchers focus on how architecture contributes to smart space. Hence the challenge of this research is to clarify the new inter-relationship between physical and digital elements in smart space.

The goal of this research is to create a new inter-relationship smart space system integrating both architectural and HCI aspects, and then implement a system prototype—"Personalized Smart Living Room" based on the new system framework in a real space. This system explores a way to arrange and represent digital elements (such as smartphone messages, music, and photos) between multiple users and their living environment, especially in a living room.

3   Methodology and Steps

The methods of this research can be divided into four steps:

In the first step, two case studies establish the new inter-relationship system framework based on both architecture and HCI.

The second step applies a scenario to the system prototype: Based on the previous system framework, we apply a scenario—"Personalized Smart Living Room" to test the system in a real living room. The concept of the scenario can be separated into three parts: user 'a' mode (Saori), user 'b' mode (Scottie) and user 'a&b' mode (multiple users).

The third step implements the system: The "Personalized Smart Living Room" is composed of two main components. First, physical elements include walls, a sofa, a table and, smartphones; Second, virtual elements include interactive wallpaper, personalized digital messages, photos and music.

Table 1. System components

Components	Sub-components (elements)
Physical Elements	Wall
	Sofa
	Table
	Smartphone
Virtual Elements	Interactive wallpaper
	Personalized message
	Personalized photos
	Personalized music

4   Results

4.1   New Inter-relationship System Framework Establishment

In order to provide a new inter-relationship system framework, two smart spaces were used as case studies based on their architecture and HCI:

Case 1: BCI studio [16]
To enable people to interact with a space more naturally, the space senses the mood of the occupant and responds appropriately by adjusting the environment. BCI studio proposes a brain-computer interface (BCI) system. This smart space enables the user to work in a more energized way via the BCI system. When the space "perceives" (by monitoring the user's brainwaves) that someone is getting sleepy, it will take appropriate action, such as providing specific background music or adjusting the lighting and temperature in the room as subliminal reminders to the user in order to make him/her stay alert and productive.

Case 2: Time Home Pub [17]
To facilitate more intuitive use of space, "Time Home Pub" senses changing events and activities by adjusting the background lighting pattern to provide a suitable ambience. The "Time Home Pub" not only adjusts the environment according to human activities, but also solidifies the connection between human feelings and memories.

This case used the whiskey glass as an atmospheric control switch in a real living room. This system consists of three main devices: an interactive table, the whiskey glass, and Liveframe.

Architecture View of Smart Space. Over time, classical architectural elements such as walls, columns, and floors have exceeded their original use by combining structural and ornamental functions into one element. This is exemplified in the modernist architecture of the early of 20th century [18]. At the end of the 20th century, with the development of human-computer interaction (HCI), a new "floating" element appeared in the interior space of buildings — the "digital element". This kind of element enhances the connection between physical elements in a space (Figure 1). The HCI-embedded physical elements are communication interfaces that can display/output or record/input digital elements (Figure 1). Therefore from an architectural view of smart space, two different elements exist, "digital elements" and "transformed physical elements". Digital elements can freely navigate between physical elements, buildings, or even the cities, but physical elements are restricted to edifices.

Traditional structural elements + new digital elements
Compared to the traditional studio, BCI embedded physical space not only provides a working space for users but also automatically perceives their needs and gives appropriate feedback by monitoring brainwaves. In Time Home Pub, a HCI embedded wall not only preserves its original functions of 'support', but it can also adjust the environment according to a user's activities.

Transformed physical elements + new digital elements
In smart space, some HCI embedded physical elements (such as furniture or appliances) transform their original functions into a dual channel interface. These transformed physical elements are able to input/output to digital elements, creating a bridge between two previously disconnected features of a room. For example, in Time Home Pub, by applying HCI, the tea table not only preserves its original appearance and function but also communicates with a whiskey glass and Liveframe. This augmented table can record friends' time-marks, track whiskey glasses with tracking marks, adjust music patterns responding to bar mode, and make a perfect connection with old photos from Liveframe.

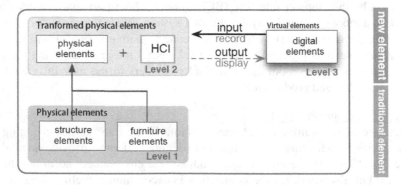

Fig. 1. Architecture view of smart space

HCI View of Smart Space. The HCI view of smart space focuses on the relationship between a user and objects in a physical space. In traditional architecture (Figure 2), a user can directly interact with objects such as the stove, TV, or a pen . However the object cannot respond to the user with feedback of any kind. On the contrary, in the smart space (e.g. Case 2), the user can connect with other elements such as animated wallpaper, a whiskey glass and Liveframe through the new interface – an interactive table. Also, the smart space system can appropriately give multiple types of feedbacks to its users. In Figure 2, we can clearly understand the interaction loop between the user and space based on the HCI view.

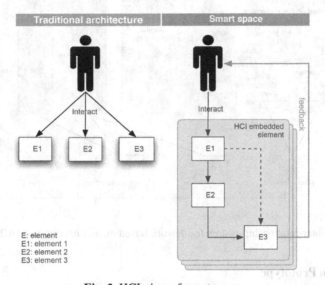

Fig. 2. HCI view of smart space

New System Framework Establishment. The new inter-relationship system framework integrating both architecture and HCI is shown in Figure 3 (from the bottom to top): Different types of physical space (e.g. living room, kitchen or bedroom) are constructed of different elements. The HCI-affected "physical elements" become "transformed elements" which are able to output/display and input/record "virtual elements". In other words, the virtual elements can be transferred, or navigate, between physical elements. Also the space provides new functionality to satisfy users' needs. This new relationship between user and space is achieved by monitoring the user's brainwaves or behavior. The space can observe the user's intention and physical status and adjust itself to adapt to the user's needs. Figure 3 clearly demonstrates the new inter-relationship based on both architecture and HCI view of smart space, and the detail relationship between 'human', 'space' and 'elements (physical elements and digital elements)' (figure 3).

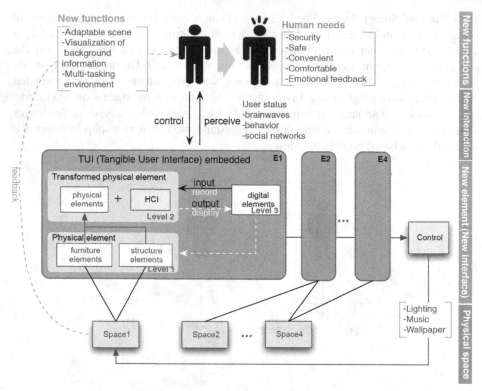

Fig. 3. New inter-relationship system framework based on architecture and HCI viewpoint

4.2   System Prototype

Based on our new framework, we tested the new system in a physical living room. With so much electronic information everywhere, "digital elements" (such as digital messages, photos or music) will become as important as physical elements in smart space. Therefore the smart space has to take into account how digital elements are presented and arranged onto physical elements, and the environment must recognize whether users are in a personal or public space by using smartphones to identify surrounding people as friends/family or strangers. The system can then appropriately and comfortably transfer personal information such as notifications or messages via different interfaces such as computers, cellphones, walls, or tables in a location dependent manner. Thus, the system can rearrange digital elements and find a comfortable way to present information in different physical elements.

Scenario Demonstration. Our new system framework, the"*Personalized Smart Living Room*" executed three scenarios: Scenario 1) user Saori; Scenario 2) user Scottie; Scenario 3) multiple users.

Scenario 1: User Saori
After work, Saori comes home and lies down on the sofa. The system immediately detects that Saori is in the space. Since the sensors of the sofa recognize that Saori is now tired, the room's interactive wallpaper displays Pop Art, and the room plays Saori's favorite music from her smartphone to help her relax. Since Saori is browsing through photos she has taken with her cell phone, the table transforms into a large photo frame and displays a slide show of photos to provide more comfortable feedback.

Scenario 2: User Scottie
Scottie comes home and usually sits down on the left side of the sofa. The system immediately perceives that Scottie is home. The wallpaper responds to his posture by presenting an animated pattern on the wall. Meanwhile, the room plays Scottie's favorite music from his smartphone. Suddenly, he notices that there is an important unread message on the table—"Meeting is changed to 9 am". After 10 minutes, he feels tired. He stands up from the sofa, and the environment changes back to normal living room.

Scenario 3: Multiple users
When Saori and Scottie come back home together, the system immediately recognizes that there are two people in the living room. In order to reflect the joyful and harmonic atmosphere, the environment changes to its bar mode. Spots on the wallpaper change color according to the users' movements, and the space plays Jazz music.

Scenario 1: Saori   Scenario 2: Scottie   Scenario 3: multiple users

Fig. 4. Scenario demonstration: scenario 1) The space presented user Saori's the pictures she took today; scenario 2) The space presented Scottie's important message through the tea table; scenario 3) In order to reflect multiple users, the space changed into bar mode

Scenario Applied System Framework. In order to evaluate the new system framework, the "Personalized Smart Living Room" was applied to the existing system framework (Figure 6). Through this prototype, we can clearly understand how different users interact with the elements in the space and the relationship between physical elements, transformed physical elements, and digital elements. For instance, the space can wirelessly grab users' personal information (personal photos, messages, and music) from their smartphones, and the table will then display personalized information according to different users' habits. Furthermore, this kind of system framework (Figure 6) can illustrate the new functions the smart space provides and how it gives appropriate feedback by changing the atmosphere (e.g. ambient music and interactive wallpaper). The users can easily and comfortably read their personal information any-where around the physical surface depending on their locations (private or public space) instead of being limited to reading messages from their smartphones.

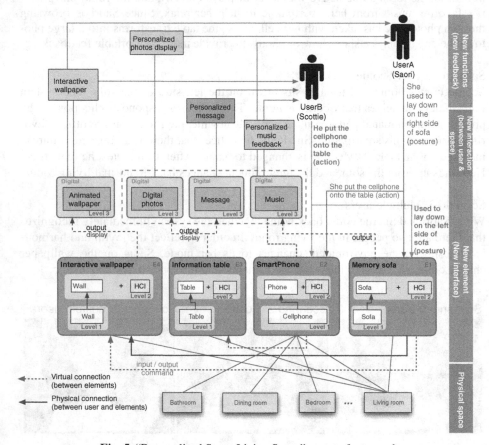

Fig. 5. "Personalized Smart Living Space" system framework

4.3   System Implementation

The system hardware was controlled by two computers (PC1 and PC2) and can be separated into three parts: personalized ambient music, interactive wallpaper and personalized information table display. Personalized ambient music is controlled by a force sensor resister (FSR) embedded in the living room's sofa. This sensor recognizes a user's pose and weight and sends this data to PC1 through an Arduino controller board to evaluate the user's status.   PC1 will then process this information and send commands to play the user's favorite music (choosing from their personal smart phone) around the space. The interactive wallpaper (pop style) was generated by processing information from real-time video (by webcam) and previous weight values (from FSR). For personalized information display, lighting sensors (photocell) embedded in the system's tea table can recognize if there is a smartphone on the table and then send a signal to PC2 to evaluate results through the Arduino board. The processing from PC2 projects personal information (smartphone: Line, message or photos) onto the table in a user-specific manner.

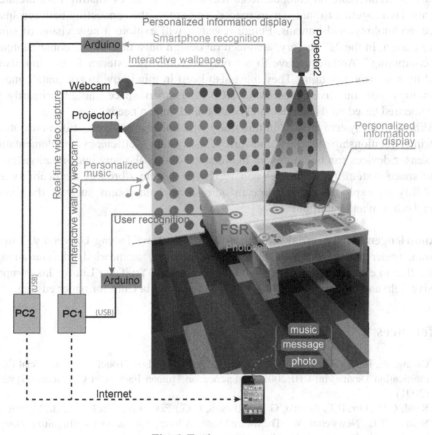

Fig. 6. Environment setup

5   Concluding Remarks

The profound difference between a traditional space and a smart space is in HCI, which enhances the functional and structural elements of architecture. However, most smart space cases have overly focused on computational technology such as system efficiency. In order to create a "new inter-relationship system framework" of smart space, this research used two case studies to address smart space from both architecture and HCI perspectives. From the architecture perspective, adding scenarios to the new system framework allow us to observe of the composition of elements in a space (Figure 3) and the connections between different layers of elements. From the HCI aspect, we can understand how users interact with the environment and how the space provides feedback (e.g. music, images, and notifications).

This new inter-relationship system framework also dually contributes to both the architect and HCI researcher. It can help elucidate the evolution of building technology and the building morphing from the exterior and the layout changing from the interior if I only stand from architecture view to smart space. It is difficult to know the impact of architecture on computational technology. Thus, evaluating both architecture and HCI together to study smart spaces can explore the connection between smart space, technology, and humans. Future research will explore a new vision of smart space design. In the 21st century, architectural design must take into account "ubiquitous computing". Architects have to not only consider the exterior forms, but also a building's interior functions. They must also keep in mind how to adequately merge technology into our lives. Therefore, HCI in a smart space should primarily be implemented based on its architectural context and human needs.

Although the system created in this study was only a prototype, it demonstrates a new inter-relationship system framework. This system's efficiency, implementation and sensor devices can be improved. In order to solidify the new inter-relationship of smart space system, future studies will verify the system's broader applicability and feasibility by exploring smart space in other household rooms such as the dining room, bedroom and bathroom.

Acknowledgement. Financial support of this research by Tatung University, Taipei, Taiwan, under the grant B101-DD03-078 is gratefully acknowledged. The authors would like to express our sincere gratitude to Professor Yu-Tung Liu for his comprehensive help and guidance and Chun-Chieh Lin and Sonia Chin for paper editing.

References

1. Chang, A., Resner, B., Koerner, B., Wang, X., Ishii, H.: LumiTouch: An Emotional Communication Device. In: CHI 2001 Conference on Human Factors in Computing Systems (2001)
2. Kidd, C.D., Orr, R.J., Abowd, G.D., Atkeson, C.G., Essa, I.A., MacIntyre, B., Mynatt, E., Starner, T.E., Newstetter, W.: The aware home: A living laboratory for ubiquitous computing research. Cooperative Buildings, 1991–1998 (1999)
3. Orr, R.J., Abowd, G.D.: The Smart Floor: A Mechanism for Natural User Identification and Tracking. In: Proceedings of the 2000 Conference on Human Factors in Computing Systems (CHI 2000), April 1-6. The Hague, Netherlands (2000)
4. Kientz, J.A., Patel, S.N., Jones, B., Price, E., Mynatt, E.D., Abowd, G.D.: The Georgia Tech aware home. In: The Proceeding of CHI 2008 (2008)
5. Ishii, H., Wisneski, C., Brave, S., Dahley, A., Gorbet, M., Ullmer, B., Yarin, P.: AmbientROOM: Integrating ambient media with architectural space. In: CHI 1998 Conference Summary on Human Factors in Computing Systems, Los Angeles, California, United States, April 18-23, pp. 173–174. ACM, New York (1998)
6. Crabtree, A., Hemmings, T., Rodden, T.: The social construction of displays. In: O'Hara, K., et al. (eds.) Public and Situated Displays: Social and Interactional Aspects of Shared Display Technologies, pp. 170–190. Kluwer, The Netherlands (2003)
7. Ruyter, B.D. (ed.): 365 Days Ambient Intelligent in Home. Philips Research. Royal Philips Electronics (2003)

8. Ruyter, B.D., Aarts, E.: Ambient intelligence: visualizing the future. In: AVI 2004: Proceedings of the Working Conference on Advanced Visual Interfaces, pp. 203–208 (2004)
9. Kim, S.H., Chung, A., OK, J.H., Myung, I.S., Kang, H.J., Woo, J.K., Kim, M.J.: Communication enhancer—appliances for better communication in a family. The Journal of Personal Ubiquitous Computing 2004(8), 221–226 (2004)
10. Raskar, R., Welch, G., Cutts, M., Lake, A., Stesin, L., Fuchs, H.: The office of the future: A unified approach to image-based modeling and spatiallyimmersive displays. In: Proceedings of SIGGRAPH 1998. ACM Press (1998)
11. Lee, C.H.J., Bonanni, L., Espinosa, J.H., Lieberman, H., Selker, T.: Augmenting kitchen appliances with a shared context using knowledge about daily events. In: The Proceedings of the 11th International Conference on Intelligent User Interfaces, pp. 348–350 (2006)
12. Jeng, T.S.: Sentient Buildings that Sense, Think, and Adapt. NCKU BANYAN Research Express 2(10) (2008)
13. Takeuchi, Y.: Weightless walls and the future office. In: CHI 2010: Writing in the Real World, Proceedings of the 28th International Conference on Human Factors in Computing Systems, pp. 619–628 (2010)
14. Weiser, M., Brown, J.S.: The Coming Age of Calm Technology (1996),
    http://www.ubiq.com/hypertext/weiser/acmfuture2endnote.htm;
    Revised version of: Weiser, M., Brown, J.S.: Designing Calm Technology. PowerGrid Journal 1(01) (July 1996), http://powergrid.electriciti.com/1.01
15. Mitchell, W.J.: City of Bits: Space, Place, and the Infobahn. The MIT Press (August 1, 1996)
16. Huang, Y.C.: A Space Make You Lively: A Brain-Computer Interface Approach to Smart Space. In: The Proceedings of the 11th International Conference on Computer Aided Architectural Design Research in Asia (CAADRIA 2006), Kumamoto, Japan, pp. 303–312 (2006)
17. Huang, Y.C., Wu, K.Y., Liu, Y.T.: Future home design: An emotional communication channel approach to Smart Space. Personal and Ubiquitous Computing 17(6), 1281–1293 (2013)
18. Summerson, J.: The Classic Language of Architecture. MIT Press, Cambridge (1996)

Digitally Enhanced Utensils:
Designing Dynamic Gustation

Yui Kita[1] and Jun Rekimoto[1,2]

[1] Graduate School of Interdisciplinary Information Studies,
The University of Tokyo, 7-3-1 Hongo, Bunkyo, Tokyo Japan
[2] Sony Computer Science Laboratories, 3-14-13 Higashigotanda, Shinagawa, Tokyo, Japan
yuikita21@gmail.com, rekimoto@acm.org

Abstract. While modern cuisine uses various materials such as powder, oil and chemical materials, time-sensitive materials such as bubbles or temperature are still not considered as part of the design of cuisine, due to their temporal nature. Although these time-sensitive gustation play an important role in cuisine, it is difficult to serve them with human hands and static utensils. In this paper, we will introduce sensing and actuation mechanisms to maintain and enhance time-sensitive gustation. We will explore the design space of digitally enhanced utensils through three research prototypes.

Keywords: food, utensil, cutlery, kitchen, cooking, cuisine, dining, wet materials.

1 Introduction

The history of cuisine is also the history of the discovery of tools and technology. For example, fire enables humans to make raw foods edible, and yeast is essential for breads or fermented food. Novel tools of cuisine were also developed as the industry has been grown. Motors contribute to affordable mousse or whipped cream, and stainless steel is necessary for modern tools in cuisine. In this sense, the development of cuisine emerged from the development of technology. On the other hand, the history of cuisine is also based on heuristic process, and scientific knowledge on cuisine's methods or reasons for recipes has not been explored. Absence of scientific viewpoint and technology for metrology is one of the reasons of this. In fact, French cuisine had been focusing on only the ingredients for a long time before chefs began to indicate the amount of ingredients.

Molecular Gastronomy

Recently, science has begun to explore these little-understood parts of cuisine [17]. This field, called molecular gastronomy [9][10], investigates the physical and chemical transformations that ingredients undergo while cooking. Knowledge based on this investigation not only unveils the cooking process, but also contributes new cooking methods. With the development of a scientific point of view on cooking, chefs began to use digitally augmented cuisine methods. One example is sous-vide. Sous-vide is a

N. Streitz and P. Markopoulos (Eds.): DAPI 2014, LNCS 8530, pp. 48–57, 2014.

cooking method for heating foods with accurate heat management. It uses thermostat chambers to heat ingredients evenly [17]. For example, when cooking meat with sous-vide, by heating meat in oil heated 70 Celsius, the lowest pasteurization temperature, chefs can cook the meat rarer than possible with other cooking methods. As another example, when chefs extract the flavor from herbs, they must be careful of the time and temperature, because one degree or one second of error produces bitterness Thus, chefs can control physical parameters to maximize the quality of the food in the kitchen.

Food in Dining
However, the quality of foods is out of the chef's control when they are served from kitchen to the diner (Fig 1). As time passes, the temperature or taste changes, or in-gredients are mixed when the guest eats them, and the food changes into something which is far from what the chef intended. This means that foods are not as designed when they are on the table, even though the chef prepares them carefully in the kitch-en. The quality of dishes decreases as time passes. For example, protein and oils in meat get hard and it loses its juicy flavor as the steam escapes. Clam soup or sherbet also loses its quality because of temperature changes. Some methods use heated uten-sils to maintain the quality of food. For example, while the temperature of steak starts to get lower when it is served, by serving it on a heated iron plate, chefs can prevent the decrease of temperature to some extent. Another example is using cooled glasses to prevent cold drinks from lose their quality as the temperature rises.

However, heated iron plate is not effective when it is not hot is not enough, and the foods are overcooked when the temperature is too high. Cooled utensils have same problem. The way of eating is also another problem that changes the taste of food which chefs cannot control. This means that the act of eating is not the part of the design of cuisine, even though careful and precise design is possible in the kitchen.

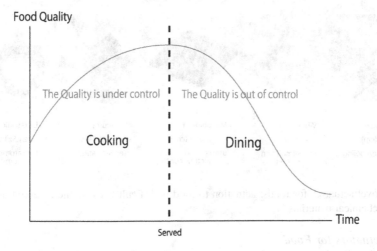

Fig. 1. Food quality after serving dishes: while the food quality is carefully and precisely con-trolled in kitchen, they are losing quality after serving and out of the control while dining

Thus, while dining, the quality of food and taste is difficult to maintain, and often the food is far from what chef has designed in the kitchen. This paper introduces digitally enhanced utensils that actuate ingredients to make the consumption of foods part of their design. We introduce three prototypes and discuss how sensing and actuation mechanisms can contribute to cuisine design.

2   Related Work

HCI and Food

Dinning Presenter [14] is a system that augments dining experience. This system shows images or changes the color of food. SpotLight [1] is a system implemented in a desk light to enhance the quality of food from its visual and sound aspect. These systems that use projector in dining context is effective only on its visuals and not on the gustation. One of the advantages of these systems is that they can be implemented in distant place by using roofs or lighting devices that naturally exist around the normal dining. On the other hand, distant from chemical materials of foods, they are not useful for augmentation of the gustation itself.

Some studies leverages physiological aspects of gustation. The gustation is composed by multiple senses such as visuals, sounds or texture. MetaCookie [12] modifies the gustation of cookie by augmenting its visuals using HMD and providing scent using an olfactory display. Another system changes the texture of food by providing the chewing sound when the user is eating food of another texture [4]. These systems can change the gustation of food, but they require large-scale devices that are often difficult to be accepted in the current dining setup.

Thus, existing studies for augmenting gustation has two divided research approach: one is fine for the dining context with less effects, and the other uses large scale devices with effective augmentation on the gustation.

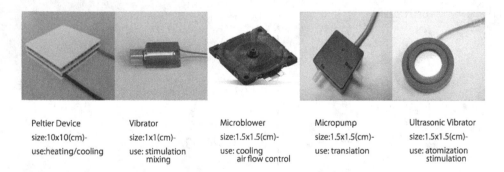

Peltier Device	Vibrator	Microblower	Micropump	Ultrasonic Vibrator
size:10x10(cm)-	size:1x1(cm)-	size:1.5x1.5(cm)-	size:1.5x1.5(cm)-	size:1.5x1.5(cm)-
use:heating/cooling	use: stimulation mixing	use: cooling air flow control	use: translation	use: atomization stimulation

Fig. 2. Novel actuators for foods: actuation to food is difficult because the essential of food is based on chemical materials

Novel Actuators for Food

One of the disadvantages of existing research products for food augmentation is that they requires large scale devices to actuate food itself including the chemical materials in the ingredients. To overcome this difficulty and design devices that effectively augment food with minimum complexity and smaller system, we surveyed actuators available for food augmentation. In this section, we explore the actuators that can effect to chemical materials or structures of food (Fig 2).

Peltier device can create a heat flux that is useful for cooling or heating materials attached on the device. It requires heat sink because it does not create heat itself but move heat from one part to the other part.

Vibrator is one of the smallest devices that can effects on foods. The taste changes not only by its temperature but also by mixing ingredients.

Microblower is useful when quiet and small blow is required. This device is used as one kind of fans in a small space. Using this device, chefs can control the flow of aroma or dry and cool the food.

Pumps are also effective to change the food's situation. They are not only available for moving ingredients, but also create a dynamic gustation changes while eating.

Ultrasonic vibrator can mix ingredients as the normal vibrators. In addition, it is effective for chemical changes without sound, in some cases. For example, when using ultrasonic vibrators for liquid materials, it can atomize the liquid, in other words turns liquid into mist. This is useful to change gustation without large-scale devices.

We designed three prototypes based on this survey, considering its size, effects on food and its cost. Actuators used in the prototypes are smaller than the quarter size of a normal dish for one guest, effect directly on the chemical materials and cost lower than one normal dish.

3   Research Prototypes

3.1   Heat

Temperature is one of the most important elements that create the gustation of food. Heating food is effective to make rising aroma and soft texture of foods especially they contain fat. HEAT is our first prototype designed to maintain the temperature of the food. For example, it maintains the temperature of meat just lower than its melting point, serving soft putty.

Mechanism
Heat consists of Peltier device, thermo sensor, and microcontroller under a stainless plate. The Peltier device heats the plate when the temperature of plate gets lower than the setting temperature. The sensors and switches of Peltier device are contoled by the microcontroller, and it also records the temperature changes while eating. The Peltier device can not only heat, but also cool the plate. The amount of the device is dependent on the plate, so the system can provide heated food and cooled heat on the same plate maintaining each temperature.

Evaluation
To confirm the effectiveness of HEAT, we conducted a study. In this study, we used cooked pork and used HEAT to maintain the temperature of pork. We measured the

temperature of pork with and without the device. In both measurements, we set the temperature of the air around the pork (room's temperature) and other conditions that may effect to the result. The desired temperature is 30 Celsius, and the temperature of the room is 25 Celsius. We repeated the measurement for five times.

The graph (Fig 3. (d)) shows the average of the results. It shows the pork on HEAT keeps around the 30 Celsius that is the desired temperature, while the pork without the system gets 25 Celsius in 10 minutes. The over shoot was with in 3 Celsius.

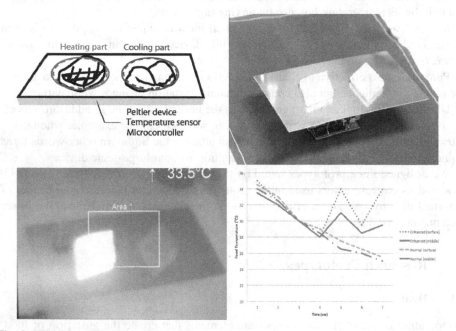

Fig. 3. HEAT: a) HEAT can provide heating and cooling part on one plate. b) Appearance of the device. c) Thermal image of HEAT. d) Evaluation of heat transition.

3.2   Pafuma

Stimulation by vibration
While bubbles in Champagne carries its aroma [6], 80% of them are disappearing to the air. PAFUMA serves bubbles before they are lost while we are just holding the glass. PAFUAM with vibrator stimulate the beverage and enhance the aroma of champagne. It stimulates the beverage just before the guest approaches to the glass when drinking.

Transformation by atomization
Aroma emerges from the surface of liquid material. PAFUMA with atomization device actuate the beverage and transforms it into moist and strengthen the aroma. It uses ultrasonic vibrator to atomize the liquid when the guest approaches to the glass when drinking.

Mechanism

A photo reflector was provided on the edge of the glass works as a proximity sensor. As the guest drinks the beverage and approaches the sensor, it detects the drink action and turns on the vibration or atomization. The time and power of actuator are programmed in the microcontroller in advance.

Evaluation

We conducted a study to investigate the effect of atomization device. In this investigation wine was used as the example of beverage. We used wine because it has strong and complex aroma. Complex aroma is useful to investigate detailed effects on the aroma.

We approximated the flow of aroma to the alcohol because the airflow is the strongest factor for each material. We used TGS2450 [8] as the sensor to investigate the density of the aroma. This sensor detects several gases including alcohol. We measured the density of alcohol in the air while user drinks 100ml wine using the sensor attached on the edge of a wine glass. We measured the density with and without the device. The sensor on the edge is located where the user's nose approaches when drinking wine to investigate the air the guest actually smells.

The figure (Fig 4. (e)) shows the result. It shows the density of alcohol has been enhanced when with the device. The waves seen in the graph is because of the airflow around the glass.

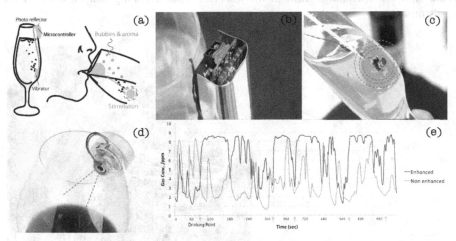

Fig. 4. PAFUMA: (a) PAFUMA stimulate/atomize liquid in the glass and enhance the aroma when drinking. (b) Approximate sensor and microcontroller. (c) A vibrator attached with magnet (d) Atomization device with ultrasonic vibrator. (e) Evaluation result.

3.3   Midas Spoon

In French cuisine, course is a normal way of serving dishes. The course can design the order of the gustation by limiting the edible foods for guest. It usually serves appetizer first, and desert last to provide satiety.

This is a technique of restaurant to design the gustation while dining invented by Escoffier, a French chef. Before the invention of course, appetizer and desert had been provided at the same time, and the dining was chaos of gustation. However, even with this technique, chefs cannot design the gustation changes on one dish. The order, amount and the changes of gustation are dependent on the gust.

MIDAS SPOON is an augmented spoon to control the changes of gustation while cooking. It changes the taste of food by adding seasoning while eating by pumping flavored sources for each bite.

Mechanism
The system consists of seasoning pumps, nozzles from pumps and shooting needle to shot the seasonings. The needle is also a touching sensor and shots seasonings as it detects the eating gestures. The types and amount of seasonings are programmed in advance and the system changes them referring the eating process detected by a weight sensor provided under the dish. GUI to program the timing and amount of seasonings are provided for chefs. The GUI consists of icons that represent the seasonings, and a programming field which consist eating process in the horizontal axis and the amount of the seasonings in the vertical axis. Chefs can program the types and the amount of seasoning by putting icons on the field. The program can be installed in the microcontroller. The microcontroller actuate the seasoning pumps according to the eating sensor and the eating process. As the microcontroller actuate the pump, the needle shot the seasonings through the nozzles. The seasoning can be done in the guest's mouse.

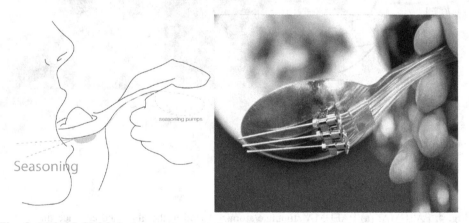

Fig. 5. MIDAS SPOON changes the gustation while eating by shooting seasoning when the guest eat food and touch the needles

4   User Study

To confirm the effect of each device on the gustation, we conducted user studies for each device. The user study has two parts: one is to investigate if guests prefer foods enhanced with the device for HEAT and PAFUMA, and the other is to investigate the detailed changes by atomization of food for PAFUMA. For the first part, 3 males and 2 females were recruited. No professional for food (e.g. sommelier) was included. Participants were asked to eat lunch 3 hours before the user study to eliminate the effect of satiety. They were encouraged to be relaxed to eliminate the effect of the metal condition.

The user study for HEAT is to investigate the effect of the gustation changes when the food is heated from the bottom by the Peltier device. Participants were asked to eat two pieces of pancake. Temperature of one piece was maintained 30 Celsius, and other was provided without the temperature management (as served naturally on the plate). We asked participants to comment on the device as an eating utensil, and asked to eat and compare the taste, then decide more preferable one. The order of eating two pancakes was randomized for each participant to eliminate the effect of after tastes.

The appearance of PAFUMA is more complex and thus unnatural compared with ordinal eating utensils or HEAT. So we tried to investigate the effect of the visual aspect of the device. The hearing process of user study is same as HEAT, although we encouraged participants to comment on the visual aspect of the device.

The study of PAFUMA has two parts because PAFUMA has two different actuations: vibration and atomization. For vibration, participants were asked to compare the taste of the aroma with and without the device, and for atomization, more detailed changes of aroma (including how it changed) was investigated.

To evaluate the stimulation, participants were asked to compare the taste of champagne with and without the vibration, and decide more preferable one. The order in the comparison was randomized for each participant. To evaluate the atomization, participants were asked to drink wine with and without the device and compare the taste, and decide which is more preferable. In addition to the evaluation, we investigated detailed aroma changes by the device. We used LIEDEL's evaluation sheet and asked participants to evaluate 5 elements that creates the complex aroma of wine in the range from 1 to 9. For comparison of evaluation of 5 elements, we prepared normal wine and decantaged (enriched by mixing air) wine in addition to the atomized wine. Participants were asked to compare the three wines with blind and fill the evaluation sheet.

Result

The result shows that both of the devices have certain effect on the gustation of food. On HEAT, the result shows significant effect and 4 in 5 participants preferred the piece with temperature was managed with the device. Visual aspect was also confirmed to be acceptable. All participants did not feel uncomfortable or it is unnatural as an eating utensil. Some participants were not even aware of the device under the plate although the height of the device is much higher than the ordinal eating utensils.

On PAFUMA, as for vibration, 4 in 5 participants preferred the champagne with the device. As for atomization, while all participants felt that the aroma was strengthened with the device, some participants commented that the aroma smelled different. In other words, the aroma was not simply strengthened by atomization but some particular parts of the aroma were enhanced.

According to the comments by participants, the large-scale devices can discomfort the user even with the size of the prototype. This is because the current ordinal utensils are so sophisticated in its visual aspects and most of them are simple on the contrary that the prototypes that include microcontroller or sensing mechanisms are not.

In HEAT, which consists all complex mechanism under one simple stainless plate, has been accepted naturally for the participants. In this sense, PAFUMA can be improved in the visual aspect, by implementing the device in the bottom of the glass.

On the other hand, MIDAS SPOON which is a directory digitally enhanced eating utensil, requires materials or shapes which is usually not used in the dining and makes participants uncomfortable. This is because the texture of surface is different from the eating utensils used in the ordinal dining. Surface covering with another material can be help to overcome this problem.

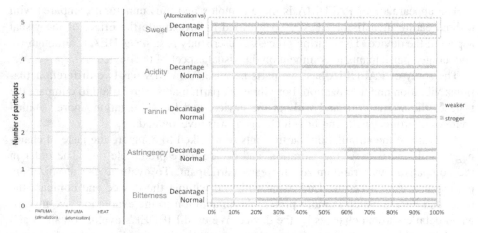

Fig. 6. Result of the user study. Over half participants preferred food supported with each device (left). We investigated detailed response to PAFUMA of atomization (right). The result shows sweet and bitterness gets stronger with atomization.

5   Discussion

Recent science reviles the relationships between the shapes or materials of utensils that effects the gustation of food. In the study, scientists found that the taste of foods differs when participants eat with different shape of spoon. They also investigated the effects of colors of eating utensils. Some eating utensils are carefully designed so that the shape of them maximizes the food quality. Glasses for wine, for example, are designed for the type of wine. In this case, for some type of wine, the glasses are designed so that it maintains the aroma in the body of glass. Glasses that maintains aroma in the body are developed for some types.

However, the design is still heuristic, and the viewpoint of metrology has not been provided as in the industrial design (e.g. automobile). In this sense, it is possible to introduce the viewpoint of metrology by investigating the food or gustation changes that differs in the shape of eating utensils. Simulation and sensing techniques are useful to design the effective shape of eating utensils. In this case, the computation works the background of the design of eating utensils thus the results consists only with the materials that are used in the ordinary dining.

6   Conclusion

Three prototypes are introduced and evaluated as the digitally enhanced utensils. The evaluation proved actuations for foods are effective to augment quality of food, although the visual complexity affects negatively on the gustation. We discussed the possibility of computation, sensing and actuation mechanisms on designing eating utensils to enrich food.

References

1. Kita, Y., Rekimoto, J.: Spot-Light: Multimodal Projection Mapping on Food. In: Stephanidis, C. (ed.) HCII 2013, Part II. CCIS, vol. 374, pp. 652–655. Springer, Heidelberg (2013)
2. Schoning, J., Rogers, Y., Kruger, A.: Digitally enhanced 49 food. IEEE Pervasive Computing 11(3), 4–6 (2012)
3. Harrar, V., Spence, C.: The taste of cutlery: How the taste of food is affected by the weight, size, shape, and colour of the cutlery used to eat it. Flavour 2(1), 1–13 (2013)
4. Koizumi, N., et al.: Chewing jockey: Augmented food texture by using sound based on the cross-modal effect. In: Proceedings of the 8th International Conference on Advances in Computer Entertainment Technology, ACM (2011)
5. http://www.riedel.co.jp/about-riedel/whyriedel (accessed: January 10, 2014)
6. Liger-Belair. Uncorked: The Science of Champagne, Revised Edition. Princeton University Press (2013)
7. http://www.tanita.co.jp/products/kurashi/thermohygrometer.html (accessed: January 10, 2014)
8. http://www.figaro.co.jp/en/top.html (accessed: January 10, 2014)
9. Adria, F., Adria, A., Soler, J.: A Day at elBulli. Phaidon (2010)
10. This, Herve. "Molecular gastronomy." Angewandte Chemie International Edition 41.1, 83–88 (2002)
11. Frank, R.A., Byram, J.: Taste-smell interactions are tastant and odorant dependent. Chemical Senses 13(3), 445–455 (1988)
12. Narumi, T., et al.: Meta cookie. ACM SIGGRAPH 2010 Posters (2010)
13. http://jjhyun.com/ (accessed: January 10, 2014)
14. Mori, M., Kurihara, K., Tsukada, K., Siio, I.: Dining Presenter: Augmented Reality system for a dining tabletop. In: Ajunct Proceedings of Ubicomp, pp. 168–169 (2009)
15. http://www.riedel.co.jp/enjoy-wine/2010/ (accessed: January 10, 2014)
16. Grimes, A., Harper, R.: Celebratory technology: New directions for food research in HCI. In: Proceedings of the SIGCHI Conference on Human Factors in Computing Systems. ACM. APA (2008)
17. Myhrvold, N., Young, C., Bilet, M.: Modernist cuisine: The art and science of cooking. Cooking Lab (2011)

Towards a Design Space for Ubiquitous Computing

Ilya Shmorgun and David Lamas

Institute of Informatics
Tallinn University
Narva Rd. 29, 10120 Tallinn
Estonia
{ilja.shmorgun,david.lamas}@tlu.ee

Abstract. The purpose of this paper is to illustrate the use of design space analysis for structuring the state of the art in a selected domain. The resulting design space was created based on a literature review and is an analytical tool that can help interaction designers identify the goals, characteristics, challenges, enabling technologies, and quality attributes that are relevant to the design and development of ubiquitous computing systems. This paper describes the procedure of selecting the design space categories, provides examples of using the design space, and discusses the limitations and perspective.

Keywords: Ubiquitous computing, design space analysis, design rationale.

1 Introduction

Over 20 years have passed since the publication of Mark Weiser's seminal article on ubiquitous computing [13]. While the technical solutions necessary for the creation of ubiquitous systems already exists, the design community is still lacking robust analytical tools devoted to the field. Currently design issues are being solved on a case-by-case basis in small teams, where members are able to sufficiently easily convey their ideas [3]. Yet, as the field matures, so do the requirements for analytical tools that can support the design and development process.

The design space proposed in this paper aims to help ubicomp interaction designers to better understand the potential design options and reasons for choosing them, as well as find suitable approaches to solving their particular design challenges within the space [8].

Following is a description of the procedure of constructing the design space, an overview of the main concepts, examples of the potential ways of using the tool, and a discussion of the limitations and perspective.

N. Streitz and P. Markopoulos (Eds.): DAPI 2014, LNCS 8530, pp. 58–65, 2014.

2   Procedure

The ubiquitous computing design space is a result of a literature review, which was triggered by an attempt to answer the question "What constitutes the field of ubiquitous computing?" Additional questions were related to the main challenges, issues, focus areas, and technologies being used. The article on "Visualizing the research on pervasive and ubiquitous computing" by Zhao and Wang [14] provided a starting point for the review, as it described a meta-analysis of papers published between 1995 and 2009 on the topics of ubiquitous and pervasive computing. The article provided an overview of key researchers, highly cited papers, as well as keywords related to the main research foci in the field.

A search for articles was conducted through several online digital libraries, mainly ACM Digital Library, IEEE Computer Society, and SpringerLink, as those were the resources accessible in Tallinn University. Additional search was done using Google Scholar. A combination of keyword search and backward searches was used [7] to find articles published in international peer-reviewed conference proceedings and journals. The articles were selected based on the titles, abstracts, and keywords, as well as the fact that the articles themselves were being cited in previously read publications.

While the analysis of articles facilitated the exploration of certain directions in depth, using the Amazon.com search with the keyword "ubiquitous computing" helped select several books, which provided an overview of the historical development of the field, a description of relevant research methods, directions, and undertaken research projects, thus adding a dimension of breadth. The selected publications included those by Krumm et al. [4], Poslad [10], Kuniavsky [5], Dourish [1,2], and Greenfield [3]. The criteria for selecting these books was based on customer ratings and reviews, the titles being cited in previously read articles and books, and reading the introductory sections.

During the work on the literature the initial list of questions was expanded to include those related to finding out what goals ubicomp designers set, what challenges they try to solve, what technologies they use to bring their ideas to life, and what quality attributes they focus on in their designs.

The notes collected from the readings were combined into several clusters, such as characteristics, enabling technologies, and design issues. Further, 18 projects were selected from the readings, which spanned a period between 1992 and 2013 and provided a glimpse of the development of research agendas over the two decades since Weiser's seminal article was published. The publications used for identifying the relevant research projects were those by Krumm [4] and Rogers [11,12]. An additional rationale for selecting these particular projects was that they addressed a spectrum of issues and challenges that ubicomp designers attempted to solve. An initial step was to provide a brief description of each project and attempt to characterize it with the concepts identified previously. This was an iterative process during which new concepts were added, while several existing ones were merged and removed. The result was 5 main categories and 31 subconcepts. The main categories are: characteristics, enabling technologies, design challenges, design goals, and quality attributes. The sub-concepts for characteristics are: invisibility, calmness, embeddedness, context-awareness, mobility, wearability, connectivity, and tangibility. The sub-concepts for enabling technologies are: displays, multimedia, alternative forms of input, low-power high-performance processors, communications, web technologies, machine-readable data formats, sensors, physical object identification, haptics, and databases. The sub-concepts for design challenges are: understanding user needs, designing for multiple interfaces, designing for smartness, selecting appropriate technologies, and developing ubicomp design conventions. The sub-concepts for design goals are: augmenting existing practices, creating engaging experiences, and creating technological infrastructure. The sub-concepts for quality attributes are: usability, accessibility, privacy, and security.

The main categories and sub-concepts were further structured by following an approach proposed by Maclean et al. [9], which uses a semi-formal Questions, Options, and Criteria notation for representation. The Questions refer to the important dimensions in the design space, Options provide possible answers to the Questions, and Criteria argue for or against the Options. In some cases Options can also lead to subsequent Questions, which help to elaborate specific details of the design [8].

By following the selected approach Questions were formed based on the main categories. The 5 Questions were: "What are the characteristics of ubiquitous computing?", "What are the ubiquitous computing enabling technologies?", "What are the ubiquitous computing design challenges?", "What are the ubiquitous computing design goals?", and "What are the quality attributes of ubiquitous computing?". The sub-concepts were used as Options for the corresponding questions. The Criteria were formed as explanations for each of the Options. Finally, the Criteria were linked to the Options through positive or negative connections based on their underlying relationships.

3   Visualizing the Design Space

As a result of applying the QOC notation the design space is visualized as node-and-link diagram where the relationships between the elements are illustrated with lines acting as links between Questions and the corresponding Options. Options are linked to corresponding Criteria with either a full line, which signifies that a Criteria argues for the particular Option, or with a dashed line, which signifies that a Criteria argues against an Option [9].

However, as Maclean et. al [9] point out, this approach to visualizing the design space is suitable for diagrams with a limited amount of nodes, as larger diagrams can quickly become messy and difficult to manage. To address this limitation a tabular form can be used (an example is shown in Table 1) where the connections between Options and Criteria are specified with "+" and "-" signs [8].

Table 1. A fragment of the design space for the ubiquitous computing design challenges presented in tabular form

Q: What are the design challenges?	C: Improving ease and convenience of use	C: Facilitating interactions with a wide variety of devices	C: Increasing user control in the interaction	C: Selecting technologies appropriate for the design task	C: Developing a robust design practice
O: Understanding user needs	+		+	+	+
O: Designing for multiple interfaces	+	−		+	−
O: Designing for smartness	+	+	+	+	+
O: Selecting appropriate technologies	+	+	+	+	+
O: Developing ubicomp design conventions	+			+	+

4 Examples of Use

Identifying the Options having the most positive Criteria suggested what a potential ubiquitous computing system could be. According to the findings a ubicomp system could be foreseen as a connected solution enabled by web technologies, machine-readable data formats, and physical object identification technologies, aimed at creating engaging experiences with a focus on privacy and security of stored information. The design challenges needing to be addressed are designing for smartness and selecting appropriate technologies.

A similar analysis, focused on identifying the Criteria with the most positive connections to Options, lead to the conclusion that ubicomp interaction designers should turn their attention to providing access to information resources while improving ease and convenience of use and ensuring users' safety and well-being, making them proactive by facilitating new interaction scenarios while also embracing existing social boundaries and conventions, and selecting technologies appropriate for the design task that can provide rich means for creating applications and services.

In addition, the ubiquitous computing design space was recently used in the LearnMix project [6], which aims to re-conceptualize the e-textbook as a collection of professional and user-contributed content available on a wide variety of devices. In this case the selection of Options was based on the project design values, which were informed by the insights from recently conducted ethnography and Delphi studies. The design values used where: integration with existing artifact ecology; sustainability; good user experience; and support for new educational scenarios. A concept map was produced to provide specific examples of related concepts as the initial design values were too general.

Further, the design values and the Options from the ubiquitous computing design space were put into a table and a 3-point scale was used to rank Options based on the design values. 1 point was assigned if the Option had no relation to the design value, 2 points - if having the Option would be useful in the project, and 3 points - if the Option was considered very important to have. Finally, averages were calculated to identify the Options, which were ranked the highest. An example of the ranking is shown in Table 2, where the highest ranked Option is "Understanding user needs".

The results of the ranking suggested that in the context of the LearnMix project it is important to focus on designing a system reliant on embedded infrastructure, enabled by multimedia, alternative forms input, low-power high-performance processors, communications, and web technologies. The main design challenge is to understand user needs with a goal of augmenting existing practices and with attention to usability.

Table 2. Ranking design space Options based on the project values

Q: What are the design challenges?	D: Integration with existing artifact ecology	D: Sustainability	D: Providing a good user experience	D: Supporting new educational scenarios	Average
O: Understanding user needs	3	2	3	3	2.75
O: Designing for multiple interfaces	3	1	3	3	2.5
O: Designing for smartness	2	2	3	2	2.25
O: Selecting appropriate technologies	3	2	3	2	2.5
O: Developing ubicomp design conventions	1	2	3	1	1.75

5   Discussion

The proposed design space is meant to help ubiquitous computing interaction designers reason about the particular choices they are aiming to make in their project circumstances by presenting different options and criteria for selecting those options. It is important to note that while all options have a certain number of criteria arguing for or against them, it does not mean that an option with the most positive connections wins [8]. It is up to the designer to select the criteria and options based on a particular context and the aspects of a system that appear to be more important than others.

The design space described here attempts to map the status quo of ubiquitous computing and offer designers a way to explore potential directions while avoiding premature commitment. However, this design space does not intend to provide a definitive answer to all possible issues in the field of ubiquitous computing, as new technology and ideas are constantly emerging along with the changing requirements of users [8].

One approach to improving the selection of base concepts included in the design space can be done by using them to describe existing ubiquitous computing projects. This effort could help identify if the initial concepts are sufficient or whether new ones need to added to more thoroughly describe the projects that are being analyzed. Another possible approach is improvement of the design space through use in actual ubiquitous interaction design scenarios.

6   Conclusion

The ubiquitous computing design space is proposed as a means for helping HCI researchers and practitioners interested in developing ubicomp systems to identify the potential design goals, characteristics, challenges, technologies, and quality attributes suitable for their work.

The analytical tool described here should be matured further by clarifying the concepts and the relationships between them. Additionaly, it can be beneficial to create an interactive application that can enable users to explore the relationships between different Options and Criteria in an interactive way. Still, we hope that the proposed design space can serve as a step towards producing better ubiquitous computing systems.

Acknowledgements. We would like to thank Sonia Sousa, Arman Arakelyan, Triinu Jesmin, Joanna Kwiatkowska, Abioudun Ogunyemi, Ulkar Bayramova, and Avar Pentel for providing valuable feedback and helping develop our ideas.

References

1. Dourish, P.: Where the Action Is: The Foundations of Embodied Interaction. MIT Press, Cambridge (2001)
2. Dourish, P., Bell, G.: Divining a Digital Future: Mess and Mythology in Ubiquitous Computing. The MIT Press (April 2011)

3. Greenfield, A.: Everyware: The Dawning Age of Ubiquitous Computing, 1st edn. New Riders Publishing (March 2010)
4. Krumm, J. (ed.): Ubiquitous Computing Fundamentals. Chapman and Hall/CRC (September 2009)
5. Kuniavsky, M.: Smart Things: Ubiquitous Computing User Experience Design, 1st edn. Morgan Kaufmann (September 2010)
6. Lamas, D., Väljataga, T., Laanpere, M., Rogalevits, V., Arakelyan, A., Sousa, S., Shmorgun, I.: Foundations for the Reconceptualization of the e-Textbook. In: Proceedings of the International Conference on e-Learning ICEL 2013, p. 510 (August 2013)
7. Levy, Y., Ellis, T.J.: A systems approach to conduct an effective literature review in support of information systems research. Informing Science Journal 9, 181–212 (2006)
8. MacLean, A., Young, R.M., Bellotti, V., Moran, T.P.: Design Space Analysis: Bridging From Theory to Practice Via Design Rationale. In: Proceedings of Esprit 1991, pp. 720–730 (1991)
9. MacLean, A., Young, R.M., Bellotti, V., Moran, T.P.: Questions, Options, and Criteria: Elements of Design Space Analysis. Human–Computer Interaction 6(3-4), 201–250 (1991)
10. Poslad, S.: Ubiquitous Computing: Smart Devices, Environments and Interactions, 1st edn. Wiley (August 2011)
11. Rogers, Y.: Moving on from Weiser's Vision of Calm Computing: Engaging Ubi-Comp Experiences. In: Dourish, P., Friday, A. (eds.) UbiComp 2006. LNCS, vol. 4206, pp. 404–421. Springer, Heidelberg (2006)
12. Rogers, Y.: The Changing Face of Human-Computer Interaction in the Age of Ubiquitous Computing. In: Holzinger, A., Miesenberger, K. (eds.) USAB 2009. LNCS, vol. 5889, pp. 1–19. Springer, Heidelberg (2009)
13. Weiser, M.: The computer for the 21st century. SIGMOBILE Mob. Comput. Commun. Rev. 3(3), 3–11 (1999)
14. Zhao, R., Wang, J.: Visualizing the research on pervasive and ubiquitous computing. Scientometrics 86(3), 593–612 (2011)

A Game Design Workshop to Support the Elaboration of Game Ideas

Christos Sintoris, Nikoleta Yiannoutsou, and Nikolaos Avouris

University of Patras, Department of Electrical and Computer Engineering, Rion
Patras, Greece
{sintoris,nyiannoutsou,avouris}@upatras.gr

Abstract. In this paper we present a set of game design workshops in
the context of which we investigate design practices and elaboration of
game ideas. The workshops aimed at engaging participants in crafting
designs for location-based mobile games. We analyse the rationale underlying the workshops and describe their structure and the involved
material. Next we outline the characteristics of six cases where these
workshops were implemented and finally we present a representative set
of games produced by the participants.

1 Introduction

In this paper we describe a game design workshop for creating conceptual designs
for multiplayer, hybrid reality, location based mobile games supporting informal
learning in cultural heritage sites. The workshop was implemented in six different
cases with different participants in each case who produced 32 conceptual designs
for the site of Pompeii. Multi-player location-based mobile games for learning are
a multifaceted field of study. Modern mobile technology and the accompanying
infrastructure that is weaved in our surroundings are becoming a new reality that
needs to be studied and understood. The theoretical base of how to transform
this technological potential into a form that can support playful learning can be
considered nascent. In part this stems from a lack of common ground as to what
elements of this hybrid space, the result of merging the digital and the physical,
can contribute to learning. Of particular interest is the possibility to employ the
motivational potential of games in this endeavour [3]. In the past decade there
has been increased interest on how to tap on this potential of technology as a
platform for location-based gaming activities with regard to learning [10,13].

Hybrid reality location-based mobile games are playful mobile activities situated in real-world contexts. They are believed to be conductive to learning,
that may lead to acquisition of skills like critical thinking, curiosity, creativity,
collaboration, consideration of multiple perspectives, social awareness, responsibility and media fluency [14]. These games are mobile, in the sense that they
require that the players move in the physical domain as part of the gameplay and
not that the players 'carry' the game on them as in 'games for mobile devices'.
The underlying idea is that with these games the players interact with the real

N. Streitz and P. Markopoulos (Eds.): DAPI 2014, LNCS 8530, pp. 66–75, 2014.

world and perform physical activities situated in it. From a learning perspective, location based mobile games focus on generating knowledge in relation to their surroundings , especially in sites with cultural interest like historic city centres and/or archaeological sites. As noted in a survey of location-based games [4], these games are conceived as tools that employ the fun of a game, so that the players can be engaged with a specific location.

The design and construction of such games can be a challenge in engineering, a challenge of balancing between playing and learning, of integrating the physical context in a meaningful way, of engaging the players, of highlighting aspects related to the importance of the site etc. It thus becomes apparent that we are confronted with a complex problem which can be approached at a social, cognitive, media-theoretic, interaction or game theoretic level. This complexity is a barrier for the wider use of games in education [9,15].

The work presented here describes the structure of a game design workshop and investigates its value as a methodological instrument /tool for designing hybrid reality location based games supporting informal learning. We mentioned earlier that the workshop was implemented in six different occasions. Designers with different backgrounds (e.g. game-based learning, engineering, management of cultural heritage, education etc.) worked in groups of 3-5 persons to create a game concepts for a hypothetical location-based mobile multi-player game for the site of ancient Pompeii. The game design task that was devised for the workshops was comprised of a fixed procedure and accompanied by material and information related to the archaeological site. During the workshops, we asked each design team to use the provided materials and to generate a game concept for the site.

2   Background

Game design workshops are not an uncommon approach in regard to investigating game design [6,12]. They possess a number of characteristics that make them a suitable research tool [12]: a) they are a focused, low-cost practice that can involve a large number of participants, b) they can generate rich data for analysis and they can function as empirical tools to study the production of game designs and they do, in fact, produce new designs, and c) they can be studied rather easily (in contrast to other methods such as for example observing game designers in their workplace).

The theoretical framework on which the structure of the game design workshop was based involved a) interaction modalities with the real world, b) an understanding of game mechanics as "the various actions, behaviors and control mechanisms afforded to the player within a game context" [8], c) the learning dimension of the cultural experience [7] [5], d) the role of technology in enriching this dimension of cultural experience [16].

Table 1. An overview of the game design workshops that have been analysed. In the third column is shown the number game concepts that were generated.

Participant characteristics in each case	Game concepts
1 2011, HCI Class in xxxxx, xxxxx Engineering students, 8th semester, programming experience, little or no game design experience	5
2 2011, PAKE training class in xxxxx, xxxxx Education specialists, partly members of design teams for ICT in education, experience in ICT in education	4
3 2011, DEG Workshop – "Involving End Users and Domain Experts in the Design of Educational Games" in Torre Cane, Italy Postgraduate students, professional designers, experts in educational technology, experts in design science	2
4 2011, GBL Summer School in Autrans, France Game based learning professionals and academics, partly experts in mobile games and mobile learning	13
5 2012, HCI Class 2 in xxxxx, xxxxx Engineering students, 8th semester, programming experience, little or no game design experience	3
6 2013, CHM Summer School in Pécs, Hungary Postgraduate students in engineering, cultural management	5

3   Research Setting

Partipants. The designers who participated in the workshops had varying backgrounds. They were recruited on six different occasions (Table 1): a) 8th semester engineering students who participated in the workshops as part of a on human-computer interaction class (cases 1 and 5), b) researchers and professional designers who participated in workshops related to game based learning and/or cultural heritage management (cases 3, 4 and 6), c) public education specialists who were training as instructors for the application of ICT in education (case 2). The participants cover a range of professional backgrounds that is expected to provide a varying perspective, while at the same time the profiles cover typical backgrounds for multidisciplinary design teams for location-based games for learning: Cases 3 and 4 are comprised of more experienced interaction and game designers, while cases 2 and 6 cover expertise leaning more towards educational and cultural heritage experts.

Workshop Layout. The design process is based on unpacking mobile games into their components, each of which is addressed separately but also in relation to the other components. This approach is grounded in a framework of design principles for location-based games defined by [2] and it partially draws elements from the Mechanics-Dynamics-Aesthetics framework (hereafter MDA) by [8]. In the workshops, the designers form teams of 3–5 members and attempt to sketch out a game design in two phases (Figure 1). During each phase the teams use the available tools (which are described below) to generate their conceptual design. At the end of both phases, all teams present their conceptual designs. The two phases are similar, with the difference that there is more time available for the second phase. The rationale for this is to use the first phase in order to get acquainted with the process and the tools and the second phase in order to work out and describe more thoroughly the game idea. At the end of each phase, each team specifies its concept by filling out a worksheet. One of the team members takes the role of the rapporteur, who presents the team's design. During the presentations the designers are allowed to comment and appropriate the presented ideas in their own designs. After the first phase, the process is repeated and the workshop session ends after the second round of presentations. The duration of the workshop is between 1 and a half and 2 hours.

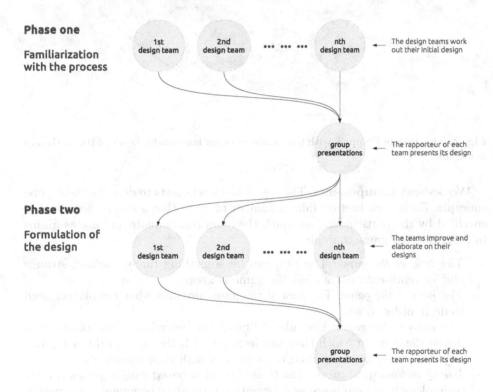

Fig. 1. The structure of a game design workshop. The workshop runs in two similar phases. First a familiarization phase and then the main design phase. The total duration of a workshop session is 1:30 to 2:00 hours.

Workshop Material. The material created for the game design workshop concerned the archaeological site of ancient Pompeii. It contains descriptions of selected landmarks, main ideas or concepts (from the economy and everyday life in Pompeii) and a map of the archaeological site. At the beginning of the workshop session the participants receive the following material: a) **a worksheet with the main components of the conceptual design (see worksheet components) which are expected to be specified by the designers in order to create the design of a specific game**, b) a map of the archaeological site of Pompeii (Figure 2), c) a description of interesting sites in ancient Pompeii, d) concept cards that describe aspects of the live in the ancient city and e) an instruction card (the material is available at `censored`).

Fig. 2. This map of Pompeii, with the locations of six landmarks, is one of the workshop materials

Worksheet Components. The teams use worksheets to describe their game concepts. Each worksheet contains a number of items that are to be described or specified by the participants, on which they can contemplate and use as fill-ins to describe their game concept:

- *The title of the game*: The title can be something funny, curious, strange and/or representative of what the game is about.
- *The goal of the game*: The goal of the game involves what the players need to do in order to win.
- *The rules of the game*: The rules delineate the behaviour of the players and define the ways in which they can interact with the (real-world or digital) objects of the game with their co-players or with their opponents.
- *Use of technological means and tools*: Location-based mobile games employ technology in various ways: as information screens, as communication media, as barcode scanners, as GPS devices, as map displays etc.
- *Mechanisms*: The mechanisms of the game involve mainly the pacing of the game and the type of interaction between players.
- *Behaviours and aesthetic result*: This item involves how the game will evolve over time and what is the envisaged player experience.

Design Task and Data Collection. The workshops were realized in six different occasions (Table 1). The profiles of the participants varied in most of the cases. While the design task was kept constant, the resulting designs reflected the profiles of the designers. In two occasions 8th semester engineering students participated in the workshop sessions, another two sessions were conducted during summer schools, one during an international workshop on game design and one were the participants were education professionals. The most productive session took place during the Game Based Learning Summer School (case 4, Table 1) where the participants had a variety of profiles (both academic and industrial) and were strongly related to a game studies background.

Each workshop session started with a brief presentation of the design task, the materials and context about Pompeii. The design scenario prescribed that the participants are impersonating game designers with the task of designing a game for visitors of the archaeological site of Pompeii. The game should thus have the characteristics of a location-based mobile game, adapted for this site. The participants were asked to design a game that can be played in a "physical space" by multiple players, who will use mobile devices or smartphones as interaction tools. They were also asked to make use of pervasive computing technology in their game, in any manner they can envisage, such as physical hyperlinks (e.g. QR or NFC tags), unrestricted wireless communication, location-sensing, augmented reality etc., without constraints. Finally the designers were asked to engage the players in learning about the specific site — i.e. ancient Pompeii. In all, the design task involved sketching out a game concept by describing its main components: the rules, the mechanics, the typical player behaviours , the available technology and the way it should be used. The requirements for this task were to create a game supporting interaction with a place of high information density, achieving any kind of learning outcome and taking into account the profiles of prospective players. The designers were allowed to assume that they have unlimited resources for their game concept. These "ideal designers" had thus to cope with a number of issues such as a) to specify how the technological means will be used in their game concept, b) how to connect the domains of the digital and the real world and c)how to employ playful interaction in the game concept.

4   Conceptual Game Designs

In this section we discuss the output of these workshops. We present in detail one example and we offer an overview of the main characteristics of the total 32 designs that were generated. Data was collected mainly by digitizing the generated worksheets. During some of the workshops it was possible to keep audio or video recordings of the discussions (cases 2, 3, 4, 5). The game concepts were subsequently analysed by employing a content analysis approach. Content analysis is not a singular method but rather a set of methods in the social sciences that are used to analyse communication and texts. Content analysis offer a number of methodological means. We employed ethnographic content analysis [11, p. 16, 21] [1], a data-driven content analysis method. Next, we will describe the specific approach with more detail.

Fig. 3. A team contemplating on their design, during the 2011 Game Based Learning Summer School in Autrans, France

Table 2. The titles of the conceptual game designs that were produced in the workshops. The contents of these concepts have been posted at **censored**

Game title
1   HCI Class in xxxxx, xxxxx
1.1 Fauns agains Vetti
1.2 A day in Pompeii
1.3 Pandora's Box
1.4 I was in Pompeii too: Fire and Lava (episode I)
1.5 Find Pompeii's Secret
2   PAKE training class in xxxxx, xxxxx
2.1 Searching in Pompeii
2.2 Touring Pompeii
2.3 Mortuus Pompeiis
2.4 I live my place some place else
3   DEG Workshop in Torre Cane, Italy
3.1 The Day of the Eruption
3.2 Reveal the Story
4   GBL Summer School in Autrans, France
4.1 No Panic in Pompeii
4.2 Inspector Peritus
4.3 Pompeii Apocalypse
4.4 Last Party under the Volcano
4.5 Pompeii Total War
4.6 Swap and Survive
4.7 Bloody Pompeii

Table 2. *Continued*

4.8 Roads of Lava
4.9 Back to the Future: Back to Pompeii
4.10 Murder Mystery Pompeii
4.11 The Volcano Strikes Back
4.12 Dionysos' Wild Party or Vesuvio's God
4.13 The Mystery of Pompeii
5   HCI Class 2 in xxxxx, xxxxx
5.1 Murder in Pompeii
5.2 Hunting in Pompeii
5.3 Murder at Faun's
6   CHM Summer School in Pécs, Hungary
6.1 Dionysus Puzzle
6.2 Soul of Pompeii
6.3 Legendary Game
6.4 Treasure Hunting in Pompeii
6.5 The Golden Treasure of Pompeii

A total of 32 game concepts were produced by the design teams (one design in case 3 was not documented in the final worksheets).

4.1 An Example: "Pompeii Total War"

"Pompeii Total War" is one of the concepts from the workshop at the Game Based Learning Summer School in 2011. Below follows the complete document that the participants delivered after the 1.30 hour session. The designers are clearly inspired by the "Total War" series of video games and have modelled their design accordingly. The language of the original design has been preserved.

The Aim. Conquer and protect flag of/from every team (other players). Your devices assist you: You can see buildings and NPCs through it. It also features a dynamic map of your camp flags and conquered flags. NPCs will give you hints and help you to solve puzzles and enigmas through a dialogue interface. Beware, you will often need to gather several clues to solve puzzle in the same time in different places. So split the team and use the simplified com-system to stay in touch

The Rules. You must protect and conquer flags by answering puzzles: - a foreign flag can be captured when resolving the puzzle that an NPC guard gave to the team. - you can recapture your own captured flags by answering a new enigma to the NPC guardian - you can recapture a lost flag by answering again to the guard (another enigma of course). You have 2 hours for the contest.

Use of Means and Tools. Tablets/smartphones with GPS (location), camera (augmented reality) dynamic map of Pompeii with list of team flags (conquered) network connection to a ?? (*–unintelligible*) (Real time changes on the world).

Game Mechanics. - RTS, capture the flags - several located enigmas - time challenge (capture the most flags) - collaborative resolution (ubiquitous problems for teams) - building strategies with several roles in the team - communication with legendary known NPCs (gods, generals, famous).

Some enigmas: on the same flags there are several possible enigmas. They are asked in a progressive way: the easier first, the harder last. Puzzle: the mosaic with Alexander and find the place where the mosaic is. A non playing character asks the players to find a picture in the pool. But to see the pic, the pool must be full. So they have to split into 2 groups. One must stay near the pool, the other has to find the valve. Once the valve is found, they open it and tell the others to look at the pool. Attention, the valve must be shut down whether the other teams can find it. Then all players have to go back to the NPC and explain who is on the pic and his role in the mythology (Dionysos, god of wine). If they are wrong, the NPC explains them but they loose the flag.

Player Behaviour and Aesthetic Result. - competition and pressure – discovery of amazing [places — people (NPCs)] - self efficacy improvement when a cooperative problem is solved - fun! - Learning a lot about past Pompeii.

5   Final Remarks

The workshop presented here is based on an understanding of location-based mobile games as complex entities that can be synthesized in a component-based manner. The workshop functioned as tool for contemplation and it allowed the participating designers to elaborate on game concepts for location-based mobile games. The analysis of the game concepts that were produced highlighted common design practices such as drawing elements from known games or genres, or employing narrative as a gameplay element. Finally, the design documents allowed us to extract a set of design patterns which could be used as building blocks for creating new games.

References

1. Altheide, D.L.: Reflections: Ethnographic content analysis. Qualitative Sociology 10(1), 65–77 (1987), http://link.springer.com/article/10.1007/BF00988269
2. anonymised. "anonymised". In: anonymised, 2(2), 53–71 (2010)
3. anonymised. "anonymised". In: anonymised, anonymised (May 2013)

4. Avouris, N., Yiannoutsou, N.: A review of mobile location-based games for learning across physical and virtual spaces. Journal of Universal Computer Science 18(15), 2120–2142 (2012)
5. Dodd, J.: The generic learning outcomes: A conceptual framework for researching learning in informal learning environments. In: Vavoula, G., Pachler, N., Kukulska-Hulme, A. (eds.) Researching Mobile Learning: Frameworks, Tools, and Research Designs, Peter Lang. (2009),
   http://www.google.com/books?hl=el&lr=&id=8IFXjRhfwdQC&oi=fnd&pg=PR&dq=
   The+Generic+Learning+Outcomes:+A+Conceptual+Framework+for+
   ResearchingLearning+in+Informal+Learning+Environments,&ots=lu4zBsgSso&
   sig=SISXxGPTVAegZhQBmjNVBfBtQGo
6. Fullerton, T., Swain, C., Hoffman, S.: Game Design Workshop: Designing, prototyping, and playtesting games. Focal Press (2004)
7. Hein, G.E.: The constructivist museum. Journal of Education in Museums 16, 21–23 (1995)
8. Hunicke, R., LeBlanc, M., Zubek, R.: MDA: A formal approach to game design and game research. In: Proceedings of the AAAI 2004 Workshop on Challenges in Game AI, pp. 1–5 (2004)
9. Kelle, S., Klemke, R., Specht, M.: Design patterns for learning games. International Journal of Technology Enhanced Learning 3(6), 555–569 (2011), http://inderscience.metapress.com/index/FT68358132155713.pdf
10. Klopfer, E.: Augmented Learning: Research and Design of Mobile Educational Games, reprint edn. The MIT Press (August 2011) ISBN: 0262516527
11. Krippendorff, K.: Content analysis: An introduction to its methodology. SAGE Publications, Incorporated (2004)
12. Kultima, J.P.A., et al.: GameSpace: Methods for design and evaluation for casual mobile multiplayer games. In: GameSpace (2009)
13. Kurti, A., Milrad, M., Spikol, D.: Designing innovative learning activities using ubiquitous computing. In: Seventh IEEE International Conference on Advanced Learning Technologies, ICALT 2007, pp. 386–390 (2007)
14. Schrier, K.: Using augmented reality games to teach 21st century skills. In: ACM SIGGRAPH 2006 Educators Program, p. 15 (2006), http://dl.acm.org/citation.cfm?id=1179295.1179311
15. Westera, W., et al.: Serious games for higher education: A framework for reducing design complexity. Journal of Computer Assisted Learning 24(5), 420–432 (2008), http://onlinelibrary.wiley.com/doi/10.1111/j.1365-2729.2008.00279.x/full
16. Yiannoutsou, N., Avouris, N.: Mobile games in museums: From learning through game play to learning through game design. Museum Education and New Media 23, 79–86 (2012)

Prototyping Distributed Physical User Interfaces in Ambient Intelligence Setups

Gervasio Varela, Alejandro Paz-Lopez, Jose Antonio Becerra Permuy, and Richard J. Duro Fernandez

Integrated Group for Engineering Research, University of A Coruña, C/ Mendizabal S/N, 15403, Ferrol, A Coruña
{gervasio.varela,alpaz,joseantoniobecerrapermuy, richard}@udc.es

Abstract. Ambient Intelligence systems require the development of highly customized distributed UIs adapted to the user and environment characteristics. They make use of many different devices, from different manufacturers, technologies and modalities. Supporting this wide variety of devices and technologies increases the complexity of a system, affecting its costs and development time. The objective of Dandelion, the solution presented in this paper, is to alleviate this complexity and reduce development costs. Dandelion provides a development framework for distributed physical UIs. It is capable of decoupling the system logic from the characteristics and specifics of the interaction devices, and supports the easy prototyping of different physical realizations of a distributed UI.

Keywords: physical user interfaces, distributed user interfaces, ambient intelligence, ubiquitous computing, user interfaces, model-driven engineering.

1 Introduction

The implicit nature of Ambient Intelligence systems, and specially the intrinsic requirements of these systems, such as environment integration, proactivity or natural interaction [1][2][3], makes designing and implementing user interfaces for AmI systems a costly process. A lot of effort must be devoted to the design and testing of highly customized UIs that must be adapted to the user and environment characteristics in order to be perceived as natural.

Those customized UIs are usually conceived as distributed physical user interfaces that make use of many distributed hardware devices [1][4]. These devices come from different manufacturers, use heterogeneous technologies, and in some scenarios, even employ custom hardware that is especially built for the system. Furthermore, if the system is going to be deployed in different scenarios, with different users or environments, many different configurations of the UI may be required.

Designing and implementing the support to this multitude of technologies and devices introduces a lot of complexity in a system, increasing the development costs and the cost of adapting it to new environments. Reducing this complexity and cost is the

N. Streitz and P. Markopoulos (Eds.): DAPI 2014, LNCS 8530, pp. 76–85, 2014.

main objective of the solution presented in this paper, the Dandelion framework. It provides a development framework for distributed physical UIs, where the system logic and interaction logic can be physically and logically decoupled from the devices and technologies used to build the UI. Taking advantage of this decoupling, Dandelion can be easily cast as a prototyping tool that facilitates the testing of different implementations of physical user interfaces.

Dandelion follows a model-driven approach that allows developers to build UIs using abstract interaction components. At deploy time, the abstract UI is connected to a selection of physical distributed devices. This connection is achieved by the Generic Interaction Protocol (GIP) [4], a device abstraction technology that, implemented as a distributed communications protocol, encapsulates the specific behavior of physical devices behind a generic interface of user interaction actions. Model-driven approaches have been widely adopted by the Human-Computer-Interaction (HCI) community since Thevenin and Coutaz [5] proposed the use of models to support UI adaptation to context changes [6][7][8]. Furthermore, the usefulness of model-driven approaches has been recognized within the Ubiquitous Computing and Ambient Intelligence fields, which are starting to use models in order to improve the adaptation capabilities of their system to context changes [8][9].

The Dandelion framework design has been inspired in the CAMELEON-RT [6] and UsiXML [7] projects, and their four UI abstraction levels. Nevertheless, Dandelion relies only on two abstraction levels, the abstract UI level and the final UI level. Besides, Dandelion shares some similarities with the iStuff project [10], as both provide distributed access to smart physical objects and rely on proxy-like components to encapsulate the specific behavior of each device. However there are important differences. First, Dandelion allows the utilization of model-driven techniques to build distributed physical UIs. Second, Dandelion provides an abstraction technology for user interaction devices. Consequently, multiple heterogeneous devices can be accessed using the same homogenous API.

This paper is organized as follows. Section 2 provides a brief overview of the Dandelion framework design and implementation. Section 3 provides an overview of the prototyping capabilities of Dandelion, and Section 4 shows an illustrative example of how to use the Dandelion framework to prototype a distributed physical UI. Finally section 5 discusses some conclusions.

2   Dandelion: A Development Framework for Distributed Physical User Interfaces

This paper presents Dandelion, a development framework for Distributed Physical User Interfaces (DPUIs) in Ambient Intelligence (AmI) environments. The main characteristic of this framework is its ability to increase the decoupling between a digital system and the particularities and specifics of the multiple technologies required by a distributed UI, especially when physical user interfaces are involved. Developers can take advantage of this characteristic to easily prototype and test different physical configurations of the UI. In this section, we are going to show the conceptual architecture and some implementation details of the framework.

The ability to decouple system logic, and more specifically, the system interaction logic, from the particular technologies and hardware devices used to interact with the user is an important characteristic for any system. However, it becomes especially relevant when the interaction system may change depending on the scenario. This is the case of Ambient Intelligence systems, which are expected to provide their functionality in very different scenarios, with their interaction systems adapted to the environment and user characteristics. In these kinds of systems, the devices and technologies used, and even the shape and behavior of the UI may change, not only for different physical environments, but also for different users in the same physical environment.

Dandelion has been conceived as a UI development framework for AmI systems, and as such, it has been designed to facilitate the development of distributed physical UIs capable of changing their shape depending on the use scenario. Figure 1 shows a block deployment diagram of a system using the Dandelion framework. As can be seen, the system logic and the interaction devices operate in a distributed manner, with Dandelion in the middle decoupling them through a UI management system (the Dandelion UI Controller) and a device abstraction layer (the Dandelion FIO layer and GIP protocol). This decoupling is provided at two different levels. First, they are logically decoupled, so that UIs can be built independently of the APIs or technologies used by specific devices. Second, they are physically decoupled, so that the system logic can be run without knowing where the devices implementing the UI are going to be physically deployed.

Dandelion uses a device abstraction layer in order to provide these two levels of decoupling. It is called the Generic Interaction Protocol (GIP), and it encapsulates the specific behavior of each device behind a generic interface of user interaction operations. GIP is a distributed communications protocol that defines a reduced set of interaction actions and creating a generic remote interface to any kind of interaction device. Any device or interaction resource that implements this interface can be remotely accessed using the same set of concepts and operations, thus decoupling the application from the underlying interaction technologies.

On top of this abstraction layer, Dandelion provides a user interface management system that allows developers to take advantage of the GIP in order to isolate their systems from the physical implementation of the UI. Dandelion uses a model-driven approach inspired on the CAMELERON-RT framework and the UsiXML models. The UIs are implemented at an abstract level using a UI Modeling Language, and then, at deploy-time or runtime, they are transformed into a Final UI.

A more detailed description of the Dandelion framework is provided in Figure 2. Dandelion uses the UsiXML Abstract UI model as the modeling language for the definition of UIs. This language allows developers to describe the UI of a system using a reduced set of generic user interaction operations, like input, output or trigger. These interaction operations, called Abstract Interaction Units (AIUs) are an abstract representation of the typical widgets found in graphical user interface toolkits. In Dandelion they represent any kind of interaction element capable of interacting with the user, such as physical devices like appliances or sensors, or even gestures or GUIs.

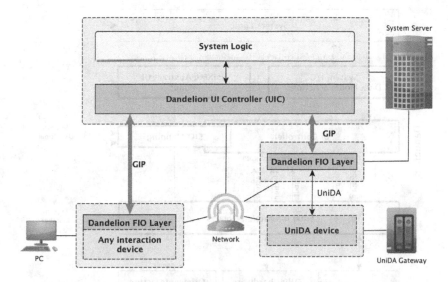

Fig. 1. Block and deployment diagram of a system using the Dandelion framework

Once a developer has implemented the system logic and described the UI using the Abstract UI model, she has to establish a relationship between the system logic and the elements forming the UI. For this purpose, Dandelion treats the AIUs as interaction black boxes capable of performing a specific kind of interaction with the user, for example obtaining data from the user or presenting data. The interface between the system logic and the UI is based on this concept, so the UI Controller uses the observer pattern to monitor some system logic objects specified by the developer. When it detects changes in those objects, the UIC notifies those changes to the AIUs that will translate them into interaction actions performed by the resources implementing the final UI, and vice versa. The data and action objects that must be monitored by the UIC are called the system I/O interface, and developers associate them to AIUs by using an API of the UIC.

In Dandelion, the interaction resources, the real devices used to interact with users, are represented by the Final Interaction Objects (FIOs) concept. They are software representations of the physical devices that encapsulate the specific logic and characteristics of each device behind the General Interaction Protocol interface. Thus, the abstraction of devices is conceptually provided by the GIP and physically realized by the Final Interaction Objects (FIOs).

The GIP is used by the UIC to establish a decoupled distributed connection between the AIUs of the user interface and the FIOs, the end devices that realize the abstract interactions specified by the AIUs. It is an event-based protocol following a publish/subscribe model and it is designed to match the set of interaction operations supported by the UsiXML Abstract UI model, so that it can easily translate between the AIUs of the UI definition and the actions performed by the FIOs. As shown in Figure 2, the GIP defines five different types of events: input, output, selection, action and focus. The UsiXML AUI model directly inspires the first four.

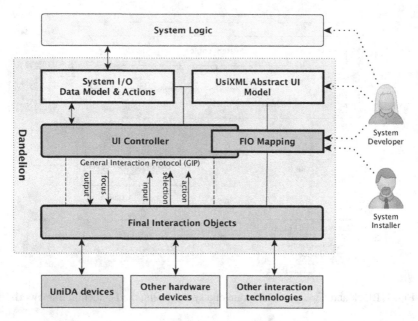

Fig. 2. Architecture diagram of the Dandelion framework

Final Interaction Objects implement the GIP as their interface to external systems. On the one hand, they receive GIP events from the UIC and translate them into specific actions, like showing a text, lighting up a LED, activating a servo, etc. On the other hand, they publish GIP events when a user performs an action in a device. These last events are received by the UIC, which, using a mapping between FIOs and AIUs, transfers them to the AIUs associated to a specific FIO. Finally, the AIUs transform those events into modifications to the data of a system logic object, or the activation of a system logic action.

When using Dandelion to build a distributed physical UI, developers are only required to implement the system logic, describe the UI requirements of the system at an abstract level with the UsiXML Abstract UI model, establish an I/O interface between the system logic and the UI, and finally, at deploy time, select the physical devices that implement the different interaction operations required by the UI. These devices can be physically distributed and use heterogeneous technologies. Dandelion integrates support for the UniDA framework [11][12], an open source framework that provides remote access to heterogeneous devices like home automation systems, so that devices supporting UniDA can be directly used. In the case of custom physical UIs, developers will be required to implement a series of FIOs to adapt their devices to the GIP interface.

Dandelion is implemented as a JAVA library that can be used by any JAVA application to build distributed UIs. It uses STOMP [13] as the supporting technology to implement the GIP protocol. STOMP allows the implementation of FIOs with any programming technology. Furthermore, Dandelion provides a FIO development framework for JAVA to facilitate the implementation of new FIOs in order to support custom interaction resources (new hardware devices or GUIs), and has integrated support for devices compatible with the UniDA device access framework.

3 Dandelion as a Prototyping Framework for Physical Distributed User Interfaces

Dandelion has been designed and is being implemented as an UI development framework for AmI systems. Therefore, the main idea behind it is to support the changes in the shape of a UI at runtime, so that ubiquitous systems can adapt their UI to changes in the users and changes in the environment. Because of this, it has been designed to integrate, in the future, support for the autonomous selection of the FIOs at runtime as illustrated in [3]. Nevertheless, in its current implementation the selection of FIOs is the responsibility of the developer or the installer of the system.

In this state, Dandelion can be a very useful tool for the prototyping of distributed physical user interfaces. As shown in Figure 3, by taking advantage of the physical and logical decoupling capabilities of Dandelion, developers of the system logic can focus on the system intelligence, while the developers of the UI can focus on the development of custom devices and FIOs. They can thus easily try very different physical configurations of the UI for different combinations of user and environment characteristics.

The use of the GIP and the FIO concept combined with the UsiXML language makes it easy to test a system using devices from different manufactures, with different physical distribution schemes and even try different and multiple simultaneous interaction modalities for the same interaction action. Developers are only required to change the mapping between the AIUs of the user interfaces and the FIOs. A change that can be easily implemented at deploy time, as the mapping is specified in an XML configuration file.

With the idea of using Dandelion for distributed UI prototyping, basic user monitoring capabilities are being integrated into the framework. For each system run, Dandelion generates a log file with the actions of the user and the UI, specifying which interaction has been activated, in which FIO and the time of the activation. Developers can use this information to compare different UI implementations and how the users respond to them.

In the next section, we are going to present a simple illustrative example of how Dandelion can be used to prototype and implement a distributed physical UI.

4 Using Dandelion for DPUI Prototyping: An Example Use Case

In our laboratory we been working on the implementation of a life assistant application for elderly people. This assistant is an AmI system that can be deployed in the different environments where the user lives, like her own home and the home of her relatives. In order to engage elderly people to use the system, it is very important that they find the system natural and easy to use. Because of this, the interaction must be adapted to the user needs and characteristics, without forgetting the environment characteristics. Therefore, the system will not use the same devices and interaction technologies in the case of a blind user or a deaf user, and it will not use the same devices in the user home as in a relative's home, as probably the former will have dedicated devices that are not available in the latter.

To simplify the presentation we have selected the UI of a small subsystem of this life assistant application. It is the notification system of the assistant, which is in charge of notifying events, alarms or messages to the users, for example if they have a meeting with the doctor, they are going to receive a visit at home or they have to take some medications.

The UI of the system is a fairly simple one. It only needs to output a message to the user and receive a confirmation. In a classical PC system, it could be a simple notification dialog with a label and a button to accept the message. But if we think of this UI in the terms of Dandelion, that is, in terms of abstract interaction operations, it needs an output interaction to show the message to the user, and an action interaction coming from the user to represent the action of confirming the message. The following code shows how this simple interface could be described using UsiXML. It only requires an output AIU and a trigger AIU that are related inside a container using a compound AIU.

```
<AbstractCompoundIU id="1" shortLabel="Notif. Dialog">
 <AbstractDataIU id="2" shortLabel="Notif. Label">
  <AbstactOutputIU\>
 <\AbstractDataIU>
 <AbstractTriggerIU id="3" shortLabel="Discard action">
  <AbstractOperationIU\>
 </AbstractTriggerIU>
</AbstractCompoundIU>
```

[UsiXML code describing the user interface of the example confirmation dialog.]

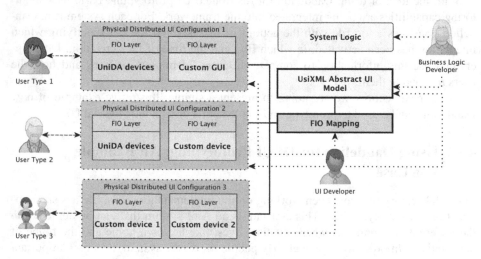

Fig. 3. Different physical configuration of the UI can be easily developed and tested. It is only necessary to implement new FIOs and change the FIO mapping of the application.

The next step for the developer is to connect the application logic with the UI. As described in section 2, this is achieved programmatically at runtime. The developer associates application data or action objects to the different AIUs described in the UsiXML file. In this example, a string object, that will contain the message that must be shown, is associated to the AIU with id '2', and a callback action, that must be executed when the user confirms the reception of the message, to the AIU with id '3'.

Until now, the developer has implemented the system logic and the system UI, and all has been done at an abstract level. The system now needs some FIOs that implement the real interaction with the user, and the developers can now take advantage of the decoupling between the UI definition and its realization in order to test different physical configurations of the UI.

For the illustration of this example, two different configurations have been implemented and tested: First a configuration of the UI for blind users, and then a configuration for deaf users. Figure 4 shows a picture of the physical setup and the relation between the physical interaction devices and the application through the FIO mapping process. As can be seen, five FIOs have been implemented to support these scenarios:

- *outputs*: colored lights using UniDA, an overlay GUI shown in a TV display, and voice synthesis using Festival [14]
- *inputs*: a light switch connected to a KNX network [15] accessed using UniDA and a hand gesture detected by a Kinnect like device

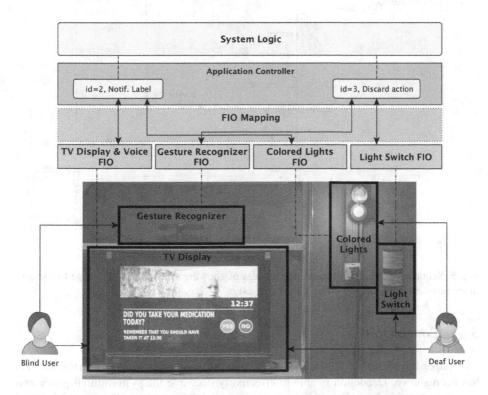

Fig. 4. Notification UI of the life assistant application adapted for deaf and blind users

In the home of a deaf user, the output AIU could be mapped simultaneously to a colored light and to a TV display. As shown in Figure 5, when the application changes the value of the message object, the UIC will send an output GIP event to the colored light and TV FIOS. When the event is received by the FIOs, the colored light will be turned on, so that the user knows that there is a notification, and can go to the living room to read it on the TV. To confirm the message she could activate a light switch deployed in the wall, which will publish an action GIP event that will be received by the UIC. While in the home of a blind user, the output AIU will be associated to the voice synthesizing FIO, and the trigger AIU to the Kinnect hand gesture recognizer.

```
10:43:34.413 | changeIO(message) | AIU(2)('Notif. Label')
10:43:34.867 | output(message) | FIO(1)('colored light')
10:43:34.985 | output(message) | FIO(2)('display')
10:46:17.146 | action() | FIO(3)('switch')
10:46.17.227 | trigger('msgConfirmationCallback')
```

[Example of UI monitoring log generated for the example described.]

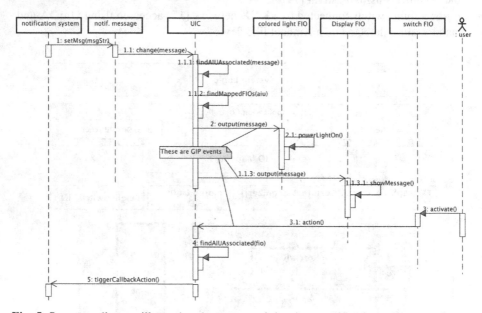

Fig. 5. Sequence diagram illustrating the process of showing a notification message to the user in the physical configuration of the UI for deaf users

5   Conclusions

This paper has presented the Dandelion framework and its prototyping capabilities. As has been shown, Dandelion is able to effectively decouple the system intelligence and system interaction logic from the complexities, modalities and specific control logic of the devices (physical or not) used to implement the user interaction. It does so by using a distributed device abstraction layer that encapsulates the behavior of devices behind a remote interface of generic interaction actions, and a distributed UI management system that allows the easy modification of the final UI at deployment time.

The ease in changing the physical implementation of the UI without affecting the system and interaction logic makes Dandelion an interesting tool for prototyping user interaction in distributed systems, especially when physical user interfaces are involved, like in Ambient Intelligence systems or Ubiquitous Computing systems.

References

1. Augusto, J.C., McCullagh, P.: Ambient Intelligence: Concepts and Applications. Int'l J. Computer Science and Information Systems 4(1), 1–28 (2009)
2. Dadlani, P., Peregrin Emparanza, J., Markopoulos, P.: Distributed User Interfaces in Ambient Intelligent Environments: A Tale of Three Studies. In: Proc. 1st DUI, pp. 101–104. University of Castilla-La Mancha (2011)
3. Varela, G.: Autonomous adaptation of user interfaces to support mobility in ambient intelligence systems. In: Proceedings of the 5th ACM SIGCHI Symposium on Engineering Interactive Computing Systems, EICS 2013, pp. 179–182. ACM, New York (2013)
4. Varela, G., Paz-Lopez, A., Becerra Permuy, J.A., Duro, R.J.: The Generic Interaction Protocol: Increasing portability of distributed physical user interfaces. In: Revista Română de Interacțiune Om-Calculator, vol. 6(3), pp. 249–268. ACM SIGCHI Romania (2013)
5. Thevenin, D., Coutaz, J.: Plasticity of user interfaces: Framework and research agenda. In: Proc. INTERACT 1999, pp. 110–117. IOS Press (1999)
6. Balme, L., Demeure, A., Barralon, N., Calvary, G.: Cameleon-rt: A software architecture reference model for distributed, migratable, and plastic user interfaces. In: Markopoulos, P., Eggen, B., Aarts, E., Crowley, J.L. (eds.) EUSAI 2004. LNCS, vol. 3295, pp. 291–302. Springer, Heidelberg (2004)
7. UsiXML, http://www.usixml.org, http://www.usixml.eu
8. Blumendorf, M., Lehmann, G., Albayrak, S.: Bridging models and systems at runtime to build adaptive user interfaces. In: Proc. 2nd EICS 2010, pp. 9–18. ACM (2010)
9. Abascal, J., Fernández de Castro, I., Lafuente, A.L., Cia, J.M.: Adaptive interfaces for supportive ambient intelligence environments. In: Miesenberger, K., Klaus, J., Zagler, W.L., Karshmer, A.I. (eds.) ICCHP 2008. LNCS, vol. 5105, pp. 30–37. Springer, Heidelberg (2008)
10. Ballagas, R., Ringel, M., Stone, M., Borchers, J.: iStuff: A physical user interface toolkit for ubiquitous computing environments. In: Proceedings of the SIGCHI Conference on Human Factors in Computing Systems, pp. 537–544. ACM, New York (2003)
11. Varela, G., Paz-Lopez, A., Becerra, J.A., Vazquez-Rodriguez, S., Duro, R.J.: UniDA: Uniform Device Access Framework for Human Interaction Environments. Sensors 11(10), 9361–9392 (2011)
12. UniDA: Uniform Device Access framework, http://www.github.com/GII/UNIDA
13. STOMP, Simple Text Oriented Messaging Protocol, http://stomp.github.io/
14. The Festival Speech Synthesis System, http://www.cstr.ed.ac.uk/projects/festival/
15. KNX Technology, KNX Association, http://www.knx.org/knx-en/knx/technology/introduction/index.php

Natural Interaction

Expression Recognition Driven Virtual Human Animation

Junghyun Cho[1], Yu-Jin Hong[1,2], Sang C. Ahn[1], and Ig-Jae Kim[1,2]

[1] Imaging Media Research Center, Korea Institute of Science and Technology, Korea
[2] Dept. of HCI & Robotics, Korea University of Science and Technology, Korea
{jhcho,hyj,asc,kij}@imrc.kist.re.kr

Abstract. Since the character expressions are high dimensional, it is not easy to control them intuitively with simple interface. So far, existing controlling and animating methods are mainly based on three dimensional motion capture system for high quality animation. However, using the three dimensional motion capture system is not only unhandy but also quite expensive. In this paper, we therefore present a new control method for 3D facial animation based on expression recognition technique. We simply utilize off-the-shelf a single webcam as a control interface which can easily combine with *blendshape* technique for 3D animation. We measure the user's emotional state by a robust facial feature tracker and facial expression classifier and then transfer the measured probabilities of facial expressions to the domain of *blendshape* basis. We demonstrate our method can be one of efficient interface for virtual human animation through our experiments.

Keywords: 3D facial animation, control interface, blendshape, facial feature tracking, expression recognition.

1 Introduction

Controlling 3D avatar, especially its emotional expression, is widely used in a variety of applications such as teleconference, movies, real-time avatar game, and human computer interaction. Therefore, it is very important to provide intuitive control interface for avatar animation. Due to high complexity of human expressions, however, it is difficult to control over three dimensional facial animation with simple interface.

Traditionally, we should use a facial motion capture system to express the detail emotional variation of virtual avatar. The facial motion capture is the process of electronically converting the movements of a user's face into a digital database using multiple cameras. A facial motion capture database describes the coordinates of reference points on the user's face.

Typical marker based motion capture systems apply up to 100 markers to the users face and track the marker movement with high resolution cameras to get accurate movements of facial parts so that we can express facial expression finely that has high degree of freedom. Unfortunately these systems are expensive, complicated, and

N. Streitz and P. Markopoulos (Eds.): DAPI 2014, LNCS 8530, pp. 89–96, 2014.
© Springer International Publishing Switzerland 2014

time-consuming to use. Marker-based systems are accurate but cumbersome and do not allow full expression for the actor due to the attached markers.

Nowadays, researchers focused on markerless technologies use the features of the face such as the corners of the lips and eyes, and wrinkles and then track them. This technique is much less cumbersome, and allows greater expression for the actor but accuracy is less than the one of marker based.

Two dimensional capture can be achieved using a single camera but this produces less sophisticated tracking, and is unable to fully capture three dimensional motions.

To overcome these drawbacks when we apply two dimensional capture method, Chai et al. [9] proposed the system to extract a small set of animation control parameters from video. Because of the nature of video data, these parameters may be noisy, low-resolution, and contain errors. Their system used the knowledge embedded in motion capture data to translate these low-quality 2D animation control signals into high-quality 3D facial expressions. To adapt the synthesized motion to a new character model, they introduced an efficient expression retargeting technique whose runtime computation is constant independent of the complexity of the character model.

Although this method enabled us to get a real-time facial animation but it needs large 3D motion dataset in advance.

So, we propose a new method which use only a single webcam but doesn't require large 3D motion database. Once we set the animation control interface, we have to choose animation production method. In terms of 3D facial animation production, the most popular approach currently is the blendshape technique, which synthesizes expressions by taking a linear combination of a set of pre-modeled expressions.

A fundamental question in developing a blendshape-based facial animation system is how to form the expression basis. A casual approach is to use an expression basis comprised of manually modeled, intuitively recognizable key expressions. In our approach, we build each member of the expression basis beforehand according to the shapes of emotional expressions that we could classify [3]. Here, we set the number of basis is equal to the number of emotional expressions that we could recognize.

Another fundamental issue that must be solved when developing a blendshape technique is how to assign the weights to each member of the expression basis set in order to produce the desired expression sequences. As we set the same number of expression basis to the emotional expression, we can simply assign the recognition result, in terms of probability, of each pre-trained expression to the weight of each member of basis at every video frame.

The remainder of this paper is organized as follows. Section 2 explains the facial expression recognition technique we used. Section 3 presents the procedure for avatar animation. Section 4 reports the experimental results, and Section 5 concludes the paper.

2   Facial Expression Recognition

An automatic facial expression recognition system needs to solve the following problems: detection and location of faces in a cluttered scene, facial feature extraction, and facial expression recognition.

2.1 Face Detection

Face detection has been regarded as the most complex and challenging problem in the field of computer vision, due to the large intra-class variations caused by the changes in facial appearance, lighting, and expression. Such variations result in the face distribution to be highly nonlinear and complex in any space which is linear to the original image space.

Face detection techniques have been researched for years and much progress has been proposed in literature. Most of the face detection methods focus on detecting frontal faces with good lighting conditions. These methods can be categorized into four types, such as, knowledge-based, feature invariant, template matching and appearance-based.

Any of the methods can involve color segmentation, pattern matching, statistical analysis and complex transforms, where the common goal is classification with least amount of error. Bounds on the classification accuracy change from method to method yet the best techniques are found in areas where the models or rules for classification are dynamic and produced from machine learning processes.

Viola and Jones [2] presented a fast and robust method for face detection which is 15 times quicker than any technique at the time of release with 95% accuracy. The technique relies on the use of simple Haar-like features that are evaluated quickly through the use of a new image representation. We used this technique in this work.

2.2 Facial Feature Tracking

In recent years, research for facial feature extraction and tracking methods became popular among computer vision society, such as SDM [6], CLM [7, 8], Shape Regression [10], and so on. Owing to these developments, we could get very robust facial feature tracker under various situations. Among them, we developed our algorithm to locate facial features based on tree-regression concept. We simply extract facial feature candidates based on intensity difference of two pixels in the image which are randomly selected. The selected pixels are indexed by the same local coordinate have the same semantic meaning. This enables the tracker to work better under geometric distortion. To select the effective features from a large number of features, we used *correlation based feature selection* method, then simplify the formula which decrease the cost of computations. For every node of the tree in every level one feature would be selected. Maximum $L^2 - 1$, here L is the number of maximum level of tree, features will be selected for every tree. Discriminative features are highly correlated to the regression target. The target $\Delta \hat{S}$ is vectorial delta shape which is the difference between the ground truth shape and current estimated shape, $\Delta \hat{S} = \hat{S} - S^{t-1}$. Good features would have highest correlation value. The following steps to find the features for each tree node which we want to build:

- Project regression target ΔS to a random direction to produce a scalar.
- Select the feature with highest correlation to the projection.
- Repeat step 1 and 2 for every node to obtain new features.
- Select optimum thresholds to generate tree.

Once we build the tree, we search facial features as follows. Face candidate area in an image will be detected by a Viola-Jones face detector, and then a mean shape will be located at the area. High correlated features that had been calculated in training phase will be extracted from the area for every tree. These features will lead to a leaf of the tree and they are led to predict a delta shape ($\Delta\hat{S}$) that will be added to the mean shape. This updates the facial feature shape in every regressor. Fig. 1 shows our search process.

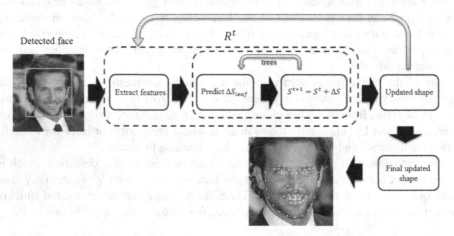

Fig. 1. Search block diagram of tree based facial feature extractor

2.3   Facial Expression Classification

We used a Gaussian Mixture Model (GMM) for our facial expression recognition. A GMM is a parametric probability density function represented as a weighted sum of M component Gaussian densities [1] as given by the equation,

$$p(\mathbf{x}|\lambda) = \sum_{i=1}^{M} \omega_i \, g(\mathbf{x}|\,\boldsymbol{\mu}_i, \boldsymbol{\Sigma}_i) \qquad (1)$$

where $\mathbf{x}$ is a D-dimensional continuous-valued data vector, ω_i, i=1,....,M, are the mixture weights, and $g(\mathbf{x}|\,\boldsymbol{\mu}_i, \boldsymbol{\Sigma}_i)$, i=1,.....,M, are the component Gaussian densities. Each component density is a D-variable Gaussian function of the form. In our experiment, we extract 68 facial feature points and classify six expressions that are defined in FACS [11], such as happiness, sadness, surprise, anger, disgust and neutral, so D and M are 136 and 6, respectively.

Given training data and a GMM configuration, we estimate the parameters of the GMM, which matches the distribution of the training feature vectors. There are several techniques available for estimating the parameters of a GMM. Among them, we used maximum likelihood estimation. We capture T frames per each expression, here we set T=90, for learning each one. For a sequence of T training vectors $X = \{\mathbf{x}_1, ..., \mathbf{x}_T\}$, the GMM likelihood, assuming independence between the vectors, can be written as,

$$p(X|\lambda) = \frac{1}{T}\sum_{t=1}^{T} \Pr(i|\ \mathbf{x}_t, \lambda) \qquad (2)$$

To solve a non-linear function of the parameter λ, we estimate ML parameter iteratively using a special case of the expectation-maximization(EM) algorithm. On each EM iteration, the following re-estimation formulas are used which guarantee a monotonic increase in the model's likelihood value,

Mixture Weights

$$\bar{\omega}_i = \frac{1}{T}\sum_{t=1}^{T} \Pr(i|\ \mathbf{x}_t, \lambda) \qquad (3)$$

Means

$$\bar{\mu}_i = \frac{\sum_{t=1}^{T} \Pr(i|\ \mathbf{x}_t, \lambda)\ \mathbf{x}_t}{\sum_{t=1}^{T} \Pr(i|\ \mathbf{x}_t, \lambda)} \qquad (4)$$

Variances (diagonal covariance)

$$\bar{\sigma}^2_{\ i} = \frac{\sum_{t=1}^{T} \Pr(i|\ \mathbf{x}_t, \lambda)\ x^2_{\ t}}{\sum_{t=1}^{T} \Pr(i|\ \mathbf{x}_t, \lambda)} - \bar{\mu}^2_{\ i} \qquad (5)$$

3   Avatar Animation

The principle of blendshape interpolation is similar to basis member interpolation. In this case, more than 2 base members can be used at a time, and the interpolation is for a single static expression, rather than across time. Each blendshape can be modeled using a variety of different methods. The amount of detail in each expression can also vary, as long as the resulting faces can be 'combined' in some manner. While this method is popular for specifying facial animation, it requires manual specification, and designing a complete animation can be quite time consuming [4].

3.1   Building Expression Basis

Building appropriate key shapes is an important part of shape decomposition. Each key shape adds flexibility and expressiveness to the model, suggesting that many key shapes should be used. However, the user must create a target model for each key shape. In order to reduce user burden the number of key shapes should be kept small. An ideal method would balance these requirements to find the minimal set of key shapes that maintains the desired animation expressiveness [4]. Here, we propose simple but very efficient way for building our expression basis. We select six representative expressions which our classifier can tell more separately and build the same number of expression basis with the shape of corresponding expression of the subject.

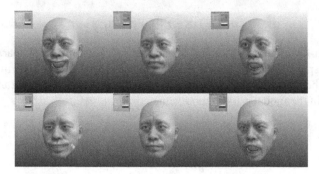

Fig. 2. Six expression basis used in our experiment

4   Experimental Result

For our experiment, we let two test subjects train pre-defined six expressions using a webcam which is installed in front of the monitor. For this, we allow each subject to capture image sequences during three seconds (T=90 frames) for each expression and input them the training engine to build our Gaussian mixture model. We modeled two different avatars which have six different expression bases like Fig. 2. Then we evaluate our proposed system can make the virtual avatar visualize natural expression according to the subject's performance.

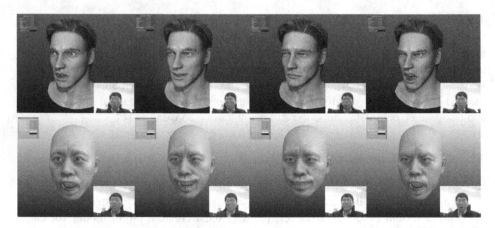

Fig. 3. Example animation sequences with different expressions

Once each subject trained his/her expressions, our classifier showed high performance of recognition over all so we could get avatar's natural expressive animation along with the performance of each subject. Fig. 3 shows two different characters make same expressions following the subject's performance. This example also shows our method can easily control any other different characters without modifying interface. If there's a falling off in recognition quality due to some noises, abrupt expression changes may be occurred. As a consequence of that, we might have weird avatar's expression. Just in case of that, we applied Kalman filter [5] which enables us to get smooth transition. We could get realistic expression of the avatar even though we applied different virtual character to the subject simply by transferring the basis weights. Through our test, we could confirm our proposed system can be efficient and useful interface for controlling a virtual avatar.

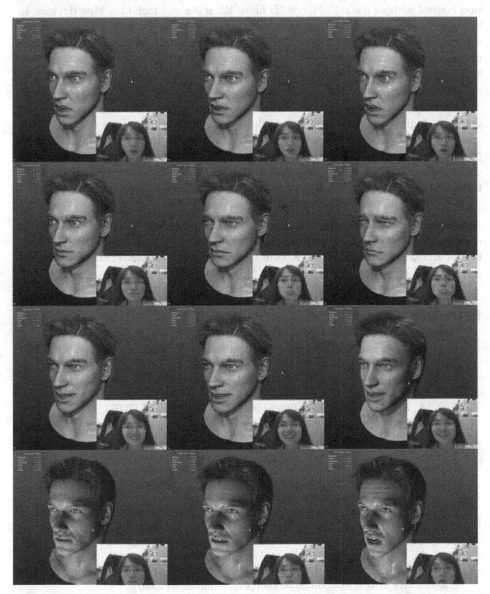

Fig.4. Another example sequences following female subject's expression. Top row shows surprise, second rows show the transition from neutral to sad, third row shows happy state. Especially, bottom row sequences show the stressed expression results by real-time rendering technique.

5   Conclusion

In this paper we propose a new efficient method for facial animation of virtual avatar. By combining the facial feature tracking and facial expression classifying methods with the blendshape interpolation technique, we can obtain the real-time facial animation control without the aid of large 3D facial database and facial tracking devices. In here, our control interface is based on only six expression clusters. Since these pre-selected expressions are not enough to span all the expression space, some possible expressions may not be shown. If we could improve our classifier's performance so that we could tell subtle expression change more precisely, we may expand the coverage of expression space. This may increase the quality of our control interface.

Generally, the controlling of virtual avatar, especially its expression, is not easy due to its high complexity. Our system classified emotional state by a single webcam and can visualize almost possible expression by simple transferring the measured probability of each expression to the weight of each blendshape basis. Through our experiment, we believe our expression based interface can be one of efficient solutions for controlling virtual avatar animation with inexpensive equipment.

Acknowledgement. This work was supported by the Global Frontier R&D Program on <Human-centered Interaction for Coexistence> funded by the National Research Foundation of Korea grant funded by the Korean Government (MEST) (2012M3A6A3055705) and the KIST Institutional Program (Project No. 2E24790).

References

1. Reynolds, D.A.: A Gaussian Mixture Modeling Approach to Text-Independent Speaker Identification., PhD thesis, Georgia Institute of Technology (1992)
2. Viola, Jones: Rapid object detection using a boosted cascade of simple features. In: Computer Vision and Pattern Recognition (2001)
3. Kim, I.J., Ko, H.: Intuitive Quasi-Eigen Faces. ACM GRAPHITE (2007)
4. Chuang, E., Bregler, C.: Performance driven facial animation using blendshape interpolation, Stanford Technical Report CS-TR-200202 (2002)
5. Kalman, R.E.: A new approach to linear filtering and prediction problems. Journal of Basic Engineering 82(1), 35–45 (1960)
6. Xiong, X., Torre, F.: Supervised Descent Method and its Applications to Face Alignment. IEEE Computer Vision and Pattern Recognition (2013)
7. Cristinacce, D., Cootes, T.: Feature detection and tracking with constrained local models. In: BMVC (2006)
8. Saragih, J.M., Lucey, S., Cohn, J.F.: Face Alignment through Subspace Constrained Mean-Shifts. In: IEEE International Conference on Computer Vision (2009)
9. Chai, J., Xiao, J., Hodgins, J.: Vision-based Control of 3D Facial Animation. In: Eurographics/SIGGRAPH Symposium on Computer Animation (2003)
10. Cao, X., Wei, Y., Wen, F., Sun, J.: Face alignment by explicit shape regression. IEEE Computer Vision and Pattern Recognition (2012)
11. Ekman, P., Friesen, W.: Facial Action Coding System: A Technique for the Measurement of Facial Movement. Consulting Psychologists Press, Palo Alto (1978)

Ambient Gesture-Recognizing Surfaces with Visual Feedback

Tobias Grosse-Puppendahl[1], Sebastian Beck[2], Daniel Wilbers[1], Steeven Zeiß[1], Julian von Wilmsdorff[1], and Arjan Kuijper[1,2]

[1] Fraunhofer IGD, Fraunhoferstr. 5, 64283 Darmstadt, Germany
{tobias.grosse-puppendahl,daniel.wilbers,steeven.zeiss,
julian.von-wilmsdorff,arjan.kuijper}@igd.fraunhofer.de
[2] Technische Universität Darmstadt, Hochschulstr. 10, 64289 Darmstadt, Germany
s.beck@stud.tu-darmstadt.de

Abstract. In recent years, gesture-based interaction gained increasing interest in Ambient Intelligence. Especially the success of camera-based gesture recognition systems shows that a great variety of applications can benefit significantly from natural and intuitive interaction paradigms. Besides camera-based systems, proximity-sensing surfaces are especially suitable as an input modality for intelligent environments. They can be installed ubiquitously under any kind of non-conductive surface, such as a table. However, interaction barriers and the types of supported gestures are often not apparent to the user. In order to solve this problem, we investigate an approach which combines a semi-transparent capacitive proximity-sensing surface with an LED array. The LED array is used to indicate possible gestural movements and provide visual feedback on the current interaction status. A user study shows that our approach can enhance the user experience, especially for inexperienced users.

Keywords: gesture recognition, capacitive sensing, proximity sensing.

1 Introduction

Society is very inhomogeneous in itself - possible users' backgrounds differ vastly in age, education, household income and technology experience. Nowadays, technological progress is more rapidly changing than it has ever before and complexity raises simultaneously with growth. The generation of people that did not grow up with computers or touch technology often has difficulties in their first steps of using new technology. Younger people experience difficulties, too, but they are more used to finding their way around these mediums and can generally adapt to new technology faster.

Gesture recognition is a highly promising technology in the field of smart environments, however, it requires training and instruction beforehand. Considering a user's capability to remember gestural movements and the sheer number of interfaces already in use today, high demands arise in terms of cognitive ability. Feedforward and feedback mechanisms for gesture recognition devices may simplify a user's interaction with components and help with memorization.

N. Streitz and P. Markopoulos (Eds.): DAPI 2014, LNCS 8530, pp. 97–108, 2014.

Fig. 1. Low-cost gesture-recognizing surfaces with visual feedback can be employed to control a wide variety of devices within an intelligent environment - reaching from interaction with an entertainment system (left) to interaction with a smart door that can be controlled via gestures, for example in public restrooms (right)

Data acquisition for gesture recognition can rely on different sensing technologies, such as cameras. In our paper, we investigate an alternate low-cost data acquisition approach - an interactive surface equipped with capacitive proximity sensors. It is able to sense hand gestures at distances of up of 20 cm. Rainbowfish' surface can illuminate its surface in different colors, as shown in Figure 1.

Capacitive proximity-sensing gesture recognition systems are able to detect the position of a human body part by combining measurements of many sensors. Each sensor is a combination of a measuring circuit and a sensing electrode made of a variety of materials, depending on the application and the required resolution. An array of capacitive sensors can be used to detect passive interaction patterns, e.g. a person's presence, but also explicit interaction, for example gestures performed by a user over an equipped surface. Besides the low cost compared to cameras, the sensing modality is very suitable in this domain, as sensors can be easily integrated and hidden in walls or furniture [5,16,11]. Moreover, we argue that a user's perception of privacy is higher compared to cameras.

Every gesture recognition system faces the challenge of exposing its affordances and providing feedback to a user. For example, users new to a specific system are often not aware of the supported interaction methods. Therefore, it is necessary to deliver interactive feedback on the interaction status and feedforward information about the gestures a user is able to perform. Figure 1 shows our gesture-recognition device projecting a visual feedback directly on its surface. For example, a glowing shadow can follow a user's hand to make interaction barriers more apparent. Moving arrows or stripes can indicate the possibility of performing a horizontal swipe gesture into a certain direction.

In summary, we provide the following contributions:

1. We present a new capacitive gesture recognition system with visual feedback.
2. In a detailed user study we evaluate the approach for its applicability in smart environments.
3. We identify new interaction paradigms and applications that can be realized with the presented technology.

The remainder of this paper is structured as follows: First, Section 2 deals with related work considering capacitive sensing and gesture recognition in intelligent environments. We present our custom-built hardware in Section 3. The user study and the experimental setup is described in Section 4. We conclude the paper with a summary of our findings in the evaluation and identify potential future research activities.

2   Related Work

The success of gesture-based interaction in the context of entertainment systems initiated an increasing trend towards natural interaction paradigms in intelligent environments. Gesture recognition systems in smart environments represent an intuitive and easy way of interaction with the surrounding, for example allowing the user to control everyday devices using simple gestures. There are several technologies that are suitable to act as an input modality for gesture recognition. Commercial camera-based systems, such as the Microsoft Kinect [9], are able to capture gestures and movements within a room. Other approaches employ the environmental noise in an environment [3] or use mobile phones for gesture recognition [1]. Stationary installed capacitive sensors can act as both, touch-sensitive and proximity-sensitive gesture-recognizing input modalities. They can be used to detect the way we touch objects [11], or infer hand positions in proximities of up to 40 cm [5].

Capacitive sensing is a fairly old and well established technology. The sensing principle was firstly applied by a Russian physicist called Leon Theremin in the 1920s [4]. Later, in the 1990s, capacitive proximity sensing was employed to create 3D user interfaces like the LazyFish [12]. These user interfaces are able to recognize objects like human hands within a proximity of up to 50 cm [12,5].

Today, capacitive sensing found its way into many applications in intelligent environments. Sato et al. use swept frequency capacitive sensing to identify human activities by the way a person touches an object [10]. Especially in smart environments, this approach can recognize how a person touches an object, for example a smart door knob that triggers locking and unlocking of a door [11]. Moreover, the technique can be employed to identify users at the time they touch a screen [7]. Recent activities also include analyzing electro-magnetic noise from household devices to recognize gestures [3].

Proximity sensors based on capacitive sensing are especially suitable for recognizing user interactions within a well-defined interaction space. For example, stationary installed capacitive sensors underneath the floor were used to realize floor localization systems [15,14]. Moreover, capacitive sensors deployed in furniture can be used to build interactive applications, for example by recognizing interactions above a table [16]. Recently, an open-source toolkit for rapid prototyping of capacitive sensing applications was presented, that can be used to realize scenarios like 3D gesture recognition, localization and fall detection [5]. Using this toolkit, objects such as human hands can be recognized within a distance of up to 50 cm, depending on the electrode size.

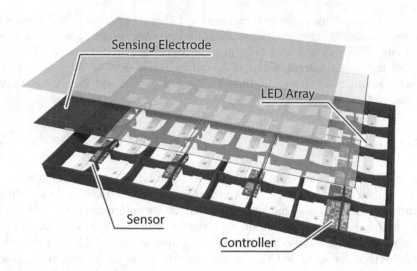

Fig. 2. The device consists of four main components: the sensors, the shielded electrodes made of transparent ITO, an LED array and a controller board. All components are interconnected by an I2C bus.

In order to extract information from low-level capacitive proximity sensing data an object recognition method is essential. These methods range from fast geometric processing [2] to sophisticated object recognition methods like Swiss-Cheese Extended [6].

Considering scenarios that require gesture recognition without a graphical user interface, it is challenging to provide a suitable and meaningful feedback on the current interaction state to the user. This feedback can be provided by different modalities, for example visually or acoustically. Majewski et al. use a laser spot that visualizes a user's pointing direction perceived by the environment to disambiguate device selection [8]. When a device is selected, the spot delivers additional feedback on the successful selection by blinking. The authors of [13] project a visual feedback directly on the user's body. The presented system provides hints on recommended hand movements and delivers feedback on the movements performed. To our knowledge, capacitive proximity sensing devices have not been directly augmented with visual techniques to give feedback on the current interaction status and indicate possible interaction paradigms.

3   Hardware and Processing Chain

A conceptual drawing of Rainbowfish is depicted in Figure 2. It employs 12 sensors which measure the capacitance between the sensor's electrode and its surroundings, also known as a loading-mode measurement [12]. The sensing electrode's surface builds up an electric field to any object in its surrounding. When a human hand approaches the sensing electrode, the capacitance increases.

This effect allows for determining an approximate hand distance based on each sensor's measurement. By combining measurements of all 12 sensors, the hand's position can be inferred by triangulation or weighted-average calculations. In order to conduct the measurement, the resulting capacitor between the electrode and the surrounding objects is charged and discharged with a frequency of 500 KHz. The sensing electrodes are transparent PET foils with a conductive layer of Indium-Tin-Oxide (ITO), a material widely used in modern capacitive touchscreens. They have a size of 10 cm by 8 cm and consist of two layers: a sensing and a shielding layer. The shielding layer is necessary to avoid electronic interferences with the underlying hardware, such as the sensors and the LED array. All components are embedded into a 3D-printed grid structure. The electrodes are adhered underneath the device's top surface - a 3 mm thick layer of semi-transparent Plexiglas.

The device has a central Inter-Integrated-Circuit (I2C) bus used for interconnecting the sensors with a controller board. This controller board is responsible for scheduling the sensors and controlling the LED array. The measurements are performed concurrently to achieve a suitable temporal and spatial performance. However, when sensor electrodes are located side-by-side, a parallel measurement would affect the neighbouring sensor. Therefore, in each measurement step only three sensors are activated in parallel to avoid interference. Using this method, we currently obtain 20 measurements per second for each sensor. Rainbowfish's controller sends the sensor values to a PC through a USB connection. The PC executes additional processing steps, like drift compensation and normalization, and determines the position of a user's hand. Based on this information, an application is able to send information on its execution state or supported gestures back to Rainbowfish. Instead of sending pixel-related data with a high update rate, the application sends lightweight function calls to trigger pre-defined visualization profiles. These profiles include illuminating the whole surface in a specified color and for a certain time, animating a swiping gesture, drawing colored rectangles, and glow effects on continuous 2D coordinates.

4   User Study

The overall goal of the user study is to explore the applicability of visual feedback on a gesture-recognizing surface in smart environments. We stated a number of hypothesis, which were investigated in the study: (*H1*) visual feedback increases the interaction speed, (*H2*) a novice user is able to handle an unknown system more easily, (*H3*) a user is able to recognize usage and system errors immediately, and (*H4*) the perception of visual feedback depends on the familiarity with the system. Therefore, we conducted a user study with 18 participants. The study consisted of four main parts: (1) which gestures would a user perform to trigger a certain action, (2) imitate gestures based on visual feedforward animations, (3) interpret visual feedback and (4) use Rainbowfish in two exemplary applications for smart environments.

4.1 Perception of Feedback and Feedforward Visualizations

In order to investigate if users are able to handle a system more easily with visual feedback and feedforward clues (*H2*), we conducted an experiment consisting of two parts. First, the participants were asked to perform certain gestures to reach an application specific goal without any animations shown on Rainbowfish's service - for example by giving instructions like *'raise the volume of a media player'* or *'switch the light off'*.

The variety in which the gestures were carried out turned out to be very high and coherent. However, they showed substantial analogies to smartphone and tablet PC usage. Eventually some general statements can be made for certain goals, for example for instructions like *select an object*. This instruction mainly resulted in grabbing, tapping on the device's surface, or hovering over the object. When considering smart environments, it can be concluded that gesture-recognizing surfaces are very hard to handle without feedforward information if only the functional goals are known to a user.

In the second experiment, the test persons were asked to imitate gestures based on feedforward visualizations projected on the Rainbowfish's surface. Again, we investigated the variety of gestures which were carried out. The feedforward animations are shown in Figure 3. Therefore, we exploited analogies to common touchscreen gestures (pinch-to-zoom, rotate, etc.), which led to a vast majority of

Fig. 3. Feedforward animations for gestures in front of Rainbowfish. The first column shows a swipe gesture from left to right, the second indicates a rotate gesture with a single hand, whereas the third visualization shows a two-handed rotate gesture.

correctly performed gestures (93.5 %). This supports the assumption that the presented feedforward animations are a suitable way of representing the affordances of a gesture-recognizing surface.

In the following experiment, we presented each participant a number of feedback expressions displayed on Rainbowfish's surface. This experiment was conducted to explore how visual feedback provided by an application is perceived by a user (*H3*). Figure 4 shows a subset of feedback animations which were evaluated. As expected, a short green flash was associated with the acknowledgement of an action by almost all users. On the other hand, a red flash was associated to neglection or rejection. Yellow and blue flashs were mainly associated to a wide variety of meanings, such as *waiting* or *in progress*, which does not allow for any generalizable statement. Interestingly, more users were able to associate a green flash with a positive outcome when the complementary red flash was shown afterwards.

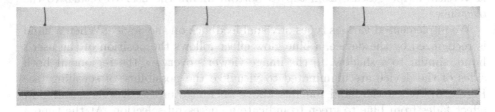

Fig. 4. Different types of feedback can be used to indicate certain application-specific outcome. In our study we asked the users to associate a meaning to the animations shown in the three images.

4.2 Evaluation of Applications in Smart Environments

In the next part of our user study, we investigated to exemplary applications which we developed for Rainbowfish. In the first application the participants controlled a home entertainment application - an image viewer - with gestures. This application consists of our gesture recognition device, as well as a screen for displaying the images. The second experiment solely employs the gesture recognition device without providing an additional graphical user interface. In this part of the evaluation, the users were asked to open, close and lock an automatic door by performing gestures.

Home Entertainment. In this experiment, an image viewer as an exemplary home entertainment application was evaluated. We placed our gesture recognition device in front of a screen that showed the image viewer application. In this setup, depicted in Figure 5, the user is able to manipulate the application's cursor by the position of her or his hands. The participant is able to scroll to both sides by placing a hand near the edges of the device. In the detail view, horizontal swipe gestures are employed to switch to the next or previous image.

Fig. 5. In the image viewer application, a user is able to select and browse between images using gestures which are enriched with feedforward animations and interactive feedback

A vertical swipe gesture from top to bottom allows the user to return to the overview.

We implemented various types of visual feedback on the device. When a hand is recognized by the device, a blue glow effect follows the position of the user's hand, similar to a shadow. In the image viewer's overview the regions at both sides of the device are illuminated to visualize the possibility of scrolling (see Figure 6). When the hand remains above an image in the overview, the glow effect fades from blue to green to indicate a successful selection. At the time a gesture is performed, the device indicates the successful recognition by shortly lighting up in green (see Figure 7).

Fig. 6. Interactive regions are visualized with a glow effect. When the hand moves over the corresponding region, an application-specific action is triggered (e.g. scrolling in the image viewer).

Fig. 7. When a gesture is recognized successfully, the device lights up in green. Moreover, it is possible to indicate unrecognized or unsupported gestures by lighting up in red.

Every participant was instructed to perform a set of tasks, one group obtaining a visual feedback by the device and one without. In order to find out if visual feedback speeds up the interaction ($H1$) and makes usage or system errors visible faster ($H2$) we recorded the number of unsuccessfully recognized gestures and the resulting interaction speed by counting the number of actions in a given time span. Additionally, we asked qualitative questions on a Likert scale from 1-10 to investigate if the perception of visual feedback depends on the familarity with a system ($H4$) and the interaction becomes easier for novice users ($H3$).

The participants were asked if they paid attention to the visual feedback provided by the Rainbowfish. One test person did not observe any feedback at all, because she was focused on the application shown on the television. Many other participants had a similar experience: they were not able to interpret the different effects and colors of the board because they focused on the application itself. Some could not associate their actions with a color or animation. Overall, the participants only showed a slight tendency to pay attention to the device's visual feedback (5.65/10 points) and supported them in their initial steps with the device (6.44/10 points). Despite the limited perception of visual feedback, the majority of users did not feel disturbed by the illuminated surface (3.00/10 points).

In conclusion, the evaluation of a home entertainment application showed that two visual feedback mechanisms - the graphical user interface and the gesture recognizing board itself - were not necessary for the majority of users. Nevertheless, novice users or users who experienced problems during the interaction benefitted from the visual feedback and feedforward animations ($H4$). An additional positive aspect can be seen in the influence of the Rainbowfish's multicolor lightning on the intrinsic motivation of a user. It was mentioned by many participants that they liked the device and especially the colors, and were motivated to start interacting with it ($H3$). The interaction speed could not be increased by providing feedback and feedforward information ($H1$).

Contactless Door-Closing Mechanism. We also conducted an experiment on controlling parts of an intelligent environment without using a graphical user interface. Therefore, Rainbowfish may be incorporated into walls, doors, or home appliances like cooking plates. We built an automatic door that can be controlled using gestures - for example to be used in public restrooms. A user is able to lock, unlock, close and open the door by performing horizontal movements in front of the device. The device delivers interactive feedback on the interaction state and gestures that can be performed. The automatic door control has three possible states, with the related colors: open (green), closed (yellow), and locked (red).

We compared two different types of visual feedback. First, a minimalistic feedback is provided by illuminating the device with the color of the current door state (see Figure 8). Second, we also visualized the gestures that are required to switch to the next state (see Figure 9). For example we visualized a red swipe gesture within the 'closed' state of the door to indicate that the door can be locked. Therefore, the corresponding colors of all states were used to visualize the required gesture.

Rainbowfish's output was essential to recognize the state of the door, as the *closed* and *locked* state cannot be differentiated by the user. The participants acknowledged that they directly focused on the visual feedback (8.48/10 points), even if they were not novice users ($H4$). At the same time, the users felt slightly

Fig. 8. The minimalistic feedback shows the state of the door - which is currently locked (red)

Fig. 9. The extended feedback also indicates when a hand approaches the gesture-recognizing surface

more disturbed by the visual feedback than in the first experiment (3.67/10 points). Nevertheless, most of the participants could interpret the correct meaning of color and animation correctly. However, the interaction speed did not improve (*H1*). The opinions about the two provided modes varied strongly among the participants. Some of them mentioned that it was not necessary to animate swipe gestures because of their convenience, and a simple state-dependent feedback was sufficient for this use-case. However, the majority of all participants experienced the animated feedback to be very helpful.

4.3   User Study Summary

It can be concluded that feedforward animations and feedback can help novice users to control devices by gestures in a smart environment (supporting *H2*). Visual feedback and feedforward information helps this group of users when experiencing usage problems (support *H3*). Users who are familiar to a system do not benefit substantially from feedforward animations (supporting *H4*). Moreover, the visualizations on Rainbowfish's surface had no influence on the interaction speed (not supporting *H1*). When providing an additional graphical user interface, the perception of feedback and feedforward animations is very limited. This supports the assumption that a system with visual feedback should be deployed as a stand-alone input modality within a smart environment.

Many users also criticized time delay as well as limited interaction distance. These problems are mainly related to technical issues, which resulted from the transparent electrode material. Mechanical deformations of ITO foil can lead to slight damages of the coating, and thus, a decreased conductivity. This effect resulted in several problems months after building the device. Furthermore, when the material is deformed due to mechanical influences (e.g. by a tap on the surface), the capacitance may change rapidly and lead to unexpected behaviour. In the future we will strongly focus on more resilient materials, for example thin conductive layers of silver on PET foil. Also, we aim to achieve interaction distances of 30 cm increasing the voltage levels from 3.3 V to 12 V.

5   Conclusion and Outlook

In this paper, we presented Rainbowfish, a novel capacitive gesture recognition system capable of delivering interactive visual feedback and feedforward information. The system was implemented with custom-built hardware and a two demonstration applications focusing on different aspects in a smart environment. In a detailed user study, we investigated the usefulness of the proposed method and possible inferences for the usage within a smart environment.

Our user study showed that visual feedback and feedforward information are very helpful for novice users who are not familiar with the corresponding gesture recognition system. When a graphical user interface is employed, experienced users often do not notice visual feedback provided on the gesture recognizing surface. On the other hand, when no GUI is provided, visual feedback also helps experienced users to interact with the gesture-recognizing surface. Having completed the experiments, participants looked forward to use our applications - resulting in a multitude of ideas where technology could be used in the future. Especially public sanitary installations, like toilet flushes, toilet doors or doors in general were mentioned. Besides that, a water tap with a gesture-controlled temperature and water regulation was the most popular idea. Moreover, many applications within a living environment were mentioned, especially in the kitchen and the bathrooms where hygienic requirements are needed. Situations in which the user has sticky hands or carries things can be simplified by gesture-recognizing fridge doors, cookers or drawers. Various other ideas included the control of ambient lightning, gaming, multimedia applications and interactive furniture.

In future work, we will aim at achieving an increased interaction distance, which is currently quite low (≤ 20 cm). Enhancing the interaction distance will allow for recognizing sophisticated 3D gestures, instead of 2D in-the-air gestures. This possibility raises new research questions on possible visualizations, as a 2D projection surface is mapped to 3D movements. Moreover, we will work on different types of user feedback, in particular by providing additional sounds when a gesture is recognized.

Acknowledgments. We would like to thank the students, visitors of the university fair *Hobit*, employees of Fraunhofer IGD and Technische Universitaet Darmstadt who took part in the user study.

References

1. Ballagas, R., Borchers, J., Rohs, M., Sheridan, J.G.: The smart phone: A ubiquitous input device. IEEE Pervasive Computing 5(1), 70–77 (2006)
2. Braun, A., Hamisu, P.: Using the human body field as a medium for natural interaction. In: PETRA 2009, pp. 50:1–50:7 (2009)

3. Cohn, G., Morris, D., Patel, S., Tan, D.: Humantenna: Using the body as an antenna for real-time whole-body interaction. In: CHI 2012, pp. 1901–1910 (2012)
4. Glinsky, A.: Theremin: Ether Music and Espionage. University of Illinois Press (2000)
5. Grosse-Puppendahl, T., Berghoefer, Y., Braun, A., Wimmer, R., Kuijper, A.: Opencapsense: A rapid prototyping toolkit for pervasive interaction using capacitive sensing. In: PerCom 2013, pp. 152–159 (2013)
6. Grosse-Puppendahl, T., Braun, A., Kamieth, F., Kuijper, A.: Swiss-cheese extended: An object recognition method for ubiquitous interfaces based on capacitive proximity sensing. In: CHI 2013, pp. 1401–1410 (2013)
7. Harrison, C., Sato, M., Poupyrev, I.: Capacitive fingerprinting: Exploring user differentiation by sensing electrical properties of the human body. In: UIST 2012, pp. 537–544 (2012)
8. Majewski, M., Braun, A., Marinc, A., Kuijper, A.: Providing visual support for selecting reactive elements in intelligent environments. In: Gavrilova, M.L., Tan, C.J.K., Kuijper, A. (eds.) Transactions on Computational Science XVIII. LNCS, vol. 7848, pp. 248–263. Springer, Heidelberg (2013)
9. Microsoft: http://www.xbox.com/kinect/ (accessed June 20, 2013)
10. Poupyrev, I., Yeo, Z., Griffin, J.D., Hudson, S.: Sensing human activities with resonant tuning. In: CHI 2010 EA, pp. 4135–4140 (2010)
11. Sato, M., Poupyrev, I., Harrison, C.: Touché: Enhancing touch interaction on humans, screens, liquids, and everyday objects. In: CHI 2012, pp. 483–492 (2012)
12. Smith, J.R., Gershenfeld, N., Benton, S.A.: Electric Field Imaging. Ph.D. thesis, Massachusetts Institute of Technology (1999)
13. Sodhi, R., Benko, H., Wilson, A.: Lightguide: Projected visualizations for hand movement guidance. In: CHI 2012, pp. 179–188 (2012)
14. Sousa, M., Techmer, A., Steinhage, A., Lauterbach, C., Lukowicz, P.: Human tracking and identification using a sensitive floor and wearable accelerometers. In: PerCom 2013, vol. 18, p. 22 (2013)
15. Valtonen, M., Vuorela, T., Kaila, L., Vanhala, J.: Capacitive indoor positioning and contact sensing for activity recognition in smart homes. JAISE 4, 1–30 (2012)
16. Wimmer, R., Kranz, M., Boring, S., Schmidt, A.: Captable and capshelf - unobtrusive activity recognition using networked capacitive sensors. In: INSS 2007, pp. 85–88 (2007)

Smart Wristband: Touch-and-Motion–Tracking Wearable 3D Input Device for Smart Glasses

Jooyeun Ham[1], Jonggi Hong[1], Youngkyoon Jang[1],
Seung Hwan Ko[2], and Woontack Woo[1]

[1] Korea Advanced Institute of Science and Technology, Deajeon, South Korea
{yeon1001,koreahjg,y.jang,wwoo}@kaist.ac.kr
[2] Seoul National University, Seoul, South Korea
maxko@snu.ac.kr

Abstract. The smart wristband is a novel type of wearable input device for smart glasses, and it can control multi-dimensional contents by using touch and motion. The smart wristband uses a touch-and-motion–tracking system with a touch screen panel (TSP) and inertial measurement unit (IMU) to help users control the smart glasses' interface accurately and quickly without environmental noise, distortion, and multi-leveled pattern recognition tasks.

This paper presents the availability and usability of the smart glasses; how exactly and quickly users can manipulate the smart glasses' multi-dimensional contents and augmented reality (AR) system by selecting, moving, and changing contents via touching and dragging a finger and rotating the wrist; the device's point-and-click capacity; and its navigation, program switchover, zoom in and out, undo and redo for interactions, and 3D virtual object manipulation aspects for application.

Keywords: Distributed, Ambient and pervasive interactions, Interactive matter and physical computing, Wearable computing, Input Device, Smart device, Smart glasses, Head-mounted display, touch-aware, motion-aware, multimodal/multisensory interaction, Symmetric interaction in real and virtual worlds.

1   Introduction

The use of interactive 3D environments has increased the demand for ubiquitous technologies [1]. The continuous research on ubiquitous environments demands the development of wearable computers to control the system. Although various approaches were investigated to overcome the limitations of interaction between humans and wearable computers, products have had difficulty maintaining a foothold in the smart device market, and research has been limited due to the absence of a fast and accurately responsive system.

A see-through head-mounted display (HMD) can provide a transparent display area within a user's field of view, enabling a user to view both physical objects in the user's surroundings and visual elements on the display. In some situations, however, such as when the user is navigating a busy environment, displayed visual elements can be

N. Streitz and P. Markopoulos (Eds.): DAPI 2014, LNCS 8530, pp. 109–118, 2014.

distracting and/or may impair the user from viewing physical objects in his or her surroundings [2]. Though a head-mounted display has a highly responsive output system, there is no stable input device that understands a user's command quickly and accurately without distraction or that enables multi-dimensional manipulation to interact with the 3D environment of the real world or virtual world.

The new input device in this project, a wristband-type motion-aware touch panel, is designed to resolve these problems, allowing for stability of input and a greater degree of freedom. In order to utilize a familiar input device, we chose a touch panel that has been popular since smartphones as a main input channel began to dominate the market for mobile devices. Obviously, using a touch panel for pointing is a more stable input method than using hand gestures or voice recognition because it is less influenced by the surrounding environment. Another problem of limited DOF can be mitigated by this device because it provides a higher degree of freedom by utilizing the rotation of users' wrists. The additional DOF can be efficiently used to deal with various GUIs available through the HMD.

The finger and wrist have an advantage as the position for the wearable device because these are the most familiar parts of body for manipulating devices, and they have the greatest range of space to control. A large portion of the population already uses their fingers and wrists to manipulate devices, manipulating devices that range from drills to computers. Since using the suggested motion-aware touch panel utilizes this familiar interaction, a motion sensor, and a touch pad with a cursor, users will not be confused and find the use of this device unappealing. Also, a wristband-type device is less likely to make people irritated, since the wearing sensation is similar to a watch, and they will find the device less likely to misplace compared to a wallet or a phone. The wrist is a very attractive body part for this device because it is connected to the finger, which is the most delicate part of the human body, and also to the shoulder and elbow, which have the largest range of motion among the body parts. The shoulder and elbow increase the wrist's position freely and widely. Although the wristband form factor requires a relatively small screen size, people can use the intuitive and delicate device without complicated procedures.

This paper presents a wristband-type 3D input system called *smart wristband*, which applies users' commands exactly by implementing the concepts above.

2   Prior Work

Smart devices have advanced rapidly. From the introduction of the first smart phone, "Simon," to the commercialization of the first wearable HMD took only twenty years. HMDs are simply reinvented wearable computing for a new era; many researchers are conducting research focused on HMD and related applications. HMD is a display device worn on the head or as part of a helmet. A typical HMD has either one or two small displays with lenses and semi-transparent mirrors embedded in a helmet, eye-glasses, or visor [3]. To widen the range of applications of HMD, including operation in cluttered environments and human-computer interaction on-the-move, a variety of input systems for HMD have been invented; however, due to limited input systems, these devices are not yet a perfect tool for human-computer interaction or wearable computing.

One of the input systems for HMD, speech recognition that enables human interaction with computers through a voice/speech platform in order to initiate an embedded service or process has been advanced. Apple's Siri and Google's Voice Search can find directions and set important reminders. Moreover, research on gesture recognition, which recognizes and identifies sign language by using cameras and computer-vision algorithms, allowing humans to communicate with a computer by hand-tracking and hand-posture recognition [4], has been conducted at research fields through computer vision and image processing. Speech- and gesture-activated control offer limited accuracy that varies from user to user and depends on ambient noise levels. Speech and image input also raise user-privacy concerns when used in public spaces and speed concerns for multi-processing tasks [5]. Even though hand-held point-and-click controllers or one-handed keyboards like the Twiddler [6] are a more stable input method, their degree of freedom is limited because of physical constraints.

Recently, as interest in wearable computers has increased, the method to utilize a wearable input device in the mobile environment has also investigated. Thomas et al. endeavored to discover what part of the body is the most appropriate position if a TSP can be attached to the body [7]. In this study, they showed that the thigh is the position where a TSP made the best performance among the body parts. However, a thigh is hard to utilize in the mobile environment because it is not easy to be reached by the hands. The wrist, by contrast, is reached easily by the hand even while a user is running. More-over, using a TSP attached to the wrist showed similar performance to that of a thigh. Therefore, we could conclude that the wrist is a proper position for a wearable TSP. The wrist is a very attractive body-part that is connected to the finger, which is the most delicate part on the human body. The degree of freedom of the wrist is six, which means users can manipulate six directions intuitively, and this range of motion is the highest among the body parts. When the anatomical position is considered as 0°, around our wrist there are two major exceptions: (1) shoulder rotation—arm abducted to 90°, elbow flexed to 90°, with the position of the forearm reflecting the midpoint 0° between internal and external rotation of the shoulder; and (2) supination and pronation—the arm next to the body, elbow flexed to 90°, and the forearm in mid-position 0° between supination and pronation [8]. The shoulder and elbow increase the range of the wrist's motion, which indicates that a wrist has a wide range of input variables such as position, speed, and acceleration, even while the user is on the move.

3   Implementation

3.1   User Interface

The user interface is composed of the 3D HMD and the smart wristband, and the smart wristband consists of three inputs and one output: TSP, IMU, HMD camera, and HMD projector. In the wearing HMD environment, a user controls implanted modes (applications), augmented information, and augmented objects with a smart wristband. First, augmented computing information is projected on the glasses. Second, as the user moves his or her head, a camera takes information from an object. Third, the TSP assists as a touch sensor for drawing an image or moving a cursor to select an object of the screen projected on the glasses to search for information on the object. Fourth, an IMU functions as a motion sensor to control the selected object to switch program mode or to scroll the projected screen. Finally, the input information transfers to a computer, and the processed information is displayed on the glasses.

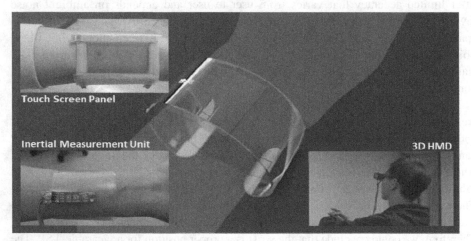

Fig. 1. Concept sketch (Back) and actual implementation (Front) of the smart wristband

Touch Screen Panel. The touch screen panel (TSP) is fabricated by nano-device processing. The indium tin oxide (ITO) on a flexible substrate and a multi-layer composite of silver nanowires and carbon nanotubes on a glass substrate are used as upper and lower electrodes, respectively [9]. The resistances of four sides on electrodes are translated by the "eGalaxTouch" program to apply finger-touch on the TSP to move the cursor, write text, or draw shapes on the projected display.

Inertial Measurement Unit. The inertial measurement unit (IMU) is the Sparkfun 9DOF Sensor Stick [10]. The values from the accelerometer, magnetometer, and gyroscope sensors are fused by the razor-9dof-ahrs method [11]. The dimension of the IMU is 34.8 mm * 10.7 mm * 2.4 mm.

Fig. 2. Implementation of TSP (Left) and IMU (Right)

3.2   Tools and Commands

All of the interactions of the smart wristband are composed of two basic interactions: between the HMD and finger touch and between the HMD and wrist rotation.

The function of TSP is similar to a touch pad on a laptop. While users see a display from the HMD, they can move a pointer to a certain location on the screen and then tap, with a short touch, on the TSP, which is recognized as a click-of-a-mouse input.

IMU is used to detect the motion of the wrist. Users can manipulate the wearable computer system through a quick or slow rotation of the wrist. The position, velocity, and acceleration of the motion of the wrist are measured and reproduced on the projected screen, as is the motion of the wrist.

The following interactions are combined for different applications of 1-dimensional, 2-dimensional, and 3-demensional interactions in various ways.

Finger Touch – Point and Click. The first application is a 1 and 2-dimensional interaction; users point and click the GUI interface on the screen through finger-touch interaction with the TSP. The TSP is a specialized surface that can translate the motion and position of a user's fingers to a relative position on the operating system that is outputted to the projected screen [12]. The TSP has features in common with the touch pad of a laptop, a substitute for a mouse where desk space is scarce. "Point" is the way that users move a pointer, and "click" is the way that they select or enter the target.

Wrist Rotate – navigation. The second application is a 2-dimensional interaction; people can scroll the screen. When users want to see the other side of the screen displayed on the HMD, they scroll augmented information by rotating the wrist. As the size of a head-mounted display is small, the contents shown to a user at once are limited. Therefore, it is probable that users will have to scroll the contents. Here, scrolling through the TSP would trigger fatigue because it would require repetitive clutching. In contrast, scrolling with wrist rotation allows users to control the augmented information easily and intuitively. This interaction can expand the range of contents and application of HMD by extending the screen that users can see and control.

Fig. 3. Navigate screen by using wrist rotation

Quick Wrist Rotate – Program switchover. The third application is a 1-dimensional interaction; users can switch contents with the device. When a user needs to switch the display to show different contents, this can be done by rotating the wrist quickly. The different speed of rotation can be used to trigger the change of contents on the display. Contents implemented in this project are search screen, wallpapers, schedule, and email. In addition, HMD users feel embarrassed when they must speak or gesture in public to change contents. To rectify this, the smart wristband provides private and natural interaction.

Fig. 4. Switch program by using quick wrist rotate

Wrist Rotate with Finger Touch – Zoom in and out. The combination of wrist-rotate and finger-touch tasks results in a zoom-in or zoom-out function. When a user rotates the wrist clockwise and touches the finger on the TSP at the same time, the user will gain a close-up view of contents on the HMD to see the enlarged page at a reduced size. Contrary to this, a counterclockwise rotation with finger touch results in zooming out quickly. To adjust the percentage of zoom setting, a user controls the degree of rotation of the wrist.

Quick Wrist Rotate with Finger Touch – Undo and Redo. When a quick wrist rotation and finger touch occur at once, undo and redo tasks are performed. While touching the finger on the TSP, a quick rotation of the wrist counterclockwise undoes the last action or actions that the user made. In addition, when a user quickly rotates his or her wrist clockwise with a finger touch on the TSP, the system redoes the last action or actions that the user made. To undo/redo several actions at the same time, the user would repeat the quick rotation several times.

4   Results

To emphasize the usability of the interface and interaction, we developed an application—3D virtual object manipulation. A 3D-augmented reality (AR) environment was constructed by Qualcomm Vuforia SDK [13]. For selection, a user can click on the 3D object and then use drag-and-drop for translation of the object by using the TSP. When the user wants to rotate the 3D virtual object, he or she can rotate the wrist, making the 3D object rotate according to the wrist rotation. As a test, we created a target picture paper augmented on a table, and then had a user attempt to fit the target with randomly distributed 3D virtual objects. As the demo shows, the user seemed confident in using the device and correctly matched the objects to the pictures. This application suggests that the smart wristband is a 3D input device that can control a 3D virtual environment. Moreover, by combination of TSP and IMU, people can control the devices in more than three dimensions; for example, by moving the wrist and touching on the screen at once, people can control other functions at once, such as depth, time, and so on. This multi-dimensional control presents development possibilities as a 3D-drawing tool.

To confirm usability, we conducted several experiments to analyze how fast and accurately users can react with this input device. We hired three subjects from our university (two males and one female, with an average age of 27). The goal of this experiment was to estimate the precision and task-completion time of using the wristband-type TSP, depending on the degree of freedom given to be controlled by wrist rotation. The task was for the subjects to rotate their wrists to the given angles of yaw, pitch, and roll; to help the participants understand the target position and actual position of their wrists, a physical target and a physical object rotated by the given yaw, pitch, and roll angles were displayed. When participants believed their wrist positions corresponded to the given angles, they were required to click the screen by tapping the TSP on their wrists. Through the experiment, we were able analyze the behavior of users with regard to how fast and accurately users can utilize our device. We estimated the time and error to complete each trial. The result shows that task completion time increases as the number of DOF increases, as shown in Figure 3d.

We additionally analyzed the task completion time within the same numbers of DOF, as shown in Figures 3a, 3b, and 3c. We also estimated errors of angles, the difference between the target angles and the angles at the moment when the user finishes a trial. The result shows that 1 DOF produces significantly fewer errors than 2 or 3 DOF cases. However, 2 DOF produced more errors than 3 DOF. According to these results, although higher DOF provide more variables to control, the experimental results illustrate that it is not more effective than a lower DOF in speed and accuracy. Therefore, the interaction should not have the highest DOF, but rather has to have the minimum DOF following the number of variables of each different control. As a result, the 1D, 2D, and 3D interactions use 2, 2, and 3 DOF of control, respectively [14].

Fig. 5. Applications for the 3D input device: 3D virtual object manipulation

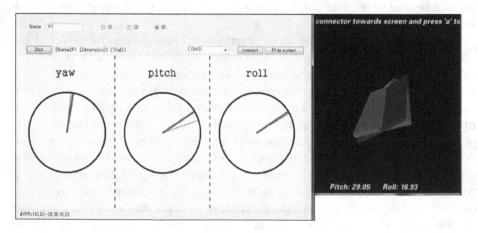

Fig. 6. Survey task: participants rotated wrist to the given angles of yaw, pitch, and roll, and then to click on the screen with the TSP on the wrist

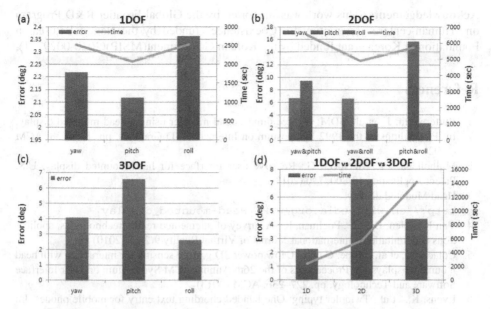

Fig. 7. Precision and task completion time in each dimension of (a) 1 DOF, (b) 2 DOF, and (c) 3 DOF, as well as (d) overall task completion time and error for each DOF

5   Conclusion

In this research, to improve the low degree of freedom and the instability of wearable input devices, we presented a new input device with the ability to select and command correctly, directly, and easily through the use of tactile and wrist motion: a wristband-type motion-aware touch panel. It was demonstrated that users were able to effectively use the wearable 3D input device for HMD-display object selection and control it by using tactile input via a finger to select the correct object and by using gestures and wrist rotation to control the screen or point at objects. In addition, five kinds of interactions—tools and commands—have been implemented, and one application—results—has been realized; these were point and click, navigation, program switchover, zoom in and out, undo and redo for the interactions and 3D virtual-object manipulation for the application.

We humans have a lifetime of experience in perceiving our environments and interacting with physical objects with our fingers and wrists. As a higher level of technologies has been continuously developed, our human requirements have grown exceedingly challenging and include high spatial accuracy and resolution, low latency, and high update rates. Therefore, this 3D-input device would satisfy our desires for an intuitive and simple but delicate interaction by using cursor movement (TSP) and a hand-gesture awareness system (IMU).

Acknowledgements. This work was supported by the Global Frontier R&D Program on "Human-centered Interaction for Coexistence" funded by the National Research Foundation of Korea grant funded by the Korean Government(MSIP)(2010-0029751).

References

1. Butterworth, J., et al.: 3DM: A three dimensional modeler using a head-mounted display. In: Proceedings of the 1992 Symposium on Interactive 3D Graphics, pp. 135–138. ACM (1992)
2. Mulholland, J.J., Maciocci, G.: Reactive user interface for head-mounted display. U.S. Patent Application 13/800, 790 (2013)
3. Head Mounted display, http://en.wikipedia.org/wiki/Head-mounted_display
4. Van Krevelen, D.W.F., Poelman, R.: A survey of augmented reality technologies, applications and limitations. International Journal of Virtual Reality 9(2), 1 (2010)
5. Colaço, A., et al.: Mime: Compact, low power 3D gesture sensing for interaction with head mounted displays. In: Proceedings of the 26th Annual ACM Symposium on User Interface Software and Technology, pp. 227–236. ACM (2013)
6. Lyons, K., et al.: Twiddler typing: One-handed chording text entry for mobile phones. In: Proceedings of the SIGCHI Conference on Human Factors in Computing Systems, pp. 671–678. ACM (2004)
7. Thomas, B., et al.: Where does the mouse go? An investigation into the placement of a body-attached touchPad mouse for wearable computers. Personal and Ubiquitous Computing 6(2), 97–112 (2002)
8. Code of federal regulations, Title 38 - Pensions, Bonuses, and Veterans' Relief, CHAPTER I–DEPARTMENT OF VETERANS AFFAIRS, Part 4–SCHEDULE FOR RATING DISABILITIES, Subpart B—Disability Ratings, The Musculoskeletal System, § 4.71 Measurement of ankylosis and joint motion (2002)
9. Lee, P., et al.: Highly stretchable and highly conductive metal electrode by very long metal nanowire percolation network. Advanced Materials 24(25), 3326–3332 (2012)
10. Sparkfun™, https://www.sparkfun.com/
11. Razor 9DOF AHRS, https://github.com/ptrbrtz/razor-9dof-ahrs/wiki/Tutorial
12. Touchpad, http://en.wikipedia.org/wiki/Touchpad
13. Qualcomm Vuforia, https://www.vuforia.com/

A Comparative Study of User Dependent and Independent Accelerometer-Based Gesture Recognition Algorithms

Aya Hamdy Ali, Ayman Atia, and Mostafa Sami

HCI Lab, Faculty of Computer Science and Information Systems
HelwanUniversity, Cairo, Egypt
Aya.hamdy@fcih.net, Ayman@fci.helwan.edu.org,
Mostafa.sami@fci.helwan.edu.eg

Abstract. In this paper, we introduce an evaluation of accelerometer-based gesture recognition algorithms in user dependent and independent cases. Gesture recognition has many algorithms and this evaluation includes Hidden Markov Models, Support Vector Machine, K-nearest neighbor, Artificial Neural Network and Dynamic Time Warping. Recognition results are based on acceleration data collected from 12 users. We evaluated the algorithms based on the recognition accuracy related to different number of gestures from two datasets. Evaluation results show that the best accuracy for 8 and 18 gestures is achieved with dynamic time warping and K-nearest neighbor algorithms.

Keywords: Gesture recognition, Accelerometers, Human Computer Interaction.

1 Introduction

Hand gesture is a form of non-verbal communication for human, people use gestures to express their intentions and deliver particular message [1]. Hand gesture interaction considered a natural way of interaction between humans and computers. It was a motivation to build gesture recognition systems to interpret and explain hand gestures as meaningful command for more natural communication between humans and computers. Hand gesture recognition has great impact on designing an efficient natural interface. Hand gesture based interface used in controlling TV like Samsung SMART TV or play console games like Nintendo Wii and Microsoft Xbox Kinect.

Hand Gesture recognition has many techniques, there are two main techniques for hand gesture recognition: vision based and sensor based [2] [3]. Vision-based technique based on camera as input device, this technique extract information about the user's hand gestures from a visually captured stream (camera) [4]. In a second step, the position of the hand and its fingers are calculated and used for recognizing predefined gestures by use of statistical methods. Vision-based technique has some limitations such as the quality of the captured images, which is sensitive to lighting conditions, cluttered backgrounds and camera facing angles. Thus it is usually not able to detect and track the hands robustly which highly affects the system performance.

N. Streitz and P. Markopoulos (Eds.): DAPI 2014, LNCS 8530, pp. 119–129, 2014.

In addition, it is also inconvenient if users are always required facing the camera directly to complete a gesture. On the contrary, Sensor based technique required only a wearable or portable accelerometer equipped device. The majority of personal electronic devices like the Apple iphone and Wiimote's are embedded with accelerometer. Sensor based gesture recognition system tracking the hand by gathering information about the hand position and orientation from the accelerometer for gesture recognition. Sensor based technique is resistant for changing environment, as it's not affected by lighting conditions or cluttered backgrounds. Accelerometer-based gesture recognition system can be used in control home appliances [5], computer applications such as media player and play games.

Gesture recognition systems can be implemented and evaluated for user-dependent and user-independent or both of them. In user dependent case, each user is required to train system before using it by performing number of training samples. In user independent user do not perform any gesture training samples for the system before using it. The user-independent gesture recognition is more difficult than the user-dependent since there is variation for the same gesture from user to another user.

Hand gesture recognition recently became a highly active research area with motivating applications such as sign language recognition [6], interact with medical instrumentation in operation room [7] and control through facial gestures [8]. Another application for accelerometer-based human motion capture and classification is in the monitoring of elderly at home for detection of falls or other abnormal ambulation patterns [9]. Moreover, this approach applied for driving awareness system [10].

Hand gestures are powerful human interactive tool. However, their fluency and intuitiveness have not been utilized as computer interface. Recently, hand gesture applications have begun to emerge, but they are still not robust and are unable to recognize the gestures in a convenient and easily accessible manner by the human. Thus, the main challenge of the gesture recognition systems is to recognize hand gestures in a fast, accurate, robust and easily accessible manner. To achieve this goal, there's many requirements need to be met by the gesture recognition system such as: accuracy, scalability and user-independence. First, accuracy means a hand gesture recognition system should be able to recognize different hand gestures without confusion among them. Second, scalability means a large gesture vocabulary can be included into system and recognized with high accuracy. Third, user-independence means the system should be able to work for different users rather than a specific user. Several gesture recognition systems based on accelerometer have been developed using a well known algorithms such as Hidden Markov Models [11] [12] and Dynamic Time Warping [13] [14]. However, most of the systems in the literature being target user-dependent or user-independent using single algorithm, or have a small dictionary size.

In this work, we evaluated the accuracy of these gesture recognition algorithms: Hidden Markov Models (HMMs), Artificial Neural Networks (ANNs), Dynamic Time Warping (DTW), Support Vector Machine (SVM) and K-nearest neighbor (k-NN) for 18 gestures dataset shown in figure 1(a) obtained from [15] and 8 gestures dataset shown in figure 1(b) obtained from [13]. We conducted two experiments to measure the accuracy of each algorithm in the case of user-dependent and user-independent recognition with 18 and 8 gestures datasets.

This paper is organized as follows. Related work is discussed in section 2, Section 3 describes datasets and the studied algorithms, the evaluation of experiments and its results has been determined in section 4, discussion about the experiments is given in section 5, and finally, section 6 summarizes our conclusion and future work.

2   Related Work

Accelerometer-based gesture recognition systems design can follow a user-independent or a user-dependent approach. The difference lies in whether the user has to train the system before utilize it. User-independent systems are oriented to general users and do not needs a training phase before being usable; conversely, user-dependent systems require the user to repeat the gesture movements several times to train the system.

User-dependent gesture recognition was stated in several literature papers. Liu et al. [13] presented personalize gesture recognition algorithm based on 3D-Accelerometer data. uWave recognized user-defined gestures with 98.6% accuracy for a gesture vocabulary with eight gesture patterns. uWave required a single training sample for each pattern. Its results show that DTW and template adaptation is effective with limited training data and a small vocabulary. Niezen presented in [14] implementation of gesture recognition system using dynamic time warping on mobile phone. They use 8 gestures with 10 samples per gesture were collected using mobile accelerometer. Results show that dynamic time warping algorithm recognizes 77 out of the 80 samples with accuracy of 96.25%. Joselli et.al presented in [12] a framework for touch and accelerometer gesture recognition for mobile games. They used HMMM algorithm for user-dependent recognition. Recognition accuracy was 89% for ten different gesture patterns. Schlömer et al. presented in [11] gesture recognition with a Wii controller for 3D hand gesture recognition using K-mean algorithm, classic Bayes-classifier and HMM for small vocabulary of five gesture patterns. The recognition results were between 85 to 95%.

Some literature work target user-dependent and user-independent or user-independent only. Arce et al presented in [16] accelerometer-bases gesture recognition system using Artificial Neural Networks. They evaluated ANN algorithm for user-independent. ANN achieved 83.33% accuracy for five gesture patterns. Zhenyu et al. [17] developed gesture recognition system based on single 3-axis accelerometer mounted on mobile phone. It use three feature extraction methods discrete cosine transform (DCT), fast Fourier transform (FFT) and a hybrid approach which combine wavelet packet decomposition (WPD). Recognition of gestures performed using Support Vector Machine for 17 gestures from 67 users. Results showed that the best recognition accuracy is achieved with wavelet-based method by 87.36% and DCT and FFT are achieved 85.16% and 86.92%. Pylvänäinen presented in [18] accelerometer-based gesture recognition recognizer using continuous HMMs algorithm. Data was collected using an accelerometer embedded in a mobile phone and gesture recognition performed on desktop PC. Recognizer tested on 10 gestures and 20 samples per gesture from 7 users with 8 states model. Results show that recognizer accuracy 99.76%

with user independent and mixed user recognition. Most of previous work described so far, depended on user-dependent recognition or small gesture vocabulary. In this paper, we aim to evaluate the accuracy of different algorithms with different datasets for user-dependent and user-independent gesture recognitions.

3   Experiments Setup

3.1   Dataset

Sensor data were collected using Wiimote's embedded 3-axiz accelerometer. We used two predefined datasets [13] and [14] gestures libraries. First dataset shown in figure 1 (a) consists of 1,800 gestures for 4 users. Each user repeated each gesture 25 times with total 450 for 18 gestures per user. Second dataset shown in Figure 1(b) consists of 4,480 gestures for 8 participants collected over days per multiple weeks. Each user repeated each gesture 10 times with total 80 for 8 gestures per day for 7 days. Data features are represented by feature vector consists of X, Y, Z readings.

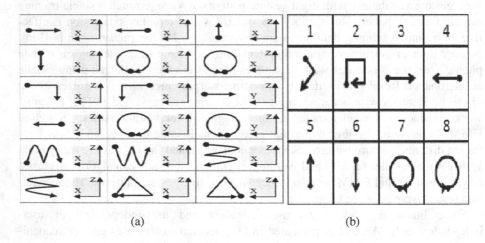

(a)   (b)

Fig. 1. Datasets vocabulary

3.2   Gesture Recognition Algorithms

Hidden Markov Model. Hidden Markov Models algorithm is a probabilistic model representing a process with states and only the output of the model is visible and states are hidden. Hidden Markov Models used in many applications such as speech recognition, sign language recognition [19] and biometric gait recognition [20]. For building and training Hidden Markov Models, we used Hidden Markov Model Toolkit [21]. It has helped in the training and testing of Hidden Markov Models. Data represented by matrix of 3 columns x, y and z acceleration values. A 4-state HMM was used for user-dependent recognition and 8-state HMM was used for user-independent recognition.

Support Vector Machine. Support vector machine is a supervised machine learning method that is widely used for data analyzing and pattern recognizing. The algorithm was invented by Vladimir Vapnik and the current standard incarnation was proposed by Corinna Cortes and Vladimir Vapnik [22]. SVM has been widely used in various applications, such as face detection [23] and activity recognition [24].Support Vector Machines (SVM) is originally designed for solving binary classification problems [25]. A gesture recognition system is supposed to recognize more than two types of gestures. For this reason, a multi-class SVM is required. The conventional way to extend binary-class SVM to multi-class scenario is to decompose an M-class problem into a series of two-class problems, for which one-against-all is the earliest and one of the most widely used implementations [26]. We extended the Matlab SVM binary classifier to implement the multi-class SVM.

K-nearest Neighbor. K-nearest neighbor (k-NN) is one of the oldest and simplest machine learning algorithms for pattern classification [27]. K-Nearest Neighbor is a supervised learning algorithm where the result of new instance query is classified based on majority of K-Nearest Neighbor category. k-NN used in many applications such as Handwritten Digit Recognition [28] and breast cancer diagnosis[29]. An object is classified by the distance from its neighbors, with the object being assigned to the class most common among its k distance nearest neighbors in the training set. We used Matlab k-NN classifier; K was empirically fixed to 5 a value that turned out to be optimal. Euclidean distance used to compute the distance between pairs of data points.

Dynamic Time Warping. Dynamic time warping [30] is an algorithm used to measure similarity between two different two sequences in time or speed. Dynamic Time Warping (DTW) is based on the Levenshtein distance algorithm. It has been used in video, audio and graphics or any data which can be turned into a linear representation such speech recognition [31]. Dynamic time warping matches gesture sample against the template gestures. Every gesture represented by sequence of feature vectors. Assume that S is sample and T is template, where S= $\{s_1,...,s_i\}$ and T=$\{t_1,...,t_i\}$ and each feature vector consists of the x, y, z-axis acceleration values. The matching cost by DTW(S, T) must be calculated. The first step is construct distance matrix D by compute the distance between each vector in S and T using formulation 1 foreach S(x, y, z) and T(x, y, z).

$$d(s_i, t_j)=(s_i - t_j)^2 \tag{1}$$

After that we compute the matching cost: DTW(S, T) using this formulation 2, Sample is then recognized as the gesture corresponding to the template with the lowest matching cost.

$$D(i, j) = d(s_i,t_j) + \min\{D(i-1, j), D(i-1, j-1), D(i, j-1)\} \tag{2}$$

Artificial Neural Networks. An artificial neural network is an algorithm based on simulation of the brain. Artificial neural networks have been applied to problems ranging such as speech recognition, predictions of time series, classification of cancers and gene prediction. We have used ANN Encog2.5 for C# [32] during our experiments. Neural network required a fixed length feature vector; the data need to re-sampled and normalized between 0 and 1 for Sigmoid activation function. Data normalized using Encog's normalization class. Data re-sampled using an algorithm described in [33] to 100 points. With 100 points each for the three x, y and z. Feature vector of size 300 points was used as input to neural network. We used backpropagation neural network and desired error 0.001. Neural network architecture depends on the number of gestures. The configuration parameters of the neural network can be seen in Table 1 used for user-dependent and independent recognitions.

4   Experiments

This section presents the implementation and evaluation of HMM, ANN, k-NN, SVM and DTW algorithms for user-dependent and user-independent recognitions with 18 and 8 gestures datasets shown in Figure 1.

4.1   User-dependent Recognition

Hidden Markov Model: In this experiment, we evaluated HMM for user-dependent recognition with 18 gestures dataset and 8 gestures dataset. In case of 18 gestures dataset, we used 20 samples for training and 5 samples for testing per gesture. For 18 gestures samples were correctly classified with accuracy 99%. In case of 8 gestures dataset, Data selected from different 7 days over multiple weeks. We used 50 samples for training and 20 samples for testing. For 8 gestures and 4 users, testing samples were correctly classified with accuracy 96.01%. HMM user-dependent results are shown in Figure 2.

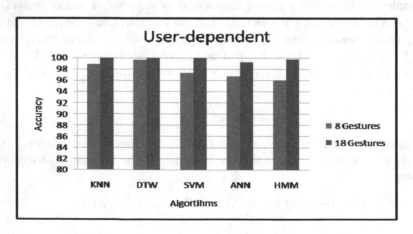

Fig. 2. Algorithms results for User-dependent Recognition

Support Vector Machine: We evaluated SVM with 18 gestures dataset and 8 gestures dataset for user-dependent recognition. In case of 18 gestures dataset, we used 20 sample for training and 5 for testing per gesture. For 18 gestures, testing samples were correctly classified with accuracy 100%. In case of 8 gestures dataset, data selected from different 7 days over multiple weeks. We used 50 samples for training and 20 samples for testing per gesture for every user. For 8 gestures, testing samples were correctly classified with accuracy 97.3%. SVM user-dependent results are shown in Figure 2.

k-nearest Neighbor. We evaluated k-NN with 18 gestures dataset and 8 gestures dataset for user-dependent recognition. As k-NN builds its classification decision based on the distances between the training dataset samples and the test sample(s) there's no actual training is performed. A certain number (k) of nearest neighbors is selected based on the smallest distances and the labels of these neighbors samples are fed into a voting function to determine the labels of the test sample. In case of 18 gestures dataset, we used one sample for training and 5 gestures for testing per gesture for every user. For 18 gestures, testing samples were correctly classified with accuracy 100%. In case of 8 gestures dataset, data selected from different 7 days over multiple weeks. We used 7 samples for every gesture, every template represent day and 20 samples for testing per gesture. For 8 gestures, testing samples were correctly classified with accuracy 98.9%. k-NN user-dependent results are shown in Figure 2.

Artificial Neural Networks. We evaluated ANNs with 18 gestures dataset and 8 gestures dataset, ANNs used backpropagation neural network. The ANNs architecture has 300 input layers, 1 hidden layer, number of hidden neurons and output layers depend on the number of gestures as shown in table 1.In case of 18 gestures dataset, we used 20 sample for training and 5 for testing per gesture. For 18 gestures, testing samples were correctly classified with accuracy 99.2%. In case of 8 gestures dataset, data selected from different 7 days over multiple weeks. We used 50 samples for training and 20 samples for testing per gesture for every user. For 8 gestures, testing samples were correctly classified with accuracy 96.7%. ANN user-dependent results are shown in Figure 2.

Table 1. Conguration parameters of the neural network

	8 gestures	18 gesture
Number of input layers	300	300
Number of output layers	8	18
Number of hidden layers	1	1
Number of hidden neurons	80	180

4.2   User-independent Recognition

Hidden Markov Model. In this experiment, we evaluate HMM with 18 gestures dataset 8 gestures dataset. In case of 8 gestures dataset, Data selected from different 7 days over multiple weeks for all the users. We used 400 samples for training and 160 samples for testing. For 8 gestures, testing samples were correctly classified with accuracy 95%.In case of 18 gestures dataset for user-independent recognition; we used 80 samples for training and 20 samples for testing per gesture selected from all the users. For 18 gestures samples were correctly classified with accuracy 90%. HMM user-independent experiment results are shown in Figure 3.

Support Vector Machine. We evaluated SVM with 18 gestures dataset and 8 gestures dataset. In case of 18 gestures dataset, we used 80 sample for training and 20 for testing per gesture selected from all the users. For 18 gestures, testing samples were correctly classified with accuracy 96%. In case of 8 gestures dataset for user-independent recognition, data selected from different 7 days over multiple weeks. We used 400 samples for training and 160 samples for testing per gesture for all the users. For 8 gestures, testing samples were correctly classified with accuracy 96.9%. SVM user-independent results are shown in Figure 3.

k-nearest Neighbor. We evaluated k-NN with 18 gestures dataset and 8 gestures dataset. In case of 18 gestures dataset, we used one sample for training and 20 samples for testing per gesture for all the users. For 18 gestures, testing samples were correctly classified with accuracy 99.8%. In case of 8 gestures dataset, data selected from different 7 days over multiple weeks. k-NN used 8 samples for every gesture from different days and users, for testing we used 160 samples per gesture for all the users. For 8 gestures, testing samples were correctly classified with accuracy 99%. k-NN user-independent results are shown in Figure 3.

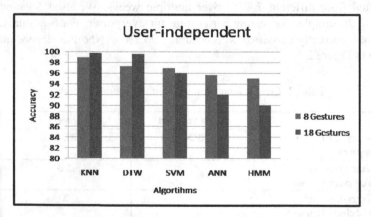

Fig. 3. Algorithms results for User-dependent Recognition

Dynamic Time Warping. In case of 18 gestures dataset, Dynamic time warping algorithm used one template matching for training per gesture for every user and 20

samples for testing. For 18 gestures, testing samples were correctly classified with accuracy 99.7%. In case of 8 gestures dataset, data selected from different 7 days over multiple weeks. DTW used 8 templates for every gesture selected from different days and users, for testing we used 160 samples for testing per gesture for all the users. For 8 gestures, testing samples were correctly classified with accuracy 97.3%. DTW user-independent results are shown in Figure 3.

Artificial Neural Networks. We evaluate ANNs with 18 gestures dataset and 8 gestures dataset. The ANNs architecture is the same as the user-dependent architecture. In case of 18 gestures dataset for user-independent recognition, we used 80 sample for training and 20 for testing per gesture selected from all the users. For 18 gestures, testing samples were correctly classified with accuracy 92%. In case of 8 gestures dataset, data selected from different 7 days over multiple weeks for all the users. We used 400 samples for training and 160 samples for testing per gesture for all the users. For 8 gestures, testing samples were correctly classified with accuracy 95.6%. ANN user-independent results are shown in Figure 3.

5   Discussion

According to [14] 8 gestures dataset show that there are variations between gestures samples by the same user collected over different days. However, according to [16] 18 gestures collected with some restrictions in order to avoid variation in gestures for the same user. Therefore, all participants are asked to perform the gestures without any, or with minimal, tilting of the remote. We conducted ANOVA test for sample from algorithms (DTW and HMM) results per users with 8 gestures in case of user-dependent recognition. P-value was 0.000305 which mean there is a difference in the algorithm accuracy, depending on user. Despite of these limitations, k-NN and DTW achieved the best recognition accuracy for user-dependent and user-independent datasets with 18 and 8 gestures. However, In case of user independent HMM, SVM and ANNs achieved the best accuracy with 8 gestures and in case of user independent they achieved best accuracy with 18 gestures.

6   Conclusions and Future Work

We have evaluated accelerometer-based gesture recognition algorithms: Hidden Markov Models (HMMs), Artificial Neural Network (ANNs), Support Vector Machine (SVM), K-nearest neighbor (k-NN) and Dynamic time warping (DTW) based on accuracy. Our evaluation based on two predefined datasets [16] and [14] gestures libraries. First dataset consists of 1,800 gestures for 4 users. Second dataset consists of 4,480 gestures for 8 participants. User-dependent gesture recognition experiment's results and User-dependent gesture recognition experiment's results showed that Dynamic time warping and K-nearest neighbor algorithms achieved the best accuracy for user-dependent and user-dependent gesture recognitions. In future work, we look forward evaluate the best accuracy algorithms on Smartphone in order to use them in developing abnormal driving behavior detection system using accelerometer.

References

1. Daugman, J.: Face and gesture recognition: Overview. IEEE Transaction on Pattern Analysis and Machine Intelligence 19, 675–676 (1997)
2. Baatar, B., Tanaka, J.: Comparing Sensor Based and Vision Based Techniques for Dynamic Gesture Recognition. In: APCHI 2012, Matsuecity, Shimane, Japan (2012)
3. Zama, R., Adnan, N.: Survey on Various Gesture Recognition Technologies and Techniques. International Journal of Computer Applications 50, 38–44 (2012)
4. Reifinger, S., Wallhoff, F., Ablassmeier, M., Poitschke, T., Rigoll, G.: Static and Dynamic Hand-Gesture Recognition for Augmented Reality Applications. In: Jacko, J.A. (ed.) HCI 2007. LNCS, vol. 4552, pp. 728–737. Springer, Heidelberg (2007)
5. Wu, J., Pan, G., Li, S., Wu, Z., Zhang, D.: Geeair: Waving in the Air to control home Appliances. In: UIC-ATC 2010 Proceedings of the 2010 Symposia and Workshops on Ubiquitous, Autonomic and Trusted Computing, Xian, Shaanxi, China (2010)
6. Fang, G., Gao, W., Zhao, D.: Large-Vocabulary Continuous Sign Language Recognition Based on Transition-Movement Models. IEEE Transactions on Systems, Man and Cybernetics, Part A: Systems and Humans 37, 1–9 (2007)
7. Wachs, J., Stern, H., Edan, Y., Gillam, M., Handler, J., Feied, C., Smith, M.: A hand gesture sterile tool for browsing MRI images in the OR. Journal of the American Medical Informatics Association 15, 321–323 (2008)
8. Nishikawa, A., Hosoi, T., Koara, K., Negoro, D., Hikita, A., Asano, S., Kakutani, H., Miya-zaki, F., Sekimoto, M., Yasui, M., Miyake, Y., Takiguchi, S., Monden, M.: FAce MOUSe: A novel human-machine interface for controlling the position of a laparoscope. IEEE Transactions on Robotics and Automation 19, 825–841 (2003)
9. Zouba, N., Boulay, B., Bremond, F., Thonnat, M.: Monitoring Activities of Daily Living (ADLs) of Elderly Based on 3D Key Human Postures. In: Caputo, B., Vincze, M. (eds.) ICVW 2008. LNCS, vol. 5329, pp. 37–50. Springer, Heidelberg (2008)
10. Fekry, M., Hamdy, A., Atia, A.: Anti-Bump: A Bump/Pothole Monitoring and Broadcasting System for Driver Awareness. In: Kurosu, M. (ed.) Human-Computer Interaction, Part II, HCII 2013. LNCS, vol. 8005, pp. 561–570. Springer, Heidelberg (2013)
11. Schlmer, T., Poppinga, B., Henze, N., Boll, S.: Gesture recognition with a Wii controller. In: Proceedings of the 2nd International Conference on Tangible and Embedded Interaction (TEI 2008), New York, NY, USA (2008)
12. Joselli, M., Clua, E.: gRmobile: A Framework for Touch and Accelerometer Gesture Recognition for Mobile Games. In: SBGAMES 2009 Proceedings of the 2009 VIII Brazilian Symposium on Games and Digital Entertainment. Rio de Janeiro, Brazil (2009)
13. Liu, J., Zhong, L., Wickramasuriya, J., Vasudevan, V.: uWave: Accelerometer-based personalized gesture recognition and its applications. Journal Pervasive and Mobile Computing 5, 657–675 (2009)
14. Niezen, G., Hancke, G.P.: Gesture Recognition as Ubiquitous Input for Mobile Phones. In: International Workshop on Devices that Alter Perception (DAP 2008), Conjunction with Ubicomp (2008)
15. Akl, A., Valaee, S.: Accelerometer-based gesture recognition via dynamic-time warping, affinity propagation, & compressive sensing. In: IEEE International Conference on Acoustics Speech and Signal Processing (ICASSP), Dallas, TX (2010)
16. Arce, F., Mario, J., Valdez, G.: Accelerometer-Based Hand Gesture Recognition Using Artificial Neural Networks. Soft Computing for Intelligent Control and Mobile Robotics 318, 67–77 (2011)

17. Pylvänäinen, T.: Accelerometer Based Gesture Recognition Using Continuous HMMs. In: Marques, J.S., Pérez de la Blanca, N., Pina, P. (eds.) IbPRIA 2005. LNCS, vol. 3522, pp. 639–646. Springer, Heidelberg (2005)
18. Starner, T., Pentland, A.: Visual Recognition of American Sign Language Using Hidden Markov Models (1995)
19. Nickel, C., Busch, C., Rangarajan, S., Mobius, M.: Using Hidden Markov Models for accelerometer-based biometric gait recognition. In: IEEE 7th International Colloquium on Signal Processing and its Applications (CSPA 2011), Penang (2011)
20. Young, S., Kershaw, D., Odell, J., Ollason, D., Valtchev, V., Woodland, P.: The HTK Book, version 3.4. Cambridge University Press (2006)
21. Cortes, C., Vapnik, V.: Support-Vector Networks. Machine Learning 20, 273–297 (1995)
22. Osuna, E., Freund, R., Girosi, F.: Training support vector machines: An application to face detection. In: Proceedings of IEEE Computer Society Conference on Computer Vision and Pattern Recognition, San Juan (1997)
23. Ravi, N., Dandekar, N., Mysore, P., Littman, M.: Activity recognition from accelerometer data. In: Proceedings of the 17th Conference on Innovative Applications of Artificial Intelligence (IAAI 2005), Pittsburgh, Pennsylvania (2005)
24. Kecman, V.: Learning and Soft Computing: Support Vector Machines, Neural Networks, and Fuzzy Logic Models (2001)
25. Suykens, J.A.K., Van Gestel, T., De Brabanter, J., De Moor, B., Vandewalle, J.: Least Squares Support Vector Machines. WorldScientific (2002)
26. Cover, T.M., Hart, P.E.: Nearest neighbor pattern classification. Institute of Electrical and Electronics Engineers Transactions on Information Theory (1967)
27. Lee, Y.: Handwritten digit recognition using k nearest-neighbor, radial-basis function, and backpropagation neural networks. Neural Computation 3, 440–449 (1991)
28. Sarkar, M., Leong, T.Y.: Application of k-nearest neighbors algorithm on breast cancer. In: Proc AMIA Symp. (2000)
29. Ratanamahatana, C.A., Keogh, E.: Exact Indexing of Dynamic Time Warping. Knowledge and Information Systems 7, 358–386 (2005)
30. Sakoe, H., Chiba, S.: Dynamic programming algorithm optimization for spoken word recognition. IEEE Transactions on Acoustics, Speech and Signal Processing 26, 43–49 (1978)
31. Heaton, J.: Programming Neural Networks with Encog2 in C# (2010)
32. Wilson, A.D., Wobbrock, J.O., Li, Y.: Gestures without libraries, toolkits or training: A $1 recognizer for user interface prototypes. In: Proceedings of the 20th Annual ACM Symposium on User Interface Software and Technology (UIST 2007), Newport, Rhode Island, USA (2007)

AiRSculpt: A Wearable Augmented Reality 3D Sculpting System

Sung-A Jang, Hyung-il Kim, Woontack Woo, and Graham Wakefield

Graduate School of Culture Technology, KAIST, Republic of Korea
{mumblefish,hikim91,wwoo,grrrwaaa}@kaist.ac.kr

Abstract. In this paper, we present a new kind of wearable augmented reality (AR) 3D sculpting system called AiRSculpt in which users could directly translate their fluid finger movements in air into expressive sculptural forms and use hand gestures to navigate the interface. In AiRSculpt, as opposed to VR-based systems, users could quickly create and manipulate 3D virtual content directly with their bare hands in a real-world setting, and use both hands simultaneously in tandem or as separate tools to sculpt and manipulate their virtual creations. Our system uses a head-mounted display and a RGB-D head-mounted camera to detect the 3D location of hands and fingertips then render virtual content in calibration with real-world coordinates.

Keywords: Augmented reality, virtual sculpting, direct 3D manipulation, embodied interaction.

1   Introduction

With affordable consumer-level 3D printing there is more demand than ever for fast and intuitive tools for 3D modeling. Attempts to fill this gap have provided simplified adaptations of professional 3D modeling tools, but by duplicating the interaction design they do not contribute advances in fluid and intuitive interaction with what we are making. No matter how accustomed we have become to the 2D mouse and keyboard combination, it remains ill-suited to 3D spatial tasks of modeling.

We present a wearable AR 3D sculpting tool (AiRSculpt) that allows users to draw expressive sculptural forms in mid-air, transforming fingertips into scalable 3D brushes or erasers, and hands into gestural controllers, manipulating virtual content with bare hands like a lump of clay: melding the immediacy of freeform sketching and gesticulation with the exploratory craft of molding material into sculptural form.

A video-see-through head-mounted display (HMD) presents the real view augmented with sculptural content. An RGB-D head-mounted camera (HMC) detects hand and fingertip locations. Users thus communicate gestures to a camera that moves with them as an extension of their own bodies. They are able to see their hands, unencumbered by gloves or devices, directly interacting with their malleable sculptures within a real, personal environment; gaining an accurate sense of scale and depth with respect to their hands, and a preview of how a 3D-printed copy will appear in-context.

N. Streitz and P. Markopoulos (Eds.): DAPI 2014, LNCS 8530, pp. 130–141, 2014.

Since the augmented space is fixed to real space coordinates, users can naturally shift their head to view what they are making from different positions and angles. Nevertheless, users retain advantages of virtual media including easy copying, scaling, and access to the object's interior. Transitioning between tools via gestures and finger postures interleaves more naturally with continuous sculpting than using menus. Selected tools and modal states are indicated by the color of augmented spheres at the fingertips. Gesture and posture design derives where possible from research on intuitive, natural hand gestures for spatial interaction and direct 3D manipulation [1, 2, 3, 4], and effective vision-based hand tracking and gesture recognition [5, 6].

The paper is organized as follows: Section 2 describes a user survey that confirmed the need for an easy-to-learn, intuitive 3D form-making interface with an interaction design divergent from existing systems, and compares our system to related works similar in spirit to our approach. Section 3 describes the system and interaction design, while Section 4 evaluates its effectiveness via an in-depth user study of a first prototype and a follow-up study of a second prototype. Section 5 draws conclusions from these results, suggesting potential applications and directions of further research.

2   Needs and Related Work

2.1   Preliminary Survey

We conducted a preliminary survey to ascertain demand for more intuitive alternative 3D modeling tools and to identify the demographic with the strongest need of this research. We gathered anonymized responses from 62 people (60% male, 40% female) from diverse backgrounds (53% science/engineering, 26% arts/design /humanities, 15% interdisciplinary). 80% of participants were in their 20s and 56% had experience using 3D modeling software. 82% said they enjoy sketching or doodling, and 84% chose pencil and paper as their preferred tool for quickly sketching out ideas. Although respondents were almost equally divided in whether they were satisfied with 3D sketching tools available today, those with prior 3D modeling experience formed 68% of the dissatisfied.

74% of respondents indicated that they have felt the need for a more intuitive modeling tool, again dominated by those with prior 3D modeling experience (constituting 91% of whom responded "definitely", 73% of whom answered "usually"). The circumstances in which this need was felt fell into five broad categories: when users get discouraged by the unintuitive interface (36%) and/or steep learning curve (20%) of existing systems, or find them inadequate for immediate or rough sketching (18%), or when they feel that drawing is difficult or not enough (15%), or desire an interaction more integrated with reality (10%).

People who expressed frustration with existing systems said they find it difficult to express the shape they want (especially smooth surfaces and natural, organic shapes), and time-consuming or painful to edit. Some explicitly stated a desire to experience their 3D virtual content in a real-world context and observe it from multiple angles. 63% of participants with 3D modeling experience did not find it comfortable to draw 3D objects with a mouse and keyboard, while only 20% did find it comfortable

(17% unsure). We observed similar results for whether it was easy to draw organic shapes using a computer (63% "no", 17% "yes", 20% "unsure").

The results of this survey clearly indicated that people from diverse backgrounds were overall dissatisfied with existing 3D modeling software options and felt strong needs for more intuitive and accessible interfaces. The people who felt this need the most were participants with 3D modeling experience. The majority (87%) were excited at the prospect of being able to draw directly in 3D space.

2.2   Related Work

Commercial digital sculpting software such as Autodesk® Mudbox®, Pixologic® Sculptris®, and ZBrush® offer an alternate approach to computer-based 3D form-making which incorporates physical sculpting techniques into the creative process. While they provide a more accessible, intuitive way of working than traditional 3D modeling tools, they are designed for a desktop environment typically accessed via a 2D interface. While some packages such as Geomagic® Freeform® are designed to work with haptic 3D input devices such as the Geomagic® Touch™, they remain generally confined to a 2D display that restricts its immersive capacity.

Most free-form 3D sketching or sculpting systems that had previously been implemented in a VR environment for 3D interaction research also utilize input devices, such as 6-axis spacemouse, sensors, physical props, or special VR gloves to track finger trajectory or hand movement [7, 8, 9, 10, 11, 12], permitting rich levels of interactive experience; however mediation via devices puts users at a visual and spatial remove from the virtual content.

Leap Motion's recent launch of Freeform, a free 3D sculpt application that allows users to create digital sculptures by manipulating a clay-like object with their fingers and hand gestures, shows industry advances made in the embodied interaction approach to 3D modeling. Although Leap's Freeform lets users sculpt with their bare hands, from the user's view their hands are physically removed from the site of creation, since it is not their hands but virtual representations of their fingertips as spheres that directly interact with virtual clay. With AiRSculpt, users can spontaneously create and manipulate virtual content directly in 3D with unencumbered hands. Also unlike Freeform, AiRSculpt is a HMD-based AR system that allows users to naturally explore and interact with virtual objects from various angles and distances within their personal environment. The benefits of moving to a 3D display for 3D modeling has been outlined well by Butterworth et al. in [13].

Many gesture-based modeling systems have also used physical input devices or wearable sensors. Gesture-controlled modeling systems such as methods using superquadrics proposed by Yoshida et al. [14] and Nishino et al. [15], or Marshall's Virtual Sculpture system [1] are glove-based approaches focused on effective hand gesture mapping and control. AiRSculpt is driven by vision-based bare-handed interaction that uniquely integrates 3D free-hand input for 3D shape formation (Draw/Erase) with a gestural interface for tool transitioning and object manipulation (Scale/Rotate/Move). Attempts to use non-instrumented hand gestures for spatial interaction such as flying through terrain or composing a 3D scene in GestureVR [4], or basic 3D manipulation operations in Kolaric et al.'s Mixed Reality application [6] and Kim's Tangible 3D [3], are centered around mapping gestures to simple manipulation tasks such as selection and scaling and do not involve direct, expressive form-making operations like sculpting. Also unlike GestureVR and Tangible 3D, which use a VR platform, and Kolaric et al.'s application, which does not have depth occlusion, in AiRculpt users see virtual content within their real-world context and know where their hands are in relation to any virtual object, allowing them to naturally and fluidly interact with their virtual creations.

Our system uses a voxel-based sculpting method introduced by Galyean and Hughes [12], which mainly consists of an additive tool that adds material to 3D space like toothpaste being squeezed out of a tube and a subtractive tool that removes material. As far as we know, the volumetric sculpting approach has not been attempted in an AR environment with direct hand interaction.

3 Sculpting System

AiRSculpt is a 3D AR system in which users wear a video-see-through HMD with an attached RGB-D camera to create clay-like forms through bare-hand interactions.

3.1 System Modules

Tracking Modules. The software includes four tracking modules (hand tracking, gesture recognition, object detector, and coordinate calibration), a sculpting module, and a renderer (Fig. 1). The hand tracking module analyzes the HMC's depth image to derive 3D positions of hands and fingertips relative to the camera. The gesture

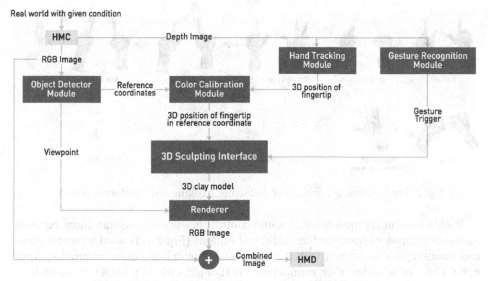

Fig. 1. High-level data-flow diagram of the AiRSculpt system

recognition module continuously analyzes the depth image to identify gestures by the user. The object detector analyzes the HMC's RGB image to detect a wall-mounted calibration image, using its reference coordinates to derive the position and orientation of the HMD. The coordinate calibration module combines hand-tracking and object-detection data to derive 3D hand and fingertip positions in reference coordinates.

3D Sculpting Module. The 3D hand and fingertip positions along with gestural input are used by the sculpting module to create, navigate, and manipulate malleable 3D virtual content (as described in section 3.2 below). We found voxel based geometry to be most suitable for freely generating and subtracting volume in 3D space, since it deals with the volume of the object directly [12, 16]. The volume is rendered as an isosurface via the marching cubes algorithm.

3.2   Sculpting Interface

The sculpting system operates between a system menu mode and a content creation mode. The system boots initially into the system menu mode, which can be used to start a new project, open an existing project, save, share, or print the current project, or exit the system. The menu consists of 2D buttons superimposed over the user's view, which are selected by moving their hand to the button's 2D position and making a grabbing gesture. Selecting the "New" button enters content creation mode, which starts with a clay-like ball by default. The system remains in creation mode until the target image is no longer in view; thus users can easily switch between modes by facing or turning away from the target image. This division rids the sculpting zone of bulky or intrusive menu interfaces and allows users to fully focus on creation.

Fig. 2. The postures and gestures of AiRSculpt's editing and transformation tools

Within content creation mode, gestural controls allow seamless transitions between various functions without needing additional buttons (Fig 2.). Toward a more natural and intuitive way to interact with the augmented content, we drew inspiration from natural human behavior when manipulating real objects where possible. Nevertheless, due to difficulties of finger tracking with the depth camera we restricted the scope of the project to mainly utilizing the user's index fingers and thumbs; and due to limitations in the gesture recognition module, certain gestures (such as the gesture for toggling tools) appear unnatural.

Cursor. Opening the index finger and thumb in each hand activates the cursor function. Spheres augmented on the fingertips display the mode of each hand by color.

Draw/Erase. By touching thumb to index finger in one hand, Draw/Erase mode will be activated. If the hand is in Draw mode, the system will add volume along the trajectory of the index finger, with the shape of the selected brush and the thickness of its stroke. If the hand is in Erase mode, the system will remove volume along the trajectory of the index finger. When index finger and thumb are apart again, Draw/Erase mode is deactivated and the hand returns to cursor mode.

Toggle Draw/Erase. Opening three fingers triggers the switch between the two tools.

Brush Size Control. The brush size controls the amount of adding or erasing volume. The brush size function is activated when users move one hand to the upper-left corner of the screen. The system changes the brush size according to the degree of openness of the hand. Accessing the corner with a fist and gradually opening the fist increases brush size, whereas closing an open hand decreases it.

Select & Move. The user can select an object by making a grabbing gesture toward it with one hand. A selected object will follow the hand as long as the fingers remain closed, becoming anchored to the location at which the grip is released.

Scale. Users can activate the scale function by making two fists (and deactivate it by releasing them). While activated, the system scales the object in proportion to the distance between the two fists.

Rotate. A swiping gesture rotates the object 45 degrees in the direction the hand moves in (up, down, left, or right).

4   Experimental Results

4.1   Implementation

We used an Accupix mybud HMD, which supports 852x480 WVGA resolution and 35° diagonal FOV. For the RGB-D camera we used Creative Senz3D, which supports 1280x720 HD 720p RGB video, 320x240 QVGA IR depth video up to 30fps, and 74° FOV. We used Unity3D for software implementation, with the Intel® Perceptual Computing SDK 2013 R6 for hand/gesture recognition, and the Qualcomm® Vuforia™ SDK for image detection. At the time of evaluation, the brush size control, undo, select & move functions and the system menu mode were not yet implemented.

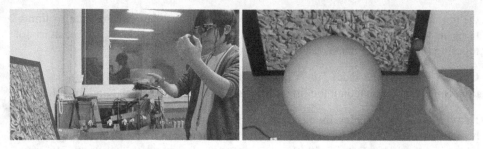

Fig. 3. AiRSculpt evaluation environment (left), and user's view at startup (right)

4.2   Evaluation Method

We selected six representatives of our target audience to participate in a small-scale, in-depth user study. The group included three males and three females, two from the arts, two from math and sciences and two from engineering backgrounds (four were also involved in interdisciplinary work). Half were experienced users of 3D modeling software (of which one had experience with virtual sculpting), while the other half had almost no 3D modeling experience at all. Two had experience in ceramic sculpture, and one was a media artist combining digital and physical media. None of the participants had experience using HMDs or VR/AR environments.

The evaluation of each participant was approximately an hour long and consisted of the following five different stages. First we gave an introduction to the gestural interface and had users practice gestural input and fingertip tracking with the Intel Perceptual Computing SDK Gesture Viewer (5 minutes), after which we gave a brief demo of AiRSculpt (3 minutes) and some practice time for the users to get familiar with its environment (5 minutes). Once the users felt ready, we gave them a series of tasks to be completed from simple to increasingly complex (10-15 minutes), and lastly when they finished we asked them to use AiRSculpt to create any form they please (15-20 minutes). Next we asked them to rate the difficulty level for all completed tasks and fill out a comprehensive questionnaire that combined sections from the most recent version of QUIS (Questionnaire for User Interaction Satisfaction) with elements from the standard USE (Usefulness, Satisfaction, and Ease of Use) Questionnaire. This was followed by a semi-structured interview assessing user experience.

The aim of this study was to gauge user reactions to our system, identify its strengths and weaknesses, and gain valuable quantitative and qualitative insight into how we could improve the experience, to better meet our objectives and expectations. All user tests were videotaped and interviews voice-recorded and transcribed with users' permission for subsequent analysis and documentation.

4.3   System and Task Performance

Users succeeded in accomplishing scaling tasks 100% of the time, having no trouble scaling an object up to twice its size or down to half or a third of its original size. Users also found it fairly easy to create a doughnut shape encircling the default ball,

	VERY HARD					VERY EASY
Depth Perception	1	2	2	0	0	1
Tool Transition	0	0	4	1	1	0
Scaling	0	0	1	1	4	0
Rotation	0	2	0	3	1	0
Rotation & Marking	0	1	2	3	0	0
Creating a donut	0	0	1	1	3	0
Creating a cone	1	2	2	0	0	0
Creating your own work	1	2	0	1	1	1

Fig. 4. Task difficulty assessment. Darker grid shading indicates higher frequency.

by either adding mass around the mid-point of the ball then rotating the ball until they came around full circle, or simply moving their fingertip 360 degrees around the ball. User performance was mixed when it came to rotation-centered tasks. Some users performed rotations effortlessly with great accuracy, whereas others only succeeded in getting the object to rotate half of the time at best. Rotations worked best when users made large, swift sweeping motions with their hands as close to their eyes (and camera) as possible. Most users improved rotations with time and guided practice.

Depth perception, i.e. determining the exact position of the virtual object relative to the user's hand, proved difficult for most users. Most often the virtual object was much further away from the hand than expected. Although users slowly improved in judging the relative distance with guidance and through trial and error, it remained a major source of frustration. Tool transition also took some getting used to, since the system had difficulty identifying how many fingers were extended. On average, users were able to transition from one tool another 7 out of 10 times throughout the evaluation process. Hand recognition worked best when the users placed their whole hand fully in view and their finger(s) extended enough to be distinguished from the palm of the hand. Consciously doing so disrupted instinctive natural interaction. Users found it challenging to make specific geometric shapes such as a cone or a pyramid, which took twice or three times as long as making a donut. Most users stated that AiRSculpt was not optimal for performing deliberate tasks of precision control; they found it much more enjoyable and satisfying to explore with task-free creativity.

4.4   Observations

All users quickly became adept at navigating the interface and transitioning between tools with gestures, and had a lot of fun playing and experimenting with the tool. Most users showed dramatic improvement over time through trial and error. Most also liked that they had a default clay ball to start out with.

Different users used AiRSculpt in surprisingly different ways. One person we evaluated moved around a lot to interact spatially with what she was making, busily viewing and changing things from different angles, even going down on her knees for a significant time to explore the interior, plunging deep into her virtual creation and reaching for things in a way not possible with a mouse and keyboard. Some users on the other hand preferred to stay relatively still, accessing different areas of the virtual object through rotation. Many preferred to sculpt standing, while some alternated between standing and sitting. However all users naturally moved toward the object for closer examination and away for an overall view.

Users also showed marked individual differences in how they used their fingers to draw or switch modes. One user tried to draw with her thumb instead of her index finger, and one user tried to use his pinky finger instead of his middle finger to transition between tools. One of the participants could not physically achieve a recognizable finger posture for toggling Draw/Erase. Some users preferred to draw with their palms facing toward them, while others facing away. The former had an easier time than the latter, since their hands were much less likely to suffer self-occlusion. Users primarily relied on visual feedback (change of colors) to discern state or selected tool, and hardly noticed the corresponding changes in text superposed on their hands.

4.5   Qualitative Evaluation Results

The qualitative evaluation was composed of a questionnaire and a semi-structured interview. The questionnaire was divided into five parts: 1) demographic; 2) overall user reaction; 3) system capabilities; 4) learnability (usefulness, ease of use, ease of learning, satisfaction); and 5) the top three positive and negative aspects of the experience. Parts 2, 3, and 4 used a 9-point rating scale. Questionnaire results showed the highest ratings for learnability, in ease of learning and satisfaction. All users easily remembered how to use it (8 point average), were able to accomplish tasks easily with few commands (7), and thought that steps to complete a task followed a logical sequence (7.2). Most users found it useful (6.9) and quickly became skillful with it (6.8). The poorest ratings were received for error correction and mistake recovery (4.5), since the prototype had no "undo" function. Users all enthusiastically agreed that AiRSculpt was fun to use (7.8), stimulating (7.5), and wonderful (7), but difficult overall (4.2).

Users most frequently used the words "fun" and "fast and easy to learn" in describing the most positive aspects of AiRSculpt. Some expressed appreciation for how well the head movement worked, and the two from the arts especially loved the bare-hand interaction. Other positive words users listed include "intuitive", "awe-inspiring", "chaotic", and "satisfying". Positive attributes they mentioned include easy tool transition, easy applicability, and conducive to creativity. In negative aspects, users most frequently mentioned discomfort of the HMD/HMC, with some expressing eye fatigue, unstable hand recognition interrupting the creative flow (by forcing the adoption of unnatural postures). Many pointed out the difficulty of judging depth, especially since our prototype did not use stereoscopic rendering nor depth occlusion of the see-through RGB video image. The only available depth cues were parallax due to head motion, and depth occlusion of the colored spheres on the user's fingertips.

The interview process helped us to contextualize the responses we observed and gain a deeper understanding of each user's experience with our system.

One particularly bold and exploratory user said she could probably "do this all day", even though she usually found it hard to be creative via computational means. She observed that AiRSculpt was apt for creating artistic work. Although she embraced the elements of unpredictability our system, some users found the lack of precise control frustrating, while others found it amusing but still wanted finer control. The media artist wanted fine-tuned control in the style of ZBrush (brush shape, type, size, material), but above all an "undo" capability. As an advanced user of 3D modeling software, he said that compatibility with other modeling software would be a critical factor in choosing a system. Another user indicated that the hardware quality and performance would be more decisive.

4.6 Preliminary Follow-Up User Study

We made several updates to our first prototype and conducted a short unstructured follow-up user study with this second prototype and four of the six participants from the former study. One significant change to address users' depth cue issues was the addition of depth occlusion by the hands over the virtual content, such that hands can appear in front of or behind parts of the virtual object according to the relative depth. Another change was the addition of a 2D button in the right-hand corner of the interface as an alternate method to toggle the Draw/Erase tools (triggered by 3D collision test), to address the difficulties some users found with the gesture-based trigger. The button also reflected the active tool by color. Other adjustments included making the initial size of the clay ball smaller to extend the available space of play, and using a more realistic clay-like rendering. The primary interests of the follow-up study was whether the added depth occlusion resolved previous perceptual errors, and whether any changes had meaningful impact on the quality of the user experience.

All participants agreed that depth occlusion was a major improvement that made AiRSculpt significantly easier and more intuitive to use. Although other parts of the system were unchanged, users perceived it as more robust and reliable. They felt that they had more control over what they were doing, allowing them to work much faster and be more ambitious with their creations than before, which made the process of making more immersive and satisfying. We were surprised at participants' skill-retention from the last experiment two months prior; most were immediately familiar with the gestural interface and hardly needed re-training or guidance. Only one participant clearly preferred the touch button over gestural input for toggling Draw/Erase, but all thought having both options was positive. All participants relied on the color of the augmented fingertip sphere to identify the active tool, and found the additional color cue of the button unnecessary. Users reported that having a bigger canvas to work with gave them a greater creative scope. Most preferred the smoother more clay-like texture, but some requested the option of choosing different kinds of materials. Criticisms centered on the discomfort of the glasses, and the distracting way they let in ambient light at the sides. The system had difficulty recognizing the smaller-than-average hands of one user. Users experienced difficulties due to the limited rotation options and range of scale; it was easier to physically move to view the object from a desired angle. Many users expressed that need for brush size control is essential for finer detail and expressive potential.

Fig. 5. User creations made with the second prototype

5   Conclusions and Future Work

Preliminary evaluation results confirm that AiRSculpt is fun, playful, intuitive, quick to learn, and a stimulating tool that encourages creative exploration and experimentation, especially suitable for artistic work. The element of play proved to be a significant factor that appealed to all users, and everyone agreed that the 3D interface and bare hand interaction made the experience of making more intuitive, immersive and satisfying. Remaining frustrating aspects derived from unreliable hand and gesture recognition and the uncomfortable or nauseating head-mounted hardware. All participants agreed robustness would dramatically increase the creative potential. Surprisingly, only one of six users observed the lack of tactile or haptic feedback.

We were encouraged by the detailed feedback we received from our participants, and are eager to forge ahead with intuitive interaction design for 3D virtual sculpting via HMD. What we seek is something not only fun and engaging, but also creatively liberating and useful. AiRSculpt seeks to seamlessly integrate the virtual realm with our physical environment as if one were a natural extension of the other: using AR technology to sculpt beyond the screen through natural bare-hand gestures. We want to provide users with the ability to create virtual matter anywhere within a more expansive sculpting zone, as opposed to being limited to manipulating pre-existing mass. It will be useful to give users the freedom of setting custom gestures for certain functions. We plan to move onto a stereoscopic view for enhanced immersion and depth perception. A comprehensive user study on a bigger scale will also be conducted to further improve our system.

Potential Applications. Interesting potentials of a portable AR sculpting system include the ability to prototype and compare 3D forms within a user's desired physical setting before fabrication, and collaborative working within a shared physical space or remote locations. We also envisage potential use for creative empowerment in arts education and art therapy.

References

1. Marshall, M.: Virtual Sculpture Gesture Controlled System for Artistic Expression. In: ConGAS Symposium on Gesture Interfaces for Multimedia Systems, AISB 2004, Leeds, UK (2004)

2. Cutler, L.D., Fröhlich, B., Hanrahan, P.: Two-handed direct manipulation on the responsive workbench. In: Proceedings of the 1997 Symposium on Interactive 3D Graphics, pp. 107–114. ACM (1997)
3. Kim, H., Albuquerque, G., Havemann, S., Fellner, D.W.: Tangible 3D: Hand Gesture Interaction for Immersive 3D Modeling. In: IPT/EGVE, pp. 191–199 (2005)
4. Segen, J., Kumar, S.: Gesture VR: Vision-based 3D hand interface for spatial interaction. In: Proceedings of the Sixth ACM International Conference on Multimedia, pp. 455–464. ACM (1998)
5. Abe, K., Saito, H., Ozawa, S.: 3-D drawing system via hand motion recognition from two cameras. In: 2000 IEEE International Conference on Systems, Man, and Cybernetics, vol. 2, pp. 840–845 (2000)
6. Kolaric, S., Raposo, A., Gattass, M.: Direct 3D manipulation using vision-based recognition of uninstrumented hands. In: X Symposium on Virtual and Augmented Reality, pp. 212–220 (2008)
7. Sachs, E., Roberts, A., Stoops, D.: 3-draw: A tool for designing 3d shapes. IEEE Computer Graphics and Applications 11(6), 18–26 (1991)
8. Deering, M.F.: Holosketch: A virtual reality sketching/animation tool. ACM Transactions on Computer-Human Interaction 2(3), 220–238 (1995)
9. Schkolne, S., Pruett, M., Schröder, P.: Surface drawing: Creating organic 3D shapes with the hand and tangible tools. In: Proceedings of the SIGCHI Conference on Human Factors in Computing Systems, pp. 261–268. ACM (2001)
10. Mäkelä, W.: Working 3D meshes and particles with finger tips: Towards an immersive artists' interface. In: IEEE Virtual Reality Conference on New Directions in 3D User Interfaces Workshop, pp. 77–80 (2005)
11. Keefe, D.F., Feliz, D.A., Moscovich, T., Laidlaw, D.H., LaViola Jr, J.J.: CavePainting: A fully immersive 3D artistic medium and interactive experience. In: Proceedings of the 2001 Symposium on Interactive 3D Graphics, pp. 85–93. ACM (2001)
12. Galyean, T.A., Hughes, J.F.: Sculpting: An interactive volumetric modeling technique. ACM SIGGRAPH Computer Graphics 25(4), 267–274 (1991)
13. Butterworth, J., Davidson, A., Hench, S., Olano, M.T.: 3DM: A three dimensional modeler using a head-mounted display. In: Proceedings of the 1992 Symposium on Interactive 3D Graphics, pp. 135–138. ACM (1992)
14. Yoshida, M., Tijerino, Y., Miyasato, T., Kishino, F.: An interface system based on hand gestures and verbal expressions that generates shapes for 3D virtual objects. In: Tech. Report of IEICE, MVE95-64, pp. 33–40 (1996)
15. Nishino, H., Utsumiya, K., Korida, K.: 3D object modeling using spatial and pictographic gestures. In: Proceedings of the ACM Symposium on Virtual Reality Software and Technology, pp. 51–58. ACM (1998)
16. Wang, S.W., Kaufman, A.E.: Volume sculpting. In: Proceedings of the 1995 Symposium on Interactive 3D Graphics, p. 151–156. ACM (1995)

Children's Collaborative Storytelling on a Tangible Multitouch Tabletop

Anna Helen Leversund, Aleksander Krzywinski, and Weiqin Chen

Department of Information Science and Media Studies,
University of Bergen, P.O. Box. 7802, N-5020 Bergen, Norway
{Anna.Leversund,Aleksander.Krzywinski,
Weiqin.Chen}@infomedia.uib.no

Abstract. According to the literature, tangible multitouch tabletops provide natural and intuitive interaction and afford face-to-face collaboration. Storytelling is an effective method for building conceptual skills and using reasoning to solve problems. This paper reports the evaluation of a tangible multitouch tabletop application (RoboTale) in supporting children's collaborative storytelling. By examining how children use RoboTale to create and tell stories, this study showed the positive effects and potential improvement in the design of RoboTale.

Keywords: Tangible user interface (TUI), multitouch tabletop, collaborative storytelling.

1   Introduction

Tangible user interfaces (TUIs) augment the real physical world by coupling digital information to everyday physical objects and environments [1]. A tangible multitouch tabletop allows multiple users to interact with physical and virtual objects simultaneously and affords natural and intuitive social interactions.

Storytelling helps to build conceptual skills such as understanding a narrative and using inductive reasoning to solve problems. The creation of digital stories also requires the creator to build technology skills through the use of software and other tools [2]. Through storytelling, children can develop 21st-century skills such as creativity, problem-solving, decision-making, communication, and collaboration.

Earlier research has shown that TUIs and multitouch tabletop interfaces have great potential for supporting collaborative storytelling [3-5]. We argue that the potential has not yet been fully explored. The goal of this research is to study how a tangible multitouch interface can enable and facilitate children's storytelling process. To achieve this goal, we have developed and evaluated RoboTale—a tangible multitouch interface supporting children creating and telling stories that focus on a robot protagonist.

N. Streitz and P. Markopoulos (Eds.): DAPI 2014, LNCS 8530, pp. 142–153, 2014.
© Springer International Publishing Switzerland 2014

2   Related Work

Collaborative storytelling is an important element in children's lives. Listening to stories and sharing their own stories and ideas with others are activities through which children make sense of their world and practice their language skills [6]. Previous research has recognized storytelling as a learning activity that allows children to develop skills such as creative problem-solving, collaborative learning, expressive design, development of multiple forms of literacy, and exploration of knowledge [7]. Recent years have seen a growing body of research focusing on using computers to support children's collaborative storytelling, for example, KidPad [8], the Klump [9], PageCraft [10], and TellTale [11].

The use of tangible technologies has also been explored to support storytelling among children in systems such as KidsRoom [12], StoryRooms [13], StoryMat [14], PuzzleTale [15], StoryTent [16], and KidStory [3]. TellTable [4] is a storytelling system for children based on a multitouch table. Children tell stories by drawing directly on the tabletop or by taking photos of objects that are uploaded to the table and used in the stories.

Very little research has been conducted with robots in children's storytelling. Chen et al. [17] conducted a survey on storytelling with robots in an educational context. They identified a few possibilities of mixing children and a robot among storytelling, including the following: giving a robot a storytelling feature to perform before the children; children do programming and story designing for the robot to perform; a robot is designed to motivate children to do storytelling; children are facilitated to assemble a robot character and its environment, and they create a story for the robot to act on; and a robot is programmed by a teacher to perform teaching assistantship (including storytelling). Sugimoto [18] developed GENTORO to support children's storytelling activities in physical spaces using a handheld projector and a robot. The possibility of manipulating a robot increases children's involvement and participation. Studies with school children indicated that GENTORO could effectively support children in designing and expressing creative and original stories.

The RoboTale system presented in this paper differs from the previous works in many aspects. First of all, it allows children to combine physical and virtual objects in their story creation and storytelling on a tabletop. Secondly, a robot protagonist whose movements can be controlled by the children is used as the main figure in the stories. Thirdly, the physical objects created by the children can interact with virtual objects or other physical objects, including the robot.

3   RoboTale

RoboTale is an application for story creation and storytelling based on the RobotTable framework for tangible interaction with robots in a mixed reality [19]. Using RoboTale, children can collaboratively create a story revolving around a robot protagonist. The story unfolds on a multitouch table, with the robot travelling on the touch surface between objects placed and moved by the children, thus forming the physical backdrop on which the children may expose the details of their story.

Children can interact with the robot and the touch surface by manipulating physical objects and touching virtual objects on the surface. The fiducial symbols (see Table 1) tagged underneath the physical objects allow them to be uniquely identified (Fig. 1). The table tracks the symbols and touch inputs, and the robot reacts accordingly. Children can tag the different objects they want to use in their story, such as Lego creations and stuffed animal toys. These objects can represent characters, locations, and sceneries. The robot can carry and transport virtual and physical items. It can also follow and avoid tracked objects, and the children can also create bridges or gates to influence the paths chosen by the robot.

Table 1. Fiducial symbols used in the evaluation

id	Use in storytelling	Symbol
0	Sun	
1	Rain	
2	Thunder	
3-6	Background	
7-10	Push marker	
11	Robot	
12-17	Drag marker	

The design goal of RoboTale is to facilitate children's storytelling by providing necessary plot elements in the context of the story. It is up to the children to use the context elements to explain what the actions of the robot signify and the intentions, motivations, and causality of the actions. Thus, in the story creation mode, the children define the relationships between the robot protagonist and other characters or locations in the story by using the tools and objects provided by RoboTale. In the story presentation mode, the robot reacts to the objects placed on the table surface by the children based on the predefined relationship. The children are free to choose which objects to put on the table, and when, to tell their story; thus, the story can become something completely different from what the children originally imagined when defining these relationships.

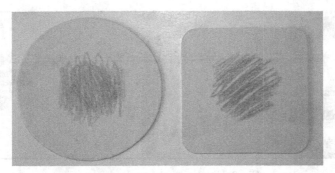

Fig. 1. Red push marker and green drag marker

4   Evaluation

In the evaluation, we focused on three research questions:

- How easy or difficult is it for the children to use RoboTale?
  This question covers whether the children can understand and make use of the different elements in the interface.
- How do children use the different tangible objects in their storytelling?
  This question covers what roles the tangible objects have and how the children use and relate to the robot.
- How do the children collaborate in storytelling, and how does RoboTale facilitate the process?
  This question covers the collaboration patterns among children and what elements in RoboTale affect and facilitate the collaboration.

The evaluation of RoboTale includes two pilot studies and one formative evaluation. All of the evaluations were conducted in a university lab in which the table was positioned in one end of the room. One side of the table was along the wall while there were chairs along the other three sides. Because the table was rather high for the children, the chairs were positioned with the back to the table so that the children could kneel on the chairs and interact with the table. The long conference table in the room was used for children to draw backgrounds and figures. The backgrounds were loaded to the table as the background for storytelling, while the figures were stuck to different physical objects.

Two cameras were used to record the activities during the evaluations (see Fig. 2). One was a web camera positioned directly above the table focusing on the interactions on the table. The other was a video camera positioned in the other end of the room, capturing the activities inside the room. Both cameras recorded audio. The interviews with participants and the teacher were also recorded with a video camera.

Each session was planned to last 40 minutes in order to fit into an ordinary class (45 minutes) and included the following steps:

Fig. 2. Views from the two cameras

1. Introduction. The researchers presented themselves to the children and asked their names and ages and what they expected. Then the researchers told the children about RoboTale and the evaluation.
2. Exploration/Tutorial. The children explored the table, checking out the robot and trying out the drag and push gestures, so that they learned how to control the robot. Explanation and help was provided when necessary.
3. Brainstorming about the characters in the story and/or backgrounds. The children were presented with the task of telling a story about the robot's first day in a new school, along with the number of characters and backgrounds that should be included. The researchers also helped them to determine which characters and backgrounds they would include in their history.
4. Distribution of tasks. After the characters and backgrounds were determined, the children discussed among themselves and agreed on who was going to draw what. The teacher assisted in this process.
5. Drawing story elements and/or backgrounds. The children sat at the conference table in the room and drew the backgrounds and characters to be used in the story (Fig. 3). The physical objects were attached with fiducial markers. The backgrounds were photographed with a smartphone and loaded to the system.
6. Storytelling. The children gathered around the table with the robot and story elements. One of the children began to tell a story, and other children joined in.

Fig. 3. Story elements drawn by children (figures with the drag effect)

7. Introduction of weather objects (Fig. 4). At a stage during the storytelling, weather objects were introduced, and children could use these objects in their stories. By introducing the weather objects in the middle of the storytelling, the researchers could observe the effects of these objects on the storytelling.

Fig. 4. Weather objects: sun, thunder, and rain

8. Continuation with the story. After all of the story elements were introduced, the children continued telling their story.
9. Debriefing. After the storytelling, the children, their teacher, and the researchers sat at the conference table and had a short interview session. The children also had opportunities to comment and ask questions.

In addition to video- and audio recording, notes were taken during the sessions. An interview with the teacher was conducted after the session and at the end of the evaluation after all sessions were finished.

The following sections give more details about these evaluations.

4.1 Pilot Studies

The two pilot studies were conducted with one adult and with a group of three children, aiming at identifying possible technical problems of RoboTale and validating the design for the formative evaluation.

One master student in information science participated in the first pilot study. The participant had never seen or used RoboTale before. Some technical problems were identified during this study. For example, the movement of the robot was not very accurate. When using the green drag marker, the robot did not stop at the exact place of the drag marker but a little bit farther away from it. Some functions in RoboTale were not very visible to the user. For example, RoboTale allows multiple character markers on the table at the same time, and it is the last placed marker that triggers the movement of the robot. The participant was not aware of this, and he put one at a time on the table. The thunderstorm was programmed so that the sound and graphics were first activated when the user shook the thunder object, not when the user put the object on the table, which was also found to be somewhat confusing to the participant. For the evaluation procedure, the planning and drawing stage was found to take most of the time, thus the thought process was predetermined with little left for improvising.

After the first pilot study, some technical improvements were made. The movement of the robot was made more accurate, the planning and drawing time was reduced, and more opportunities for improvising were provided.

Three children (8–9 years old) participated in the second pilot study, and their teacher was present during the evaluation. Technically, the drag marker (round shape) and the push marker (square shape) were not self-explanatory, and the children had to ask which one did what. The children were found to make many story elements and figures beforehand and put them on the table, and many of them were not used in the storytelling. With so many elements on the table, the movements of the robot were affected. In addition, the use of RoboTale and the storytelling was very unstructured at first, largely depending on individual activities. The teacher had to intervene to tell the children about turn-taking and provide them with some structure. With more structure and interventions from the teacher and the researchers, the children proceeded with the story. For the evaluation procedure, we found that we should not ask children questions that were not relevant to the story during their activities. The presence of the cameras was largely ignored and did not interfere with the children's activities. The debriefing was useful and worked well.

After the second pilot study, more technical improvements were made. We added colour to the drag markers and push markers, so they became more easily recognizable and memorable. Because it is difficult for children to manage the process themselves, the structure of the storytelling process was made clearer. Story elements and figures were introduced gradually to avoid cluttering the table and the cognitive load for children to handle all of the elements at the same time.

4.2   Formative Evaluation

The formative evaluation was conducted with 18 children (8–9 years old) divided into six groups and their teachers. We were conscious that all groups should include both girls and boys.

In this evaluation, there had been variations in the use of tangible objects, as summarized in Table 2.

Table 2. Variations in the use of tangible objects

	Group1	Group2	Group3	Group4	Group5	Group6
Robot	X	X	X	X	X	X
Background	X	X	X	X	X	X
Sun	X	X	X	X	X	X
Rain	X	X	X	X	X	X
Thunder	X	X				
Figure marker	X	X			X	
Control markers (red and green)			X	X		X
Figures without functions						X

Interface. Most of the children seemed to understand how the different objects worked after a short time. However, some usability problems with the tangible objects were also identified. The red and green control markers were not found to be self-explanatory. The children had to learn and remember the differences. Although the children could learn and remember them rather quickly, we could see that when the number of such objects increases, the level of difficulty would increase as well. This confirms that it is important to design tangible objects so that the functionality and the scope of their usage are clear [20]. The lack of convention within TUI makes this particularly challenging.

The children assumed that red and green control markers would affect the movements of the robot in a similar way. However, the trigger distance for the drag marker (red and round) is much longer than the push marker (green and square). This resulted in the children adopting a trial-and-error method to learn the distance between the marker and the robot. The same happened with the weather markers. The children expected that all of the weather markers would work in similar ways. They found out that the thunder marker did not give continuous feedback like the other two markers (sun and rain). The conflict between the design model and the children's mental model caused some frustration and confusion.

Although the number of tangible objects in the evaluation was not very high, we had already observed that the table was full of objects. This kind of physical clutter of objects [21] affected the movement of the robot. If we make the objects smaller, it would be difficult for the camera inside the table to identify the objects. If we make the table bigger, it would take more space and would be difficult to get hold of the objects across the table. This scalability problem is considered to be one of the biggest challenges with TUI [21].

Children's Relation to the Tangible Objects. All of the children seemed to like the robot. They personalized it, although the robot could not move without the children using the push markers and drag markers. A girl said, "Hello you" ("Hei du" in Norwegian) to the robot while stroking its head gently. After a child picked up the robot and placed it on the table, the robot went towards the figure standing on the table. The child giggled and moved the figure away. The robot continued to follow the figure. One of the children exclaimed, "He was crazy about it (the figure) there" ("Han var helt vill etter den der" in Norwegian). When children wanted the robot to come to them, they used expressions such as the following: "Now you are mine" and "Come to me" ("Nå er du min" and "Kom til meg" in Norwegian). The interview also confirmed the children's positive attitude towards the robot. They used sweet, tough, kind, and other words describing personal qualities to describe the robot. The teacher thought that the children saw the robot as a kind of hero and therefore it appealed to them.

The children showed great interest in the weather objects. They thought these objects were "cool". These objects became the centre of their attention and were used very frequently. We observed that the weather objects with the combination of sound and visual effect had positive effects on the children's imaginations. The following conversation and activities show how the children used the weather objects in the storytelling.

E11: *Out in the playground, they are playing* (E12 put on the sun marker). *It was good weather. But suddenly, it started – Take that off* (pointing at the sun marker), *suddenly it started to rain – Can you give me that?* (putting down the green marker and pointing at the red push marker). (E12 passed the red marker to her) *...rain* (putting the rain marker and the red push marker). *Then he (the robot) went away. Now he had nobody to be with.*

The weather objects had great influence on the content of the stories. Some of the children almost forgot all of the other elements. Many were inspired by these objects, and their stories turned to a new path. Some children were so engaged in playing with the weather objects that they later realised they had forgotten about school, which was the main theme set up in the beginning of the story. The weather objects were used not only to describe the weather but also to describe feelings and emotions: When the sun was shining, everything was good, but when the rain marker was on, the robot suddenly felt lonely and abandoned. The thunder marker often gave the story a darker twist. Such use of the weather objects was observed in most of the group stories where the sun marker represented positive events and feelings while the rain and thunder markers represented dark and negative feelings. Some boys had special interest in the thunder marker and liked to play a high thunder sound. In some cases, this caused disruption in the storytelling. Therefore, after two sessions, the thunder object was removed from the elements. Nonetheless, some groups still used thunder in their story even when the thunder object was not available. Some groups also used the sun marker as a disco light. When spinning the marker around quickly, it could look like the rotating light in a disco. During the interview, the children also expressed their wishes for other weather objects such as rainbow, day and night, and so on.

The robot and the weather objects differed from the rest of the system because they were dynamic and gave feedback in the form of sound and movement, which made them more popular among the children.

Collaboration among the Children. Face-to-face collaboration is one of the most important affordances of a multitouch table. The children were found to be mostly good at sharing the tangible objects and taking turns to tell stories. The interaction level was high among the children. The table was rather large, which made it difficult for the children to reach to the other side. They often helped each other to move tangible objects when the others had difficulties reaching them. During the sessions, there were not enough objects so that each child could have his or her own object. They were "forced" to work together, share, and take turns. Providing different numbers of objects on the table was found to promote collaboration, as also shown by Stanton et al. [3] in KidStory. Some children felt ownership towards the background and figures they themselves created, which resulted in some children having to ask the others to "borrow" their figures. The children not only took turns to tell the story but also intervened in each other's stories and collaborated in the content of the story by giving suggestions. In some groups, the children expressed that the next person should continue with the story. It also happened that the children did not agree on what was going to happen in the story and how the characters in the story should react to different events. Sometimes, they overruled each other by determining what was allowed or not allowed. In some cases, when the group did not come to an agreement, one of the children kidnapped the story and continued as she or he wanted because the tangible objects were accessible to everyone [21]. This often resulted in several small stories with different themes and various degree of coherence. Some children were found to be better collaborators than others. The interview with the teachers revealed that the class was working more with collaboration methods, and individual differences in maturity had an impact on their collaboration skills. Harris et al. [22] found clear gender- and age-related tendencies in a study of children and their use of multitouch tables versus single-touch tables. The study showed that there could be significant differences between the ability to use an interface and the ability to collaborate on a task. When using RoboTale, although the children individually had no problems interacting with the system, it did not mean that children could work together to make and tell a story. During the evaluation, some children showed leadership and organized the group work, which was considered very positive by the teachers.

5   Conclusion and Future Work

The evaluation results show that the RoboTale interface is easy to learn, and children were able to understand how to use the system in a very short time. The design of the tangible objects was essential for the children. Dynamic objects that gave feedback in the form of sound or movement were important sources of inspiration and creativity. The robot was given human traits such as being kind, evil, and so on. The results also indicate that although the tangible tabletop affords collaboration, intervention and facilitation were still necessary to ensure productive collaboration. The evaluations have also provided recommendations for further development of RoboTale.

In addition to technical improvements based on the feedback from the evaluations, we have identified many directions to pursue in future research. For example, we can conduct research focusing on the role of the robot in children's story creation and storytelling. Comparative studies can be conducted to investigate whether there are differences in children's interactions with and without the multitouch table or with and without the tangible objects. We can also investigate whether RoboTale can help children with special needs. Through collaboration with teachers, we plan to integrate the RoboTale into classroom activities so that children can use RoboTale over longer period in school activities. A longitudinal study in schools will provide more insight into the effects of RoboTale.

References

1. Ishii, H., Ullmer, B.: Tangible bits: Towards seamless interfaces between people, bits and atoms. In: Proceedings of the ACM SIGCHI Conference on Human Factors in Computing Systems (CHI 1997), pp. 234–241. ACM, New York (1997)
2. Czarnecki, K.: How Digital Storytelling Builds 21st Century Skills. Library Technology Reports 45(7), 15–19 (2009)
3. Stanton, D., Bayon, V., Neale, H., Ghali, A., Benford, S., Cobb, S., Ingram, R., et al.: Classroom Collaboration in the Design of Tangible Interfaces for Storytelling. In: Proceedings of the SIGCHI Conference on Human Factors in Computing Systems (CHI 2001), pp. 482–489. ACM, New York (2001)
4. Cao, X., Lindley, S.E., Helmes, J., Sellen, A.: Telling the Whole Story: Anticipation, Inspiration and Reputation in a Field Deployment of TellTable. In: Proceedings of the 2010 ACM Conference on Computer Supported Cooperative Work (CSCW 2010), pp. 251–260. ACM, New York (2010)
5. Mi, H., Krzywinski, A., Sugimoto, M., Chen, W.: RoboStory: A Tabletop Mixed Reality Framework for Children's Role Play Storytelling. Paper presented at the Proceedings of Workshop on Interactive Storytelling for Children (IDC 2010), Barcelona, Spain (2010)
6. Miller, P.J., Sperry, L.L.: Early talk about the past: The origins of conversational stories of personal experience. Journal of Child Language 15, 293–315 (1988)
7. Peterson, C., McCabe, A.: Developmental psycholinguistics: Three ways of looking at a child's narrative. Plenum, New York (1983)
8. Hourcade, J.P., Bederson, B.B., Druin, A., Taxén, G.: KidPad: Collaborative storytelling for children. Paper presented at the CHI 2002 Extended Abstracts on Human Factors in Computing Systems, CHI EA 2002 (2002)
9. Benford, S., Bederson, B.B., Akesson, K., Bayon, V., Druin, A., Hansson, P., Hourcade, J.P., Ingram, R., Neale, H., O'Malley, C., Simsarian, K., Stanton, D., Sundblad, Y., Taxén, G.: Designing Storytelling Technologies to Encourage Collaboration Between Young Children. In: Proceedings of CHI 2000, pp. 556–563. ACM, New York (2000)
10. Budd, J., Madej, K., Stephens-Wells, J., de Jong, J., Katzur, E., Mulligan, L.: PageCraft: Learning in context a tangible interactive storytelling platform to support early narrative development for young children. In: Proceedings of the 6th International Conference on Interaction Design and Children (IDC 2007), pp. 97–100. ACM, New York (2007)
11. Ananny, M.: Supporting children's collaborative authoring: Practicing written literacy while composing oral texts. In: Stahl, G. (ed.) Proceedings of the Conference on Computer Support for Collaborative Learning: Foundations for a CSCL Community (CSCL 2002), pp. 595–596. International Society of the Learning Sciences (2002)
12. Bobick, A.F., Intille, S.S., Davis, J.W., Baird, F., Pinhanez, C.S., Campbell, L.W., Ivanov, Y.A., Schütte, A., Wilson, A.: Perceptual user interfaces: The KidsRoom. Commun. ACM 43(3), 60–61 (2000)
13. Alborzi, H., Druin, A., Montemayor, J., Platner, M., Porteous, J., Sherman, L., Boltman, A., Taxén, G., Best, J., Hammer, J., Kruskal, A., Lal, A., Schwenn, T.P., Sumida, L., Wagner, R., Hendler, J.: Designing StoryRooms: Interactive storytelling spaces for children. In: Boyarski, D., Kellogg, W.A. (eds.) Proceedings of the 3rd Conference on Designing Interactive Systems: Processes, Practices, Methods, and Techniques (DIS 2000), pp. 95–104. ACM, New York (2000)
14. Ryokai, K., Cassell, J.: StoryMat: A play space for collaborative storytelling. In: Proceedings of CHI 1999 Extended Abstracts on Human Factors in Computing Systems (CHI EA 1999), pp. 272–273. ACM, New York (1999)

15. Shen, Y.T., Mazalek, A.: PuzzleTale: A tangible puzzle game for interactive storytelling. Comput. Entertain. 8(2) (2010)
16. Green, J., Schnädelbach, H., Koleva, B., Benford, S., Pridmore, T., Medina, K., Harris, E., Smith, H.: Camping in the digital wilderness: Tents and flashlights as interfaces to virtual worlds. In: CHI 2002 Extended Abstracts on Human Factors in Computing Systems, pp. 780–781. ACM, New York (2002)
17. Chen, G.-D., Nurkhamid, Wang, C.-Y.: A Survey on Storytelling with Robots. In: Chang, M., Hwang, W.-Y., Chen, M.-P., Müller, W. (eds.) Edutainment 2011. LNCS, vol. 6872, pp. 450–456. Springer, Heidelberg (2011)
18. Sugimoto, M.: A Mobile Mixed Reality Environment for Children's Storytelling using a Handheld Projector and a Robot. IEEE Transactions on Learning Technologies 4(3), 249–260 (2011)
19. Krzywinski, A., Mi, H., Chen, W., Sugimoto, M.: RoboTable: A tabletop framework for tangible interaction with robots in a mixed reality. In: Proceedings of the International Conference on Advances in Computer Enterntainment Technology (ACE 2009), pp. 107–114. ACM, New York (2009)
20. Ishii, H.: Tangible bits: Beyond pixels. In: Proceedings of the 2nd International Conference on Tangible and Embedded Interaction (TEI 2008). ACM, New York (2008)
21. Shaer, O., Hornecker, E.: Tangible User Interfaces: Past, Present, and Future Directions. Found. Trends Hum.-Comput. Interact. 3(1-2), 1–137 (2010)
22. Harris, A., Rick, J., Bonnett, V., Yuill, N., Fleck, R., Marshall, P., Rogers, Y.: Around the table: Are multiple-touch surfaces better than single-touch for children's collaborative interactions? In: O'Malley, C., Suthers, D., Reimann, P., Dimitracopoulou, A. (eds.) Proceedings of the 9th International Conference on Computer Supported Collaborative Learning (CSCL 2009), vol. 1, pp. 335–344. International Society of the Learning Sciences (2009)

An Optical Guiding System for Gesture Based Interactions in Smart Environments

Martin Majewski[1], Tim Dutz[2], and Reiner Wichert[1]

[1] Fraunhofer Institute for Computer Graphics Research IGD, Darmstadt, Germany
{martin.majewski,reiner.wichert}@igd.fraunhofer.de
[2] Multimedia Communications Lab, Technische Universitaet Darmstadt, Germany
tim.dutz@kom.tu-darmstadt.de

Abstract. Using gestures to control Ambient Intelligence environments can result in mismatches between the user's intention and the perception of the gesture by the system. One way to cope with this problem is to provide the user with an instant feedback on what the system has perceived. In this work, we present an approach for providing visual feedback to users of Ambient Intelligence systems that rely on gestures to control individual devices within their environments. This paper extends our previous work on this topic [1] and introduces several enhancements to the system.

Keywords: Gesture-based Interaction, Visual Feedback, Ambient Intelligence.

1 Introduction

Since Mark Weiser formulated the vision of ubiquitous computing systems embedded pervasively in our everyday environments [2] back in 1991, the amount of intelligent networked-devices has grown significantly. They are present in the form of smart entertainment systems such as TVs and HiFi sets, embedded in home automation systems and white ware, or part of communication devices such as tablet computers and smartphones. Every single of these devices provides its own, specific user interface and this can make it difficult for the user to keep track of the wide variety of functionalities provided. Consequently, there is a growing interest for more comprehensive interaction methods [3]. In the past couple of years, scientists invented and examined different approaches to provide a more natural and unified way of interacting with smart environments [4], and a very convenient way of selecting and interacting with devices within smart environments are gestures [5].

Because gestures are often used in interactions between humans and usually correctly interpreted by a human counterpart, interacting with smart environments via gestures feels natural and intuitive. However, there can be a significant mismatch between the understanding of a gesture when performed by a person and the interpretation of the same gesture by a computer system. This mismatch results from a variety of reasons:

N. Streitz and P. Markopoulos (Eds.): DAPI 2014, LNCS 8530, pp. 154–163, 2014.

- An incorrect positioning of the gesture tracking sensors
- An insufficient tracking precision
- A wrong interpretation of the gathered tracking data by the computer system
- The user's misleading self-assessment when performing unambiguous gestures
- The user's erroneous believe in an unlimited adaptivity of the computer system

The creation of failsafe gesture recognition systems that are capable of covering large areas (such as the entire living room) is an enormous challenge as these systems have a high implementation complexity. An interim solution on the way towards this goal might be to develop systems that can provide users with instant, sophisticated feedback on what the system has perceived, thus enabling them to better adapt their behavior to the system's capabilities. To this end, we have developed an optical guiding device that acts like an omnipresent environmental cursor. This laser-based device visualizes the current interpretation of the user's gesture to her, thus allowing her to adapt accordingly. Furthermore, we implemented a highly customizable and flexible software solution that connects multiple economy-priced gesture and position tracking devices such as Microsoft's Kinect, the Leap Motion Tracking bar, and the CapFloor system for the provision of reliable multi-resolution user localization and gesture tracking.

2   Related Work

The research on whole-body gestures can be traced back to at least the early 1960s [6, 7]. The current efforts in this area concentrate mainly on virtual reality and entertainment applications [8, 9]. To perform gestural interaction, a human body pose recognition system is needed and since the release of Microsoft's Kinect sensor, 3D cameras that sell at a reasonable price have become widely available.

This text is an addition to our earlier work [1]. For this, we have found inspiration mainly in the research of Wilson et al [8], who first introduced the dedicated XWand input device based on inertial measurement units and infrared LEDs. These allow for the determination of the XWand's position and orientation in order to calculate the location that it is currently being pointed at by the user. Although not being a marker free whole-body interaction method in its own right, it led to Wilson's later work, the WorldCursor [1]. This laser-pointing device highlights the location currently selected by the XWand in the environment, thus improving the selection process.

The Beamatron project of Wilson et al. [2], published by Microsoft Research in 2012, shows a marker free interaction approach using several Kinect cameras, a microphone array setup, as well as a high definition projector mounted on a stage-light robot arm. Although being heavily related to our works with respect to the character of the utilized input and output devices, the Beamatron project is not a feasible solution for everyday home setups. The stage-light robot arm makes it a costly product, and it is too voluminous for the average ceiling height. Furthermore, although it relies on complex algorithms to identify and follow the user's location, it is relatively static and inflexible. Figure 1 shows pictures of both the WorldCursor (to the left) and the Beamatron (to the right).

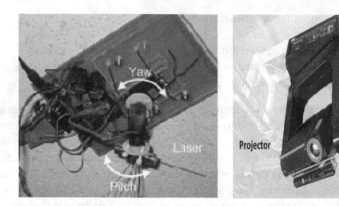

Fig. 1. WorldCursor, left [11] and Beamatron, right [12]

The effectiveness of locating the user in a real word environment highly depends on the sensor technology used. Camera based location is a common method nowadays. Since the introduction and the gaining popularity of smartphones and tablet computers, the focus of gesture recognition research oftentimes lies on capacitive sensory empowered gesture interaction. The transition from small screens to large areas capable of not only tracking smaller limbs, but the whole body was performed by Grosse-Puppendahl et al. [3] in 2013 with the OpenCapSense tookit and Braun et al. [4] with the CapFloor system – a highly affordable floor setup for locating people's position and approximating their posture within a given area. Another accurate solution for detailed limb tracking can be found with the LeapMotion IR sensor bar, although it is limited to a small spatial room.

With our solution, we show a compact, affordable, and relatively flexible visual feedback system. We additionally use the CapFloor technology for providing more accurate position estimation and combine this location approach with both a Kinect camera for low-resolution entire body gesture recognition and a LeapMotion device to support finger gestures.

3   The Perception Gap

The gap between a user's intention when performing a gesture and the system's interpretation of this gesture was already described at length in the predecessor work of Majewski et al. [1]. Due to this, we will only briefly summarize our findings here. In the subsequent paragraphs of this section, we will then introduce the modifications to the system as described in our previous paper. These modifications should help to close the perception gap to an even greater extent than the original system.

To use the index finger as a pointer and to thus generate an immaterial cone that spreads towards the pointing location is a common choice by humans when trying to point at something, but such a gesture can hardly be comprehended by gesture interpretation systems that only rely on simplified skeleton models, such as the Kinect camera. Based on such a simplified skeleton model, only the orientations of the larger limbs of the human body can be perceived the system and as such, when the user is pointing at something with her finger, the system actually bases its interpretation of the pointing location on the orientation of the user's shoulder and wrist. This often results in a significant mismatch between the intended pointing location and the gesture interpretation by the system. Figure 2 visualizes this problem.

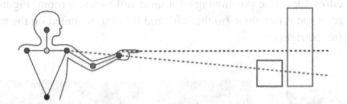

Fig. 2. Pointing mismatch

A second challenge for the computer-based interpretation of gestures is the parallax between gaze and arm angle that is affecting the perceived direction of a pointing gestures. Figure 3 shows this effect from a bird's perspective. There is a considerable difference between constructing the ray that spreads towards the pointing location from the shoulder and wrist on the one hand, and from the iris on the other. The closer the target object is, the larger the effect. In certain situations, this parallax is reduced, as highlighted on the right side of the figure. However, already a small offset angle results in a several centimeters large shift when pointing at something within a few meters distance. More specifically, an offset of merely five degrees between the user's gaze and her shoulder-wrist-line will result in a deviation of 17 cm when pointing at something in a distance of two meters. This error can make pointing on several relatively small devices in close proximity to each other very difficult.

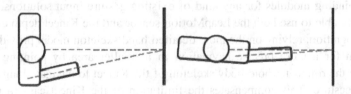

Fig. 3. Parallax mismatch

A third problem occurs when the time delay between performing a pointing action and the reaction by the system exceeds a certain time interval. According to a study by Kammer et al. [5], only delays of less than 100 milliseconds are perceived to be acceptable by users. As such, a user will be inclined to find a slow gesture interpretation system unsatisfactory, even if her gestures are interpreted correctly by the system and trigger the intended effects.

4   Visual Feedback System

4.1   Visual Feedback Robot

The visual feedback robot was introduced in 2012 by Majewski et al. [1] and is based on an Arduino microcontroller board, operating a small laser mounted on two servo-motors that allow for a free positioning of a laser dot inside a room. Figure 4 shows both an image of the robot alone (to the left) and it being mounted on the ceiling of a living room (to the right).

Fig. 4. Visual Feedback Robot (left) and mounted on living room ceiling (right)

4.2   Visual Feedback Framework

The software framework that supported the original feedback robot was completely redesigned, resulting in a modular architecture that allows extending functionality by providing binding modules for any kind of existing gesture input solutions. Through this, we were able to use both the LeapMotion sensor and the Kinect depth camera for gesture recognition, relying on the more detailed hand skeleton model provided by the LeapMotion for a more precise navigation in a smaller area by pointing a finger, while using the rougher whole-body skeleton of the Kinect to navigate long distances using arm gesture. This compensates the limitation of the Kinect camera not being able to track small limb joints. The tracking module of our approach abstracts the input devices and generates a unit ray representation. Every input device is associated with a priority ID to generate a hierarchical ordering of the provided tracking accuracy. Figure 5 provides an overview of the architecture of our framework. The various tracking methods used in our system are detailed in the next section.

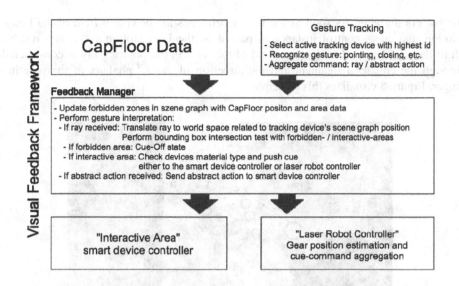

Fig. 5. Visual Feedback Framework architecture

5   Tracking and Localization Methods

5.1   Low-Resolution Whole-Body Gestures

While in the progress of orientation and navigation, the user tends to use less accurate gestures to bypass larger spatial areas and provoke an immediate response from the system. For these situations, we use a less detailed motion tracking approach based on the Kinect camera and create the resulting pointing ray from the shoulder-wrist-line. This is sufficiently accurate for many types of gestures, although it forces the user to adapt her gestures to the system's perception, suffering from the problems described in chapter 3. This is where the supporting effect of the instant feedback that is provided by the visual feedback robot as introduced in chapter 4 is the largest.

5.2   High-Resolution Hand-Based Gestures

Excessive limb motions, which are required for interacting with the low-resolution system, can be tedious or even impossible, when the spatial area available is highly limited. Furthermore, the ray construction by way of the shoulder-wrist-line is not as precise as in case of using the finger. For this reason, we have extended our gesture tracking system with a LeapMotion infrared sensor bar. Alas, the sensor bar has severe limitations in terms of detection range, which is an area of only about 0.226 m³ above the bar. Consequently, the amount of use cases that depend on this kind of sensor is strongly limited. We chose to use the LeapMotion as a stationary tracking device on the armrest of a sofa, were it is comfortable to use while sitting next to it. In this position, the lower arm is supported by the armrest, making the interaction with the bar comfortable. As soon as the user approaches the detection field of the Leap-Motion, the cue's control instance is passed to the LeapMotion's skeleton results. Until the user leaves the detection field of the device, the pointing ray is constructed through the collateral ligament and the direction of the 3rd phalanx of the pointing finger. Figure 6 visualizes this principle.

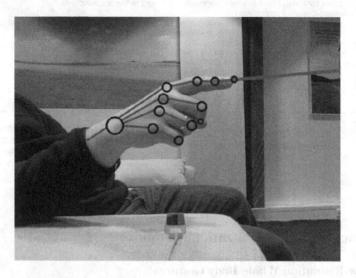

Fig. 6. High-resolution pointing gestures with LeapMotion

5.3   CapFloor User Position Detection

Camera-based tracking systems have their limitations in terms of field of view and tracking distance, and are also a cause for privacy concerns for many users. Further-more, even powerful depth tracking camera systems have their limitations when it comes to the quantity of detectable users. To both provide for a better coverage of the user detection area and address these concerns, we have investigated a possibility to detect users through the CapFloor capacitive sensor based floor [13, 14].

The hardware demands of CapFloor suite our interest in delivering an economy-priced solution very well. The CapFloor uses thin copper wires as antennas, which are orthogonally arranged under a carpet or integrated into tile joints. These antennas are connected to a sensor bus system in the room's baseboard and the gathered data is processed within the CapSense framework. This framework, being capable of detect-ing and classifying standing or lying objects, provides us with the required data for our setup. We use this to realize two uses cases as described in the next two sections.

5.4   Dynamic Forbidden Area Determination

For obvious security reasons, we have designed our laser-based visual feedback sys-tem to avoid user eye contact. To this end, the system tracks the position of all users using and will not point the laser beam to any of such locations. Different to static objects like furniture, users tend to move through the room and as such, there position needs to be constantly updated. However, camera-based tracking approaches such as ones based on the Kinect are only of limited use for this, as the can move out of sight of their tracking area. To this end, we rely on the CapFloor sensor to reliable inform our system of the user's position. More specifically, we use the classification of the detected objects to make body size estimation. If the CapFloor software classifies the detected person as standing, we use a cylindrical bounding box and set its height to 200 cm. This height dimensions accords to the door's height in our environmental model. The width is set to the significantly detected floor proximity area's long side of the detected person, but not less than 50 cm in diameter to ensure the head coverage even if the person bends its head sideways. If the CapFloor software classifies the detected person as lying, we use a rectangular bounding box and set its height to 50 cm. The width and depth dimensions are determined by the side length sum of the active antenna cells. These bounding boxes are updated in real-time in our environmental model and ensure the dynamic creation of forbidden areas not to be highlighted by the visual feedback robot.

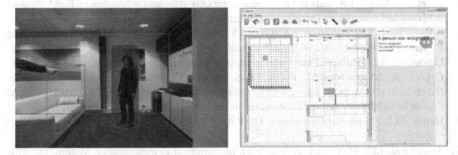

Fig. 7. Forbidden area determination

5.5 Selective Device Activation

If a system is supposed to cover a larger with visual pointing feedback, it requires multiple cameras and projectors. Leaving all those devices active and just waiting for the user to enter the camera's field of view is certainly not a satisfying situation. Based on the user location detection with CapFloor, our approach allows the activation of cameras and projectors only when the user is close enough to benefit from the functionalities that they can provide.

6 Conclusion and Future Work

In this contribution we have introduced three important additions to our visual feedback system that compensate the limitations of the low detail skeleton reconstruction of the Kinect camera, made possible through the development of a highly flexible visual feedback framework. Furthermore, we have increased the security and usability aspect of the system by providing static and dynamic forbidden areas that avoid unwanted cue projection.

To measure the benefits of our current work, we intend to perform an extensive user evaluation of our system in the near future. The users' feedback will then be used to improve the system further. We also plan to investigate a richer cue provision with portable multimedia projectors, as well as more complex laser setups where we focus on affordability and suitability for daily use.

Acknowledgments. This work is partially financed by the European Commission under the FP7-ICT-Project Miraculous Life (grant agreement no. 611421).

References

1. Majewski, M., Braun, A., Marinc, A., Kuijper, A.: Visual support system for selecting reactive elements in intelligent environments. In: Cyberworlds (CW). IEEE, Darmstadt (2012)
2. Weiser, M.: The Computer for the 21st Century. Scientific American 265(3) (1991)
3. Sears, A., Jacko, J.A. (eds.): The human-computer interaction handbook: Fundamentals, evolving technologies and emerging applications. CRC Press (2007)
4. Reeves, L.M., Lai, J., Larson, J.A., Oviatt, S., Balaji, T.S., Buisine, S., Collings, P., Cohen, P., Kraal, B., Martin, J.-C., McTear, M., Raman, T.V., Stanney, K.M., Su, H., Wang, Q.Y.: Guidelines for multimodal user interface design. Communications of the ACM 47 (2004)
5. Grguric, A., Mosmondor, M., Kusek, M., Stockloew, C., Salvi, D.: Introducing gesture interaction in the Ambient Assisted Living platform universaal. In: ConTEL 2013: Proceedings of the 12th International Conference on Telecommunications, Zagreb (2013)
6. Heilig, M.L.: Sensorama Simulator. US Patent 3050870, US Patent Office, Long Beach (1962)
7. Sutherland, I.E.: Sketchpad: A man-machine graphical communication system. In: Afips Conference Proceedings, vol. 2(574). ACM, New York (1963)
8. Kessler, G.D., Hodges, L.F., Walker, N.: Evaluation of the CyberGlove as a whole-hand input device. ACM Transactions on Computer-Human Interaction 2(4) (1995)
9. Gallo, L., De Pietro, G., Marra, I.: 3D interaction with volumetric medical data: Experiencing the Wiimote. In: Proceeding Ambi-Sys 2008, Proceedings of the 1st International Conference on Ambient Media and Systems, vol. (14). ICST, Brussels (2008)
10. Wilson, A., Shafer, S.: XWand: UI for intelligent spaces. In: Proceedings of the ACM Conference on Human Factors in Computing Systems, vol. (5). ACM, NewYork (2003)
11. Wilson, A., Pham, H.: Pointing in intelligent environments with the worldcursor. In: INTERACT International Conference on HumanComputer Interaction. IOS Press, Ohmsha (2003)
12. Wilson, A., Benko, H., Izadi, S., Hilliges, O.: Steerable Augmented Reality with the Beamatron. In: Proceedings of the 25th Annual ACM Symposium on User Interface Software and Technology. ACM, NewYork (2012)
13. Große-Puppendahl, T.A., Berghoefer, Y., Braun, A., Wimmer, R., Kuijper, A.: OpenCapSense: A rapid prototyping toolkit for pervasive interaction using capacitive sensing. In: PerCom 2013, San Diego (2013)

14. Braun, A., Heggen, H., Wichert, R.: CapFloor - A Flexible Capacitive Indoor Localization System. In: Chessa, S., Knauth, S. (eds.) EvAAL 2011. CCIS, vol. 309, pp. 26–35. Springer, Heidelberg (2012)
15. Kammer, D., Keck, M., Freitag, G., Wacker, M.: Taxonomy and Overview of Multi-touch Frameworks: Architecture, Scope and Features. In: Workshop on Engineering Patterns for Multitouch Interfaces, Berlin (2010)

Paint-It: A Children's Habit Revised

Nikolaos Partarakis[1], Margherita Antona[1], and Constantine Stephanidis[1,2]

[1] Foundation for Research and Technology – Hellas (FORTH)
Institute of Computer Science
Heraklion, Crete, GR-70013, Greece
[2] University of Crete, Department of Computer Science, Greece
{partarak.antona,cs}@ics.forth.gr

Abstract. Ambient Intelligence technologies can play an important role in enriching the education and learning experience. Such technologies offer students increased access to information within an augmented teaching environment which encourages active learning and collaboration, enhancing their motivation to learn. This paper focuses of transferring painting into the Ami environment through the usage of an augmented digital surface as a painting canvas, and offering interaction through augmented physical painting material such as paint tubes, brushes, physical palettes of color, etc. This enriched painting experience is targeted to support the development of artistic skills for young artists through employing artistic concepts such as color theory, color mixing for artists, brush type information, etc.

Keywords: Ambient Intelligence, Serious Games, Learning, Painting, User Interfaces for children.

1   Introduction

Undoubtedly painting is considered one of the most joyful activities for children, and it has important impact on child development as well. Research conducted in the field has depicted that cutting, pasting and painting are the most frequently occurring pre-school activities [21]. The benefits of painting activities for children are well known in the pedagogical domain and will not be discussed here. This paper aims at transferring the children's painting experience in modern digital environments while maintaining all the benefits and fun of physical painting, by exploiting ambient intelligence techniques. This is achieved through the development of a serious game named Paint-it, which combines an augmented digital surface for painting with physical objects such as brushes, paint tubes, and painting palettes, which maintain in the digital world their meaning and functionality of the physical world.

2   Background and Related Work

Innovative learning environments such us Serious Games (SGs) and simulations provide an applied context in which novel skills can be learned, applied, mastered,

N. Streitz and P. Markopoulos (Eds.): DAPI 2014, LNCS 8530, pp. 164–171, 2014.

integrated and transformed into new concepts and application areas. The fact that people learn from digital games is no longer in dispute. Research [6,7,8,9,10,11] has shown that serious games can be a very effective as instructional tools and can assist learning by providing an alternative way of interacting and presenting instructions and content, with enhanced efficacy over traditional learning. A learner's motivation impacts the learning outcome more than any other factor [5], and SGs seem to be very effective to this purpose [25]. As a consequence, such environments are becoming increasingly popular as vehicles of knowledge transfer and learning. Additionally, SGs have become both a growing market in the video games industry [1,2] and a subject of academic research [3], receiving attention from many diverse fields such as computer science, business studies, psychology, cultural studies, sociology and pedagogy [4].

One of the main characteristics of a serious game is the fact that the instructional content is presented together with fun elements. Such a game makes learners become personally involved with playing in an emotional and cognitive way. By engaging learners emotionally and cognitively, attention and motivation are increased, thus supporting learning.

The usage of ICT technology to offer entertainment painting experiences to children has been considered in the past in a number of different variations. A collaborative, computer-based finger painting program for children has been proposed in the past facilitating an input surface called MultiTouch Surface (an input device that is separated from the computer screen used to transfer signals on a pc and then display the results on the screen) [24]. The evolution of ICT technology and its penetration to everyday activities has today made this form of painting available through mainstream devices such as smart-phones and tablets.

This paper propose a novel form of digital painting where traditional painting materials reappear and play a crucial role in the way that children understand and interact with the application.

3   Building a Collection of Augmented Physical Objects for Painting

The Paint-it system builds on the Tag recognition facilities offered by the Microsoft Surface SDK and the Samsung SUR-40 Microsoft Surface device to create a number of augmented physical objects to be exploited by children while painting (see Fig. 1). These objects either emulate the feeling of painting using actual art supplies or act as easy to understand and use control elements (physical game controls).

Brushes are an important tool for painting. There are different shapes and sizes of brushes. A number of different brushes are available in the Paint-it application (see Fig. 1 section A), exhibiting different behaviours depending on the blob tracking capabilities of the device. More specifically, the blob that the brush creates when placed on top of the painting surface is used to produce the brush size used. This allows starting a stroke with a large stroke weight but adjust it accordingly while moving on the surface by simply reducing the pressure applied on the brush. In this sense any size, filament and shape of brush can be used. Currently, a set of children's painting brushes are used in Paint-it.

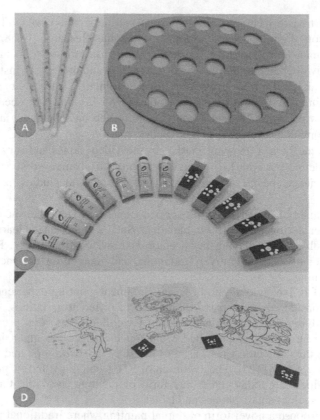

Fig. 1. Collection of augmented physical objects for painting

A painting palette is the item used by children for mixing colours. The augmented palette used by Paint-it is a standard wooden palette with slots in the areas where colours are placed or colour mixing occurs (see Fig. 1 section B). When placed on top of the surface, the device presents the available colours for mixing through the slots. Children can therefore select and mix colour from their "magical" palette of colours that becomes alive when placed on the surface.

Learning colour mixing is an essential part of the educational benefits of painting. Paint-it aims at facilitating this learning curve both through the palette (mixing colours using the palette) and through the selection of paint tubes so as to mix or create a colour. To do so, a collection of tagged painting tubes were created (see Fig. 1 section C). Each of these tubes can be selected as colour when placed on the surface or mixed with other tubes when selected concurrently.

Printed tracing sketches are introduced in the Paint-it application for supporting children's typical colouring activities. Sketches can be downloaded from the internet, printed on transparent film and tagged (see Fig. 1 section D). Tags are used so as to move the painting canvas together with the sketch (for example when a child rotates the sketch, the painting canvas get rotated accordingly) to select the desired sketch and then paint on top of it.

Paint-it also provides a set of augmented physical objects that act as control elements and therefore provide access to the functionality of the game (see Fig. 2). Several control elements are employed: (a) a **Canvas** representing an empty painting canvas, a Palette representing the color mixing palette, (c) a **Transparency** wheel rotated to adjust the transparency of brush strokes and (d) a **Color wheel** offering access to a color wheel where children can make their first steps into color theory.

Fig. 2. Collection of augmented physical objects acting as control elements

4   Paint-It

Paint-it aims at creating a pleasant and joyful application for children that could act both in favour of entertainment and learning. In Paint-it, playing gets the primary focus, while learning happens seamlessly through mixing and pairing colours to achieve the desired by the game results. A typical instantiation of the game is presented in Fig. 3. Children have the option to select among a number of different sketches, which are contained in the application's library bar. The library bar only requires that the children navigate within the collection and no text is used. The selection of a sketch from the collection results in displaying on the surface three items. The coloured sketch presents to children the desired outcome, the black and white canvas define the area to be painted, and the palette is meant to be used for colour selection or colour mixing (taping a colour results into selection, tapping another one results into mixing). Children should use their painting palette to generate the colours presented on the completed sketch, and then use their physical paint brushes to fill the area of their canvas. Alternatively, colour selection and mixing can be performed by placing paint tubes on the surface. When the physical palette of colours is placed on the surface, it replaces the digital one.

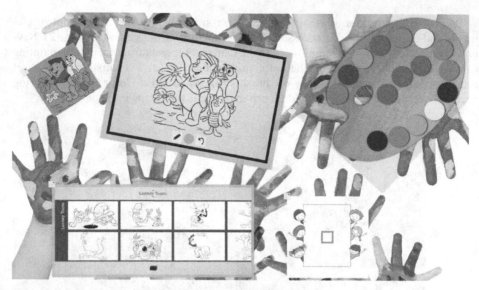

Fig. 3. The Paint-it variation for children

The full range of facilities provided by Paint-it include: (a) the colour mixing palette with two different instantiations (a digital mixing palette and a mixed reality physical palette), (b) a collection of sketches offering a variety of alternatives, (c) an unlimited collection of printed sketches created by end user , (d) a colour wheel to help children understand the fundamentals of colour theory such as primary, secondary and complimentary colours and (e) a transparency wheel for experimenting with the overlay of transparent over opaque colours.

Paint-it is currently deployed for demonstration purposes on a Samsung SUR40 [14] at FORTH-ICS Ami facility [13]. Fig. 4 presents Paint-it for children running on the aforementioned device, showing the use of the presented physical augmented objects.

Fig. 4. Paint-it for children on a Samsung SUR40 Microsoft® Surface® device

5   Implementation

The implementation of Paint-it was conducted using Microsoft Visual C# [15] and Microsoft Surface 2.0 SDK [16]. The painting canvas was based on one of the control elements provided as sample by the SDK. The built-in tag recognition facilities provided by the SDK were used, and all physical items were tagged using the tag series supported by the device. Knowledge of colors, pigments and paints was modeled in the form of an ontology that has been defined using RDF [17] and was developed with the Protégé ontology editor [18]; SemWeb [19] was adopted for querying the ontology using the SPARQL syntax [20]. Color space transformations for the conversion of color representations between different color spaces and mixing algorithms in a linear color space for reproducing actual pigment mixing were developed in the form of class libraries to be used by Paint-it.

6   Heuristic Evaluation

Heuristic evaluation was adopted as first evaluation method for Paint-it. It is one of the most popular usability inspection methods for identifying usability problems in a user interface design. Heuristic evaluation involves an inspection from a small group of expert evaluators who examine the interface and judge its compliance against recognized usability principles (the heuristics). The evaluation of Paint-it was conducted by three usability experts based on ten general heuristic rules [22]. A scoring scale from 0 (not a usability problem) to 4 (usability catastrophe) was used [23]. In total, nine issues were identified and the most critical are presented below:

- Issue 1. Severity score= 3.5:
  - Problem definition: In order for children to start painting they should place the Paint-it tag on the surface and then select the collection to get access to ready to use sketches. This is too complex for young children especial under the age of six.
  - Suggestion: Consider having the collection of sketches active on the surface when the application starts.
- Issue 2. Severity score= 3.5
  - Problem definition: It is not certain that children can understand what is written and then use the tag's menu.
  - Suggestion: Consider eliminating the tag and the menu and don't present action buttons.
- Issue 3. Severity score= 3
  - Problem definition: The way that the palette is working is misleading (in order to mix colors users should select the color and then select one of the mixtures of the palette.
  - Suggestion: Color mixing should happen silently. When a child selects a color the paint brush is filled with that color. When another color is selected the brush is filled with a color resulting from the mixing of the previous with the current selection.

- Issue 4. Severity score= 3
  - — Problem definition: It is not clear to children how to clean their brush.
  - — Suggestion: Provide a metaphor such as a glass of water that when touched clears the currently created mixture.
- Issue 5. Severity score= 2.5
  - — Problem definition: A palette of color is available both on the surface and on the canvas. This sometimes is confusing.
  - — Suggestion: Consider providing only the large palette of colors and remove the one from the painting canvas. A metaphor such as a glass of water that when touched clears the currently created mixture.

7   Discussion and Future Work

This paper has presented the development and instantiation of a painting game for children. Several augmented physical objects were employed to produce a more joyful and playful environment and to emulate aspects of the actual painting process. The main underlying objective was assisting childrens' development and facilitate learning through experimentation which is considered an important part especially for the preschool age. Regarding future improvements, the results of the heuristic evaluation are going to be addressed prior to conducting larger scale user-based evaluation with children.

Acknowledgements. This work is supported by the FORTH-ICS internal RTD Programme 'Ambient Intelligence and Smart Environments'.

References

1. Susi, T., Johanesson, M., et al.: Serious Games - An Overview (Technical Report). Skövde, Sweden, University of Skövde (2007)
2. Alvarez, J., Michaud, L.: Serious games: Advergaming, edugaming, training and more. Montpellier, France, IDATE (2008)
3. Ritterfeld, U., Cody, M., et al.: Serious Games: Mechanisms and Effects. Routledge, New York (2009)
4. Breuer, J., Bente, G.: Why so serious? On the Relation of Serious Games and Learning. Eludamos. Journal for Computer Game Culture 4(1), 7–24 (2010)
5. Norman, A.D., Spohrer, C.J.: Learner-centered education. Communications of the ACM 39(4), 24–27 (1996)
6. Squire, K., Jenkins, H.: Harnessing the power of games in education. Insight 3, 5–33 (2003)
7. Squire, K.: Replaying History: Learning World History through playing Civilization III. Instructional Systems Technology. Indiana University, Indiana (2004)
8. Egenfeldt-Nielsen, S.: Beyond Edutainment: Exploring the Educational Potential of Computer Games. IT. University of Copenhagen, Copenhagen PhD: 1-280 (2005)

9. Liarokapis, F., de Freitas, S.: A Case Study of Augmented Reality Serious Games, Looking Toward the Future of Technology Enhanced Education: Ubiquitous Learning and the Digital Native. In: Ebner, M., Schiefner, M. (eds.), ch. 10, pp. 178–191. IGI Global (2010) ISBN: 978-1-61520-678-0

10. Prensky, M.: Don't bother me mom, I'm learning. Paragon House, St. Paul (2006)

11. de Freitas, S., Neumann, T.: The use of 'exploratory learning' for supporting immersive learning in virtual environments. Computers and Education 52(2), 343–352 (2009)

12. FORTH-ICS Ambient Intelligence Programme: http://www.ics.forth.gr/index_main.php?l=e&c=4

13. Art Games: http://www.ics.forth.gr/ami/education/Art_Games.html

14. Samsung SUR40: http://www.samsunglfd.com/product/feature.do?modelCd=SUR40

15. Microsoft Visual C#: http://msdn.microsoft.com/en-us/vstudio/hh388566

16. Microsoft® Surface® 2.0 SDK and Runtime: http://www.microsoft.com/en-us/download/details.aspx?id=26716

17. RDF Vocabulary Description Language 1.0: RDF Schema, W3C Recommendation (February 10, 2004), http://www.w3.org/TR/rdf-schema/

18. http://protege.stanford.edu/

19. SemWeb.NET (Semantic Web/RDF Library for C#/.NET): http://razor.occams.info/code/semweb/

20. SPARQL Query Language for RDF: http://www.w3.org/TR/rdf-sparql-query/

21. Rubin, K.H.: The social and cognitive value of preschool toys and activities. Canadian Journal of Behavioural Science/Revue Canadienne des Sciences du Comportement 9(4), 382 (1977)

22. Nielsen, J., Landauer, T.K.: A mathematical model of the finding of usability problems. In: Proceedings of ACM INTERCHI 1993 Conference, Amsterdam, The Netherlands, pp. 206–213 (1993), http://www.useit.com/papers/heuristic/

23. Karat, C., Campbell, R.L., Fiegel, T.: Comparison of empirical testing and walkthrough methods in user interface evaluation. In: Proceedings ACM CHI 1992 Conference, Monterey, CA, May 3-7, pp. 397–404 (1992)

24. Browne, H., et al.: Designing a collaborative finger painting application for children (2000)

25. Ritterfeld, U., Cody, M., Vorderer, P. (eds.): Serious games: Mechanisms and effects. Routledge (2009)

Robot-Supported Pointing Interaction
for Intelligent Environments

Mark Prediger[1], Andreas Braun[2], Alexander Marinc[2], and Arjan Kuijper[1,2]

[1] Technische Universität Darmstadt, Darmstadt, Germany
mark.prediger@stud.tu-darmstadt.de
[2] Fraunhofer Institute for Computer Graphics Research IGD, Darmstadt, Germany
{andreas.braun,alexander marinc,arjan.kuijper}@igd.fraunhofer.de

Abstract. A natural interaction with appliances in smart environment is a highly desired form of controlling the surroundings using intuitively learned interpersonal means of communication. Hand and arm gestures, recognized by depth cameras, are a popular representative of this interaction paradigm. However they usually require stationary units that limit applicability in larger environments. To overcome this problem we are introducing a self-localizing mobile robot system that autonomously follows the user in the environment, in order to recognize performed gestures independent from the current user position. We have realized a prototypical implementation using a custom robot platform and evaluated the system with various users.

Keywords: Gesture recognition, service robots, smart environments.

1   Introduction

The notion of smart environments has started to slowly affect our daily lives. Ever more technical devices and computers are placed into our surroundings, providing comfort functions, security features and entertainment to a variety of users - overall trying to improve the individual quality of life. However, the increased number and functionality of devices causes an increased cognitive load on the user, trying to keep an overview and staying in control. One method to reduce this load is implicit control of the environment, e.g. by automatically controlling the lighting when the user enters a new room. While this non-intrusive form of environmental control can be powerful, there are various interactions that have to be performed in an explicit way, either if the user wants to stay in control, or if the system did not engage in the desired actions. Traditionally this explicit interaction is performed using devices like as switches or remote controls, or in modern applications using central control units that communicate with a smartphone or tablet.

An intuitive approach to this explicit control is natural interaction that relies on interpersonal communication tools - speech and gestures [1]. In terms of interacting with an environment this can be realized by performing a pointing gesture on a specific device, indicating the desire for manipulation, followed by a specific command,

N. Streitz and P. Markopoulos (Eds.): DAPI 2014, LNCS 8530, pp. 172–183, 2014.
© Springer International Publishing Switzerland 2014

e.g. using speech or certain gestures [2]. A popular method to recognize full-body gestures is the Microsoft Kinect that provides skeleton tracking using depth imaging [3]. While this allows reliable recognition, the detection range is limited to the field of view of a single camera, making it difficult to equip entire areas with such technology. Although Caon et al. [4] presented a gesture recognition system using multiple Kinects and proved the advantages over a single one, the general limited scalability will remain when attempting an area-wide solution.

Instead we propose an alternative solution, placing the depth camera on a mobile robot system that is integrated with the smart environment and able to follow the user, thus realizing a permanent gestural control of appliances throughout larger areas.

Mobile service robots are capable to directly interact with its physical world and such help humans to perform different tasks. Service robots are used for vacuum-cleaning [5], healthcare and assistance [6] and telepresence applications for motor-disabled people [7]. Nickel et al. presented and evaluated a visual pointing gesture recognition system to improve human-robot interaction [8].

To enable safe robot navigation, a simultaneous mapping and localization mechanism (SLAM) is required. For domestic environments, which are highly unstructured and dynamic, Grid Mapping [9] is a common and robust approach. Grid Mapping uses Rao–Blackwellized particle filters to create a grid map of desired resolution and localize the robot in it based on range sensor readings coming from laser range finders or depth cameras such as the Kinect. Newer approaches utilize the 3D capabilities of depth cameras and high GPU computing power to create full 3D maps of the environment [10] in real-time.

Following humans to maintain communication and interaction is also a common task in robotics. Doisy et al. [11] presented and evaluated different human following strategies using a Kinect depth camera and the lane-curvature [12] obstacle avoidance algorithm. Similar research with a laser range scanner was performed by Gockley at al. [13]. Hiroi et al. showed a human-following robot for carrying charges and capable riding an elevator [14].

Altogether much successful research has been done in fields of intelligent environments, natural interaction and robotics. However, our combination of a human-following robot providing a gesture recognition system to control intelligent environments is unique, and introduces a novel interaction scheme. We extended previous human-following approaches to enable the robot estimating user's location after tracking loss and seamlessly recover without user's explicit help. Our method was implemented and evaluated in a prototype system combining a robot platform, the Kinect and an intelligent environment.

2   Device Selection and Gesture Control

To enable the user selecting and controlling devices utilizing only hand or arm gestures, the user's location, pointing direction and spatial position and shape of all devices have to be known. As a first step we need to acquire the robot-relative pointing direction. For that we can use the joint positions provided by a skeleton tracker, e.g. taking a ray between shoulder and wrist joints. The Kinect is using fast methods for body pose estimation from depth image data, as presented by Shotton et al. [3]. A discussion about choosing appropriate joints for pointing gestures and user preference of different gesture types has been provided by Majewski et al. [15].

The next step in enabling interaction requires determining the global pointing direction, achieved by registering the local ray to the global coordinate system using the robot's current location. In order to select the device we are pointing at, we are checking for intersections with the ray. Therefore each device needs to have a spatial region assigned to it that should include all geometry, i.e. a bounding volume. This can be an oriented bounding box [16], a sphere or a 3D Gaussian blob [17] amongst other methods. Since it can't be simply assumed that the ray will intersect the desired device at all times, strategies to deal with ambiguous and occluded devices are required, a few of which have been presented by Braun et al. [18].

After successfully selecting a device, the user has to communicate the desired intention to the system. For simple devices that solely rely on binary states, such as lamps, the pointing gesture itself, in combination with some temporal threshold can be considered sufficiently expressive. A higher amount of functionality would require additional control mechanisms. However, an exhaustive examination of all demands for any type of devices is out of scope of this work.

3   Person Tracking Using a Mobile Robot

3.1   Mapping and Localization

In section 1 we already presented some common 2D and 3D SLAM approaches. Energy and computation power saving is crucial on mobile robots, thus the less demanding Grid Mapping is a reasonable choice here. It can be used in our application without further adaptation since it is already designed to operate in unstructured and dynamic environments. Of course other SLAM approaches are also applicable.

3.2   Person Following

The person following problem can be divided in three parts - Target detection and tracking, actual target following and the recovery behavior on tracking loss [13].

Since detecting and tracking the target is already provided by the gesture control system we only need to care about the last two topics. For actually following a person we use the *direction following* strategy [11] [13] which showed the best results. On direction following, the followed person is set as a movement target and the robot tries to rotate in its direction while simultaneously moving towards it. The method is combined with an obstacle avoidance approach to enable robust navigation.

The third part is the behavior the robot exhibits when it loses the human. Previous approaches neglect this problem and implement very basic recovery behavior, like either stopping the robot completely [13] [14] or drive it to the last observed user location and hope to re-detect the human from there [11]. This behavior can be suitable for industrial environments with wide hallways where tracking loss occurs rarely and a predictable robot movement is desired. In home environments however ways can be very narrow, thus the followed person can quickly disappear from robot's view. Stopping the robot each time and calling back the user would severely impact the interaction experience.

Instead we propose an approach which enables the robot to autonomously recover from a tracking loss without explicit help of the user. Therefore we try to predict multiple potential locations of the user based on knowledge of the environment, and let the robot explore those locations sequentially. Location prediction is done using a variant of the particle filter [19]. A particle filter in general tries to estimate a system's state by sequentially simulating multiple possible system states at the same time. To implement a particle filter two functions are required – a system model and an observation model. The system model is a probabilistic function predicting a particle's next state in a simulation step, given its current state and environment observations. The observation model tells us the likelihood of an observation given the current state. At each point t the system has a set $S_{t-1}^{(n)}$ of n particles with importance weights $w_{t-1}^{(n)}$ from the previous step, and creates a new particle set $S_t^{(n)}$ with importance weights $w_t^{(n)}$. To allow particles to quickly disappear when inside the robot's view, we use the *Sequential Importance Resampling* (SIR) version of the algorithm with resampling at every step:

1. Randomly sample a subset of particle $S'^{(n)}$ out of $S_{t-1}^{(n)}$ with replacement, using their importance weights $w_{t-1}^{(n)}$ as selection probabilities.
2. Predict the next state of each particle in $S'^{(n)}$ according to the system model and save the new particles in $S_t^{(n)}$.
3. Assign each particle in $S_t^{(n)}$ a new importance weight w_t^k given current observations.
4. Normalize the importance weightings to have a sum of 1.0.

A suitable system model for predicting a next possible state was developed by testing and improving different configurations. For our current version the system state contains the person's location p, indirected movement speed $\dot{p}$, its orientation θ and the rotational speed $\dot{\theta}$. Following listing shows the steps to compute the next state x_t from x_{t-1}:

$$p_t \sim N\left(p_{t-1} + \frac{3}{4}\dot{p}_{t-1} \cdot \Delta t, 0.04\right) \qquad (1)$$

$\dot{p}_t \sim N(\dot{p}_{t-1}, 0.16 \cdot \Delta t \cdot \max_{\dot{p}})$, and limit its value to lie in $[0, \max_{\dot{p}}]$.

$\theta_t \sim N(\theta_{t-1} + \dot{\theta}_{t-1} \cdot \Delta t, 0.16)$, and limit its value to lie in $[-\pi, \pi[$.

$\dot{\theta}_t \sim N(\dot{\theta}_{t-1}, 0.16 \cdot \Delta t \cdot \max_{\dot{\theta}})$, and limit its value to lie in $[0, \max_{\dot{\theta}}]$

Note that $\max_{\dot{p}}, \max_{\ddot{p}}, \max_{\dot{\theta}}$ and $\max_{\ddot{\theta}}$ denote upper bounds of the fastest possible particle movement.

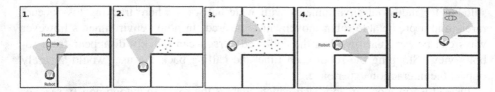

Fig. 1. Particle filter illustration. **1.** Robot sees human going into the hallway. **2.** Robot loses track of human and begins to estimate his position with multiple particles (red dots). **3.** Robot approaches the estimated points. **4.** Robot notices that the human is not in the hallway and clears out the corresponding particles. **5.** Robot moves to remaining particles and finds human.

Since the skeleton tracker is the only used observation source we only can tell if a human is detected in front of the Kinect or not. Thus we used two different importance weights: 0.95 if the particle represents a person inside Kinect's view and 1 if not. 0.95 might sound a little high but is appropriate when considering that the particle filter step is done around 10 times per second and the skeleton tracker needs 1 – 2 seconds before resuming the tracking after the person re-appeared.

As can be seen in Fig. 1, using our approach the robot is able to re-detect the human even if he has significantly moved from his last observed location. However, since each single particle represents a potential human location, there must be a policy which selects the following goal from the set of all particles. As depicted in Fig. 2, choosing the centroid of all particles can lead to unreasonable goals, e.g. an empty space or even impassable terrain.

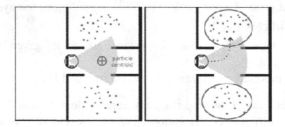

Fig. 2. Two separated particle regions with invalid centroid (left). Clustered particles and an appropriate movement path (right).

Therefore it is required to divide the particles into separated clusters and explore them one after other ignoring the remaining ones at a time. In our approach we used the k-means [20] algorithm for clustering, and take the centroid of the nearest cluster as movement target. More sophisticated approaches which minimize the movement of the robot are conceivable, however, our solution showed to provide good results on the real robot.

4   Prototype System

To investigate the simple feasibility of a human-following robot providing gesture recognition to control environmental devices, a prototypical system was implemented. Implementation and evaluation took place in the Living Lab of Fraunhofer Institute for Computer Graphics Research. It consists of multiple rooms including a kitchen, living room and sleeping room, all equipped with corresponding furniture. Since it represents an Intelligent Environment, it contains several remotely controllable devices such as lights, power sockets, roller shutters and consumer electronics. The lab's computer system does already know the locations and capabilities of each device, and provides a generic API to control them. The devices' locations and sizes are represented by oriented bounding boxes in 3D space and are entered relative to the lab's intern coordinate system.

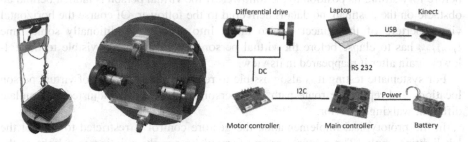

Fig. 3. Pictures of robot platform, right - components of mobile robot platform

The used hardware platform is a small custom robot powered by a differential drive with two motorized wheels. Each wheel can be controlled independently allowing the robot to drive forward or rotate in place. The wheels are equipped with odometry sensors to measure the driven way and provide hints to the localization algorithm about how the robot probably did moved at last (Fig. 3- left). To perceive its environment a Microsoft Kinect is mounted on a rack on top of the robot and can be tilt up and down by a servo motor if needed.

The robot software is based on the open source robot framework ROS [21]. ROS provides many different robotics-specific components such as communication, device drivers, libraries for localization and mapping, visualization and simulation.

In our work we used the ROS package *slam_gmapping*, which implements the Grid Mapping [9] algorithm to create a 2D grid map of the lab, and the *amcl* package to localize the robot within the map during a run.

To detect and track users with the Kinect the NITE skeleton tracker of the OpenNI framework is used. It can handle up to 16 users and extract 24 joint positions of each person in full 3D space. With help of the ROS *Transformations* library and robot's position on the map the joints are transformed to global map coordinates for gesture control and following.

To follow a person we used the navigation stack of ROS which is able to safely drive the robot to a specified target location on the map, which in our case is either the tracked person position or a prediction given by the particle filter. Therefore a *costmap* of the environment is created and permanently updated during the run. The costmap collects information about free space and potential obstacles the Kinect observes and allows computing a safe trajectory to the target point. For trajectory generation we use the *base_local_planner* package implementing the dynamic window approach DWA [22] which considers the physical dynamics of the robot such as current speed and maximum acceleration rate.

To enable faster testing and evaluating the person following performance independent from the used skeleton tracker, a software component called virtual target provider was developed. It can replace the tracker and allows entering the target coordinates manually trough a GUI instead. To be comparable with a real skeleton tracker the virtual target provider checks whether the robot has a clear view on the target before forwarding its position to the follower. If the virtual person is hidden behind an obstacle on the costmap, no data is delivered to the follower. Of course the horizontal view aperture of the Kinect is also taken into account. Additionally some time $t_{redetect}$ has to elapse before the virtual person becomes actually visible to the follower again after it reappeared in its view.

For systematic testing it is also possible to record or create a path of virtual person locations and replay the route path. The person's speed can be adjusted to simulate different walking behavior.

In the prototypical implementation the gesture control is restricted to control the lab lightings only. The gestures are performed by simply pointing to a light at the ceiling with the right arm. The light is then turned on or off depending on its pervious state. To be recognized as a gesture the arm angle must be greater than 45° up from horizon and the arm movement may not exceed a certain threshold for some frames.

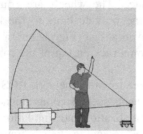 

Fig. 4. Effects of different tilt angles on skeleton and gesture recognition of the Kinect

A particular challenge is the narrow vertical field of view of the Kinect infrared sensor and its lack of tracking skeletons that are too close to the sensor. This requires an appropriate placement of the sensor on the mobile robot. The important parts of the skeleton are the arm and hand joints, which are typically held considerably high. Fig. 4 illustrates this effect. In consequence a high angle should be used. However, this has a negative effect on the Kinect's ability to monitor the environment - low obstacles can't be recognized for now.

5   Evaluation

To investigate the person following performance and global pointing gesture recognition, we have performed a live evaluation of our implementation with distinct users. We have focused on following aspects - number of tracking losses and recovery failures, driven distance and average speed and gesture recognition reliability. The evaluation was performed in two rounds, one with real persons and one with virtual targets. For the first round 13 test candidates, uninvolved in the details of this work, were invited and should interact with the robot in a predefined manner. The robot should follow them, recognize their gestures and control the corresponding lights. Since the used NITE skeleton tracker showed to be unreliable during preliminary tests, a second round with a virtual target provider was performed, evaluating following and recovery performance only.

The candidates for the real-person-round consisted of 11 male and 2 female users ranging in age between 14 and 55 years. In an initial interview they were asked a few questions. Using a scale from 1 to 9 in average they estimated their experience with service robots at 2.1 and experience with gesture control systems at 3.9.

The candidates were instructed to walk a predefined route at their own preferred speed. The route had a length of about 23.9 meters and was marked by numbered paper notes on the floor representing checkpoints. At each checkpoint the candidates should stop and wait for the robot to capture them, before proceeding to the next checkpoint. To communicate the candidates whether they are currently tracked by the robot, the robot indicated its state showing different colors on its laptop's display. Fig. 5 gives an overview of the checkpoints and their locations in the lab on the left, and the areas for headlights, as well as collected pointing directions on the right. For avoiding frequent tracking loss the robot's maximum speed was set to 0.2m/s.

If the robot failed to re-detect the user after losing him and spent more than 20s in searching state, a timeout occurred and the robot stopped immediately. If the robot still failed to detect the user after 5 more seconds, it was manually adjusted by the evaluation supervisor.

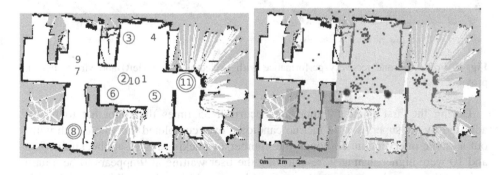

Fig. 5. Left - checkpoint locations. Right - Colored areas of headlights, collected pointing results as red dots and the critical checkpoints 5 and 6 as larger blue dots.

The paths between checkpoint (7, 8), (8, 9), (9, 10) can be considered as most critical, since the candidates likely disappear from robot's view here. At some checkpoints denoted by red circles the candidates had to perform a gesture by pointing to the ceiling and such toggling the state of the light in the corresponding room. If the robot fails to recognize the gesture, it had to be performed up to 2 more times. Critical checkpoints here are 2, 5 and 6, since lying near the kitchen-living room transition. Light above 2 belongs to the living room but those above 5 and 6 to the kitchen.

The second round consisted of the same route and same number of runs as the first one. The round also was performed with the real robot, except that it now should follow a target given by the virtual target provider instead of real persons. The view aperture for the virtual target provider was set to about 50° and re-detection delay to 0.7 sec. The virtual walking speed between two consecutive checkpoints was set to 0.8 m/s. Since the person's virtual route was recorded and thus exactly the same at each run, the time when the virtual person began to walk from one checkpoint to other was manually chosen to introduce some variance. Because previous tests has shown good results concerning the following performance with the virtual target, the robots maximum moving speed was increased to 0.3 m/s. Following data was automatically recorded during each run: the robots average driving speed and distance, number of timeouts at each checkpoint, number of interventions by the operator after timeout at each checkpoint and times when arriving at and leaving a checkpoint.

The driving speed and distance driven has considerably improved using the virtual target provider. The average driving speed almost doubled from 0.12m/s to 0.20m/s. The distance the robot had to drive each round was reduced from 21.6 to 15.5 meters in average.

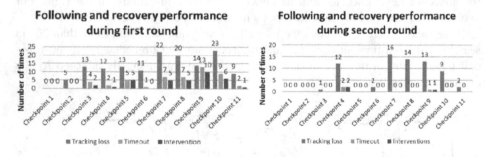

Fig. 6. Following and recovery performance with skeleton tracker (left) and virtual person provider (right)

During the first round 50 timeouts occurred, 35 times the robot hat to be re-adjusted by the supervisor. In fact no candidate ever completed the whole path without a single intervention. Although the number of tracking losses at checkpoint 7, 8 and 10 were higher than at 9, re-detecting the user waiting at 9 appears to be a hard task for the robot, hence most interventions happened here. A possible explanation is that when the robot is moving towards 9, the user is seen through the narrow doorway between sleeping and living room, which confuses the skeleton tracker.

It is remarkable that in 15 of the 50 timeouts the robot managed to re-detect the user after stopping at current pose. Apparently the particle filter provided a good estimation about the user's position so the robot was indeed facing the person but the skeleton failed to actually detect it before timeout.

During the complete second round only 3 interventions occurred. Two times the robot tried to backup into the kitchen and got stuck at a ground threshold which cannot be detected by the Kinect for now. The third time the particle filter estimated a wrong user location and the robot couldn't correct it before timeout. Altogether the robot completed 10 of 13 runs without any interventions, and two of the three recovery failures were caused by physical incidents.

The user experience was evaluated in a questionnaire using Likert-scales from 1 to 9. Significant agreement is a number of 7 or more on average while disagreement is indicated by 3 or less on average. In general the users found the robot's behavior appropriate, but a majority of eleven users felt at least a little bit disturbed by the robot. While six of the thirteen candidates were actually willing to adapt the living environment to the robots needs, ten stated that they wouldn't like to change their walking behavior. A correlation between the acceptance and the user's experience with service robots or gesture control could not be determined.

Since the robots maximum speed was limited to a fraction of normal walking speed some users experienced the robot blocking the doorway when they tried to move from checkpoint 8 to 9. A better avoidance behavior and prediction of the user's next possible movement was desired. Another common proposal was to increase the maximum searching time of the robot. The timeout of 20 seconds seems to be chosen as to small, at least with respect to the low robot speed. The choice was mainly motivated by attempting to limit the maximum time an evaluation run takes. For real applications there is no problem in increasing the timeout threshold. The results show that the following performance is mainly restricted by the skeleton tracker and not the following algorithm and particle filter itself. Assuming a good person tracker, the proposed recovery approach is able to find the user after tracking loss in the very most cases. Besides less recovery failures a better tracker will also cause a reduction of the driven way. At same time the driving speed of the robot can be safely increased, further improving the following performance. The global user localization by itself is quite accurate, but the pointing direction precision suffers from the user's self-awareness.

6   Conclusion and Future Work

In this work we have designed and presented a flexible gesture recognition system applied on a mobile robot platform and enabling human-machine-interaction in intelligent environments. We have presented a generic methodology that allows simultaneous person tracking, following and gesture control. Existing methods for person following have been adapted for indoor scenarios, enabling fast loss recovery using a particle filtering algorithm that estimates potential user location and provides a stepwise exploration of candidate areas. The system has been implemented in a prototypical form using a custom mobile platform, a Kinect and a regular PC. Combining this with an existing model of an actual living lab that includes all controllable appliances, a full prototype realizing following a user, recognition of pointing gestures and control of appliances has been created. We have evaluated the following performance in a study with multiple users in a real setting and virtual targets for reference. We were able to verify the feasibility of such a system using this approach.

Nevertheless there is still room for improvement. First of all a better skeleton tracker which doesn't rely on background subtraction is required to allow a more reliable tracking of users. Pure optical trackers show good results, thus a combination of both depth and color trackers is reasonable. It also is conceivable to use different person trackers for gesture recognition and following, since following does not require joint extraction but needs more robust human detection instead. The particle filter for estimating the user's position can be improved by using additional information sources, such as motion detectors already applied in the intelligent environment. Further the hardware of the robot needs to be adjusted to improve operation in real home environments. Better mechanics would allow overcoming carpet edges and enable faster robot movement; additional range sensors can help in capturing very low obstacles. Another aspect is the human-robot interaction. For actual usage methods have to be provided allowing the user to give different instructions to the robot, for example for stopping or driving to a specific location. Regarding devices that have multiple controllable properties, e.g. sound volume and track number on a stereo system, further investigation is necessary. The device selection itself can be improved by providing direct feedback about the pointing direction computed by the robot, for example with a moving laser pointer mounted on the robot [15].

Allowing multiple users can be considered. Simultaneously tracking two or more humans is mainly restricted by the optical view aperture and spatial position of robot and users, therefore algorithms for a smarter positioning of the robot have to be developed. Context acquired by the intelligent environment can be taken into account as well. For example the robot can be instructed to ignore sleeping or otherwise busy users.

Acknowledgments. We would like to thank all the participants in the studies that were performed. This project was partially funded under EC grant no. 610840.

References

1. Valli, A.: The design of natural interaction. Multimed. Tools Appl. 38, 295–305 (2008)
2. Braun, A., Kamieth, F.: Passive identification and control of arbitrary devices in smart environments. In: Jacko, J.A. (ed.) Human-Computer Interaction, Part III, HCII 2011. LNCS, vol. 6763, pp. 147–154. Springer, Heidelberg (2011)
3. Shotton, J., Fitzgibbon, A., Cook, M., Sharp, T., Finocchio, M., Moore, R., Kipman, A., Blake, A.: Real-time human pose recognition in parts from single depth images. Commun. ACM. 56, 116–124 (2013)
4. Caon, M., Yue, Y., Tscherrig, J., Mugellini, E., Abou Khaled, O.: Context-aware 3d gesture interaction based on multiple kinects. In: Ambient 2011, First Int. Conf. Ambient Comput. Appl. Serv. Technol., pp. 7–12 (2011)

5. Forlizzi, J., Disalvo, C.: Service Robots in the Domestic Environment: A Study of the Roomba Vacuum in the Home. In: Proceedings of the 1st ACM SIGCHI/SIGART Conference on Human-Robot Interaction, pp. 258–265 (2006)
6. Graf, B., Parlitz, C., Hägele, M.: Robotic home assistant Care-O-bot® 3-product vision and innovation platform. In: Jacko, J.A. (ed.) HCI International 2009, Part II. LNCS, vol. 5611, pp. 312–320. Springer, Heidelberg (2009)
7. Tonin, L., Carlson, T., Leeb, R., Millán, J.d.R.: Brain-controlled telepresence robot by motor-disabled people. In: Conf. Proc. IEEE Eng. Med. Biol. Soc., pp. 4227–4230 (2011)
8. Nickel, K., Stiefelhagen, R.: Visual recognition of pointing gestures for human–robot interaction. Image Vis. Comput. 25, 1875–1884 (2007)
9. Grisetti, G., Stachniss, C., Burgard, W.: Improved Techniques for Grid Mapping With Rao-Blackwellized Particle Filters. IEEE Trans. Robot. 23, 34–46 (2007)
10. Newcombe, R.A., Davison, A.J., Izadi, S., Kohli, P., Hilliges, O., Shotton, J., Molyneaux, D., Hodges, S., Kim, D., Fitzgibbon, A.: KinectFusion: Real-time dense surface mapping and tracking. In: Proceedings of the 2011 10th IEEE International Symposium on Mixed and Augmented Reality, pp. 127–136. IEEE (2011)
11. Doisy, G., Jevti, A., Lucet, E., Edan, Y.: Adaptive Person-Following Algorithm Based on Depth Images and Mapping*. In: Proceedings of Workshop on Robot Motion Planning (2012)
12. Ko, N., Simmons, R.: The lane-curvature method for local obstacle avoidance. In: Proceedings of IEEE/RSJ International Conference on Intelligent Robots and Systems, pp. 1615–1621 (1998)
13. Gockley, R., Forlizzi, J., Simmons, R.: Natural person-following behavior for social robots. In: Proceeding of the ACM/IEEE International Conference on Human-Robot Interaction - HRI 2007, pp. 17–24. ACM Press, New York (2007)
14. Hiroi, Y., Matsunaka, S., Ito, A.: Mobile Robot System with Semi-Autonomous Navigation Using Simple and Robust Person Following Behavior. J. Man, Mach. Technol. 1, 44–62 (2012)
15. Majewski, M., Braun, A., Marinc, A., Kuijper, A.: Visual Support System for Selecting Reactive Elements in Intelligent Environments. In: International Conference on Cyberworlds, pp. 251–255 (2012)
16. Marinc, A., Stockloew, C., Tazari, S.: 3D Interaction in AAL Environments Based on Ontologies. Fourth Ambient Assisted Living Congress (2012)
17. Wilson, A., Shafer, S.: XWand: UI for intelligent spaces. In: Proceedings of the ACM Conference on Human Factors in Computing Systems, pp. 545–552. ACM (2003)
18. Braun, A., Fischer, A., Marinc, A., Stocklöw, C., Majewski, M.: Context-based bounding volume morphing in pointing gesture applications. In: Kurosu, M. (ed.) Human-Computer Interaction, Part IV, HCII 2013. LNCS, vol. 8007, pp. 147–156. Springer, Heidelberg (2013)
19. Arulampalam, M.S., Maskell, S., Gordon, N., Clapp, T.: A tutorial on particle filters for online nonlinear/non-Gaussian Bayesian tracking. IEEE Trans. Signal Process. 50, 174–188 (2002)
20. MacQueen, J.: Some methods for classification and analysis of multivariate observations. In: Proceedings of the Fifth Berkeley Symposium on Mathematical Statistics and Probability, p. 14 (1967)
21. Quigley, M., Conley, K.: ROS: An open-source Robot Operating System. ICRA Work. Open Source Softw. 3 (2009)
22. Fox, D., Burgard, W., Thrun, S.: The dynamic window approach to collision avoidance. IEEE Robot. Autom. Mag. 4, 23–33 (1997)

BlowBrush: A Design of Tangible Painting System Using Blowing Action

Yang Ting Shen[1] and Pei Wen Lu[2]

[1] Department of Architecture, Feng Chia University, Taichung, Taiwan
yatishen@fcu.edu.tw
[2] Department of Urbanism, Faculty of Architecture,
Delft University of Technology, Delft, The Netherlands
Peiwen.Lu@tudelft.nl

Abstract. This paper presents a novel tangible interaction system called Blow-Brush that enables people to create leaf collage paintings on a digital canvas by blowing at a toy windmill. We couple the metaphorical mapping between wind and blow to facilitate the interaction that uses digital leaf inks for drawing. The windmill-shape device functions as a brush that transforms users' blowing and grasping actions into painting commands. Four kinds of digital leaf inks can be used alternately via swapping the physical RFID sheets. Uses manipulate the tangible brush and inks to compose a digital leaf collage intuitively as well as artists. We carefully review the related literature of tangible interaction and abstract the critical criteria as our design guideline. In the end of this paper, we conduct the comparative evaluation to assess the effectiveness between Blow-Brush, TouchBrush, and MouseBrush based on the criteria.

Keywords: Tangible User interface, Embodied Facilitation, Affordance, RFID.

1 Introduction

The use of real world metaphor for the intuitive interface design is getting more attention due to the development of HCI (Human-computer Interaction). Instead of designing regular interfaces such as a mouse or a keyboard, the researchers have diverse focus on the concepts of multi-modality rather than uni-modality, target-driven interfaces rather than command-based ones, and finally active rather than passive interfaces [15]. *Embodied interaction* is an approach to understand HCI that apply complex interplay of mind, body, and contextual environment in interaction. Dourish defines the term embodied interaction as a proper way to exploit our familiarity with the everyday world [5]. The way in which we experience the world is through directly interacting with it, and we act in the world by exploring the opportunities for action that it provides to us. Dourish believes the experience that we gain from daily life should be designed as clues to increase our engagement with abstract computing process. This approach usually refers to the *tangible computing* technology due to the shared idea of embodiment. In the article of Tangible Bits, Ishii and his group in MIT design TUI (Tangible User Interfaces) which employ physical objects, surfaces, and spaces as

N. Streitz and P. Markopoulos (Eds.): DAPI 2014, LNCS 8530, pp. 184–195, 2014.
© Springer International Publishing Switzerland 2014

tangible embodiments of digital information [12], [13]. Their early project called Urp [37] provides an example to explain how to involve the daily experience in the implement of TUI. In short, people are used to mapping their analogous conventions with unfamiliar stuffs.

This concept called affordance are first proposed by Gibson [7] and appropriated by Norman [18], [19] in the context of HCI. According to Norman's definition, affordance is the design aspect of an object which suggests how the object should be used. In the field of TUI, the concept of affordance is particularly matched with the design of user's interaction derived from the daily experience. However, it doesn't mean all TUIs can carry well affordance spontaneously. Affordance relies on the embodied metaphor [1], which means the associable mapping or connection between things that help us understand one thing in terms of another. In view of intuitiveness approach, metaphorical mapping efficiently borrows the prefabbed knowledge to facilitate the familiarity of new stuff immediately. Therefore, the TUIs with well embodied metaphor may suggest the intuitive interaction without any prior instruction.

In this paper, we propose a novel painting system that uses the natural *"blowing"* action as the tangible interaction tool. The painting system called BlowBrush enables people to create leaf collage paintings on a digital canvas by blowing at a toy windmill. We try to couple the metaphorical mapping between wind and blow to facilitate the interaction that uses digital leaf inks for drawing. We carefully review the related literature of tangible interaction and abstract the critical criteria as our design guideline. In the end of this paper, those criteria of tangible interaction also play the important role for our evaluation. We conduct the comparative evaluation based on the criteria to assess the effectiveness between BlowBrush, TouchBrush, and MouseBrush.

2 Literature Review

Direct manipulation, guided by affordance, is commonly argues to support "ease to use" in terms of tangible interaction [10]. The intention of most of tangible interaction design is to take the advantage of natural physical affordance [19] to achieve a legible and seamless interaction between users and information. This concept highly links to the intuitive behaviors derived from direct manipulation. What makes direct manipulation intuitive is the essential question in terms of affordance applied to tangible interaction. In the following section, we make careful studies and review several researches and projects to reveal the design thinking from tangible manipulation to metaphorical affordance.

2.1 Tangible Manipulation of Digital Information

Shneiderman first used the term *direct manipulation* to refer to an emerging class of highly usable and attractive systems and proposed three principles in 1993 [32]. The concept was originally proposed in the context of GUI (Graphical User Interfaces). Some researchers like Ishii inherited this concept and further applied it to the theory of TUI (Tangible User Interface) in 1999 [35]. Ishii run the tangible media group at MIT media lab and conducted serial researches related to tangible interaction. The early case metaDESK [36] supported interaction with a geographical map through the direct manipulation of several physical tokens. Triangles [8] designed a set of triangle-shape triangle panels for exploring stories in a non-linear way. PuzzleTale [29] made use of tangible puzzle pieces on tabletop surface for dynamic storytelling interaction. In the PuzzleTale system, assembling the tangible puzzle pieces could affect the digital characters and create a flexible story context. Other famous research projects such as Resnick's Programmable Bricks and Crickets [22], [23], Raffle's Topobo [21], and Kaltenbrunner's reacTIVision [14] employed sensible components, assembly robots, and tabletop surfaces as haptic mediations to manipulate digital information directly.

Another approach for direct manipulation regarded the tangible technology as an assisted tool for full-body interaction. Schlömer and his teammates employed the Wii controller to support the sensor-based gesture recognition [27]. Users could define personal gestures to interact with the computer like a photo browsing on a home TV. The Surface Drawing project [26] developed a drawing system that allowed users to draw 3D shapes with bare hands and tangible tools. Tangible Comic [25] created an immersive environment where users controlled their digital avatars in the narrative scene via the full-body motion mapping. Blui [20] supported the hands-free interaction with blowing motion to directly control certain interactive applications. The Sound Maker project [1] allowed users to output ambient sounds according to their full-body input. All of the researches or projects we mentioned above shared the common argument: design tangible manipulation complied with relevant digital information for more *intuitive* interaction.

2.2   Natural Metaphor for Affordance

What made tangible interaction so intuitive? Was "affordance"[19]   the consequent result while things were tangible? A keyboard, strictly speaking, was tangible but not intuitive at all. Fishkin argued metaphor [6] was the key chain to which the users' actions were analogous to the real-world effect of similar actions. He cited Bit Ball [22] as a negative sample which had the well tangible interface design but no analogous metaphor mapping.

The mapping between real-world experience and designed actions effectively helped users borrow the prefabbed experience and then apply them to new stuffs directly. That is intuitive affordance coming from. In I/O Bulb project [37], every building model casted a digital shadow corresponding to the real solar shadow. Users moved or rotated the building models to check the inter-shadowing problems. In addition, the graphical wind needles were distributed on the screen surface to visualize the airflow. Those tangible stuffs and visualized phenomena helped users to effectively apply their experience to the interactive manipulation. Another example called I/O Brush [24] used the metaphor of painting brush to trigger the associable and intuitive painting interaction. I/O Brush was a drawing tool which captures real-world colors and textures as the painting materials. Users move the brush over the target material surface and capture its color and texture, and then drew with them on the canvas. Users could quickly engage with the interaction process without training because the tangible brush inherited the metaphorical mapping of general paintbrush functions. Those two projects we mentioned above successfully imitated our natural cognitions and embedded them to target interaction. The invisible connection facilitated the emergence of familiarity to support affordance while we manipulated the metaphorical stuffs.

3   BlowBrush

We present a novel tangible interaction system called BlowBrush [30] that enables people to create leaf collage paintings on a digital canvas by blowing at a toy windmill. The BlowBrush system is inspired by the experience of natural wind-shaped leaf collages. Through the daily experience of nature, people associate leaf collages with wind and blowing intuitively. Using blowing action as a trigger leverages the cognitive benefits of using articulated joints that facilitates mappings and reflections of the real world metaphor [31]. We try to implement people's natural action in the interaction design to reduce the training process and invite more intuitive manipulation. In this paper, we create a novel blowing interaction play to simulate the wind's painting, to bring out one's creative genius, and perhaps to capture a little bit of the glory of the wonderful fall colors on the digital canvas for all to enjoy.

3.1   The BlowBrush System

The BlowBrush system uses the blowing action as the primary interactive painting tool to draw leaf inks in the digital canvas. In order to receive the blowing action and to guide the drawing directions on the digital world, we develop the tangible object that imitates the windmill form. It consists of three parts for drawing command input: 1.Blowing detection, 2.Rotating detection, and 3.Ink detection (Fig. 1). The combination of blowing and rotating detection functions as a tangible brush. There is a microphone embedded in the blowing detection part to measure the intensity of blowing force. With the increase of wind pressure, the opacity of digital leaf ink will deepen progressively, and vice versa. The blowing time duration controls the amount of leaves being painted on the canvas. Secondly, the body of windmill is rotatable to simulate the different directions of wind. A rotating sensor and a microprocessor are embedded under the root of windmill body to measure the degree of rotation. Uses can rotate the windmill body to distribute the digital leaf ink in the target location of canvas.

Leaves are the metaphorical painting ink of our BlowBrush system. Using leaves as painting ink has two advantages. First, it relates our real world experience in the nature to an artful painting interaction. Users can easily recognize the concept of a wind shaped painting by drawing from their daily experience. Secondly, having leaf-shape ink assures a recognizable painting outcome. Users can then focus their attention on playing with leaf-shape stencils without worrying about their painting skills.

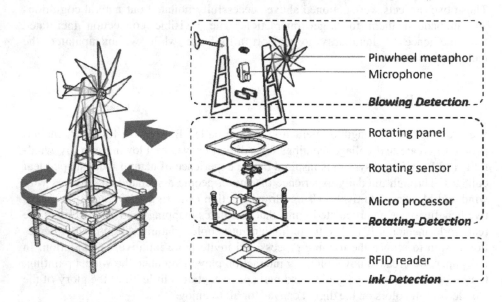

Fig. 1. BlowBrush consists of blowing, rotating, and ink detection functions

Four kinds of leaves (Sugar Maple, White Oak, Hickory, and Sugar Maple) attached on transparent RFID sheets function as different ink categories. Users can choose the target leaf ink by placing the corresponding RFID sheet under the windmill. In addition, they can swap different RFID sheets to change leaf inks during the interaction process just like a real painter doing.

3.2   The Tangible Drawing Interface

The leaf collage painting is instantly displayed on the digital canvas when a user blows at the windmill (Fig. 2). In the initial scene (Fig. 1 left), the canvas shows an image with some footprints and tree shadows on the snowfield to provide the context of a real world environment. When the users start to blow the pinwheel, one kind of digital leaf inks appear on the canvas with different opacities and accumulated amounts according to the blowing intensity and duration. For example, high intensity and long duration renders high opacity and more amounts of leaves. The position of digital leaf inks is determined by the rotation degree of windmill. Users can grasp the windmill body and rotate it in clockwise or anti-clockwise direction to distribute the digital inks in target locations. In addition, users can switch four kinds of painting leaves by putting one kind of RFID sheet under the toy windmill at a time.

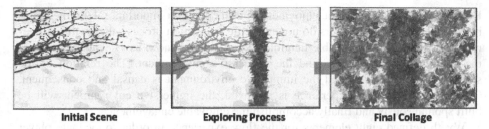

| Initial Scene | Exploring Process | Final Collage |

Fig. 2. The digital canvas design and the drawing process

4 Evaluation

The primary goal of our evaluation is to validate the effective design of BlowBrush for the tangible interaction. Some previous researchers have contributed significant works related to the theories and methodologies of tangible interaction evaluation [1, 11, 12, 17, 18]. Here we draw out the critical points of view from those researches and conclude six criteria for the evaluation of tangible interaction. Based on the evaluation criteria we adopt, the comparative evaluation between BlowBrush, Touch-Brush, and MouseBrush is conducted with 13 subjects. The quantitative and qualitative results are addressed to provide robust evidences from subjects.

4.1 Evaluation Criteria for Tangible Interaction

In this section we carefully review widespread theories and researches related to tangible interaction and conclude them into six criteria: *Metaphorical Affordance, Enjoyable Engagement, Tangible Manipulation, Spatial Interaction, Embodied Facilitation, and Expressive Representation*. The six criteria not only function as the design guideline for the development of tangible interaction design, but also provide the assessable measures in the phase of evaluation.

Metaphorical Affordance. Affordance is the design aspect of an object which suggests how the object should be used [18, 19]. The essential question is why people have the sense or knowledge to comprehend the manipulation of objects designed by affordance? What makes things intuitive enough? Actually, affordance design borrows the concept of metaphor. Metaphor is the inherent attribute of human derived from the mapping ability of daily experience and new stuffs.

Metaphorical affordance focuses on building the direct mapping and the seamless coupling between pre-existing experience and tangible object design. Then we can take advantage of natural physical affordances to achieve a heightened legibility and seamlessness of interaction between people and information [12, 13]. Based on this view, the critical successful factor is to simulate or duplicate our pre-existing experience and apply it to the tangible interaction design. The appropriation of our daily experience can bring the intuitive behaviors according to the metaphorical affordance.

Enjoyable Engagement. The enjoyment of users plays an important role in the tangible interaction design. If users do not enjoy the interaction process, they will not interact with it [33]. An enjoyable tangible interaction enhances users' engagement via the smooth flow experience and the immersive environment. The relation of the smooth flow experience and the immersive environment is causal and consequent. Once the smooth flow experience is achieved, the immersive environment will be built spontaneously and finally accomplish the enjoyable engagement.

Wyeth defined eight elements for the flow experience in order to evaluate player enjoyment in games [33]. Here we slightly modify his scheme to adapt to the tangible interaction and conclude the following protocol [1, 33, 38]: In the beginning, the tangible interaction needs to set up the clear goal and appropriate challenges which match users' skill level. During the interaction process, users should feel a sense of control and feedback over the tangible objects for the concentration and immersion demands. If the tangible interaction allows multi-users access, the opportunity of social interaction should also be supported.

Tangible Manipulation. The term tangibility means the attribute of being easily detectable with the senses. When it is applied to tangible interaction scenarios, the creature from this concept is generally defined as a tangible object. The tangible object represents the physical object which serves as a special purpose interface for a specific application using explicit physical forms [12]. The tangible object mediates between users and their target digital information and partially shares the similar idea with HCI. However, the critical difference between tangible interaction and HCI is that the tangible object itself is coupled with computational resources to allow users' direct manipulation [11].

Tangible manipulation involves directly manipulating material objects that represent the objects of interest [34]. Users physically grab, feel, and move tangible objects to "interact" (input, output, or both) with target information [9, 11]. In addition, if possible, the manipulation of user and the feedbacks from system should be close bound with tangible objects together to provide the cognitive mapping. This kind of integration bridges the gap between cause and effect and provides legible relations of them. For example, when we design a tangible brush for digital drawing, the slight vibration which simulates the contact of brush and paper should occur on the tangible brush. If the vibration feedback doesn't couple with the brush or replaces by other effects such as a beep from the speaker, the users may have the difficulty to inherit the metaphorical sense from experience.

Spatial Interaction. Spatiality is an inherent attribute of tangible interaction. The tangible objects which are manipulated by users for interaction are embedded in the physical space. Sharlin[28] argues that manipulating tangible objects exploits the intuitive spatial skills of human. He concludes that a good spatial mapping coupling between objects and its task determines the fundamental quality of tangible interaction.

Spatial interaction embeds tangible objects in the real space and interaction thereby is triggered by users' spatial engagement of movement and perception [9, 11]. Here the tangible objects have broader definition which contains the physical parts and their consequent user actions. Both of them are regarded as spatial clues to evoke the spatial experience in order to enhance the intuitive bodily interaction. For example, the boxing machine usually hangs a punching bag from the top of machine. The suspended bag hints users to interact with it rather than any other button on the machine. Furthermore, in some situations like the boxing machine case, users even have the chance to employ full-body movement and perception called full-body interaction [3, 11]. The full-body interaction encourages users to use as many senses as possible. It creates the immerse environment to attract users' engagement of interaction.

Embodied Facilitation. The term facilitation in the tangible interaction field is defined as the interrelated structure of physical space and metaphorical system which prohibits some actions in order to facilitate target purposes [9, 11]. To be more embodied, the term "constraint" replaces facilitation and expresses straightforward about how to design the tangible interaction via embodied facilitation: ease some activities via limiting others. The following question is how could we determine which kind of activities should be blocked and vice versa?

Human has the inherent facilitation knowledge to reason from analogy. This kind of ability is derived from our daily experience and helps us to build the predetermined movement paths. Therefore, the design logic of embodied facilitation only needs to follow the common sense: block and hinder the functions which make people confused and mistaken. The embodied facilitation is supposed to provide the configuration of material objects or spaces affects and directs emerging behaviors [11]. For example, when we design the plug device, triangular shape is better than rectangular one due to the metaphorical mapping. This kind of concept also refers to the Nielson's error prevention [17] and Norman's affordance [18, 19].

Expressive Representation. In tangible interaction, representation has the meaning of the interrelation between physical and digital performances and how users can perceive them [11]. Ishii also uses the term representational significance [13] to express the importance of physical tokens, which embody the abstract system status for users' legibility. Nielsen's heuristics also introduce the criteria called visibility of system status to keep users informed about what is going on, through appropriate feedback within reasonable time [17].

Expressive representation emphasizes the existence of tangible objects. Users need to be aware of the tangible objects and keep utilizing them during whole interaction process. In addition, the legibility of tangible interaction should be built through coupling the uses' action and the system reaction; moreover, keep it perceivable.

4.2   Evaluation Methodology

As noted in Section 4.1, in order to study the performance of BlowBrush in the six criteria, we conduct the comparative evaluation that compares the blow-based interface (BlowBrush) with our familiar commercial interfaces including touch-based interface (TouchBrush) and mouse-based interface (MouseBrush).

The evaluation compares the performance between three kinds of interfaces by the questionnaire. The development of our questionnaire is based on the six criteria of tangible interaction (4.1). For the comparison purpose, each interface has individual section but share the similar questions. The questions in the questionnaire consist of quantitative and qualitative parts. Five-point Likert scale [12] is applied to the quantitative questions with the scale from 1(strongly disagree) to 5(strongly agree). In addition, subjects also can write down their comments under each question to provide us qualitative information. Twenty-one subjects are selected from diverse backgrounds including design, art, computer science, engineering, and material etc. Their ages are distributed in the 18-40 years range. All subjects use touch-based and mouse-based computers regularly or alternatively in their daily life.

4.3   Evaluation Result

We map three diagrams in Fig. 3 right for the further comparison in individual criteria. Through the mapping diagram, we can quickly realize that BlowBrush performs well in the criteria of Metaphorical Affordance, Enjoyable Engagement, Tangible Manipulation, and Expressive Representation. However, in the criteria of Spatial Interaction and Embodied Facilitation, the BlowBrush have approximate or even lower score than other two interfaces (Fig. 3 left: Embodied Facilitation is approximate and Spatial Interaction is lower).

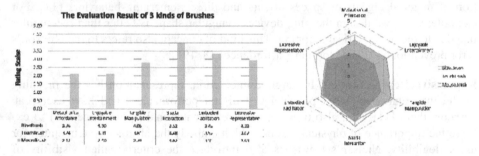

Fig. 3. Left: The bar chart illustrates the comparative scores of 3 brushes in each criterion. Right: The mapping radar chart of 3 brushes

In order to probe into the cause, we retrieve the qualitative feedbacks of subjects in the questions of Embodied Facilitation and Spatial Interaction. For the Embodied Facilitation part, subjects show a lot of interests about the constraint of blowing action. Most of subjects appreciate the limited input method to prevent errors or mistakes triggered by unintentional actions. However, they also say the extra training or practice is necessary due to the unconventional input method. Some subjects expect they can add other natural actions such as gestures and combine them with the blowing action to make interaction more customized.

The BlowBrush interface causes more problems and receives lower score than two other interfaces in the criterion of Spatial Interaction (3.52 v.s. 4.48 & 4.02). Most subjects feel confused about the spatial mapping of digital leaf inks. They believe the

TouchBrush and MouseBrush provide better spatial mapping when they are drawing. While drawing by TouchBrush, digital inks are directly mapped with subjects' finger positions on the screen. The Mouse interface has no direct manipulation on the screen but uses the virtual cursor to locate the targeted area. However, BlowBrush has no spatial mapping or indicator between input and output interaction to assist subjects to locate their target positions precisely.

5   Discussion

In this paper we present the BlowBrush system for interactive painting artistic creation via natural blowing action and assess it through the comparative evaluation. According to the overall statistical result, the BlowBrush (3.82) has higher score than TouchBrush (3.56) and MouseBrush (2.92) in the average score. This result suggests that the overall performances of BlowBrush and TouchBrush are effective for the painting task (over 3 in 5 scales). However, the mapping of radar charts also indicates that BlowBrush and TouchBrush have different superior performances in the six criteria.

The further analysis shows that BlowBrush performs well in the criteria of Metaphorical Affordance, Enjoyable Engagement, Tangible Manipulation, and Expressive Representation. It suggests two primary conclusions: 1. The design of blowing action as the tangible input method successfully associates the nature metaphor with the painting process. Subjects can couple their experience of nature (Wind blows fallen leaves) with the manipulation of tangible interaction (Human blows digital leaf inks). 2. The novel interface successfully engages subjects with fun. Most of subjects show a lot of interests when they play with BlowBrush. The enjoyable interface derived from blowing action keeps subjects engaging in the interaction and enjoying their play. However, BlowBrush may have inferior performances in the criteria of Embodied Facilitation and Spatial Interaction. We try to draw out the causes through the qualitative analysis of subjects' heuristic feedbacks. For the Embodied Facilitation criterion, we believe one of the reasons which make BlowBrush ineffective is familiarity. Subjects generally have sufficient skills to manipulate the TouchBrush and MouseBrush interfaces because two of them have been used in our daily life regularly. Using blowing action as an input method may be unconventional and need extra training or practice. For the Spatial Interaction criterion, the difficulty of BlowBrush is derive from the mapping between the input and output locations. According to the feedbacks of subjects, two potential solutions for the disadvantages in spatial mapping are proposed. First, we can add a clear virtual cursor on the digital canvas to locate the commands from the remote input windmill. Second, maybe we can make the input method more straight via blowing on the digital canvas directly. Of course, the new proposal needs further considerations and tests based on the six criteria of tangible interaction.

References

1. Antle, A.N., Corness, G., Droumeva, M.: What the body knows: Exploring the benefits of embodied metaphors in hybrid physical digital environments. Interacting with Computers 21, 66–75 (2009)
2. Blythe, M., Overbeeke, K., Monk, A.: Funology: From usability to enjoyment, vol. 3. Kluwer Academic Pub. (2004)
3. Buur, J., Jensen, M., Djajadiningrat, T.: Hands-only scenarios and video action walls: Novel methods for tangible user interaction design. In: The 5th Conference on Designing Interactive Systems: Processes, Practices, Methods, and Techniques, pp. 185–192 (2004)
4. Desurvire, H., Jegers, K., Wiberg, C.: Evaluating fun and entertainment: Developing a conceptual framework design of evaluation methods. In: Facing Emotions: Responsible Experiential Design INTERACT 2007 Conference, Rio, Brasil (2007)
5. Dourish, P.: Where the action is: The foundations of embodied interaction. The MIT Press (2004)
6. Fishkin, K.: A taxonomy for and analysis of tangible interfaces. Personal and Ubiquitous Computing 8, 347–358 (2004)
7. Gibson, J.: The concept of affordances. Perceiving, Acting, and Knowing, 67–82 (1977)
8. Gorbet, M., Orth, M., Ishii, H.: Triangles: Tangible interface for manipulation and exploration of digital information topography. In: Proceedings of the SIGCHI Conference on Human Factors in Computing Systems, pp. 1–8. ACM Press/Addison-Wesley Publishing Co. (1998)
9. Hornecker, E.: A design theme for tangible interaction: embodied facilitation. In: ECSCW 2005 (2005)
10. Hornecker, E.: Beyond affordance: Tangibles' hybrid nature. In: Proceedings of the Sixth International Conference on Tangible, Embedded and Embodied Interaction, pp. 175–182. ACM (2012)
11. Hornecker, E., Buur, J.: Getting a grip on tangible interaction: A framework on physical space and social interaction. In: Proceedings of the SIGCHI Conference on Human Factors in Computing Systems. ACM (2006)
12. Ishii, H.: Tangible bits: beyond pixels. In: Proceedings of the 2nd International Conference on Tangible and Embedded Interaction. ACM (2008)
13. Ishii, H., Ullmer, B.: Tangible bits: Towards seamless interfaces between people, bits and atoms. In: Proceedings of the ACM SIGCHI Conference on Human Factors in Computing Systems, pp. 234–241. ACM (1997)
14. Kaltenbrunner, M., Bencina, R.: reacTIVision: A computer-vision framework for table-based tangible interaction. In: Proceedings of the 1st International Conference on Tangible and Embedded Interaction. ACM (2007)
15. Karray, F., Alemzadeh, M., Saleh, J., Arab, M.: Human-computer interaction: Overview on state of the art. International Journal on Smart Sensing and Intelligent Systems 1, 137–159 (2008)
16. Likert, R.: A technique for the measurement of attitudes. Archives of Psychology (1932)
17. Nielsen, J.: Heuristic evaluation. Usability inspection methods 17, 25–62 (1994)
18. Norman, D.: Affordance, conventions, and design. Interactions 6(3), 38–43 (1999)
19. Norman, D.: The design of everyday things. Basic Books, AZ (2002)
20. Patel, S., Abowd, G.: Blui: Low-cost localized blowable user interfaces. In: Proceedings of the 20th Annual ACM Symposium on User Interface Software and Technology. ACM (2007)

21. Raffle, H., Parkes, A., Ishii, H.: Topobo: A constructive assembly system with kinetic memory. In: Proceedings of the SIGCHI Conference on Human Factors in Computing Systems. ACM (2004)
22. Resnick, M., Martin, F., Berg, R.: Digital manipulatives: New toys to think with. In: Proceedings of the CHI 1998 Conference on Human Factors in Computing Systems, pp. 281–287 (1998)
23. Resnick, M., Martin, F.: Programmable bricks: Toys to think with. IBM Systems Journal 35(3.4), 443–452 (1996)
24. Ryokai, K., Marti, S., Ishii, H.: I/O brush: Drawing with everyday objects as ink. In: Proceedings of the SIGCHI Conference on Human Factors in Computing Systems, pp. 303–310. ACM (2004)
25. Samanci, Ö., Chen, Y., Mazalek, A.: Tangible comics: A performance space with full-body interaction. In: Proceedings of the International Conference on Advances in Computer Entertainment Technology, pp. 171–178. ACM (2007)
26. Schkolne, S., Pruett, M., Schröder, P.: Surface drawing: Creating organic 3D shapes with the hand and tangible tools. In: Proceedings of the SIGCHI Conference on Human Factors in Computing Systems. ACM (2001)
27. Schlömer, T., Poppinga, B., Henze, N., Boll, S.: Gesture recognition with a Wii controller. In: Proceedings of the 2nd International Conference on Tangible and Embedded Interaction, pp. 1–4. ACM (2008)
28. Sharlin, E., Watson, B., Kitamura, Y.: On tangible user interfaces, humans and spatiality. Personal and Ubiquitous Computing 8(5), 338–346 (2004)
29. Shen, Y.T., Mazalek, A.: PuzzleTale: A tangible puzzle game for interactive storytelling. Computers in Entertainment (CIE) 8, 11 (2010)
30. Shen, Y.T., Do, E.Y.L.: Fun with blow painting!: Making leaf collages by blowing at toy windmill. In: Proceeding of the Seventh ACM Conference on Creativity and Cognition, pp. 437–438. ACM (2009)
31. Shen, Y.T., Do, E.Y.L.: Making digital leaf collages with blow painting! In: Proceedings of the Fourth International Conference on Tangible, Embedded, and Embodied Interaction, pp. 265–268. ACM (2010)
32. Shneiderman, B.: Direct manipulation 97 (1993)
33. Sweetser, P., Wyeth, P.: GameFlow: A model for evaluating player enjoyment in games. Computers in Entertainment (CIE) 3, 1–24 (2005)
34. Ullmer, B.: Tangible interfaces for manipulating aggregates of digital information. PhD Thesis. Massachusetts Institute of Technology (2002)
35. Ullmer, B., Ishii, H.: Emerging frameworks for tangible user interfaces. IBM Systems Journal 39, 1–15 (2000)
36. Ullmer, B., Ishii, H.: The metaDESK: Models and prototypes for tangible user interfaces. In: The 10th Annual ACM Symposium on User Interface Software and Technology. ACM (1997)
37. Underkoffler, J., Ishii, H.: Urp: A luminous-tangible workbench for urban planning and design. In: Proceedings of the SIGCHI Conference on Human Factors in Computing Systems, pp. 386–393 (1999)
38. Wiberg, C.: A measure of fun: Extending the scope of web usability. PhD Thesis. Umeå University (2003)

DETI-Interact: Interaction with Large Displays in Public Spaces Using the Kinect

Tiago Sousa[1], Igor Cardoso[1], João Parracho[1], Paulo Dias[1,2],
and Beatriz Sousa Santos[1,2]

[1] DETI/UA- Department of Electronics, Telecommunications and Informatics
[2] IEETA- Institute of Electronics and Telematics Engineering of Aveiro
University of Aveiro
Campus Universitário de Santiago, 3810-193 Aveiro, Portugal
{tiagosousa,idc,parracho,paulo.dias,bss}@ua.pt

Abstract. The problem of interaction with large displays in public spaces is currently of interest given the large number of displays available in such spaces (as lobbies, train stations, waiting rooms, etc.) that are only showing information with no possibility to interact with the contents. Several works have been developed in order to allow interaction with these displays using technologies such as infrared, Bluetooth, GPRS, digital compasses or touch screens. Some only intend to provide information, while others emphasize on capturing users' attention eventually leading them to some action. This paper describes DETI-Interact, a system located in the entrance hall of a University department allowing users to interact with a large display without the need to carry any electronic device since a Kinect is used to capture different user's gestures. In this work, special attention was given to another issue intrinsically linked to the presentation of information on large public displays 'How to call the user's attention?'

Keywords: Large displays, natural interfaces, attention catching.

1 Introduction

With the reduction of weight and cost of computer and television screens, we are witnessing a proliferation of large digital displays in public spaces [1], such as lobbies, train stations, waiting rooms, etc. These displays often only show information not offering the possibility to interact with the contents. At the same time, new products in the field of human-computer interaction have started emerging, allowing more natural user interfaces. Examples of such are innovative controllers, like the Wii Remote, PlayStation Move, Kinect and other less known devices, which have been widely accepted by the community [2]. Combining these controllers with large displays opens interesting new possibilities to address relevant issues in the study of interaction with large public displays, which have been tackled through the use of different technologies such as smartphones or RFIDs, implying that users would use some

N. Streitz and P. Markopoulos (Eds.): DAPI 2014, LNCS 8530, pp. 196–206, 2014.

piece of hardware, precluding a more natural and general usage of this type of systems.

This paper describes a project that started by studying different possibilities of interaction with public displays using mobile phones. As a test bed, we developed a system running an application to provide useful information for students of our department deployed in the entrance hall. Despite several differences, since our system is currently limited to one display and the main focus of the research is on the interaction, it has some similarities with other public display systems, such as the E-CAMPUS project [3].

Our system, DETI-Interact, has already been through several stages. As mentioned, initially the possibility of using smartphones (Android equipped with compass, accelerometer and touchscreen) to control the display was explored, and different interaction techniques were developed and tested [4]. However, given the necessity to download an application into the user phone, the system was underused when deployed for real usage. This caused a redesign and a new version of the system was developed using a Kinect[1] to allow gesture interaction, and was installed in the entry hall of our department, providing access to potentially relevant information for those who walk in the department, such as faculty members' contacts, schedules of the courses offered at the department, as well as several promotional videos of the department activities. This idea meets the issue raised by McCarthy, "how an interactive display can be used in the background to enrich casual interactions of the people nearby, by sensing the presence of those people" [5].

This version is working and was evaluated with our students, and as part of university activities promoting science education (such as Science Week and a Summer Academy for high school students); however, the environment is error prone, since different gestures or movements may be detected (for example other people passing by) leading to involuntary interactions. Therefore, in the latest version we used tools made available by the Kinect SDK[2] (tracking of a particular user, smoothing parameters, etc.) so that the gestures produced where easy to use, but at the same time difficult to be replicated involuntary.

Since the system is deployed in a passageway, an important problem is how to get the attention of those passing showing the possibility of interaction. Otherwise potential users may not realize that the system is interactive. As Agamanolis wrote, "Half the battle in designing an interactive situated or public display is designing how the display will invite that interaction" [6]. In order to solve this problem a method capable of capturing the user's attention to DETI-Interact and to the fact that it is possible to interact with it through gestures was devised.

The system is currently being tested and preliminary results of tests indicate that it is already self-explainable and is a viable solution to provide interaction with displays in public spaces.

---

[1] http://www.microsoft.com/en-us/kinectforwindows/
[2] http://go.microsoft.com/fwlink/?LinkID=247735

In what follows the architecture of DETI-Interact is presented as well as the applications available, the interaction and the attention catching methods are briefly described, and some conclusions are drawn.

2   Architecture and Available Applications

The current architecture of the application is presented in Fig.1. Regarding user interaction, the system uses a Kinect sensor to capture the gestures that are sent to the application and trigger associated actions. The information presented by DETI-Interact comes from different sources. Information related to the Department is obtained through already existing web services available at the university. The system also has a local repository of videos that can be visualized on the screen.

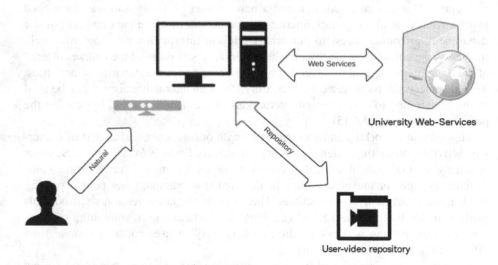

Fig. 1. General Architecture of the DETI-Interact

DETI-Interact is an extensible framework that currently encompasses multiple modules, each with its own requirements and user interface layout. As of now from a main screen (Fig. 2) four applications can be selected: a faculty member list, arranged in a vertical grid list, where users can use all three gestures developed to interact with it (described in the next section); a course schedule list (Fig. 3); a video player (Fig. 4) that allows playing videos from the local repository; and a ping pong game (Fig. 5).

Fig. 2. DETI-Interact main screen (application/module list)

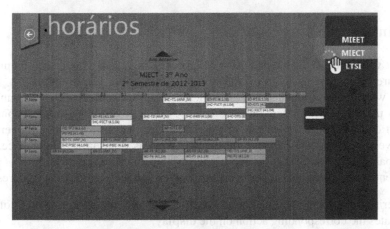

Fig. 3. Table DETI-Interact class schedule list

Fig. 4. DETI-Interact video player

Fig. 5. Ping Pong game

3   Interaction

The first version of DETI-Interact using Microsoft Kinect had a large and complex set of gestures, thus leading to an overall difficult interaction. For instance, the "Push" gesture, which consisted in a strong and quick forward movement of the hand and arm [7], was used to select an item on the display. Although very responsive if done correctly, it could produce a high rate of false positives due to involuntary movements, made even worse by the fact that the interaction was done in a public space, with people passing by near the sensor and triggering this unwanted behavior.

Currently, the interaction is performed through a set of three different gestures:

- Hovering – holding the hand in a specific position for a short period of time activates the corresponding action on the display;
- Hand up – Allows ascendant scroll by holding the hand near the top position;
- Hand down – Allows descendant scroll by holding the hand near the bottom position;

This interaction method has been selected taking into account the recommendations from Kinect for Windows Human Interface Guidelines [8], which advise that there shouldn't be too many gestures, especially if they are very alike, and that they should be easy to learn and carry out.

The use of "Hovering" instead of "Push" was envisioned to prevent, or at least greatly diminish, the number of false positives happening during interaction. Given that the users who will be interacting need to stay in a specific position for a certain amount of time, the probability of an involuntary selection will decrease, as they will have time to notice and avoid completing the action. The efficiency of use slightly decrease, however, application robustness is more relevant than speed of use.

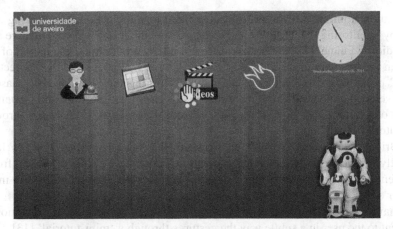

Fig. 6. Progress bar shown to give feedback concerning "Hovering"

We believe that "Hovering", besides reducing the number of interaction errors, is easier to learn, which is relevant as most users of DETI-Interact will not be much familiarized with the system, yet they need specific information at a specific moment and thus the system should be very intuitive. A progress bar is shown to give users feedback regarding how much time has elapsed since the hovering has started (Fig. 6). This seems an important advantage when compared with the "Push" gesture since in informal tests with users we noticed that most of them needed some explanation to be able to use correctly the "Push" gesture.

The quick learning curve was also one of the main reasons for selecting the "Hand up" and "Hand down" gestures, when scrolling vertically. The "grab and drag", suggested in the Microsoft Kinect for Windows SDK, was also a possibility as it is a realistic and nice performing metaphor of many day-to-day actions involving physical objects [9]. In fact, our tests with "grab and drag" were mostly positive in a user interface with content arranged horizontally. However, when the content was vertically oriented users tended to have greater difficulty and higher fatigue, mostly due to the fact that the list was long. Because the faculty member module of DETI-Interact was already arranged vertically, we opted for a vertical scrolling enabled by "Hand up" and "Hand down", thus reducing much of the fatigue felt by the users. When the interaction hand is above the user's shoulders, an upwards scroll is triggered, while below the user's waist, a downwards scroll is triggered.

4   How to Call the Users' Attention

Catching attention of users for this kind of application is a known problem [1] [10] [11]. If no attention catching method is provided, potential users may not even realize that the system is interactive.

Some other papers report the attempt to solve this problematic, like the Proxemic Peddler [6], an interesting implementation of a public advertising display, is based on a framework (the Proxemic Framework) aimed at acquiring and maintaining interest and attention from users, eventually leading them to some action, like making a purchase, by monitoring their interest and trying to lead them into a more attentive stage. The Audience Funnel [12] defines six different interaction phases, where two of them are taken into account in DETI-Interact: the "Passing by" phase and the "Direct interaction" phase. Thus, to capture users' attention during the "Passing by" phase, we have developed a module whose main focus is to attract people's attention when they pass by our system and, in a subtle way, present the gestures to the users through a 'mini-tutorial'.

As Brignull described, "social embarrassment has been identified as a key factor, especially in determining whether people will interact with a public display in front of an audience" [1]. To overcome this barrier, it was decided to use the skeleton instead of a user's real image for psychological reasons.

We have developed a method, whose main focus is to attract people's attention and to present to the user in a subtle way the gestures through a 'mini-tutorial' [13].

Fig. 7. Calling the users' attention

When users pass in front of the display, a skeleton that replicates their movements is shown ("Passing by" phase [12]) as shown in Fig. 7. It was decided to use the skeleton (making use of the potential of the Kinect) instead of a user's real image for psychological reasons [1], as the image of a person projected on a public place may cause some discomfort. In addition to the user(s) skeleton(s), a virtual ellipse similar to a target appears on the screen. When the user places their feet inside the target, the ellipse changes its color indicating the beginning of interaction. This also allows delimiting the area where the user should be in order to have better performance. According to the human interface guidelines for the Kinect [9], this device should be used in a spatial range between 40cm and 4m away from the equipment, yet we reached empirically the conclusion that for the environment of DETI-Interact, the appropriate distance is between 1,8m and 2m.

This approach also allows tracking a specific user, enabling the application to respond only to the gestures performed by the user who is inside the interaction area.

When a user is detected inside this area, a 'mini-tutorial' of the application is triggered. A virtual hand is projected over the skeleton's hand and an area indicating where the user should put his/her hand to start the application appears, effectively committing to the "Direct interaction" phase [12]. The projected virtual hand matches the general cursor of the application; therefore, the user has the perception that he/she can control any application with the right hand.

When the user puts the right hand on the indicated area, besides an illustrative message indicating that the user must wait to select the application (consistent with all the available applications of DETI-Interact), a progress bar appears elucidating the user that he/she must wait to trigger the wanted action.

5   Tests with Users

Our first test with the current version of DETI-Interact took place during the Summer Academy event (Academia de Verão) of 2013, organized by the University of Aveiro. A total of 12 students aged 16 years old, 8 males and 4 females, were able to qualitatively test DETI-Interact. They were given some objectives that needed to be fulfilled using DETI-Interact replicating real world scenarios where a user reaches the department and needs to obtain some kind of information that may be available on the entry hall display. The task were to find the email of a particular teacher, in the list of teachers, check a schedule of a particular course and open a specific video. No help was given.

Although these users are not University students, we can consider that they have a quite similar profile, since a good portion of them will probably be admitted at the University in the following year.

In order to evaluate the performance and satisfaction of the users, a direct observation was performed during testing, followed by a survey that included mainly questions about the usability of the system. The answers to these questions were given in a 5 level Likert-type scale with 1 being the worse value and 5 the best value.

As previously stated, the number of users was not significant enough to perform a statistical analysis of the data. Therefore, these tests should be seen as qualitative and not quantitative results.

Two of the most relevant issues were related to the attention calling module and the methods used for interaction. Fig. 8 and Fig. 9 show the results for these two questions.

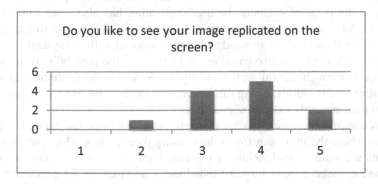

Fig. 8. Results obtained regarding the question: "Do you like to see a skeleton replicating your movements?" (1- not at all, 5- very much)

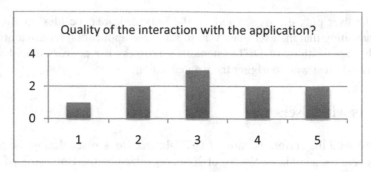

Fig. 9. Results obtained regarding the question: "The application presents a good interaction?" (1- not at all, 5- very much)

In general, results were positive both concerning the interaction and the attention catching method. Another very interesting aspect was that 11 in 12 users said that they would like to have a similar system in their own schools.

Some of the less positive results (as apparent in Fig. 9) may be due to an observed problem during the tests related to the high luminosity present in the entry hall, which led to a decrease in the accuracy of the Kinect sensor. This problem can be improved if the user is nearer the sensor.

Other less positive aspect that became evident was that smaller users had more difficulty in reaching certain areas of the screen, since they do not have a large range of upper limbs as compared to taller users.

6   Conclusions and Future Work

This paper presents DETI-Interact a system that allows interaction through gestures with a large display situated at the entrance hall of our department. This system has been used as a test bed to develop and test new interaction methods with this type of displays that should be intuitive to retrieve relevant information to people entering the department. The issue of catching the user's attention has also been studied and a method was developed that seems effective enough to entice people to interact also showing potential users where to stand and how to interact with the system.

Alongside this work and also based in DETI-Interact, the possibility of manipulating 3D objects through natural gestures using the Kinect is being studied, as well as the navigation in 3D worlds. Using this interaction method we expect a more natural interaction than currently existing approaches.

New entertainment applications are planned, such as a Pac-Man game, and a paint application where the users can freely draw using their bodies. Moreover, some improvements are under consideration for the near future, as allowing interaction using the left hand to make it easier for left-handed users, and making the interaction adaptable to the user's height.

The ability to turn users into contributors to the system, e.g. by recording and showing their activity in a timeline (as seen in [10]), either anonymously or by submission, which could then be used to automatically rank the most important contents or applications, or even provide score rankings for the Pac-Man game, is another point we consider important for a future implementation.

DETI Interact has been evolving according to the feedback obtained from organized user tests and from informal feedback given by passersby as it has been running for some time; it is a framework that has the potential to encompass much more applications, and it will continue to be used to study other relevant issues concerning interaction with large public displays, as well as to motivate students' assignments.

Acknowledgments. We thank the students who contributed to DETI-Interact in any way. We also thank DETI (Department of Electronics, Telecommunication and Informatics) of the University of Aveiro, as well as IEETA (Institute of Electronics and Telematics Engineering of Aveiro), which supported the project from the beginning, allowed prototype deployment in the department's entrance hall, and provided the research initiation grants.

This work was partially funded by FEDER through the Operational Program Competitiveness Factors – COMPETE – by National Funds through Foundation for Science and Technology – FCT (references FCOMP-01-0124-FEDER-022682 and PEst-C/EEI/UI0127/2011).

References

1. Brignull, H., Rogers, Y.: Enticing People to Interact with Large Public Displays in Public Spaces. In: Proceedings of the IFIP International Conference on Human-Computer Interaction (INTERACT), pp. 17–24 (2003)
2. Tuukka, M.T., Rauhamaa, P., Takala., T.: Survey of 3DUI applications and development challenges. In: 3DUI, pp. 89–96 (2012)
3. Friday, A., Davies, N., Efstratiou, C.: Reflections on Long-Term Experiments with Public Displays. IEEE Computer 45(5), 34–41 (2012)
4. Duarte, F., Dias, P., Sousa Santos, B.: Deti-interact: Interacting with public displays through mobile phones. In: 6a Conferência Ibérica de Sistemas e Tecnologias de Informacão (CISTI 2011), Workshop on Information Systems for Interactive Spaces, pp. 787–792 (2011)
5. McCarthy, J.: Using Public Displays to Create Conversation Opportunities. In: Workshop on Public, Community and Situated Displays at ACM Conference on Computer Supported Cooperative Work (2002)
6. Agamanolis, S.: Designing displays for Human Connectedness. In: Workshop on Public, Community and Situated Displays at ACM Conference on Computer Supported Cooperative Work (2002)
7. Cardoso, I., Dias, P., Sousa Santos, B.: Interaction with large displays in a public space using the Kinect sensor. In: 20º Encontro português de Computação Gráfica - EPCG 2012, pp. 81–88 (2012)
8. Hespanhol, L., Tomitsch, M., Grace, K., Collins, A.: Investigating intuitiveness and effectiveness of gestures for free spatial interaction with large displays. In: Proceedings of the International Symposium on Pervasive Displays (PerDis 2012), article 6, 6 p. ACM, New York (2012)

9. Human Interface Guidelines v1.8 – Kinect for Windows – Microsoft Corporation, http://go.microsoft.com/fwlink/?LinkID=247735 (last accessed on January 24, 2014)
10. Sawhney, N., Wheeler, S.: Aware Community Portals: Shared Information Appliances for Transitional Spaces. Personal Ubiquitous Comput. 5(1), 66–70 (2001)
11. Wang, M., Boring, S., Greenberg, S.: Proxemic Peddler: A Public Advertising Display that Captures and Preserves the Attention of a Passerby. In: Proceedings of the International Symposium on Pervasive Displays, vol. 3 (2012)
12. Michelis, D., Müller, J.: The Audience Funnel: Observations of Gesture Based Interaction with Multiple Large Displays in a City Center. Int. J. Human-Computer Interaction 27(6), 562–579 (2011)

A Gesture-Based Door Control Using Capacitive Sensors

Steeven Zeiß, Alexander Marinc, Andreas Braun, Tobias Große-Puppendahl,
and Sebastian Beck

Fraunhofer-Institut für Graphische Datenverarbeitung IGD,
Fraunhoferstraße 5, 64283 Darmstadt
{steeven.zeiss,andreas.braun,
tobias.grosse-puppendahl}@igd.fraunhofer.de,
alexander.marinc@gmail.com, s.beck@stud.tu-darmstadt.de

Abstract. In public places sanitary conditions are always of concern, particularly of surfaces that are touched by a multitude of persons, such as door handles in rest rooms. Similar issues also arise in medical facilities. Doors that open based on presence are common in environments such as shopping malls; however they are not suited for sensitive areas, such as toilet stalls. Capacitive proximity sensors detect the presence of the human body over a distance and can be unobtrusively applied in order to enable hidden gesture-based interfaces that work without touch. In this paper we present a concept for a gesture controlled automated door based on this sensor technology. We introduce the underlying technology and present the concept and electronic components used in detail. Novel interaction patterns and data processing methods allow to open, close, lock and unlock the door using simple gestures. A prototype device has been created and evaluated in a user study.

Keywords: Ambient Assisted Living (AAL).

1 Introduction

The importance of proper sanitation is a well-understood principle to help prevent the spreading of diseases. Door handles in public spaces can be used by hundreds of people in the scope of the day and may act as a source of infection by passing bacteria or different virus between persons [1]. Ideally, these surfaces should either be cleaned or contact be avoided. Automated doors are commonplace in modern environments, e.g. in front of shops, to allow easy entrance and minimize heating cost. However, these are limited to detecting the presence of persons and usually rely on a simple timer to close again. This prevents application in scenarios where the door requires more than one mode of operation, e.g. if it has to be locked and unlocked. In this paper we present a method for a gesture-based door control relying on a set of capacitive sensors that are able to detect the human body over a distance. Using a few simple hand gestures in front of an unobtrusively applicable box it is possible to control an automated door without touching any surface, thus considerable reducing associated health risks. We consider three different potential applications. Public toilets in

N. Streitz and P. Markopoulos (Eds.): DAPI 2014, LNCS 8530, pp. 207–216, 2014.

crowded areas can be visited by a large number of persons each day and have numerous lockable stalls. There are various technologies that improve sanitation, including automated flushing and self-cleaning seats, controlled using presence sensors. However, in order to lock and unlock the stalls it is still necessary to use a handle, as mere presence sensors do not have the required expressiveness to control the locking process. This can be achieved using a set of gestures and our proposed system. The second application area is hospitals. Sanitation is a major concern here and often doors have to be controlled without the use of hands, e.g. using foot switches. The automated doors typically only allow opening and self-close after a preset amount of time. Using our system it is possible to use dedicated opening and close gestures that could be also controlled with a foot-based system. A final application would be door controls for persons with physical disabilities. When there are limitations to the fine motoric skills of the user it is possible to configure the system in a way that it can be controlled by coarse gestures that are specifically tailored to a user.

On the following pages we will briefly introduce the technological basis of capacitive proximity sensors and discuss the related works before detailing the system design and gesture sets available to control the system. We will describe the components of the prototype we created, including components used. Finally, the results of a user evaluation testing the usability of the system will be presented.

2   Related Works

Capacitive proximity sensing is a fairly old technology, first introduced by Russian physicist Leon Theremin around 1918, who created an early electronic instrument – the eponymous Theremin [2]. It allows controlling pitch and volume of a generated sine wave by moving the hands in the range of two distinct antennas.

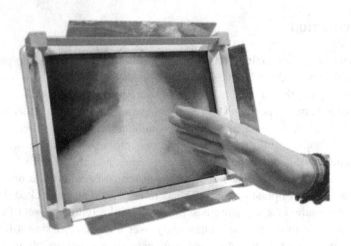

Fig. 1. Thracker prototype attached to a display [3]

The potential applications in HCI have been a research interest at the MIT in the 1990s [4]. Additionally, the technology has been used for different interaction devices in the last years [5, 6]. A closely related application is Thracker, developed by Wimmer et al. and shown in Figure 1 [3]. Using four sensors that are placed on the corners of a monitor it is possible to track the position of a hand moving in front of it and detect grasp gestures, in order to control typical UI functions, such as scrolling and zooming.

3   Capacitive Proximity Sensing

Capacitive sensors measure the capacitance of an electric system. Both the sensor and the human body act as a part of an electric field that is generated with regard to a common ground. Using a simple plate condenser model this relationship can be described using the following equations for capacitance C, charge Q, electrode area A, distance between plates d, vacuum permittivity ε_0, dielectric constant ε_r and electric field strength E [7].

$$C = \frac{Q}{U} = \epsilon_0 \epsilon_r \frac{A}{D} \quad , \quad E = \frac{Q}{\epsilon_0 \epsilon_r A}$$

Smith et al. distinguish three different measurement modes of capacitive proximity sensing of the human body [8, 9]. Transmit mode uses a dedicated sender and receiver electrode, whereas the sender is placed close to body creating a capacitive coupling, resulting the body to act as sending electrode. This allows the sender and receiver to be placed further apart. The second mode is shunt mode using a field created between a dedicated sender electrode and a dedicated receiver electrode. The human body entering this field causes a displacement current, reducing the overall capacitance that can be associated to a distance from the center point between the two electrodes. The final method is loading mode that uses a single electrode creating an oscillating electric field with regards to the environmental ground. If the human body enters this area, the capacitance of the system increases with regards to the proximity between electrode and body. The latter is used as method of choice for our proposed system. Loading mode allows for a simpler technical setup and increased detection distances on a planar and dense electrode layout.

4   System Design

As described in the previous sections, capacitive proximity sensors are employed when hand gestures close to the door have to be recognized. For a simple-to-build and low-cost setup, four sensors are sufficient and provide basic gesture recognition. These sensors allow for recognition of circular gestures and horizontal or vertical movements, also known as swipe gestures. The four sensor electrodes are arranged in a diamond shape, as depicted in Figure 2. For swipe gesture detection, only two sensors will be active: either the horizontal, or the vertical ones. The door lock is installed as a stand-alone, as it can be opened manually from one side only.

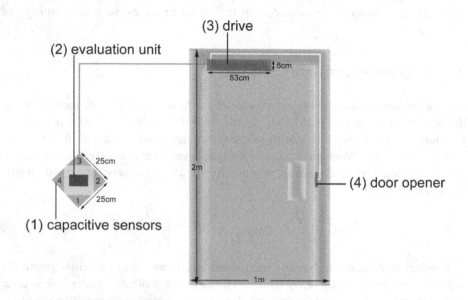

Fig. 2. Simple schematic of the installation

4.1 Gesture Control

The general process of recognizing gestures is depicted in a state diagram, shown in Figure 3. The microcontroller stays idle until one of the sensors' measurements exceeds a threshold value. Once that has occurred, the sensor's current ID is written into a buffer. Depending on the start- and endpoints of a gesture, e.g. when leaving and entering the interaction area, the buffer's values are matched to pre-defined sequences, similar to Dynamic Time Warping. In case no pattern was recognized, the microcontroller is turned back into idle mode and waits for the next gesture trigger. When a pattern has been recognized successfully, succeeding actions can be executed – for example opening of the door.

In order to recognize gestures, sets of predefined patterns are defined *a priori*. These patterns contain the sequential activation orders of the four sensors. As a simple example, pattern 12341 would represent a circular gesture, whereas pattern 1111444 would represent a vertical swipe gesture.

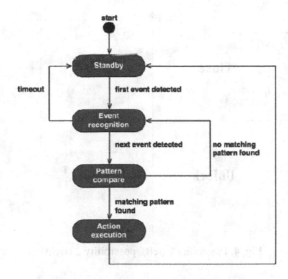

Fig. 3. State diagram of the event detection

4.2   Gesture Set and Triggerable Actions

A door can be reduced to four basic functions: Opening, closing, locking and unlocking. We diagramed these function as six different gestures: swiping horizontally, from left to right, and vice versa; swiping vertically up or down; and a circular gesture from left to right, and vice versa. In the following, we describe four different ways of matching these gestures to the actions the door can executed.

Method 1. Circular gestures are used to open and close the door, while vertical and horizontal swipe gestures lock and unlock the door. Method 1 bears the advantage that it is hard to open and close the door on accident. The necessity of this can easily be determined when considering application in a public restroom. For example, the gesture could accidentally be triggered when a person turns her back to the gesture recognizing surface. Circular gestures may happen less frequently by accident. In order to avoid unintended unlocking of the door, vertical swipe gestures are applicable.

Method 2. In this approach, circular gestures are mapped to locking and unlocking the door. This approach was developed in analogy to ordinary doors, as keys or door knobs are also turned around to lock and unlock the door. Moreover, the direction of locking and unlocking is also given by a natural mapping and habits. Thus, we argue that this is the most intuitive approach, and will prove this assumption in our evaluation. On the other hand, opening and closing the door is initiated by a horizontal or vertical movement. As explained in method 1, this bears the danger of opening or closing the door by accident when there is limited space around the gesture recognition. However, when the door is locked, an open gesture can be restricted: The door must then be unlocked prior to opening it.   Figure 4 depicts the two different methods which are evaluated in our user study.

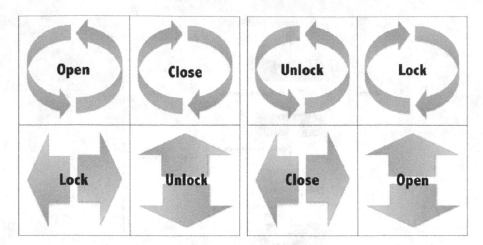

Fig. 4. Possibility 1 (left), possibility 2 (right)

4.3   Functionality and Implementation

Locking and Unlocking the Door. As described in the previous section, the setup does not depend on a dedicated door lock. When the door is closed, it may only be opened by manually turning the door knob on the inside of the restroom, or by gestures. To keep the option of manually opening the door is very important in case people find it hard to cope with gesture recognition systems, or in the event of electricity blackouts and evacuations within a building. Locking and unlocking the door is realized in software with the possibility of indicating the current state by a status LED attached to the gesture recognition device. Even though locking and unlocking is not really necessary, we argue that the psychological effect cannot be neglected with the intention of people feeling more secure when the door is locked. It is also imaginable to extend the setup by an additional capacitive sensor on the outer part of the door. This would allow for additional security when the door is opened after unlocking it.

Opening and Closing the Door. In the previous sections, we described the door motor-control with two input lines for mechanical buttons. Therefore, the enable signal is pulled to 3.3V. In order to trigger the motor control, two succeeding impulses must follow during the next second. Unfortunately, there is no way to distinguish between the actual door, as it is not communicated to the peripheral components (either open or closed). Therefore, an internal marker is used that saves the current state and may trigger a different system behavior.

5   Prototype

We have created a prototype of the system, as shown in Figure 5. It is a portable system with the door applied on a stand. Sensor and evaluation electronics are integrated into a single unit that only requires a power supply and a single connection to the

motor control of the door. We are using a set of motor and locking mechanism provided by DORMA PORTEO.

Fig. 5. Overview of the prototype system. Left - door full view. Middle - door close-up of locking mechanism. Right - control unit open and closed view.

5.1   Sensor Electronics

The basic sensor is based on an oscillating circuit that changes frequency based on the
capacitance of the system. The layout of the board is shown in on the left and is based
on the IC TLC555 provided by Texas Instruments [10]. The system is grounded upon
the OpenCapSense rapid prototyping toolkit for capacitive proximity sensing developed by Grosse-Puppendahl et al. [11].

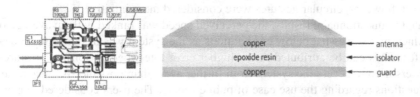

Fig. 6. Left: board layout of sensor module. Right: layer model of sensor electrode

Some features of this toolkit include different filtering algorithms, such as moving
average or median filtering with a variable sample count. In this project we use a
combination of arithmetic mean and moving average to generate a smooth signal for
further processing. Additionally, we employ a guard electrode to prevent external
electric fields from disturbing the measurements.

5.2   Motor Control

In order to control the different functions of the door, an interface between the control unit and an input channel of the motor control is used. As we are only in need of four of the eight provided sensor channels of OpenCapSense it is possible to use one of the free channels to control a relay attached to the door switches, as shown in Figure. 7. We employ a FTR-B4 provided by Fujitsu-Takamisawa that has low power consumption and can be controlled using the board supply of 5 V.

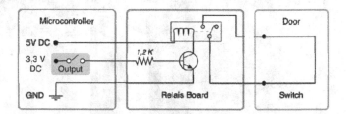

Fig. 7. Circuit diagram of the simulated switch

6   Evaluation

We have evaluated the usability of the system using our prototype. The control unit was placed at a height of about 1.20 m on the left part of the door frame. We wanted to compare both of the presented gesture sets and get a general feedback on the system concept. There were 16 users participating in the study (2 female) between the ages 21 and 35 (mean 27). They were randomly assigned an order of the two sets to avoid learning bias. Afterwards the users had to fill out a small questionnaire with various Likert-scale questions (scale 1-10). The error results are shown in Fig. x. There is a visible and fast learning effect from first to last gesture regardless of set, as the users were trying out the system at this point. The error rate on the second set was generally lower, implying a significant learning effect. There is no obvious preference for any set, however, circular gestures were considered more intuitive.

Related to questionnaire results, the perceived speed was ranked with an average of 7.13, which was somewhat below expectations as the system was designed to be usable swiftly. This can be attributed to the higher error rate when performing gestures. Many users tried to access the system from further away than possible. We also asked some questions regarding the use case of public toilets. The users considered hygiene to be very important in those areas, with a rating of 8.88. Finally the users would like a system such as this to be available in public toilets with a score of 9.25, indicating that the current hygienic standards may be insufficient.

The questionnaire also included open questions where users could state potential improvements of the system. Drawing from this, users would prefer a more concise visual feedback of the current system status. Our system used a single LED, which was not considered sufficient. The error rate was considered too high. It has to be determined whether an angled setup or optical feedback once the hand enters the detection area is more reasonable. Additionally, there should also be an acoustic or visual warning for people standing in the swing area of the door when it is moving automatically.

7 Conclusion and Future Work

In this paper we presented a gesture-based door control system based on capacitive proximity sensors that allows controlling doors in public spaces without touching any surface. We have provided the system concept and two sets of gestures that can be used to control the door. The system was implemented in prototypical form and evaluated in a study with 16 participants. The results show that the system is intuitive to use and that the subjects would strongly prefer this system to touching door handles in public toilets, indicating that this system is a viable alternative to current solutions. However, our system signifies only a first step in this direction and there are numerous improvements that can be applied to future iterations.

The door system we use does not provide its current state to our control unit, thus it has to be tracked with software. In the future, we plan on switching to a system providing this functionality, or integrate additional sensors that measure the state.

Another addition to the system, suggested by study participants, is providing a better visual feedback. It is particularly interesting to display whether a door is closed or open. We are considering using a LCD display that could provide an iconic representation of the system state if an error has occurred or if the hand is obstructing the gesture area. This feedback should ideally be available on both sides of the door. Finally, we would like to investigate other interaction systems that provide an even higher expressiveness. The Leap Motion allows for a fine detection of finger and hand locations [12]. This enables detecting actual gestures associated with doors, such as grabbing a virtual door handle or moving an imaginary key. Particularly for user groups that are often using these gestures, this might increase the intuitiveness and acceptance.

References

1. Barker, J., Vipond, I.B., Bloomfield, S.F.: Effects of cleaning and disinfection in reducing the spread of Norovirus contamination via environmental surfaces. J. Hosp. Infect. 58, 42–49 (2004)
2. Glinsky, A.: Theremin: Ether music and espionage. University of Illinois Press (2000)
3. Wimmer, R., Holleis, P., Kranz, M., Schmidt, A.: Thracker - Using Capacitive Sensing for Gesture Recognition. In: 26th IEEE International Conference on Distributed Computing Systems Workshops (ICDCSW 2006), pp. 64–64. IEEE (2006)
4. Zimmerman, T.G., Smith, J.R., Paradiso, J.A., Allport, D., Gershenfeld, N.: Applying electric field sensing to human-computer interfaces. In: Proceedings of the SIGCHI Conference on Human Factors in Computing Systems - CHI 1995, pp. 280–287. ACM Press, New York (1995)

5. Braun, A., Hamisu, P.: Using the human body field as a medium for natural interaction. In: Proceedings of the 2nd International Conference on PErvsive Technologies Related to Assistive Environments - PETRA 2009, pp. 1–7. ACM Press, New York (2009)
6. Grosse-Puppendahl, T., Braun, A.: Honeyfish - A high resolution gesture recognition system based on capacitive proximity sensing. In: Embedded World Conference 2012, p. 10. WEKA Fachmedien, Haar (Design & Elektronik) (2012)
7. Baxter, L.K.: Capacitive Sensors. Sensors Peterbrgh, 1–17 (1996)
8. Smith, J.R.: Electric field imaging (1999)
9. Smith, J., White, T., Dodge, C., Paradiso, J., Gershenfeld, N., Allport, D.: Electric field sensing for graphical interfaces. IEEE Comput. Graph. Appl. 18, 54–60 (1998)
10. Schnabel, P.: Elektronik-Fibel. Elektron. Bauelemente, Schaltungstechnik, Digit 4 (2007)
11. Grosse-Puppendahl, T., Berghoefer, Y., Braun, A., Wimmer, R., Kuijper, A.: OpenCapSense: A Rapid Prototyping Toolkit for Pervasive Interaction Using Capacitive Sensing. In: IEEE Int. Conf. Pervasive Comput. Commun., vol. 18, p. 22 (2013)
12. SparkFun: Leap Motion Teardown, https://learn.sparkfun.com/tutorials/leap-motion-teardown

PaperIO: Paper-Based 3D I/O Interface Using Selective Inductive Power Transmission

Kening Zhu

School of Creative Media, City University of Hong Kong
keninzhu@cityu.edu.hk

Abstract. In this paper, we introduce *PaperIO*, a paper-based 3D I/O interface, in which a single piece of paper can be sensed and actuated at the same time in three dimensions using the technology of selective inductive power transmission. With this technology, paper material with multiple embedded receivers, can not only selectively receive inductive power to perform paper-computing behavior, but also work as input sensors to communicate with power transmitter wirelessly. In addition, due to the simplicity, this method allows users to easily customize their own paper I/O devices. This paper presents the detailed implementation of the system, results of the technical experiments, and a few sample applications of the presented paper-based 3D I/O interface, and finally discusses the future plan of this research.

Keywords: Paper Computing, 3D User Interface, Tangible User Interface.

1 Introduction

Throughout the evolution of paper, artists and designers have created various art forms through techniques such as folding, bending, and pop-up [13]. Today, paper craft is used in many other areas, such as storytelling, education, and medical treatment [6]. Paper craft can also be used to enhance in-class communication among teachers and children [2]. In addition, researchers who are interested in paper material to bring up the concept of Paper Computing [3], which explored paper as input or output in human computer interaction. However, few of them allow paper to both control and be controlled physically by digital contents at the same time, which separated the usage of paper as input and output in different contexts.

This paper presents *PaperIO*, a new type of paper-based I/O interface based on the technology of selective inductive power transmission [8]. It is able to selectively provide inductive power to different receivers in the context of multiple receivers embedded in paper material, and further actuate the shape-changing of paper as an organic output method. Based on this technology, we developed a technique to enable power receivers to send feedback back to power transmitter while receiving power wirelessly at the same time, thus allow the system to sense the 3D information (Here we define 3D information as the presence, the positions and the orientations) of power receivers, integrating both output and input interfaces in paper material with

N. Streitz and P. Markopoulos (Eds.): DAPI 2014, LNCS 8530, pp. 217–228, 2014.

embedded power receivers. Compared to existing research, *PaperIO* doesn't required complex electrical sensor and actuator circuit embedded in the paper where power receivers are the sensors themselves, and it is real-time and camera-free to avoid the problems such as lighting and hand occlusion.

In the rest of this paper, an overview and comparison of the related work in paper input and output will be presented and discussed in the next section. As follow, the detailed implementation of *PaperIO* will be presented with experimental results of technical performance. Then a few examples of interaction will be described as using *PaperIO* as a 3D input interface for pure virtual reality, and using *PaperIO* as both input and output interfaces at the same time for paper-based interaction. Finally, the paper concludes with the discussion and the future work of *PaperIO*.

2   Related Work

PaperIO falls on the general research of Paper Computing, which using the 3D information of paper as input and output interfaces. This section will review and compare *PaperIO* with these related works.

2.1   Paper as Input

The presented system is highly related to using paper material as an input medium based on hardware implementation. In order to overcome the shortage of computer-vision-based paper input, researchers started to explore the hardware based solution for 3D paper input. RFID [14] is one of the earlier hardware-based paper input technologies. However, it can only sense the presence of the paper-like tag, instead of more advanced information such as position and orientation. Yingdan Huang et al. [16] developed Easigami, a tangible user interface which embeds potentiometers on the edge of paper, so that users can construct different shapes of paper models by combining paper which is then reflected in a 3D virtual representation. In Pulp-based Computing [11], Marcelo Coelho et al. developed a paper-based bending sensor by infusing carbon resistive ink in between two layers of paper. Therefore, the resistance of the paper bending sensor would change while the paper is being bended. Byron Lahey et al. [1] developed PaperPhone, which is the combination of a flexible E-Ink display and a bending sensor connected to the external processing circuit. Paper-Phone allows users to navigate the digital content through a set of pre-defined bending gestures.

While the existing works in hardware-based paper input required complex processing circuit either embedded in or connected to the sensors and the paper material, *PaperIO* doesn't contain any complex circuit in the paper, besides the flat power receiving coils which are providing the 3D input. This fact simplifies the design of *PaperIO* sensors, and makes it possible for end-users to design and implement their own *PaperIO* sensors.

2.2   Paper as Output

PaperIO is also motivated by how to actuate paper output automatically. Greg Saul et al. [4] developed a set of interactive paper devices with embedded electronics, which can actuate light, sound and movement in paper. In these paper devices, conductive paths are inkjet-printed on the paper to form the complex schematics of circuits, and electrical components, such as microprocessor, speaker, and shape memory alloy, are soldered to the conductive paths. In Pulp-based Computing, the circuits are screen-printed on the paper material with components embedded during pulp making process. Using Pulp-based Computing and LilyPad [9], Jie Qi et al. developed Electronic Popables [5], the interactive pop-up books that integrates electronics and pop-up mechanisms as a complete user interface. Animated Paper [12] was presented as a versatile platform created from paper and shape memory alloy (SMA), which is easy to control using a range of different energy sources from sunlight to lasers. In Animated Paper, the paper craft attached with SMA can be controlled to move with a high-power laser pointer. More recently, AutoGami [7] was developed as one step forward for allowing end-users to create their own automated movable paper-craft.

In summary, there are three main contributions we claimed for *PaperIO* technology over existing paper interfaces. Firstly, compared to computer-vision-based paper input, *PaperIO* doesn't rely on any light condition, and it allows users to manipulate the paper with embedded receivers with hands directly and freely. These features overcome the disadvantage of lighting and hand-blocking. Secondly, while comparing with most of the existing hardware-based solutions for paper input and output, *PaperIO* utilizes the technology of selective inductive power transferring, and only simple coils are embedded in paper material. We believe these could enhance the tangibility and the customizability of the paper interface. Finally, in the technical aspect, *PaperIO* could provide a wide range of variations in the input of 3D information, including gradual changes in position and orientation, as shown in the experiments.

3   System Description

3.1   Overview of Theoretical Principle

The basic principle of *PaperIO* is based on the theory of inductive power transmission. As shown in Figure 1, the power receiving coil is connected to a capacitor C1, which tunes the resonant frequency of the receiving coil to a specific value, and a diode D1, which will be turned on only when the receiving coil is closed enough to the power transmitter for receiving enough power. When D1 is turned on, the negative part of the AC current in the receiving coil would be cut-off, and the receiving coil generates a new magnetic flux with almost twice of its resonant frequency. Therefore, the power feedback sensor with the capacitor C2 could sense the change of the magnetic flux, as its resonant frequency is tuned by C2 to the twice value of the resonant frequency of the power receiving coil.

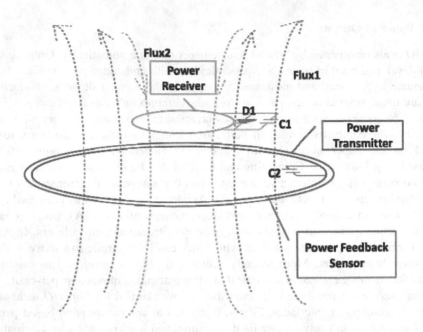

Fig. 1. Basic theoretical principle of *PaperIO*

The magnetic flux generated by the power receiver (Flux2 in Figure 1) would change when the power receiver's position and orientation are changed. Therefore, this sensor should be able distinguish the difference when the receiver is moving, and further enable it as a 3D input device. In addition, by controlling the value of C2, the power feedback sensor can have multiple resonant frequencies to differentiate the presence of different power receivers. Finally, receivers with simple actuators, such as shape memory alloy, embedded in paper material, make paper as both input and output devices.

3.2   Simulation

Based on the theoretical hypothesis described above, we first simulated *PaperIO* in SPICE software environment [10]. As shown in Figure 2, there are three resonant circuits in the schematic: transmitter (L1), receiver (L2) and feedback sensor (L3), while L1 and L2 are linked by coupling coefficient K1, L2 and L3 are linked by coupling coefficient K2, and L1 and L3 are linked by coupling coefficient K3. On the left side of the simulated schematic, the transmitting coil is excited by a sinusoid power source with the amplitude of 12V. For the purpose of simulation, we picked 510 kHz for the value of transmitting frequency. The transmitter is modeled as a two-turn coil (L1) with the diameter of 10cm and the resistance (R1), and the feedback sensor is modeled as a two-turn coil (L3) with the diameter of 5cm and the resistance (R2), and placed 2mm above L1. The right side of the schematic shows the model of power receiver, which is a 2-turns circular coil with the diameter of 5 cm, and it is connected to diode D1 and capacitor C1 for the resonant frequency of 510 kHz. In this model, we assume the closest distance between L1 and L2 is 1 cm. According to the equations in [8], we calculated the values of L1, L3 and K3 as shown in Figure 2. Additionally, Fast Fourier Transform (FFT) was employed to process and analyze the raw signal from the feedback sensor in the frequency domain in the simulation.

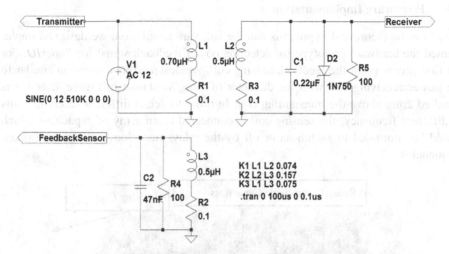

Fig. 2. Simulation Schematic for *PaperIO*

When the receiver is not present near the transmitter, there is only one active coupling K3 between the feedback sensor and the transmitter. The simulation results of this situation are shown in Figure 3(a), where the signal detected by the sensor only shows one peak value in the frequency domain at the frequency of 510 kHz. When the receiver is moving closer to the transmitter and the sensor, the coupling K1 and K3 are activated. The simulated results (Figure 3(b)) show that different values of amplitude occur in the frequency domain at the value of 1.02 MHz, which is twice of the value of the resonant frequency of the receiver.

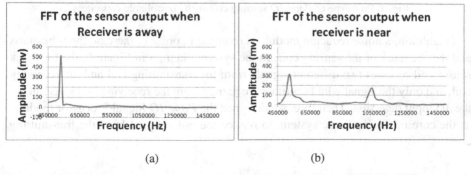

(a)   (b)

Fig. 3. (a) The FFT result of sensor signal when the receiver is away; (b) The FFT result of sensor signal when the receiver is near

When the values of K1 and K2 are changed, due to the change of the receiving coil's position or orientation, the amplitude at the frequency of 1.02 MHz would also change. Therefore, we can develop a circuit prototype to detect this value-changing in the frequency domain, and further map this change to the 3D information of the power receiving coil.

3.3   Hardware Implementation

Based on the theoretical hypothesis and the software simulation, we designed implemented the hardware prototype for detecting power feedback signal for *PaperIO*. For the first prototype of the feedback sensing coil, we designed its dimension similar to the power receiving coil with the diameter of 5cm, as shown in Figure 4, and it is installed 2mm above the transmitting coil. In order to detect different receiving coils in different frequency, the sensing coil is connected to an array of capacitors which would be controlled to switch on or off by the relays, to achieve different resonant frequencies.

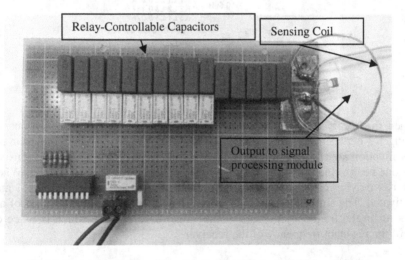

Fig. 4. Prototype of *PaperIO* sensing coil with controllable capacitors

In addition, a noise-reducing module is required in order to increase the robustness and the accuracy of the sensing coil. In the system diagram in Figure 5, the feedback sensor coil receives two different signals from the transmitting coil and the receiving coil, and only the signal with two-times frequency from the receiving coil is useful for the 3D input detection. Therefore, we designed the *PaperIO* Signal Processor module, as the core of the hardware system, to reduce the noise signal from the transmitting coil.

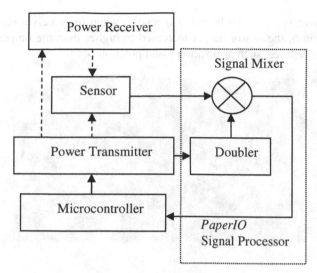

Fig. 5. System Diagram of *PaperIO*

The *PaperIO* Signal Processor module contains two main units: the frequency doubler and the signal mixer. As the raw signal from the sensing coil is a mixed signal with the frequency whose value is twice of the transmitting frequency, a double-frequency signal is required, in order to reduce the noise using digital operational mixer circuit. The frequency doubler is designed based on the theory of Phase-Locked Loop (PLL), and the doubled signal is passed to one input of the signal mixer which is an operational subtractor, while the other input signal is the raw signal detected by the feedback sensing coil. Finally, the output result from the signal mixer is the signal detected only from the power receiving coil. Furthermore, the de-noised signal is passed to the anlog-to-digital module of the microcontroller to control the power transmitter.

4   Performance Experiment

4.1   3D Input: Horizontal Translation

In the experiments of sensing the horizontal translation of the receiver, the target was to find out whether the sensor output would change when the receiver is moved on the horizontal level. The receiver was placed at the starting 1 positions not aligned with the sensor, as shown in Figure 6(a). During this experiment, the receiver was placed closed to the transmitter, and moved from the position 1 to position 6 through the center position for the distance of 15 cm, and the sensor output was recorded accordingly.

The results in Figure 6(b) show that the sensor gives different output when the receiver is at different horizontal positions. When the receiver is moving from center to the other position, the transient pattern of the sensor output can be recorded as the input for interactive systems. To be noted specially, when the receiver reached position 2 and position 5, the sensor output increased to higher than the output when the receiver was not presence, such as position 1 and position 6.

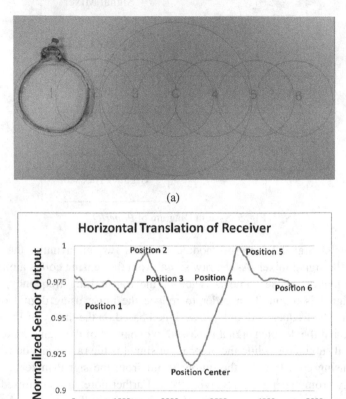

(a)

(b)

Fig. 6. (a) Experiment to detect the horizontal movement of receiver, (b) *Paperio* sensor output of the horizontal movement of receiver

4.2   3D Input: Vertical Translation

For the experiment of moving the receiver vertically, we aimed to determine to which height the receiver can be sensed by the sensor and different sensor output for different height of the receiver. The set-up of the experiment is shown in Figure 7(a). The acrylic box contains slots for inserting a flat and thin plastic sheet to hold the receiver at a certain height, and the vertical distance between two nearby slots is 5mm. This structure allowed us to control the vertical distance between the receiver and the sensor. When the distance was changed, the receiver was removed from the scene and placed back after changing the distance. In this experiment, the vertical distance was changed from 0mm to 20mm.

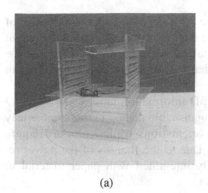

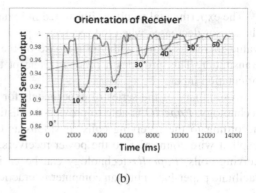

Fig. 7. (a) Experiment setup for sensing vertical translation of receiver; (b) *Paperio* sensor output of the vertical movement of receiver

Figure 7(b) illustrates the results of sensing the vertical translation of the receiver. The normalized sensor outputs were clearly distinguished as the receiver was placed at different height above the sensor. Therefore, the concept of using *PaperIO* as a height sensor is proofed.

4.3   3D Input: Orientation

For the setup of sensing the orientation angle of the receiving, a set of angle models with the specific values of 5°, 10°, 20°, and 30°were made using acrylic material as shown in Figure 8(a), and other values of angle can be realized by stacking these models together.

During this experiment, the angle model was placed on the surface right above the sensor, and the receiver was fixed on the model as shown in Figure 8(a). The model would be changed from 0° to 60°, in order to measure sensor output in different values of orientation angles of the receiving coil.

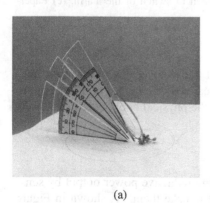

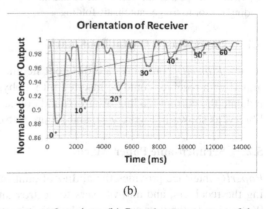

Fig. 8. (a) Experiment setup for sensing orientation of receiver, (b) *Paperio* sensor output of the tilting of receiver

The experimental result, as illustrated in Figure 8(b), shows that the output value of the sensor decreases when the receiver is present near the transmitter, and the output value increases along with the increase of the angle between the receiver and the transmitter. This provides a proof of concept that *PaperIO* can also be used as an orientation input.

In summary of the series of experiments for 3D information input using *PaperIO* technology, *PaperIO* is able to provide the distinguishable analog output continously according to the receiving coils' positions and orientations while it doesn't require explicit wire connection to the power receivers. Due to the flatness of the power receiving coils, *PaperIO* technology can be easily integrated with paper material to facilitate paper-based human computer interaction.

5   Example Interaction

For the application of *PaperIO* sensor, we focused in paper-based ubiquitous computing, mainly daily activities, gaming entertainment, and social networking. As the proof of concept, we designed four examples of the interaction, Paper Controller for Virtual Reality, Paper-based Digital Bookmark, Scrunch-able Paper Alarm, and Origami Interaction.

(a)   (b)   (c)   (d)   (e)

Fig. 9. (a) Using *Paperio* as a bookmark, (b) *Paperio* senses the reading progress of the book, (c) LED and speaker are turned on to alarm; (d) Scrunch to switch of the alarm, (e) Paper-folding sensor to trigger automatic folding

5.1   Paper-Based Digital Bookmark

As the *PaperIO* could indicate different height of the receiver, the paper sheet integrated with receiver could be inserted into a physical book as a piece of bookmark, to indicate the current reading progress, and connect the physical book with digital book library, as shown in Figure 9 (a) and Figure 9 (b).

5.2   Scrunch-able Paper Alarm

PaperIO interface provides the ability of controlling inductive power output by sensing the receivers, and allows users to destroy and remake them. As shown in Figure 9(c) and 9(d), the user can easily "destroy" the presence of the input receiver and stop the alarm by scrunching the paper alarm, if he or she is woken up or wants to continue sleeping.

5.3   Physical Origami Interaction

The ability of detecting the orientation of receiver makes *PaperIO* a origami-folding interface. As shown in Figure 9(e), the *PaperIO* sensor can detect the folding of one corner which contains a receiving coil being tilted due to the folding, and control the power transmitter to provide power to the receiver in the other part of the paper, to activate the connected shape memory alloy and trigger the automatic paper-folding. This origami interaction provides users a physical and tangible feedback of origami making, and gives the possibility of physical creative interface for origami co-designing between human and computer.

6   Discussion and Future Work

Since *PaperIO* is in the early stage of prototyping for the proof of concept, there are still a few limitations and space for improvement in the current system. Firstly, although the experiments showed that *PaperIO* could provide quite accurate results for the 3D information of the power receiving coils, the results are still affected by the environmental noise, either from the peripheral electromagnetic signals or from the unstable hand movements by the users. Therefore, a better noise-reducing module is required for more accurate results from the *PaperIO* system. Secondly, it is difficult for the current version of *PaperIO* to work as translation input and orientation input at the same time. Therefore, advanced interaction skills would be employed to support *PaperIO* interface.

In conclusion, we have developed *PaperIO*, a paper-based 3D I/O interface using the technology of selective inductive power transmission, and proved its performance through a series of hardware experiments. *PaperIO* is able to sense the 3D information of power receivers when they are closed to the power transmitter, and convert the input to further control the output of the power transmitter. In addition, *PaperIO* can be easily integrated with flexible paper material for paper-based human computer interaction. Various examples of interaction were presented as the proof of concept. We believe *PaperIO* provides a new venue for creating paper-based human computer interaction.

References

1. Lahey, B., Girouard, A., Burleson, W., Vertegaal, R.: PaperPhone: Understanding the use of bend gestures in mobile devices with flexible electronic paper displays. In: Proceedings of the 2011 Annual Conference on Human Factors in Computing Systems (CHI 2011), pp. 1303–1312. ACM, New York (2011)
2. Foreman-Takano, D.: Origami and Communication Strategies. Doshisha Studies in Language and Culture 1-2, 315–334 (1998)
3. Kaplan, F., Jermann, P.: PaperComp 2010: First international workshop on paper computing. In: Proceedings of the 12th ACM International Conference Adjunct Papers on Ubiquitous Computing (Ubicomp 2010, Adjunct), pp. 507–510. ACM, New York (2010)

4. Saul, G., Xu, C., Gross, M.D.: Interactive paper devices: End-user design & fabrication. In: Proceedings of the Fourth International Conference on Tangible, Embedded, and Embodied Interaction (TEI 2010), pp. 205–212. ACM, New York (2010)
5. Qi, J., Buechley, L.: Electronic popables: Exploring paper-based computing through an interactive pop-up book. In: Proceedings of the Fourth International Conference on Tangible, Embedded, and Embodied Interaction (TEI 2010), pp. 121–128. ACM, New York (2010)
6. Shumakov., K., Shumakov, Y.: Functional interhemispheric asymmetry of the brain in dynamics of bimanual activity in children 7-11 year old during origami training. PhD dissertation, Rostov State University (2000)
7. Zhu, K., Zhao, S.: AutoGami: A low-cost rapid prototyping toolkit for automated movable paper craft. In: Proceedings of the SIGCHI Conference on Human Factors in Computing Systems (CHI 2013), pp. 661–670. ACM, New York (2013)
8. Zhu, K., Nii, H., Fernando, O.N.N., Cheok, A.D.: Selective inductive powering system for paper computing. In: Proceedings of the 8th International Conference on Advances in Computer Entertainment Technology (ACE 2011), article 59, 7 p. ACM, New York (2011)
9. Buechley, L., Eisenberg, M., Catchen, J., Crockett, A.: The LilyPad Arduino: Using computational textiles to investigate engagement, aesthetics, and diversity in computer science education. In: Proceedings of the SIGCHI Conference on Human Factors in Computing Systems (CHI 2008), pp. 423–432. ACM, New York (2008)
10. LTSPICE IV, http://www.linear.com/
11. Coelho, M., Hall, L., Berzowska, J., Maes, P.: Pulp-based computing: A framework for building computers out of paper. In: Proceedings of the 27th International Conference Extended Abstracts on Human Factors in Computing Systems (CHI EA 2009), pp. 3527–3528. ACM, New York (2009)
12. Koizumi, N., Yasu, K., Liu, A., Sugimoto, M., Inami, M.: Animated paper: A toolkit for building moving toys. Comput. Entertain. 8(2), Article 7, 16 pages (2010)
13. Sloman, P. (ed.): Paper: Tear, Fold, Rip, Crease, Cut. Black Dog Publishing (2009)
14. Radio-frequency identification (RFID), http://en.wikipedia.org/wiki/Radio-frequency_identification
15. Mackay, W.E., Pothier, G., Letondal, C., Boegh, K., Sorensen, H.E.: The missing link: Augmenting biology laboratory notebooks. In: Proceedings of the 15th Annual ACM Symposium on User Interface Software and Technology (UIST 2002), pp. 41–50. ACM, New York (2002)
16. Huang, Y., Eisenberg, M.: Easigami: Virtual creation by physical folding. In: Spencer, S.N. (ed.) Proceedings of the Sixth International Conference on Tangible, Embedded and Embodied Interaction (TEI 2012), pp. 41–48. ACM, New York (2012); Sloman (ed.): Paper: Tear, Fold, Rip, Crease, Cut. Black Dog Publishing (2009)

Cognitive, Perceptual and Emotional Issues in Ambient Intelligence

Collecting Behavior Logs with Emotions in Town

Kenro Aihara

National Institute of Informatics / The Graduate University for Advanced Studies
2-1-2 Hitotsubashi, Chiyoda-ku, Tokyo 101-8430, Japan
kenro.aihara@nii.ac.jp

Abstract. This paper proposes a new methodology for collecting visitors' behavior and their emotions in town by using smartphones.

Existing social information services, such as Facebook and Twitter, are expanding to attach location data to users' content. To capture situations of town, such as events what happens there or how people feel, the author believes that it's not enough to collect tweets and behavior logs of locations in the town, because in fact the number of geotagged tweets is limited. Especially for microscopic analysis of town situations in small resolution of time and space, more information sources reflecting strollers' behaviors and emotions are needed.

The paper proposed a function of LBS smartphone application to collect users' behavior and emotions. When a user installs and uses an application with the function in town, the function records and transmits not only his/her locations but also his/her facial expressions by using front-facing camera.

An experiment was made in the beginning of November 2013. 55 subjects participated in the experiment. In addition to using the application in town, subjects were requested to provide correct data of facial expressions in 9 classes such as excited, fun and tired.

The function extracts 66 feature points of face by using Saragih's model. As a quick result, the overall precision of 9 class-classification is 91.1% at 10-fold cross validation. The author believes that the result supports that the proposed application can collect facial expressions of not only active users who post microblogs but also read-only users.

Keywords: Context, Human activity modelling and support, Sensor-augmented environments, Smart and hybrid cities, behavior log, emotion, facial expression.

1 Introduction

In recent years, the amount of geotagged information, which contains geographical data, has been rapidly growing. GPS-equipped smartphones facilitate users to embed location data in their content, such as tweets and photos, and to post them to social services like Facebook[1] and Twitter[2].

---

[1] http://www.facebook.com/
[2] http://twitter.com/

N. Streitz and P. Markopoulos (Eds.): DAPI 2014, LNCS 8530, pp. 231–240, 2014.

To capture situations of town, such as events what happens there or how people feel, the author believes that it's not enough to collect tweets and behavior logs of locations in the town, because in fact the number of geotagged tweets is limited. In previous work of the author, only 1% of LBS users posted microblogs while strolling in town. Therefore, for microscopic analysis of town situations in small resolution of time and space, more information sources reflecting strollers' behaviors and emotions are needed.

This paper proposes a new methodology for collecting visitors' behavior and their emotions in town by using smartphones. When a user installs and uses an application with the function in town, the function records and transmits not only his/her locations but also his/her facial expressions by using front-facing camera.

2 Background

A lot of network services with location data are proposed, and some of them, such as foursquare[3], are getting popular. Usually location information is given as geographical coordinates, that is, latitude and longitude, a location identifier such as ID for facilities in geographical information services (GIS), or a postal address. Google has launched Google Places[4], which gathers place information from active participating networkers and delivers such information through Google's web site and API (application programmable interface). Google may try to grasp facts and information on activities in the real world where it has not enough information yet even though it seems to have become the omniscient giant in the cyber world. Google already captures some real world phenomena in its own materials. For example, it gathers landscape images with its own fleet of specially adapted cars for the Google Street View service[5]. However, the cost of capturing and digitizing facts and activities in the real world is generally very expensive if you try to obtain more than capturing photo images with geographical information. Although Google Places may be one of the reasonable solutions to gathering information in the real world, it's not guaranteed that it can grow into an effective and reliable source reflecting the real world.

Existing social information services, such as Facebook and Twitter, are expanding to attach location data to users' content.

Crowdsource-based services on real world, such as FixMyStreet[6] or Waze[7], are getting popular these days. Although these services seem effective for collecting current issues in town, there is a common problem how to promote posts and how to give incentives to users. Only if a service covers rich and exhaustive information of each local area, the service gets very attractive for users.

---

[3] http://foursquare.com/
[4] http://www.google.com/places/
[5] http://www.google.com/streetview/
[6] http://www.fixmystreet.com/
[7] https://www.waze.com/

However, only if a lot of users participate and post information of events happened around them exhaustively, the service can provide rich local information.

3   Nicott: An LBS for Explorers in Town

3.1   Service Description

The author has developed and provides an LBS called "Nicott" since November 2013[8]. Nicott has the function of collecting behavior logs and facial expressions.

Nicott is designed for explorers who visit Futako-tamagawa area, which is being redeveloped as a smart city in Tokyo and consists of complexes including shopping malls, supermarkets, offices, and residential areas around the Futako-tamagawa station. The service can be accessed via iOS application. When visitors arrive in the service area and access the service, they can get information about scheduled events and user-generated contents.

Major functions of the service are as follows.

3.2   User Functions

Event Information. When the Nicott application is invoked, it shows the list of hot events around the area (Fig. 1(a)). Contents of each event are supplied by local business users.

By selecting one event in the list, the information of the event is given (Fig. 1(b)). The information includes not only basic items, such as time and place, but also contents that are posted by Nicott users. Viewing related users' contents to the event, users may be able to have a viewpoint of other visitors and realize how to enjoy it.

Sharing Posted Contents. Users can switch to browse shared posted contents in the page of event list (Fig. 1(c)). They also can sort them in the order of posted time and popularity. Popularities are given as the number of "like" declaration of other users.

The detail of the content is called by tapping it in the content list (Fig. 1(d)). It includes a photo, comment, related event, location in the map, and popuarity.

Posting Content. Menu button is located at the top left corner (Fig. 1(e)). Menu consists of "Camera", "Event Calendar", "My Album", "Map", and "Settings".

By selecting "Camera" mode in the menu, users are requested to take a new photo or select one stored image. After they determined a photo, input form appears. Users have to input comment and select one emoticon in nine candidates as follows:

---

[8] https://itunes.apple.com/jp/app/nicott/id730354076

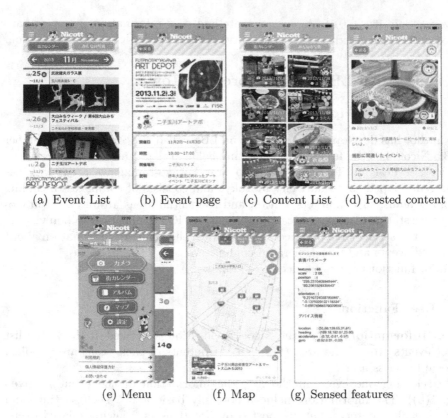

(a) Event List   (b) Event page   (c) Content List   (d) Posted content

(e) Menu   (f) Map   (g) Sensed features

Fig. 1. Snapshot images of the Nicott application

- Excited! Need more! (a)
- Exhilarated! (b)
- Relaxed and soothed. (c)
- Nice. Want better. (d)
- So so. (e)
- Need a break. (f)
- Not good. Displeased. (g)
- Tired. (h)
- Exhausted. (i)

The author assumes that Lang's model of emotions, which emotional affect has been conceptualized along two dimensions: valence, which describes the extent of pleasure or sadness, and arousal, which describes the extent of calmness or excitation[8,6]. Each dimension is divided into three sections, so that nine emotional classes are defined. Corresponding label and emoticon is given for each class.

Declaring a relative event and exporting the same content to other SNSs, such as Twitter and Facebook, are optional. They can also set the post private.

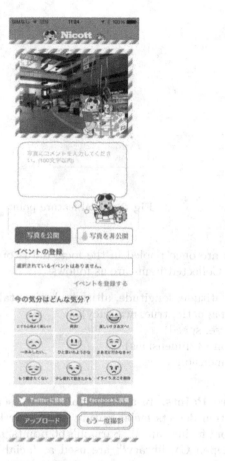

Fig. 2. Posting content

Map. Map mode can be used for check the places of events and contents with current user's location (Fig. 1(f)).

3.3 Sensing Functions

User Data. The Nicott service collects the following user attributes:

- gender
- generation
- zip code

The service collects users' demographic attributes at the first access.

Onboard Location and Motion Sensors. The Nicott application gets location and motion data from onboard sensors even in the background mode.

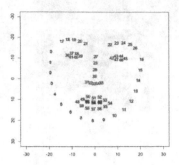

Fig. 3. Facial feature points

Collected data are once pooled in the local datastore and then transmitted to the log server. Collected items are as follows:

- Location (latitude, longitude, altitude, horizontal/vertical accuracies)
- Heading (magnetic, true, accuracy)
- Move (course, speed)
- Acceleration (3 dimensions)
- Gyro (3 dimensions)

Facial Feature Points. In addition to onboard sensors described above, the Nicott application detects facial feature of its user by processing photo image captured by front facing camera. Saragih's 66 points[9] detected by Face Tracker[9] software and Open CV library[10] are used as facial feature (Fig. 3). Fig. 1(g) shows the page for users to realize what data are being sensed by the application.

4   Experiment

An experiment using the Nicott application was made in two days.
    The objectives of the experiment are as follows:

- collecting sensor logs and users' contents
- creating training data set to learn classifiers of facial expression
- interviewing preferences of private information with subjects

In the experiment, more than 24,000 behavior logs and 90,000 facial feature data were collected. And also 911 contents were posted by users.

---

[9] https://github.com/kylemcdonald/FaceTracker
[10] http://opencv.org/

Table 1. Subjects of a Nicott Experiment

age	# of subjects	percentage
20–29	15	25.9
30–39	26	44.8
40–49	12	20.7
over 50	5	8.6

Table 2. Result of Question "Please answer apps that you use often with your smartphone. (multi answer)"

applications	# of answers	percentage
game	21	38.2
SNS	46	83.6
music	29	52.7
movie	33	60.0
transporation, navigation	44	80.0
reservation	10	18.2
e-commerce	21	38.2
ebook	7	12.7
finance	11	20.0
camera	37	67.3
misc.	5	9.1
never use any applications	1	1.8

4.1 Subjects

55 subjects participated in the experiment; 33 males and 22 females. Age distribution is shown in Table 1. The result of the question what applications they often use in Table 2.

4.2 Creating Training Data Set

In addition to using the application in town, subjects were requested to provide correct data of facial expressions in nine emotional classes. They made their facial expression, while they were creating their dummy contents for each corresponding emotional class.

4.3 Preliminary Test of Classifying Facial Expressions

Using training data set of facial features, a classifier of nine emotional classes was learned. LIBSVM[11][3], which is an implementation of Support Vector Machines[4], is used as a classifier.

---

[11] http://www.csie.ntu.edu.tw/~cjlin/libsvm/

Table 3. Result of Classification of Facial Expression

	a	b	c	d	e	f	g	h	i
a	278	0	0	65	0	2	0	0	4
b	1	243	0	82	0	3	0	0	0
c	0	0	110	104	0	0	0	0	0
d	0	2	0	516	0	1	0	0	2
e	0	0	0	86	372	0	3	0	0
f	2	2	0	76	0	375	0	0	0
g	0	0	0	62	5	0	376	2	0
h	0	0	0	78	0	0	1	377	0
i	4	0	0	68	1	0	0	0	367

The classifier was made by using all training data set, that is, the classifier is independent of individuals. The performance of the classifier with 10-fold cross validation is shown in Table 3. For example, 65 training data of class a are classified into class d. As a result, overall precision is 91.1% and recall is 82.1%. Precision of class d (516/1137, 45.4%) and recall of class c (110/214, 51.4%) is relatively much lower than the other classes. Class d corresponds to "Nice. Want better." and is located in the middle range of arousal. The typical facial expression of class d may be neutral or "emotionless". The author thinks that that is one of the reasons of this low accuracy.

Considering the training data set includes some noise data because the settings of creation of the data was not stable and face of subjects had to fluctuate during the process, the author believes that the result supports that the proposed application can collect emotions of users by processing their facial images. It is important that the application can collect emotions of not only active users who post contents but also read-only users, compared to sentiment analysis[7] methods based on natural language processing of posted contents.

Facial expressions are currently classified on the server by using facial feature points transmitted from the application. The author, however, thinks that the classifier can be onboard and emotional classes are determined on the fly, because the classifier may be independent of individuals.

4.4   Interview

After the experimental usage, subjects were interviewed on preferences of providing private information: personally identifiable information (PII), emotions, locations, environmental camera such as surveillance camera, environmental sensors (Table 4).

PII is a category of sensitive information that can be used to uniquely identify, contact, or locate a single person, such as full name, home address, and email address. The others are "de-identified" and not considered sensitive.

As a result, subjects tend to resist to provide their PII to private services, even though they permit that their PII is used for public benefits. In contrast,

Table 4. Conditions of Providing Private Information (single answer)

condition	PII	emotion	location	camera	sensor
when my private information may contribute to improve public benefits, such as prevention of disaster or crime	41.8%	10.9%	20.0%	52.7%	34.5%
when quality of the service gets improved	5.5%	38.2%	21.8%	5.5%	12.7%
when given information is improved and gets more useful	47.3%	49.1%	54.5%	34.5%	43.6%
I don't want to provide my private information in any conditions	5.5%	1.8%	3.6%	7.3%	9.1%

emotions are permitted for private services. The author thinks that this result supports our application that collects emotions of users can be accepted by them.

Considering "I don't want to provide my private information in any conditions", there may be more oppositive feelings than PII, although the result of environmental cameras and sensors seems like PII.

5   Conclusions

This paper proposes a new methodology for collecting visitors behavior and their emotions in town by using smartphones. The service called Nicott has been developed. As a result of an experiment, the author believes that the result supports that the proposed methodology can collect facial expressions on the fly. In addition, the methodology that collects emotions can be accepted by users.

The author continues to develop and provide these services. To evaluate the effectiveness of the model, experiments are being planned. Analysis of user behavior logs and the development of methods to exploit emotions to enhance user experience in town are future issues.

Acknowledgments. The author thanks KDDI R&D Laboratories, Shibasaki Laboratory of Center for Spatial Information Science of the Univerisity of Tokyo, Tokyu Corporation, the National Institute of Advanced Industrial Science and Technology (AIST), and JIPDEC for their cooperation with this research.

This work was supported by the Grant-in-Aid for IT Integration-based New Social System Development and Demonstration Project of the New Energy and Industrial Technology Development Organization (NEDO) of Japan.

References

1. Aihara, K.: Do strollers in town needs recommendation?: On preferences of recommender in location-based services. In: Streitz, N., Stephanidis, C. (eds.) DAPI 2013. LNCS, vol. 8028, pp. 275–283. Springer, Heidelberg (2013)

2. Aihara, K., Koshiba, H., Takeda, H.: Behavioral cost-based recommendation model for wanderers in town. In: Jacko, J.A. (ed.) Human-Computer Interaction, Part III, HCII 2011. LNCS, vol. 6763, pp. 271–279. Springer, Heidelberg (2011)
3. Chang, C.-C., Lin, C.-J.: Libsvm: A library for support vector machines. ACM Transactions on Intelligent Systems and Technology 27, 27:1–27:27 (2011)
4. Cortes, C., Vapnik, V.: Support-vector networks. Machine Learning 20(3), 273–297 (1995)
5. Ducheneaut, N., Partridge, K., Huang, Q., Price, B., Roberts, M., Chi, E.H., Bellotti, V., Begole, B.: Collaborative filtering is not enough? experiments with a mixed-model recommender for leisure activities. In: Houben, G.-J., McCalla, G., Pianesi, F., Zancanaro, M. (eds.) UMAP 2009. LNCS, vol. 5535, pp. 295–306. Springer, Heidelberg (2009)
6. Lang, P.J.: The emotion probe: Studies of motivation and attention. American Psychologist 50(5), 372–385 (1995)
7. Pang, B., Lee, L.: Opinion mining and sentiment analysis. Foundation and Trends in Information Retrieval 2(1-2), 1–135 (2008)
8. Russell, J.A.: A circumplex model of affect. Journal of Personality and Social Psychology 39(6), 1161–1178 (1980)
9. Saragih, J.M., Lucey, S., Cohn, J.F.: Deformable model fitting by regularized landmark mean-shift. International Journal of Computer Vision 91(2), 200–2015 (2011)
10. Zheng, V.W., Cao, B., Zheng, Y., Xie, X., Yang, Q.: Collaborative filtering meets mobile recommendation: A user-centered approach. In: Proceedings of the 24th AAAI Conference on Artificial Intelligence, pp. 236–241 (2010)

Panic Room: Experiencing Overload and Having Fun in the Process

Björn Bankowski, Thiemo Clausen, Dirk Ehmen,
Maximilian Ernestus, Henning Hasemann, Tobias Jura,
Alexander Kröller, Dominik Krupke, and Marco Nikander

Technische Universität Braunschweig, Germany
{b.bankowski,t.clausen,d.ehmen,m.ernestus,h.hasemann,t.jura,a.kroeller,
d.krupke,m.nikander}@tu-bs.de

Abstract. We present the "Panic Room", an ambient system in the
form of a game, where a player has to perform an ever-growing number
of parallel tasks until he is overloaded. The game is built in a way to
deduce construction and design principles for pervasive environment, as
it allows for experimenting with design anti-patterns, disguised as game
elements.

1 Introduction

Recent advances in embedded devices allow for a simple integration of everyday
household objects with the Internet, forming the Internet of Things. In the very
near future, smart objects will become ubiquitous, allowing people to build complex ambient intelligence (AmI) systems at very low cost. Such systems could be
used for a number of innovative and everyday tasks, such as influencing human
behavior to help overcome certain disorders [Fog02,KMRA09], help in assisted
living for elderly people [Dem08,GAL]. This requires the user can handle them
properly, even when stressed or overstrained. Important challenges in the design
of such systems are the cognitive, emotional and action-oriented effects on the
user. Many people already feel helpless and stressed when working with traditional computing devices. AmI systems could increase this, with the user feeling
surrounded and controlled by an automatic system. Knowing the associations
between different types of design and the users emotional, cognitive and behavioral responses, is thus essential for designing systems that are accepted by the
user.

The Panic Room is used to study this process, by turning this goal on its
head. It presents itself as a game for one or more players; see Fig. 1. The players
interact with smart objects by performing actions and gestures. According to
the background story, this is necessary to prevent a submarine from sinking.
The game cannot be won however; the submarine always sinks. The objective is
to design the room and the interactions in a way which keep the players engaged
while they are asked to perform more and more tasks, of increasing complexity,
until they are finally overburdened and fail.

N. Streitz and P. Markopoulos (Eds.): DAPI 2014, LNCS 8530, pp. 241–252, 2014.

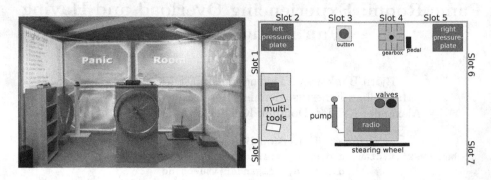

Fig. 1. The Panic Room. Left: View of an entering player. Right: Top-view schematic of object placement.

2 Design

The central goal in the design is to keep the players engaged in what they experience as fun, but at the same time to overload them with an overwhelming number of tasks. To ensure a positive experience however, avoiding frustration or a feeling of powerlessness is absolutely essential. Observing and interviewing players allows drawing conclusions about the influence and rank of different aspects of AmI systems.

In addition to observing players during the game, we interviewed players after the game and tailored the experience to balance the complexity of the game. Our observations allow linking of design choices to reactions, and the deduction of design and construction principles for usable ambient systems.

2.1 Environment

The room consists of three semi-opaque walls, covering a space of about 3×1.5 meters. Back-projection is used to display a submarine interior and an underwater environment on the walls, the overall visual impression was tailored to resemble a playful submarine impression and supported by an acoustic background with watery effects and typical submarine "pings".

Interaction with the system happens through smart objects which were placed at different locations all over the room, in a way that will require the players to move through the room in order to reach different objects. This effect is supported by the console in the center of the room. It constitutes an obstacle that must be walked around when trying to reach other objects.

The projection surface is large enough so it cannot be observed completely by a player interacting with one of the smart objects, which forces players to turn their heads in order to notice all upcoming tasks.

2.2 Smart Objects

All smart objects in the room are battery powered and operate wirelessly. They are robust enough so that a player can interact with them freely without having to be worried about breaking things. In addition to the movable smart objects, the environment is fitted with a number of RFID tags which are hidden at different places to allow device localization. While most objects allow the user to give input to the system by pushing buttons or levers, turning wheels, and even dispositioning objects, some of the objects also provide additional ways of feedback from the system to the player. This is particularly useful when it comes to overloading a player, because it makes it possible to demand the player's attention at different places and/or objects at the same time.

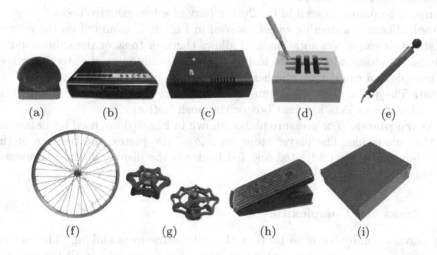

(a)   (b)   (c)   (d)   (e)

(f)   (g)   (h)   (i)

Fig. 2. Smart objects used in the Panic Room: Pushbutton (a), Radio (b), Multitool (c), Gearbox (d), Air Pump (e), Steering Wheel (f), Valves (g), Foot Pedal (h) and Pressure Plate (i)

In total there are twelve objects to interact with, chosen from nine different types:

Push-Button. The push-button object, shown in Fig. 2(a) consists of a large emergency-stop button mounted on a pillar at waist level. Due to its simplicity it is mainly used in introductory tasks and tasks which consist of interactions with multiple objects.

Radio. The radio, as seen in Fig. 2(b), is one of the more complex objects in the room. It is equipped with a card reader, five toggle switches and a rotary knob. The card reader can be used to recognize colored ID cards. It furthermore features a small 2-line text display and a beeper. Altogether the radio allows complex interactions and thus has the potential to draw the user's whole attention to this single object. It is placed on the steering wheel console and is freely movable (although no tasks require it to be moved). Surveying the users revealed that the radio was considered the most "interesting" object, perhaps a consequence of it being the only smart object in the guise of an every-day object.

Multitools. We provide three Multitool objects like the one depicted in Fig. 2(c). These are hand-sized boxes in different colors, especially suitable for moving them around in the whole room. The boxes can detect when they are placed at specific locations within the room. Additionally, each box can determine its orientation. The boxes are equipped with a small push button and a multicolor LED to provide feedback to the player.

Gearbox. The gearbox, shown in Fig. 2(d) is a wooden box with a lever which can assume twelve different positions, mimicking an over-complicated version of the shift-stick in a car.

Pump. The pump, as seen in fig. 2(e) is part of a few exertive tasks.

Wheel. There is a steering wheel, as seen in Fig. 2(f), mounted on the central stand. It can detect rotation, and allows the user to steer the submarine.

Valves. The two valves, shown in Fig. 2(g) are mounted on the steering wheel console and can detect whether they are in an open or closed state.

Pedal. The pedal (Fig. 2(h)) can detect pressure and is used in conjunction with other objects like gear box or the push button.

Pressure plates. The pressure plates, shown in Fig. 2(i) are used for balancing the submarine. The player steps on one of the plates, the balance of the submarine is then adjusted and fed back via the display of the underwater landscape.

2.3 Tasks and Complexities

The players' main task is to prevent the submarine from sinking. The players are given a certain time amount which elapses continuously, until the game is over. The user can increase the remaining time by solving tasks; not solving a task leads to time loss. The total number of concurrent tasks increases during the game so that the player will eventually not be able to complete tasks quickly enough to prevent the time from running out.

At the beginning of the game, the players are given a short series of tutorial tasks to familiarize them with the various smart objects in the room and their associated activities. These tutorial tasks are not intended to be stressful; the players are given as much time as they need to complete them. Once all tutorial tasks have been completed successfully, the actual game begins.

Even at the beginning of the actual game phase, the players are still learning how to play the game. While the objects in the room are now familiar to the players due to the tutorial, the actual tasks which they have to perform, are not all familiar to them (many tasks require interacting with multiple objects for instance). Early testing revealed that some players feel that a lengthy tutorial mode, which presents no challenge as such, is boring, so the remainder of the learning process was integrated into the main phase of the game itself.

Initially only a limited selection of relatively easy modules is present in the pool of modules which can be started. Whenever a task is started which has not been successfully completed by the players a single time yet, it is presented with an explanatory text in addition to the name and image associated with the task. When the task has been completed once, the lengthy explanatory text is left out, leaving the images, the name of the task, and in some cases a short description. The players are thus always presented with a selection of tasks, a few of which are new to them, but most of which are already known. This ensures that already learned tasks are not forgotten, that the players are not totally overwhelmed by a huge number of tasks which are unfamiliar to them, and it ensures continually increasing variety throughout the course of the game.

In general, tasks in the main phase of the game are designed to be very diverse to raise the game's overall complexity. Often more than one object is involved and the tasks' character reaches from being permanently in background ('avoid obstacles') over short-timed ones ('press the button 10 times') to tasks requiring object movement ('put the red box into the blue shelf'). Deliberately confusing tasks (*do not press the button*") are also started in order to increase cognitive load and further confuse the player. Due to the tasks complexity, sound is not used to announce them. Acoustic feedback however is given to indicate success or failure after the task ended. A tasks complexity is defined by various influences:

Task Announcement. Most of the tasks are presented as a box on wall with a short text and up to two pictures. These boxes "fall down" to indicate the task's deadline if any. The radio uses a beeper and its small display to announce radio-related tasks. Obstacles are announced by a calm but salient voice.

Cognitive Complexity. The amount of thinking required to understand and perform tasks varies from task to task ('enter a number sequence by gear' is much more difficult to accomplish than 'shake the multitool').

Spatial Extent. Some tasks involve no movement while some (e.g. 'shift gear then press button') require moving several meters or even make the player search for objects.

Duration. While some tasks can be solved in a sub-second interval some take a lot of time. Tasks with long duration can be further subdivided into long continuous actions (the pumping task) and tasks that do not necessarily require constant action but constant attention ('use pedal to keep speed in a specific zone', using the steering wheel to avoid obstacles).

Besides the tasks posed to the user, the system creates overload by several other means as well:

Locus. The locus of tasks announcements widens over time: Initially all tasks are presented in the center of the front wall; later on all of the wall space is used, as is a small display on the radio.

Parallelism. The number of parallel requests increases from one to about 8 during the course of a game.

Task Difficulty. The cognitive complexity of tasks increases: Initial tasks are
very simple ("press the red button"), whereas later tasks require more processing and complex actions ("shift gear to 8, then press button", "do *not*
press the red button", "hold the red box against all hull screws until the
scanner shows red, then repair by clicking").

Time Pressure. Each task is given a deadline in which the user has to solve
it. After deadline expiration the tasks is considered failed and the remaining
time is decreased.

Immersion. Due to shape and size of the room and projective walls, the experience is designed to be immersive in the sense that the field of vision of
the player is usually completely covered with tasks and game objects, while
still ensuring an unthreatening experience by always allowing the player to
naturally step backwards out of the room.

Audio. An increasing amount of alarm sounds, explosions, and countdowns
further distract the player.

We will now briefly introduce our game tasks. Where not otherwisely stated,
tasks will be announced via task announcement textboxes on the projection walls
and have to be completed within a given timeout.

Switches. The radio will display a switch configuration which the player has to
set up on the radio. This task is communicated only through the radio.

Pump. A bubble is displayed which gets bigger with pumping until it bursts.

Balance. The submarine is tilted to one side and the player has to step on the
opposite pressure plate to rebalance it.

Shake, Shake2. The player has to shake one or two multitool boxes.

Charge Multitool. A multitool has to be hold against a power symbol on a
specific position. The position is shown in the task announcement.

Listen. A specific multitool has to be hold to the players ear.

Steer Tasks, Shift and Steer. There will be different commands like 'steer
to the left' or 'hold the steer' or 'engage gear X and use the steering wheel'.

Shelf. A specific multitool has to be put onto a specific place in the shelf,
marked by different colors.

Authorization. Out of a set of authorization cards the correct one has to be
chosen and placed on the radio. Additionally the switch configuration on the
card has to be entered. This Task is solely communicated via the radio.

Radio Switches. The rotary knob on the radio has to be turned into a specific
direction.

Radio Tune. The radio will display a relative signal quality. The player has to
find the right rotary knob position to achieve a signal quality of 100%. This
Task is solely communicated via the radio.

Gear. Different gears have to be shifted in the correct order.

Gear and Pedal. A gear has to be engaged while holding the foot pedal.

Button x10. The Push Button has to be hit 10 times.

Button Confusion. The player can do what he wants, but not press the Push
Button. The resource manager will ensure that no tasks require a button
press as long as this task is active.

Pedal. A gauge is displayed in the lower right corner of the front wall, the player
has to control the pedal in order to keep the gauge in a defined range.

Power Failure. The walls will tint red and the user has to press a button to
end the situation. Will not influence the time account.

3 Technical Background

In order to provide an immersive experience, Smart Objects in the panic room
need to be able to robustly detect events without delay such that they be processed by the game logic and turned into visual feedback. Even slighly noticable
delays or inconsistent behavior due to faults would immedietaly disrupt the
game experince. In this section we present our Smart object hardware and the
accompaning software stack that obeys these constraints.

3.1 Smart Objects

The interactive objects contain sensors and actuators, connected to an Arduino [Ban05] microcontroller platform. Each object contains a custom set of
sensors such as accelerometers, buttons, light and pressure sensors and their respective electronic interfaces in addition to the battery. The location of movable
objects can be determined using embedded RFID modules. Sensor data is pre-
processed by the embedded device to ensure a reliable and responsive wireless
connection to the server, using a fast, interaction-based protocol which is also
used for hardware-control (e.g. writing data to a display or activating a beeper).

The low-level connection is established using wireless 2,4 GHz XBee modules
using the 802.15.4 protocol [IEE11] in a point-to-point topology. Each object is
powered by a lithium polymer battery, allowing runtimes of up to three hours.

3.2 Software Architecture

Communication. The micro controllers communicate with the server using
custom middleware, which not only handles all of the communication, but also
provides plug-and-play sensor management and failure handling. In order to
provide quick reaction times and convey the feeling that player actions have an
immediate effect, we developed a lightweight protocol, tailored for short response
times. The protocol also provides auto-configuration of the smart objects and
high reliability communications.

The protocol not only defines message types for sensor data, but also for
maintenance purposes such as low power warnings or confirming that an object
is still functioning. Each sensor type is managed by a driver which handles the
sensor specific messages and provides sensor objects with a high level API to the
game application. The server automatically uses the matching driver to create
sensor objects, which can be used by the various game modules from then on.

When a game module requires sensor data, it requests a sensor object and
registers a listener for the event it is interested in. The middleware transfers this
listener to the micro controllers, which will respond as soon as the event occurs.

Error Handling. Since all of our smart objects are battery-powered, communicate wirelessly with the server and are exposed to the players, some failures and faults are inevitable. Player actions which remain unprocessed due to faults with the hardware would disrupt the immersive game experience and have to be detected and handled. If an Arduino fails to send three consecutive *Alive* messages, sent every 50ms, then the Arduino and all its sensors are considered temporally unavailable. Any running tasks which require the unavailable sensors are aborted, and modules which require those sensors can then no longer be started. As soon as the connection is re-established, the server notifies the Smart Object about the decisions it made due to the failure.

Resource Management and Scheduling. To avoid conflicting use of a single sensor device (e.g. by different tasks using the same object), tasks have to request the abstract sensor objects from the resource manager. Since tasks that only require a few sensors to run are more likely to get their resource demands fulfilled instantly, a scheduler takes special care of tasks with more dependencies, ensuring the desired balance of complex and simple tasks. If a task was not able to start for a certain amount of time because the needed resources were blocked by other game modules, the scheduler will correct the situation by not allowing other tasks to allocate the demanded resources. This way, the overdue task gets the chance to execute. The scheduler starts with a small pool of simple tasks, which is extended by new, more complex tasks one at a time, so the player does not have to learn multiple new tasks at a once in short succession.

Graphics. The graphical interface which is projected on the walls is implemented using the Java Processing framework [pro01]. Graphical objects are rendered in three different layers, dependant on their role in the game:

The topmost layer displays the task announcements. Each announcement consists of a box with text and images that explain to the player what needs to be done in order to solve the task. It appears at the top of the screen, falls down and has to be completed before it reaches the bottom.

The middle layer shows the interior of the submarine consisting of windows, control panels and other decorative elements. Its purpose is to simulate the submarine environment, but no direct user interaction with this layer is possible. A simple physics engine, based on verlet integration [Ver67], is used to gradually destroy the interior of the submarine. First the elements of the interior become partially detached from the 'walls' of the submarine, and start to swing with the movements of the submarine. Later they become completely free and move about within the submarine, according to its movement, to distract the players.

The background layer is rendered in 3D using OpenGL [SA94] and shows the underwater environment which can be seen through the windows of the submarine. The submarine is cruising through a landscape of hills that need to be evaded by the player, to avoid time penalties and damage to the submarine. Besides the partially broken interior elements which are swinging around, the tilting horizon is the main visual clue of the rocking movements of the submarine. Tilting of the submarine is induced by interactions with the pressure plates, collisions with undersea mountains or special tasks that involve restoring the horizontal trim.

4 Observations

Data was collected by integrating a logger routine into the system for recording when the player succeeds or fails at a task. Additionally, players were asked to wear a pulse and blood oxygen analyzer in form of a fingerclip during gameplay which would allow us to get an indication of the physical effects of the game.

Players were also asked to fill in a questionnaire after having played the game. Capturing a video of each game (with allowance of the players) enabled us to analyze individual game situations and behaviors in detail.

4.1 Observations per Game

To get an idea of a typical run of a game we compiled the data from all the games into a single "average game" shown in Figure 3. The tutorial mode was cut out, an average number of active tasks was computed, and the pulse data was averaged into a single typical pulse curve. The increasing pulse shows, that using the Panic Room affects the players physical and/or emotional state to a degree that is measurable with a biomedical pulse sensor. Although the total number of tasks increases over the course of the game, the number of solved tasks stays constant, indicating the existence of an upper bound beyond which the players cannot perform better, despite increasing load.

Contrary to our initial assumptions, players did not primarily focus on the tasks appearing on the front wall. The screens haven been vertically divided into slots as seen in Figure 1. We recorded the failure rates of tasks depending on the slot they were announced in. The result is shown in Figure 4. The failure rate for slot 3 stands out notably low. This can be explained by the fact that the big red push-button, which is part of many tasks, is placed right in front of it and that most of the interactive objects in the room are within the range of a lunge, when standing right in front of slot 3. We thus suspect that players tend to focus on tasks announced close to their current position and will avoid moving.

4.2 Observations per Tasks

Figure 5 lists a ranking of the failure rates of the different tasks, depending on the phase of the game. We observe that the ranking of high-failing tasks changes drastically between the two game phases: For instance *Authorization*, one of the most complex and time-consuming tasks had a higher success rate in the later game. Steering tasks on the other hand seem to decrease in success rate. Since these two tasks are usually – due to the location of their respective

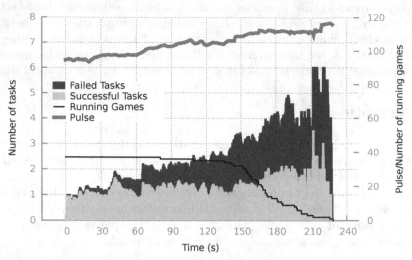

Fig. 3. An average game. The filled curves show the average number of visible tasks on the screen depending on the duration of the game. The portion of those tasks that were eventually solved is indicated in green. Not all games lasted equally long, thus data from later game phases averages over fewer samples.

objects – executed by the same person, this could indicate that the attention has shifted from observing the landscape and avoiding obstacles, to explicit task announcements. This impression is supported by the observation that the failure rates of the other tasks involving the radio have also become better or at the very least stayed similar, in spite of the higher overall task load.

The *Gear* and *Pedal* tasks increase in success rate, while the combined tasks using the gear has become worse. This could be explained by the fact that most of the combined tasks such as *Gear and Button* or *Shift and Steer* , where the objects are located remote, are done cooperatively, which becomes more difficult with increasing game speed.

The failure rate of *Button Confusion* has gone to zero, either meaning that it is ignored in a high-load situation or indicating a training effect on the players.

The Task *Listen* has become the worst of all although there are more complex tasks utilizing the multitools. This could indicate that the players perceive the task as more involving or demanding more commitment due to the incorporation of other body parts. It is also possible that the players are confused by the fact that although they are asked to listen, the multitool will not produce any sound.

We categorize tasks by "Task Announcement", "Cognitive Complexity", "Spatial Extent" and "Duration" as mentioned in Chapter 2.3. Figure 6 shows the resulting failure rates grouped by these categories. In the earlier phase of the game (before 2.5 minutes) when less tasks are active simultaneously a ranking of influences to the failure rate can be seen. It is most important that the task is communicated to the players in a clear manner. If they are not aware of the task, they are not able to perform it, and it is counted as "failed" in that case. The tasks' content is less important: If they are easy to understand, do not last

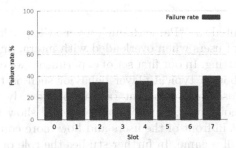

Fig. 4. Failure rates per slot during seconds 75 to 150. See Fig. 1 for slot placement.

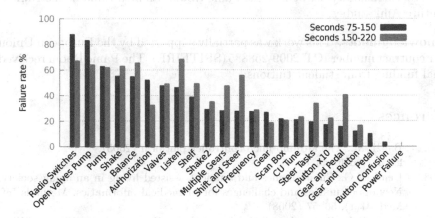

Fig. 5. Failure rate by task (second 75 - 150 and second 150 - 220)

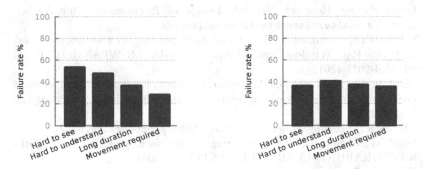

Fig. 6. Failure rates by category (second 75 - 150 and second 150 - 220)

too long, and do not require movement (in this order) their possibility of being accomplished increases. In the later game parts of the game (after 2.5 minutes) the influence of these factors on the failure rate seems to be almost equal. This is caused by the fact that players get to know the tasks and learn how to solve them efficiently.

5   Conclusion

In this work we presented the "Panic Room", a versatile platform that allows to observe the reaction of users when overloaded with interacting with ubiquitous systems in a playful setting. In our first set of experiments we could already draw several conclusions about a typical player behavior such as the average player being able to solve tasks at a constant rate independently from the load by ignoring spatially remote tasks. Furthermore we could show the importance of task descriptions right in front of the users and how more complex tasks can be learned in the course of a game. In further studies the role of acoustic feedback for the user experience in overload situtaions could be evaluated in more detail. Due to its extensibility, we believe the Panic Room can be a valuable instrument for future AmI studies.

Acknowledgments. This work was partially supported by the European Union under contract number ICT-2009-258885 (SPITFIRE). The Panic Room received partial funding from student tuitions.

References

Ban05.   Banzi, M.: The arduino microcontroller platform (2005),
           http://arduino.cc/
Dem08.   Demiris, G.: Smart homes and ambient assisted living in an aging society.
           New opportunities and challenges for biomedical informatics. Methods Inf.
           Med. 47(1), 56–57 (2008)
Fog02.   Fogg, B.J.: Persuasive Technology: Using Computers to Change What
           We Think and Do (Interactive Technologies), 1st edn. Morgan Kaufmann
           (December 2002)
GAL.   Lower Saxony Research Network Design of Environments for Ageing,
           http://www.altersgerechte-lebenswelten.de
IEE11.   IEEE. IEEE Standard for Local and metropolitan area networks – Part
           15.4: Low-Rate Wireless Personal Area Networks (LR-WPANs). IEEE Std
           802.15.4-2011 (2011)
KMRA09.   Kaptein, M., Markopoulos, P., Ruyter, B., Aarts, E.: Persuasion in ambient
           intelligence. Journal of Ambient Intelligence and Humanized Computing (1),
           43–56 (2009)
pro01.   The Java Processing Framework (2001), http://processing.org/
SA94.   Segal, M., Akeley, K.: The opengl graphics interface. Technical report, SIL-
           ICON GRAPHICS COMPUTER SYSTEMS (1994)
Ver67.   Verlet, L.: Computer "experiments" on classical fluids. i. thermodynamical
           properties of lennard-jones molecules. Phys. Rev. 159, 98–103 (1967)

Ontology Based Simulation Framework: Studying of Human Behavior Changes Impacted by Accessibility of Information under Building Fire Emergency

Chaianun Damrongrat and Mitsuru Ikeda

School of Knowledge Science
Japan Advanced Institute of Science and Technology, Ishikawa, Japan 923-1211
{chaianun.d,ikeda}@jaist.ac.jp
http://www.springer.com/lncs

Abstract. In gerneal, human behavior under emergency situation is considered as irrational behavior. However, recent research studies showed that evacuees had rational decision making process even though they said they were panic at that time. Evacuees behaved rationally based on information they could access at that moment and then selected the best option for response. This research is interested in relationship between human behavior and accessibility of informaiton under the restricted information situation, emergency in this case. We propose an ontology-based simulation framework as a tool to find out the relationship. Even though it is hard to claim that human will behave as same as the simulation outcome, we could study the relationship by observing trend and tendency of human behavior changes in the simulation by varying simulation parameters. For this purpose, the simulation models should be easy to modify. Then ontology plays a key component for this issue.

Keywords: ontology based simulation, human behavior, accessibility of information, emergency situation, restricted information.

1 Introduction

In restricted information situation, such as a building fire emergency, there were many people injured and died because they did not know and/or overlooked vital information [1],[2]. In this such situation, people should evacuate to safe places as fast as they could. However, due to the lack of accessible information, incorrect information and time limit, this situation is hard for evacuees to make a right decision to respond the situation effectively.

Research studies showed that occupants behave rationally under emergency. Some behaviors might look irrationally and hesitantly but that was because they were lack of important information in their hand. It made they had a hard time to make a good decision. Research experiment showed that ones who did not know where the emergency exits were will escape to the entrance they entered

N. Streitz and P. Markopoulos (Eds.): DAPI 2014, LNCS 8530, pp. 253–261, 2014.

even though there was a nearer emergency exit in the area. On the other hand, ones who know the information of emergency exits selected to escape by the nearest exit [2], [3]. This showed that occupants responded differently if they have different accessibility of information.

This research interested to know how accessibility of information can make an impact to human behavior. We have a hypothesis following existing findings that occupants have rational behavior under the critical situation [4], [5], [6]. They react based on the information they have at that time. In another word, their behavior is based on accessibility of information. To extend the existing findings, we aims to find hidden relationship among human behaviors changes and accessibility of information under restricted information situation. This research proposes an ontology-based simulation framework to find the relationship between human behavior and accessibility of information under restricted-information situation. We use an indoor building fire emergency as an example for our research domain. Even though we could not claim that human behavior will react exactly the same as simulation outcome; however, we could find trend or tendency of human behavior changes by varying simulation parameters. Since the research study is rely on tendency of the simulation outcome, it is better to have an approach that flexible enough in modifying the behavior models. Then the ontology is used in this research describing models of human behaviors and environment's character such as fire development. The ontology is mainly used for three purposes. The first is a tool to transfer knowledge from domain experts such as interviewing of fire fighters or safety guidelines to become machine-readable data which is used in simulation system. The second is using ontology reasoning to find the hidden relation among human behavior and accessibility of information. The last one is flexibility of reusing and sharing knowledge. We can edit or change situation model or behavior model easily with new ontology. Moreover, this ontology-based simulation framework could be used as a tool to verify hypotheses of finding relationship among an accessibility of information, human behavior and critical situation in different interested problem.

Understanding this relationship could help us, researchers, to understand how to maximise benefit of accessibility of information effectively. For example, in a limited time and resources we cannot provide all information the sensors have to occupants. The knowing could point out what type of information is a vital information and when to provide that information to the right ones who need them to escape the emergency.

2   Human Behavior under Emergency

Human behavior under emergency, in general, is considered as irrational behavior because of panic. However, research studies showed that evacuees in an indoor emergency took action with rational behavior based on information they had at that time even though they said themselves they were panic at that moment [4], [5], [6].

2.1 Behaviors under Overloading Information Situation and Restricted Information Situation

Research studies on human behavior under overloading information situation mostly based on research of natural disasters. People tried to contact to others for informing and checking current situation from the both ends of communication [7] [8]. This behavior might not so relate with this research because natural disaster and building fire have different characters. However, it could reflex some problem of human behavior under rich information situation. Another case study is overuse the alarms could make people immune and ignore them when the emergency is really happened [9]. This showed that individuals have behavior to ignore the information if they believe the information is abused. For restricted information situation, there are many research studies and reports showed that evacuees tried to escape the emergency by the main entrances or normally-used exits but overlooked the emergency exits which might be nearer ones [2], [3], [10].

2.2 Human Behavior in Psychological Perspective

Research studies showed that there are many behaviors the evacuees might express under the critical situation. For example, herding behavior and altruistic behavior. Herding behavior is often observed during an evacuation of a room, for example, with two exits. One exit is crowded with evacuees while another exit is not fully utilized. There were many event that herding behavior happened such as a fire in the Station nightclub, 211 Cowesett Anenue, West Warwick, Rhode Island which the evacuees tried to escape by the main entrance of the building and caused approximately one hundred people died [10]. Altruistic behavior is happened when the individual feel empathy to another. The individuals are more willing to help ones in need if they observed that others initiate help [11]. However, these behaviors require to observe other individuals' behavior. This research will focus on modeling an individual behavior, and will let the social behavior in the future work.

3 Methodology

To studying the human behavior changes impacted by accessibility of information, we propose a simulation framework which use ontology to enhance an ability of modifying the behavior models. To find out what are the behavior changes, we have to compare two simulation outcomes. These two simulations have to processed under the same controlled set of simulation parameters such as agents properties, decision making process, group size of agents and environment's properties. The only difference between the two simulations is level of information accessibility. One simulation has limited accessibility of information, another one has better level of information accessibility.

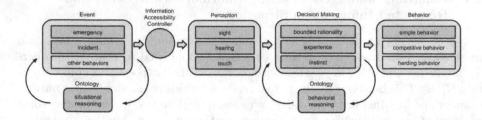

Fig. 1. In this simulation framework we focus on individual behavior only, as be showed with dark blue color. Behavior interacting with social such as competitive behavior or herding behavior are not include in this research study yet, as be showed with light blue color. Ontology is used to model the emergency situation, simple behavior such as avoiding to be close to dangerous area, and model the consequence of emergency situation and human behavior by its reasoning. In this research we are interested in how information accessibility have impacted to human behavior. Then we have a module controlling level of information to human agents in simulation.

3.1   Simulation Framework

In studying relationship between human behavior and information accessibility, we have intension to propose a simulation framework which flexible enough to handle to evaluate new hypotheses. This means the framework should be comfort to modify modules such as behavior models. To achieve this purpose we embeded ontology to the existing study to utilize the advantages of ontology such as flexibility of modifying the human behavior models, reuse and reshare knowledge in the framework. The research study proposed a process model describing emergency behaviors has four major modules, cues or event, perception, decision making and behavior [12] as showed in Fig.1. Without ontology module, the simulation framework would be highly depend on modelers or domain experts who normally might not familiar with IT such as simulation model. Ontology could be a tool to overcome this gap because it is a human-and-machine readable language. Since this research focus on study relationship between individual behavior and information accessibility. The social behaviors, as showed in light blue in Fig.1, will be omit at this time.

3.2   Ontology

This simulation framework uses ontology to model an agent behavior, relationship among agents, relationship between agent and environment. For example, an agent should avoid to go to dangerous areas. However, this research is an initial state of using this framework, the complex concept models are not applied to this work yet. In the near future we could utilize the benefit of using ontology to conceptualize knowledge to make more complex model. Moreover, ontology is good to separate domain knowledge from the operation knowledge [13]. This means we can define our behavior model more complex and more realistic from assistance of domain experts such as fire fighters who may not well understanding how the simulation system works. Without ontology, the domain experts may have to understand how the system works while making a new model. It is not convenient for domain experts and take time.

Ontology Design. The research goal is to study the relationship among human behavior and information accessibility under a critical situation. However, this research considers on individual behavior. The interaction behavior among agents will be left to the future work. This section describe how the ontology is designed. The ontology is used to describe concepts of human behavior, information accessibility and critical situation, respectively. The overview ontology is showed in Fig.2 which some social behaviors in the fureture work are prepared. In this paper, the individual behavior is considered based on what behaviors that an agent can do in the simulation. The two main behaviors are *Avoid* and *Escape*. An agent should have behavior to avoid dangerous places, and should escape to safe places in evacuation. After that we consider what the information accessibility is. We make a *Perception* concept to describe how to access information. However, this research considers on the simple simulation. The information accessibility in this research is not complex yet. It is only on and off statement. For the critical situation, we have to define concepts of *Dangerous* and *Safe* to define dangerous place and safe place in the simulation. In this paper, we define fire as relating to danger. Any place with fire is a dangerous place, otherwise is safe place.

3.3   Simulation Methods

There are some research studies related to evacuation in emergency situation. Crowd behavior was proposed to represent the human behavior under emergency. Research studies compared human behavior with fluid and particle motion analogy [14]. However, Later studies showed that fluid analogies of crowd were untenable[15]. Herding behavior was proposed instead based on the observation that in a room with two exits, one exit was clogged while the other was not fully utilized [16]. This behavior represents human behavior in real situation which the fluid analogy model could not explain this behavior properly. These research studies focus on social behavior. They required high computational power since the model had to concern about each agents movement in the simulation environment and interaction among agents. To avoid the high computation of agents' movement, another model such as matrix-based simulation was proposed [17]. it discretized a floor area into cells. This approach was simple and easy to understand to model the environment scene; however, the model highly depended on the modelers skill. In our research we attempt to use simple part of a small unit, such as behavior of an individual agent, to explain complex phenomena. This research do not consider about the detail of how an agents movement is in the simulation environment. We consider the outcome of its action such as

Fig. 2. The overview of ontology design in this research

an agent A move from room R_a to room R_b with time T_1. Rooms and entire building elements are represented in node-based representation [18]. The building elements such as rooms, corridors and exits, are considered and modeled on their physical accessibility. For example, room R_a physically connects to room R_b as showed in Fig.4. In this simulation, each agent has the same behavior and decision making process. Behavior model is described by an ontology which is comfortable to change when we want to edit the behavior model.

Simulation Scenario. This scenario aims to find the impact of accessibility of information toward human behavior changes. In the simulation, an evacuee is represented as an agent in simulation system. The agent assumed to be able to make a decision based on information it has at that time to respond the emergency situation. To find out the behavior changes impacted by information accessibility, this research observes the different outcomes between two simulation set. The first simulation set represents behaviors of evacuees whom can access necessary and updated information. For example, knowing of location of emergency exits and how the fire development is. The second simulation set is ones who can access limited and/or outdated of information. For example, knowing only some nor completely no idea of emergency exit locations, and knowing of an outdated of fire development in twenty minutes ago.

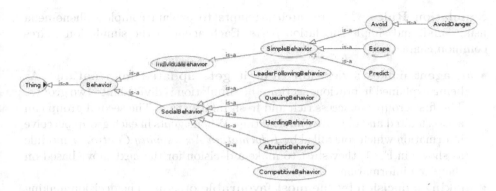

Fig. 3. Example of ontology design describing behavior concept in this simulation framework. However, in this research we focus on only IndividualBehavior.

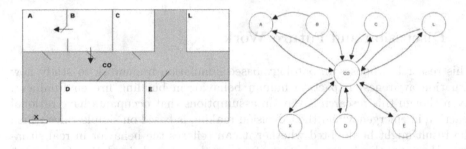

Fig. 4. The building's elements are modeled based on their accessibility [18]. A node represents to an element of building. For example, a floor plan has rooms A, B, C, D, E, elevator L, corridor CO and an exit X which are represented their physical accessibility graph.

Simulation Parameters. In the real emergency situation, there are many factors that is hard to be predicted or calculated in advance. For example, fire development's speed, processing time for an individual to take for a decision making. We design these factors as adjustable parameters in the simulation. Some parameters are described as the following list below.

- **time limit** - exceeded time means the building is too dangerous to survive. In that case, remaining individuals who got stuck in the building are fail to escape the building fire.
- **individuals information processing time** - each individual requires a period of time to process information they have to make a decision. The more information an individual perceive, the more processing time it take.
- **fire development** - it is a speed of fire spreading from one location to neighbor locations. All fire in the building have the same speed.

Simulation Rules. This research attempts to explain complex phenomena using small and simple simulation parts. Each agent in the simulation shares common characters.

- **an agent makes a decision right it gets updated information** - As being explained in previous section, the simulation is divided into two groups. The first group can access rich and fresh information. The second group can access limited and outdated information. When agents in each group perceive information which controlled by *Information Accessibility Controller* module as shown in Fig.1, they start to make a decision for the next move based on the given information.
- **making a decision by the most favourable option** - The decision making process will scan for all possible options an individual has, then predict the consequence for each option, and finally select the most favourable option. The criteria to make a decision is described in the ontology. For example, to avoid dangerous places and select the shortest path to the nearest safe exit.

4   Discussion and Future Work

This research proposes an ontology based simulation framework to study how situation awareness impact to human behavior in building fire environment. Even though this research is rely on assumptions that occupants have rational reaction in emergency and their decision making is based on simple rules which the result might be doubted whether it can reflexes the behavior in real situation. However, this is a good start of an ontology based simulation framework for studying human behavior changes impacted by information accessibility in an indoor emergency. In the near future, we can improve the rules to handle with more complex condition. Using ontology also has advantage of reuse and sharing knowledge from experts or other existing research studies. These make this research more flexible to adapt with different study purposes. For example, studying other information affecting human behavior, what will happen if occupants have some preference such as prefer to help other impaired occupants and evacuate the building together. These issues can be done by changing ontology and simulation rules. Moreover, the more understanding of relationship between human behavior and information accessibility could improve the indoor sensing technology in the near future. For example, under the critical situation which each individual could not process all information with the limited time. This knowledge might help us to prioritize which typ of information is the vital information to escape the emergency.

References

1. Hasofer, A.M., Thomas, I.: Analysis of fatalities and injuries in building fire statistics. Fire Safety Journal 41(1), 2–14 (2006)
2. Ouellette, M.: Visibility of exit signs. Progressive Architecture 74(7), 39–42 (1993)

3. Kobes, M., Helsloot, I., de Vries, B., Post, J.G., Oberijé, N., Groenewegen, K.: Way finding during fire evacuation; An analysis of unannounced fire drills in a hotel at night. Building and Environment 45(3), 537–548 (2010)
4. Kobes, M., Helsloot, I., de Vries, B., Post, J.G.: Building safety and human behaviour in fire: A literature review. Fire Safety Journal 45(1), 1–11 (2010)
5. Fahy, R.F., Proulx, G.: Human behavior in the world trade center evacuation. In: Fire Safety Science–Proceedings of the Fifth International Symposium, pp. 713–724 (1998)
6. Fahy, R.F., Proulx, G., Aiman, L.: Panic or not in fire: Clarifying the misconception. Fire and Materials 36(5-6), 328–338 (2012)
7. Manoj, B.S., Baker, A.H.: Communication challenges in emergency response. Communications of the ACM 50(3), 51–53 (2007)
8. Vanderford, M.L., Nastoff, T., Telfer, J.L., Bonzo, S.E.: Emergency communication challenges in response to hurricane katrina: Lessons from the centers for disease control and prevention. Journal of Applied Communication Research 35(1), 9–25 (2007)
9. Joe Wilson, F.S.: Addressing diverse human behavior issues in the new era of multi-layered emergency communications. Copyright: 9-1-1 Magazine, Feature Content, http://www.federalsignal-indust.com/news/addressing-diverse-human-behavior-issues-new-era-multi-layered-emergency-communications
10. Grosshandler, W.L., Bryner, N., Madrzykowski, D., Kuntz, K.: Report of the technical investigation of the station nightclub fire. National Institute of Standards and Technology Gaithersburg, MD (2005)
11. Batson, C.D., Powell, A.A.: Altruism and prosocial behavior. In: Handbook of Psychology (2003)
12. Pan, X.: Computational modeling of human and social behaviors for emergency egress analysis. PhD thesis, Stanford University (2006)
13. Noy, N.F., McGuinness, D.L., et al.: Ontology development 101: A guide to creating your first ontology (2001)
14. Helbing, D., Farkas, I., Vicsek, T.: Simulating dynamical features of escape panic. Nature 407(6803), 487–490 (2000)
15. Still, G.K.: Crowd dynamics. PhD thesis, University of Warwick (2000)
16. Low, D.J.: Statistical physics: Following the crowd. Nature 407(6803), 465–466 (2000)
17. Ketchell, N., Holt, A., Kinsella, K.: A technical summary of the aea egress code. tech. rep., Tech. Rep. 1, AEA Technology (2002)
18. Damrongrat, C., Kanai, H., Ikeda, M.: Increasing situational awareness of indoor emergency simulation using multilayered ontology-based floor plan representation. In: Yamamoto, S. (ed.) HIMI/HCII 2013, Part II. LNCS, vol. 8017, pp. 39–45. Springer, Heidelberg (2013)

My Smart TV Agent: Designing Smart TV Persona for Linguistic UX

Seyeon Lee, Jiwon Moon, Hokyoung Im, Chung-Kon Shi, and Bong Gwan Jun

Graduate School of Culture Technology, KAIST
291 Daehak-ro(373-1 Guseong-dong), Yuseong-gu, Daejeon 305-701, South Korea
{birdkite,moon.jiwon,imagine21c,bonggwan,chungkon}@kaist.ac.kr

Abstract. Linguistic UX design for Smart TV has been creating much heap as a means of new TV control. Since human voice displays powerful social presence, the issue with defining a Smart TV agent that interacts with users has a big impact in users' satisfaction. The purpose of this study is to analyze the linguistic patterns in vocal commands of TV users and to suggest underlying personas of Smart TV agent that appears when users interact with a Smart TV. First, we analyzed most common TV viewing situations and the patterns of users' behavior through a survey. Then, we collected 867 vocal data through a cultural probe method in which 10 families, each representing a typical type of TV viewers, by asking them to record what they would like to say to the TV while watching it for about a week. We suggest 6 different type of Smart TV personas, such as expert, assistant, colleague, slave, machine and pet, based on the relationship that the user and TV exhibited. With the collected vocal data, we analyzed the participants' speech pattern and style to examine which type of Smart TV persona was most prevalent. As a result, there were slight difference in types that emerged according different functions of Smart TV and we found that the assistant type appeared most frequently followed by the colleague type.

Keywords: Affective communication, Smart TV agent, Linguistic UX, Voice command.

1 Introduction

We no longer expect our TV to just change the channel and adjust the volume for us. TVs can now perform a lot more functions with the birth of Smart TV which is capable of bringing the internet to the TV screen [1]. However, it is difficult to encourage users to actively engage with them just because there are more functions to operate since TV is the longest standing Lean Back media in people's mind. That is why there is a steady effort to find the most appropriate way to encourage users to engage in active control of TV utilizing a touch remote control, a motion control, smartphones, motion capture and vocal command etc.

The most attractive attribute of vocal command technology is that users can easily pick it up without particular training. However, at the moment, it fails to meet the standard people expect to get from the experience. Of course, the level of communication

N. Streitz and P. Markopoulos (Eds.): DAPI 2014, LNCS 8530, pp. 262–271, 2014.

with high level of cognitive ability to understand context only existed between human to human communications. Therefore, users will experience something different when commanding TV using vocal communication compared to using a remote control or a key board.

For linguistic UX design, there is a strong emphasis in affective approach based on the understanding of human psychology and behavior. The machine that is interacting with the user is now perceived as a machine that can understand the user's intent and communicate with a personality [2]. Then, which persona of Smart TV most likely to satisfy the user and overcome the barrier of uncanny valley? What type of relationship should this persona (or the agent) should represent? The goal of this research is to look at different types of implied listener that seems to appear in the communication process between the user and Smart TV. Also, we will suggest appropriate persona of the TV agent that the users will be most likely to be satisfied with.

2 User - Smart TV Relationship

According to Chatman, S.B., there is a certain narrative-communication situation model that describes the author and the reader in story and discourse [3]. In case of users' effort to vocally command Smart TV, there is an implied speaker and a listener representing the user and the Smart TV. It can be said that this implied listener who implements what user wants as the agent inside of a Smart TV. Then, how can we define the relationship between the user and the Smart TV agent?

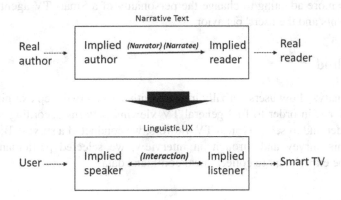

Fig. 1. "Narrative-Communication Situation Model" applied in linguistic UX for Smart TV

The human-computer relationship can be described with three examples: One-up vs. One-down vs. One-across. First, by One-down they argued that the computer is just another tool and that it should just follow the command of the user. Secondly, One-up implies that the computer is a master with high knowledge that is able to carry out difficult things the user cannot otherwise. Finally, One-across suggests a team-work between the computer and the user come together equally as a team [4]. In this case, the researchers found out that the user and the computer felt a sense of connectedness [5]. Such relationship between a user and a computer can be defined by the language the users use when interacting with a computer. Therefore, through a linguistic analysis of TV viewers' situation, we can examine how the users of Smart TV define their relationship with the machine.

Personalities of Smart TV agent are also important for building a relationship with the users, and it can also affect user satisfaction. Among five important factors of defining personalities that psychologists suggested [6], the two most important categories of media personalities are categories like dominance/submissiveness and friendliness/unfriendliness [4] [7] [8]. Users will show different types of speech style according to not only their own personality but also in accordance to the personality of the Smart TV agent they interact with. This is relevant to the suggested relationship between the Smart TV and the users. For example, if a Smart TV shows dominant trait over the user, the user will respond with more respectful tone of speech and if submissiveness is the set personality of the machine, then users will talk down or use direct commands. When the Smart TV displays friendliness, users will use intimate style of speech and not when the machine shows unfriendliness. Therefore, we can figure out the personality of the Smart TV agent when we look into the words and speech style of the TV users.

In addition to specify the persona of a Smart TV, factors such as gender and age must be examined. It is typical of users to respond in regard to their own stereotype that differs by gender and age of the counterpart [9]. This is why it is important to find which gender and age would be most appropriate for a Smart TV agent in order to satisfy the expectation of the users. In this line of examination, we need to look at whether it is more adapting to change the personality of a Smart TV agent according the TV contents and the users' behavior.

3   Method

In order to analyze how users verbally interact with a TV, a two-step examination was conducted. First, in order to find general TV viewing patterns according to viewers' age and gender and to select typical TV viewers, we conducted a survey. Based on the results of this survey and through an interview, we selected participants for our cultural probe experiment to collect vocal command data.

3.1   Survey

An online survey was released aimed at gathering data on TV viewers' behavior and the choice of content inherent to the moment of watching TV based on age and gender. For 2 weeks, 173 participants (m: 76, f: 97) each described 5 most common TV viewing behaviors at home. We were able to collect 722 data on TV viewing situation and observed different type of TV viewing behavior based on age and gender.

We divided TV viewers into 9 groups according to their age and explored which type of TV programs were most frequently watched by each group, with whom, and what they usually did when they were watching TV. As for the children under 10, kids programs were most frequently watched with their parents accompanying them. For teenagers, they usually played games or spent time engaging with social networking services while watching TV. Many in their 20's and 30's said that their TV was on during resting moments at home, before going to bed and while eating as well. Gender divided the preference of TV programs among young people with sports/game and entertaining TV contents preferred by males and drama and entertainment programs for women. As for men in their 40's, many watched the news. Women in their 50's watched drama with an exceptionally high preference. Based on these results and interviews, we recruited participants who showed similar typical TV viewing patterns and conducted a Cultural Probe Research.

3.2   Cultural Probe Research

In order to extract natural voice commands from participants as if they were interacting with a Smart TV in real life, cultural probe methodology was utilized to collect such data. Cultural probe methodology is a useful way to collect data by allowing participants to record their own behavior, situations and their ideas freely in everyday lives [10]. We were able to recruit appropriate candidates for our Cultural Probe research based on collected information of the TV viewers' characteristics of age, gender and behavior from our survey. Eleven selected participants (m: 4, f: 7/age under 10: 1, 10's: 1, 20-30's: 6, 40-50's: 2, over 60: 1) were given a kit with a voice recorder and a journal to record the family's TV viewing environment. Specifically, they were asked to write down the names of the TV programs, who were watching with them and what they were doing while watching TV. Also, the families were asked to record whatever they wish to say to the TV they were watching. From this observation we were able to collect 867 vocal data from 10 families.

4   Results

4.1   Smart TV Function and Four Sentence Types

First, we categorized the vocal command data into 6 different types of Smart TV functions: Basic Function, Search Function, Recommend Function, Additional Function, and Social talk. Basic function refers to functions that can be performed by the TV remote control such as adjusting the TV volume and changing the channel etc. Search function allows the user to explore information. Vocal commands for asking for the weather and a specific TV program schedule etc. would be such case. Recommend function enables the user to get a recommendation from the TV. Vocal data such as "Turn on some music program" and "Put on a documentary about pets" can be classified as commands for such function. Additional function implements the user's request that is different with the previously mentioned functions and is new to the TV experience. Vocal commands like "Capture this scene", "Show me from the beginning", and "Skip advertisements" are some of the examples. Social talk refers to innocent utterances of the user with no intention of commanding the TV.

Second, with the vocal data, we examined the frequent use of the 4 types of speeches such as the declarative, imperative, interrogative, exclamatory type. Then we cross-examined it with the 6 Smart TV functions.

Table 1. Number of vocal data in different function and sentence types

	Declarative	Imperative	Interrogative	Exclamatory
Basic Function	11	143	1	0
Search Function	9	154	169	0
Recommend Function	7	55	24	0
Additional Function	43	203	19	0
Social Talk	13	1	9	6
Total	83	556	222	6

Overall, the use of the imperative sentences were dominating in all functions, however, there were some differences in each function. For the basic function, the imperative sentence covered 92.3% and other types of sentences were rare to find. Interrogative sentences took up 50.9% of the search function request, implying that users generally requested to get more information from the Smart TV while watching something. Imperative and interrogative sentences each scored 64% and 27.9% for the recommend function. As for the additional function, imperative sentences highly used with 76.6%, however, declarative sentence type followed that number with 16.2%. Social talk was rare to detect, however, declarative and interrogative sentences were most frequent and it was the only function to attract exclamatory sentences.

Although we were able to find out which function had the most frequent request when users were watching TV and which style of speech they were using, such results were not sufficient in finding out which Smart TV persona the users were engaging with. Therefore, in the next step of our research, we analyzed the users' speech style in detail and drew out 6 types of TV agent personas according to how the users were verbally implying their relationship with the Smart TV.

4.2   Six Types of Smart TV Persona Analysis

Users' vocal commands were divided into 6 different styles of speeches by two factors, respect and intimacy. First, when there is lack of intimacy and high respect, people use honorifics. In Korean language, there are certain grammar rules to be applied when speaking with an elder person or those who you respect making the style of speech significantly different. Such unique characteristic allowed us to pick out vocal data for the first speech type. Second, when there is strong intimacy and respect, people use an expression like "let's" while using informal language and more intimate words. The third type of speech style is when both intimacy and respect are average, typical vocal commands would include the word "please" and the expression "can you..." translated in English. When the level of intimacy and respect are both low, users use expressions that have no respect for the listener, a typical vocal command would sound like "(just) do it." The fifth speech type appears when there is strong intimacy but little respect. There is no expectation of the other to respond but the speaker uses friendly form of speech. Finally, the last type of speech shows when there is almost no sense of intimacy and respect for the other. The speaker addresses the other as a non-human being and commands as if they would type in a command on a computer.

Table 2. Six type of Smart TV agent categorized by speech style

Type	Intima-cy	Respect	Speech style	Example (Translated in English)
Expert	Low	Very High	Honorific language	· It would be great if you could provide translated subtitle. · Could you please show me the shopping channel? · I would be happy if you could add the share function.
Colleague	High	High	Let's~ I hope~ Do you Know~?	· Let's change the music. · I hope the TV turned off when I fall asleep. · Do you know where I can buy it?
Assistant	Neutral	Neutral	Please, do~ Will you~? Can you~?	· Please change the channel. · Let me know the location of that café. · Will you tell me the price of those shoes?
Slave	Low	Low	(just) do~	· Change to channel 5. · Turn up the volume. · Record this song.
Pet	High	Low	Monologue /Utter	· I will came back after eat some food. · The ghost is typing Morse code. It's scary! · I hope to go there. · It looks delicious!
Machine	Very Low	Very Low	Word /Command (not a sentence)	· KBS (name of the channel). · Alarm. · Forward.

By categorizing the vocal data into 6 different types, we can glimpse how the users are defining their relationship with the Smart TV. We named each type according to their features as the following: Expert, Colleague, Assistant, Slave, Pet, and Machine. We then checked the frequency of these types in our vocal data.

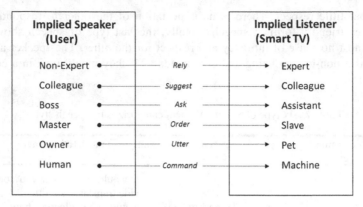

Fig. 2. User-Smart TV relationship and implied verbal manners

Out of 867 vocal commands that we collected, the most prevalent command was "please do (this)" with 391 cases, which is about 45% of the whole data. And the Assistant type with such wording took up 51%. The second most frequent type was the Colleague type with 29%. Generally, expressions like "let's do…", "I would like you to…", and "I want to do…" that were indirectly commanding the TV and questioning about a TV program were included in this case. Therefore, many users were interacting with an underlying TV persona by showing low level of intimacy and respect but feeling comfortable with an Assistant type who can help them or a Colleague type who is an equal being to them.

In addition, we found that there were only a handful of cases indicating a Machine type which has no humanistic feature; and there was hardly a case for the disrespected Slave type as well. This may indicate that when people use their own voice as an input device to control Smart TV, they are treating it as a human being that has a sense of respect. The Expert type took up 7% of the data; however, we discovered that it was one particular participant who has been mainly using honorific type of speech. Therefore, it is difficult to generalize using formal type of speech to a Smart TV.

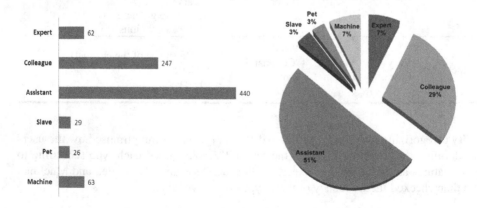

Fig. 3. Number and percentage of vocal data appearing six different types of agent

4.3   Smart TV Functions and Six Types of Smart TV Personas

In this step, we wanted to find different types of Smart TV personas for the TV functions we categorized in the previous section. As a result, the Assistant type was dominant in most functions. The Assistant type appeared most frequently with 72%, especially in the basic function.

On the other hand, for the search function, the Colleague type appeared most frequently with 50% and followed by 41% of Assistant type. As we analyzed in the previous section, interrogative sentences are used mostly for the search function. Since many participants used causal tone of asking for information or to control, which is relevant to the Colleague type, this type dominates almost the half of all data. Even though these kinds of expressions are more closed to the Colleague type, they also can be used to refer the Assistant type.

Table 3. Number of vocal data in different functions and six types of agent

Function	Expert	Colleague	Assistant	Slave	Machine	Pet
Basic Function	7	5	111	14	17	1
Search Function	10	167	137	0	18	0
Recommend Function	10	26	45	3	1	1
Additional Function	35	40	146	12	28	4
Social Talk	0	9	1	0	0	19

Even if the number of vocal data for the "Pet" type was very small, 66% of them appeared as social talk function. In this experiment, participants would say something to the TV, but the TV couldn't provide a feedback. Thus, such dialogue becomes a monologue similar to talking to a pet. If a Smart TV is developed to a certain degree so that they can give a witty answer to users' sporadic expressions, we can assume that the level of intimacy and respect would increase, making it easier for the Colleague (friend) type to appear more often.

5   Discussion and Conclusion

This study is the first step of developing appropriate Smart TV personas from the linguistic UX point of view. From this study, we were able to find a certain linguistic tendency of users' voice commands and several implied personas in users' general situation of TV viewing.

Our research showed that many users didn't regard Smart TV as just a machine or a tool. Instead, they seemed to interact with it as if it were a living thing. In addition, most of data represented that users regarded Smart TV as an assistant, who has a lower status than the user, or as a colleague who has the same level of status with the user. Furthermore, we were able to find a possibility that the relationship between the user and Smart TV could be developed to provide more equal sense of the relation in the future if advanced Smart TV provides more valuable experience to the users. Natural language processing in the electronic equipment such as computers, mobile phones, and Smart TVs has not been developed to the level of reproducing human-like natural linguistic communication, and users are not yet accustomed to the linguistic UX. Since users have a low expectation of the Smart TV's ability to have a natural conversation, we can assume why the percentage of "Social talk" among the whole functions was very low.

The limitation of our study is that the collected vocal data does not reflect the real life interaction between a Smart TV and a user; the participant recorded their vocal command without hearing the response of the TV. We considered using an existing Smart TV which is applied in linguistic UX researches for collecting vocal data, but since the role of Smart TV is yet ambiguous, we wanted participants to freely imagine the role of the TV and record their dialogues. In the next step, we can analyze various dialogues and feedbacks from the users when they experience a two-way communication with Smart TV.

In addition, we conducted the experiment with only Korean participants and all the collected vocal data was in Korean language. Since we analyzed the vocal data based on the linguistic rules of Korean language, it may be difficult to generalize the findings when translated into other languages. Lastly, this research did not cover to suggest the preferred age, gender, and detailed personalities of a Smart TV agent depending on different groups of viewers. Therefore, for future work, we will look at the preferences of Smart TV personas depending on different age and gender groups. Furthermore, we will develop TV agent characters that reflect users' preferences and evaluate the users' level of satisfaction and affection with them.

Acknowledgments. This research was supported by Samsung Electronics Co., Ltd.

References

1. Shin, D.H., Hwang, Y., Choo, H.: Smart TV: Are they really smart in interacting with people? Understanding the interactivity of Korean Smart TV. Behaviour & Information Technology 32(2), 156–172 (2013)
2. Nass, C., Steuer, J., Tauber, E.R.: Computers are social actors. In: Proceedings of the SIGCHI Conference on Human Factors in Computing Systems, pp. 72–78. ACM (1994)
3. Chatman, S.B.: Story and discourse: Narrative structure in fiction and film. Cornell University Press (1980)
4. Reeves, B., Nass, C.: The Media equation: How people treat computers, television, and new media. Cambridge University Press (1997)
5. Nass, C., Fogg, B.J., Moon, Y.: Can computers be teammates? International Journal of Human-Computer Studies 45(6), 669–678 (1996)
6. John, O.P., Donahue, E.M., Kentle, R.: The "Big Five. Factor Taxonomy: Dimensions of Personality in the Natural Language and in Questionnaires". In: Pervin, L.A., John, O.P. (eds.) Handbook of Personality: Theory and Research, pp. 66–100 (1990)
7. McCrae, R.R., Costa, P.T.: The structure of interpersonal traits: Wiggins's circumplex and the five-factor model. Journal of Personality and Social Psychology 56(4), 586 (1989)

8. Nass, C., Moon, Y., Fogg, B.J., Reeves, B., Dryer, C.: Can computer personalities be human personalities? In: Conference Companion on Human Factors in Computing Systems, pp. 228–229. ACM (1995)
9. Nass, C., Moon, Y., Green, N.: Are Machines Gender Neutral? Gender-Stereotypic Responses to Computers With Voices. Journal of Applied Social Psychology 27(10), 864–876 (1997)
10. Gaver, B., Dunne, T., Pacenti, E.: Design: Cultural probes. Interactions 6(1), 21–29 (1999)

UbiComp Applications for Assisting Visually Impaired People Live an Independent Life: A Participatory Conceptualization Design Phase

Anna Leda Liakopoulou and Irene Mavrommati

Hellenic Open University School of Applied Arts Athens, Greece
lliakop@yahoo.com, mavrommati@eap.gr

Abstract. This paper presents a classified set of proposals of Ubiquitous Computing Applications aimed for the wellbeing of the visually impaired, and the initial design analysis and conceptualization process that led to them. Domestic applications for the visually impaired have been conceptualized and evaluated, with insight from participatory design approaches. Thirty two total proposals resulted from brainstorm sessions between the designer and a focus group of blind end users. The proposals were then ranked by a broader focus group of visually impaired end users. Top ranked scenaria are further evaluated in order to identify strengths and weaknesses and make further improvements. Such classified scenarios can provide valuable input towards a ubiquitous computing system that is designed from its very conception based on the needs of the visually impaired.

Keywords: Scenario based design, Visually impaired, Ubicomp applications.

1 Introduction

Visually impaired people face daily great difficulties in living an independent life. The main reason for this is the almost exclusive use of visual information in our environments. Aiming to assist this group's independent living, a set of Ubiquitous Computing (UbiComp) application scenarios reported here were defined, evaluated, and prioritized, using Participatory Design methods.

The iterative process of user-centred design for the blind starts in the first design phases: analysis and preliminary concept phases. The setting assumed from the analysis is the domestic environment. Thirty two total proposals resulted from brainstorm sessions between the designer and a focus group of end users. Many of these scenarios addressed the replacement of printed information with other forms that can be reachable and usable from blind people within their domestic environment, aiming to their safe and independent living. The proposed ideas-scenarios were focusing on activities such as cooking, dressing, entertaining, washing, cleaning and also more specific needs such as security alerts, finding of things and obstacles, medicine information and many more. The proposals were then ranked by a broader focus group of visually impaired end users. "Talking Eyes", a top ranked scenario was further

N. Streitz and P. Markopoulos (Eds.): DAPI 2014, LNCS 8530, pp. 272–281, 2014.

evaluated in order to identify its strengths and weaknesses and further improve it. This prioritized set of scenarios, presented here as a result of concept design research, can serve as valuable input towards a ubiquitous computing system that is designed from its very conception based on the needs of the visually impaired.

2   Related Work

The Chatty Environment [4-7], and iCARE [9], [11], were the two most notable research environments related to the research presented here. Both approaches are addressed to visually impaired users and are using augmented everyday objects, aiming to a better, safer and more independent living of the visually impaired. The approaches are similar to the design concept research approach presented in this paper. The Chatty Environment is an environment where the world uses an alternative audio channel, to reveal itself to the user. A prototype was built which consisted of several components: a large number of tagged entities in the environment, a world explorer in form of a portable device and a tag reader connected to the world explorer to pick up the tags. iCARE on the other hand proposes 5 different applications: iCARE Reader, iCARE Information Assistant, iCARE Interaction Assistant, iCARE Haptic Interface and iCARE Accessible Environment. Both of these projects used participatory design methods. Inspired by these projects and the work described in [12], research presented here, followed some methods of requirements analysis: interviews, focus groups and questionnaires- and cross checked the resulted requirements and feedback that the users gave to all these researches. Scenarios were used in all these projects as a testing method for the proposed ideas. A new approach in this research, compared to the existing projects, was the combined evaluation method of Cognitive Dimensions of Notations framework (CD) questionnaires [3] with Bellotti's questions [2]. Other differences are the large number of proposed scenarios and the absence of any assisting devices that users would have to carry in order to achieve their goals.

3   Towards a Taxonomy of Ubiquitous Application Scenarios

Participatory design methods (brainstorming, interviews, questionnaires, and observation) were adopted as a user centered design approach most suitable for defining a UbiComp application for the visually impaired. Scenario based design was used for the presentation of the application proposals; scenarios were described in the form of textual descriptions.

A primary team of five people was formed as a focus group; four of the participants were visually impaired and represented the future users of the system and one, the author, who was sighted and had the role of informing, inspiring and organising the whole process. The age of the team was ranging between 20-45 years old. Every member of the team had a high or higher education level and they were all active members of the society. Two of the members are actively involved in the "Panhellenic Association of the Blind" which appeared very helpful through the process. The process was formed in three stages -Analysis, Idea, Evaluation- as they are defined in user centered design processes and according to ISO 3407 [1]. At this point we have to emphasize that this research is focused on the concept of a suitable ubicomp application and not the actualized or prototyped application and that's the reason why the stage of "design" is in fact the "idea generation".

4   Design Analysis Phase

At the stage of the Analysis, information was gathered about visually impaired users and their needs and requirements. In order to do so personal interviews were conducted, and visits on location / domiciles of visually impaired were realized. Observation was direct in their environments, but also via videotaped sessions of blind living at their homes. A live interview with the visually impaired was used, based on a questionnaire text script in order to facilitate understanding of the everyday living habits of blind people. A focus group was formed in order conduct a brainstorming and exchange ideas, problems, thoughts and probable solutions that would lead us to ideas that would meet the needs and requirements of more than one user.

The methods of user-analysis were based on [8],[15] and were similar to the ones used in related research such as «The Chatty Environment» [4-6]. Through the initial analysis the environment of the proposed applications was identified as the domestic environment, being of primary importance to the focus group; it is also more contained in terms of the technology involved, and thus more likely to be better suited for currently available Ubiquitous computing infrastructure. Within the augmented domestic environment the identified needs and requirements of the blind were addressed through participatory proposals. A user persona (fig.1) was described, in order to facilitate design research during the concept phase. The persona transfers abstract concepts to a human figure [13]. In this way, the requirements of different users will take the form of a specific future user.

Resulting from the initial analysis, the needs and requirements of the users were clarified, along with the users' environment. The primary wish of members of the group was to be able to have an independent life and not needing to depend on other people. More specifically, the proposed ideas would have to:

- replace the environment's visual information
- preferably focus in domestic environment
- allow the user to be independent
- not enforce their disability and make them stand out more than it already happens. That means that **blind people don't want to have any extra visible appliance that they would have to use or carry around.**

Two extra facts that appeared through the interviews were the memory factor and the vocal information. **Blind people have a strong memory and they don't want an application that would minimize the exercise of this sense** and also they are very familiar and open to speech, as their preferred output medium.

FEW WORDS	I am Marios. I am 24 years old, blind, master's student at Law School and member of the "Panhellenic Association for the blind" (P.A.B). I have a very good relation with my parents and my sister but the last few years I live by myself. I am very social, I have a lot of friends, I like going out, travel and reading. Generally I'm very optimistic despite all the difficulties that my disability could cause me. Through P.A.B. we examine problems and difficulties of visually impaired, we take part in researches and we believe in a better future.
MY DAY	I wake up early, I always take my breakfast and I leave for the university where I spend many hours of the day. At the afternoon I spend some time at the P.A.B., I go for a walk or a bit of exercise. At the evening I go back home for studying, relaxing and dinner.
TRANSPORT	Wherever I go, I use the white cane. It helps me move around in known & unknown places, indoors or outdoors. If I need to take a transportation, I use the subway or I take a taxi.
HEALTH	My health is in great condition. Blindness is something I was born with and I'm used to live with it. I believe it's easier for me than for some people who lose their site in a later age.
VALUES	I want to be independent and self-sufficient. I don't want to be treated differently.
PERSPECTIVES	I get informed about progress & evolution. I fight for my beliefs. I'm very optimistic that in the future, technology will be able to help me live a more independent life.

Fig. 1. The persona description

5   Ideas – Concepts

After the gathering of information, the identified requirements transform into ideas – proposals through scenario based design. Scenarios may come up from brainstorming and they can be very effective when users are involved for their creation [14]. Thirty-two (32) proposals were created and presented with a scenario based design process. As the length of this paper does not allow us to present the full scenarios, these are briefly outlined in Fig.2.

	NAME	Context	USER REQUIREMENT	GRADE
1	Talking Eyes	Domestic	Food Products' information	6 (#1)
	Smart Outfit	Domestic	Dressing up – Finding of requested clothes	31
3	Smart Mirror	Domestic	Dressing up – Affirmation of good result from another person	91
4	Smart Clothes	Domestic	Dressing up – Matching clothes	62
5	Let me Know	Domestic	Safety at home (Left appliances and lights in «on» mode)	70
6	AmbiFeelings	Domestic	«Watching» visual mediums (TV, Projections, etc)	81
7	Welcome	Domestic	Get informed when someone arrives home	105
8	Best Friend	Domestic	Taking care of a pet	101
9	EnLighten me	Domestic	Get informed for a burnt bulb	84
10	Weathy	Domestic	Weather information – Sunny or cloudy day	61
11	Stain Free	Domestic	Get informed about stains on the clothes	58
12	Reminder	Domestic	Get informed upon request for proposed home-works	103
13	Super Clean	Domestic	Cleaning – Information about forgotten spots	78
14	Home Deblock	Domestic	Avoiding blocks	71
15	Street Deblock	Outdoors	Avoiding blocks	85
16	Warning	Domestic	Informartion about damaged cooking utensils	55
17	Talking Eyes Med	Domestic	Medicine products information	38
18	Measure	Domestic	Measuring during cooking	57
19	Show me the way	Outdoors	Recognition of routes	47
20	Digit Reader	Domestic	Vocal digit reader for bills	30 (#3)
21	Finder	Domestic	Finding of lost items	49
22	Map Reader	Domestic	Map reading through haptic and vocal input and output	89
23	Make my day	Domestic	Boiling	97
24	Shopping List	Domestic	Information about ending consumable goods	61
25	New Data	Domestic	Information for updated research results	93
26	Compass	Domestic / Outdoors	Orientation help	67
27	Separate it	Domestic	Separating clothes for washing	71
28	Scan It	Domestic	Recognising visitors and people who ring bell	70
29	Spot It	Domestic	Finding of displaced items	65
30	Eat It	Domestic	Information about food denaturation	26 (#2)
31	Informer	Outdoors	Information about the exact amount of taxi bill	38
32	Dust Off	Domestic	Information about dust on clothes and fabrics	72

Fig. 2. All the 32 scenarios were created together with the focus group as a response to some of the problems that blind people meet in their everyday life. The grading shows the preferences of the users. The smaller the number, the more preferable the scenario, e.g. Talking Eyes was ranked as first priority from 3 users and as third priority from the fourth user (1+1+1+3=6).

6   Most Prominent Scenarios

The scenarios were discussed and re structured to reach their final form, which was given to the users of the team for ranking at the stage of evaluation.

The ranking was made based on the following criteria: personal priority preference, degree of addressing the needs of each user, degree of facilitating his/her autonomy.

The most widely preferred application scenario, as it came up through ranking, was «Talking Eyes». It describes an application that informs the user about the identity of a food product, the expiry date and any other related information that might appear on the packaging. As the user grabs the product and removes it from the storage place, he/she can hear a voice that announces the identity of the product and the expiry date, e.g. Spaghetti Barilla, July 2011. At this stage the user doesn't have to do anything in order to be informed. The basic information of the identity and the expiry date are "given" to him/her without having asked for them. If the user needs some extra information about the specific product, he/she may ask the application for this information by saying for example: "Ingredients". Then the application announces again to the user the requested information. The specific application pre-assumes the existence of embodied RFID tags on food products that hold all the necessary data of a product as it appears on its packaging. The data stored in the RFID tags is recognized by an RFID reader that turns digital data into vocal and announces it to the user.

The next four top ranked scenarios were the following:

Ranked second in the Focus Group preference was «Eat it»:   an application scenario, set in the domestic environment, that informs the user about denaturation of food. There are certain types of food products, such as cheese for example, where some level of denaturation may appear without making the food dangerous. «Eat it» uses a sensor that can spot the denaturation, a vocal device through which the user is informed and an augmented "smart" knife that can «guide» the user to cut off the denaturated piece of the product.

Third in preference was «Digit Reader»: an application scenario, set in the domestic environment, that informs the user about numeric information on documents such as bills, food delivery checks, etc. As the user takes the document and places it on the augmented table, the table vocally informs him/her about the total amount he/she is supposed to pay. In that way, blind people may be sure that nobody is taking advantage of their disability by overcharging them.

Ranked forth was «Smart Outfit». This is a domestic application scenario, whereby blind people can choose the clothes they want to wear without the help of another person. The user opens the closet and asks for a specific garment, e.g. Gray suite. Tagged sensors on the clothes recognize the demanded cloth and the hanger of the specific cloth comes out of the closet. The user may continue in the same way asking for his whole outfit such as shirt, shoes, etc.

In the fifth place was «Talking Eyes Med». A scenario for a domestic application that informs the user about all the necessary information of the medicine he/she uses. The application works in exactly the same way as «Talking Eyes» through RFID tags and RFID reader.

7   Evaluation

After ranking the scenarios and selecting the preferred ones, the next process step was to explore those in more depth. Questionnaires were given to the users in order to evaluate «Talking Eyes», that was the widely preferred application scenario. At the initial conceptual stages of the system design, the aims of the evaluation were to test:

- the awareness of the users according to the purpose of the future system
- the understanding of the needs they may fulfill through it
- the expected necessity and frequency of its use
- the level of difficulty they expect to meet by its use
- the easiness of understanding its functionality.

Through open type questions we expected them to share with us their concerns – if there were any- about problems of the system, trust, privacy, benefit and their overall expected satisfaction. The questionnaire of the evaluation was based on the Cognitive Dimensions of Notations framework [3], a questionnaire optimized for users. The questionnaire was accompanied by the scenario of the application idea which we have tested by answering the five questions that Bellotti [2] suggests for designers and researchers, before giving it to the users for the final evaluation. For the evaluation an additional three new people were added to the initial focus group; these people were also visually impaired but had not participated into the previous concept creation stages.

8   Results of Evaluation for Talking Eyes Scenario

The outcome of the evaluation showed that the users believe that the proposed application (as part of an overall system) can meet their needs and requirements but also pointed out at the following new facts:

- All users understand the needs they can fulfil through this application.
- 6 out of 7 total users believe that the particular application would be quite to absolute necessary to them.
- Most of them mentioned that they could use it 1-3 times per week.
- All users believed that it would be quite easy for them to use the application (based on the description provided).
- All users believed that the functionality of the application was clear.
- 5 out of the 7 total users couldn't find any problems with the application described.
- All users stated that they would trust the application.
- 6 out of the 7 total users didn't have a privacy issue. (There are more benefits to them than privacy concerns).
- All users stated the importance of the health benefit that the particular application accomplishes.
- All users believe they would be quite satisfied by such application.

The existing team and the new team of evaluators differentiated on two key-points: the address and the action as they are defined by Bellotti [2]. Two out of the seven total users (28%) expressed doubts concerning those two areas. They specifically mentioned an "on-off" function of the system as well as the choice of not being informed of the type of the product as for some food products they can recognize them from their packaging.

According to Bellotti, and by keeping in mind the results of the evaluation, the following challenges arise: For addressing the system: a) How to disambiguate intended target system, b) How to not address the system. Regarding action towards the system: a) How to avoid unwanted selection. The aspects described by Bellotti are worth taking into account for the creation of future system application proposals, as well as for detailing the ones of this study.

Bellotti's framework was used in two different phases. First the proposed scenario was checked by designers, before giving it to the focus group for validation. This appeared very helpfull in order to test the parameters of the application and it's meeting to the stated users' needs and requirements. At the next step, we assessed the proposed idea according to the Bellotti framework. The framework of Bellotti presents five design challenges inspired by analysis of human-human communication that are mundanely addressed by traditional graphical user interface designs (GUIs) [2] . In conjunction with the questions from the Cognitive Dimensions framework [3], the Bellotti design framework appeared to be very helpful and accurate for leading the design process. The Cognitive Dimensions evaluation results pointed out the very specific areas of Bellotti's framework that needed to be re-examined: the areas of address and action. More details in process and results is reported in [10].

9   Conclusions

The design research in the initial concept phase advocates that visually impaired people wish and need to be autonomous, independent and safe. They don't want to be depended on others or behave differently than the sighted. UbiComp systems comprising of specific applications, that are evaluated and ranked from their conception phase through a design process as the one described in this paper, can help to meet this goal, so that the scenario-ideas that get realized into applications are suitable for this specific group's needs. Such Ubicomp applications should aim to enhance the capabilities of blind people, give them new prospects, and allow them to live an independent life and to take advantage of the same information as sighted people do. All the applications presented in section 2 were created according to the blind users' requirements and presented a solution to their specific problems. What is important in this approach is that, compared to similar projects such as "The Chatty Environment" [6],[5],[7],[4] that we mentioned earlier, the focus was on keeping the applications simple and without any extra required effort from the users. The use or carrying of any extra appliances was not adopted, which was an important point that the blind users themselves stated from the interviews during the analysis phase.

All the applications concepts generated in this design process (reported more extensively in [10]), after being improved and revised via focus group appraisal, can be used as use cases or initial requirements in a domestic UbiComp System that aims to facilitate the safe and independent living of blind people.

References

1. Akoumianakis, D.: Human Computer Interaction - Διεπαφή Χρήστη – Υπολογιστή, μια σύγχρονη προσέγγιση. Klidarithmos Publications, Athens (2008)
2. Bellotti, V., Back, M., Edwards, W.K., Grinter, R.E., Henderson, A., Lopes, C.: Making Sense of Sensing Systems: Five Questions for Designers and Researchers. In: Proceedings of the SIGCHI Conference on Human Factors in Computing Systems: Changing our World, Changing Ourselves, Minneapolis, Minnesota, USA, pp. 415–422 (2002)
3. Blackweell, A.F., Green, T.R.G.: A Cognitive Dimensions Questionnaire Optimised for Users. In: 12th Workshop of the Psychology of Programming Interest Group, Cozenza Italy (April 2004)
4. Coroama, V.: Experiences from the Design of a Ubiquitous Computing System for the Blind. In: Adjunct Proceedings of the CHI 2006 Conference on Human Factors in Computing Systems, Montréal, Canada, April 22-27 (2006)
5. Coroama, V., Kapic, T., Röthenbacher, F.: Improving the Reality Perception of Visually Impaired through Pervasive Computing. In: Ferscha, A., Hoertner, H., Kotsis, G. (eds.) Advances in Pervasive Computing, pp. 369–376. Austrian Computer Society (OCG), Vienna (2004) ISBN 3-85403-176-9
6. Coroama, V., Röthenbacher, F.: The Chatty Environment – Providing Everyday Independence to the Visually Impaired. In: Workshop on Ubiquitous Computing for Pervasive Healthcare Applications at UbiComp 2003, Seattle, Washington (October 2003)
7. Coroama, V., Röthenbacher, F.: The Chatty Environment. In: Demo at the Second Conference on Pervasive Computing and Communications (PerCom 2004), Orlando, Florida, March 14-17 (2004)
8. Dix, A., Finlay, J., Abowd, G., Beale, R.: Human-computer interaction, 3rd edn. M. Giourdas Publications, Athens (2004)
9. Krishna, S., Little, G., Black, J.A., Panchanathan Jr., S.: iCARE Interation Assistant: A Wearable Face Recognition System for Individuals with Visual Impairments. In: 7th International ACM SIGACCESS Conference on Computers and Accessibility (ASSETS 2005), Baltimore, MD (2005)
10. Liakopoulou Anna Leda, Postgraduate Diploma Thesis in Graphic Arts Multimedia MA, Hellenic Open University (2009)
11. Panchanathan, S., Black, J.A., Rush Jr., M., Iyer, V.: iCare – A user centric Approach to the development of assistive devices for the blind and visually impaired. In: 15th IEEE International Conference on Tools with Artificial Intelligence (ICTAI 2003), Sacramento, CA (2003)
12. Panchanathan, S., McDaniel, T., Balasubramanian, V.: Person-centered accessible technologies: Improved usability and adaptation through inspirations from disability research. In: Proceedings of the ACM Workshop on User Experience in e-Learning and Augmented Technologies in Education (2012)
13. Pruitt, J., Adlin, T.: The Persona Lifecycle: Keeping People in Mind Throughout Product Design. Morgan Kaufmann (2006)

14. Rosson, M.B., Carroll, J.M.: Scenario-Based Design. In: The Human-Computer Interaction Handbook: Fundamentals, Evolving Technologies and Emerging Applications, pp. 1032–1050 (2002)
15. Strömberg, H., Pirttilä, V., Ikonen V.: Interactive scenarios—building ubiquitous computing concepts in the spirit of participatory design. Personal and Ubiquitous Computing 8(3-4), 200–207 (2004)

Using Eye-Gaze and Visualization to Augment Memory
A Framework for Improving Context Recognition and Recall

Jason Orlosky[1], Takumi Toyama[2], Daniel Sonntag[2], and Kiyoshi Kiyokawa[1]

[1] Osaka University, Osaka, Japan
{orlosky@lab.ime,kiyo@ime}cmc.osaka-u.ac.jp
[2] German Research Center for Artificial Intelligence, Kaiserslautern, Germany
{takumi.toyama,sonntag}@dfki.de

Abstract. In our everyday lives, bits of important information are lost due to the fact that our brain fails to convert a large portion of short term memory into long term memory. In this paper, we propose a framework that uses an eye-tracking interface to store pieces of forgotten information and present them back to the user later with an integrated head mounted display (HMD). This process occurs in three main steps, including context recognition, data storage, and augmented reality (AR) display. We demonstrate the system's ability to recall information with the example of a lost book page by detecting when the user reads the book again and intelligently presenting the last read position back to the user. Two short user evaluations show that the system can recall book pages within 40 milliseconds, and that the position where a user left off can be calculated with approximately 0.5 centimeter accuracy.

1 Introduction

It has been long known that humans often fail to convert short term memory into long term memory, and are inherently forgetful. We often mistakenly judge certain events as being unimportant, but which turn out to be important at a later time or in a different context. To help cope with this memory deficiency, technology has been used as a form of cognitive offloading to assist and sometimes even function as a substitute for memory intensive tasks. Good examples include digital calendars, reminder systems, life logging applications, and the use of search engines for information not committed to long term memory [1], [4], [7], [8]. Our research builds on this idea by augmenting memory through the use of eye-tracking and an AR display as shown in Figure 1. When a user returns to the situation in which a memory occurred, eye gaze can be used to detect context and more accurately present the user with previously stored information. Eye tracking is first used to identify a user's point of attention and to outline an area for recognition, such as text or an environmental object. That text or object is then inserted into a database along with relevant tags such as date, time and location. "Memories," represented by an array of contextual and temporal tags in the database, can be recalled later with keyword searches or object detection triggers.

N. Streitz and P. Markopoulos (Eds.): DAPI 2014, LNCS 8530, pp. 282–291, 2014.

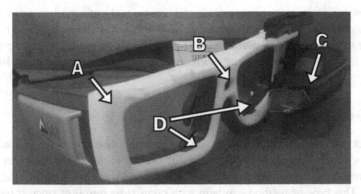

Fig. 1. Hardware setup showing A) 3D printed connector, B) outward facing camera, C) head mounted display, and D) inward facing eye-tracking cameras

Examples of applications of this technology include recalling items such as forgotten page numbers in documents, the location of misplaced keys, or patient information prior to surgery. Interfaces such as this one also have the potential not only for consumer use, but for use with clinical patients suffering from memory related illnesses such as vascular dementia or Alzheimer's disease. In addition to describing a general framework that facilitates the encoding of temporal events into digital form, we describe the hardware setup shown in Figure 1 and specific software implementations within the framework. These implementations include a system that can help a user recall a lost book page and a system that can encode an event, such as placing one's keys on a desk, into the database for later recall. Though a variety of implementations within this framework are possible, we chose page recollection and simple event storage since they are prime examples of how this framework can translate to practical application. To our knowledge, this is the first attempt at introducing a combination of eye-gaze interaction and AR into this kind of memory assistive model.

2   Prior Work

2.1   Research on Memory and Context

One widely explored field of research related to memory is that of physical systems that serve as memory aids. One such example is the SenseCam, which takes intermittent photos throughout the day and serves as a retrospective memory aid [4]. Detailed studies using the SenseCam show that memory can be improved by reviewing images taken by the system, especially long term memory [13]. A similar device called the EyeTap has been used as a form of capturing life experiences and sharing these experiences with others [7]. Although a large number of other software memory aids such as calendars and reminder systems are available, a majority of them only exist as mobile or smartphone based applications. Several systems are also available that utilize sensor data in order to extract context. One such system by Belimpasakis proposes a client-server platform that enables not only life logging, but richer social experiences by extracting more meaningful contextual information from data [1]. The above systems all have the potential to be combined with or improved by various models for memory and decision making, such as those proposed by Hutter et al. [5]. They also fall into the broader goal of creating a complete database of all life events [2].

2.2   Eye Gaze and Augmented Reality

Another set of closely related studies are those which use computer vision and eye tracking for context recognition.   One major branch is the study of object recognition, which can be conducted using hysteresis, feature tracking, and other algorithms [6], [16]. This type of method can help with context recognition since it has the potential to extract semantic information from objects in one's environment.   In addition to recognizing objects, location can also be extracted using gaze and other sensors [14]. In conjunction with HMD systems, activity can also be recognized using other types of mobile sensors [12].   Once context, location, or other relevant content has been determined, information visualization methods can be used to place the information in a relevant location in the environment [10].   This can prevent information from becoming a distraction, and can make recalled information easier to view. Our framework uses a combination of elements from life logging, context recognition, memory models, and AR in order to assist users with event recall.

3   Hardware Design and Setup

We first construct a 3D gaze tracking system combined with an HMD that does not require the use of external tracking or projection hardware. The device is composed of a pair of eye tracking goggles, custom 3D printed attachment, and HMD. The devices are all connected, and can be calibrated as a single system.

3.1   Hybrid Eye Tracker and HMD

To start, we needed an apparatus for eye and vergence tracking that could be used simultaneously with a head mounted display placed near the user's eye. We decided to use a pair of SMI Eye Tracking Goggles, which can be worn like glasses and leave enough room to attach an HMD. The HMD part of our system consists of an 800 by 600 pixel AirScouter HMD, which includes digital input via USB and depth control. The focal depth can be set from 30 centimeters (cm) to 10 meters (m).

In order for gaze to be measured appropriately in the HMD, a user's eye convergence must be consistent and eye tracking hardware must provide enough accuracy to ensure consistent gaze on a target object of interest.   In addition, we needed a way to make sure that the distance between the tracker and HMD would remain at the same during use. To ensure these conditions, we created a 3D printed fastener that fixed the distance between the prototype HMD and the eye tracker as shown in Figure 1 A. This setup allows for both left and right eye configurations.

3.2   Aligning Virtual and Real Environments

In order to provide information back to the user in an intelligent fashion, in many cases we have to align digital text with objects in the scene. In the case of recalling a book page or sentence in a document, text and pointers must be displayed in line with the targeted object and text. First, when a scene image is taken from the camera, the image is blurred by a Gaussian kernel and thresholded into a binary image in order to detect the centroid of each word region. The retrieval process is done by matching extracted features to the features of books, documents, and other media previously stored in the database [17]. Since we apply an image based method, we can deal with a variety of different paper mediums, fonts, and sizes. By matching the features between the scene image and the retrieved database image, we also calculate the homography between them. Based on this homography, the pose, rotation, and transformation of text in the scene image can be is estimated. This data can also be used both for HMD calibration and correct projection of overlaid data.

3.3   Gaze Calculation, Calibration and Focus Detection

Though the calculation for aligning virtual and real environments is independent of eye tracking, calibration for the eye tracker, HMD, and document pose estimation can be done all at once. From the eye tracker, we first extract a 3D vector of the direction of each eye, represented by GL=(glx,gly,glz) and GR=(grx,gry,grz) in Figure 2. Using this data, the approximate intersection of the two gaze vectors in 3D space is calculated. Though the specific details of the eye tracking process are proprietary, there are several basic steps that occur. Images are first taken from two infrared eye cameras and one scene camera. Each eye is then illuminated by six infrared light sources and the system tracks the changes of the six reflections off of the eye. Adjustments can be made for the height and width of a user's eyes, but the distance between eye tracker and HMD will still remain constant because the two pieces are connected.

Next, we calibrate the whole system, which is done in two steps. In the first step to calibrate gaze, the wearer to looks at one or more arbitrary points in the real world, allowing the system to adjust for that specific user's eyes. After this step, the system can be used for object recognition and non-environmentally aligned display of recalled information.

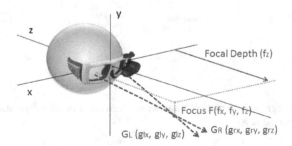

Fig. 2. Visual representation of the gaze vectors G_L and G_R used to compute gaze direction

In order to allow the HMD to align text with books or documents in the real world, a second calibration is used to determine the size and position of documents in the real world relative to the HMD camera and display screen. This calibration is done by asking a user to gaze at calibration point on a specific document, allowing the system to determine the size of the document relative to the user's field of view, thereby finalizing the entire calibration process.

When trying to extract a user's focus on an object or line of text, we utilize temporal fixation detection [16]. Once an object or document in the environment is detected, a threshold which can be set based on user preference functions as a trigger for encoding an event. In the case of recalling an item, such as a book page, detection of a book's cover or document title will trigger the display to output the last page or location viewed by the user. Next, we describe the framework for storage and recall.

4   Framework

Data processing within this framework primarily occurs in one of three steps, as shown in Figure 3. The first phase is interaction, where the primary sources of input are the position extracted from the eye-tracking interface, the environmental image from outward facing camera, and sensors such as GPS, accelerometer (for determining activity through methods such as those by Ravi et al.), and system time [12]. The second step is the encoding of this information into the database. Input data is stored in the database as an array of searchable keywords, and elements like time are stored as a chronological array. Finally, recollection of events is triggered by user initiated keyword search or by recognition of current context, and relevant database entries are displayed back to the user through the mixed-reality display.

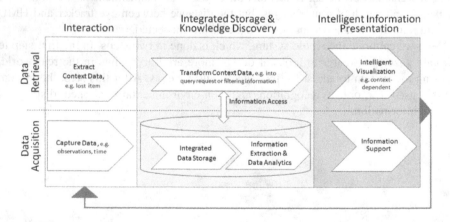

Fig. 3. Modified design of information framework showing flow of information [15]. Original image courtesy of Siemens AG.

4.1   Gaze Interaction and Context Recognition

The first and likely most important part of this framework is the method by which we recognize a user's context. Although there are a variety of methods used to detect objects in the environment such as those by Lowe et al. and Belongie et al., we use image retrieval for document recognition, and can also extract text in the environment through an optical character recognition (OCR) algorithm [2], [6]. Our system can also accept predefined markers as input, which provides a diverse test bed to show the interaction between recognizing objects in various contexts and storing/recalling information from the database. Using gaze as a form of interaction and search, we can recognize books, store names and locations, room numbers, and other text-based information that tends to be easily forgotten. We use marker tracking in place of object recognition which allows us to focus on methods for storage into the database and recall into the user's current context. As an example, recognition of text on a door plate and a marker on a set of keys can be stored in the database as an event. Alternatively, restaurant names and preferred menu items can be recognized and stored.

4.2   Database Design and Storing Events

Once an object or set of objects has been recognized, it must be stored in the database in a particular context. One important dimension for context is time, since events that occur closer to one another are likely more closely related. Time is also important in human memory, like our ability to remember procedural tasks or sequential events better than randomly distributed ones. This is the reason why many people must sing a song from the beginning in order to recall a particular phrase in the song. Other dimensions include semantic relevance, physical location, and custom input for more specific applications. These dimensions can also be cross-referenced to improve recall. Though the number of dimensions could be expanded with additional implementations, the current database elements include 1) an event, which represents the essence of the memory, 2) time, which is the moment in time when the event occurred, 3) location where the memory occurred, 4) semantic context, which includes any available information extracted from OCR or other contextual data extracted from sensors, 5) keyword, which represents an optional additional relevant contextual cue, and 6) an arbitrary field for use with specific implementations, such as the book page recollection algorithm. Though the mechanisms behind human memory are not fully replicated in our framework, these methods can serve as rough metaphor for basic storage and recall of past information.

Database queries can be manually engaged by a user, or automated based on triggers from a certain event or idea. If a user were searching for his or her keys for example, he or she would input "keys" as a keyword search and would be presented with a list of terms from the database contextually related to the word "keys," such as room numbers or objects detected in the immediate vicinity or time frame of the nearest occurrence of keys.   This method is comparable to personal information models such as those proposed by Maus et al., but takes advantage of augmented reality for reduced interaction and faster presentation [8].

4.3   Information Presentation and View Management

Once information has been recalled from the database, it must be presented to the user in an intelligent way so that it is in context and does not induce confusion. In the example of finding the last sentence a user was reading in a certain book, simply displaying the first word of the sentence in the HMD would not be enough for a user to find his or her place quickly. Instead, our system uses a document image retrieval and projective calculation to determine the position of the book, and appropriately displays a notification or pointer to where the user left off in the real world. Finally, view management can move resulting notifications to ensure that recalled information does not interfere with reading, walking, searching, or other visual tasks [10].

4.4   Software Implementation

Here we present a software implementation of our framework which accounts for a certain type of cognitive task. Like many easily forgotten events, leaving a reading task without marking the page is a frequent occurrence. By implementing one type of recollection method within our framework, we can solve this problem. Using the same steps outlined in the framework section, this particular method detects when a user is reading a specific document or book, searches the database for any memories related to reading that particular book, and displays navigation cues to the reader to show the page and location where he or she last left off, as shown in Figure 4. In addition to displaying the correct page, pointers show the user the direction of their last reading position, and a line is displayed under the last word read.

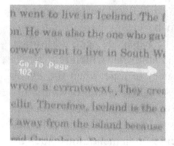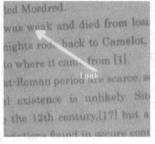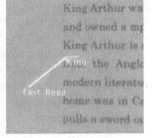

Fig. 4. Images showing recognition of an incorrect page (left), correct page with bookmarked text located above the HMD viewing field (center), and correct position with pointer (right)

Memory Logging and Recall Mechanisms. To provide a visual representation of how entries are recalled from the database, Table 1 shows how entries from a single day would appear in the database, and Figure 5 shows a view through the HMD showing a corresponding list of results using the keyword "book" as a search string queried from that database. The keyword search would be narrowed down further upon adding additional search strings such as time range or location. In the case of visual book recognition, instead of presenting search results, the document recall algorithm takes over, and displays the page and navigation instructions from Figure 4.

Table 1. Sample database entries for a single day

Event	Keyword	Time	Location	Context	Custom
book	Moby Dick	2014-01-22:21:15	home	read	pg88&x36&y773
book	Moby Dick	2014-01-22:18:22	home	read	pg5&x120&y150
magazine	Modern Art	2014-01-22:01:34	library	view	null
book	Relativity	2014-01-22:10:34	school	read	pg200&x52&y318
memo	groceries	2014-01-22:07:21	home	view	null

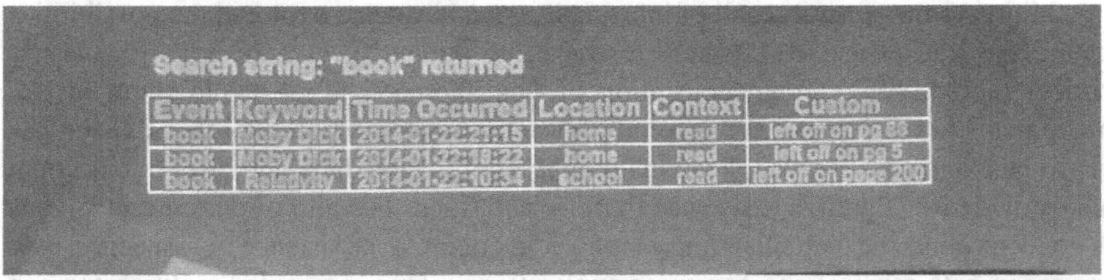

Fig. 5. Segment of an image taken through the HMD viewing screen of returned search output

5   Evaluations of Time-to-Recall and Accuracy

To provide a simple evaluation of book page recall, we conducted two short experiments. The first was designed to measure the time it takes to recognize a page when a user first looks at a document, and the second was designed to determine how accurately the exact reading position could be measured for re-display.

Time-to-Recall. The first experiment was conducted by asking 10 users to wear the display system. Each user was then presented with both a document presented on a computer monitor and a printed sheet, both of which had the same size and text. They were then asked to read each document as if they typically would any other type of text, and the recall algorithm was applied to each frame throughout both reading tasks. Reading angle was also measured for each participant to test whether we could still recall the text despite different viewpoints. Results show that for both the digital and physical documents, the recognition accuracy for each frame was 100% for reading angles between 70° and 90°. There was only a 0.54% decrease in accuracy for viewing angles between 50° and 70°. Other informal experiments showed that for over 50° of deviation from vertical, accuracy of recall decreases rapidly. However, considering that most participants chose to read the texts at between 50° and 90°, we can safely assume that the method is effective for the general viewing of text.

Reading Position Test. In the second experiment, we asked another set of 13 users to read through a document and pause at four different words over the course of two minutes. For each word, we measured the distance between the center of the requested word and the point provided by the eye tracker. On average, the deviation from each word was approximately 0.5 cm across all participants for the two minute period, and showed a minor decrease in accuracy over the first minute. This distance is equivalent to either one line of text in the vertical direction or one to two words in the horizontal direction, meaning that a user would never have to read more than one or two lines of text away from his or her last reading position. With this level of accuracy, we can conclude that recall of page and position is effective for general use.

6   Discussion

In addition to the general recall of information, we have also explored the possibilities of the eye tracker and HMD setup for recalling patient faces and virtual display of patient records [15]. A generalization of this approach is the exploitation of eye movements in the context of more complex activities for which the role of vision has yet to be explored. New application domains should take daily activities into account and provide for cognitive assistance in those activities. The aim of our current studies is to determine the potential impact of such cognitive assistance for specific user groups in both medical and consumer applications. Our augmented reality setup can also potentially be used to interpret the center of gaze and fixations of dementia patients, which can be used to recall assistive information from the database.

7   Conclusion

In this paper, we propose the use of a combined eye-tracking HMD interface for detecting context, storing events into a database, and virtually presenting those events back to the user at a later time. Within this framework, we implement both the database for storing and recalling events, and a more specific method for recognizing documents, which virtually projects a pointer to the last location in the real world where the user left off. We then conduct two short evaluations testing the accuracy of document recall and reading position, finding that both are effective for practical use. This system can function as a cornerstone for the development of other context sensing AR interfaces, and we hope it will encourage further research on memory assistive technology.

Acknowledgements. Many thanks for the support of DFKI's MedicalCPS, Kognit, and ERmed projects for their contributions to this work. Another thanks to friends, family, and mentors for continued support and encouragement.

References

1. Belimpasakis, P., Roimela, K., You, Y.: Experience explorer: A life-logging platform based on mobile context collection. In: Third International Conference on Next Generation Mobile Applications, Services and Technologies, NGMAST 2009, pp. 77–82. IEEE (2009)

2. Belongie, S., Malik, J., Puzicha, J.: Shape matching and object recognition using shape contexts. IEEE Transactions on Pattern Analysis and Machine Intelligence 24(4), 509–522 (2002)
3. Gemmell, J., Bell, G., Lueder, R., Drucker, S., Wong, C.: MyLifeBits: Fulfilling the Memex vision. In: Proceedings of the Tenth ACM International Conference on Multimedia, pp. 235–238. ACM (2002)
4. Hodges, S., et al.: SenseCam: A retrospective memory aid. In: Dourish, P., Friday, A. (eds.) UbiComp 2006. LNCS, vol. 4206, pp. 177–193. Springer, Heidelberg (2006)
5. Hutter, M.: Universal artificial intelligence: Sequential decisions based on algorithmic probability. Springer (2005)
6. Lowe, D.G.: Object recognition from local scale-invariant features. In: The Proceedings of the Seventh IEEE International Conference on Computer Vision, vol. 2, pp. 1150–1157. IEEE (1999)
7. Mann, S., Fung, J., Aimone, C., Sehgal, A., Chen, D.: Designing EyeTap digital eyeglasses for continuous lifelong capture and sharing of personal experiences. In: Alt. Chi, Proc. CHI (2005)
8. Maus, H., Schwarz, S., Dengel, A.: Weaving Personal Knowledge Spaces into Office Applications. In: Fathi, M. (ed.) Integrated Systems, Design and Technology 2012, pp. 71–82. Springer, Heidelberg (2013)
9. Montemerlo, M., Pineau, J., Roy, N., Thrun, S., Verma, V.: Experiences with a mobile robotic guide for the elderly. In: AAAI/IAAI, pp. 587–592 (2002)
10. Orlosky, J., Kiyokawa, K., Takemura, H.: Dynamic text management for see-through wearable and heads-up display systems. In: Proceedings of the 2013 International Conference on Intelligent User Interfaces, pp. 363–370. ACM (2013)
11. Pollack, M.E., Brown, L., Colbry, D., McCarthy, C.E., Orosz, C., Peintner, B., Ramakrishnan, S., Tsamardinos, I.: Autominder: An intelligent cognitive orthotic system for people with memory impairment. Robotics and Autonomous Systems 44(3), 273–282 (2003)
12. Ravi, N., Dandekar, N., Mysore, P., Littman, M.L.: Activity recognition from accelerometer data. In: AAAI, pp. 1541–1546 (July 2005)
13. Sellen, A.J., Fogg, A., Aitken, M., Hodges, S., Rother, C., Wood, K.: Do life-logging technologies support memory for the past?: An experimental study using sensecam. In: Proceedings of the SIGCHI Conference on Human Factors in Computing Systems, pp. 81–90. ACM (2007)
14. Sonntag, D., Toyama, T.: Vision-Based Location-Awareness in Augmented Reality Applications. LAM Da 2013 5 (2013)
15. Sonntag, D., Zillner, S., Schulz, C., Weber, M., Toyama, T.: Towards Medical Cyber-Physical Systems: Multimodal Augmented Reality for Doctors and Knowledge Discovery about Patients. In: Marcus, A. (ed.) DUXU 2013, Part III. LNCS, vol. 8014, pp. 401–410. Springer, Heidelberg (2013)
16. Toyama, T., Kieninger, T., Shafait, F., Dengel, A.: Gaze guided object recognition using a head-mounted eye tracker. In: Proceedings of the Symposium on Eye Tracking Research and Applications, pp. 91–98. ACM (2012)
17. Toyama, T., Dengel, A., Suzuki, W., Kise, K.: Wearable Reading Assist System: Augmented Reality Document Combining Document Retrieval and Eye Tracking. In: 2013 12th International Conference on Document Analysis and Recognition (ICDAR), pp. 30–34. IEEE (2013)

How Do We Teach Young Children
New Concepts via Sketching?

Chau Thai Truong[1,2], Duy-Hung Nguyen-Huynh[1,2], and Minh-Triet Tran[1]

[1] Faculty of Information Technology, University of Science, VNU-HCM
[2] John von Neumann Institute, VNU-HCM
Ho Chi Minh city, Vietnam
chau.truong.ict@jvn.edu.vn, hung.nguyen.ict@jvn.edu.vn,
tmtriet@fit.hcmus.edu.vn

Abstract. The authors propose a system that supports children to learn new concepts of familiar topics via their sketches on an interaction surface. The proposed system has two main subcomponents: a system of interaction surface with touch detection from depth images captured by a Kinect and a sketch recognition module based on the idea of bag-of-word model. The system provides a natural and intuitive interface for children because they can learn new concepts via sketching. With the dataset of 70 common concepts, the accuracy of the sketch recognition is 78.21% and the average response time to recognize a sketch is 0.86s. The sketch database can also be easily customized to teach new concepts to children.

Keywords: Human-computer interaction, sketch recognition, bag-of-word model, table-top, 3D interaction.

1   Introduction

Human-computer interaction (HCI) plays an important role in the evolution of computing society. Researches in the field of interaction between users and computers aim to enhance the ease of use, ergonomics, and portability as well as to save time for users. Recent researches in HCI also aim to create intelligent ambient environments that are suitable for users of different ages so that people can have much more exciting experience. Examples of these systems include the Dangerous Australians product that works as an interaction surface and shows the images of Australian species for tourists, especially children [1]; the Google Glass wearable device that operates as a mini computer and can display the information via the glass screen in front of user's eyes [2].

In the field of HCI, smart phones and tablets are becoming more and more popular. In 2013, the market share of smart phones and tablets takes up 79.7% of the worldwide smart connected device market [3]. With the appearance of these devices, children have new forms of entertainment. They spend their time playing games, drawing pictures, or surfing Internet on these devices. Therefore, we can utilize smart phones and tablets instead of books and magazines to teach kids of 10 or

N. Streitz and P. Markopoulos (Eds.): DAPI 2014, LNCS 8530, pp. 292–303, 2014.
© Springer International Publishing Switzerland 2014

under new concepts in various familiar topics such as animals, plants, transportations, buildings, etc. This motivates our proposal to devise a system on these devices to support children in learning new concepts via sketching. Our system allows children to do many interesting tasks such as drawing a colorful picture just by sketching, practicing to sketch an item, or write a letter beautifully with decoration.

To deploy our system in a large area, such as a playground for children, we intergrate our learning-via-sketching system into an interaction surface using a Kinect to transform any regular surface into an interactive one [4]. Additionally, our proposed system can also be further developed to run on many common operating systems on personal computer (Windows, Linux, Mac) or on mobile device (Android, iOS, Windows Phone).

To perform the sketch recognition function, we use the dense version of SIFT to extract descriptors and apply the spatial pyramid scheme to represent the final image feature. The accuracy of our sketch recognition method is evaluated by testing on a dataset containing 70 classes, which is a part of the dataset by Eitz et.al. in [5]. Experimental results show that our sketch recognition method has the accuracy of 78.21%. Besides, with this dataset, the average response time to recognize an arbitrary sketch is 0.86s, which is acceptable for the system to run in real time.

The content of the paper is as follows. In Section 2, the authors briefly review the researches in the field of HCI and sketch recognition. Our proposed system and experimental results are presented in Section 3 and 4 respectively. Finally, conclusions and further development are discussed in Section 5.

2   Related Work

2.1   Sketch Recognition

Sketch is an intuitive image type in real life. Because of its simplicity and ease to draw, sketch is often used to represent or remember something visible. Therefore, using a computer to teach children via sketches of some common concepts can bring the excitement and motivation to children so that they can learn more effectively. Sketch recognition approaches can be divided into two groups:

Gesture-Based Approaches: These approaches are related to gestures that people use to draw a sketch. Akshay Bhat et.al. use entropy value of the angles caused by drawing gestures to determine whether a sketch is text or hand-drawn diagram [6]. Dean Rubine uses 13 features of a gesture to encode a sketch [7]. The main disadvantage of these methods is that the accuracy depends mainly on the order of the drawn sketches. This significantly reduces the flexibility of drawing a sketch because the image is constrained to be drawn in the order of its smaller parts.

Free-sketch Approaches: these methods are based on vision-based or geometric-based features of sketches to learn and classify the group to which a sketch belongs. Heeyoul Choi et.al. use Isomap kernel to compute the dissimilarity between two sketches [8]. Paul Corey et.al. integrate both gesture-based and geometric-based techniques to perform a hybrid method for sketch recognition [9]. Specifically Mathias Eitz et.al. use bag-of-features representation of a sketch and run multi-class support vector machines to classify sketches [5]. Unlike gesture-based systems, these systems do not depend on how a sketch is drawn. Therefore, we follow this trend, particularly the bag-of-feature representation to develop our method.

2.2   Interactive Surface

Interactive products have become more and more popular for users to communicate with digital devices and systems. Depending on the needs of users, there are many products with many different sizes, designs, materials and technologies. Medium-sized products such as tablets, ATM vending machines, smartphones are designed with small touch screens for the sake of mobility.

Many research approaches of interactive products have been presented, especially tabletops. Tobias Schwirten et.al. use laser to determine touch events in radarTOUCH system [10]. Nicolai Marquardt et.al. detect the actions of hands and fingers with or without markers/gloves via single or multiple traditional cameras [11]. Andrew Wilson uses depth data from a Kinect touch sensor to find out touched points [12]. Especially, Björn Hartmann et. al. propose eight interaction methods that are used in a working desk that supports interactions with real keyboards and mice [13]. We apply this idea to develop our interaction surface. Users interact through virtual devices projected by a projector over any relatively-flat surface and touch events are detected from depth data captured from a Kinect.

3   Proposed System

This section shows the main components and operations of our system. The overview of our system is presented in Sec.3.1. The touch event detection module is described in Sec.3.2. Finally, Sec.3.3 shows the sketch recognition method using bag-of-word model to recognize sketches drawn by a user on an interaction surface.

3.1   Overview of the System

Fig.1. demonstrates the overview and main structures of our proposed system. User draws sketches on a flat normal surface. In our system, during the interaction process, the surface and a Kinect device are held in fixed positions. A single computer collects depth data images captured from a Kinect to filter the drawn sketches and classify those sketches. The image of sketches and the result class name are shown on the surface via a projector. These functions are divided into two parts: touch detection and sketch recognition.

Touch detection: A Kinect device operates continuously to capture depth images of the surface. Depth information is processed by the computer and touched points are detected from this process. Then, appropriate touch events are generated. Finally, the projector shows the images of sketches.

Sketch recognition: this subcomponent is the main function of our system. When a user draws a virtual image of a sketch, the touch detection subcomponent shows the real image while the sketch recognition subcomponent classifies the class to which this sketch belongs. With the recognition result, a child can learn new concepts by doing the following tasks:

– Drawing and completing a picture by the corresponding image returned after each time a sketch is drawn. Corresponding images can be retrieved from the local storage of the system or from the Internet via web APIs. The returned image can then be re-sized and moved to the appropriate place (see Fig.2. (b), (c), (d), and (e)).

– Practicing how to sketch beautifully an item (a tree, a plane, a car…) or a letter. To support this task, the system lists many predefined concepts in the order of the similarity with the sketch.

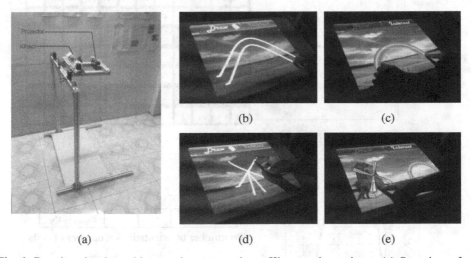

(a)   (b)   (c)   (d)   (e)

Fig. 1. Drawing sketches with a touch system using a Kinect and a projector (a) Overview of the system (b) A user draws a sketch on the touch surface (c) This sketch is recognized and replaced by the real image (d) More sketches are drawn. (e) The drawing is completed gradually by many images recognized from the sketches.

3.2   Touch Event Detection

In this module, we reuse our touch event detection module proposed in [4] to perform the interaction process. In reality, this module can be substituted by any device that has touch function such as smart phones or tablets. The sketch recognition module is designed as a program that can be modified to run on common operating systems such as Windows, Android, or iOS.

3.3   Sketch Recognition Method

In section 3.3, we present the process to recognize sketches. The main structure is based on the concept of bag-of-word model [14]. The main steps of this method are densely sampling on images, building visual word dictionary or codebook, descriptor vector quantization, building final image descriptor based on the codebook and using Support Vector Machines learning model to train and test data.

Densely sampling on images

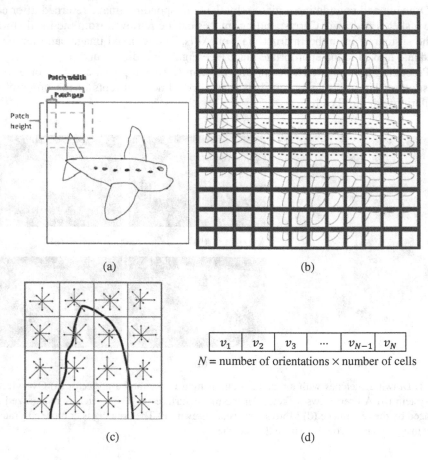

Fig. 2. Computing patch descriptors. (a) Example of 3 overlapping patches with different border colors (red, blue, orange); (b) All patches in an image; (c) The gradient orientations and magnitudes in the cells of each patch; (d) The total descriptor vector from (c).

To represent an image as a feature vector, the common approach is to locate regions of interest, or keypoints in the image, with different keypoint detectors, among which SIFT detector [15] is widely used. However, in sketch images, there are very few keypoints as an image mostly contains strokes and curves, not textures. Therefore, instead of using regular SIFT detector, we calculate the dense SIFT descriptor, which sample in all regions of an image to generate overlapping 16-by-16 pixels subimages or patches. Each patch is subdivided equally into non-overlapping 4×4 cells.

Two adjacent patches have a gap of 4 pixels horizontally or vertically. The number of patches in each image is:

$$\frac{(width_{image} - width_{patch})}{patch\ gap} \cdot \frac{(height_{image} - height_{patch})}{patch\ gap}.$$

The descriptor vector is the gradient orientation and amplitude map of that 16×16 pixel patch. In each cell, the image orientation previously computed is quantized into 8 bins depicting 8 different gradient directions over the range $0 - 360^o$ resulting in a histogram of 8 orientations weighted by the pixel's gradient amplitude and the pixel's distance from the center of the patch. Finally, histograms of $4 \times 4 = 16$ cells are concatenated to make a final descriptor of the patch as a single vector of 128 dimensions (16 cells $\times$ 8 dimensions). The descriptor is normalized afterwards. This process is demonstrated in Fig.2.

Visual dictionary construction
The main purpose of this step is to find the patch patterns that appear most frequently in the dataset and then calculate the frequent of each pattern in the dataset. These patches form the visual dictionary of the dataset or the codebook. The training step, testing step as well as the final product use this codebook to quantize the patch descriptors of input images. We use a common algorithm for clustering problems – the k-means algorithm.

Vector quantization
The purpose of this step is to quantize the large set of the visual descriptors to a smaller set of visual words, i.e. consider an image in terms of visual words rather than visual descriptors. Each D-dimensional descriptor is encoded to a K-dimensional vector that belongs to the space of the codebook. The main criterion to encode a descriptor is the Euclidean distance between that descriptor and each visual word in the codebook. We use the soft vector quantization method for each descriptor V. Let distance D_i be the distance from the ith visual word to V, we get k nearest visual words and assign the following Gaussian function values of D_i's to the corresponding dimensions of the code vector:

$$d_i = e^{\frac{-D_i^2}{\sigma^2}}$$

Therefore, the weight for each dimension of a patch's code vector depends mainly on the similarity between that patch and each visual word.

Using spatial pyramid scheme and average pooling to build an image descriptor
Pyramid matching [16] is a scheme used to estimate the approximate similarity between two sets of feature vectors, i.e. the distance between these two set in the same feature space. The idea of this scheme is to combine the representations of smaller set partitions in the feature space at multiple resolutions and compare resulting multi-resolution representations of sets. More specially, this scheme makes a sequence of increasingly coarser grids in the feature space and takes a weighted sum of the number of matches for each resolution. Two points are considered as a match if they belong to the same grid cell at the same resolution. Matches found at finer resolutions

are weighted more because those matches are more highly expected than matches at coarser resolutions are.

After the quantization step, for each image $s^{(t)}$, we achieve the set of codes $C^{(t)} = [c_1^{(t)}, ..., c_N^{(t)}]$ corresponding to the set of descriptors $V^{(t)} = [c_1^{(t)}, ..., c_N^{(t)}]$ where N is the number of descriptors for $s^{(t)}$. The histogram of each spatial region of the spatial pyramid is calculated by the average pooling on the codes as follows:

$$z_j^{(t)} = \frac{1}{Q} \sum_{i=1}^{Q} c_{ij}^{(t)}, j = 1, ..., K$$

where Q is the number of descriptors in that region of $s^{(t)}$ and K is the dimensions of image code $c_i^{(t)}$. The final image descriptor is formed by concatenating the histograms of all spatial regions and has the number of dimensions as:

$$M = K \sum_{l=1}^{L} 4^l = K \frac{1}{3}(4^{L+1} - 1)$$

where L is the number of spatial pyramid levels.

Training and testing steps using Support Vector Machines (SVM) model
The two main processes in this method are training and testing. In the training process, the final sketch descriptors of training images are learned by SVM. The testing images are then verified on the trained SVM model to determine the accuracy of the system. In real application, the trained SVM models are also used to predict the class of an input sketch from a user.

4   Experimental Results

Experiments of the touch detection accuracy are already mentioned in [4]. In this section, we present three experiments. The first experiment in Sec.4.1 determines the accuracy of the sketch recognition module. The feasibility of the system to run in real time is mentioned in Sec.4.2. Finally, Sec. 4.3 shows the efficiency of the system in teaching children. The first two experiments are performed on the system using CPU core i7 2.2Ghz with 8GB RAM.

4.1   Sketch Recognition Accuracy

In the first stage of our system, we conduct the experiment of the sketch recognition module. We reuse a part of the dataset published by Mathias Eitz in SIGGRAPH 2012 [5]. Our dataset consists of 70 classes with total 5600 1111-by-1111 images of many familiar topics. Each class contains 80 images. Some images in our dataset and their corresponding real images are demonstrated in Fig.3. We resize all images to 128×128 pixels and extract 16-by-16 patches and the numbers of overlapping pixels

8. Each class is divided into 2 parts for training and testing. The training part is also divided into 4 equal parts for cross-validation (CV) testing.

Since the images in each class can be very different (see Fig.4), we find the class of a test image by voting from 10 different SVM models. The final predicted class is the one that has the largest sum of probabilistic estimate scores of 10 models. Each SVM model is chosen randomly from the CV parts as well as the final training part.

Fig. 3. Some sketch images in the dataset (1st row) and corresponding images (2nd row)

Fig. 4. Some classes that have very different images: the plane (1st row) and the butterfly (2nd row)

To build the visual dictionary, we use the k-means algorithm with 300 clusters. The final image descriptors are calculated at 3 spatial pyramid levels, which results in $300 \times (4^0 + 4^1 + 4^2) = 6300$ dimensions for each descriptor. The cross-validation accuracy of k-fold test (with $k=4$) is presented in Fig.5.

After the cross-validation test, we train the system with the whole training set and evaluate the accuracy of sketch recognition function with the test set. The accuracy for each of 70 classes is demonstrated inFig.6.. Although there are still 4 classes with low accuracy of less than 50%, most of the classes can achieve high accuracy   and the average accuracy of our system is 78.21%. The confusion matrix for 70 classes is illustrated in Fig.7.

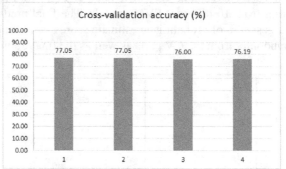

Fig. 5. The cross validation accuracy of k-fold test (with k=4)

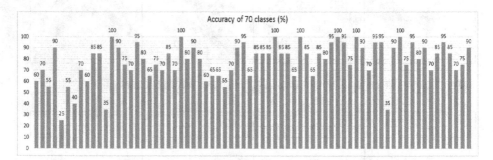

Fig. 6. The accuracy of 70 classes in the total test. There are 4 difficult classes with the accuracy below 50%.

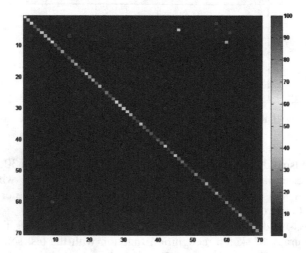

Fig. 7. Confusion matrix for 70 classes

4.2 Feasibility of the System to Recognize the Sketches in Real Time

We test the feasibility of the system to run in real time by taking the average running time of test images in the final test (after the CV test). The running time of the stages are shown in Table 1. This experiment is conducted in the same system configuration and parameters as in Sec.4.1.

Table 1. The average running time of sketch recognition

Calculating patch descriptors	0.458s
Calculating final image descriptor	0.139s
Testing on SVM models	0.263s
Total	**0.860s**

4.3 Efficiency of the System in Teaching Children

The second stage of our proposed system is to evaluate the attractiveness and efficiency in teaching new concepts for young children. 20 young Vietnamese children of the ages from 6 to 8 are divided into two groups to learn English words of common concepts. Children in the first group learn with traditional teaching method and printed books of pictures while those in the second group learn by playing with our system and sketches. From the observation, kids in the second group can quickly remember new words and can save up to 30% time to learn words in a category in comparison with those in the first group. Furthermore, children in the second group spend 50-70% more time in studying than those in the first group and can study more concepts.

5   Conclusions

In this paper, we propose a system that can be intergrated to an interactive product to teach children new concepts via their sketch images. The system can be deployed on our interaction surface using Kinect or on any other mobile device.

To perform the sketch recognition module, we extract the dense SIFT descriptors that is computed by densely sampling all regions of a sketch; the idea of bag-of-word model and spatial pyramid scheme to represent the image feature. Additionally, we also use Support Vector Machine for the training and testing steps and real application.

Experiments of this system are about the accuracy of a large set of sketch images with 70 different types and the time respond that enables the feasibility to run in real time. Results from the experiment show that our system meets the requirement to be a real-time system that runs with high accuracy. The dataset can also be changed to diversify the concepts that can be taught to children.

Further developments of this system include the system functions such as: sharing on social networks, more intuitive interfaces; and the sketch recognition algorithms such as: more sketch types, instant feedback from users to improve the accuracy.

References

1. Lightwell,
   http://lightwell.com.au/projects/dangerous-australians/
2. Fig. 8, http://www.google.com/glass/start/
3. Enterprise Irregulars, http://www.enterpriseirregulars.com/66218/idc-87-connected-devices-2017-will-tablets-smartphones/
4. Truong, C.T., Nguyen-Huynh, D.-H., Tran, M.-T., Duong, A.-D.: Collaborative smart virtual keyboard with word predicting function. In: Kurosu, M. (ed.) Human-Computer Interaction, Part IV, HCII 2013. LNCS, vol. 8007, pp. 513–522. Springer, Heidelberg (2013)
5. Eitz, M., Hays, J., Alexa, M.: How do humans sketch objects? ACM Transactions on Graphics (TOG) - SIGGRAPH 31(4) (July 2012)
6. Bhat, A., Hammond, T.: Using entropy to distinguish shape versus text in hand-drawn diagrams. In: IJCAI 2009 Proceedings of the 21st International Jont Conference on Artifical Intelligence, San Francisco (2009)
7. Rubine, D.: Specifying gestures by example. In: SIGGRAPH (July 1991)
8. Hammond, T., Heeyoul, C.: Sketch recognition based on manifold learning. In: AAAI 2008 Proceedings of the 23rd National Conference on Artificial Intelligence (2008)
9. Corey, P., Hammond, T.: GLADDER: combining gesture and geometric sketch recognition. In: AAAI 2008 Proceedings of the 23rd National Conference on Artificial Intelligence (2008)
10. Schwirten, T.: radarTOUCH., http://www.radar-touch.com/
11. Marquardt, N., Kiemer, J., Greenberg, S.: What caused that touch?: Expressive interaction with a surface through fiduciary-tagged gloves. In: ITS 2010 ACM International Conference on Interactive Tabletops and Surfaces (2010)
12. Andrew, W.D.: Using a depth camera as a touch sensor. In: ITS 2010 ACM International Conference on Interactive Tabletops and Surface (2010)
13. Hartmann, B., Morris, M.R., Benko, H., Wilson, D.A.: Augmenting interactive tables with mice & keyboards. In: UIST 2009 Proceedings of the 22nd Annual ACM Symposium on User Interface Software and Technology (2009)
14. Li, F.-F., Fergus, R., Torralba, A.: Recognizing and Learning Object Categories
15. Lowe, D.G.: Distinctive Image Features from Scale-Invariant Keypoints. International Journal of Computer Vision 60(2), 91–110 (2004)
16. Grauman, K., Darrell, T.: The Pyramid Match Kernel: Discriminative Classification with Sets of Image Features. In: ICCV 2005 Proceedings of the Tenth IEEE International Conference on Computer Vision (2005)
17. Lin, L., Luo, P., Chen, X., Zeng, K.: Representing and recognizing objects with massive local image patches. Pattern Recognition 45(1), 231–240 (2012)
18. Cortes, C., Vapnik, V.: Support-Vector Networks. Machine Learning 20(3), 273–297 (1995)
19. Tuddenham, P., Davies, I., Robinson, P.: WebSurface: An interface for co-located collaborative information gathering. In: ITS 2009 Proceedings of the ACM International Conference on Interactive Tabletops and Surfaces (2009)
20. Klinkhammer, D., Nitsche, M., Specht, M., Reiterer, H.: Adaptive personal territories for co-located tabletop interaction in a museum setting. In: ITS 2011 Proceedings of the ACM International Conference on Interactive Tabletops and Surfaces (2011)
21. Dippon, A., Echtler, F., Klinker, G.: Multi-touch Table as Conventional Input Device. In: Stephanidis, C. (ed.) Posters, Part II, HCII 2011. CCIS, vol. 174, pp. 237–241. Springer, Heidelberg (2011)

22. Grauman, K., Darrell, T.: The Pyramid Match Kernel: Efficient Learning with Sets of Features. The Journal of Machine Learning Research 8, 725–760 (2007)
23. Lazebnik, S., Schmid, C., Ponce, J.: Beyond Bags of Features: Spatial Pyramid Matching for Recognizing Natural Scene Categories. In: CVPR 2006 Proceedings of the IEEE Computer Society Conference on Computer Vision and Pattern Recognition (2006)
24. Bosch, A., Zisserman, A., Muñoz, X.: Scene classification via pLSA. In: Leonardis, A., Bischof, H., Pinz, A. (eds.) ECCV 2006. LNCS, vol. 3954, pp. 517–530. Springer, Heidelberg (2006)
25. Morris, M.R., Lombardo, J., Wigdor, D.: WeSearch: Supporting collaborative search and sensemaking on a tabletop display. In: CSCW 2010 Proceedings of the 2010 ACM Conference on Computer Supported Cooperative Work (2010)

User Experience in
Intelligent Environments

Design and Evaluation of a Smart Library
Using the APEX Framework

Tiago Abade[1,2], Tiago Gomes[1,2], José Luís Silva[3], and José C. Campos[1,2]

[1] Departamento de Informática, Universidade do Minho, Braga, Portugal
[2] HASLab / INESC TEC, Braga, Portugal
[3] Madeira-ITI/Universidade da Madeira, Funchal, Portugal
{pg20691,pg19814}@alunos.uminho.pt,
jose.l.silva@m-iti.org, jose.campos@di.uminho.pt

Abstract. User experience is a key point for successful ubiquitous computing (ubicomp) environments. The envisaged design should be explored as soon as possible to anticipate potential user problems, thus reducing re-design costs. The development of ubicomp environments' prototypes might help, providing feedback on the users' reaction to the environments. This paper describes the design and evaluation of ubicomp environments using APEX, a rapid prototyping framework providing user experience via a 3D application server and connected physical devices. APEX prototypes allow users to explore and experience many characteristics of a proposed design, in a virtual world. The paper focus in particular the design and evaluation of a smart library in the APEX framework.

Keywords: ubiquitous computing, 3D environments, prototyping, evaluation.

1 Introduction

The design and engineering of interactive systems presents several challenges. The presence of a human factor means that the impact of design decisions is hard to predict and assess without being tested with actual users. This assessment, however, must be done as early as possible, before too many resources have been invested and too much time elapsed. Even though tools have been proposed that automate specific aspects of interactive systems' analysis [2,9], the use of prototypes remains the main approach to support early evaluation through user testing. Prototypes allow a system to be explored and/or analysed at an early stage avoiding the costs of producing a complete enough system to be ready for user testing.

Ubicomp environments pose specific challenges in terms of prototyping. Due to their physical and spatial nature, prototypes to enable an assessment of the experience of using (being in) those systems can become costly to develop and deploy. The acquisition of adequate resources (e.g. physical devices, sensors), deployment to its intended target location, and subsequent experimentation,

N. Streitz and P. Markopoulos (Eds.): DAPI 2014, LNCS 8530, pp. 307–318, 2014.

all have expensive associated costs. Design decisions, once committed to, can be difficult to reverse [4]. In some cases, fielding a system for the purpose of testing might not be possible. Prototypes based on simulations in 3D virtual environments provide designers with a way of checking proposed design solutions with relatively low investment.

This paper illustrates the use of APEX [17,18] which is a framework for rapid prototyping of ubicomp environments. The framework reduces the costs of development by providing, among other features, the means to experience the system before physical deployment, based on the 3D environment delivered. The framework is being used to demonstrate the value of the approach for early evaluation of ubiquitous environments including aspects of user experience before physical deployment *in situ*. The paper describes the approach and illustrates it through the design and evaluation of the prototype of a smart library. The evaluation aims to check and understand whether the envisaged design suits the goals and correctly adapts to the needs and expectations of users.

The paper is structured as follow: Section 2 presents related work and describes the APEX platform. Section 3 presents the case study used. The prototype is presented in Section 4. Section 5 describes a user study made and Section 6 summarised with conclusions and future work.

2   APEX Framework and Related Work

Although several approaches that aim to prototype ubicomp environments can be identified (3DSim [11], UbiWorld [3], the work of O'Neill et al. [13], and VARU [7] are examples), they are mainly focused on helping ubiquitous system designers to identify unwanted behaviour in their systems, and to support informed decision making in an iterative design cycle. Other approaches (UbiWise [1], UbiREAL [12], d.tools [6] or Topiary [10]) focus on prototyping ubicomp applications or isolated devices and not on the prototyping of ubicomp environments as a whole. Some approaches allow an exploration of user experience but not of the whole ubicomp environment. Silva [14] provides an in-depth overview of the various approaches.

The absence of an approach that focuses on the experience that users will have of the design of the whole ubicomp environment, and which supports a formal and exhaustive analysis is remedied by APEX. The APEX framework is described in detail in [14,18]. Here, we provide a brief outline of its main characteristics.

The framework brings together an existing 3D Application Server (OpenSimulator[1]) with a modelling tool (CPN Tools[2]). APEX-based prototypes enable users to navigate and interact with a virtual world simulation of the envisaged ubiquitous environment. By this means users can experience many of the features of the proposed design. Prototypes are generated in the framework to help

---

[1] http://opensimulator.org (accessed: 6 December 2013).
[2] http://cpntools.org/ (accessed: 6 December 2013).

the developer understand how the user might experience the system. The two main features of APEX are:

- Allowing the rapid prototyping of ubicomp environments;
- Providing a 3D virtual environment as a basis to represent the system to be developed that can be explored by users in a realistic way.

3D application servers, such as SecondLife[3] or OpenSimulator provide a fast means of developing virtual worlds. OpenSimulator in particularly, has the advantage of providing access to the source code, thus supporting extensibility and better configurability.

APEX uses the formal notation, Coloured Petri Nets (CPN) [8], to describe the behaviour of the virtual environment. This behavioural model drives the virtual environment running OpenSimulator. This process is achieved using a specially designed APEX component. Using a combination of purpose built components[5], object warehouses, and an appropriate off-the-shelf viewer (e.g. Cool VL viewer[4]) APEX supports the construction of interactive and rich environments, providing users with an experience close to that of being in the real environment. Several users can establish connections simultaneously using different points of view in the OpenSimulator server. The users experience the proposed solution by navigating and interacting with the simulation as an avatar controled by mouse/keyboard, wiimote or smartphone.

The overall architectural view of the framework is presented in Figure 1. The five main components are:

1. a behavioural component, responsible for managing the behaviour of the prototype, including the description, analysis and validation of the virtual environment's behaviour;
2. a virtual environment component, responsible for managing the physical appearance and layout of the prototype, including managing the 3D simulation and the construction of the virtual environment;
3. a physical component, responsible for supporting connections to physical external devices, such as smart phones and sensors;
4. a communication/execution component, responsible for the data exchange among all components and for the execution of the simulation;
5. a configuration tool component, responsible for supporting the setting up and management of the framework.

These components support an approach to prototyping based on layers: Simulation layer, using OpenSimulator; Modelling layer, using the CPN models; Physical layer, using external devices and real data.

Developers can choose the level of abstraction they need to understand the design while prototyping the environment. APEX allows developers to switch between layers to evaluate different characteristics of the prototype. These characteristics might include the experience of the user using a physical device, or

---

[3] http://secondlife.com/ (accessed: 6 December 2013).
[4] http://sldev.free.fr/ (accessed: 6 December 2013).

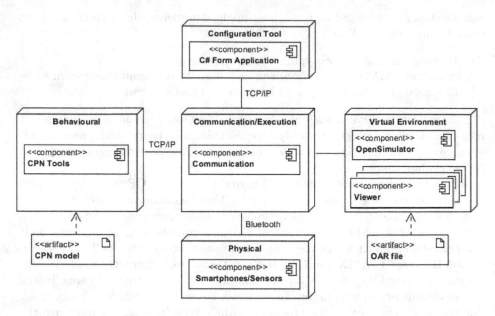

Fig. 1. APEX architecture

using the physical layer or alternatively providing an analysis of the behaviour of the system using the Modelling layer. For further information about the APEX framework, see [15,17,16,14,18].

3   Prototyping a Smart Library

The introduction of ubiquitous computing technology into an existing library was explored using the facilities provided by APEX. The prototype included displays to provide information about the availability of seats, and sensors to determine which seats are occupied. The proposed design was assessed through user tests. The costs involved in deploying the solution to the actual library, including the potential for disruption, means that performing such tests on the actual system was not possible.

3.1   The Library

The system is based on a specific library at the University of Minho, located in the Gualtar campus in Braga (Portugal). The building has 3 floors, including a ground-floor where the main reception is located. The other two floors are identical and have reading and study rooms (see Figure 2). Each of these two floors is composed of a reception (on the right in the figure) surrounded by doors that give access to the reading/study rooms. These rooms have 6 table sections (marked with circles in Figure 2).

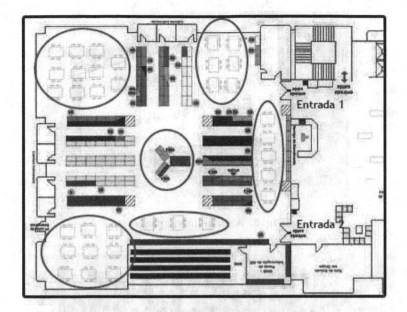

Fig. 2. Table sections of the Gualtar's library

The library is equipped with authentication systems for books and material requests. It does not currently provide any counting system to keep track of seat availability. The proposed enhancement of the library with ubicomp technology enables indication of seat availability. It is designed to illustrate the APEX approach.

4   The Prototype

A 3D model of the library was built using OpenSimulator. The virtual environment was then enriched by introducing simulated technological solutions (sensors and public displays) to help users to identify available seats. CPN models that drive the ubicomp environment were added to support the additional services provided by the library.

Two types of information panels were simulated to provide information about seats in the library. The first type shows an alphanumeric message with a sentence followed by the number of seats available (see figure 3). Several alphanumeric panels were placed on every floor, at the main entrance and in the centre of every reading/studying room. The second type of information panel uses the floor plan of the library and indicates the availability of seats using LEDs (see figure 4). This type of panel indicates the location and availability of seats with red and green lights. In the library, LED panels are intended to be located at the entrance of each floor.

The design and location of the panels were chosen with a view on maximizing their value to the users of the library. Figure 5 shows the location of the panels.

Fig. 3. Alphanumeric panel

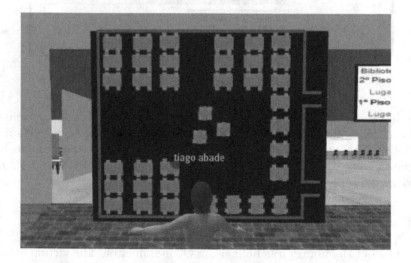

Fig. 4. LED panel

Two types of sensors were used to determine seat availability: pressure sensors and movement sensors. The pressure sensors make it possible to identify occupied seats. The movements sensors, located in the ceiling, can be used to determine the availability of seats by detecting people near the tables.

The design equips chairs with pressure sensors that are triggered by users as they sit down. Every time such an action occurs, this information is sent to every screen present in the building to refresh the data displayed. Movement sensors detect the presence of users when they are close to the seat, and modify the numeric counter when the user gets in or out of their range. The value of the counter is reflected in the screens.

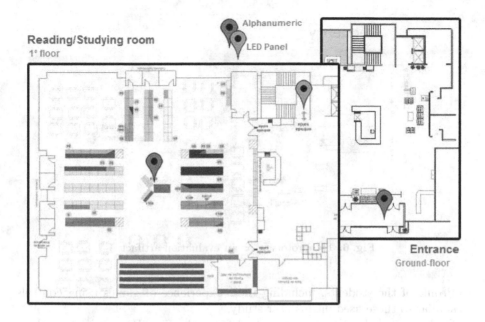

Fig. 5. Painels location

5 User Study

The user study was designed to evaluate users preferences in relation to the type, location and number of panels. The aim of the study was to predict the utility of the system once fielded. Considering that students are the largest group of users of the library, test subjects were recruited from the student population.

5.1 Procedure

The students were briefed with a short introduction about the purpose of the prototype and the information they would find in the simulation. They were asked to enter the library and find an available seat (as they were used to do in the physical library), but this time using the screen panels' assistance.

Each student used the simulation individually but bots were introduced in several seats to improve the realism of the experience. Students were free to explore the environment without being disturbed. No time restrictions were placed in relation to accomplishing the designated task of finding a place to seat.

While in the virtual environment, students were observed, noting their movements and the steps they took to find a place to sit. After completing the tasks, students were asked to answer a questionnaire. The questionnaire was composed of 36 questions, addressing not only the characterisation of the test subjects, and topics related to the screen panels, but also topics related to the use of the virtual environment as a prototype. The questionnaire was divided into the following sections:

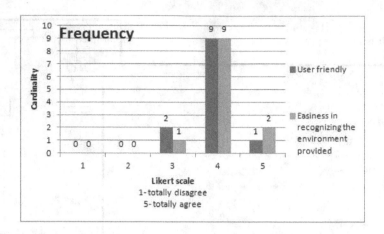

Fig. 6. The prototype as an evaluation artifact

- Profile of the students, including their experience of games using controls similar to those used in this user study.
- Evaluation of the prototype as a tool for evaluation. Here, aspects such as immersion, utility and user satisfaction were measured.
- Evaluation of the prototyped solution, including questions concerned with the location, design and behaviour of the screen panels.

Answers were given in a 5 points Likert scale.

5.2   Results

The two main aspects addressed in the study will now be discussed. To simplify presentation, only the more relevant/illustrative questions are addressed.

Twelve students, with an average age of 23 years, participated in the study. Of the 12 students that participated in the study, 10 declared they were familiar with third-person gaming.

The Prototype as an Evaluation Artifact. There was positive reaction to the use of a virtual environment as a means of prototyping a ubiquitous system. Students responded positively to whether the environment was easy to use, and whether they were able to recognise the environment that was being evaluated. The mode of responses was 4 (Agree). 9 replies were provided in each case (see Figure 6).

Questions relating to how well the environment supported the identification of alternative solutions, and how effective the environment was in providing an understanding of the design before physical construction, obtained a mode of 5.

Very high results were obtained for user satisfaction. Whether the approach could be used to validate other environments, and how well this method could be used to explore problems in other areas, obtained modes of 5 (see figure 7).

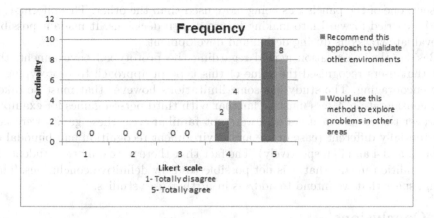

Fig. 7. User satisfaction - frequency graphic

These values demonstrate user satisfaction and a clear understanding of the framework proposed. This is consistent with a previous study where the use of the framework by software engineers was addressed [18].

Screen Panels' Evaluation. All but one of the participants totally agreed with the value of producing a real implementation of the proposed panels in the library on the basis of their evaluation of the simulation. When questioned about the possibility of using the LED panel only, 9 users replied with a mark of 3 or less, clearly showing preference for the joint use of the two types of panels. However, from the observations made during the simulation the participants spent more time watching the LED panel. In reality, during the simulation, in which both panels were available, the tendency of almost every user was to ignore the numeric panel. This suggests that the LED panel might be sufficient, and the preferred source of information.

The location of the panels was another topic addressed in the questionnaire. Here a mode of 3 was obtained regarding the appropriateness of their current location. From the comments collected, and despite several distinct opinions, the most general view was that the panels should be located at the reception on each floor. In addition it was thought that an LED panel should be placed at the centre of each reading/study room so that the students present might be aware of changes in seats availability.

5.3 Discussion

The results of the study helped better understand how a system of panels, to help users find available seats in a library, would be used in practice by users of the space. The virtual environment simulation not only helped users get a feel for what the system would be, enabling them to later answer the questionnaire, but also helped us realize that while users were keen to have both types of panels present, one of the panels was being more used than the other. This information can be carried forward into making future design decisions. It made it possible to evaluate tradeoffs during design and development.

Besides the information gained regarding the prototyped environment, the fact that users recognised the value of this type of approach to prototyping is also encouraging. The study has some limitations however that must be taken into consideration. Users must be familiar with third person games for example. However the results of users who were not familiar with these games were not substantially different (ease of use and environment recognition had bimodal of 3 and 4, and 4 and 5, respectively). The fact that there were only two students in this condition means that it is not possible to draw definitive conclusions. This is an aspect that we intend to address in further user studies.

6 Conclusions

Experience is difficult to capture as a requirement that could be shown in a system. With the aim to support the design and evaluation of ubicomp environments, a framework for the rapid development of these environments was developed: the APEX framework. This paper describes the application of this framework to a library, exploring the introduction of technology that allows its users to identify available seats. The proposed solution is based on the introduction of sensors and public displays in the library.

A user study was carried out with users of the library. The subjects explored a virtual environment simulation of the proposed smart environment, through avatars who represented them. This approach enabled the evaluation of the environment, but also of the framework itself. The results of the user study indicated the validity of the prototype as a basis for providing early experience to users, helping in the identification of how the system is likely to be used, thus supporting the discovery of aspects that should be improved or modified.

The repetition of these experiments in a CAVE environment, using a 3D stereoscopic projection system, is being carried out. The goal is to check whether immersion has a direct influence on the results. We plan to identify the role of the level of immersion provided by the prototype in the evaluation of ubicomp environments.

As future work, we plan to re-evaluate the location of the panels in the library, considering the avatars' movements in addition to the personal opinions provided. After the redesign, the new results will be compared with the ones reported herein.

Acknowledgments. The authors wish to thank Michael Harrison for his comments on a previous version of this paper.

This work is funded by the ERDF - European Regional Development Fund through the COMPETE programme (operational programme for competitiveness) and by National Funds through the FCT – Fundação para a Ciência e a Tecnologia (Portuguese foundation for science and technology) within project FCOMP-01-0124-FEDER-015095.

References

1. Barton, J.J., Vijayaraghavan, V.: UBIWISE, A simulator for ubiquitous computing systems design. Hewlett-Packard Laboratories, Palo Alto, HPL-2003-93 (2003)
2. Campos, J.C., Harrison, M.D.: Interaction engineering using the ivy tool. In: ACM Symposium on Engineering Interactive Computing Systems (EICS 2009), pp. 35–44. ACM, New York (2009)
3. Disz, T., Papka, M.E.: UbiWorld: An environment integrating virtual reality, supercomputing, and design. In: Computing Workshop, pp. 46–57 (1997)
4. Garlan, D., Siewiorek, D.P., Smailagic, A., Steenkiste, P.: Project aura: Toward distraction-free pervasive computing. In: Law, E., Hvannberg, E., Cockton, G. (eds.) Pervasive Computing, pp. 22–31. IEEE (2002)
5. Gomes, T.: Master Thesis: 3D Virtual Environments Generation. Master, Universidade do Minho (2013)
6. Hartmann, B., Klemmer, S.R., Bernstein, M., Abdulla, L., Burr, B., Robinson-Mosher, A., Gee, J.: Reflective physical prototyping through integrated design, test, and analysis. In: Proceedings of the 19th Annual ACM Symposium on User Interface Software and Technology, pp. 299–308. ACM (2006)
7. Irawati, S., Ahn, S., Kim, J., Ko, H.: Varu framework: Enabling rapid prototyping of VR, AR and ubiquitous applications. In: IEEE Virtual Reality Conference, VR 2008, pp. 201–208. IEEE (2008)
8. Jensen, K., Kristensen, L.M., Wells, L.: Coloured petri nets and cpn tools for modelling and validation of concurrent systems. In: International Journal on Software Tools for Technology Transfer (STTT), ch. 9(3-4), pp. 213–254 (2007)
9. John, B.E., Prevas, K., Salvucci, D.D., Koedinger, K.: Predictive human performance modeling made easy. In: Proceedings of the SIGCHI Conference on Human Factors in Computing Systems, CHI 2004, pp. 455–462. ACM (2004)
10. Li, Y., Hong, J.I.: Topiary: A tool for prototyping location-enhanced applications. Proceedings of the 17th Annual ACM 6(2), 217–226 (2004)
11. Nazari, S.A., Klar, A.: 3DSim: Rapid Prototyping Ambient Intelligence. In: SOc-EUSAI Conference, pp. 303–307. ACM (2005)
12. Nishikawa, H., Yamamoto, S., Tamai, M., Nishigaki, K., Kitani, T., Shibata, N., Yasumoto, K., Ito, M.: UbiREAL: Realistic smartspace simulator for systematic testing. In: Dourish, P., Friday, A. (eds.) UbiComp 2006. LNCS, vol. 4206, pp. 459–476. Springer, Heidelberg (2006)
13. O'Neill, E., Lewis, D., Conlan, O.: A simulation-based approach to highly iterative prototyping of ubiquitous computing systems. In: 2nd International Conference on Simulation Tools and Techniques. ICST (Institute for Computer Sciences, Social-Informatics and Telecommunications Engineering), pp. 56–66 (2009)
14. Silva, J.L.: PhD Thesis. Rapid prototyping of ubiquitous computing environments. PhD thesis, Universidade do Minho (2012)
15. Silva, J.L., Campos, J.C., Harrison, M.D.: An infrastructure for experience centered agile prototyping of ambient intelligence. In: Symposium on Engineering Interactive Computing Systems, pp. 79–84. ACM SIGCHI (2009)
16. Silva, J.L., Campos, J.C., Harrison, M.D.: Formal analysis of ubiquitous computing environments through the apex framework. In: Symposium on Engineering Interactive Computing Systems, pp. 131–140. ACM SIGCHI (2012)

17. Silva, J.L., Ribeiro, Ó.R., Fernandes, J.M., Campos, J.C., Harrison, M.D.: The apex framework: Prototyping of ubiquitous environments based on petri nets (chapter 6409). In: Forbrig, P. (ed.) HCSE 2010. LNCS, vol. 6409, pp. 6–21. Springer, Heidelberg (2010)
18. Silva, J.L., Campos, J.C., Harrison, M.D.: Prototyping and analysing ubiquitous computing environments using multiple layers. International Journal of Human-Computer Studies (accepted)

Fairness Properties for Collaborative Work Using Human-Computer Interactions and Human-Robot Interactions Based Environment: "Let Us Be Fair"

Myriam El Mesbahi[1], Nabil Elmarzouqi[1,2], and Jean-Christophe Lapayre[2]

[1] National School of Applied Sciences of Marrakech, ENSA Marrakech
Cadi Ayyad University, UCA
Avenue Abdelkarim Khattabi, BP 575, Guéliz, Marrakech, Morocco
[2] Laboratoire d'Informatique de l'Université de Franche-Comté, LIFC
FEMTO-ST/DISC UMR CNRS 6174, Computer Science for Complex Systems Dept. (DISC)
Franche-Comté University, UFC
16 route de Gray, 25030 Besançon Cedex, France
m.elmesbahi@edu.uca.ma, elmarzouqi@uca.ma,
jean-christophe.lapayre@univ-fcomte.fr

Abstract. Fair human-computer interactions and human-robot interactions in distributed environments are inspected, and it is suggested that humans, computers and robots may have to achieve overlapping tasks. Permission-based and token-based algorithms are used to ensure fairness in interactions between humans, computers and robots. Results of simulation experiments are used to illustrate the impact of several environment properties including a variety of processes, sent messages, received messages, collaboration stratum, average waiting time, and the average execution time. Actual experiments efforts are discussed and the convenient properties involved in designing fair human-computer and human-robot interactions in distributed systems are considered.

Keywords: Human-Computer Interaction, Human-Robot Interaction, Collaboration, Fairness, Distributed Environment.

1 Introduction

Human beings environment has always been full of objects with which they had to interact. And over the years, technology has known a great development. Nowadays, the human is discovering new ways of interaction with his new surroundings among which computers and robots come on top. Since the advent of computers and robots technology, its use has progressed very rapidly. In fact, one can easily admit that our era is heavily based on man-machines interactions.

Through the past decades, Human-Computer Interaction (HCI) emerged as a focal area of computer science research, and has made great strides toward understanding and improving interactions with computer-based technologies. There betterments more than anything else have triggered this explosive development. Indeed, some of the reasons for its success are forthrightly interaction related, since HCI evoked many difficult problems and elegant solutions such as collaborative work.

N. Streitz and P. Markopoulos (Eds.): DAPI 2014, LNCS 8530, pp. 319–328, 2014.

Now, advances in computer technology are leading to breakthroughs in robotic technology that offer significant implications for the Human-Robot Interaction (HRI) field. The latter has recently received considerable attention in research. Mainly HRI researchers are striving to develop systems that allow multiple robots and multiple humans to interact with each others.

In fact, how to ensure those interactions in the same environment has been a central issue for researchers. Nevertheless, rare are the works related to important theoretical common points and distinctions between HCI and HRI. In literature review, most of the studies deal with the applications of HCI and HRI separately in collaborative environments [1-2]. Indeed, an important remaining bottleneck is the need for computers as well as robots to interact efficiently with human team members. In the light of the development interactions has known, collaboration can be easily stated as the best option, however it is not as easy as it sounds. Coming together to work toward a common vision does not just happen on its own. We believe that by necessity, successful collaboration depends on developing relationships in which collaborators should be treated as equals. In fact, if fairness is found in a group, collaboration becomes an ideal concept, far more effective than an entity working alone.

It is well-known that one of the most significant concepts in collaborative environments in general [3], and in interactions in particular is that of fairness. In order to support the work on collaborative tasks within groups, the necessity for a fair collaborative environment arises. Within a given situation, there is usually a great deal of agreement as to how given humans, computers and robots ought to be treated identically, and what properties matter to the fairness. Indeed, the most difficult tasks can be accepted if collaborators are convinced to be treated fairly, inversely, gainful interactions may be rejected if they feel unfairly treated.

This leads to the questions of "given a group of humans, a group of computers, a group of robots, an environment, and a task, how should fair collaborative behavior arise?", and "what properties should be taken into account in order to ensure fair interactions?" The idea presented in this paper is how to amalgamate HCI and HRI in a fair way in order to collaborate in a distributed system. Our approach differs from other approaches in the way that our platform deals with distributed environment integrating both HCI and HRI and considers different interaction stratums. The practicality of our platform is proven by an implementation facilitating fair interactions.

The next section presents related work in the field of HCI compared to HRI as well as their relation to fairness. We analyze some significant similarities and differences that have been proposed to date by considering them to be a basis for finding a fair collaboration based solution. In section 3 we present our concept of interaction stratums and their connection with fair collaboration. Section 4 introduces the distributed Java platform upon which the prototype for a collaborative fair interaction is built. Before we conclude this paper in section 6, section 5 gives a summary and a brief discussion illustrating ideas for potential extensions of our work and future development of the collaborative platform.

2   HCI vs. HRI Merging towards Fairness

HRI is an interesting topic of research since it is strongly driven by innovation, characterized by enormous potential and growth opportunities. Hence, the question that will need to be discussed is therefore whether robots as a new interactive technology can grasp with traditional HCI assumptions, models and processes. Thus, this section introduces existing similarities and substantial differences to clarify the relationship between HCI and HRI, embellished by fairness properties and collaboration estates.

In fact, Kiesler and Hinds [4] noted that in HRI three new aspects appear. First, they maintain that the human perception of robots is different from other computer technologies. People tend to anthropomorphize robots taking them as peers and fellows. A second major point is that of mobility. They argue that robots are in multiple cases mobile, negotiating interactions in dynamic environments. Finally, robots are able to learn about themselves and their surroundings and act correspondingly.

Another vision was given by Thrun [5] advancing that the main difference between HCI and HRI is autonomy. He explains that robots are able to make their own decisions in a broad range of situations; yet it is not the case for computational devices.

Han et al. [6] addressed the difference between computer-based contents and robot-based contents. They believe that HCI is static and restrictive; whereas in HRI, robots are expected to offer dynamic interactions, to be more interactive with humans and more user-friendly than computers.

Breazeal [7] believes that HRI can be classified into four interaction paradigms. She argues that the robot can be perceived as a tool used to perform a task, a cyborg extension physically merged as a part of the human body, an avatar being a person projection or as a social partner discerned as an artificial being. These paradigms lead to a differentiation between HCI and HRI in terms of duration, interaction intensity, decision making, and adaptability to new challenges.

Fong, Thorpe and Bauer [8] addressed the existing differences between HCI and HRI. They believe that computers are always controlled by humans, but robots have a certain degree of autonomy. They also think that the major components of a HCI are a human and a computer, while HRI components are a man, a robot and an environment. They do believe that HCI is simple whereas HRI is complex. They assume that computers are in general fixed or portable such as Smartphones, while robots are able to move. Finally, they advance that on the one hand, HCI are mostly based on vision and audio, and on the other hand, HRI can provide different means of interactions.

Likewise, Scholtz and Bahrami [9] argue that HRI requires different relationships than those in HCI and propose five roles of interaction: supervisor who monitors robots, operator who helps the robot accomplish a particular task, mechanic or programmer who applies a software or hardware fix to the robot, peer or teammate who interacts with the robot at a task level and bystander who has no training but needs to co-exist in the same environment as the robot.

Feil-Seifer and Matarić [10] believe that the key difference between the two types of interactions is that HRI allows embodied systems to utilize physical context and mobility. They argue that unlike PDAs for example, robots do have the ability to take decision and they are mobile.

Table 1 summarizes the general views as introduced above. Indeed, a description of the relationship between HCI and HRI in all embracing and concluding argumentation currently seems inevitable.

Table 1. Summary of similarities and differences between HCI and HRI

Research Study	HCI	HRI
Kiesler and Hinds [4]	— Robots Perception (robot as a peer) — Robots Mobility — Robots Decisions Making	
Thrun [5] Han et al. [6]	The main difference between HCI and HRI is autonomy	
	— Static and Restrictive Interaction — Mostly Mouse and Keyboard Inputs — Output to Human : Audio, Animation, Moving	— Dynamic and User-Friendly Interaction — Voice, Face, Touch Screen, Gesture and Sensing Inputs — Output to Human : Audio, Video, Animation, Voice, Gesture, Facial Expression
Breazeal [7]	— Short/Medium Term Interaction — Restricted Environment — Interface layer/Control layer — Superficial Interaction with People — Less Possibilities of Learning	— Long Term Interaction — Survival in the Real Environment — Deeply Integrated "Interface" and "Control" — Intense Interaction with People — Learning in the Human Environment
Fong, Thorpe and Bauer [8]	— Controlled by Humans — 2 dimensions (human + computer) — Simple — Static User Model — Fixed or Portable — Mostly Vision and Audio	— Autonomy — 3 dimensions (human + robot + environment) — Complex — Dynamic User Model — Movable (mobility) — Vision, Audio and Tangibleness — Face to Face — Learning and Decision Making
Scholtz and Bahrami [9]	5 roles of interaction in HRI : supervisor, operator, mechanic, peer, bystander	
Feil-Seifer and Matarić [10]	The main differences are physical embodiment and mobility	

Most of the approaches presented above focus on simple differences between the two types of interactions but they do not consider how in their presence, entities could fairly collaborate. In our own conceit, we believe that surely some properties should be taken into account, to which, fairness should be added for the sake of establishing good collaboration. First of all, we deem that an important point is that of movement: computers are generally in fixed positions or may be portable, while robots are usually in movement. Another point is that of teams' creation, we think that both computers and robots could be part of homogenous or heterogeneous teams of different sizes. Moreover, the number of collaborators interacting may vary from one to many in both HCI and HRI. This final point will be discussed in details while talking about collaboration stratums in next section. The study of such systems is of great importance since they are different from other traditional distributed systems in terms of fairness requirements. Hence, the study of fairness algorithms for collaboration is paramount.

3   HCI vs. HRI within Interaction Stratums

In this section, the focus is on the type of interaction which should be chosen in order to ensure collaboration between several humans, several computational machines and several robots.

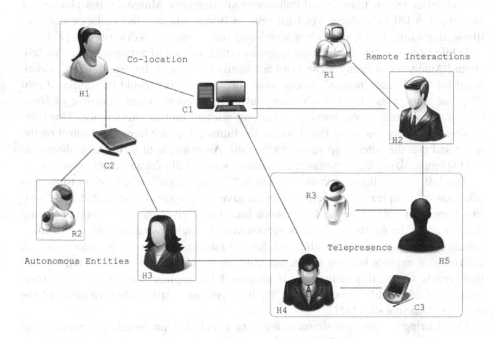

Fig. 1. Interaction stratums in collaborative environment

In [3] authors define collaboration as being a continuity of the collaborative workspace which is spread out over three dimensions going from coordination to collaboration while passing by cooperation. In order to ensure a good collaboration it is necessary to define and understand the different possibilities and situations that may occur during HCI and HRI. In fact, during collaboration the general topology of collaborators may change while moving in the environment. Thus, only one or a mixture of four interaction states could occur as illustrated in Fig. 1. We distinguish between "Co-location", "Remote Interaction", "Autonomous Entity", and "Telepresence" stratums. It is a simplified illustration of the multi-stratum interaction environment. Other dimensions should also be taken into account, such as the roles that collaborators might have during an interaction and the communication modalities involved in it.

Co-location is one of the spatio-temporal conditions making spontaneous collaborative interactions possible [11], and is a recurrent theme in research concerning collaboration and fairness. Having two or more collaborators co-located in a physical environment is the most typical catalyst for interaction because where there is proximity there is often social engagement to interact. This closeness allows more interaction but also emphasizes requirements onto the communication and interaction ways.

In the situation of "Remote Interaction", collaborators are separated by physical barriers but linked via telematic technologies, denoting a wide range of distances and thus panoply of interactions. Indeed, collaborators share the same visual perspective using a "what you see is what I see" interaction metaphor [12]. Yet, this distance has a great influence on fairness and collaboration strategies. Moreover, the plethora of mobility has led to a global trend for remote interaction and fair collaboration. An illustrating example is that of urban search and rescue robots, as discussed in [13].

While adding to this remote interaction a certain amount of autonomy, we then talk about "Autonomous Entity". The word autonomy consists of the words "auto", Greek word for "self", and "nomos", Greek word for "law", which could be translated into "the one who gives oneself his/her own law". It concerns systems capable of some degree of self-sufficiency, moving and acting without human interference. This interaction situation is shown in Fig. 1 where the human does not have any control on the robot and that the latter is operating on its own. An example of this case, is discussed in [14] emphasizing the importance of autonomy especially for air vehicle systems.

The last case of interaction as depicted is "Telepresence", which refers to the application of complex video technologies to give geographically separated collaborators a sense of being together in the same location It gives the experience of "going there without being there". This is represented by demonstrating that the primary collaborator is at a remote location and that the remote collaborator is collocated with the robot. It enables humans to interact with an environment that is spatially out of their reach. Often, this technology is proposed for applications involving environments that are hostile or unreachable for humans: outer space, deep recesses of the ocean, radioactive sites [15].

Considering the previous stratums, it can be concluded that humans, computers and robots must be endowed with fair mechanisms in order to ensure the aimed collaboration. In the next section, four algorithms are visited along the way taking into account two approaches: permission-based approach and token-based approach.

4   Simulation Results

The algorithms proposed by Lamport [16] and by Ricart and Agrawala [17] which fall
into permission-based algorithms category, and the algorithms proposed by Naimi, et
al. [18] and by Suzuki and Kasami [19] falling into token-based algorithms category
are compared in this section, in order to choose the best approach for a fair collaboration. In this paper, humans, computers and robots are supposed co-located, thus we
focus on the co-location interaction stratum. The simulation prototype is a Java programming language based platform, implementing algorithms using TCP sockets.
During each experiment, all collaborators will have access once to the shared resource. To obtain statistically reliable results we made long-time simulations executing 100 collaborations. On each experiment we vary the total number of collaborators
between 3 and 50. Figures 2 and 3 show the results of the simulations for the permission-based and token-based algorithms.

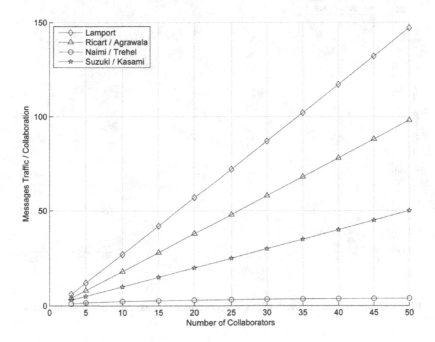

Fig. 2. Traffic intensity in accordance with the number of collaborators

To assess fairness performance of the collaborative algorithms, it is crucial to consider the impact of traffic intensity. Fairness performance making a comparison between permission-based and token-based algorithms in terms of messages traffic with
a single sub-task per collaborator is critical. Fig. 2 shows messages traffic as a function of the number of collaborators. It is evident that the behavior of the four
algorithms changes while the total number of collaborators increases. In fact, the

token-based approach algorithms [18-19] outperform the permission-based approach algorithms [16-17] in fairness aspects according to the total number of collaborators. In other words, token-based algorithms guaranty fairness with a less traffic intensity.

Satisfying fairness, delay constraints are also important. Thus, we focus next, on the delay generated for different waiting times. The value of the collaboration delay should be small as much as possible in order to guarantee a fair collaborative environment. According to Fig. 3 the delay incurred represents different changes for different collaborative message propagation times. It shows delays in collaboration as a function of the message propagation time between any two collaborators. Under all values of the latter, permission-based algorithms showed better results and outperformed token-based algorithms.

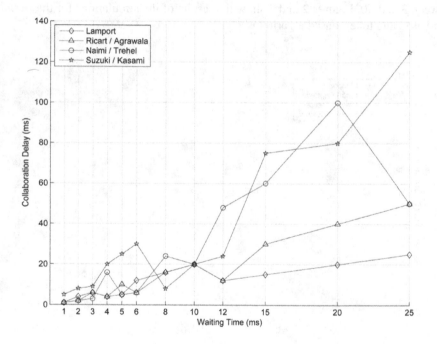

Fig. 3. Collaboration incurred delays in accordance to message transmission times

5   Discussion

In our research study, we support fairness in a distributed collaborative environment. In fact, we consider our work as a part of HCI and HRI and their relation to fair collaboration. Moreover, we identify fairness as the major performance criteria in evaluating the effectiveness of collaboration. Traffic intensity and delay are important fairness metrics but often contradicting. Further, fairness is a trade-off between traffic intensity, delays incurred and participation. Permission-based algorithms as presented, outmatched token-based ones in terms of collaboration delays performance. Yet, the latter outperformed permission-based algorithms in terms of traffic intensity. Moreover, token-based algorithms adapt to multiple topologies and offer extensibility possibilities. While permission-based algorithms are static, token-based ones are dynamic in terms of adding or removal of collaborators and the general topology and of the humans, computers and robots in the co-located collaborative HCI and HRI based environment. Thereby, we believe that token-based algorithms are more suitable to ensure fairness in our case of study. Nevertheless, a compromise in terms of collaboration delay should be assured. This result comes as a first step towards a quantitative verification of fairness properties. Thus, this study uncovered the need to incorporate a wide range of algorithms with the aim to choose the best for the HCI and HRI. For the future development of the platform, a number of extensions of the current prototype are planned. Indeed, there are several directions of further work possible from here. In fact, integrating the other interaction stratums is a highlight target and a challenging issue of our work.

6   Conclusion

In this paper, we present a comparative study between HCI and HRI emphasizing the similarities and differences between both interactions. We also tackle the way in which those interactions take place into a collaborative environment. A broad range of fair collaboration strategies were visited along the way. The goal of this work is not to propose new fairness algorithms and collaboration techniques but to adapt existing ones to this novel application domain. While many researchers have established the correlation between fairness and collaboration within distributed systems, no quantitative large studies have ever been attempted to consolidate the credibility of this theory within a HCI and HRI based environment. Moreover, to the author's knowledge, there have been few attempts to provide a formal classification of what fairness properties a HCI and HRI based collaborative environment requires. In this paper, we have shown how the fairness-based platform allows for enhanced interactions and better collaboration of distributed collaborators. The realization is based on the Java programming language as well as permission-based and token-based algorithms. This work represents the first steps towards an algorithmic vision of true fair team work between humans, computers and robots. The hope is that this work may provide a basis for a new algorithm responding to all of the already discussed problems. The ideas described in this paper are now facing the field reality through the experiments we are conducting. The preliminary results are encouraging, but the integration of other interaction stratums is still a great confrontation in our study.

References

1. Kartoun, U., Stern, H., Edan, Y.: A Human-Robot Collaborative Reinforcement Learning Algorithm. Journal of Intelligent & Robotic Systems 60(2), 217–239 (2010)
2. Królak, A., Strumiłło, P.: Eye-blink detection system for human-computer interaction. Universal Access in the Information Society 11(4), 409–419 (2012)

3. Elmarzouqi, N., Garcia, E., Lapayre, J.-C.: CSCW from Coordination to Collaboration. In: Shen, W., Yong, J., Yang, Y., Barthès, J.-P.A., Luo, J. (eds.) CSCWD 2007. LNCS, vol. 5236, pp. 87–98. Springer, Heidelberg (2008)
4. Kiesler, S., Hinds, P.: Introduction to This Special Issue on Human-Robot Interaction. Human-Computer Interaction 19(1), 1–8 (2004)
5. Thrun, S.: Towards A Framework for Human-Robot Interaction. Human-Computer Interaction 19(1), 9–24 (2004)
6. Han, J., Jo, M., Jones, V., Jo, J.H.: Comparative Study on the Educational Use of Home Robots for Children. Information Processing Systems 4(4), 159–168 (2008)
7. Breazeal, C.: Social Interactions in HRI: The Robot View. IEEE Transactions on Systems, Man, and Cybernetics - Part C: Applications and Reviews 34(2), 181–186 (2004)
8. Fong, T., Thorpe, C., Baur, C.: Collaboration, Dialogue, and Human-Robot Interaction. In: Jarvis, R.A., Zelinsky, A. (eds.) Robotics Research. STAR, vol. 6, pp. 255–266. Springer, Heidelberg (2003)
9. Scholtz, J., Bahrami, S.: Human-Robot Interaction: Development of an Evaluation Methodology for the Bystander Role of Interaction. IEEE International Conference on Systems, Man & Cybernetics 4, 3212–3217 (2003)
10. Feil-Seifer, D., Matarić, M.J.: A Multi-Modal Approach to selective Interaction in Assistive Domains. In: IEEE International Workshop on Robot and Human Interactive Communication, pp. 416–421 (2005)
11. Lawrence, J., Payne, T.R., De Roure, D.: Co-presence Communities: Using pervasive computing to support weak social networks. In: 15th IEEE International Workshops on Enabling Technologies: Infrastructure for Collaborative Enterprises, pp. 149–156 (2006)
12. Stefik, M., Bobrow, D.G., Foster, G., Lanning, S., Tatar, D.: WYSIWIS revised: Early experiences with multiuser interfaces. ACM Transactions on Information Systems 5(2), 147–167 (1987)
13. Wang, X., Zhu, J.: A Mixed Reality Based Teleoperation Interface for Mobile Robot. Intelligent Systems, Control and Automation: Science and Engineering 1010, 77–93 (2011)
14. Roberts, J.F., Stirling, T.S., Zufferey, J.-C., Floreano, D.: Quadrotor Using Minimal Sensing For Autonomous Indoor Flight. In: 3rd US-European Competition and Workshop on Micro Air Vehicle Systems & European Micro Air Vehicle Conference and Flight Competition (2007)
15. Xin, M., Sharlin, E.: Exploring Human-Robot Interaction Through Telepresence Board Games. In: Pan, Z., Cheok, D.A.D., Haller, M., Lau, R., Saito, H., Liang, R. (eds.) ICAT 2006. LNCS, vol. 4282, pp. 249–261. Springer, Heidelberg (2006)
16. Lamport, L.: Time, Clocks, and the Ordering of Events in a Distributed System. Communications of the ACM 21(7), 558–565 (1978)
17. Ricart, G., Agrawala, A.K.: An Optimal Algorithm for Mutual Exclusion in Computer Networks. Communications of the ACM 24(1), 9–17 (1981)
18. Naimi, M., Trehel, M., Arnold, A.: A log(N) Distributed Mutual Exclusion Algorithm Based on the Path Reversal. Parallel and Distributed Computing 34(1), 1–13 (1996)
19. Suzuki, I., Kasami, T.: A Distributed Mutual Exclusion Algorithm. ACM Transactions on Computer Systems 3(4), 344–349 (1985)

ENGAGE! EMPOWER! ENCOURAGE!—Supporting Mundane Group Decisions on Tabletops

Mirko Fetter and Tom Gross

Human-Computer Interaction Group, University of Bamberg, Germany
mirko.fetter@uni-bamberg.de

Abstract. This paper presents an interaction model to support groups making decisions, aiming to ENGAGE the group in the interaction, EMPOWER all users to put forth their opinion, and ENCOURAGE the group to discuss the options. Based on the tabletop application MTEATSPLORE, we show how the interaction model helps to design a system to structure the decision making process and thus can lead to an effective and efficient yet inclusive support for mundane decisions.

Keywords: Group Decision Support, Interactive Tabletop, Multi-touch.

1   Introduction

Decision-making processes in organisations are getting more and more complex. The involvement of different stakeholders, highly specialised decision makers, as well as the increasing complexity of the decision environments, the high costs of subpar decisions and the factor time as a competitive resource, all lead to an increasing complexity when trying to find optimal decisions. Group Decision Support Systems (GDSS) are designed to help groups of people to reach consensus when looking for the best-fitting solution for an unstructured problem [3, 5]. They achieve this by inter alia structuring discussions, outlining procedures, and supporting the exploration of alternatives. GDSS are therefore applied in different settings from supporting merger and acquisition decisions of an executive board to helping a community find consensus on the best location for a new industrial estate.

GDSS are rarely applied in mundane group decision-making processes—that is, supporting those everyday, small decisions that are made in dyadic or polyadic settings of small groups (e.g., choosing a movie with friends; deciding on sights to visit on a family vacation; choosing a restaurant for a lunch with colleagues). While the actual costs of suboptimal decisions in these cases are not as high as in the first examples, still the perceived costs can lead to a poor movie experience, or a ruined vacation, maybe preceded by lengthy, exhausting and ineffective discussions.

In the following we introduce MTEATSPLORE (cf. Fig. 1), a system supporting small groups with the mundane decision of choosing a restaurant together. We layout the design rationale of MTEATSPLORE that is based on three phases (ENGAGE, EMPOWER and ENCOURAGE), which aim to structure the process of group decisions making, yet do not automate and patronise the final decision. We conclude with an outlook to future work.

N. Streitz and P. Markopoulos (Eds.): DAPI 2014, LNCS 8530, pp. 329–336, 2014.

Fig. 1. Users interacting with the MTEATSPLORE on a multi-touch setup

2   Related Work

The diverse behavioural patterns of people when making decisions have been extensively researched for individuals as well as for groups [2, 9, 14]. A variety of studies assessed the consumer behaviour of groups in the marketing field [15] and shed light on what the critical factors are when small groups make mundane decisions. However, the number of systems currently available that support groups with making such mundane decisions is very low.

Business review sites—like Yelp[1] for restaurants, tripadvisor[2] for hotels and sightseeing, or IMDB[3] for movies—allow users to extensively inform themselves about a product or service and so provide some help to form an opinion on the best available alternatives for mundane decisions like hotel booking or restaurant selection. But, such services do not offer convenient functionalities to enable groups to explore such information together, which would be a prerequisite for making a group decision. Even single users are not well supported throughout the decision making process, as besides filters and search functions mostly no additional tools to structure the decision making process are offered. There are no tools that allow to easily store a selection of promising alternatives, to rank or compare them directly.

While recommender systems [12]—which provide users with suggestions on the basis of their personal preferences—better support decision-making process as a whole, there are only few systems that provide recommendations for groups [1, 7]. The group

---

[1] http://www.yelp.com
[2] http://www.tripadvisor.com
[3] http://www.imdb.com/

recommender system CATS (Collaborative Advisory Travel System) [10] had a focus on designing an interaction concept for a group of people when collaboratively deciding for a skiing vacation. Further group recommenders supporting mundane group decisions are an extension to e-Tourism [4] to recommend tourist activities, as well as PolyLens [11] and AGReMo [1] for the selection of a movie in a group. However, those group recommender systems share two of the disadvantages that most recommender systems share: First, a high degree of automatisation, that at the end only provides one single option without further explanation, is often perceived by the users as to patronising [6]. Second, in order to be able to generate recommendations recommender systems need to know the preferences of the individual users upfront. This often requires an extensive phase of providing the system with the data (e.g. by rating a number of previously seen films). In ad-hoc scenarios, as we imagine them for MTEATSPLORE, such an approach is not feasible.

Finally, while there are already a number of more universal guidelines for developing interaction designs for applications on interactive tabletops, like, for example, the system guidelines for co-located, collaborative work on a tabletop displays by Scott et al., [13] the focus of our interaction model is on a higher level of specific applications—that is, applications that support groups with making mundane decisions.

3   ENGAGE! EMPOWER! ECOURAGE!—A Model for Interaction

The rationale behind using GDSSs in organisations are well documented, including phenomena like groupthink [8], where individual critical thinking is replaced by a thinking that leads to a preference of harmonic in-group consensus, although the decision made might be irrational from the own perspective. Yet, phenomena like the pressure to conform, individual domination, differing communication styles or differing group and individual goals also play a role when choosing a dining opportunity or a cinematic experience in a small group. For example, some people might find it difficult to put forward their own preferences out of politeness, shyness, or cautiousness. This might be especially true in combination with other group members that tend to be bolder, rash, or in other ways dominating. This might lead to suboptimal decisions, where some group members feel left behind or cause lengthy decisions. We, therefore, suggest systems that support groups with mundane decision-making.

By studying work done in the field of GDSS and the related area of group recommenders, we identified three basic requirements for successfully supporting mundane decision-making. First, such systems should make the process of reaching a decision more efficient and effective, yet should not constrain and automate the process, but ultimately leave the group in charge. Second, such systems should equalise member participation by giving a voice to each group member. And third, the application of such systems should be effortless and support a smooth, persuasive access.

In order to address these requirements, we propose a three-phase model for the design of GDSS that support mundane decisions: ENGAGE, EMPOWER and ENCOURAGE.

ENGAGE—this first phase aims to engage the group in using the system. The goal is to persuade and invite the group into using the tool, although some of its members may be reluctant. We, therefore, suggest designing this phase in a way that it first proposes interaction possibilities for a single user. However, the goal is to design these first interactions of a facilitator or informal leader in a way they gradually draw in the other members of the group (e.g. by making the first user ask questions like "In which area to we want to eat?" or "At what time to we plan to go to the cinema?"). This phase is finished when all group members are interacting with the system.

EMPOWER—this second phase should be designed to equalise the users and to give all users a voice. In this phase all users are using the system. However, the focus in this phase is less on collaboration, but more on the individual exploring of alternatives, deciding on the preferred options based on the presented information, and putting forward the own preferences by actively choosing options. The design of this phase should optimally support structured individual work in order to boost the effectiveness and efficiency of the overall decision-making process. One goal in this phase is to not yet encourage to much discussion among the members, but at the most short chats like for example "This seems to be a nice option here…". When everybody feels informed and had the chance to put forth their preferences, this phase ends.

ENCOURAGE—the last phase aims to animate the group to have a conversation and to foster a discussion. Instead of presenting an automated decision based on the individual preferences, this phase should offer more freedom of decision but at the same time structure and guide the discussion of the members until they reach consensus. Therefore, the design should help to gradually reduce the options alongside the discussion process paving the way to the final decision and the end of the last phase.

In the following we describe the interaction concept of the MTEATSPLORE table based on theses three phases.

4   MTEATSPLORE—Supporting Mundane Group Decision

MTEATSPLORE is a multi multi-user, multi-touch tabletop application, designed to support a group of up to four users in finding a restaurant, which best fits the preferences of all group members. It is designed with various settings in mind including the placement of the tabletop in a hotel lobby, a tourist information office, or a conference centre. As one design goal was to empower participants that usually do not put there self forward in an unfamiliar setting, MTEATSPLORE is targeted towards ad-hoc formed, not well-acquainted groups of people (e.g., business partners, workshop participants at a conference). Additionally, it should satisfy the needs of more close-knit groups (e.g., colleagues, family members), with participants that know each other preferences better. In the following the interaction concepts and details on the design and implementation are outlined.

4.1   The Interaction Concept of MTEATSPLORE

The interaction design of MTEATSPLORE is based on the three phases ENGAGE, EMPOWER and ENCOURAGE and is depicted in Fig. 2.

Accordingly, the first phase (1) is designed to ENGAGE the group in the interaction with the table. We designed it to be operated by one user, who, by taking action motivates the group to use the table. This person can be seen as an informal leader or facilitator, for starting the decision process. By setting a location and a radius with one combined gesture (A) this user defines the area for which MTEATSPLORE suggests restaurants.

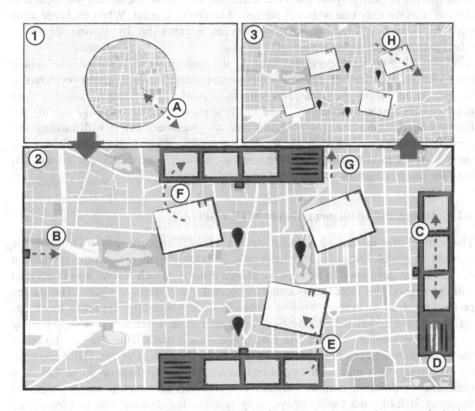

Fig. 2. Three phases of the MTEATSPLORE interaction concept presented counter clockwise representing the phases: 1) ENGAGE, 2) EMPOWER and 3) ENCOURAGE

This action leads to the next phase (2), which aims at EMPOWERing all users to freely and actively express their preferences by individually selecting restaurants they would like to visit. The group members place themselves at the four sides of the tabletop and drag out (B) their user workspaces. Each user now can individually go through the available restaurants with a swiping gesture (C). By activating filters (D) on the basis of personal preferences (e.g., only restaurant with outdoor dining options) the users can reduce the number of restaurants in their user workspace. If users find a restaurant interesting they can drag it (E) to the map in the centre—which serves as a shared workspace—to express this interest. When a restaurant sheet is dragged out, it offers more information, indicates the location on the map with a marker, and can be freely moved around in the shared workspace. Furthermore, a coloured marker in the colour of the users workspace indicates who is interested in this restaurant. If another user drags out the same restaurant, an animation visually merges the two restaurant sheets, and adds the coloured marker of this user. By dragging a restaurant sheet back in their workspaces (F) the users can reverse their choices. This action removes their coloured marker from the restaurant sheet if more users are interested in this restaurant, or respectively removes the restaurant sheet from the shared workspace, if the user was the only one who was interested in this restaurant. When users are done with the individual selection process, they can express this by closing their user workspace with a dragging gesture (G).

When all user workspace are closed, the last phase (3) starts. This phase ENCOURAGES an informed discussion among the users. While it would be technical feasible to only show the restaurants with most markers, our design explicitly does not have this sort of automatism. Like the first phase aims at smoothly starting the interaction, this phase wants to gently see the members off. By discussing the preferred restaurants based on the markers, the members can gradually reduce the number of restaurants removing them one by one with a strike-through gesture (H) until the reach consensus with one restaurant left.

4.2   Design and Implementation of MTEATSPLORE

The aim of the interaction concept design of MTEatsplore was to transfer the interaction model ENGAGE, EMPOWER and ENCOURAGE to a concrete application design. It was developed in an iterative design process, which always was concerned with how good the interaction design supported the respective phase. The design process involved several prototyping stages from storyboarding, via paper mock-ups (cf. Fig. 3) and mid-fi design prototypes to an interactive wireframe prototype leading up to the final implementation. The final application is implemented in Java based on the Multitouch for Java Framework MT4j[4] , and makes usage of the TUIO protocol[5] for receiving touch input. This combination allows the application to be run on a multitude of different commercial and non-commercial tabletop setups (e.g., the Samsung SUR40) on a variety of operating systems. For development and testing we used a low-cost setup consisting of a 40" LCD screen in combination with a Kinect camera and the software running on an 2,7 Ghz Quad-Core Intel Core i5 iMac with OS X 10.8.2. For the final system we used our custom tabletop consisting of a 1080p

---

[4] http://www.mt4j.org
[5] http://www.tuio.org/

42" LCD screen and a combination PQ-Labs G4 42" Multi-touch Overlay with 32 simultaneous touch points and the software running on an 3,3 GHz Intel Core i3 with Ubuntu 12.04 LTS.

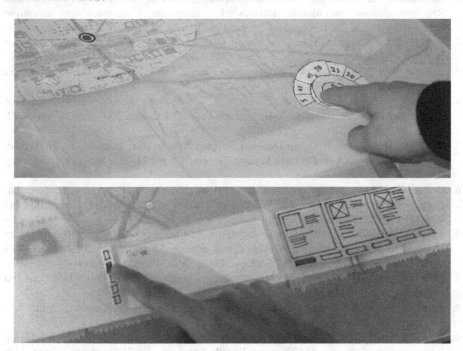

Fig. 3. Evaluation of paper prototypes of MTEATSPLORE: early design for the selection of the area in the first phase, and for applying filters in the second phase

5   Conclusions and Future Work

We presented MTEATSPLORE with three phases for supporting mundane group decision support: ENGAGE, EMPOWER and ENCOURAGE. How well MTEATSPLORE works, and whether the three phases will lead to better, more inclusive and more efficient decision making needs to be shown in a thorough evaluation. We plan to conduct studies that compare the performance and experience of groups choosing a restaurant together with and without MTEATSPLORE. Our aims are twofold. First, we are interested in how well MTEATSPLORE is able to convey the concept of ENGAGE, EMPOWER and ENCOURAGE, to trigger the intended behaviour, and to lead to the envisioned outcomes for each phase. Second, we are interested in how the concept supports the decision making process by analysing the satisfaction of the users with decision as well as with the decision process. Further observations of people using the table in the local tourist information will give additional insights.

Acknowledgments. We thank the members of the Cooperative Media Lab, especially Sascha Leicht and David Bimamisa.

References

1. Beckmann, C., Gross, T.: AGReMo: Providing Ad-Hoc Groups with On-Demand Recommendations on Mobile Devices. In: European Conference on Cognitive Ergonomics, ECCE 2011, August 24-26, pp. 179–183. ACM Press, N.Y. (2011)
2. Castellan, N.J. (ed.): Individual and Group Decision Making: Current Issues. Lawrence Erlbaum, Hillsdale (1993)
3. DeSanctis, G., Gallupe, R.B.: A Foundation for the Study of Group Decision Support Systems. Management Science 33(5), 589–609 (1987)
4. Garcia, I., Sebastia, L., Onaindia, E., Guzman, C.: A Group Recommender System for Tourist Activities. In: Di Noia, T., Buccafurri, F. (eds.) EC-Web 2009. LNCS, vol. 5692, pp. 26–37. Springer, Heidelberg (2009)
5. Gray, P.: The Nature of Group Decision Support Systems. In: Burstein, F., Holsapple, C.W. (eds.) Handbook on Decision Support Systems 1, pp. 371–389. Springer, Heidelberg (2008)
6. Gross, T.: Supporting Effortless Coordination: 25 Years of Awareness Research. Computer Supported Cooperative Work: The Journal of Collaborative Computing and Work Practices 22(4-6), 425–474 (2013)
7. Jameson, A.: More Than the Sum of its Members: Challenges for Group Recommender Systems. In: Proceedings of the Working Conference on Advanced Visual Interfaces, AVI 2004, Gallipoli, Lecce, Italy, May 25-28, pp. 48–54. ACM Press, N.Y. (2004)
8. Janis, I.L.: Victims of Groupthink: A Psychological Study of Foreign-Policy Decisions and Fiascos. Houghton Mifflin, Boston (1972)
9. Janis, I.L., Mann, L.: Decision Making: A Psychological Analysis of Conflict, Choice, and Commitment. Free Press, N.Y. (1977)
10. McCarthy, K., Salamo, M., Coyle, L., McGinty, L., Smyth, B., Nixon, P.: Group Recommender Systems: A Critiquing Based Approach. In: Proceedings of the 11th International Conference on Intelligent User Interfaces, IUI 2006, Sydney, Australia, January 29-February 1, pp. 267–269. ACM Press, N.Y. (2006)
11. O'Connor, M., Cosley, D., Konstan, J.A., Riedl, J.: PolyLens: A Recommender System for Groups of Users. In: Proceedings of the Seventh European Conference on Computer-Supported Cooperative Work, ECSCW 2001, Bonn, Germany, September 16-20, pp. 199–218. Kluwer Academic Publishers, Dordrecht (2001)
12. Resnick, P., Varian, H.R.: Recommender Systems. Communications of the ACM 40(3), 56–58 (1997)
13. Scott, S.D., Grant, K.D., Mandryk, R.L.: System Guidelines for Co-Located, Collaborative Work on a Tabletop Display. In: Proceedings of the Eight European Conference on Computer-Supported Cooperative Work, ECSCW 2003, Helsinki, Finland, September 14-18, pp. 159–178. Kluwer Academic Publishers, Dortrecht (2003)
14. Tindale, R.S., Kameda, T., Hinsz, V.B.: Group Decision Making. In: Hogg, M., Cooper, J.M. (eds.) The SAGE Handbook of Social Psychology, pp. 381–406. SAGE Publications, London (2003)
15. Ward, J.C., Reingen, P.H.: Sociocognitive Analysis of Group Decision Making among Consumers. Journal of Consumer Research 17(3), 245–262 (1990)

Constructing the Immersive Interactive Sonification Platform (iISoP)

Myounghoon Jeon[1,2], Michael T. Smith[3], James W. Walker[2], and Scott A. Kuhl[1,2]

[1] Cognitive & Learning Sciences, [2] Computer Science, [3] Electrical and Computer Engineering
Michigan Technological University
Houghton, MI, USA
{mjeon,mtsmith,jwwalker,kuhl}@mtu.edu

Abstract. For decades, researchers have spurred research on sonification, the use of non-speech audio to convey information [1]. With 'interaction' and 'user experience' being pervasive, interactive sonification [2], an emerging interdisciplinary area, has been introduced and its role and importance have rapidly increased in the auditory display community. From this background, we have devised a novel platform, "iISoP" (immersive Interactive Sonification Platform) for location, movement, and gesture-based interactive sonification research, by leveraging the existing Immersive Visualization Studio (IVS) at Michigan Tech. Projects in each developmental phase and planned research are discussed with a focus on "design research" and "interactivity".

Keywords: design research, interactive sonification, interactivity, visualization.

1   Introduction

Speech may be the most obvious means of communication using an auditory channel, whereas it is not the entirety of an auditory display just as text is not the only feedback in a visual channel. As compensating for the weakness of speech display (e.g., overall slowness [1] or interference with the current dialogue), auditory researchers have spurred research on sonification, which is defined as the use of non-speech audio to convey information [2]. Since the birth of international community of auditory display (ICAD) [3], the taxonomy and theory of sonification have been developed, categorized, and refined [e.g., 4, 5, 6]. Audification is a common sonification technique, where a series of data is converted to samples of a sound signal [7]. It plays sounds without interruption, so it is just as hearing music. However, there is no interaction in such a type of sonification. With terms, 'interaction' and 'user experience' being pervasive, interactive sonification [8] has also been introduced and its role and importance has rapidly increased. Interactive sonification can be defined as "the use of sound within a tightly closed human-computer interface where the auditory signal provides information about data under analysis, or about the interaction itself, which is useful for refining the activity" [9]. As an interactive sonification technique, parameter mapping [e.g., 4] has often been used, where data features are mapped onto acoustic attributes such as pitch, tempo, timbre, etc. Parameter mapping enables users to navigate through the (big) data,

N. Streitz and P. Markopoulos (Eds.): DAPI 2014, LNCS 8530, pp. 337–348, 2014.

to adjust the mapping on prerecorded data, or to mold the sonification of data in real time [e.g., 10, 11]. Another framework for interactive sonification is model-based sonification [4]. In this approach, the data are used for a dynamic system setup. In this configuration, interacting with sonification models could have similar characteristics to interacting with physical objects such as musical instruments [9].

In the current paper, we introduce our unique sonification research platform, "iISoP" (immersive Interactive Sonification Platform). In this platform, researchers can conduct any type of sonification research, including audification, interactive sonification (parameter-based and model-based), as well as visualization, depending on their research goals. To double our research capability, we have made up of a multidisciplinary constituents, including cognitive scientists (empirical research based on embodied cognition paradigm), computer scientists (sonification and visualization system implementation), sound designers (sonification design), and visual and performing artists (performance and art research).

1.1   Areas of Interactive Sonification

Interactive sonification can be incorporated into multiple areas, such as user interface design, interactive learning, and novel user experience design including accessibility issues.

First, interactive sonification facilitates the design and implementation of natural user interfaces (NUIs) given that it implies dynamic elements [12]. As human-machine systems get more complicated, the demand for NUIs has increased (e.g., successive NUI workshops at the AutomotiveUI conference, 2011, 2012, 2013). When NUIs are rendered, however, they often lack interface visibility or physical feedback, which makes natural UIs unnatural [13]. Interactive sonification could offer appropriate feedback, and complement interface visibility by providing ambient affordance, or even guide users' activities [e.g., 14]. Research has supported that interactive sonification is an effective technique in exploring map data [15] and multivariate data in tangible computing [16], in desktop [17], or in ubiquitous computing contexts [18].

Second, interactive sonification enhances learning effects. For example, embodied interaction based on interactive sonification has shown effective in various learning areas. To illustrate, Antle et al. [19] developed a computational system that helps children understand musical concepts in the form of intuitive, physical analogs. Ferguson [20] showed the potential that interactive sonification can be used for communicating real-time acoustic analysis results to singers and instrumentalists. Howison et al. [21] also introduced the instructional design which helps students develop an understanding of proportional equivalence through perceiving, planning, and performing actions with the body with embodied-interaction based on interactive sonification. Recently, movement-sonification projects have also been introduced in sports training [e.g., aerobics, 22, rowing in a boat, 23]. All of these projects have suggested that fully engaging embodied interaction with sonified feedback is effective in enhancing the learning effects.

Finally, interactive sonification improves overall user experiences. To illustrate, recent research on the aquarium scene sonification project [24] made informal learning environment (e.g., aquariums, zoos, etc.) more accessible to diverse populations and improved user experiences, simply by adding sonification of audience's gestures, which leads to a musical fugue with fish movement-based sonification [11, 14]. Results suggest that interactive sonification could improve visitors' learning and overall experiences by letting them to play a more constructive and interactive role.

2   System Configuration and Visualizer

For those promising applications of interactive sonification, we have developed a multi-purpose interactive sonification platform. We use 12 infrared cameras (using the Vicon tracker) attached around the Immersive Visualization Studio (IVS) walls to track users' location, movement, and gesture. The sonification system (based on JAVA, specifically, a JFugue library) generates speech, music, and sounds in real-time via a 5.1 speaker system, based on tracking data. 24 multivisions on a display wall visualize corresponding graphical user interfaces (GUIs) via OpenGL. More detailed system configuration is described below.

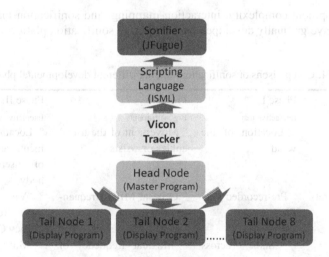

Fig. 1. The Vicon tracker sends the signal to (1) the visualizer (head node), which distributes it to 8 tail nodes, each of which is connected to 3 multivisions; and (2) the sonifier via the scripting language

The visualization component of the iISop (immersive Interactive Sonification Platform) provides visual feedback to users as an accompaniment to the audio component. Input data can be acquired by interfacing with the Vicon tracking system, or by reading data dumps in order to run prerecorded sessions. The visualization is shown on the display wall of 6x4 42" television screens which are powered by a cluster of 8 computers, each with 2 high-end graphics cards. The Vicon tracking system consists of 12 infrared cameras with sub-millimeter accuracy running at approximately 120 Hz. The system tracks special reflective markers, which can be attached to objects and configured to be tracked as a single entity. We have constructed six trackable objects for the use with the system: one wand, one hat for the head, and four straps, one for each wrist and ankle. Tracking these five parts of the body and a wand is sufficient to discern a wide variety of movements and allows for sophisticated data analysis.

The visualizer code is written in C++, using the OpenGL framework. It works by running a master program on the head node of the cluster, then launching a copy of the display program on each tail node. The master either receives Vicon tracking data or reads from a prerecorded data dump and then, broadcasts the positional data of each object being tracked across the network via UDP (User Datagram Protocol) packets. The display programs receive these UDP packets and decode them to determine what data to display. In this way, the visualization remains synchronized across all nodes in the cluster. Each copy of the display program actually displays the same scene, but is given a different view frustum corresponding to its physical position on the display wall such that all of the programs running a single, coherent image in tandem display.

3   Phased Sonification Projects

Taking development complexity, interaction-mapping, and sonification-mapping into account, we have gradually developed our interactive sonification platform to be more fine-grained.

Table 1. Comparisons of sonifications among different developmental phases

	Phase I	Phase II	Phase III
	Interactive map	Big instruments	Interactive sonification
Tracking	° Location of the wand	° Movement of the users' ankles or wrists	° Location, movement, and gesture of users' whole body
Sound Generated	° Pre-recorded wav file (speech)	° General MIDI (frequency)	° Virtual instruments (e.g., Korg Legacy Cell)
Sonification Information	° Same across languages	° Musical frequency or type of instrument	° Multiple sound profiles
Sonification Mapping	° Horizontal Location: Language ° Distance to Map: Amplitude ° Wand flip: Gender of voice	° Horizontal Location: Musical scale ° Distance to Map: Whole (white)/semi (black) key, ° Hopping height: Velocity	° Many to many mappings
Visualization Mapping	° Distance to Map: Zoom	Horizontal Location: Highlight of the keyboard	Many to many mappings
Level of Interactivity	° Reactivity	° Reactivity	° Full Interactivity

3.1   Interactive Map

Overall Concept. Because there was no sound equipment or software in the original Immersive Visualization Studio at Michigan Tech, we first developed an interactive map for Michigan Tech introduction as a sonification test bed. Users can listen to the pre-recorded (i.e., wave files) MTU introduction in multiple languages (e.g., USA English, UK English, Hindi, Chinese, Japanese, Korean, German, French, Spanish, Persian, etc.) based on their *location* in front of the big world map (Fig. 2). Depending on their distance from the map, the amplitude of voice clip changes (e.g., 6dB increases when the user approaches the map by one unit) with the automatic zoom function of the visual map. In addition, depending on their horizontal location, panning of the sound is applied using a 5.1 speaker system. As a basic platform, this phase has a *discrete* one-on-one mapping between users' location and speech sounds. Information given by the sound (Michigan Tech introduction) is always the same across users' locations, but only the format (language) changes. This can be called a "responsive" system [25], rather an interactive system because it involves only a one- way communication.

Fig. 2. Users can listen to Michigan Tech introduction in different languages based on their relative location to the world map

Sonification Implementation. The interactive map program takes inputs of the object (in this case, a wand) location from the visualizer program to play Michigan Tech introduction in multiple languages. The location of the wand is kept as an x, y, z point in the Cartesian coordinate, along with the wave file in question that is prepro-grammed into the executable. The program then takes the information of the wand's location to determine the amplitude of the wave files that are being played. If the users back up from the display wall, they would hear all voices at a softer level. If the users get closer and point to a certain country, they would hear the introduction in the language that corresponds to the closest country. Depending on the up/down spin orientation of the wand, either male or female voice was amplified and the opposite voice was muted.

3.2   Big Instruments

Overall Concept. Next, we implemented big virtual instruments (e.g., keyboard, percussions, etc) that respond to the users' movements. For example, the display wall show a "Big Piano" (Fig. 3.) on the screen and the user can play the piano by hopping in front of the display wall just as in a famous film, "Big". The sound is generated using the general MIDI with different velocity depending on users' height of hopping. The pressed key is highlighted on the screen accordingly. In the second phase, the sonification system starts to generate real-time sounds using MIDI, which is different from the first phase using prerecorded files. Further, each location contains musically different semantics, frequency information, which is towards a mapping with more continuous variables than in the interactive map.

Fig. 3. Users can play big instruments by movements in front of the display wall

Sonification Implementation. This program again receives inputs of the sensing object (e.g., markers of the ankles) locations. In a constants file, it can be updated to take in as many objects as one wishes to track. In other words, several people can play together. Given that an object crosses a pre-defined plane in z (z being from the floor to the ceiling), a sound would play based on the calculated location corresponding to a note, and a calculated velocity based on the current sample and the sample before it (used as a distance covered over time calculation). The instrument was set in the constants file, allowing for easy change of instruments between running the application.

3.3   Interactive Sonification

Overall Concept. For a more advanced design research, we have developed a fine-tuned interactive sonification system in the third phase. In contrast to one-on-one mapping used in the previous two phases, this interactive sonification phase

Fig. 4. Users can improvise real-time sonification and visualization based on their location, movement, and gesture. They can change multiple mappings via the scripting language.

allows for many-to-many mappings. In this phase, users can wear a number of trackable objects simultaneously. The positions of these objects are matched with multiple parameters of sonification and visualization systems. For researchers without programming background to configure these mappings, we created a web-based scripting language [for more details, see 26]. Note that we integrated analytical mappings and holistic mappings [e.g., 16]. For example, the system logs time passed, average velocity, and average acceleration (mapping with accumulated time); and proximity to other objects (mapping with the relationship between objects). These holistic mappings are expected to provide an additional aesthetic dimension [see 18] to the real-time sonification and visualization as well as full interactivity [25]. Whereas the first two projects show only responsiveness of the system, the holistic mappings in the third phase enable more interactive communication between the system and users, by reflecting and recurring to the previous messages when generating new messages [see 11].

This system could be used as not only a scientific research platform, but also an experimental artistic performance research platform. Our first on-going project is an interactive ballet performance. Ballerinas can improvise their own music and sound based on their dance, rather than dance based on predefined music. Here, we obtain two different meanings simultaneously: their action (dance) and the conversion of their action into musical meaning [27]. To this end, we have invited ballerinas and analyzed their movements. To extract and analyze key patterns of their movements, we have used video recordings and a cognitive task analysis. Extracted key patterns have informed the sound designers' iterative mapping configurations. The behavioral patterns are being categorized and matched with a certain emotional state [c.f., laban movement 28] and then, will be mapped onto sound profiles accordingly. In addition to real-time art performance, this interactive sonification system can be used for training and learning purposes. The interactive sonification could generate target sounds and guidance sounds to help dancers, instrumentalists, or athletes get to their target behaviors. The visualizer will also help them monitor their own actions.

Table 2. Example of Sonifier Parameter Mappings in Phase III

	X	Y	Z	Velocity	Acceleration	Proximity	Time passed	Average velocity	Average accel.
Frequency	√				√				√
Frequency Range		√			√				
Panning	√								
Tonality							√		
Rhythm				√				√	
Rhythmic Stability						√			√
Beat per Minute					√		√		
Intensity				√				√	
Instruments	√				√				

Sonification Implementation. A scripting language (ISML: Interactive Sonification Markup Language, http://cs.mtu.edu/~jwwalker/isml-creator/ISML-Creator.html) was created to allow for researchers to create a script to define how the program would react to positional inputs of worn arm and leg bracelets, etc. The scripting language was implemented to allow for the researchers to define specific events where the sonification mappings have changed. The script also allows for the researchers to generate sounds based on statistics such as position, velocity, acceleration, proximity to other objects, time passed, average acceleration, average velocity, or any equation that uses these inputs to generate an output. Within the implementation of the scripting language, the researchers also have the ability to store values for later use, allowing for almost any event to be described by the scripting language.

Visualization Implementation. The visualization responds to user movements in a number of aspects (Fig. 4). A colored sphere is drawn at the location of each object being tracked. The color of the spheres changes in response to the objects' average proximity to each other, using warmer colors the greater the distance between the objects. Trailing afterimages are rendered for each sphere, with the afterimage elongating the greater the velocity of that object. Each sphere also regularly emits particles which fly in the same direction and velocity as the sphere that created them at the point in time when they were spawned. The background includes multiple intersecting, rotating wireframe spheres whose rotation speed and color are tied to the average velocity of the tracked objects, while the background itself grows brighter and darker in response to tracked objects' average proximity. Transparency effects are used to blend the various visualization components.

4   Discussion and Future Work

Given that interactive sonification has such big potential in a number of research do-mains, our goal is to make a design research platform that allows researchers to con-duct all of the experimental sonification research in a single platform. Before we describe our phased developments in detail, we would first examine design research taxonomy which outlines our design research approaches.

Design can be defined as "a plan for arranging elements in such a way as to best accomplish a particular purpose" [29]. On the other hand, research can be defined as "a systematic investigation that establishes novel facts, solves new or existing prob-lems, proves new ideas, or develops new theories." Taken together, "design research" can be referred to as "the investigation of knowledge through purposeful design." When we agree that sonification is a purposeful mapping between sound and meaning [30] or making an organized sound from the semiotics perspective (Panel discussion at ICAD 2012), the mapping or organizing sound could involve diverse research, aiming at ease of use (perspective of user interface), coaching (perspective of learning and training), or aesthetics (perspective of user experience), depending on its purpose.

Faste and Faste [31] proposed a new framework of the relationship between design and research, and classified design research into four categories: (1) "Design through research" or studious design research is similar to traditional research; (2) "Design of research" or formative design research refers to a meta-process, including the creative activities of planning and preparing for subsequent empirical or theoretical research; (3) In "research on design" or diagnostic design research, researchers investigate their design processes to enhance the future practice of design; and (4) in "research through design" or embedded design research, designers practice their craft to seek new know-ledge and to gain insight for the possible outcomes.

All of those four design research approaches have been integrated in our sonifica-tion design research using a single platform, iISoP. In other words, (1) Visual, sound, and performing artists and researchers conduct their empirical experiments and based on those research data, they have iteratively redesign their works; (2) Con-structing our platform per se can be said as a creative design to prepare for future research design. To this end, we tried to reflect several sonification dimensions (one-on-one mapping vs. many-to-many mapping) and interactivity dimensions (e.g., responsiveness vs. full interactivity) in our phased projects. Accordingly, a project in each phase has been designed in a systematic way for conducting differentiated em-pirical research; (3) By achieving (2), researchers can look back on and diagnose how they practice their design in terms of goals, variables, and methods. For exam-ple, by showing clear distinctions in each project layer, designers can consciously recognize the elements of each layer; and replicate, extend, and combine those in-gredients in their future design; (4) Designers' new outcomes can pose unique ques-tions and thus, inspire researchers' future direction again. Therefore, we envision to seeing the harmony and resonance of all these different approaches in our design research platform.

Planned research projects include training and learning (e.g., instrumentalists and athletes [e.g., 23]) and natural user interfaces for exploring and manipulating large-scale data (e.g., geographical [15] or social networks [16]). Developing a sonification-inspired story-telling system for children is also considered. To investigate "interactivity" further, we plan to conduct a number of studies about the interactions among humans, animals, and robots in the iISoP environment. To devise a fully interactive system, we cautiously review the possibility of anthropomorphism [32] of the iISoP. To this end, it needs to evolve further with higher intellectual capability. Finally, the iISoP could be developed for virtual museums and galleries for better accessibility of audience with diverse disabilities and for enhanced user experience for all populations [11].

References

1. Jeon, M., Gupta, S., Davison, B.K., Walker, B.N.: Auditory menus are not just spoken visual menus: A case study of "unavailable" menu items. Journal of the Audio Engineering Society 60(7/8), 505–518 (2012)
2. Kramer, G., Walker, B.N., Bonebright, T., Cook, P., Flowers, J., Miner, N.E.A.: The sonification report: Status of the field and research agenda. Report prepared for the National Science Foundation by Members of the International Community for Auditory Display. International Community for Auditory Display (ICAD), Santa Fe (1999)
3. Kramer, G.: An introduction to auditory display. In: Kramer, G. (ed.) Auditory Display: Sonificaiton, Audification, and Auditory Interfaces, pp. 1–77. Addison-Wesley, MA (1994)
4. Hermann, T.: Taxonomy and definitions for sonification and auditory display. In: Proceedings of the 14th International Conference on Auditory Display (ICAD 2008), Paris, France (2008)
5. Hermann, T., Hunt, A., Neuhoff, J.G.E.: The Sonification Handbook. Logos Publishing House, Berlin (2011)
6. Walker, B.N., Kramer, G.: Sonification. In: Karwowski, W. (ed.) International Encyclopedia of Ergonomics and Human Factors, 2nd edn., pp. 1254–1256. CRC Press, New York (2006)
7. Walker, B.N., Kramer, G.: Auditory displays, alarms, and auditory interfaces. In: Karwowski, W. (ed.) International Encyclopedia of Ergonomics and Human Factors, 2nd edn., pp. 1021–1025. CRC Press, New York (2006)
8. Hermann, T., Hunt, A.: The discipline of interactive sonification. In: Proceedings of the International Workshop on Interactive Sonification, Bielefeld, Germany (2004)
9. Hermann, T., Hunt, A.: An introduction to Interactive Sonification. IEEE Multimedia 12(2), 20–24 (2005)
10. Walker, B.N., Kim, J., Pendse, A.: Musical soundscapes for an accessible aquarium: Bringing dynamic exhibits to the visually impaired. In: Proceedings of the International Computer Music Conference (ICMC 2007), Copenhagen, Denmark, August 27-30 (2007)
11. Jeon, M., Winton, R.J., Henry, A.G., Oh, S., Bruce, C.M., Walker, B.N.: Designing interactive sonification for live aquarium exhibits. In: Stephanidis, C. (ed.) HCII 2013, Part I. CCIS, vol. 373, pp. 332–336. Springer, Heidelberg (2013)
12. Jeon, M., Walker, B.N., Bruce, C.M.: Science or art? "Sonification in the age of biocybernetic reproduction": A case study of the accessible aquarium project. In: Proceedings of the International Conference on Auditory Display (ICAD 2013), July 6-10 (2013)

13. Malizia, A., Bellucci, A.: The artificiality of natural user interfaces. Communications of the ACM 55(3), 36–38 (2012)
14. Jeon, M., Winton, R.J., Yim, J.-B., Bruce, C.M., Walker, B.N.: AquariumFugue: Interactive sonification for children and visually impaired audience in informal learning environments. In: Proceedings of the 18th International Conference on Auditory Display, ICAD 2012 (2012)
15. Zhao, H., Smith, B.K., Norman, K., Plaisant, C., Shneiderman, B.: Interactive sonification of choropleth maps. IEEE Multimedia 12(2), 26–35 (2005)
16. Hermann, T., Bovermann, T., Riedenklau, E., Ritter, H.: Tangible computing for interactive sonification of multivariate data. In: International Workshop on Interactive Sonification (ISon), York, UK. (2007)
17. Stockman, T.: Interactive sonification of spreadsheets. In: Proceedings of the International Conference on Auditory Dislay (ICAD 2005), Limerick, Ireland, pp. 134–139 (2005)
18. Fernström, M., Brazil, E., Bannon, L.: HCI Design and interactive sonification for fingers and ears. IEEE Multimedia 12(2), 36–44 (2005)
19. Antle, A.N., Droumeva, M., Corness, G.: Playing with the sound maker: Do embodied metaphors help children learn? In: Proceedings of the Conference on Interaction Design and Children, Chicago, IL, USA, pp. 178–185 (2008)
20. Ferguson, S.: Learning musical instrument skills through interactive sonification. In: International Conference on New Interfaces for Musical Expression (NIME 2006), pp. 384–389 (2006)
21. Howison, M., Trninic, D., Reinholz, D., Abrahamson, D.: The mathematical imagery trainer: From embodied interaction to conceptual learning. In: Proceedings of the SIGCHI Conference on Human Factors in Computing Systems (CHI 2011), Vancouver, BC, Canada, pp. 1989–1998 (2011)
22. Hermann, T., Zehe, S.: Sonified aerobics: Interactive sonification of coordinated body movements. In: Proceedings of the International Conference on Auditory Display (ICAD 2011), Budapest, Hungary (2011)
23. Schaffert, N., Mattes, K., Effenberg, A.O.: The sound of rowing stroke cycles as acoustic feedback. In: Proceedings of the International Conference on Auditory Display (ICAD 2011), Budapest, Hungary (2011)
24. Walker, B.N., Godfrey, M.T., Orlosky, J.E., Bruce, C., Sanford, J.: Aquarium sonification: Soundscapes for accessible dynamic informal learning environments. In: Proceedings of the Conference on Auditory Display (ICAD 2006), London, UK, pp. 238–241 (2006)
25. Rafaeli, S.: Interactivity: From new media to communication. Sage Annual Review of Communication Research: Advancing Communication Science 16, 110–134 (1988)
26. Landry, S., Jeon, M., Ryan, J.: A broad spectrum of sonic interactions at immersive interactive sonification platform (iISoP). In: Proceedings of the 21st IEEE Virtual Reality Conference (Workshop in Sonic Interactions in Virtual Environments), Minneapolis, Minnesota (2014)
27. Roddy, S., Furlong, D.: Emobided cognition in auditory display. In: Proceedings of the International Conference on Auditory Display (ICAD 2013), Lodz, Poland (2013)
28. Camurri, A., Lagerlöf, I., Volpe, G.: Recognizing emotion from dance movement: Comparison of spectator recognition and automated techniques. International Journal of Human-Computer Studies 59, 213–225 (2003)
29. Neuhart, J., Neuhart, M., Eames, R.: Eames Design: The work of the office of Charles and Ray Eames. Harry N. Abrams, New York (1989)

30. Jeon, M.: Two or three things you need to know about AUI design or designers. In: Proceedings of the International Conference on Auditory Display (ICAD 2010), Washington D.C. (2010)
31. Faste, T., Faste, H.: Demystifying "design research": Design is not research, research is design. In: Proceedings of the IDSA (2012)
32. Le Groux, S., Manzolli, J., Verschure, P.F.M.J.: Interactive sonification of the spatial behavior of human and synthetic characters in a mixed-reality environment. In: Proceedings of the 10th Annual International Workshop on Presence, pp. 27/388–34/388 (2007)

Human–Computer–Biosphere Interaction: Beyond Human - Centric Interaction

Hill Hiroki Kobayashi

Center for Spatial Information Science, The University of Tokyo
5-1-5 Kashiwanoha, Kashiwa-shi, Chiba
277-8568, Japan
kobayashi@csis.u-tokyo.ac.jp

Abstract. Current human–computer interaction (HCI) is primarily focused on human-centric interactions. However, people experience many non-human-centric interactions during the course of a day. Interactions with nature, such as experiencing the sounds of birds and trickling water, can reinforce the importance of our relationship with nature. The paper presents the author's vision of Human–Computer–Biosphere Interaction (HCBI) to facilitate non-human-centric interaction with the goal of moving society towards environmental sustainability. HCBI extends HCI from countable people, objects, pets, and plants into an auditory biosphere that is uncountable, complex, and non-linguistic. This paper describes the development and integration of non-human-centric design protocols, requirements, methods, and context evaluation.

Keywords: HCBI (Human Computer Biosphere Interaction), Nature Conservation, Nature Interface, Smart Fashion, Soundscape Visualization, Sustainability, Sustainable Interaction Design.

1 Introduction

At times, human beings seem incapable of mutually beneficial coexistence with nature. The often expressed desire for sustainable relations between man and the environment may sometimes appear to be an unobtainable dream. The problem often seems so intractable that it could appear that the best way to solve all of the world's environmental problems would be to destroy all civilizations. Obviously this is not possible However, it is possible to ask whether humans and nature can be integrated more effectively and mutually in a beneficial manner. The current information technology is capable of providing people with the perception of being close to nature and can be used to promote conservation. However, even though conservation specialists have been actively advocating environmental protection by publicizing current critical situations and by trying to reach the public through state-of-the-art information technologies, such as high-resolution images and bio-acoustical recordings, such efforts can never be more than human–computer interactions, and as such, do not satisfy people's spiritual and psychological need to establish an intimate relationship with the natural world. These efforts are also not sufficient to protect endangered populations [6].

N. Streitz and P. Markopoulos (Eds.): DAPI 2014, LNCS 8530, pp. 349–358, 2014.
© Springer International Publishing Switzerland 2014

The missing factor is not knowledge or technology, it is an interface by which interaction with remote animals and the environment can be facilitated, without actual physical interaction, in a manner analogous to people's interactions with their family members at home. It is from this perspective that we introduce Human–Computer–Biosphere Interaction (HCBI).This paper presents our vision of HCBI by offering a conceptual overview, related works, currently developed interfaces, and related discussion. This study is not intended to propose a solution to any one single technological or ecological problem; however, it proposes a new viewpoint of multidisciplinary HCBI-based design and interfaces.

2   Human Biosphere Interaction

In ancient times, interactions between human societies and nature were significantly different than they are now for both technological and cultural reasons. Technological advances have allowed humans to alter ecosystems significantly. For example, heavy construction equipment can completely denude forest areas to provide sites for mining operations. Such equipment is also used to prepare sites for putatively "environment friendly" residential developments. In ancient times, humans were less capable of altering natural environments and were more spiritually and emotionally connected to nature. For example, during seasonal festivals, Japanese farmers prayed to various gods, thought to dwell in mountainous regions, for favorable weather conditions, and the general population was taught to respect the gods. In this cultural environment, wild animals and their habitats were left undisturbed. Japan's history and culture largely evolved because of benevolent interaction with nature. Although humans suffered from natural disasters, human society inflicted little damage on the natural environment.

Society and even business activities paid respect to the traditional cultural relationship with the nature until urbanization became increasingly widespread. Urbanization has occurred throughout the world. The majority of all western countries are predominantly urban. With the advent of urbanization, human society created a paradox in its relationship with nature. Assuming that a culturally rooted respect for nature endures, do we truly believe we are protecting the natural environment when we damage forested mountain areas to create "ecologically-friendly" residential areas? If humanity desires to live in ecological harmony with nature, why is it necessary to significantly alter mountain terrain and destroy forests? Very few humans now believe in the existence of gods that control weather or other agricultural conditions. We no longer imagine that wilderness areas are occupied by mythological creatures. However, because we no longer embrace the presence of such historical and cultural metaphors in our daily lives, especially in city life, there has been little outcry at the severe devastation of nature brought about by urbanization. Furthermore, the increased availability of information on delicate natural habitats has ironically increased tourism to such areas, resulting in accelerated environmental destruction [6].

Fig. 1. "Roadkill." An Iriomote cat has been struck and killed by an eco-tourist's vehicle. (Photo by Ministry of the Environment, Government of Japan.)

The situation with the Iriomote cat is a good example of how information provided to raise understanding of environmental issues has had a negative impact. As pictured in Figure 1, the Iriomote cat (Felis iriomotensis) is a wild feline, approximately the size of a domestic house cat, found solely on Iriomote, an island in the southern Ryukyu Islands, Okinawa Prefecture, Japan The species was discovered by Dr. Imaizumi in 1967 [17]. However, once information about this new species was widely disseminated, the cat gained significant economic value. A great number of eco-tourists have visited the island, which has been designated as a world heritage area, in hopes of seeing the endangered cat in the wild before it becomes extinct. Consequently, the most significant threat to that species is the possibility of being killed by a vehicle driven by eco-tourists. As the number of eco-tourists increases, so does the number of cars rented and cats killed. Perplexingly, since the news media first reported this ironic fact, there have been even more visits by eco-tourists and even more road kills. It is ironic that the vehicles driven by nature-loving tourists are a significant threat to an endangered species and could result in extinction.The situation is particularly serious, given that less than 100 members of the species are thought to exist.

If information technology could be used to provide a simulated experience of being close to nature and simultaneously promote the necessity of nature conservation, the number of road kills of the endangered species in this world heritage area might decrease. Even though conservation scientists have actively advocated environmental protection by providing information on current critical situations and reaching out to the public with state-of-the-art information technologies, a high-resolution picture of an endangered animal killed by a car, such as that shown in Figure 1, can never be more than human–computer interaction (HCI), and thus, will probably be ineffective at preventing further deaths as such information seems to attract more direct human interaction with endangered species.As noted previously, what is required is an interface that would allow people to experience a sense of connection with the nature but at a distance. To protect endangered species and threatened habitat areas, we need a methodology that allows people to experience a deeply satisfying, but remote, interaction with nature. This is important because the sense of being a part of the nature may contribute to human emotional balance. A reverent attitude towards nature can provide a starting point to a path to mental and physical well-being [14] . This is a fundamental tenet of Japanese Zen Buddhism. When we are emotionally stressed, recalling or experiencing the beauty of nature can help us recover a sense of well-being [14].

3   Goal of Human–Computer–Biosphere Interaction

Human–Computer–Biosphere Interaction (HCBI) attempts to facilitate non-human-centric interaction with nature by integrating computer systems into the global ecosystem. The key HCBI concepts are:

1. **Physical separation:** Current information technologies allow people to communicate over long distances in real time without direct contact between the caller and the receiver.

2. **Information Connectivity:** Current information technologies are capable of conveying not only explicit objects such as text and voice messages, but also nonverbal messages, even though the feelings expressed may often be unclear or open to misinterpretation. Despite limitations, application of new aspects and interfaces are advancing information communication in ways that extend human and biosphere interactions beyond the language barrier for non-human-centric interaction.

3. **Ecological Neutrality:** By combining physical separation and information connectivity, nonverbal information interaction between human beings and the biosphere is possible. These are "virtual" interactions, and their environmental impact never exceeds their virtual impact, which may be effective for nature conservation.

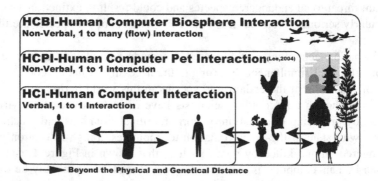

Fig. 2. Human–computer–biosphere interaction (HCBI) concept, an extension of HCI and HCPI. © 2009 [6]

Ultimately, application of these concepts allows us to create virtual impacts on wild animals without ever interacting with them physically. In doing so, we can facilitate interactions among remote animals and the environment in a manner analogous to people's interactions with their family members at home Such interaction could eliminate the need for tourism that results in the death of an endangered species, as mentioned previously. Currently, HCI research and applications, primary focus on human-centric interactions. However, there are many non-human-centric interactions in daily life. Using HCI technology to increase people's awareness of nature and facilitate benign interaction with nature is a key challenge of HCBI.

4   Related Works: Human–Computer Interaction

HCI is a discipline concerned with the design, evaluation, and implementation of interactive computing systems for human use and with the study of major phenomena surrounding them [4]. The author proposes to extend HCI and Human–Computer–Pet Interaction (HCPI) to explore HCBI [8]. The conceptual relationships between HCI, HCPI, and HCBI are illustrated in Fig 2. HCI technologies have been employed in a wide range of applications. Computer supported cooperative work uses computer systems to exchange explicit messages to support task-specific activities.

For example, we exchange ideas, thoughts, theories, and messages by encoding and decoding words through computer media, cell phones, email, and chat systems. We also consciously and unconsciously exchange non-verbal cues in our social relationships. This non-verbal information helps us to find an appropriate context during the verbalization process so that the intended message is easily received and understood by the listener. For example, "Tsunagari" communication, a concept developed to foster a sense of closeness between people, allows users to exchange non-verbal cues interactively over a network. The "Family Planter System" is a specific application of Tsunagari communication that was developed for family use [5].Implicit information communication enables non-linguistic and non-verbal interaction among humans and different species, both plants and animals, over physical distances. For example, Lee et al. proposed a novel type of physical interaction and symbiosis

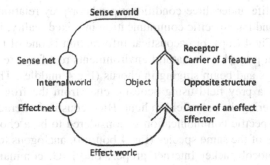

Fig. 3. Functional cycle from von Uexküll's Umwelt theory [15]

between humans and pets using a computer and the Internet [8]. Weilenmann and Juhlin [16] describe how interaction between dogs and humans is affected when new technology, such as a GPS tracking device, is introduced. The dog handler's interpretation of the GPS data supports the hunter's understanding of the dog's intentions.Botanicalls was initially developed by graduate students at New York University's Interactive Telecommunications Program. One of the original goals was to enrich people's relationships with plants and explore the value of nature in increasingly technical environments. The Botanicalls [1] project was included in the Museum of Modern Arts' "Talk to Me" Exhibition that featured projects designed to establish emotional, sensual, or intellectual connections. The Botanicalls system allows plants to phone or tweet when human help is required; for example, when a plant needs water. When people phone a plant they are given the plants' botanical characteristics. Non-human-centric interaction is also reflected in the semiotic theories of Jakob von Uexküll[15]. von Uexküll established the concept of Umwelt, from the German word meaning "environment" or "surrounding world," and suggested that all animals, from the simplest to the most complex, fit into their unique worlds with equal completeness. A simple world corresponds to a simple animal, a well-articulated world to a complex one. Jakob von Uexküll stated that relations between subject and object are the "biological foundations that lie at the very epicenter of the study of both communication and signification in the human and non-human animal" [15]. This relationship is illustrated in the functional cycle diagram presented in Fig 3.

Utilizing HCBI to interconnect the human- and the non-human-centric world can help us increase the physical distance in von Uexküll's functional cycle with ubiquitous computing systems. With HCBI, we can begin to interact with remote subjects beyond normal physical and genetic distances for a simulated direct personal experience of a particular ecology.

5   HCBI Interaction Design

The author proposes a novel cybernetic interface that uses mobile technology to create computer-wildlife bio-acoustical interaction. To establish interaction with wildlife, the monitoring system artificially creates a "prey field" to control the movement of the target wildlife under three conditions: predator-prey relationship, interspecific communication, and interspecific communication in mixed reality, illustrated in Fig 4. As illustrated in Fig 4 (top), bio-acoustical information is one of the signals used by predators to detect prey [13]. In natural environments real frogs respond to the initial call of virtual frogs and begin singing in chorus (Fig 4 middle). The predator detects the emergence of a prey field using acoustic cues from the frog chorus before approaching and entering the prey field to hunt. Bio-acoustical interaction has thus been established. Interspecific communication is considered to be a chorus produced by a group of members of the same species (Fig 4 bottom), analogous to the Internet Control Message Protocol packet Internet groper, or PING, command that is used to determine if a host on a network is reachable from another host [11].

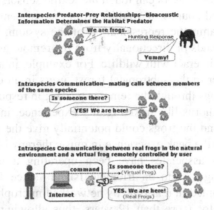

Fig. 4. Interspecies predator-prey relationship (top), intraspecies communication (middle), and intraspecies communication in a mixed reality (bottom). © 2009 [8]

Fig. 5. Wearable Forest [7] @ siggraph'08, 09 Art Gallery

The Wearable Forest [7] uses the HCBI interaction. As shown in Fig 5, Wearable Forest is a garment that bio-acoustically interacts with wildlife in a distant forest through a networked remote-controlled speaker and microphone. It is intended to emulate the unique bio-acoustic beauty of nature by allowing users to experience a distant forest soundscape. This interaction between humans and nature can occur with minimal environmental impact. The Wearable Forest received first place in a juried selection process for the 12th IEEE International Symposium on Wearable Computers, 2008.The Wearable Forest consists of a local audio-visual interactive clothing system and a remote audio I/O system, similar to the Wildlife I/O system, which is placed in a forest. The remote and local systems facilitate intraspecies communication with wildlife in a mixed reality environment, as illustrated in the bottom panel of Fig 4, through a real time bio-acoustic loop. The remote system, consisting of weather-resistant microphones and speakers, was placed in an uninhabited subtropical forest on Iriomote Island.

To interact with wildlife, users can touch the textile sensors, which transfer the user-selected, pre-recorded sounds of wildlife from the garment to the speakers in the forest presents a diagrammatic representation of the system. The bio-acoustic loop, which transfers live sounds bi-directionally from the remote and local sites, gives the user the opportunity to interact with wildlife. For example, in a relatively quiet period after a brief rain shower in the subtropical forest, users in an urban location can play back the croaking of frogs through the remote speaker; in response, actual frogs might start croaking. In this chorus-like mixed reality experience, intraspecies communication between the user and the frogs could potentially give the user a sense of belonging to nature, similar to the peak experience in music therapy [9].

The author and his associates have been operating a networked bio-acoustic streaming and recording system on Iriomote Island since 1997 [6]. Sounds have been continuously streamed in real-time by networked microphones every day, 24 h a day, 365 days a year, for more than 12 years, thus allowing users to listen to live sounds of the ecosystem over the Internet without physically going there. To maintain the remote system, the author enters the tropical forest to replace system components just once a year. Even though the author, in essence, becomes a tourist, the environmental destruction caused by one visit each year is clearly less than 3,000 visitors every day. Having information connectivity with a remote ecosystem can enable control of the extent of the impact resulting from HCBI. By turning off the computer system's power source off, the virtual impact on the remote ecosystem can be removed to maintain ecological neutrality. These are "virtual" interactions, and their environmental impact never exceeds their virtual impact. Inserting electronic technology into natural areas is moderately eco-friendly. While it is not the best solution, it is a better solution than the alternatives.

6   Discussions: Ecological Neutrality

Is inserting electronic technology into natural areas "eco-friendly?"

Yes, if done moderately. There is no right or wrong answer, but moderation is the key, just as it is the key to a sustainable society. Any activity, if conducted too often, can be destructive. An example of a behavior that is only eco-friendly in moderation would be ecotourism, which is defined as:

"Responsible travel to natural areas that conserves the environment and improves the well-being of local people." (**The International Ecotourism Society. 1990**)

However, immoderate eco-tourism can be detrimental to the ecology. For example, it is estimated that more than 3,000 eco-tourists visit Iriomote Island every day. These visitors come from urban areas to experience the island's magnificent ecosystem. They walk in the jungles and trample on plants. As mentioned previously, cars rented by eco-tourists accidentally kill members of an endangered species in areas that have been set aside for their protection. Thus, it can be contended that people who visit the island for eco-tourism purposes become "ego-eco-tourists," even if that is not their intention. Ironically, attracting tourists, which was intended to raise awareness of the need for conservation, has accelerated environmental destruction. No matter how non-intrusive, the presence of eco-tourists can disturb nature conservation efforts.

7   Contribution to HCI Community

The author and his associates initially introduced the concept of HCBI at HCI venues discussing environmental sustainability in 2009 [6]. The theory, method, and evaluation of human and wildlife interaction were not discussed in detail because the research was not sufficiently well developed. However, the future direction of HCBI has been suggested by several researchers. In 2010, DiSalvo et al. stated [2] that HCBI points out the inherent contradiction in attempting to use technology to create more intimate connections with nature and Pereira et al. cited HCBI as an example of sustainable computing [12]. Giannachi [3] stated that HCBI clothing, for example the Wearable Forest system, facilitates the creation of a human–computer environment that enables new forms of communication.Interestingly, Mancini explored animal–computer interaction that aims to foster the relationship between humans and animals by enabling communication and promoting understanding between them and emphasized that the study of interactions between animals and computing technology has never entered the mainstream of computer science [10]. Mancini also organized CHI 2012 and hosted a Special Interest Group on Animal-Computing Interaction at CHI 2012. As mentioned previously, the missing factors that would facilitate more robust studies of interactions between animals and computing technology are not knowledge or technologies. The missing factor is an interface that can facilitate human interaction with remote animals and the environment in a manner similar to the interactions with pets and their surrounding environment at home.This paper proposed intraspecies communication in a mixed reality to bridge the gap between humans, computers, and animals. The study reviews existing technologies and touches on physical separation, information connectivity, ecological neutrality, and the functional cycle in Umwelt theory. It reflects the author's multi-disciplinary vision of HCBI, which extends HCI from countable people, objects, pets, and plants into the biosphere, which is essentially uncountable, complex, non-linguistic, and non-human-centric, and potentially points the way to a sustainable society.

8   Conclusion

This study presents the author's vision and practice of HCBI to facilitate a sustainable society. HCBI extends the subject of HCI from countable people, objects, pets, and plants into a biosphere that is uncountable, complex, and non-linguistic in non-human centric scape. Utilizing HCBI to interconnect the human and non-human centric world can extend the subject of interaction based on Umwelt's functional cycle with computing systems. Currently, HCI is focusing primarily on human centric interactions in which the author and co-workers expect some perceivable feedback from others as a response to their inputs before they end an interaction. In contrast, in our daily lives, there are many non-human centric interactions. These include the sounds of birds, insects, swaying leaves, and trickling water in a beautiful forest, all of which can implicitly imprint the beauty of Nature in our minds. The ecological transition of focusing users's attention toward nature in daily lives using human–computer interaction technology is a key challenge of Human–Computer–Biosphere Interaction. This research accomplished to develop and integrate the non-human centric interaction design protocols and methods.

References

1. Bray, R., et al.: Botanicalls (2009), http://www.botanicalls.com/
2. DiSalvo, C., et al.: Mapping the landscape of sustainable HCI. In: Proceedings of the SIGCHI Conference on Human Factors in Computing Systems, pp. 1975–1984. ACM (2010)
3. Giannachi, G., et al.: Archaeologies of presence: Art, performance and the persistence of being. Routledge, London (2012)
4. Hewett, Baecker, Card, Carey, Gasen, Mantei, Perlman, Strong, Verplank: Definition of Human Computer Interaction (1992), http://old.sigchi.org/cdg/cdg2.html
5. Itoh, Y., et al.: 'TSUNAGARI' communication: Fostering a feeling of connection between family members. In: CHI 2002 Extended Abstracts on Human Factors in Computing Systems, pp. 810–811. ACM (2002)
6. Kobayashi, H., et al.: Human computer biosphere interaction: Towards a sustainable society. In: CHI 2009 Extended Abstracts on Human Factors in Computing Systems, pp. 2509–2518. ACM (2009)
7. Kobayashi, H., et al.: Wearable forest clothing system: beyond human-computer interaction. In: ACM SIGGRAPH 2009 Art Gallery, pp. 1–7. ACM (2009)
8. Lee, P., et al.: A mobile pet wearable computer and mixed reality system for human poultry interaction through the internet. Personal Ubiquitous Comput. 10(5), 301–317 (2006)
9. Lowis, M.J.: Music as a trigger for peak experiences among a college staff population. Creativity Research Journal 14(3-4), 351–359 (2002)
10. Mancini, C.: Animal-computer interaction: A manifesto. Interactions 18(4), 69–73 (2011)
11. Muuss, M.: Packet InterNet Grouper (1983)
12. Pereira, R., et al.: Sustainability as a value in technology design. In: First Interdisciplinary Workshop on Communication for Sustainable Communities, pp. 1–7. ACM (2010)
13. Saunders, S.: The Evolution of Animal Communication: Reliability and Deception in Signaling Systems. Biology & Philosophy 24(3), 405–416 (2009)
14. Suzuki, D.T.: Zen and Japanese culture, Rev. and enl., 2nd edn. Pantheon Books, New York (1959)
15. Vonuexkull, J.: A Stroll through the Worlds of Animals and Men - A Picture Book of Invisible Worlds. Semiotica 89(4), 319 (2009)
16. Weilenmann, A., Juhlin, O.: Understanding people and animals: The use of a positioning system in ordinary human-canine interaction. In: Proceedings of the SIGCHI Conference on Human Factors in Computing Systems, pp. 2631–2640. ACM (2011)
17. Yoshinori, I.: A new genus and species of cat from Iriomote, Ryukyu Island. Journal of the Mammal Society of Japan 3, 74 (1967)

Smart Objects: An Evaluation of the Present State Based on User Needs

Alessandra Papetti[1,*], Matteo Iualé[1], Silvia Ceccacci[1], Roberta Bevilacqua[2],
Michele Germani[1], and Maura Mengoni[1]

[1] Department of Industrial Engineering and Mathematical Sciences,
Università Politecnica delle Marche,
Via Brecce Bianche, 12 60131 Ancona, Italy
[2] Laboratory of Bioinformatics, Bioengineering and Home Automation,
Istituto Nazionale di Ricerca e Cura per Anziani,
Via Santa Margherita, 5 60124 Ancona, Italy
{a.papetti,m.iuale,s.ceccacci,m.germani,m.mengoni}@univpm.it,
r.bevilacqua@inrca.it

Abstract. In the last years, some attempts have been made to explore the use of smart objects, with the purpose of monitoring well-being and supporting people's independent living. However an inventory of characteristics of smart products currently available on the market is still lacking. The aim of this study is to provide an overview of such products in order to: (1) understand if their features really match users' needs, answering to the definition of assistive technology and, consequently, (2) understand if an environment embedded with SOs can be considered as assistive too, taking into consideration the attributes given by the definition of the SOs, of being embedded in familiar objects and immerse in the users' surround.

Keywords: Inclusive Design, Universal Design, Home Environment, Internet of Things.

1   Introduction

Nowadays, the most common definition of Smart Objects (SOs) describes them as everyday objects equipped with sensors, memory and communication capabilities [1, 2]. Consequently, SOs are able to capture information coming from the surrounding as well as to react on the basis of the user's needs [3]. The capability of interacting rapidly with the users represents their crucial feature, in addition to their intrinsic characteristic of being familiar tools for the users and, most of all, being "immerse" in the environment. Smart objects raise unique challenges and opportunities for designing interaction with intelligent systems, coping with the mostly limited interaction capabilities, exploring context information to provide more natural interaction, helping the user to understand the behavior and capabilities of the objects.

In a broader sense, SO are able to help people in participating in their environment through adaptation, accessibility and communication. Moreover, they can offer assistance

---

* Corresponding author.

N. Streitz and P. Markopoulos (Eds.): DAPI 2014, LNCS 8530, pp. 359–368, 2014.

to the elderly people's independent living. When applied to people with disabilities, a smart object can be considered an Assistive Technology (AT), in line with the definition given by Cowan and Turner-Smith [5]: "any device or system that allows an individual to perform a task that they would otherwise be unable to do, or increases the ease and safety with which the task can be performed".

In the last years, some attempts have been made to explore the use of smart objects, with the purpose of monitoring well-being and supporting independent living. However an inventory of characteristics of smart products currently available on the market is still lacking.

The aim of this study is to provide an overview of such products in order to:

— understand if their features really match users' needs, answering to the definition of assistive technology, and consequently
— understand if an environment embedded with SOs can be considered as assistive too, taking into consideration the attributes given by the definition of the SOs, of being embedded in familiar objects and immerse in the users' surround.

To this purpose, it was carried out a review of SOs currently available on the market. In particular the International Classification of Functioning, Disability and Health (ICF) [6] has been exploited in order to understand the ability of SOs to support people in the activities domains.

2   The Search Strategy

The first step of the research was the creation of an inventory of the smart assistive devices available on the market. For this purpose we conducted an Internet search, using the keyword "smart object". This preliminary step has highlighted a large improper use of the term "smart object", that becomes more a marketing term (e.g., any innovative product from a technical, esthetic and communicative point of view is called "smart"). For that reason, the detection of proper smart objects was complicated by the enormous quantity of retrieved tools. Consequently, several search strategies have been explored in order to select the most appropriate one, with the aim of guiding the search on the most appropriate SOs.

As a first step, we have compiled a list of household items (e.g., clothes, stairs, toilets, etc.) with which people come into contact every day. Also aids were included: in particular, we have considered the assistive device typologies collected by McCreadie and Tinker [7]. As a second step, keywords as "smart", "interactive" and "inclusive" have been selected, starting from the smart object definition. Objects and keywords have been then used together for the search, exploiting several combinations and search engines. Finally, both search engine tips and synonyms for the previous words have been considered.

For each object, it has been verified if it was compliant with the requirements and the producer company site has been investigated in order to find other products related to the search topics. At the end, the search strategy resulted in about 190 relevant smart devices. The objects can be classified in: Clothes (e.g., sweater, vest, etc.),

Clothing Accessories (e.g., shoes, elastic bands, bracelets, etc.), *Dishes* (e.g., forks, glasses, etc.), *Household Devices* (e.g. video-cameras, decorative objects, household appliances, etc.), *Medical Devices* (e.g., glucometer, sphygmomanometer, etc.), *Personal Care Products* (e.g., toothbrushes, toilet, etc.).

3   Smart Objects Evaluation Method Based on ICF

In order to systematically investigate   how the available SOs are able to satisfy users' needs, it was decided to use the International Classification of Functioning, Disability and Health (ICF). The ICF has a universal application [8], as it allows describing the health and health-related states associated with all health conditions. It not focuses only on disable people but allow to describe the condition of any person. The domains contained in ICF are described from the perspective of the body, the individual and society in two basic lists: "Body Functions and Structures" and "Activities and Participation". The domains for the Activities and Participation cover the full range of life areas (from basic learning or watching to composite areas such as interpersonal interactions or employment).

In order to understand the extent to which SOs can be adopted to support a person in each activity domains, at first the parameter monitored and the information provided by the collected SOs have been analyzed. Then the relevance of this information respect to all the activity domains have been evaluated. The results of this first evaluation are reported in. The percentage has been calculated by considering the total amount of information related to each activity domain, in relation to the total amount of parameters provided by the collected SOs. As we can see, the majority of SOs is able to provide support with respect to three domains of activity: mobility (d4), self-care (d5) and domestic life (d6). It worth to underline that the sum of percentages differs from 100%. This is due to the fact that a parameter can support several activities domains.

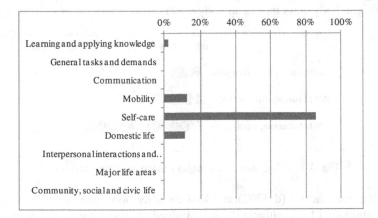

Fig. 1. Activities domain covering

As reported also in the most used tools in geriatric assessment, the Katz Index of Activities of Daily Living (ADL) [9], and the Instrumental Activities of Daily Living (IADL) [10], it is possible to assert that the ability to perform activity related to mobility, self-care and domestic life is a good predictor of elderly independence.

The shows that self-care is the most covered domain. Consequently a deeper investigation was conducted, in order to understand which activities, more related to this domain, are actually supported by SOs.

Through the analysis of the results, which are reported in, it is possible to observe that the majority of smart objects provides support to the activities related to "Looking after one's health" (d 570) and in particular they are focused on ensuring physical comfort, health and physical well-being by monitoring specific parameters, for the achievement of a better lifestyle ().

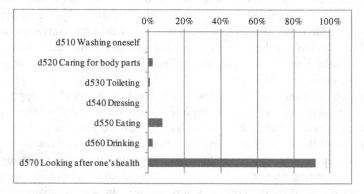

Fig. 2. Self-care domain covering

As far as the several functioning categories are concerned, these objects can help to maintain a balanced diet and an appropriate level of physical activity (d 5701) by monitoring eating habits and daily routines and by measuring physical parameters such as weight, body mass index and body water.

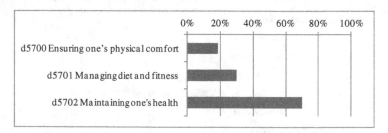

Fig. 3. Looking after one's health related activities covering

Maintaining one's health (d 5702) and looking after body parts are other important functions supported by intelligent devices. Indeed, they can support regular physical examinations, for example, by simply wearing smart clothes and/or accessories and/or using smart toilets. In this way, appropriate algorithms analyze the parameters and generate alerts only when necessary, in order to prevent risks and reduce the need of professional assistance.

Other products aim at ensuring the user physical comfort (d 5700), supporting the domestic environmental care and informing the users about the current temperature or lighting, for example, and suggesting the most appropriate ones.

As described in Fig. 3, the majority of SOs aims to support the users in activity related to the "Maintaining one's health" (d 5702) domain. Accordingly, the need of investigating the ability of these products in supporting a person is raised, in particular concerning the monitoring of the own health and the specific health needs.

To this purpose, it was decided to evaluate the significance assumed by every information provided by SOs in order to monitor the "Body Functions" (BF) defined by the ICF. According to ICF, by the term BF we mean to denote the physiological functions of the body system (including the psychological ones).

This method can be used to assess the SOs potential capabilities to support any person in monitoring its own health condition, whatever it is. In fact, impairments caused by any disease can result in problems, deviations or significant loss in one or more functions of the body.

The summary of the results of the assessment is described in Fig. 4. The graph shows the extent to which the SOs (in terms of percentage) is able to support each body function according to information respectively provided.

The correlations have been classified in three categories, according to their relevance respect to the specific BF:

— information that can be used to measure the functionality in a direct way (in black): the acquisition of such an information allow to directly monitor the loss in a specific BF. For example, the acquisition of *diastolic and systolic blood pressure* allows to determine precisely the state of the "blood pressure functions" (b 420).
— data that can be used to measure the state of the BF in an indirect way (in dark grey). For example, the occurrence of *a fall*, which can be detected thanks to a *fall detector*, can be indicative of impairment of "vestibular functions" (b 235).
— parameters that can be correlated with the state of the considered BF (in light grey): these parameters may provide information about the possible alteration of a certain BF (e.g., the detection of an abnormal *galvanic skin response* can be correlated with a change in the "heart functions" (b 410).

For more details, the correlations identified between the data provided by SOs and body functions are reported in Appendix.

By analyzing the results, it is possible to observe that the about 25% of information provided by SOs can be useful to support the user in maintaining its own weight. A lot of information can be exploited to understand the user emotional state (about 17%) and analyze his/her sleep quality (about 11%). Furthermore, several data related to heart and hematological system functions are captured and analyzed by the majority of SOs (more than 10%).

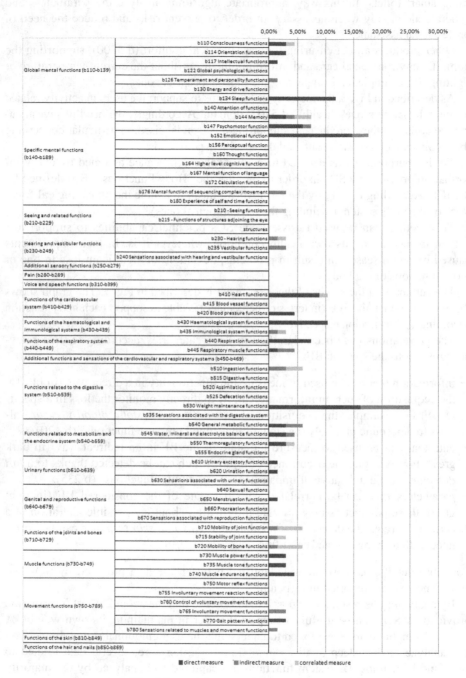

Fig. 4. Potential support for Body Function

4   Conclusions

In an ontological point of view, much evidence show that inclusiveness is a prerequisite of any assistive technology artefacts, aimed at cooperating with people, especially if they have particular needs to face, as the elderly.

To understand if the available products can be considered inclusive and if they effectively match the needs of the elderly, we have started from the analysis of the activities, that it is expected an assistive environment should be able to support.

Using ICF, we have noticed that the available SO are not able to support all the activities, most of all the ones ascribed to the cognitive domain, such as for example, learning and applying knowledge.

It seems that the implementation of more complex software architectures inside the smart objects should be stressed, in order to have a new generation of products, that can be considered more intelligent and intuitive. For example, this can strongly support cognitive processes like work memory, attention and reasoning. This, can be a key issue for assuring the success of the future generation of SO.

Probably, the reason of this defect should be found in the lack of interoperability of the SOs, which is an issue amply treated in literature [11]. In fact, the majority of the SO includes and/or requires specific apps or software to interpret the monitored information and to provide feedbacks to the users. This requirement may represents a limit when these objects have to be interconnected each other, to create an integrated assistive environment targeted on the specific user's needs. Indeed, it is necessary to develop an "intelligent management tool", essential to collect, elaborate and exploit the data generated by several objects.

Currently, it could be said that the SO are not inclusive, because a) they are not able to answer to a specific problem, but just to collect information on some parameters; b) they are not planned to be integrated in more complex systems, that can describe the extended concept of "environment".

Nowadays, the SO can be divided in system-oriented, importunate smartness and people-oriented, empowering smartness [12]. In the first case, smart objects can take certain self-directed actions based on previously collected information, so that the space would be active, in many cases even proactive. In the other case, smart objects empower users to make decisions and take mature and responsible actions.

Through the implementation of the software architectures of the SO, also inside more complex platform, this subdivision can be overcome, creating a new generation of products, that can be context-aware oriented, and finally becoming inclusive.

References

1. Ferguson, G.T.: Have your objects call my objects. Harvard Business Review 80(6), 138–143 (2003)
2. Gellersen, H.W., Schmidt, A., Beigl, M.: Adding Some Smartness to Devices and Everyday Things. In: Proc. of WMCSA 2000 – 3rd IEEE Workshop on Mobile Computing Systems and Applications. IEEE Computer Society, Monterrey (December 2000)

3. Ziefle, M., Rocker, C.: Acceptance of pervasive healthcare systems: A comparison of different implementation concepts. In: 4th International Conference on-NO PERMISSIONS, Pervasive Computing Technologies for Healthcare (PervasiveHealth), March 22-25, pp. 1,6 (2010)
4. Bohn, J., Coroama, V., Langheinrich, M., Mattern, F., Rohs, M.: Living in a World of Smart Everyday Objects—Social, Economic, and Ethical Implications. Human and Ecological Risk Assessment 10, 763–785 (2004)
5. Cowan, D., Turner-Smith, A.R.: The role of Assistive Technology in Alternative Models of Care for Older People. In: Tinker, A., et al. (eds.) Alternative Models of Care for Older People Research. The Royal Commission on Long Term Care, vol. 2, pp. 325–346. The Stationery Office, London (1999)
6. World Health Organization. International Classification of Functioning, Disability and Health, Geneva. World Health Organization (2001)
7. McCreadie, C., Tinker, A.: The acceptability of assistive technology to older people. Ageing & Society 25, 91–110 (2005)
8. Bickenbach, J.E., Chatterji, S., Badley, E.M.: Üstün TB. Models of disablement, universalism and the ICIDH. Social Science and Medicine 48, 1173–1187 (1999)
9. Lawton, M.P., Brody, E.M.: Assessment of older people: Self-maintaining and instrumental activities of daily living. Gerontologist 9(3), 179–186 (1969)
10. Katz, S., Down, T.D., Cash, H.R., et al.: Progress in the development of the index of ADL. Gerontologist 10, 20–30 (1970)
11. Perumal, T., Ramli, A.R., Leong, C.Y., Mansor, S., Samsudin, K.: Interoperability for Smart Home Environment Using Web Services. International Journal of Smart Home 2(4) (2008)
12. Streitz, N., et al.: Designing Smart Artifacts for Smart Environments. Computer 38(3), 41–49 (2005)

Appendix

Table 1. Correlation between Body Functions and parameters provided by SOs

Body Functions	Info	Activity pace	Activity speed	Activity time	Activity/Movement	Ankle-Brachial Index (ABI)	Arterial oxygen content (CaO2)	Audio	Awoke numbering	Basal Metabolic Rate (BMR)	Bed exit activity	Blood glucose	Blood lactate	Body fat	Body Mass Index (BMI)	Body water	Body weight distribution	Bone mass	Breathing Rate	Calories burned	Carboxyhaemoglobin (COHb)	Cardiac Output (CO)	Core body temperature	Daily Calorie Intake (DCI)	Daily medicines missing	Device status	Diastolic Blood Pressure	Electrocardiography (ECG)	Electroencephalography (EEG)	Electromyography (EMG)	Fall detection	Fork servings frequency	Fork servings interval	Galvanic Skin Response (GSR)	Heart Rate
b110-b139	b110																				•											•		▲	
	b114																																		
	b117																														•				
	b122																																		
	b126																																		
	b130																																		
	b134							•	•																						•				
b140-b189	b140																																		
	b144																							•		□									
	b147	•	•																													•	•		
	b152								•									•									•							•	•
	b156																																		
	b160																																		
	b164																																		
	b167																																		
	b172																																		
	b176						□																												
	b180																																		
b210-b229	b210																																		
	b215																																		
	b220																																		
b230-b249	b230						□																												
	b235																																□		
	b240																																		
b250-b279																																			
b280-b289																																			
b310-b399																																			
b410-b429	b410																							•						•				▲	•
	b415																																		
	b420				•																														
b430-b439	b430					•						•								•															
	b435																																		
b440-b449	b440																					•													
	b445																															•			
b450-b469																																			
b510-b539	b510																																□	□	
	b515																																		
	b520																																		
	b525																																		
	b530			□	□									•	•	•	•		•				•		•								□	□	
	b535																																		
b540-b559	b540										•				•	□	□																		
	b545														•																				
	b550																								•										▲
	b555																																		
b610-b639	b610																																		
	b620																																		
	b630																																		
b640-b679	b640																																		
	b650																																		
	b660																																		
	b670																																		
b710-b729	b710			▲	▲												□																▲		
	b715																□																▲		
	b720			▲	▲												□																▲		
b730-b749	b730																																•		
	b735																																•		
	b740												•																				•		
b750-b789	b750																																		
	b755																																		
	b760																																		
	b765																																□	□	
	b770	•	•																																
	b780												□																						
b810-b849																																			
b850-b869																																			

BODY FUNCTIONS		Heart Rate Variability	Hematocrit	Hemoglobin	In bed time	Indoor light level	Indoor noise level	Last sip time	Lean mass	Light on/off	Meal duration	Meal time	Metabolic Equivalent Task (MET)	Methaemoglobin (MetHb)	Muscle mass	Open/Close medicines dispenser	Oxygen saturation (SpO2)	Phonocardiogram (PCG)	Position (GPS)	Position change in the bed	R-R Interval	Skin temperature	Sleep quality	Sleep time	Spirogram	Stress level	Systolic Blood Pressure	Urine analysis	VCO2	Video	Visceral fat rating	VO2	VO2 max	Water consumption	Weight
b110-b139	b110																																		
	b114																		■												■					
	b117																																		
	b122																																		
	b126																															□				
	b130																																		
	b134				■								■					■				■	■													
b140-b189	b140																																		
	b144							▲				▲				■																				
	b147																															□				
	b152	■		■														□				■				■	■				□				
	b156																																		
	b160																																		
	b164																																		
	b167																																		
	b172																																		
	b176																															□				
	b180																																		
b210-b229	b210					▲				▲																									
	b215																																		
	b220																																		
b230-b249	b230						▲																												
	b235																															□				
	b240																																		
b250-b279																																			
b280-b289																																			
b310-b399																																			
b410-b429	b410	■																■			■														
	b415																																		
	b420																										■								
b430-b439	b430		■	■										■			■																		
	b435																									▲		□							
b440-b449	b440																								■				■			■	■		
	b445																												□			■			
b450-b469																																			
b510-b539	b510										▲	▲																							
	b515																																		
	b520																																		
	b525																																		
	b530								■		□	□																				■			■
	b535																																		
b540-b559	b540																																		
	b545					□																												■	
	b550																					■													
	b555																																		
b610-b639	b610																													■					
	b620																													■					
	b630																																		
b640-b679	b640																																		
	b650																													■					
	b660																																		
	b670																																		
b710-b729	b710																																		
	b715																																		
	b720																																		
b730-b749	b730														■																				
	b735														■																				
	b740														■																				
b750-b789	b750																																		
	b755																																		
	b760																																		
	b765																																		
	b770																																		
	b780																																		
b810-b849																																			
b850-b869																																			

■ = direct measure   □ = indirect measure   ▲ = correlated measure

Factors Influencing the Quality of the User Experience in Ubiquitous Recommender Systems

Nikolaos Polatidis and Christos K. Georgiadis

Department of Applied Informatics, University of Macedonia, Thessaloniki, Greece
{polatidisn,gxri}@acm.org

Abstract. The use of mobile devices and the rapid growth of the internet and networking infrastructure has brought the necessity of using Ubiquitous recommender systems. However in mobile devices there are different factors that need to be considered in order to get more useful recommendations and increase the quality of the user experience. This paper gives an overview of the factors related to the quality and proposes a new hybrid recommendation model.

Keywords: Ubiquitous Computing, Recommender Systems, Quality Factors, User Experience.

1 Introduction

Recommender systems are software algorithms aiming at filtering information [7]. Their job is to propose items or services using information based on user preferences. Recommender systems main algorithms are based on collaborative filtering, which is the most widely used algorithm. The items or services are recommender according to preferences of other users that have similar preferences [7]. Another important recommendation algorithm is content based filtering where the recommendations depend on previous items found in the history of the user and the top matching are proposed by the system [7]. Further recommendation algorithms include knowledge based filtering where the system uses a knowledge based attitude to generate recommendations. It is an algorithm where the user pre defines a set of requirements that the system will use to create the list of the recommendations. Moreover the knowledge database can be built by recording the user preferences while he is browsing or by asking him to complete a questionnaire [7].

Hybrid recommender systems use a combination of the above methods and look the most promising due to the fact that can take the advantage of each method and improve the overall output. The hybridization can occur in different ways such as using the output of one algorithm as the input for the other or by combining the recommendations of each algorithm at the interface level [7].

Ubiquitous recommender systems assist the user of a mobile device by providing him with personalized recommendations of items or services that are in the proximity [9]. These recommendations usually include mobile tourism related services such as tourist guides, shopping recommenders and route finders [9], [13]. A clear example of

N. Streitz and P. Markopoulos (Eds.): DAPI 2014, LNCS 8530, pp. 369–379, 2014.

ubiquitous recommendations can be found in [15] where a city guide is proposed by the authors for mobile device users that are equipped with GPS in their devices. Moreover it has been proposed that ubiquitous recommender systems can make smoother the buying process in the actual store by recommending items that are of the user interest [12]. Such recommenders can suggest items, display their ratings and comments.

The idea of ubiquitous computing as proposed by Want and Pering [16] and the main idea was to move away from traditional desktop environments to distributed computing, using a variety of devices. In addition it usually referred as pervasive computing [9], [16]. A critical part of ubiquitous recommendations is context awareness that has to be taken into consideration in order to provide accurate recommendations [2], [3], [9]. This brings us to a critical point where if we want to have quality recommendation we have to let the system use the location and at the same time have our privacy respected. Such systems aim to solve the information overload problem found nowadays on the internet and do it successfully up to a point. However different quality factors have to be ensured in order to improve the user experience and increase the overall quality.

The diagram below gives an overview of a ubiquitous context aware recommender.

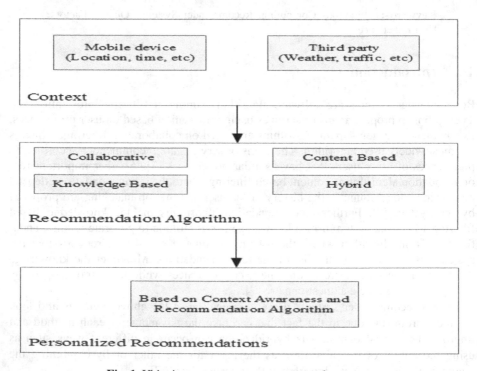

Fig. 1. Ubiquitous context aware recommender system

This work is focused on introducing ubiquitous recommender systems and how they have emerged and then a detailed description of the factors that affect the user experience follows. Although a number of different technologies has to be used the key challenge is to hide the presence of such technologies from the user and develop a smooth integrated process, which will include all the related factors as an integrated and complete framework that aims to deliver the right content to the user appropriately and securely.

The overall aim of the research is to:

- Give a clear description of the factors influencing the quality of the user experience in ubiquitous recommender systems.
- Propose a new algorithm based on collaborative filtering that utilizes data from its own database combined with information gathered from the users' social network and context.

2   Influencing Factors

Main factors include context awareness, privacy and algorithms [9]. Also a challenge that is found in traditional recommender systems but also applies to ubiquitous recommendations is the 'new user' problem, which is an important factors that plays a vital role in the development of such systems. It is noted that the factors that affect considerably the quality of the user experience in ubiquitous recommender systems are not found in other environments and are primarily to the size of the device, the physical resources and the amount of time the user is willing to use a small size device. Furthermore a less critical factor but considered essential is multilingual personalization [6].

2.1   Context Awareness

Context can be used by ubiquitous recommender systems to produce more personalized recommendations [1]. Recommender systems use collaborative and content filtering methods most of the time to produce recommendations, however this methodology does not take into consideration the contextual information and how this can be applied to the current situation and increase the overall quality of recommendations. According to the same scholars contextual recommender systems can be categorized in three main types. Fully observable, partially observable and unobservable. Moreover, a point is to discover the changes in the contextual factors and how to represent them in a mobile environment.

Ubiquitous context aware recommender systems vary and include different factors such as location, time, weather and emotional status of the user. The contextual information is very important if we want to provide recommendations that are based on Location Based Services [1].

Contextual information can be collected either explicitly, which is by asking the user directly to provide data using a questionnaire. Moreover data can collected implicitly by environment data, such as historical information and changes that occur during the use of the service [1]. Required values may be taken into the system by using the sensors of the device such as the camera and the Global Positioning System (GPS) [5].

Context is considered to be the most important aspect in ubiquitous recommender systems [1], [9]. We strongly believe that if context is utilized properly more useful recommendations will occur and the user will be highly satisfied.

2.2   Privacy

Privacy means that the user is ensured and decides on what ways his data will be processed [8], [10]. Privacy concerns direct users towards a negative behavior when they are asked to provide more data in order to receive personalized recommendations.

In Recommender Systems users are divided in three main categories [10]:

- Users that will provide any kind of information in exchange with the highest level of personalization possible.
- Users that will give some information so they can receive some kind of personalized recommendations.
- Users that will not give any kind of information due to privacy concerns.

Privacy is crucial factor that it is possible to be addressed using the right techniques. If this issue didn't exist then the user would supply any necessary information and his experience using the recommender system would be of a very high standard.

2.3   New User and Item

The new user and item problem are very important when the algorithm used is based solely in collaborative filtering (CF). They occur when a new user or item is added to the database there is no history about the user or no rating history about the item or service.

If a user wants the highest quality possible from a recommender then this is a very important issue that needs to be faced and this can only be dealt with the use of hybridization techniques.

Hybrid recommender are divided into three main categories [7]:

- Parallel
- Monolithic
- Pipelined

Parallel hybrid recommender use the same input in one or more recommendation algorithms and then combine the output of each into a hybridization step and produce a single output. Monolithic recommenders use a single recommender and combine different techniques. Finally pipelined recommender use the output from a single recommendation algorithm as the input for the next one.

Hybrid recommender can increase the quality of recommenders overall, since single algorithms have limitations, such as the new user and item problem described above.

3   Less Influencing Factors

Less important factors or else defined as challenges can be found in the literature as well.

3.1   Perceived Accuracy

A factor that needs some consideration is perceived accuracy which is a point where a user feels that the recommendations match his preferences [11]. It is considered to be a measuring assessment of how good the recommender performed and how accurate is to find the interests of a particular user.

3.2   Familiarity and Novelty

Familiarity is a description of the previous experience that user has with the recommended item or services [11]. However familiarity might mean that all the recommendation categories must be familiar to the user. Novelty must be introduced and balanced with familiarity so the user would be as satisfied as possible.

3.3   Attractiveness

Attractiveness is conserved with the process of irritating the user and evoke positive imaginations and increase the possibility of desiring. Attractiveness is concerned on how well the recommendations will be delivered to the user and not the recommendations itself [11].

3.4   User Interfaces

Limitations found in the user interface, where different devices may be used, the task would be to develop suitable and user friendly interfaces [5]. User interfaces are tightly related to the attractiveness as described above and could improve the quality. The more attractive is the user interface the user will be satisfied.

3.5   Multilingual Personalization

Given the fact that there is a vast amount of data found on the internet, these data can exist in different languages [6]. It is possible that the data requested from a user will not be available in his native language but be available in a foreign language.

Research has been done towards the field of personalized information retrieval [6]. It is a field where if suitable research occurs then more useful recommendations will be delivered.

4   Proposed Model

User experience is more and more becoming an essential part in the attention of the research community. However there isn't much work done on how the quality of the user experience in ubiquitous recommender systems can be increased and what kind of standards could be specified to work towards that direction.

The criteria need to be combined into a comprehensive framework that could be potentially used to evaluate the qualities of ubiquitous recommender systems. The framework should take into consideration all the major criteria that should be satisfied. A comprehensive model identifying all the aforementioned essential qualities must be established as a standard. That is how potential users will adapt a system.

Moreover it should be noted that the quality of recommendations and hence an increased user experience is heavily based on the algorithm used. A hybrid algorithm based on collaborative filtering is necessary due to the better prediction of hybrid algorithms. However there is a gap in collaborative filtering with the new user and item issues, which can be solved with the use of data from social media such as Facebook. In addition the proposed algorithm must incorporate contextual information to be useful in ubiquitous environments. The figure below gives an abstract representation of the model.

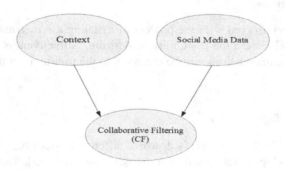

Fig. 2. Proposed hybrid model abstract representation

An issue is that in a social network different types of relationships can be found. Consider the graph and the table below that are two different social relationships.

In the above network there are different kind of relationships such as friendship, which is denoted by a double direction arrow and follower or member, which is denoted by single direction arrow.

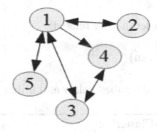

Fig. 3. Graph representation of a social relationship

At the table UxU below where a zero value is denoted it means that there is no kind of relationship and where one is denoted there is some kind of relationship.

Table 1. Representation of socials relationships

	User1	User2	User3	User4	User5
User1	0	1	1	1	1
User2	1	0	0	0	0
User3	1	0	0	1	0
User4	1	0	1	0	0
User5	1	0	0	0	0

The table below describes a ratings database of users about items or services that could be found in a social network.

Table 2. User ratings of items in a social network

	Item1	Item2
User1	2	5
User2	0	6
User3	5	5
User4	2	1

However the larger the network gets then it will become very difficult to identify relationships between that impose an actual value so they can be used. We chose the K-means algorithm [14] as the clustering algorithm due to its simplicity. K is the desirable number of clusters we want.

The users then will be clustered into N groups so the algorithm will be searching only on relevant user data.

The set of users is represented as follows:

U = {User1, User2, User3, ... , User n}

The clusters are then represented as follows:

C = {Cluster1, Cluster2, Cluster3, ... Cluster n}

Each cluster C is a set of user that are related.

Cluster1 = {u1, u2, u3, ... , un}

The proposed algorithm is described below and utilizes the k-means clustering.

Algorithm Social-Media-Clustering
Input
U: the set of people and groups related to the user
G: the graph of the user that defines the relationships
TR: the matrix with the user ratings
Output
C: The superset of the required cluster sets

Fig. 4. Social media clustering algorithm

The k-means algorithm outline is as follows:

N is the number of total users
K specifies the number of the required clusters
Sim (x, y) is the similarity function that will be used by k-means
Take the first k users and assign them as centroids
Compare the rest users to the centroid users
Assign users to clusters

Fig. 5. Outline of the K-means algorithm

We will use the Pearson correlation as the similarity measure function. The similarity between users i and j is defined as follows:

$$sim(i,j) = \frac{\sum_{u \in U}(R_{u,i} - \bar{R}_i)(R_{u,j} - \bar{R}_j)}{\sqrt{\sum_{u \in U}(R_{u,i} - \bar{R}_i)^2}\sqrt{\sum_{u \in U}(R_{u,j} - \bar{R}_j)^2}}$$

Fig. 6. Pearson correlation

4.1 Preliminary Experimental Results

At this very initial development stage of the algorithm we used a subset of the Books-Crossing [17] dataset as the collaborative filtering dataset. Furthermore we developed in the lab a realistic user rating dataset to use as the social network retrieved dataset. Then we used the Java programming language along with the Apache Mahout library [18] on the social network dataset with k=2 to get 2 clusters of data, with the algorithm described above and are available in Mahout. Then we took the first cluster and combined it with the collaborative filtering dataset. Finally we applied the algorithm described above and k=2 to get 2 clusters of data in order to use the first one by the collaborative filtering algorithm.

At this early stage it is observable that k-means can be applied to a dataset to retrieve the required subset from it. Also by getting this subset and combining in with a larger set we get more rating and have a higher probability of quality recommendations. Finally if the set is too large and the algorithm might be slow k-means can be applied again to get the required subset. Although further tests need to be conducted to show that this subset can produce satisfactory recommendations.

Moreover context parameters need to be taken into consideration and into the dataset in order to conduct more tests and see the quality, while using context.

5   Conclusions and Future Work

Recommender systems has matured to a full research area both in academia and in practice. However extended research has still to be done in ubiquitous environments and as the field grows, significant, new, challenges will be faced in terms of infrastructure and criteria. This is due to the fact that two different areas have to be researched and as ubiquitous computing and recommender system develop further many more characteristics will appear and new solutions will have to be proposed. Ubiquitous recommender systems will have to combine different characteristics to become useful to our everyday lives and provide an improved user experience.

Quality is a very important aspect found everywhere, including recommenders and ubiquitous environments. It is vital for the designer to be aware of the factors that relate to the improvement of the user experience. Most important factors that need to be addressed include context awareness, privacy and the new user and item problem found in collaborative filtering. Less important factors that if addressed could potentially improve the quality of the user experience include perceived accuracy, familiarity and novelty, attractiveness, improved user interfaces and multilingual personalization.

However mobile devices and networking infrastructures are evolving constantly and new challenges arise. Both designers and developers should be aware of new open problems and implications.

In addition it should be noted that although it is an important research field there is not much work in the literature regarding quality and serious work should be taken to define the required criteria that need to be satisfied.

Also simple case studies can be employed with the form of a questionnaire so that results from real users can be used to design better systems. The case studies should use the precision and recall methods [4]. These studies could be employed both in the prediction of the algorithm in retrieving the relevant friends and for the actual prediction system.

The overall contribution of the paper was to give a clear description of the factors influencing the quality of recommendations in ubiquitous recommender systems, highlighting that the recommendation engine itself is the most important. We also gave a first step directing towards the development of a collaborative filtering algorithm based on combined source data and by preliminary results we show that the datasets can be combined efficiently and that the final set can be clustered in order to make the algorithm faster.

References

1. Adomavicius, G., Mobasher, B., Francesco, R., Tuzhilin, A.: Context-aware recommender systems. AI Magazine 32(3), 67–80 (2011)
2. Bilandzic, M., Foth, M., Luca, A.D.: CityFlocks: Designing social navigation for urban mobile information systems. In: Proc. of the 7th ACM Conference on Designing Interactive Systems, pp. 174–183. ACM, Cape Town (2008)
3. Burrell, J., Gay, G.K.: Collectively defining context in a mobile, networked computing environment. In: CHI 2001 Extended Abstracts on Human Factors in Computing Systems. ACM, Seattle (2001)
4. Buettcher, S., Clarke, C.L.A., Cormack, G.V.: Information retrieval: Implementing and evaluating search engines. MIT Press, Cambridge (2010)
5. Gavalas, D., Konstantopoulos, C., Mastakas, K., Pantziou, G.: Mobile recommender systems in tourism. Journal of Network and Computer Applications 39, 319–333 (2014)
6. Ghorab, M.R., Zhou, D., Steichen, B., Wade, V.: Towards Multilingual User Models for Personalized Multilingual Information Retrieval. In: Proceedings of the 1st Workshop on Personalized Multilingual Hypertext Retrieval (PMHR 2011) in Conjunction with the 22nd ACM Conference on Hypertext and Hypermedia (HT 2011), Eindhoven, The Netherlands (2011)
7. Jannach, D., Zanker, M., Felfernig, A., Friedrich, G.: Recommender Systems an Introduction. Cambridge University Press (2011)
8. Kobsa, A.: Privacy-Enhanced Web Personalization. In: Brusilovsky, P., Kobsa, A., Nejdl, W. (eds.) Adaptive Web 2007. LNCS, vol. 4321, pp. 628–670. Springer, Heidelberg (2007)
9. Mettouris, C., Papadopoulos, G.A.: Ubiquitous Recommender Systems. Computing Online First Articles (2013)
10. Polatidis, N., Georgiadis, C.K.: Mobile recommender systems: An overview of technologies and challenges. In: 2013 Second International Conference on Informatics and Applications (ICIA), September 23-25, pp. 282–287 (2013)
11. Pu, P., Chen, L., Hu, R.: A user-centric evaluation framework for recommender systems. In: Proceedings of the Fifth ACM Conference on Recommender Systems (RecSys 2011), pp. 157–164. ACM, New York (2011)
12. Reischach, F.V., Michahelles, F., Schmidt, A.: The design space of ubiquitous product recommendation systems. In: Proc. the 8th International Conference on Mobile and Ubiquitous Multimedia, pp. 1–10 (2009)
13. Ricci, F.: Mobile Recommender Systems. J. of IT & Tourism 12(3), 205–231 (2011)
14. Ricci, F., Rokach, L., Shapira, B., Kantor, P.B.: Recommender Systems Handbook. Springer (2011)
15. Takeuchi, Y., Sugimoto, M.: A user-adaptive city guide system with an unobtrusive navigation interface. Person. Ubiquitous Comput. 13(2), 119–132 (2007)

16. Want, R., Pering, T.: System challenges for ubiquitous and pervasive computing. In: Proc. the 27th International Conference on Software Engineering, pp. 9–14. ACM (2005)
17. Ziegler, C.-N., McNee, S.M., Konstan, J.A., Lausen, G.: Improving recommendation lists through topic diversification. In: WWW 2005: Proceedings of the 14th International Conference on World Wide Web, pp. 22–32. ACM, New York (2005)
18. The Apache Mahout Machine Learning Library mahout.apache.org

The Experience of Spatial Interaction: Conceptualizing the User Experience of Virtual Environments

Charalampos Rizopoulos[1,2] and Dimitris Charitos[2]

[1] Department of Communication and Internet Studies,
Cyprus University of Technology, Limassol, Cyprus
c.rizopoulos@cut.ac.cy
[2] Department of Communication and Media Studies,
National and Kapodistrian University of Athens, Greece
vedesign@otenet.gr

Abstract. This paper examines the issue of User Experience (UX) as applied to immersive Virtual Reality from the standpoint of environmental psychology and related fields as a complement to principles from the fields of product design, psychology of emotion, formal aesthetics etc. Partly on account of its generality, multidisciplinary nature, and broad applicability, UX continues to defy a single commonly accepted definition, a fact which necessitates a holistic treatment of the subject of spatial interaction design. Various approaches and models of environmental psychology, as well as approaches to usability and UX are outlined in light of the need to highlight the influence and effects of particular spatial designs to particular dimensions of UX. Additionally, the concept and constituent dimensions of environmental appraisal are similarly defined and analysed, and indicative experimental designs currently under development are briefly described.

Keywords: User Experience, spatial cognition, virtual environments, environmental appraisal.

1 Introduction

Humans use spatial organizing principles in their daily lives; they are used to navigating space and communicating easily within space. Using information technology is often an abstract and complex experience due to lack of appropriate affordances [18]. Metaphors can create affordances for information technology by mapping affordances which already exist in relevant source domains [24]. Appropriately designed spatialized user interfaces may structure the domains of ICT applications through spatial metaphors. It could then be suggested that graphical interactive environments, created by following these principles, may enhance communication between humans and computers. Spatial metaphors have long been used for aiding navigation within information sets. The term "spatial interaction" refers to an interaction paradigm in which the perception and utilization of space by the user is of primary importance and resembles that of actual, physical space to a significant degree. Traditional

N. Streitz and P. Markopoulos (Eds.): DAPI 2014, LNCS 8530, pp. 380–391, 2014.

WIMP-based interfaces (e.g. Windows) make use of spatial analogies and metaphors, but they do not provide an experience that is perceptually similar to that of physical space. The use of a graphical, (3D) spatial context for visualizing information may exploit the intrinsic skills that humans have for navigating in 3D space and for detecting visual patterns there. A virtual environment, being a 3D graphical representational context, is an intrinsically spatial type of communication interface. Ellis [15] has emphasized the role of virtual reality (VR) as a communication technology or a medium of communication. Virtual reality (VR) could then be considered as the predominant manifestation of spatial interaction to date; virtual environments (VEs) – in the form of first-person computer games – are currently the most widespread applications in which users routinely navigate and act within 3D synthetic spaces. This paper aims to provide some insights into the way theoretical approaches of environmental perception, cognition, and appraisal can be interrelated with dimensions of User Experience in the context of spatial interaction, and primarily immersive virtual reality. In the sections that follow, aspects of usability and User Experience are discussed as essential parts of the process of environmental appraisal geared toward virtual space, and relevant experimental designs are outlined.

2   The Concept of User Experience in the Context of Spatial Interaction

Spatial interaction is accompanied by an enrichment of traditional usability and user experience (UX) indicators via the increased relevance of factors pertaining to environment design. 3D spaces may be seen as alternate but potentially persistent settings of human activity, as evidenced by online multiplayer games. The technological advances that make such a transition to true 3D spatial experiences possible also raise the issue of expanding the theoretical models, approaches, and frameworks that may be used for the design of spatial experiences. To date, the majority of VR-related research has focused on advancing the technological aspects that make these experiences possible, while comparatively fewer attempts have been made to investigate the impact of these experiences in relation to the design of perceptible form and interaction from a psychological aesthetic, design and communicative perspective.

2.1   Aspects of Usability in the Case of Spatial Interaction

In the context of spatial interaction, the notion of usability is augmented by the addition of constructs related to performance in spatial tasks, e.g. wayfinding, orientation, and various forms of spatial knowledge acquisition (e.g. landmark, route, and survey knowledge). For instance, Nash et al. [31] provide a number of performance indicators per sensory modality that are more suited to spatial interfaces, such as the ability to distinguish different colours and shapes, recognition of signs and symbols, estimation of distances and sizes, wayfinding and search, perception of auditory stimuli, response to kinaesthetic cues, object manipulation ability, effective locomotion through or around openings, corridors etc. To the extent that usability is influenced by user performance, factors such as spatial knowledge acquisition and performance in the context of spatial tasks become important in its assessment, as they are a manifestation of learnability and controllability. Regarding spatial knowledge acquisition, the environmental information that is acquired is stored in the form of spatial networks called *cognitive maps*. Cognitive maps provide a snapshot of an individual's perception and conception of spatial structures, which consists of spatial knowledge that has already been acquired, and continues to be extended and enriched. A cognitive map can represent several types of knowledge, e.g. topological, metric, route descriptions, fixed features, and sensory images with varying degrees of accuracy [19].

Main Types of Spatial Knowledge. Among various models of spatial knowledge acquisition, the most widely adopted is the one proposed by Siegel & White [38], according to which mental representations of space consist of three types of knowledge structures, which largely describe the process of transitioning from egocentric to allocentric frames of reference, as proposed by Piaget & Inhelder [33]:

1. *Landmark knowledge.* Certain elements of the environment acquire landmark status by virtue of their morphological characteristics (e.g. size, prominence / difference from surroundings) or socially or culturally-derived meaning (e.g.; town hall, church etc.).
2. *Route knowledge.* At this stage, the individual has been familiarized with landmarks and is able to form connections between them. The progression from point A to point B is still perceived from an egocentric perspective, but the spatial relations between landmarks are becoming more solidified.
3. *Survey knowledge.* At this stage, the individual perceives an environment from a global frame of reference disconnected from actual experience of the environment (e.g. navigation).

It is assumed that spatial knowledge acquisition begins at landmark knowledge and then progresses sequentially through the other two types of spatial knowledge. This assumption is valid only when the individual begins acquiring spatial knowledge by actual navigation in a heretofore unknown environment. However, the opposite progression may ensue if the individual's initial experience of the environment in question comes not from personal experience, but through spatial representations such as maps, which tend to offer a survey perspective of the environment ([2], [23]).

Landmark knowledge. The distinctiveness of landmarks is the result of differences in form, function, and / or symbolic meaning from their surrounding elements [27]. This distinctiveness may be due to physical form (e.g. landmark is taller / wider than surrounding elements), colour, lighting, texture, or other parameters that may be physically perceptible. Additionally, landmarks may have acquired such a status on account of the function they serve or due to their association with past events or commonly shared sociocultural values (e.g. the place of residence of a famous historical figure). It is also worth noting that landmark distinctiveness may not be limited to the visual modality [11]. The user's body, through its movement, can also accomplish a function similar to that of landmarks if the latter are sparse or do not exist (e.g. path integration) [36].

Lack of differentiation between landmarks can result in confusion and navigational errors ([29], [40]). Therefore, distinctiveness is not evaluated only against a landmark's surrounding elements, but also against other landmarks located at a relative distance, and thus can be said to correlate with its "usability", and more specifically with its effectiveness in supporting navigation.

An additional criterion for categorizing landmarks is whether they rely on the perceptible properties of their form ("object landmarks") or their placement – i.e. the spatial relationship between them and other elements – for obtaining their landmark status ("geometric landmarks") [26]. Sometimes an efficient way to turn an object into a landmark is to place it at a central and clearly visible location, or even slightly further from other objects, even if they have the same morphological characteristics. In this manner, the 'load' of endowing an object with landmark status is partially or entirely borne by spatial relations. Incidentally, this strategy aids the acquisition of route knowledge, because routes with adjacent landmarks tend to be encoded more accurately in memory because of the increased attention these landmarks receive. In this case, the congruence between the orientation of the landmark and the orientation of the route can lead to better understanding of spatial structure as opposed to a configuration in which these two orientations differ [40].

In the case of spatial interaction, the concept of landmark can be said to correspond to elements of the system which are more prominent by virtue of their importance or morphology – e.g. in a typical 'smart room' setting, a specific area which has been allocated to a specific task may attain landmark status. In VEs, to the extent that they provide an experience that is close to that of navigating a physical environment, the concept of landmarks is much closer to its original meaning.

Route knowledge. Route knowledge may be seen as a specific series of landmarks that occur at specific intervals [40]. This type of spatial knowledge is often not accompanied by knowledge of other spatial elements that lie along the route [21] – e.g. a driver may have expert knowledge of a given route but not of other elements along the road. Also not surprisingly, however, route knowledge is inflexible, as it is orientation-specific. Additionally, route knowledge acquired directly is more accurate that route knowledge acquired indirectly, leading to significant differences in performance [30]. The shape of the route itself is the element that changes as a function of the subject's active or passive role during the acquisition period [17]. In the context of a virtual environment, therefore, it can be assumed that more embodied forms of locomotion (e.g. simulated walking, treadmill-based movement, etc.) can be regarded as more active than arbitrarily defined methods (e.g. pressing keys). Therefore, the obvious recommendation is to design locomotion with embodied action in mind.

Signage can also reinforce the learning of particular routes [16]. An indicative example is colour coding, which points toward the "correct" direction. However, it could be argued that such schemes can limit the subject's exposure to the environment by promoting certain routes over others, thus potentially limiting the subject's exploratory tendencies and, ultimately, affecting spatial knowledge acquisition.

Complex routes are generally more difficult to remember than simple ones. Typically, the complexity of a route is related to the number of segments it consists of, determined by the number of intersections or decision points located along that route.

Survey knowledge. When survey knowledge actually forms the initial stage of spatial learning, distance estimation tends to be easier because in the case of direct experience more cognitive processing is required due to factors such as orientation specificity. Some elements are deemed more significant and thus serve as points around which primary networks of spatial relations are formed. Other networks near or around the primary ones are given secondary or tertiary importance [12]. Survey knowledge acquisition is also influenced by the environment's complexity; in exceedingly complex environments, the acquisition of survey knowledge without the aid of representations such as maps may be very difficult or impossible. On the other hand, in simple environments, the survey knowledge acquired from direct experience tends to be similar to that acquired indirectly [30].

It is possible to create virtual spatial experiences that are radically different to what the user is used to, to the point of being completely alien if so desired, given that there are intrinsic characteristics that space within a VE may possess and which significantly differentiate the experience afforded from a VE to the experience of physical space. For instance, a VE may comprise abstract and not iconic representational forms, may not have gravity, or teleportation points may exist, allowing users to move from point A to point B without covering the intervening distance. Space in a VE may be non-contiguous; the principles of real space may be violated; no physical constraints exist to dictate the dynamic, spatio-temporal nature of a VE; a VE does not necessarily have scale consistency [5].

A wide field of view (FOV) facilitates the acquisition of survey knowledge – it accelerates the whole learning process by allowing the subject to perceive a greater number of environmental stimuli [3]. This observation is directly translatable to Virtual Reality; the use of displays with wide FOV can be expected to result in faster and more efficient survey knowledge acquisition.

Alternative Approaches. Other approaches (for a review see [19]) highlight the qualitative changes in spatial knowledge as a result of increased experience and familiarity with an environment, thus disputing the essentially sequential nature of spatial knowledge acquisition as per the approach described above. According to approaches of this category, existing knowledge, which spans all stages proposed by Siegel & White at varying degrees, is enriched so that its quality (e.g. level of detail, precision etc.) is improved. Some approaches (e.g. anchorpoint theory) blur the line between landmarks and routes, suggesting that the most important parameter for spatial learning is the significance attributed to each environmental element by the subject [23]. According to approaches of this category, individuals tend to form a hierarchy of spatial networks, each containing all types of spatial elements (e.g. landmarks, paths, etc.)[1]. Montello et al. [30] suggest that what is initially encoded in mental spatial representations is topological (as opposed to metric) relations between elements, and that the primary alteration in spatial mental representations that results from learning is the addition of metric knowledge.

Cognitive Map Inaccuracies. The most common errors in cognitive maps, ascertainable through methods such as sketch mapping, are omissions (when parts of the environment do not appear on the sketch), distortions (when parts of the environment appear distorted on the sketch), and additions (when elements that appear on the sketches do not exist in the environment) ([2], [32]). Inaccuracies often function as heuristics aiding encoding and recall through simplification – e.g. intersection angles rounded to the nearest multiple of 90 or 45, slightly converging lines perceived as parallel, ellipsoids encoded as circles, etc. among spatial elements involve misjudging positions and distances, resulting in spatial configurations that resemble "tectonic plates" (where spatial elements are grouped together and moved as a single unit), "fisheye lens" (where distances between elements are overestimated), or "magnet" (where distances between elements are underestimated) ([19, [23]). Generally, lack of substantial inaccuracies can be an indicator of high environmental "usability".

2.2   Extending Usability: The Concept of User Experience

On a rudimentary level, hedonic factors were part of early definitions of usability offered by Shackel [37] and Stanton & Baker [39], which consisted of eight components: effectiveness, learnability, flexibility, attitude, perceived usefulness, task match, task characteristics, and user characteristics. Of these components, attitude refers to the system's ability to retain its use within acceptable margins of comfort and required effort while also increasing user satisfaction and hence the probability of future use. Perceived usefulness and task match were also indirectly related to hedonic quality, in the form of satisfaction resulting from the compatibility between system functionality and user goals. The ISO 9241-11 definition of usability refers to effectiveness, efficiency, and satisfaction within a specific context of use (which is further analyzed in users, tasks, equipment, and environment). An interesting implication of this definition is the important role of contextual factors (including the environment) in the perception of usability. Typical inaccuracies pertaining to the relations considers usability as the absence of negatively evaluated elements which, in turn, negatively impact the perceived "worth" of a system – even though the term "worth" is not explained in great detail. The main tenet of this family of approaches is that satisfaction is equated with the absence of problems rather than the generation of added value.

Hertzum [20] refers to "hedonic usability", i.e. the subjective evaluation of system use aspects that are not directly related to productivity. It can be further subdivided

---

[1] Typically, a person's primary spatial network is anchored on the home, or on the transition between home and workplace. Around the primary network, secondary and tertiary networks are formed. When navigating, individuals tend to employ these hierarchical levels in succession.

into *relief*, which refers to the minimization of negative affect resulting from system use, and *hedonic quality*, which refers to the system's ability to elicit positive affective reactions. Hertzum also refers to "perceived usability", the subjective perception of effectiveness, efficiency, and other mostly pragmatic aspects of system use. Alonso-Ríos et al. [1] refer, among others, to subjective satisfaction as the system's ability to provide users with pleasurable stimuli (perceptual aspect) and pique their interest (cognitive – symbolic aspect).

As evident from the above, the constant expansion of the traditional conception of usability is necessary so that various aspects of system use not directly related to efficiency, productivity, utility, and other pragmatically-oriented concepts are accounted for. This process of expansion leads to the wider concept of User Experience (UX), which has come to involve three broad classes of factors: the user, the object being used (i.e. the system), and the context of use, which includes 'tangible' (environmental stimuli) as well as 'intangible' (sociocultural norms, subjective values etc.) elements. As interaction design paradigms evolve and encompass elements that deviate from conventional contexts (e.g. as computation and interaction expands onto physical and virtual space), the focus inevitably shifts toward aspects that are more hedonically-oriented and would have been considered extraneous up to that point [28].

Some Indicative Conceptualizations of User Experience. The most fundamental distinction in UX is the one between pragmatic and hedonic aspects (e.g. [22]). The former refers to the system's ability to effectively support the user's basic, more productively-oriented needs, whereas the latter points to the system's ability to excite the user's interest and attention and encourage him/her to adopt its use as part of his/her identity.

Tiger (in [4], p. 497) refers to four different types of pleasure that may be derived from using a product: (i) *physio-pleasure*, resulting from the perception of sensory stimuli and bodily actions that provide kinaesthetic feedback, (ii) *socio-pleasure*, resulting from social interaction, as well as social identification processes provided or supported by the product in question, (iii) *psycho-pleasure*, which entails the subject's cognitive and emotional processes and responses during the use of the product, and (iv) *ideo-pleasure*, the product's symbolic or artistic value and its compatibility with the subject's self-identity.

Norman [41] suggests that users interact with the system on three distinct but interconnected levels: (i) *visceral or reactive level* (automatically executed actions largely dictated by biological factors; a typical example is direct sensory feedback, which can be in itself a pleasurable stimulus), (ii) *behavioral level* (actions that are automatically executed due to habituation; this is the level that most closely corresponds to 'traditional' usability), and (iii) *reflective / contemplative level* (the interpretation of a stimulus by the user based on intra-individually derived or sociocultural values and concepts, such as self-image, roles, identity etc.). Crilly et al. [10] provide a categorization similar to Norman's: (i) *aesthetic impression*, the interplay between novelty and order in the perception of the product, (ii) *semantic interpretation*, the way the product's functionality and mode of operation is communicated to the user (this dimension resembles 'traditional' usability), and (iii) *symbolic association*, the importance and meaning of the product in terms of desired and/or projected identity. Also similar is the categorization by Desmet & Hekkert [13], which consists of three types of pleasure: (i) aesthetic pleasure, (ii) attribution of [sociocultural or symbolic] meaning, and (iii) emotional response. Similarly, Rafaeli & Vilnai-Yavetz [34] mention three basic dimensions of the experience of using physical artefacts: (i) instrumentality (functional aspects), (ii) aesthetics, and (iii) symbolism. Kuniavsky [25] refers to identity as a UX dimension, construed as a combination of functionality and symbolism with respect to the user's self-image. Kuniavsky considers identity design to be the most important parameter that shapes the user's affective response toward a product.

Costello & Edmonds [7] synthesized a number of approaches of the concept of pleasure and ended up with thirteen different dimensions, some of which (i.e. exploration and discovery) have clear applications in spatial settings, while others (competition, sympathy, camaraderie) have clear social connotations. Pleasure from sensory feedback and symbolic meaning and identification is also present in this framework. The concept of value has also been analysed into a number of constituent dimensions [9] that include aesthetic, symbolic, functional, and ergonomic value, as well as categorization and attention-drawing ability.

With respect to interaction scale, three levels may be distinguished. On a macroscopic level, the user interacts with the system in its entirety (as one unit). The microscopic level, on the other hand, refers to the user's interactions with specific objects or subcomponents of the system, often in the context of larger activities. An intermediary level can also be envisioned, on which the user interacts with collections of subcomponents with shared functionality that constitute a single system component which supports a specific user activity. Furthermore, it is evident from the literature cited above that the broadest and most inclusive categorization of UX variables consists of four main dimensions: physical / sensory, cognitive, symbolic, and social. These dimensions can also be interpreted in terms of their intra-individual or social focus, ranging from the purely individual to the collectively determined.

3   Environmental Preference and UX

Environmental appraisal refers to the process of assigning an affective quality to environments and stimuli originating from them, and is closely linked with an array of cognitive, affective, and behavioural responses [8]. Essentially, it translates to assigning affective responses to environments.

As is the case with UX, environmental appraisal can occur on several levels. Four such broad levels are the physical or perceptual, the social, the cognitive, and the symbolic. The physical or perceptual level refers to the way objectively defined parameters are perceived through the appropriate sensory subsystems (e.g. lighting, colour) prior to cognitive processing. The social level entails evaluating an environment in terms of the social entities found therein and the possibilities for social (or parasocial) interaction it offers. The cognitive level refers to the impact of environmental elements on cognitive processes and is the level that most closely corresponds to 'traditional' usability. The symbolic level deals with the way environmental elements become part of the subject's self-identity. With the exception of the social level, which refers to elements that are in a way extraneous to the environment itself, the other three levels signify a progression from the more concrete to the more abstract in terms of environmental appraisal properties. Additionally, elements under appraisal can pertain to different aspects of the environment, such as the space itself (e.g. geometry, size, etc.), the objects or actors it contains (e.g. layout, presence of embodied agents etc.), and environmental circumstances (e.g. light, colour, noise level, temperature etc.). A review of relevant literature (see [35]) highlights some indicative dimensions of environmental appraisal, listed below (expanded and adapted from [35]):

- **Pleasantness.** The most fundamental dimension of environmental appraisal. Pleasant environments tend to be perceived as beneficial, safe, enjoyable, and aesthetically pleasing.
- **Size, extent, and visibility.** Whether an environment is visible in its entirety without the user having to move. There are also social connotations to size and extent (e.g. crowding).
- **Complexity.** The number of separate elements an environment consists of, the variability in their form or texture, and the number of sensory modalities involved in the perception of stimuli.
- **Coherence / unity.** The extent to which elements of an environment are similar or complementary, constituting a single overarching unit.
- **Modularity.** The extent to which an environment is segmented, i.e. consists of several interconnected parts..
- **Legibility.** A legible environment offers cues as to its functions, its constituent elements, and its properties (see Lynch 1960).
- **Utility.** The degree to which the environment can support the subject's goals.
- **Familiarity.** In a productive activity (i.e. an activity with clear goals and specific positive and negative outcomes associated with its successful or unsuccessful execution), lack of familiarity is usually interpreted as negative.
- **Predictability / clarity.** The inhabitant's ability to anticipate the form and function of environmental elements.
- **Novelty.** The extent to which an environment contains new elements or elements that had not been perceived by the individual. Novelty can be seen as the inverse of familiarity and tends to induce exploratory behavior.
- **Safety / privacy.** The extent to which the environment can provide the user with the opportunity of voluntary inaccessibility (e.g. hiding) and encourage informal behavior.
- **Malleability.** The ability of the environment to be configured by the inhabitants in accordance with their needs and goals; malleability is an aspect of personalization.
- **Natural elements.** The extent to which an environment contains natural elements or related connotations.
1. **Representational and interactional fidelity.** The extent to which sensory stimuli and behaviors that resemble those found in the real world are featured in a VE.

4   Concluding Remarks and Future Work

Interrelating UX and environmental preference variables is expected to result in a detailed categorization of the impact of elements of spatial design on the users' perception and evaluation of spatial interfaces in general and immersive VEs in particular. Such a framework will assist the design and evaluation of such interfaces from a more theoretically informed position. As a means of producing conclusive evidence of the interrelationships among the concepts outlined in the previous sections, a series of experiments are currently being designed. Among others, these experiments attempt to address the following issues:

- Assessing the impact of various degrees of embodied action within immersive VEs on the functional and emotional aspects of UX.
- Assessing the impact of environments as social entities that promote parasocial interaction with the users by appropriate changes in form, colour, lighting, and other parameters.
- Ascertaining the influence of factors related to representational and interactional realism on user performance and enjoyment.
- Investigating the correlation between stable subjective variables such as personality and spatial ability, and performance in spatial tasks or environmental preference.
- The degree to which the aforementioned relationships fluctuate as a function of immersion and presence.

These experiments are considered steps toward the formulation of a theoretical framework and a set of guiding principles for the design or synthetic spatial experiences.

References

1. Alonso-Ríos, D., Vázquez-García, A., Mosqueira-Rey, E., Moret-Bonillo, V.: Usability: A Critical Analysis and a Taxonomy. International Journal of Human-Computer Interaction, 26, 53-74 (2010).
2. Bell, P.A., Greene, T.G., Fisher, J.D., Baum, A.: Environmental Psychology, 4th edn. Harcourt Brace, Orlando (1996)
3. Billinghurst, M., Weghorst, S.: The Use of Sketch Maps to Measure Cognitive Maps of Virtual Environments. In: Proceedings of the Virtual Reality Annual International Symposium 1995, March 11-15, pp. 40–47. IEEE, Triangle Research Park (1995)
4. Buccini, M., Padovani, S.: Typology of the Experiences. In: Proceedings of "Designing Pleasurable Products and Interfaces", Helsinki, Finland, August 22-25, pp. 495–504. ACM Press, Helsinki (2007)
5. Charitos, D.: Communicating Environmental Meaning through Designing Space in Virtual Environments. In: Ylä-Kotola, M.Y., Inkinen, S., Isomaki, H. (eds.) The Integrated Media Machine: Aspects of Future Interfaces and Cross-Media Culture, Integrated Media Machine, vol. III, pp. 13–35. European Institute of Sustainable Information Society, Rovaniemi (2005)

6. Cockton, G.: Usability Evaluation. In: Soegaard, M., Dam, R.F. (eds.) Encyclopedia of Human-Computer Interaction, The Interaction-Design.org Foundation, Aarhus (2012), http://www.interaction-design.org/encyclopedia/usability_evaluation.html (accessed June 4, 2012)
7. Costello, B., Edmonds, E.: A Study in Play, Pleasure and Interaction Design. In: Proceedings of the 2007 Conference on Designing Pleasurable Products and Interfaces (DPPI 2007), Helsinki, Finland, August 22-25, pp. 76–91. ACM Press, New York (2007)
8. Craik, K.H., Feimer, N.R.: Environmental Assessment. In: Stokols, D., Altman, I. (eds.) Handbook of Environmental Psychology, 1st edn., pp. 891–918. John Wiley & Sons, New York (1987)
9. Creusen, M.E.H., Schoormans, J.P.L.: The Different Roles of Product Appearance in Consumer Choice. Journal of Product Innovation Management 22, 63–81 (2005)
10. Crilly, N., Moultrie, J., Clarkson, P.J.: Seeing Things: Consumer Response to the Visual Domain in Product Design. Design Studies 25, 547–577 (2004)
11. Darken, R.P., Sibert, J.L.: A Toolset for Navigation in Virtual Environments. In: Proceedings of ACM User Interface Software & Technology, pp. 157–165 (1993)
12. Darken, R.P., Sibert, J.L.: Wayfinding Strategies and Behaviors in Large Virtual Worlds. In: Proceedings of CHI 1996, Vancouver, BC, April 13-18, pp. 142–149. ACM Press, New York (1996)
13. Desmet, P., Hekkert, P.: Framework of Product Experience. International Journal of Design 1, 57–66 (2007)
14. Dieberger, A., Tromp, J.: The Information City Project: A virtual reality user interface for navigation in information spaces. In: Proceedings of the Vienna Virtual Reality 1993 Conference, Vienna, Austria (1993)
15. Ellis, S.R.: Nature and origins of virtual environments: A bibliographical essay. Computing Systems in Engineering 2, 321–347 (1991)
16. Evans, G.W.: Environmental Cognition. Psychological Bulletin 88, 259–287 (1980)
17. Gaunet, F., Vidal, M., Kemeny, A., Berthoz, A.: Active, Passive and Snapshot Exploration in a Virtual Environment: Influence on Scene Memory, Reorientation and Path Memory. Cognitive Brain Research 11, 409–420 (2001)
18. Gibson, J.J.: The ecological approach to visual perception. Lawrence Erlbaum Associates, Hillsdale (1986)
19. Golledge, R.G., Stimson, R.J.: Spatial Behavior: A Geographic Perspective. The Guilford Press, New York (1997)
20. Hertzum, M.: Images od Usability. International Journal of Human-Computer Interaction 20, 567–600 (2010)
21. Hirtle, S.C., Hudson, J.: Acquisition of Spatial Knowledge for Routes. Journal of Environmental Psychology 11, 335–345 (1991)
22. Karapanos, E., Zimmerman, J., Forlizzi, J., Martens, J.B.: User Experience Over Time: An Initial Framework. In: Proceedings of CHI 2009, Boston, MA, USA, April 4-9, pp. 729–738. ACM Press, New York
23. Kitchin, R., Blades, M.: The Cognition of Geographic Space. Tauris, London (2002)
24. Kuhn, W.: Handling data spatially: Spatializing user interfaces. In: Kraak, M.J., Molenaar, M. (eds.) Advances in GIS research II: Proceedings of the 7th International Symposium on Spatial Data Handling, vol. 2, pp. 13B.1–13B.23. IGU, Delft (1996)
25. Kuniavsky, M.: Smart Things: Ubiquitous Computing User Experience Design. Morgan Kaufmann, Burlington (2010)

26. Lin, C.T., Huang, T.Y., Lin, W.J., Chang, S.Y., Lin, Y.H., Ko, L.W., Hung, D.L., Chang, E.C.: Gender Differences in Wayfinding in Virtual Environments with Global or Local Landmarks. Journal of Environmental Psychology 32, 89–96 (2012)
27. Lynch, K.: The Image of the City. The MIT Press, Cambridge (1960)
28. McCullough, M.: Digital Ground: Architecture, Pervasive Computing, and Environmental Knowing. MIT Press, Cambridge (2004)
29. Montello, D.R.: Navigation. In: Shah, P., Miyake, A. (eds.) The Cambridge Handbook of Visuospatial Thinking, pp. 257–294. Cambridge University Press, New York (2005)
30. Montello, D.R., Hegarty, M., Richardson, A.E., Waller, D.: Spatial Memory of Real Environments, Virtual Environments, and Maps. In: Allen, G.L. (ed.) Human Spatial Memory: Remembering Where, pp. 251–285. Lawrence Erlbaum Associates, Mahwah (2004)
31. Nash, E.B., Edwards, G.W., Thompson, J.A., Barfield, W.: A Review of Presence and Performance in Virtual Environments. International Journal of Human-Computer Interaction 12, 1–41 (2000)
32. Oliver, K.: Psychology in Practice: Environment. Hodder Arnold, London (2002)
33. Piaget, J., Inhelder, B.: The Child's Conception of Space. Norton, New York (1967)
34. Rafaeli, A., Vilnai-Yavetz, I.: Instrumentality, Aesthetics and Symbolism of Physical Artifacts as Triggers of Emotion. International Symposium on Theoretical Programming 5(1), 91–112 (2004)
35. Rizopoulos, C., Charitos, D.: Implications of Theories of Communication and Spatial Behavior for the Design of Interactive Environments. In: Proceedings of the 7th International Conference on Intelligent Environments, Nottingham, UK (2011)
36. Ruddle, R.A., Volkova, E., Bülthoff, H.H.: Walking Improves Your Cognitive Map in Environments that Are Large-Scale and Large in Extent. ACM Transactions on Computer-Human Interaction 18, article 10 (2011)
37. Shackel, B.: Usability – Context, Framework, Definition, Design and Evaluation. In: Shackel, B., Richardson, S. (eds.) Human Factors for Informatics Usability, pp. 21–37. Cambridge University Press, New York (1991)
38. Siegel, A.W., White, S.H.: The Development of Spatial Representations of Large-Scale Spatial Environments. In: Reese, H.W. (ed.) Advances in Child Development and Behavior, vol. 10, pp. 9–55. Academic Press, New York (1975)
39. Stanton, N.A., Baber, C.: Usability and EC Directive 90/270. Displays 13(3), 151–160 (1992)
40. Vinson, N.G.: Design Guidelines for Landmarks to Support Navigation in Virtual Environments. In: Proceedings of CHI 1999, Pittsburgh, PA, pp. 278–285. ACM Press, New York (1999)
41. Norman, D.A.: Emotional Design: Why We Love (or Hate) Everyday Things. Basic Books, New York (2004)

A See-through Vision with Handheld Augmented Reality for Sightseeing

Goshiro Yamamoto, Arno in Wolde Lübke,
Takafumi Taketomi, and Hirokazu Kato

Nara Institute of Science and Technology
8916-5 Takayama Ikoma 630-0192, Japan
{goshiro,arno-w,takafumi-t,kato}@is.naist.jp
http://imd.naist.jp/

Abstract. We propose a see-through vision with augmented reality (AR) for increasing the quality of the experiences in the activities of sightseeing. In the sightseeing activities, there are certain temporal and spatial limitations when sightseers are gazing on the real objects. In this research, we aim to eliminate the spatial limitations caused by the inability to see farther objects through opaque surfaces by using see-through vision technology with alpha blending, and to make the appearance of the target objects with 3D effect based on parallax effect. We focus on the platform of handheld devices that provides AR experiences with high accurate alignment of virtual objects on pre-captured real scene images based on cube mapping method. This paper describes the engineering methodology that we have used to develop our prototype system and the implementation of the prototype system for confirming our approach. The results about how the prototype system performs on a real site are reported in this paper.

Keywords: Augmented reality, see-through vision, sightseeing, handheld AR.

1 Introduction

Mobile computing technologies have been rapidly developed and these development spreads changes to use augmented reality (AR) for general public because a handheld device provides one of the simplest AR structures with a camera and a display [Möhring et al., 2004],[Henrysson et al., 2005]. The AR technology has the potential to enhance the quality of life (QOL) in daily routines, education, work, and so forth. Sightseeing is one of the activities which is entertaining and intellectual. The essential elements of sightseeing activities include being at the location and facing towards the existing objects. In this paper, we propose a handheld see-through vision with AR technology to give sightseers better experiences. There are certain temporal and spatial limitations with sightseeing when sightseers are gazing on real objects. Temporal limitations are caused by the time constrain that sightseers can only experience the view at current time. Spatial

N. Streitz and P. Markopoulos (Eds.): DAPI 2014, LNCS 8530, pp. 392–399, 2014.

limitations are caused by the inability to see further objects through opaque surfaces. In this research we are trying to eliminate spatial limitations by using X-ray AR [Sandor et al., 2010][Santos et al., 2013] and Indirect Augmented Reality (Indirect AR) [Wither et al., 2011][Akaguma et al., 2013] technology to give sightseers more enjoyable experiences.

The activity of sightseeing can be carried out in indoor or outdoor environments. For the indoor environment, tracking and motion sensing can be achieved using motion tracking sensors. However, it is difficult to capture tracking points in outdoor environment and it is costly to install motion tracking sensors at every site. Thus, a solution for sightseeing in outdoor environment using motion sensors including accelerometers, gyroscopes, and digital compass on a handheld device is proposed. We implemented cube mapping expression with pre-captured panoramas photos inspired by Indirect AR which is proposed by Wither et al. to reduce perceptual tracking errors with motion sensing. However, 2D information of Indirect AR was not suitable for displaying objects that are close to the user. Therefore, we proposed a novel approach to use 3D effect in conjunction with Indirect AR information. Our approach takes parallax effect into consideration to make the appearance of the target objects feel like 3D with alpha blending based on X-ray AR.

The following sections describes the engineering methodology that we used developing our prototype system, the implementation of the prototype system, and the results of an user experiment using the prototype system in Todaiji temple.

2   Method

In this research, we focus on the situation where the sightseeing spot is a ruin located under the ground. After a ruin was discovered and dug up, it will be filled up within a temporary period. In this case, the sightseers are not able to view the actual scene after the period. To re-present the ruin to the sightseers with an immersive environment, we developed a see-through vision handheld AR application. The application is implemented using the proposed method which includes two phases, cubic environment map construction with alpha blending and a movable viewpoint in the cubic environment map, as shown in Figure 1.

In the first phase, we construct a cubic environment map which contains a 3D model of the ruin and panorama photos of the environment. The 3D model of the ruin is created using the information that were measured when the ruin was yet filled up. The panorama photos of the surrounding environment near the ruin were taken and used as the background of the cubic environment map. The cubic environment map was constructed by these two elements and rendered using alpha blending method.

In the second phase, we propose the method of movable viewpoint which provides parallax effect of the 3D object to the user. In the conventional methods, the relationship between the cubic environment and the view point is fixed. This caused the effect that the object has 2D appearance even it has 3D information.

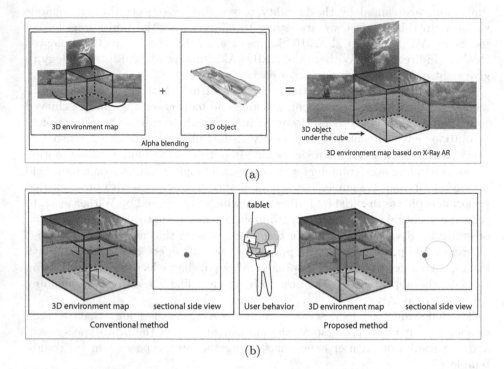

Fig. 1. Proposed method with cubic environment map construction with alpha blending and a movable viewpoint in the cubic environment map. (a) A cubic environment map was created using panorama photos and a 3D model of the ruin. The 3D model is rendered under the cubic environment with alpha blending. (b) In the conventional methods, the viewpoint is fixed at the centre of the cubic environment map. In our proposed method, the viewpoint is moved around the sphere which is located at the centre of the cubic environment according to the orientation of the devices.

Thus we improve the perception by implementing a movable viewpoint according to the orientation of the user's device. This implementation provides the parallax effect where the user is able to feel the object exists in 3D environment.

The proposed method with two phases is able to provide better perception to the user while viewing the scene. The following chapter details the implementation of the proposed method.

3   Implementation

We implemented a prototype system on iOS devices (Apple iPad/iPad mini) based on the above conceptual idea as the following. In advance, the 3D data of the target ruin is created by measuring the real ruin and using 3D modeling software, and panorama photos is also taken by omnidirectional camera.

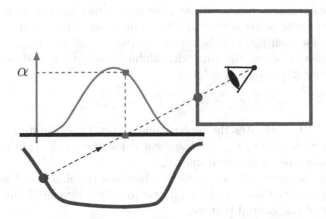

Fig. 2. Alpha lookup: To compute the alpha value that is used to combine the color of a ruin surface point (brown dot) and its occluding point of the environment (green dot) a ray can be cast and its intersection with the alpha plane (black line) can be used to look up the actual value.

The system we implemented is based on Indirect AR idea. As conventional tracking and mapping methods often prove unreliable in many outdoor scenarios, a main benefit of this approach is to avoid registration errors by substituting the commonly used video feed with pre-captured panorama photos of the surrounding environment. Although being purely virtual, the use of panoramic photos which are displayed partially depending on the users location and orientation often creates the illusion of actually seeing the actual environment.

For our prototype system, we rely on a cubic environment map which is mapped onto a cube that is centered around the virtual camera. In order to register the cubic map with the real world environment, we use the build-in sensors (namely accelerometer, gyroscope and compass) of the test device to compute the users orientation and adjust the virtual camera accordingly.

Additionally, a 3D reconstruction of an ancient ruin is part of the scene. The ruin is located below the bottom cube plane. As sketch of the virtual setup is given in Figure 2.

To create the impression that the ruin is located below the ground of the cube we follow work of Sandor et. al. [Sandor et al., 2010] and emulate a x-ray vision that renders the parts of the environment that occlude the ruin transparent. For this purpose, we blend the fragment color of a projected ruin surface point in screen space with the corresponding color of the occluding environment map pixel. The blending coefficient is chosen according to an user-generated alpha texture that is mapped onto a plane located above and oriented parallel to the ruin. Geometrically, the alpha value used for a certain surface point of a ruin can be obtained by shooting a ray from the surface point in direction of the camera origin, computing its intersection with the alpha plane, and looking up the alpha value at that point (see Figure 2).

For the implementation, we chose a two render pass approach: In the first render pass the alpha plane is rendered to an offscreen render target to determine alpha value for each pixel of the screen. In the second render pass the environment is rendered before the ruin with alpha blending enabled, where the final fragment color $\mathbf{c}_{i,j}$ is optained by

$$\mathbf{c}_{i,j} = \alpha_{i,j}\mathbf{s}_{i,j} + (1 - \alpha_{i,j})\mathbf{d}_{i,j} \qquad (1)$$

where $\alpha_{i,j} \in [0,1]$ denotes the alpha value at pixel coordinate (i,j) of the off-screen render target and $\mathbf{s}_{i,j}$ the fragment color due to the ruin and $\mathbf{d}_{i,j}$ is the fragment color due to the environment.

Following the approach of , to further increase the illusion of seeing through the environment the used alpha map was modified by combining it with edge information of the ground texture.

To amplify the user's feeling of being part of a 3D scene and to model the users potential motion, we decided to place the virtual camera on a ellipsoid that is centered around the origin. We compute the camera's position as the intersection of a ray that is given by the direction

$$\mathbf{r}(t) = t\mathbf{d} \qquad (2)$$

of the camera and the ellipsoid

$$\frac{x^2}{a^2} + \frac{y^2}{b^2} + \frac{z^2}{c^2} = 1, \qquad (3)$$

where a, b and c define the form of the ellipse and $\|\mathbf{d}\| = 1$. The position on the ellipse is then $\mathbf{p} = t_i\mathbf{d}$, where t_i is the result of substituting Equation 2 into Equation 3 and solving for t:

$$t = \left(\left(\frac{d_x}{a}\right)^2 + \left(\frac{d_y}{b}\right)^2 + \left(\frac{d_z}{c}\right)^2\right)^{-\frac{1}{2}} \qquad (4)$$

where d_x, d_y and d_z denote the components of $\mathbf{d}$.

4   Results

The prototype system is used in our experiment conducted at Todaiji temple which is the famous world cultural heritage site in Japan. In the precincts of Todaiji, the Sobo ruin, which is Monkfs lodging house, was discovered and dug up for a limited time only. At that time, we measured the ruin and use the measured information to acquire 3D model as shown in Figure 3 (a). After the ruin was filled up, we captured photos of surrounding environment of the ruin using an omnidirectional camera at the several fixed points (Figure 3 (b)). The pre-collected data is the element to create cube environment map.

As shown in Figure 4, the results of views in the conventional environment and proposed environment have good see-through vision. Both environments

(a)   (b)

Fig. 3. Pre-collected data for creating cube environment map. (a) A 3D model of the ruin based on the measurement in multiple viewpoints. (b) A pre-captured panorama photo of the real environment.

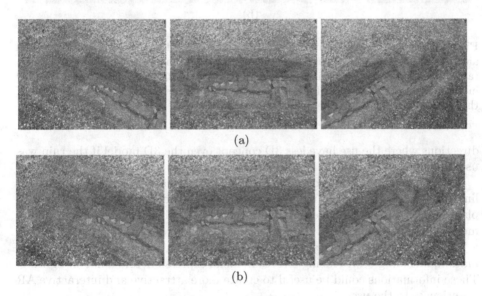

(a)

(b)

Fig. 4. The results of views of the ruins. (a) Viewing the ruin in conventional cube environment. (b) Viewing the ruin in the environment created by proposed method.

provide realistic vision to the user and create the immersive conception of gazing the ruin. Furthermore, when we display the views of the ruin in 2D pictures, the conventional methods and the proposed method yielded very similar results. However, the proposed method provides the parallax effect to the user where the distance of two viewing directions changes dynamically (Figure 5 (b)). The user is able to feel more existing in the 3D environment compare to the conventional method. The conventional method fixed the distance between two viewing

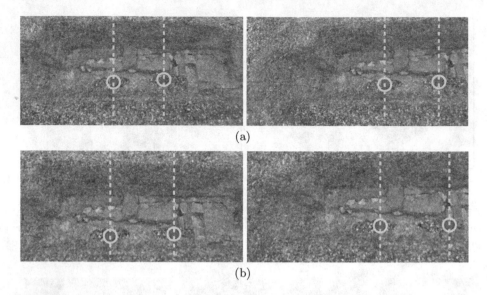

Fig. 5. The effectiveness of parallax effect between conventional cube mapping method and proposed method. The circles are located on the surface of the cube environment. (a) Conventional cube mapping method provides only 2D information even the 3D model was used. (b) Proposed method provides parallax effect between the surface of the cube environment and the 3D model.

directions where the use have less 3D concept even the 3D model if the ruin was used in the implementation (Figure 5 (a)).

The limitation of the proposed method is the reliability of the scene. This limitation is caused by the moving viewpoint where distortion happens at two plane images of the cube were merged. Instead of cube-based mapping, implement sphere mapping method might mitigate the distortion effect.

Furthermore, front camera of the device can be used to collect additional information, including userfd facing direction, facial expression, and ambient lighting. These informations could be useful to create more attractive and interactive AR experiences to the user.

5   Conclusion

This paper focus on increasing the quality of the experiences in the activity of sightseeing with AR technology. We choose the ruin which is in the ground as the target environment, and propose see-through vision technology that can provide the sightseers additional experiences than traditional touring way. To realize 3D appearance of the object, we implemented two phases, cubic environment map construction and movable viewpoint in the cubic environment map, based on Indirect AR and X-ray AR.

In the first phase, the alpha blending method is used for rendering 3D model of the object and panorama photos are used for constructing cubic environment map. The second phase, movable viewpoint in the cubic environment map, can provide a better 3D perception to the user then fixed viewpoint. However, if the viewpoint was moved farther from the center of the cubic map the corners of the cubic environment map will cause collation of the 3D effect. This drawback can be overcome by using sphere mapping instead of cubic mapping.

We also conduct an experiment at Todaiji temple using our prototype system. Future work includes adding the effect of shadow and improve stereoscopic vision with movable viewpoint.

Acknowledgements. This research was partially supported by Grant-in-Aids for Scientific Research (A), No. 23240024, the "Ambient Intelligence" project sponsored by MEXT, and NAIST Advanced Research Partnership Project. We are very grateful to Todaiji for giving us the opportunity to conduct this experiment.

References

Möhring, M., Lessig, C., Bimber, O.: Video See-Through AR on Consumer Cell Phones. In: Proceedings of International Symposium on Augmented and Mixed Reality (ISMAR 2004), pp. 252–253 (2004)

Henrysson, A., Billinghurst, M., Ollila, M.: Face to Face Collaborative AR on Mobile Phones. In: Proceedings International Symposium on Augmented and Mixed Reality (ISMARf 2005), pp. 80–89 (2005)

Wither, J., Tsai, Y.T., Azuma, R.: Indirect Augmented Reality. Computers & Graphics 35(4), 810–822 (2011)

Sandor, C., Cunningham, A., Dey, A., Mattila, V.V.: An Augmented Reality X-Ray System based on Visual Saliency. In: Proceedings of IEEE International Symposium on Mixed and Augmented Reality (ISMAR), pp. 27–36 (2010)

Akaguma, T., Okura, F., Sato, T., Yokoya, N.: Mobile AR using pre-captured omni-directional images. In: Proceedings ACM SIGGRAPH Asia 2013 Symp. on Mobile Graphics and Interactive Applications, Article No. 26 (2013)

Santos, M.E.C., Chen, A., Terawaki, M., Yamamoto, G., Taketomi, T., Miyazaki, J., Kato, H.: Augmented Reality X-ray Interaction in K-12 Education. In: Proceedings of the 13th IEEE International Conference on Advanced Learning Technologies (ICALT 2013), pp. 141–145 (2013)

A Structure of Wearable Message-Robot for Ubiquitous and Pervasive Services

Tomoko Yonezawa[1] and Hirotake Yamazoe[2]

[1] Kansai University, Osaka, Japan
yone@kansai-u.ac.jp
[2] Osaka University, Osaka, Japan
yamazoe@osipp.osaka-u.ac.jp

Abstract. In this paper, we introduce a haptic message-robot which gives user-friendly physical contacts while it tells message to the user. This robot is expected to help elderly people who need outings but have anxiety. The pervasive support of the robot via network will provide the user a human-like service as though it were a real caregiver. The system makes haptic stimili corresponding to the user's clothing and posture. We investigated two types of implementations: the first implementation combines haptic stimili and anthropmorphic motion to express the physical contact, and the second one is an simplified system for application on smartphones to provide ubiquitous services. The subjective evaluations in a course with two diverges showed the effectiveness of both the robot's motion and the haptic stimili on the intelligibleness and affective communication.

1 Introduction

Since there have been many ubiquitous and pervasive services via smartphones for users who are outing, it is important to provide services in appropriate manner for each user. Those devices have touch screens for an intuitive input method. Touch screens are intuitive way of visual-tactile interaction, but at the same time, there have been several reports on the dangers of the users who are walking during use. On the other hand, elderly people often have difficulties to use touch screen in looking for applications. Thick and small interface sometimes causes confusion to them.

In our outings, our needs for information are focused on i) push services such as email messages and ii) locational or directional services. For children, these devices can provide various messages from her/his mother, friends, and unusual information around the place at the same time. If an integrated system can provide all information in a comfortable and common manner to be easy to understand, not only small children or elderly people but also normal adults do not need to bother themselves about treatments of their devices.

To solve these problems in outings, we propose an integrated service manner by a wearable robot for anthropomorphic support like a partner. The anthropomorphism have been discussed for familiar and communicative systems [1].

N. Streitz and P. Markopoulos (Eds.): DAPI 2014, LNCS 8530, pp. 400–411, 2014.

A partner robot can provide comprehensive information by anthropomorphic expression. We adopted a simultaneous expression of both the physical contacts from the robot to the user and the whispering vocal utterance for private communication. At the same time, the robot makes its bodily motions corresponding to the physical contact. The anthropomorphism is expected to give users an integrated communication manner for various types of ubiquitous services. The system is covered by a stuffed animal to make anthropomorphic stimuli from the device. We also tried to develop a simplified system for popularization on the public uses. User's posture and situation are also one of the important factors to determine the appropriate timing and strength of the physical contacts. So we implemented the robot with a sensor device with 3D accelerometer and 3D compass. In simulating the real use in outings, we evaluated the effectiveness of the physical contact by the proposed system in a course with two diverges.

2   Related Research

There have been various approaches on haptic representations for mobile devices. The vibration stimuli on the touchscreens of mobile devices [2, 3, etc.], vibro-tactile devices [4–6, etc.], gyro moment [7, 8, etc.], and a combination of skin stretch and vibro-tactile stimuli [9] were proposed not only as push-type notifications but also as interactive feedbacks and directional indicators. Combination with other modalities is expected to provide realistic communication during the user's outings.

On the other hand, many researches have tried to anthropomorphize various information and artificial presences for familiar communication and user's understandings. The facing, gazing and pointing gestures of the robots and agents showed large effectiveness [10–13, etc.]. Tactile communications between an artificial presence and a human have also been developed to accommodate input from a user, such as physical interactions from the user toward the pet robots[14]. In order to facilitate an affective communication between human and robot, we propose to incorporate the opposite direction of the usual flow of human-robot tactile communication.

Since anthropomorphized modalities in communication-media [15, 16, etc.] can enrich human-human communication, Kashiwabara et al. have proposed a small, wearable avatar robot on the user's shoulder citeimai12. In our research, we aim to anthropomorphize haptic stimuli as physical contact and adopt them to a wearable message robot to enable the intelligible and affective expression as though the robot were touching the user. As a first step, we combined haptic stimuli and simultaneous anthropomorphic behaviors of the robot in order to generate the robot's physical contact.

To provide various messages from the robot to the user in each appropriate manners, the system needs to understand the user's context. There are many methods of the context recognition based on her/his bodily motion using accelerometers [18–20, etc.]. In order to recognize the user's activity such as "stopping", "walking", or "running", we employed an 3D accelerometer and an 3D compass inside the agent.

3   System Implementation

In order to provide ubiquitous services in familiar, intuitive, and intelligible mannar, we adopted a partner-like anthropomorphic presence. For delivering a familiar partner robot especially for children or elderly people, the robot was placed at the user's right arm to show the attitude of the robot as though it cuddles up to the user in the same way that caregivers.

3.1   Preliminary Tests for the Adequate Fixing Place

It is important to design the appropriate fixing place of the robot on the user's body. The design should be considered from the viewpoints of both the intelligibleness of the physical contact message and the comfortable place during the user's outing. The placements should be considered by the safeness and the user's sensitivity for the haptic stimuli in recognizing the physical contact form the robot. Head or neck are not adequate places to show the robot's presence to the user, and lower arms or lower legs are not adaptive while the user is walking. Accordingly we considered four places; shoulder, berry, upper arm, and ham.

As a preliminary test for the placement design of the robot, we conducted a subjective evaluation for the four types Figure 1. For each placement of a stuffed toy, the participant made an evaluation using a five-point rating scale of the relevance (5: very relevant, 4: somewhat relevant, 3: even, 2: somewhat irrelevant, 1: irrelevant) of the following statements:

p-Q1 It was easy to look at the robot.

p-Q2 You felt as though the robot looked at you.

p-Q3 You felt affection to the robot.

p-Q4 The robot seemed to feel afefction to you.

p-Q5 It was easy to walk with the fixed robot.

p-Q6 You felt as though the robot were sharing time with you.

p-Q7 You were relieved with the stuffed toy.

p-Q8 The robot seemed to be relieved with you.

p-Q9 You felt embarrassed with the fixed robot.

Figure 2 illustrates the means opinion scores (MOS). The results of ANOVA with repeated measurements are shown in Table 1. From the results of ANOVA among four conditions, the most actual and reasonable place was the arm. The p-Q3, p-Q4, p-Q6, p-Q7, and p-Q8 are regarded as the emotional evaluations, and p-Q1, p-Q2, p-Q5, and p-Q9 are the evaluations from the viewpoint of the practical use. The embarrassed feeling, p-Q9, for the upper arm was the lowest score. While the stuffed animal was attached at the user's belly, she/he felt the affection from the robot rather than that on the arm. However, the feelings for equality and existence showed the best when the robot was attached on the user's arm.

Fig. 1. Considered places

Table 1. Two-factor ANOVA for preliminary results

	F	p	significance in post-hoc test
p-Q1	7.62	$\leq.01$	shoulder–{belly,arm}
p-Q2	8.18	$\leq.01$	arm–ham
p-Q3	4.72	0.01	arm–{shoulder, ham}
p-Q4	5.44	$\leq.01$	arm–{shoulder, ham}, belly–ham
p-Q5	3.49	0.03	arm–ham
p-Q6	2.51	0.083	———
p-Q7	5.41	$\leq.01$	arm–ham
p-Q8	12.5	$\leq.01$	ham–{arm,belly}, shoulder–{belly,arm}
p-Q9	5.65	$\leq.01$	arm–{shoulder,belly,ham}

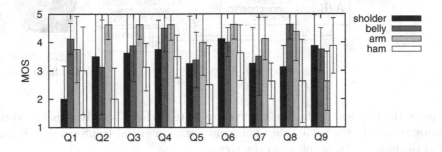

Fig. 2. Results of preliminary test

3.2 System Design

In human-human communication, we perform not only *notification* expressions to relay information easier, but also *affection* expressions to convey emotional states or affection. we assume combining both *notification* and *affection* is important to realize human-like communicative expression of agents and robots.

Here, for example, let us consider the situations that the robot support elderly's outing and want to notify them of toilet timings. In such situations, the robot should not notify the timing by loud voice. The robot should first perform *notification* behavior to draw the elderly's attention and then notify them the timings secretly and casually. In emergency case, both *notification* behavior and (audio) information should be given simultaneously. On the other hand, since *affection* expressions are shown casually to relieve the users and to build relationships of trust, we give neither meaning nor importance to *affection* expression. In our system, we combined haptic stimuli and anthropomorphic behaviors to

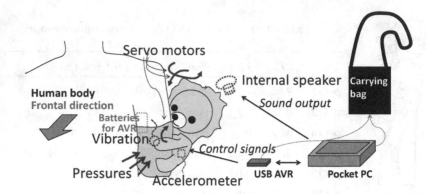

Fig. 3. Hardware structure

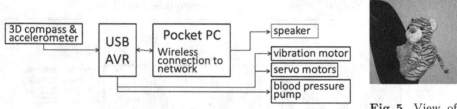

Fig. 4. System flow

Fig. 5. View of
the fixed system

express the physical contact in the system so that the robot gives us the visual-haptic stimuli at the same time. This configuration aimed to produce an illusion of anthropomorphic touch from the robot.

In order to realize the proposed robot system, we implemented two types of test-bed systems: a detailed robot for the strong anthropomorphism (Figure 3–5), and a simplified robot for popularization on the public uses (Figure 7–9).

Figure 3 shows the configuration of the detailed system. The detailed system consists of three servo motors; two for its head and one for its left arm, vibration motors, cuff of blood pressure sensor for pressing actuation, a small speaker for vocal messages, and three-dimensional accelerometer and compass sensors to detect user's situations. All devices are connected and controlled by a PC via a AVR controller (Figure 4). For appropriate behaviors of the robot, the robot detect user's situations by using accelerometer and compass sensors. In the current implementation, the robot can recognize three situations: "walking", "running", and "expanding arm forward" based on the sensor data (Figure 6).

Figure 5 shows the appearance of the system. The robot system was about 400 [g] weight and 21 [cm] height without PC. If the user needs outings, she/he must carry a small pochette. So we implemented a simplified system for popularization on the public uses.

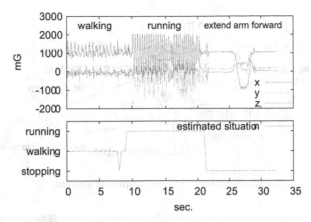

Fig. 6. Estimated situations

3.3 Simplified System Design

Figure 7 shows the configuration of the simplified system. The system consists of three servo motors: two for its head and one for its left arm, vibration motors, a small speaker for vocal messages, and three-dimensional accelerometer and compass sensors. All devices are connected and controlled by a small board PC (Figure 8).

Figure 9 shows the appearance of the simplified system. The total weight is about 250 [g] and the height is 18 [cm] including processor and battery. We can easily wear the simplified system and the presence of the robot was not so reduced compared to the previous system.

4 Evaluation

In order to evaluate the effectiveness of the physical touch from the wearable message robot, we have conducted two types of experiments in different situations: in a standing situation [21] and in a walking situation [22]. The results showed significances of both anthropomorphic motions of the robot and haptic stimuli.

In this paper, we introduce an experiment with a simulation of real outings using a labyrinth of corridors with landmark pictures in order to evaluate the effectiveness of the physical touch from the robot on guiding users while their outings. Standing, stopping, and walking situations were included in the settings of the experiment. We used the original system described in Section 3.2 to give affective expressions of the robot with using haptic pressures on the user's arm.

Hypotheses: H-1) Participants in the experiment differently evaluate the expressions of the robot by the existence of haptic stimuli. H-2) The participants differently evaluate the expressions of the robot by its behavioral motions.

Participants: Twenty-six people (thirteen females and thirteen males) aged from nineteen to twenty-five.

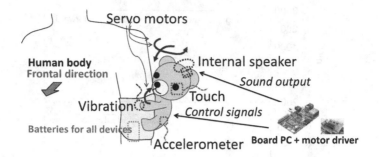

Fig. 7. Hardwares in the simplified system

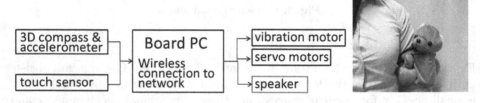

Fig. 8. System flow in the simplified system

Fig. 9. View of the simplified system

Settings: Figure 10 shows a labirinth-like setting in the experiment. The participants walked in the course with the fixed system corresponding to the indicated side at the rhombus-shaped points (◊v1 and ◊v2).

There were three pictures at the pausing places, from s1 to s3. A picture of a convenience store was put on the wall at the s1 place, a picture of a restaurant was put at the s2 place, and a picture of a park was put at the s2 place. The width of the course was about 90 cm. Figure 11 shows a view of the labirinth-like course.

We prepared the expressions of both "notification" and "affection." The notification was expressed by combining the patting motion of the robot's arm with haptic stimuli of the vibration. The affection was expressed by combining haptic stimuli of pressure on the user's arm with the motion of the robot's head as though the robot were looking up at the user's face.

Conditions: The four conditions with two factors; the first factor is the bodily motions of the robot: with motions (M) or without any motion (m), and the second factor is the haptic stimuli from the robot: with touch (T) or without any touch (t). Combinations of the factors are following four conditions.

MT : The robot moved its body with haptic stimuli.
Mt : The robot just moved its body without any haptic stimuli.
mT : The robot did not moved but with haptic stimuli.
mt : The robot did not moved and there was not any haptic stimulus.

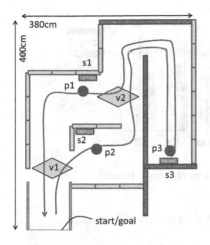

Fig. 10. Course simulating "outing"

Fig. 11. View of the experiment

Procedures: The subjects were instructed to walk around in the course or stop at the indicated place by the robot. The robot made a "notification" expression at each diverging point, ◇v1 and ◇v2 to tell the participant the way to the park. In the fronts of s1 and s2, the participant was talked by the robot with the initial physical contact prepared in the condition. The script for s1 was "Here is a convenience store," the script for s2 was "Here is a restaurant." At the place of the park, s3, the robot talked "I'm happy to come to the park." with an expression of "affection." After the session in each condition, the subject evaluated the expressions of the robot.

The participant was not instructed to react to the robot. One session included two diverging points and three places. The experiments in different conditions were held in repeated measurements for each subject with the counter-balanced orders of the conditions.

After each experiment, the subject used a five-point rating scale to evaluate the relevance (5: very relevant, 4: somewhat relevant, 3: even, 2: somewhat irrelevant, 1: irrelevant) of the following statements;

Qa The expression of the robot was comfortable.
Qb The robot's expression was easy to understand.
Qc The expression of the robot was easy to perceive.
Qd You felt affection for the robot.
Qe The robot was suitable to extend your emotion.
Qf You want to use the robot in the future.

Results: Figure 12 displays the results of means opinion scores for each statements. The results of two-factor ANOVA are shown in Table 2. From the results, we could confirm the effectiveness of both haptic stimuli and anthropomorphic motion but without strong interaction between the factors.

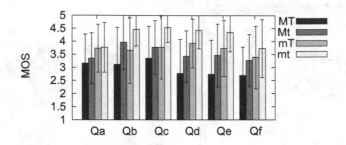

Fig. 12. MOS Results in the experiment

Table 2. Two-factor ANOVA for the experiment results

	motion		touch		Interaction with significance
	F	p	F	p	
Qa	6.92	0.014	0.38	0.54	–
Qb	9.11	<.01	10.23	<.01	–
Qc	8.89	<.01	6.77	0.015	–
Qd	28.1	<.01	14.1	<.01	–
Qe	14.9	<.01	14.0	<.01	–
Qf	21.0	<.01	8.89	<.01	–

Qb and Qc are the statements related to the intelligibleness of the robot's "notification." The ANOVA results for both statements showed the significance for anthropomorphic motion and haptic stimuli. From the results, it is confirmed that the intelligibleness is effectively elevated by the anthropomorphic behaviors and the haptic stimuli from the robot.

Qd and Qe are the statements related to the affective aspect. The ANOVA results showed the effectiveness of both factors. We could confirm that the affection from the user can also be elevated by these configurations.

Qa and Qf are the statements related to the sustainable use. The results of ANOVA for Qa showed a significance that indicates the effectiveness of the anthropomorphic motion of the robot but without any significance of haptic stimuli. From the results, it is conjectured that the comfortable use is provided by the anthropomorphic behaviors. On the other hand, the results for Qf illustrated both significances of the motion and haptic stimuli. There is a possibility of the desire for sustainable use that elevated by the intelligible and the affective communication with the robot.

5   Discussion

The results of the experiment showed the effectiveness of our system configuration of the message robot.

In the preceding experiment in a standing [21] and walking situations [22], we have confirmed the effectiveness of the physical touches expressing "notification" and "affection." From the results of the experiment described in this paper, we could confirm the possibility of the sustainable use by the mixture of the "notification" and "affection." On the other hand, we could not find any interaction between the factors. Although the combination of the haptic stimuli and the robot's motion did not bring any unique result in the evaluation statements, almost all participants said that the condition MT brought an illusion as though the robot were touching on the participants' arms in the free descriptions. Consequently we could confirm the communicability of our proposed systems.

The proposed message robot is expected to be used by elderly people who suffer from dementia or children tracking in their night outings. The evaluations in this paper and the preceding evaluations did not ask elderly people or children participants. In the future we are going to verify the effectiveness in an elderly care center to track the patients and give them the appopriate guide.

Not only for elderly people, children, or disabled people but also for normal adults, the message robot can provide a ubiquitous information instead of the actual portable devices. To popularize the message robot with appropriate anthropomorphism, we need to consider the usage of our own portable devices instead of the board PC. The system also need the personalization of the physical contact in order to build more intuitive and intimate communication between the robot and the user.

6   Conclusion

In this paper, we introduced an anthropomorphic physical-contact method for a message robot in simulating the user's outings. By using the prototype of the implementations, the subjective evaluations in a labirinth-like course with diverges showed the effectiveness of both haptic stimuli and the anthropomorphic motion of the robot.

In the future, we are also going to conduct the evaluation on the simplified system to reveal the effectiveness of anthropomorphic integration of the messages from mobile devices and ubiquitous services. It is also important to verify the effectiveness of the partner robot to bring intuitive and comprehensive information in ubiquitous environments for our comfortable outings.

Acknowledgements. This research was supported in part by KAKENHI 24300047 and KAKENHI 25700021. The authors would like to thank the participants in the experiment.

References

1. Duffy, B.R.: Anthropomorphism and the social robot. Robotics and Autonomous Systems 42(3), 177–190 (2003)
2. Fukumoto, M., Sugimura, T.: Active click: Tactile feedback for touch panels. In: CHI 2001 Extended Abstracts on Human Factors in Computing Systems, pp. 121–122 (2001)
3. Poupyrev, I., Maruyama, S., Rekimoto, J.: Ambient touch: Designing tactile interfaces for handheld devices. In: Proc. of UIST 2002, pp. 51–60 (2002)
4. Cassinelli, A., Reynolds, C., Ishikawa, M.: Augmenting spatial awareness with haptic radar. In: Proc. of ISWC 2006, pp. 61–64 (2006)
5. Kajimoto, H., Kanno, Y., Tachi, S.: Forehead Electro-tactile Display for Vision Substitution. In: EuroHaptics 2006, Paris (2006)
6. Kajimoto, H.: Electro-tactile Display with Real-Time Impedance Feedback. In: Kappers, A.M.L., van Erp, J.B.F., Bergmann Tiest, W.M., van der Helm, F.C.T. (eds.) EuroHaptics 2010, Part I. LNCS, vol. 6191, pp. 285–291. Springer, Heidelberg (2010)
7. Amemiya, T., Sugiyama, H.: Haptic handheld wayfinder with pseudo-attraction force for pedestrians with visual impairments. In: Proc. of ASSETS 2009, pp. 107–114 (2009)
8. Yano, H., Yoshie, M., Iwata, H.: Development of a non-grounded haptic interface using the gyro effect. In: HAPTICS 2003, pp. 32–39 (2003)
9. Bark, K., Wheeler, J.W., Premakumar, S., Cutkosky, M.R.: Comparison of Skin Stretch and Vibrotactile Stimulation for Feedback of Proprioceptive Information. In: Symposium on Haptic Interfaces for Virtual Environment and Teleoperator Systems, pp. 71–78 (2008)
10. Imai, M., Ono, T., Ishiguro, H.: Physical relation and expression: Joint attention for human-robot interaction. In: IEEE Int. Workshop on Robot and Human Communication, pp. 512–517 (2001)
11. Kozima, H.: Infanoid: A babybot that explores the social environment. In: Socially Intelligent Agents: Creating Relationships with Computers and Robots, pp. 157–164. Kluwer Academic Publishers, Amsterdam (2002)
12. Yonezawa, T., Yamazoe, H., Utsumi, A., Abe, S.: Gaze-communicative Behavior of Stuffed-toy Robot with Joint Attention and Eye Contact based on Ambient Gaze-tracking. In: ICMI 2007, pp. 140–145 (2007)
13. Yoshikawa, Y., Shinozawa, K., Ishiguro, H., Hagita, N., Miyamoto, T.: The effects of responsive eye movement and blinking behavior in a communication robot. In: Proc. IROS 2006, pp. 4564–4569 (2006)
14. Shibata, T., Tashima, T., Tanie, K.: Emergence of emotional behavior through physical interaction between human and robot. In: IEEE International Conference on Robotics and Automation, vol. 4, pp. 2868–2873 (1999)
15. Sekiguchi, D., Inami, M., Tachi, S.: Robotphone: Rui for interpersonal communication. In: Proc. CHI 2001 Extended Abstracts, pp. 277–278 (2001)
16. Adalgeirsson, S.O., Breazeal, C.: Mebot: A robotic platform for socially embodied presence. In: Proc. HRI 2010, pp. 15–22 (2010)
17. Kashiwabara, T., Osawa, H., Shinozawa, K., Imai, M.: TEROOS: A wearable avatar to enhance joint activities. In: Proc. CHI 2012, pp. 2001–2004 (2012)
18. Figo, D., Diniz, P.C., Ferreira, D.R.: Preprocessing Techniques for Context Recognition from Accelerometer Data. Personal and Ubiquitous Computing 14(7), 645–662 (2010)

19. Maekawa, T., Watanabe, S.: Unsupervised Activity Recognition with User's Physical Characteristics Data. In: Proc. of ISWC 2011, pp. 89–96 (2011)
20. Bao, L., Intille, S.S.: Activity Recognition from User-Annotated Acceleration Data. In: Ferscha, A., Mattern, F. (eds.) PERVASIVE 2004. LNCS, vol. 3001, pp. 1–17. Springer, Heidelberg (2004)
21. Yonezawa, T., Yamazoe, H., Abe, S.: Physical Contact using Haptic and Gestural Expressions for Ubiquitous Partner Robot. In: IROS 2013, pp. 5680–5685 (2013)
22. Yonezawa, T., Yamazoe, H.: Wearable partner agent with anthropomorphic physical contact with awareness of clothing and posture. In: ISWC 2013, pp. 77–80 (2013)

Developing Distributed, Pervasive and Intelligent Environments

Developing Smart Homes Using the Internet of Things: How to demonstrate Your System

Ioannis Chatzigiannakis[1], Jan Philipp Drude[2], Henning Hasemann[3], and Alexander Kröller[3]

[1] Computer Technology Institute and Press "Diophantus", Patras, Greece
ichatz@cti.gr
[2] Leibniz Universität Hannover, Germany
jpdrude@googlemail.com
[3] Technische Universität Braunschweig, Germany
{h.hasemann,a.kroeller}@tu-bs.de

Abstract. The Internet of Things (IoT) currently grows with great momentum offering the potential of virtually endless opportunities for new applications and services in the "Smart Home" context. Yet, regardless of the tremendous efforts made by the relevant research & development community, application development is still a very complex and error prone process as the large range of IoT devices and smart appliances often result to complex systems-of-systems interactions. In addition, we need to factor in the human behavior and interaction goals thus making it more difficult to understand and analyzing the operating principles of the new applications. It is therefore imperative to conduct experiments verifying the complex interactions of those systems, as well as to be able to demonstrate and showcase them; to give users clear evidence how the system around them will behave. In this work we present two demonstrators that we have developed during the past years in order to provide a generic environment for showcasing new applications and services in a "Smart Home" context. We have displayed these demonstrators at several occasions, which gave us numerous opportunities to receive feedback from spectators of different backgrounds. We discuss the design choices of each demonstrator, the benefits of each approach and the experience gained from each one.

1 Introduction

The Internet of Things (IoT) currently grows with great momentum. One major driving application for this is building automation, especially in the "Smart Home" context. Smart homes combine several active and passive appliances: HVAC, entertainment media, lighting control, energy profiling, and automation of mechanical tasks are just some examples. This constitutes a broad range of appliances with diverse requirements and interaction patterns making Smart Homes a challenging environment for the design of user experiences. It is therefore important to be able to design systems that detect, analyze and react to the behavior of the users and the general environment.

N. Streitz and P. Markopoulos (Eds.): DAPI 2014, LNCS 8530, pp. 415–426, 2014.

We observe two effects: while the number of interactive embedded components grows dramatically, they increasingly penetrate the lives of their users. Their widespread deployment enable significant technical achievements, and the data they deliver is capable of supporting an almost unlimited set of high value proposition applications. A central problem hampering success is that sensors are typically locked into unimodal closed systems [PRB+11]. For example, motion detection sensors in a building may be exclusively controlled by the intrusion detection system. Yet the information they provide could be used by many other applications, for example, placing empty buildings into an energy-conserving sleep mode or locating empty meeting rooms.

Recently, new means of coping with this increase of complexity from a data integration perspective have been proposed, many of them targeted at the idea of describing elements of the IoT network in a universal way. The SPITFIRE project [1] has connected the IoT with the *Semantic Web*, a vast distributed knowledge database existing in the current World Wide Web. The unique approach of SPITFIRE goes beyond a mere linkage but elevates the embedded devices of the IoT to fully self-describing smart objects. In the final abstraction step, SPITFIRE combines the descriptions of several embedded devices and form so-called *Semantic Entities* [HKK+13], to enable reasoning about descriptions of the actual observed real-world objects. This allows for a novel style of application development: An application developer does not need to address devices individually at a low-level networking layer but can rather define interactions based on semantic descriptions available from the devices or the Semantic Web. Findings of applications then can be pushed back to devices and used as input knowledge for other applications, thus providing a universal platform that allows communication about arbitrary facts between components.

Consider a smart home application that might be defined close to natural language and read "turn off all heaters that are in the same room as an open window". Additionally, the application might enhance the devices description so the according heaters hold the information why they have been turned off, which can in turn be used by a different application, which might or might not be related to home-automation. In order to fully exploit this new connectivity on a data layer, it is imperative to be able to simulate and experiment with different states of devices and real-world objects in order to evaluate the correct behavior of the application.

Application development that takes advantage of such large range of embedded devices and smart appliances have strong dependencies on IoT systems that often result to complex systems-of-systems interactions. In addition, the need to include the human behavior and interaction in the loop further complicates this situation as the applications usually need to be compliant with a plethora of often contradicting requirements. It is therefore important to test and optimize applications in a controllable environment such as real networks of limited size [BCF+11,GKN+11]. Designers need to conduct experiments verifying the complex interactions of those systems, as well as to be able to demonstrate and

---

[1] http://www.spitfire-project.eu

showcase them; to give users an idea how the system around them will behave. As Mark Weiser announced in the nineties [Wei93],

> "the research method for ubiquitous computing is standard experimental computer science: the construction of working prototypes of the necessary infrastructure in sufficient quantity to debug the viability of the systems in everyday use".

In this work we present two demonstrators that combine of IoT devices in a controllable Smart Home environment. Their focus is on allowing for interactions that make complex processes easily understandable. These demonstrators rely on testbed structures that utilize real-world networks. They provide a rich environment for interacting with the IoT network at device level, and offer visual feedback on the complex interaction patterns triggered by user actions. A wide variety of scenarios can be accommodated so that we can carefully monitor the operation of the resulting system under different settings. The user can also interact with the demonstrator in real-time by introducing external events and control the operation of the resulting system. Both demonstrators are independent of the high-level applications thus they can be used to reliably reproduce the same series of event scenarios and test how the applications react to set of external events.

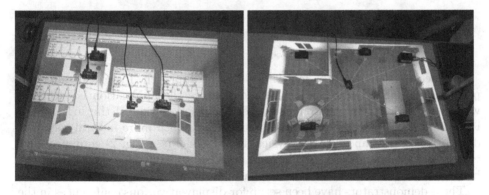

Fig. 1. The Projected House demonstrator

The first demonstrator consists of 10 iSense nodes [2] equipped with an environmental module responsible for reading the light and temperature conditions and a actuator module that can control a small fan and an LED lamp. The nodes are placed on top of a two neoFoam surfaces on designated positions. In order to monitor the status of the running demonstrator, each iSense node is connected via USB to a laptop. This connection is required in order to collect all the debug output from the nodes so that the visualization can be done at a later point. The neoFoam has been drilled so that the USB cables can be put through. The two

---

[2] http://www.coalesenses.com/

surfaces are placed side-by-side creating a combined surface of 200 x 70 cm. The laptop is also responsible for the visualization of the demonstrator. Two video projectors are connected to this machine that project the visualization on the neoFoam surface. In order to cover the whole 200 x 70 cm surface, the projectors are attached to a metal frame that allows their elevation up to 190 cm from the neoFoam, while at the same time, provides stability for the whole structure (see Fig. 1). For logistic and portability reasons, the frame consists of many smaller parts that allow its disassembly.

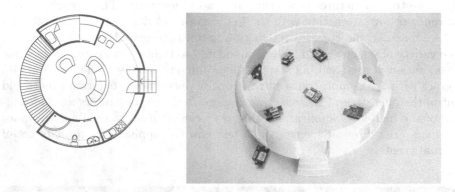

Fig. 2. The House model demonstrator: Floor plan and photo

The second demonstrator follows a different approach. Instead of having a projected visualization of the environment where the application is executed, we offer a realistic 3D environment where we the position of the IoT devices is more flexible while the interaction is done in a much more natural way. The demonstrator is composed of a physical home model (see Fig. 2) equipped with various actuators and sensors. They are attached to embedded devices and can be relocated within the model for simulating different deployment scenarios.

These demonstrators have been setup for display at various conferences in the past years, as part of a demonstration session. We have used them to show case different applications that allow the automatic control of home appliances and their configuration based on the needs and behavior of the user. Throughout all these events many visitors have had the opportunity to interact with the demonstrators in order to acquire a better understanding of the smart home applications. While both demonstrators were very valuable tools to explain the concepts of our applications and highlight the main technological characteristics, each one had different benefits and drawbacks. In this paper we present the software and hardware design of the demonstrators that we have developed and summarize the experiences gained.

2   A Complete Protocol Stack for Semantic Sensors

The generic demonstrators that we have developed offer the ability to showcase high-level user applications that utilize IoT resources connected via the Web. The actual development makes minimal assumptions on the connectivity of the IoT devices with the Web and uses well accepted standards for interacting with the devices. In this section we describe in details the software infrastructure that is used for interacting with the physical domain.

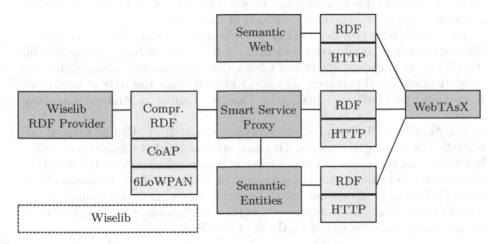

Fig. 3. Simplified software- and protocol architecture of our system. Blue boxes represent software components while khaki boxes represent communication protocols.

All of our embedded software builds on the Wiselib [BCF+10], a multi-platform embedded algorithms library. On top of that we provide the Wiselib RDF Provider [HKP12] which is responsible for managing semantically annotated data on the device such as sensor data, sensor meta data or high-level application knowledge. In order to provide these descriptions and other services (such as actuation) to the Internet, we provide a Wiselib-implementation of the standardized IPv6 interface 6LoWPAN [KMS07]. On the application layer we provide an implementation of the Constrained Application Protocol (CoAP) [FSHB11] which allows RESTful service provisioning. Together with the usage of the RDF standard for universally valid fact descriptions this allows self-describing and auto-configuring devices which connect to the Semantic Web.

In order to cache device descriptions and translate between the lightweight embedded networks protocols and Semantic Web clients that rely on protocols like HTTP, we introduce the Smart Service Proxy (SSP) [HKK+13]. The SSP collects and caches semantic descriptions produced by the devices and provides a web service endpoint for interaction with the system. An overview of these components and their interactions is given by Figure 3.

2.1   Wiselib RDF Provider

A main challenge in interacting with IoT devices is the vast variety in terms of employed hardware and available system resources. It is common to have devices with limited amount of available memory, processing power or energy – also devices have different peripheral and memory configurations (RAM, internal flash, SD cards and so forth). To overcome this heterogeneity, we adopt a storage mechanism for semantic (RDF) data that is resource-efficient, portable and provides means of grouping semantic statements into documents. This allows to make knowledge addressable and provides fine-granular control over what information is communicated for a successful retrieval of knowledge.

The Wiselib RDF provider [HKP12] provides a portable, modular and resource-efficient embedded database for the storage of RDF data. It builds on the Wiselib [BCF+10], an embedded algorithms library that focusses on modularization, resource efficiency and portability. Thanks to the Wiselib, the RDF Provider can be compiled for platforms like Contiki, TinyOS, Arduino or Android and many more.

The Wiselib RDF Provider represents the stored RDF data as a set of potentially overlapping documents. This way, statements that change on a regular basis (such as those describing the current sensor value) can be requested independently from those that change rarely or never (such as the owner of the embedded device). The documents are exported over a configurable and extensible set of encodings and protocols such as the combination of a lightweight RDF compression scheme on top of CoAP and 6LoWPAN.

2.2   Constrained Application Protocol (CoAP)

The Constrained Application Protocol (CoAP) is a IETF CoRE working group draft dealing with Constrained Restful Environments [FSHB11]. It presents a web transfer protocol suitable for machine-to-machine applications such as smart energy and building automation. The protocol is designed to operate effectively in erroneous low bandwidth environments while providing a subset of HTTP's methods (GET, PUT, POST, DELETE). By this means it offers the ability to provide RESTful web services in IoT deployments.

Using CoAP makes interaction with the IoT device as simple as invoking an HTTP resource. The communication between endpoints is based on a lightweight request/response model. The message exchange is asynchronous and is based on UDP and thus connectionless. Essentially the development of the high-level application is completely decoupled from the way the IoT devices communicate and organize their network. Furthermore, by avoiding the use of any middleware to provide access to the devices, the developer does not need to acquire additional technical knowledge in order to test and evaluate a new application using the demonstrators.

2.3   Smart Service Proxy

While our architecture provides devices that are self-describing and usable without a central authority, at some point an application developer might want to access the semantic descriptions of objects such as the deployed devices or the observed real-world objects in the very same way they use other resources on the Semantic Web, namely by issuing HTTP requests. In such a scenario, user and/or application developer will usually not want to be concerned with the peculiarities of efficient access to the embedded devices that is, request congestion, checking for presence of the device, caching, configuring push- versus pull-based mechanisms and conversion between different RDF serialization formats.

The Smart Service Proxy (SSP) fills this role and more: It provides a service endpoint to the Web which can be used to access up-to-date device descriptions and control device actuation via a RESTful HTTP interface. To the embedded network, the Smart Service Proxy provides a registration service and can negotiate observe mechanisms with the embedded devices in order to save energy by only communicating when descriptions change in a way that is considered relevant. While on the "front" side, the SSP provides different RDF encodings, on the "back" side it can communicate with embedded devices using an exchangeable and extensible protocol stack, including CoAP and 6LoWPAN, but also allowing for non-standard communication protocols to ease adaption.

2.4   Semantic Entities

While a sound, accessible semantic description of embedded devices already provides a certain degree of abstraction and ensures connectivity on a data layer, an application programmer or user will usually want to be able to describe observations, state and actions in terms of real-world objects and not be concerned with the devices monitoring them.

The *Semantic Entities Service* offers that: It can access any number of Smart Service Proxies or other data sources on the Semantic Web and combine the found semantic descriptions into a semantic description of real-world objects, the Semantic Entities (SEs). Which descriptions are to be assembled into what kind of Semantic Entities can be configured by the user using a set of rules which can be injected into the system. Examples of these rules are *"Construct one SE for each object being observed"* or *"Construct one SE for each type of sensor in each room"*.

Constructed Semantic Entities are exposed in the same standardized Semantic Web format as the device descriptions or static data on the Semantic Web and can thus be seamlessly integrated.

2.5   The WebTAsX User Interface

For these situations we provide the WebTAsX User Inferface (see Fig. 4). WebTAsX provides user-friendly web frontend that can connect to Smart Service Proxies, Semantic Entities and/or static data on the Semantic Web or provided locally by a user. WebTAsX offers the user a list of entities (that is devices, or abstract Semantic Entities), as well as other available semantic data sources and allows the straight forward creation of actuation rules.

Fig. 4. Setting automation rules with the WebTAsX tool

3 Demonstrators

3.1 The Projected House Demonstrator

Our first approach to demonstrate the system was based on projection of house shapes to a planar surface. For this, two projectors were mounted on a steel framework, projecting downwards the images of two houses onto a plane where several smart objects were placed. The projectors where connected to a PC and could thus dynamically alter the projection to reflect the state of the simulation.

The projection shows two rooms, which have been rendered by a consumer interior design software. Furniture suggests an office environment, however there was no emphasis on believability during construction. One room covers most of the available space, to account for demos where many objects have to be placed in the same room. The other room is tiny, just sufficient to have some object space that does not belong to the main room.

We provided a set of sensors and actuators based on iSense nodes that were placed at different positions the virtual building. These included a switchable fan and radio as well as several light- and temperature sensors. Via additional screens visitors could observe the semantic descriptions of objects and create rules using WebTAsX.

This approach of using projectors coving the demonstration surface completely had the following advantages:

Visulazation of Abstract Data. In addition to providing the imagy of a house as substitute for a physical model, the projectors allowed us to provide several abstract visulations, such as packet flow between objects or curves plotting the recent sensor data history. This made the state and otherwisely invisible actions of the system very visible and allowed the visitor to observe live what influence on the internal state of the system certain actions have.

Daylight Cycle Simulation. The projected house model was not just presented as a static image but rather its lighting conditions over the course of a day were visualized in form of a full-sized animation. In order to be able to discuss long-term sensor value analysis in a descriptive way, the simulated day was configured to pass in a matter of minutes.

As our smart objects were equipped with light sensors they could pick up the simulated lighting condition produced by the projector.. This allowed an interesting way of presenting: While the processed sensor values were indirectly controlled by the daylight simulation, they were still produced by actual light (from the projector) being picked up by light sensors, a process that could easily be influenced by the demonstrator or a spectator to observe the effect on the descriptions of the nodes and auto annotation system.

Tangible Objects. The smart objects could be freely moved, switched and replaced by the user. This allowed for example to demonstrate the semantic auto annotation by bringing in a new, unconfigured device, placing it in the virtual building and switching in it on. Objects equipped with light sensors could thus be moved when to a place with different light situation or influenced directly using a flashlight. This way, the user could directly observe the effects of his actions on the system.

3.2   The Model House Demonstrator

The central piece of the demonstrator is a model of a house, developed with easy interaction in mind. There is a large main room, which can hold about five smart objects. This is sufficient for complex demonstration scenarios of pervasive systems; the user can put both sensors and actuators into it, and define operational rules for them. LED lighting in the walls can be used to showcase home automation applications, where the light level automatically changes based on user-induced sensor input. There are three additional rooms. These are smaller, capable of holding one or two smart objects, with the purpose to show how a system can use location information to provide separate services for different parts of the home.

The smart objects are bare-bone sensor and actuator hardware, powered by batteries or USB connections. They are used without casing, to let the user obtain a feeling for the hardware. We used different products, including Arduino and iSense devices, as well as most Contiki- or TinyOS-driven sensor nodes.

The architectural design of the model has been extracted from futuristic architecture of the 1960s. The ideas behind those designs having always been a mechanization in living, the model is rather suitable for the topic of home automation. The model illustrates a small, independent housing unit, consisting of a bathroom, a bedroom, which is not much more than a bunk, a terrace and a larger living room with kitchenette.

In contrast to the designs from the 1960s, which came mostly out of student designs with low budgets and defective constructions, this model can actually be imagined in a technological context. Building automation and a technological construction process with prefabricated parts in small numbers are economically reasonable nowadays and could lead to inexpensive, mobile housing units.Nonetheless the simple floor-plan and design ask for adaption by a human being. In its cold self the design does not seem to inviting, but it has the big advantage, that it can be customized. In color, in material, in facilities, in furniture. This is actually an important way of thinking in contemporary architecture, that most architects lacked in the 1960s. In that time, architects would invent completely new ways of living, in new structures, taken from science-fiction novels. This would certainly lead to a synchronized society, where cities would look very much alike, containing similar housing units, which would tend to peoples every needs; a society that appears to be like Aldous Huxley's Brave New World. Having overcome this kind of thinking for good and for bad, architects nowadays think more individualized. Structures like our model are still thinkable, but only if they can be customized, very much like buying a car.

The design was very much affected by its final outcome being a model. While a simple cubic building would have been more economic, if it would have been a real building, nonetheless that was not what we were looking for, which is easy interaction and vividness. This allowed us to trade some preferrable properties for real houses for a more appealing style. The model fits its purpose: It can arouse peoples interest by looking different, however fitting.

Interactions. Through the provided hardware/software stack, our system offers a unique user experience: A device can be installed by just switching it on and placing it in one of the rooms of the building model. Through self-description and auto-configuration mechanisms, the description of the device becomes available to the system so the device is considered in future events.

Using a frontend, the user can define rules like "When the weather report says it is above 24 degrees and it is between 4pm and 8pm, turn on the air condition". All available devices will be used to fulfill this request. This way the impression of a "smart" home is completed: Without any need for technicalities, the system will try to fulfill the request of the user, incorporating available sensors and actuators as well as the knowledge available in the Semantic Web.

4 Experiences

The projected house was used at several occasions which gave us numerous opportunities to receive feedback from spectators of different backgrounds. In October 2012, the demonstrator was used to demonstrate "True Self-Configuration for the Internet of Things" [CHK+12] at the Internet of Things Challenge

Competition [3] in Wuxi, China. In a process that combined votes from a jury and the audience, the demo was awarded third prize.

In 2013, the yearly Future Internet Assembly [4] was held in Dublin. Again, the projected house demonstrator was used to show and discuss the latest advances of SPITFIRE, in this case in the *Hands on FIRE* demo session. In contrast to the former setups, for the FIA we decided to split the demo into two parts: One focussing on the specifics of our CoAP implementation, the other one – using the projecting demonstrator – focussed more on the interaction of all SPITFIRE components. This demo was again a great success, as it received the best demo award, chosen out of a total of 17 demonstrations.

More importantly, on all occasions we received valuable feedback from spectators: While the tangibility and the possibility to influence the simulation in such a direct way were positively noted. The visitors noted however that the smart objects placed on a plane surface did not really convey the message of a smart building but rather of a collection of objects. While ths is sufficient to demonstrate a protocol stack it missed out on sufficiently illustrating the amount of ubiquity and integration, SPITFIRE provides. By the use of USB cabling and because of the not location-aware visualization, displacing the objects yielded a slightly inconsistent experience: While the sensor values would adapt to the potentially changed lighting situation, the visual aids for packet flow and annotations would still be placed at the devices' original position.

From a exhibitors point of view we have to mention a notable amount of overhead in transporting (often via airplane) and assembling several bars of metal framework and two projectors.

The Model House demonstrator addresses most of these issues: By the use of RFID we can locate devices and thus have them freely movable with a consistent experience. Consisting of a single piece, it is almost trivial to transport and set up and, first and foremost provides a much more natural and believable model of a smart home: Location mechanisms are integrated into the floor, light is produced by LEDs that simulate light-bulbs, rooms can have individual (natural) lighting situation; the house itself is three-dimensional and tangible.

Acknowledgments. This work was partially supported by the European Union under contract number ICT-2009-258885 (SPITFIRE).

References

BCF+10. Baumgartner, T., Chatzigiannakis, I., Fekete, S., Koninis, C., Kröller, A., Pyrgelis, A.: Wiselib: A generic algorithm library for heterogeneous sensor networks. In: Silva, J.S., Krishnamachari, B., Boavida, F. (eds.) EWSN 2010. LNCS, vol. 5970, pp. 162–177. Springer, Heidelberg (2010)

BCF+11. Baumgartner, T., Chatzigiannakis, I., Fekete, S.P., Fischer, S., Koninis, C., Kröller, A., Krüger, D., Mylonas, G., Pfisterer, D.: Distributed algorithm engineering for networks of tiny artifacts. Computer Science Review 5(1), 85–102 (2011)

---

[3] http://iot2012.org/
[4] http://fi-dublin.eu

CHK⁺12.   Chatzigiannakis, I., Hasemann, H., Karnstedt, M., Kleine, O., Kröller, A., Leggieri, M., Pfisterer, D., Römer, K., Truong, C.: Demo: True self-configuration for the IoT. In: IoT Challenge Competition, Internet of Things International Conference for Industry and Academia, IEEE (2012) (to appear)

FSHB11.   Frank, B., Shelby, Z., Hartke, K., Bormann, C.: Constrained application protocol (CoAP). IETF draft (July 2011)

GKN⁺11.   Gluhak, A., Krco, S., Nati, M., Pfisterer, D., Mitton, N., Razafindralambo, T.: A survey on facilities for experimental internet of things research. IEEE Communications Magazine 49(11), 58–67 (2011)

HKK⁺13.   Hasemann, H., Kleine, O., Kröller, A., Leggieri, M., Pfisterer, D.: Annotating Real-World Objects Using Semantic Entities. In: Demeester, P., Moerman, I., Terzis, A. (eds.) EWSN 2013. LNCS, vol. 7772, pp. 67–82. Springer, Heidelberg (2013)

HKP12.   Hasemann, H., Kröller, A., Pagel, M.: RDF provisioning for the Internet of Things. In: 3rd IEEE International Conference on the Internet of Things, pp. 143–150 (2012)

KMS07.   Kushalnagar, N., Montenegro, G., Schumacher, C.: IPv6 over low-power wireless personal area networks (6LoWPANs): Overview, assumptions, problem statement, and goals. Technical report, IETF Secretariat (2007)

PRB⁺11.   Pfisterer, D., Römer, K., Bimschas, D., Kleine, O., Mietz, R., Truong, C., Hasemann, H., Kröller, A., Pagel, M., Hauswirth, M., Karnstedt, M., Leggieri, M., Passant, A., Richardson, R.: Spitfire: Toward a semantic web of things. IEEE Communications Magazine 49(11), 40–48 (2011)

Wei93.   Weiser, M.: Some computer science issues in ubiquitous computing. Communications of the ACM 36(7), 75–84 (1993)

Denial-of-Service Attacks in Wireless Networks Using Off-the-Shelf Hardware

Alexandros Fragkiadakis*, Ioannis Askoxylakis, and Panos Chatziadam

Institute of Computer Science,
Foundation for Research and Technology - Hellas (FORTH)
P.O. Box 1385, GR 711 10 Heraklion, Crete, Greece
{alfrag,asko,panosc}@ics.forth.gr

Abstract. Wireless network technologies offer ubiquitous broadband access to millions of users at an affordable cost. However, the broadband nature of the wireless medium make these networks vulnerable to a number of attacks. Malicious interference at the physical layer, and extended packet collisions at the medium access layer can cause significant DoS attacks. In this work, we show how off-the-shelf hardware can be used to create devastating DoS attacks in a IEEE 802.11 network. Moreover, we present two algorithms for attack detection that are based on the cumulative sum algorithm.

1 Introduction

Network proliferation has been remarkable, especially during the last decade. Technology advancements in the area of network communications have offered high performance improvement and ubiquitous Internet access. From the era of the early-stage communication protocols (e.g. Aloha) through the active networks [1], and software-defined networks [2], ubiquitous network access has been achieved thanks to the advances in wireless technologies. A number of communication protocols (IEEE 802.11, IEEE 802.15.4, IEEE 802.16, etc.) enable energy efficient communications in relatively large distances. Thousands of smart phones and other wireless clients can now enjoy any-time any-where Internet connectivity.

Nevertheless, the broadcast nature of the wireless medium make wireless communications susceptible to a number of threats. Adversaries can cause severe Denial-of-Service attacks (DoS) [3] by exploiting a number of vulnerabilities. DoS attacks pose a major threat in every communication system, often with catastrophic results as wireless communications are nowadays used in many applications (e.g. smart cards [4]). At the physical layer, adversaries can generate malicious interference resulting in heavy packet loss in the network. At the medium access (MAC) layer, malicious users can create extended packet colissions, causing severe DoS attacks in the wireless network. Throughout this work we refer to adversaries and malicious users as jammers.

---

* Corresponding author.

N. Streitz and P. Markopoulos (Eds.): DAPI 2014, LNCS 8530, pp. 427–438, 2014.
© Springer International Publishing Switzerland 2014

Our contribution focuses on showing how off-the-shelf equipment can be used to create DoS attacks at the physical, and medium access layers. We also present two algorithms for the detection of these attacks. The rest of this paper is organized as follows. In Section 2 we present the basic components of our off-the-shelf jammer. Section 3 describes how malicious interference can be used to create DoS attacks. In Section 4 we demonstrate how extended packet colissions are easily caused by jammers, and how greedy behaviors affect network's performance. Section 5 presents two algorithms for attack detection based on the cumulative-sum algorith. Finally, conclusions appear in Section 6.

2   Off-the-Shelf Hardware for Malicious Purposes

As mentioned in the previous section, wireless networks, due to their broadcast nature, are susceptible to a number of threats. A major threat referred as physical-layer jamming refers to interference created by a malicious node. There is a number of commercial devices that can be used for this purpose (e.g. [5–7]). Nevertheless, as we show in this paper, off-the-shelf hardware can be successfully used to launch severe DoS attacks in a wireless network.

Our jamming equipment is based on a mini-ITX board (Fig. 1) carrying 512 MB of RAM with a 80 GB disk. The wireless interface cards are based on the Atheros 802.11a/b/g CM9-GP mini-PCI card. Furthermore, Ath5k [8], an open source IEEE 802.11 driver is used, on Gentoo Linux.

Fig. 1. Off-the-shelf jamming device

The software part of the jammer is shown in Fig. 2. This consists of several components implemented in both the kernel and user spaces of the Linux operating system. At user-space, the *command repository* contains all the attack characteristics. These define a detailed adversary model to be used against a wireless network. Such a typical model can describe, for example, the wireless channel to be attacked, the attack intensity in terms of packet rate, transmission power, attack duration, etc. Commands are propagated through the *netlink socket interface* to kernel-space, stored in the *command trace collection* module that provides buffering capabilities. Finally, the characteristics of the adversary model are used to setup several parameters of the Ath5k driver in order to make an attack feasible.

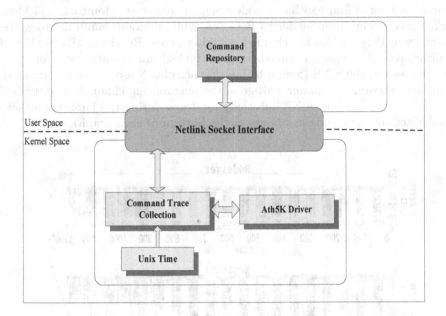

Fig. 2. Jammer software layout

3   Physical-Layer Attacks

A major threat in wireless networks is interference that is caused by signal emissions in neighboring channels. In general, interference can be characterized as malicious or non-malicious, depending on the incentives of the interferer. Non-malicious interference can be caused by nearby legitimate nodes that operate in neighboring channels ([9]). Malicious physical-layer interference (jamming) is created by signal emissions in neighboring channels. This affects both the transmitters and the receivers of a wireless network. IEEE 802.11 transmitters sense the wireless medium before any transmission takes place. If the measured noise is above a threshold, they refrain from transmission for some random time. So, if a jammer is present, the transmission operations of the legitimate nodes can be heavily disrupted, hence DoS attacks become feasible. On the other hand, legitimate receivers cannot correctly detect and decode incoming packets in the presence of jammer. This is due to the excessive noise generated in their vicinity that leads to an extensive packet loss. Moreover, as packets are lost in the network, further retransmissions by the transmitters take place causing severe network disruption.

In order to demonstrate the effects of physical-layer jamming we use a single off-the-shelf jammer with characteristics as described in Section 2. The specific type of jammer does not follow any rules of the IEEE 802.11 protocol, so it freely performs jamming even if legitimate transmissions are taking place. We setup a network of four legitimate nodes: Sender, Receiver, Monitor1, and Monitor2. Packets flow from Sender to Receiver, while periodic jamming using the frequency of the neighboring channel is taking place. Receiver, Monitor1, and Monitor2 record the packets that belong to the legitimate traffic, and for every recorded packet, the SINR (Signal-to-Interference plus Noise Ratio) is computed, taking into account the power leakage in the neighboring channels as described in [10]. Fig. 3 shows how SINR substantially drops during the jamming attacks (symbolized by the orthogonal boxes at the bottom of each graph).

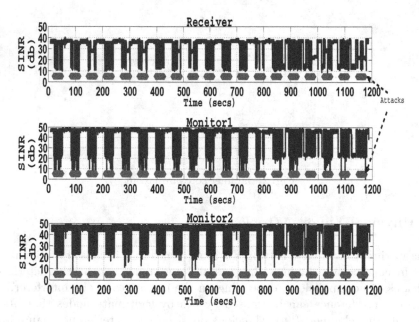

Fig. 3. SINR variations during the jamming attacks

When SINR significantly drops, a wireless receiver often becomes unable to detect and further decode a transmitted packet. This results to packet loss, throughput degradation, as well as energy waste, as transmitters keep retransmitting packets. Fig. 4 shows the retry attempts of the transmitter (Sender), the throughput at the Receiver, and the total packet loss in the network when a jammer is present. Retry attempts increase up to five times during jamming, while throughput drops to about 1 Mbps (from 15 Mbps when no jamming takes place), and packet loss increases over 60%.

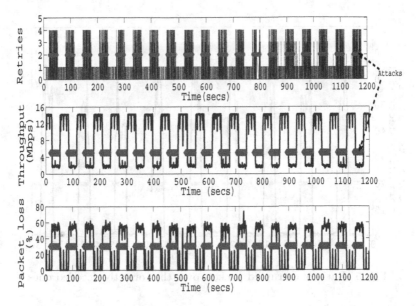

Fig. 4. Performance degradation during the jamming attacks

4   MAC Layer Attacks

IEEE 802.11 is a CSMA/CA (carrier sense multiple access with collision avoidance) based medium access protocol. Each potential transmitter has to first sense the wireless medium, and if it is free, transmission takes place. However, if the medium is occupied, it has to enter a back-off stage where it waits for some amount of time before repeating the same procedure (sensing, etc) [11].

4.1   Denial-of-Service Attacks through Packet Collisions

Attackers can exploit the CSMA/CA mechanism of IEEE 802.11 by emitting energy when the wireless medium is occupied by a legitimate node. At this point, jammer emits energy on the same channel legitimate nodes use for communication, aiming to cause packet collisions and to degrade network's performance. Packet collisions refer to captured packets that mainly suffer from CRC (cyclic redundancy check) errors. Fig. 5 shows the ratio of the corrupted packets (CRC errors) over the correctly decoded ones, captured in a single receiver when a periodic jammer is present. Jammer operates on the same channel used for the legitimate communication. Observe that the ratio exceeds 60% when jamming traffic is emitted. This is a severe DoS attack as corrupted packets are essentially lost packets that the sender will attempt to re-transmit up to a number of times (retry limit).

Next, we demonstrate how jamming on the same channel affects the performance of video transmission in the wireless network. For this reason, we set up

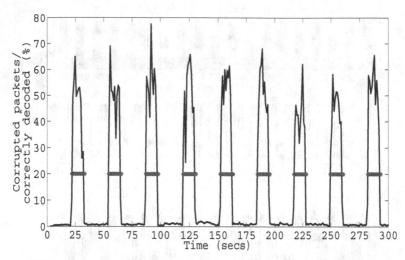

Fig. 5. Ratio of corrupted packets over the correctly decoded ones

a testbed consisting of a video server, a video client and the jammer described in Section 2. Encoded MPEG-4 video is transmitted from server to client using RTP/UDP packets. Periodic jamming takes place in the network. We measure video's performance using PSNR (Peak-Signal-to-Noise Ratio), an objective quality metric widely used to measure video performance. Supposing there are two $m \times n$ images S and D, where S is the original image and D the reconstructed image, the PSNR of this image is given by:

$$PSNR = 20 \times log_{10} \frac{V_{peak}}{\sqrt{MSE}} \qquad (1)$$

where $V peak$ is its maximum value (e.g. 255 for 8-bit encoding), and MSE is the mean squared error given by:

$$MSE = \frac{1}{m \times n} \sum_{i=0}^{m-1} \sum_{j=0}^{n-1} [S(i,j) - D(i,j)]^2 \qquad (2)$$

Fig. 6 [12] shows the PSNR for each received video frame, and for two experiments: (i) when no jamming is used (No Jam), and (ii) when jammer is active periodically for a duration of 80 seconds (Jam). Observe that PSNR significantly drops when jamming is taking place.

4.2 Greedy Behavior

The CSMA/CA mechanism of IEEE 802.11 requires that potential transmitters should wait for some time when the wireless medium is busy in order to decrease the colission probability. The waiting time (back-off time) is chosen uniformly

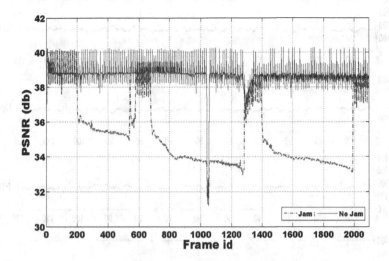

Fig. 6. PSNR per frame

in the interval $[0 - CW]$, where CW is the *contention window* size. Initially, CW equals CWmin, that is the *minimum contention window*. Each time a node finds the wireless medium busy, it doubles CW up to CWmax. When a sucessful transmission takes place, CW redues to CWmin.

This mechanism can be exploited by a malicious (or greedy) node assigning a very small value to its CWmin. With a small CWmin, the malicious node can monopolize the medium and make the legitimate nodes entering the back-off stage repeatedly. Fig. 7 shows the throughput achieved by four wireless nodes when all attempt to transmit a UDP flow of 200 Kbytes to a single access point, without the presence of a greedy node.

Next, Node1 becomes greedy by periodically assigning a very small value to its CWmin. Repeating the same experiment, in Fig. 8 we show that Node1's throughput increases from about 200 Kbytes/sec to 350 Kbytes/sec while the throughput of the rest of the nodes falls almost to 100 Kbytes/sec. Node1 becomes greedy every 10 seconds for a duration of 10 seconds. After that period, it stops behaving greedy by assigning a proper value to its CWmin.

Such greedy behaviors negatively affect legitimate nodes performance reducing the fairness of the wireless system. Fairness is related to the ability of the MAC layer to equitably share a common channel between a number of contending nodes [13]. Jain's fairness index [14] is widely used as a metric to measure the fairness of a system. Assuming that N is the number of competing flows and γ_i the fraction of packets from node i that arrived within a time window, Jain's index is defined as follows:

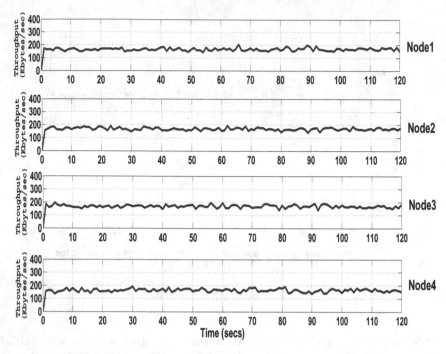

Fig. 7. Throughput with the absence of a greedy node

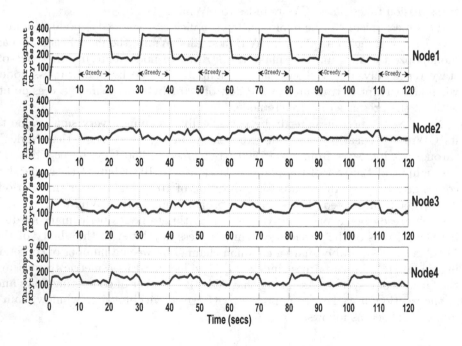

Fig. 8. Throughput with the presence of a greedy node (Node1)

$$F = \frac{(\sum\limits_{i=1}^{N} \gamma_i)^2}{N \times \sum\limits_{i=1}^{N} \gamma_i^2} \quad (3)$$

When $F = 1$ perfect fairness is achieved, while when $F = \frac{1}{N}$ absolute unfairness is achieved.

Fig. 9a shows how the fairness of the network drops when one of the nodes becomes greedy. Observe that as the number of flows decreases, the drop in fairness increases. This is because less nodes content for the medium, hence it is easier for the greedy node to monopolize it by selecting a small CWmin value. On the other hand, if no greedy node is present, fairness increases, for all flows (Fig. 9b).

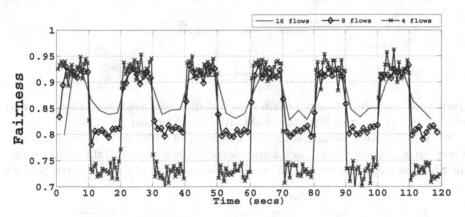

(a) When a greedy node is present

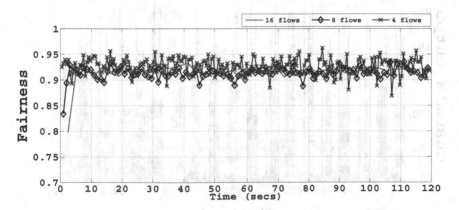

(b) When a greedy node is absent

Fig. 9. Fairness for a different number of flows

5   Attack Detection

In this section we describe techniques for the detection of physical-layer jamming, and collisions at the MAC layer. As shown in Fig. 3, jamming causes extended SINR drops. Based on this, we deploy a cumulative-sum (cusum) algorithm [15] able to detect abrupt changes of the SINR. In previous works [12, 16–18] we show that maximum performance, in terms of false alarms/detection probability, is achieved when considering the maximum minus the minimum values of SINR within a short and long windows. Cusum is defined as:

$$y_n = \begin{cases} y_{n-1} + Z_n - a & \text{if } y_n \geq 0 \\ 0 & \text{if } y_n < 0 \end{cases} \tag{4}$$

Z_n is the expectation of a specific metric that changes whenever jamming takes place (in our case the SINR-based metric), and $a \in R^+$ controls its drift. Furthermore, Z_n is given by $Z_n = D(n) - \bar{D}(n)$, where

$$D(n) = \max_{n-K+1 < i \leq n} x_i - \min_{n-K+1 < i \leq n} x_i,$$

and

$$\bar{D}(n) = \frac{\sum_{i=n-M+1}^{n} D(i)}{M},$$

During the jamming attacks, cusum's output increases as shown in Fig. 10, and when it exceeds a predefined threshold, an alarm is raised.

We use the same technique for the detection of MAC layer attacks in cases where an adversary causes packet colissions in the network. Rather than using the SINR as metric for the cusum, we consider the ratio of the corrupted packets

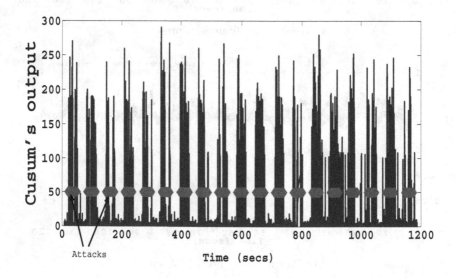

Fig. 10. Cusum's output

over the correctly decoded ones (Fig. 4). Cusum's output increases similarly as in Fig. 10 indicating the attack.

6 Conclusions

In this paper we demonstrated how commodity hardware can be used as jammer and severely affect network's performance. At the physical layer, jammer can create malicious interference that substantially degrades network performance. At the MAC layer, jammer can create extended packet collisions by energy emission when legitimate wireless traffic is being transmitted. Furthermore, a greedy node by exploiting the back-off mechanism of IEEE 802.11, can monopolize the medium, restricting network resources to the non-misbehaving nodes.

Efficient detection of these attacks is feasible by considering an SINR-based metric at the physical layer, and the ratio of the corrupted packets over the correctly decodes ones at the MAC layer. Both metrics are utilized by a cusum algorithm that signals an alarm if a predefined threshold has been exceeded.

References

1. Bartzoudis, N., Fragkiadakis, A., Parish, D., Luis-Nunez, J., Sandford, M.: Reconfigurable computing and active networks. In: Engineering of Reconfigurable Systems and Algorithms, pp. 280–283 (2003)
2. Monsanto, C., Reich, J., Foster, N., Rexford, J., Walker, D.: Composing software-defined networks. In: Proc. of the NSDI, pp. 87–98 (2013)
3. Spyridopoulos, T., Karanikas, G., Tryfonas, T., Oikonomou, G.: A game theoretic defense framework against dos/ddos cyber attacks. Computers & Security 38, 39–50 (2013)
4. Markantonakis, K., Mayes, K., Sauveron, D., Askoxylakis, I.: Overview of security threats for smart cards in the public transport industry. In: Proc. of the ICEBE, pp. 506–513 (2008)
5. Sesp jammers, http://www.sesp.com
6. Mobile device jammer, http://www.phonejammer.com/home.php
7. Software-defined radios, http://www.ettus.com/home
8. Linux wireless drivers, ath5k, http://linuxwireless.org/en/users/Drivers/ath5k
9. Tragos, E., Fragkiadakis, A., Askoxylakis, I., Siris, V.: The impact of interference on the performance of a multi-path metropolitan wireless mesh network. In: Proc. of ISCC, pp. 199–204 (2011)
10. Angelakis, V., Papadakis, S., Siris, V., Traganitis, A.: Channel Interference in 802.11a is harmful. Testbed validation of a simple quantification model. IEEE Communications Magazine, 160–166 (2011)
11. Natkaniec, M., Pach, A.: An analysis of the backoff mechanism used in ieee 802.11 networks. In: Proc. of ISCC, pp. 444–449 (2000)
12. Fragkiadakis, A., Tragos, E., Askoxylakis, I.: Video streaming performance in wireless hostile environments. In: Proc. of the 5th FTRA International Conference on Multimedia and Ubiquitous Engineering, pp. 267–272 (2011)

13. Berger-Sabbatel, G., Duda, A., Heusse, M., Rousseau, F.: Short-term fairness of 802.11 networks with several hosts. In: Belding-Royer, E.M., Agha, K.A., Pujolle, G. (eds.) Proc. of the IFIP. IFIP, vol. 162, pp. 263–274. Springer, Heidelberg (2004)
14. Jain, R.: The Art of Computer Systems Performance Analysis. John Wiley & Sons (1991)
15. Cardenas, A., Radosavac, S., Baras, J.: Evaluation of detection algorithms for mac layer misbehavior: Theory and experiments. IEEE/ACM Transactions on Networking (2009)
16. Fragkiadakis, A., Siris, V., Traganitis, A.: Effective and robust detection of jamming attacks. In: Proc. of Future Network and Mobile Summit, pp. 1–8 (2010)
17. Fragkiadakis, A., Tragos, E., Askoxylakis, I.: Design and Performance Evaluation of a Lightweight Wireless Early Warning Intrusion Detection Prototype. EURASIP Journal on Wireless Communications and Networking 12, 1–18 (2012)
18. Fragkiadakis, A., Siris, V., Petroulakis, N., Traganitis, A.: Anomaly-based intrusion detection of jamming attacks, local versus collaborative detection. Wireless Communications and Mobile Computing, 1–19 (2013)

Context Aware Collaborative Computing Model for Natural Disaster Management Systems

Hamid Mcheick[1], Raef Mousheimish[2], Ali Masri[2], and Youssef Dergham[2]

[1] Department of Computer Science, University of Quebec at Chicoutimi (UQAC),
555 Boulevard de l'Université Chicoutimi, G7H2B1, Canada
`hamid_mcheick@uqac.ca`
[2] Department of Computer Science, Faculty of Sciences (I), Lebanese University,
Rafic Hariri Campus, Hadath-Beirut, Lebanon
`{mch.raef,alimasri1991,youssefdergham}@gmail.com`

Abstract. Nowadays, natural disaster management is considered one of the critical issues, where many governments are spending a huge amount of money to master it. And to help these governmental bodies in managing this kind of situation, we used the concept of collaborative computing, to introduce an approach for mobiles to collaborate in order to act as helper agents for other ones with limited resources. Our approach is called the Disaster Pool. And in this paper we highlighted the importance of collaborative computing, have a quick look on previous work, and discuss our approach and the implemented code.

Keywords: Collaborative computing, context-aware applications.

1 Introduction

Looking at our reality, we can easily notice that every person now is counting on the mobile devices to accomplish many tasks in his life, ranging from simple basic tasks, and up to complex and business ones. The continuously evolving capabilities of mobile devices, in all their aspects, like the computational power, speed of processing, the rapidity of interactions, and the list would go on... All these technological advancements affected the mobile world and the usage of its devices, so research and industrial communities are both working on reaching the maximum benefits from these devices, and exploit their capabilities and potentials in so many domains, like military, sport, business, and especially in the field of health. Where mobile devices and counting on the fact that they are always with their users, can be really helpful in monitoring and guiding users to preserve their safety and their health, and more importantly these devices can act as a life guards in case of a disaster to help and guide the users. And this is exactly what we tried to express in this article.

When we talk about health, we can't ignore the increasing usage of mobile devices, and we can easily seethe wide spread of mobile applications, concerning fitness, monitors, and the disaster management applications. The last ones are the topic of interests now, because any person's first concern is his safety, and if we have a guide that is

N. Streitz and P. Markopoulos (Eds.): DAPI 2014, LNCS 8530, pp. 439–449, 2014.

always beside us, and we can blindly count on him, then we need to fear less about our lives, and not to mention that this last type of application is really important to highlight the concept of context-aware applications, where the device is aware of its environment and can benefit from the resources offered by the components of this environment. So after reading and surfing the current works on disaster management, we tried to leave our own mark in this field, and we merged in our approach the world of mobile and collaborative computing, and indeed we added the awareness and the smartness to our solution by using some of the context-aware techniques.

This paper is organized into five sections, we first show some previous works that are related to our approach, and then we discuss our motivation which carried us to write such a paper, we will then detail our approach with the implementation, and finally conclude with our conclusion and mention some of the future remarks.

2   Related Works

We do not intend to perform a complete review of what is context in this paper, interested reader might refer to *Brezillons*work [2]. The reader is referred to *Chen and Kotz*[4] and *Korkeaaho* [5] for a more detailed list on the projects and researches in the context-aware field.

Briefly, the definition of context is not satisfied in general. Many researchers have defined context by giving examples of contexts. Schilit divides context into three categories [11]: i) Computing context, such as network connectivity, communication costs, and communication bandwidth, and nearby resources such as printers, displays, and workstations. ii) User context, such as the user's profile, location, people nearby, even the current social situation. iii) Physical context, such as lighting, noise levels, traffic conditions, and temperature.

Dey *et al.* [10] defined context as any information that characterizes a situation of any entity. An entity is a person, place or object that is consider relevant to the interaction between a user and an application, including the user and applications themselves, and extension, the environment the user and applications are embedded in.

In *Chi-Sheng Shihet al.* [1], the authors tried to build a context-aware architecture to help users in disaster situations, by contacting some specific servers to get instructions and directions on how to act in such situations.

Some other examples on health care context awareness projects would include, the Vocera communication system [3]. Hospital of the future centre for Pervasive Health care, Denmark [6][7] where a context-aware prototype is proposed. And Context-aware mobile communication CICESE, Mexico [8].

3   Motivation

Clearly the growth of the smart-phone market is huge and is expected to continue growing, therefore, such devices have already being hailed as the next wave in computing.

Smartphones are predicted to become nearly ubiquitous and are thus a major step towards the vision of ubiquitous computing so often dreamed of. The combination of pervasive wireless networks and computational devices has created an era of mobile computing, the likes of which have never been seen before.

In large scale disasters, the network is a significant problem, and thus many of the constraints that we place on our work are centered on dealing with the loss of networking, while still enabling distributed computing when the network is available. We want to create novel distributed applications which take advantage of the distribution of the nodes in powerful ways.

Our approach suggests to make use of available resources and application almost in every smart-phone (Bluetooth, Wi-Fi, Hotspot, 3G etc.) and to collaborate the use of these resources between nodes (mobiles, cells, body sensor networks)in the disaster area (pool).

4   Disaster Pool Model

Our contribution is named The Disaster Pool Model. In the pool we could find smart-phones and/or body and wearable Sensors. The smart phones interact with the cloud through 3G, Wi-Fi and Cells. Other sensors interact through Bluetooth, Wi-Fihotspots and Wi-Fi, trying to connect with the nearby available smart phones.

If a smart phone is suffering from a lower bandwidth, no signal or internet access, it could use other phone in the area to communicate with the cloud, or to execute a code and so on. Figure 1 shows an overview of our approach.

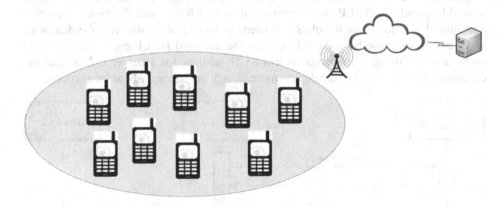

Fig. 1. A pool of collaborative mobile devices (smart phones and body sensors)

Counting on our design of the disaster pool approach, and more specifically the heavily usage of the collaborative computing concepts and the context-aware techniques, would turn so many useful fictional activities to become real, possible and feasible ones, we will count some of these activities, Let's take two smart phone A and B, and one body sensor, that is, C, the three devices are classified by the server to be in the same pool:

- **A** suffers from the lack or the speed of mobile data connection, so it can use the data from the near smart phone **B** using the Wi-Fi hotspot. So the server framework would enable automatically the hotspot on **B** and provide the password to **A**.
- **A** suffers from the lack or the speed of mobile data connection, so it can connect to a near Wi-Fi, this could be possible because the server registers the Wi-Fi provider in the area, and authenticate **A** to let it use the connection reliably.
- **A** suffers from a dead battery, and **C** usually send its monitored data to the server through **A**, in this case the server turns on the Bluetooth on **B**, and then **C** could send its data about the human handler of **A** through **B**, to continue monitor his health conditions.
- **A** suffers from the lack of computational resources, so **A** could send his data to be executed on **B**, and then get the results back.

Talked about the applicability and some of the desirable outputs of our approach, we will step now to discuss an important construct of the whole application, that is the communication protocol, and we tried our best to make it as simple as possible. So two keywords were used.

The first one is **REGISTER** and it's sent from the mobile device to the server, so in this way the server could track the mobile devices, know their locations, classify them into pools, and so in case of a disaster, and if a mobile device asks for help, the server could propose a near registered mobile device to be used.

Secondly and after mentioning the help procedure, asking for it can be done using the second keyword, i.e. **HELP**, this keyword can be sent from a mobile device to another one, and then followed by the class that needs to be executed, after this the demander could get the response from the helper. Also the keyword **HELP** could be sent to the server and in this case the server returns an IP address for a helper that is near the demander. The following figure depicts more clearly the concept of our interactions:

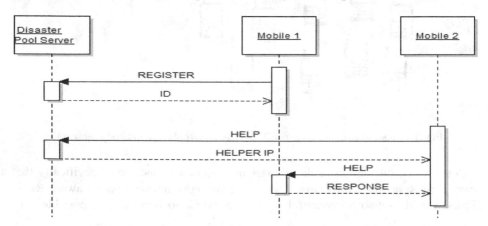

Fig. 2. The commands of the protocol depicted in a sequence diagram

5   Implementation

To put some life in our approach, we chose to implement the way of communication between the mobile phones together. Two programs where implemented using the JAVA programming language and the eclipse development environment with eclipse ADT plugin. The first one represents the disaster pool, i.e. the server, and the second one is an android mobile application.

Our implementation simply describes the fact that a mobile has a limited amount of resources in case of emergency as in disasters, and needs some other mobile to carry out the communication between it and the server or to execute the code for it. The demanding mobile is called the **demander**, the mobile used for resource sharing is called the **helper** and finally we have the old traditional **server**.

First of all, if a disaster occurs and the demander was unable to communicate with the server, it will connect to a lookup-server that can be found nearby, - A solution is that these servers could be provided by the government for this use - , then the demander asks the lookup server for a helper that is able to handle some kind of computations specified by the properties sent, and the lookup server by its way will return the desired helper. Another approach is to communicate directly with another mobile via a Wi-Fi hotspot, since at disaster time, mobiles will be alerted to open Wi-Fi hotspots for others with low resources to connect with. After selecting the helper, the demander sends it some data (files, script, parameters, etc.) to be executed, and this code communicates with the server or gets processed locally to get some data to be used. Figure 3 shows clearly our system design:

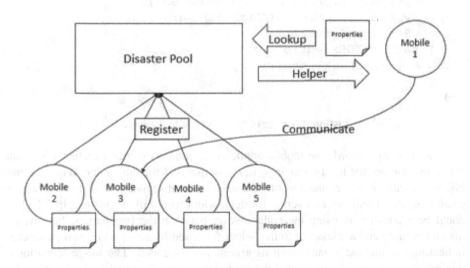

Fig. 3. The overall system design

Concerning the Disaster Pool, this java application runs as a server that keeps listening for registering clients, or for demanders that requests help. All the registered clients will be saved in a collection 'Pool' so they can become helping candidates later. When a demander requests a help, the disaster pool will seek for a helper with good resources and pass back its address. The code of the service is a little bit long, because we took into account some of the multi-threading and the authentication issues, but in the following listing, we shows how the servers works on accepting the connections from clients and creating a thread for each client.

```java
public void runServer() {
    System.out.println("Server is running...");
    while (true) {
        try {
            newClientThread(server.accept(), clients, id++);
            System.out.println("New client attached");
        } catch (IOException e) {
            e.printStackTrace();
        }
    }
}

public static void main(String[] args) {
    DisasterPooldPool = null;
    try {
        System.out.println("Creating pool...");
        dPool = new DisasterPool(1234);
        System.out.println("Pool created");
        System.out.println("Running server...");
        dPool.runServer();
    } catch (IOException e) {
        e.printStackTrace();
    }
}
```

Listing. 1. a piece of the java code of the server

Now crossing towards the mobile application, and as we stated earlier, it's an android application that has two main jobs, the helper and the demander. When the mobile phone runs it will connect to the disaster pool and registers itself to be a helping candidate, and it will run as a server for demanders who will ask it for help. The help could be requested by using the collaboration between the two parties, like the demander would send a .class file to the helper followed by some additional parameters indicating the method's name with its arguments if needed. The usage scenarios of this application are unbounded and the advantages are very good since the .class file sent is very small. But one disadvantage is the privacy, in which it may not be important in case of emergency. Where people usually, care less about their private data when they are in an emergency situation, and care more about saving their lives.

The code of the mobile application is quiet complex, this is because of the android added files, like the manifest file, the layout one, and we took into account, in our coding, the steps to create a background application that doesn't affect the resources of the android device, from all the different perspectives, like the battery, the CPU, the RAM, and so on... Thus the impact of our application on the android device was kept to minimum. Almost all the Java code for this mobile application, is important, where it's divided into separate tasks and each one of these tasks, handles an important job. The following listing for example, illustrates the helper task, where the helper is programmed, and in the background, to wait for a connection from another peer, process the help request and respond with the appropriate results.

```java
classHelperTask extends AsyncTask<Void, Void, Void> {

    @Override
    protected Void doInBackground(Void... arg0) {
      while (true) {
        output.println("REQUEST_HELPER");
        etLog.append("Requesting help...\n");
        String helperIP = input.nextLine();
        try {
          Socket socket = new Socket(helperIP, 1234);
          Scanner helperIn = new Scan-
ner(socket.getInputStream());
          // PrintWriterhelperOut = new
          // PrintWriter(socket.getOutputStream(), true);
          etLog.append("Message from helper: " +
helperIn.nextLine());
          helperIn.close();
          if (socket != null) {
            socket.close();
          }
          break;
        } catch (Exception e) {
          etLog.append("Error connecting with help-
er\nRetrying...\n");
        }
      }
      return null;
    }
  }
```

Listing. 2. The helper task android code

6   Analysis and Benefits

After implementing and trying the work we have done, we came across an analysis phase, where we clearly and practically defined the effectiveness of our solution, its light impact on the resources, its reliability and the benefits from using such approach.

Experimenting and concluding depending on two independent experiments. The experiments goals is to depict the effectiveness and the reliability of our application and the communication protocol. So two android mobile phones were registered successfully at the server, which is a java code, executed at a remote laptop. In the first experiment we tried to ask the server for help, and the server replies with the IP address of the other android device, and then a peer-to-peer connection took place between the two near devices, the demander of the help sends the HELP command to the helper device, and then the class that needs to be executed, in this way preserving the power and the resources of the demander. We didn't specify a class, because it could be anything, it could be processed locally or it could access the internet, make calls to the server and so... In the second experiment, we detected and contacted directly the helper device, and send it the class to be executed. And indeed in the two cases, we got the expected results from the operation.

Using this approach, we counted primary on the collaboration between the android devices, and so utilizing the collaborative computing concepts, and also we used the two architectural design of the network, that is, the client/server and the P2P paradigm, and by exploring the environment to detect nearby devices, we apply some context-aware techniques. The scenario could be summarized with the following figures, that shows how a demander, asks for help, and getting it. The figures illustrate the three main procedures, i.e. fetching for a helper, asking for help, and getting the response.

Figure 4 shows the running server after the two smartphone were registered to it:

Fig. 4. The disaster pool application

Figure 5 shows the demander while asking the server to locate an available helper, then sends the help request to the located smart phone, and finally get back the result.

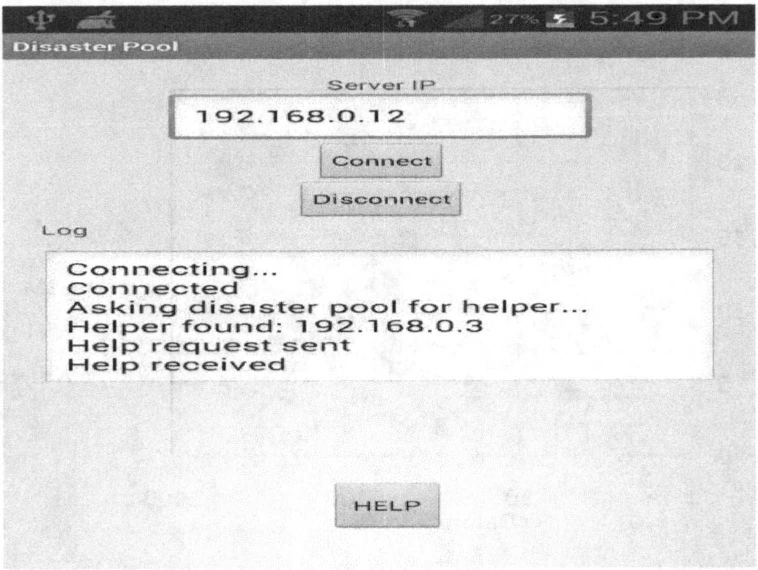

Fig. 5. The demander role

Figure 6 shows the helper after receiving a help request and returning the result.

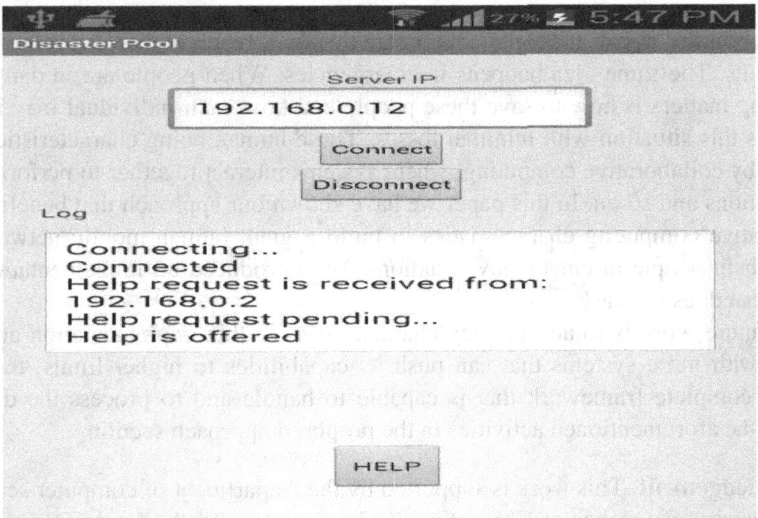

Fig. 6. The helper role

In addition to this work, it's worth to mention that using our approach, which is heavily counting on the hotspot solution, can preserve the life of the battery, and prolong the activeness of the mobile device. This figure, got from a previous study [9], can clear the idea:

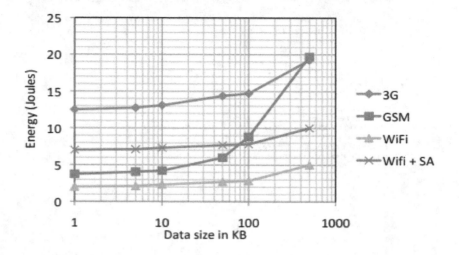

Fig. 7. The energy consumption

7   Conclusion

In any job in the world, if people collaborate they will reach higher and more significant results. The same idea happens in emergencies. When people are in danger, the only thing matters is how to save these people and how each individual may interact to bypass this situation with minimal losses. These human being characteristics were adopted by collaborative computing, where systems interact together to perform some computations and so on. In this paper we have shown our approach that benefits from collaborative computing characteristics to build a giant human-mobile network that cope to help people in emergency situations. We introduced an implementation of a system that does this task.

Our future work is to add privacy characteristics to this implementation and integrate it with more systems that can push its capabilities to higher limits, to finally create a complete framework that is capable to handle and to process the different types of the aforementioned activities in the proposed approach section.

Acknowledgement. This work is supported by the Department of computer science at the University of Quebec at Chicoutimi (QC), Canada, and the Ecole Doctorale des Sciences et de Technologie at the Lebanese University, Lebanon.

References

1. Shih, C.-S., Trieu, T.-K.: Shadow Phone: Context Aware Device Replication for Disaster Management
2. Brezillon, P.: Context in problem solving: a survey. Knowl. Eng. Rev. 14, 134 (1999)
3. Stanford, V.: Beam me up, Dr. McCoy. IEEE Pervasive Computing Mag. 2(3), 1318 (2003)
4. Chen, G., Kotz, D.: A Survey of Context-Aware Mobile Computing Research, Dartmouth Computer Science Technical Report TR2000-381, Hanover (2000)
5. Korkea-aho, M.: Context-Aware Applications Survey (2000),
   http://www.hut.fi/mkorkeaa/doc/context-aware.html
6. Bardram, J.: Applications of context-aware computing in hospital work examples and design principles. In: Proceedings of SAC, Cyprus, March 14-17 (2004)
7. Bardram, J.: Hospitals of the future ubiquitous computing support for medical work. In: Hospitals Workshop Ubihealth 2003 (2003)
8. Munoz, M., Rodriguez, M., Favela, J., Martinez-Garcia, A., Gonzalez, V.: Context-aware mobile communication in hospitals. IEEE Comput. 36(9), 3846 (2003)
9. Balasubramanian, N., Balasubramanian, A., Venkataramani, A.: Energy Consumption in Mobile Phones : A Measurement Study and Implications for Networks Applications. In: Proceedings of 9th ACM SIGCOMM Conference, New York, USA (2009)
10. Dey, A.K., Salber, D., Abowd, G.D.: A conceptual framework and a toolkit for supporting the rapid prototyping of context-aware applications. Human-Computer Interaction Journal 16(2-4), 97–166 (2001)
11. Schilit, B., Adams, N., Want, R.: Context-aware computing applications. In: Proceedings of IEEE Workshop on Mobile Computing Systems and Applications, pp. 85–90. IEEE Computer Society Press, Santa Cruz (1994)

Situated Micro-displays for Activity-Aware Systems

Esunly Medina[1], Fahim Kawsar[2], Roc Meseguer[1], and Sergio F. Ochoa[3]

[1] Department of Computer Architecture, BarcelonaTech, Barcelona, Spain
esunly@gmail.com
[2] Bell Laboratories, Alcatel-Lucent, Belgium
[3] Computer Science Department, Universidad de Chile, Santiago, Chile

Abstract. Most activity-aware systems designed to support mobile workers in dynamic environments, such as hospitals or industrial plants, typically consider the use of mobile devices and large displays. However, we envision potential benefits of using ubiquitous micro-displays as support of mobile workers activities. Particularly, in this paper we show how the use of situated micro-displays, as a mechanism for embedding information into a physical environment, can contribute to improve the performance and experience of mobile workers in those scenarios. The article also describes the prototype of a micro-display network designed to support people performing spatially distributed activities. It also presents a user study that helps understand how the spatial distribution of situated micro-displays impacts on the mobile workers performance.

Keywords: Situated micro-display, activity-centric system, mobile work.

1 Introduction

Advances in wireless communication, sensor networks and ubiquitous computing have made possible the interaction between people and numerous devices that are interconnected and physically distributed in the environment [1]. These advances have promoted the evolution of single-monitor setups towards multi-display environments [2], where it is possible to have displays embedded in a physical ambient and also in everyday objects. Several studies on workplaces have shown how instrumented environments and everyday artefacts support people cognition and collaboration [3,4]. Researchers have emphasized the need to deliver task-centric information in dynamic workplaces, such as hospitals or industrial plants, as a way to support the activities performed by mobile workers [5,6].

Typically, *situated information systems* [7] provide information of the physical environment to mobile workers, and *activity-aware systems* [8] infer the workers' activity context in order to offer them suitable supporting services. Most of these systems types rely on the use of mobile devices and large displays [9]. However, recent researches [10] advocate for the use of micro-displays to provide situated information in activity-aware systems and offer activity-specific guidance. These micro-displays are mobile and adaptive. They are distributed across the environment and provide simple visual representations of human activities that are linked to physical entities –such as objects and people– and integrated in the environment.

N. Streitz and P. Markopoulos (Eds.): DAPI 2014, LNCS 8530, pp. 450–461, 2014.

We envision the potential benefits of using micro-displays to provide instructions and activity-centric information to mobile workers in highly dynamic work contexts. Consequently, this paper describes a prototype of an activity-aware system based in micro-displays.

As stated in [10], the use of multiple micro-displays raises a number of questions regarding their spatial placement and distribution. For instance, where and how the displays should be deployed in a physical environment to optimize the information support to mobile workers? In that sense, particular studies are needed to identify the trade-off between the quality of the information provided by the micro-displays and the fragmentation of users' attention. By increasing the number of displays we can show the information in a fine-grained and situated fashion. However, too much and/or not-so-relevant information demands higher cognition and could lead to information overload, jeopardizing its assimilation by the end-users. Therefore, it is critical to understand the impact of the distribution granularity and placement alternatives of micro-displays to positively impact the effectiveness of activity-aware systems. Trying to deal with that issue, this article also reports the results from a user study aimed at understanding the impact of spatial placement and distribution of situated and activity-aware micro-displays, on the users' awareness and attention. Our results show that adding situated micro-displays to support the participants' activities enhances user experience and do not causes information overload. Both, quantitative and qualitatively results clearly show the benefits of introducing situated micro-displays. By increasing the density of micro-displays in an area, the performance of individuals improves and they also get favourable impressions after the activity completion.

Next section describes the prototype of a micro-display network. Section 3 presents the user study and section 4 discusses the obtained results. Section 5 presents several design guidelines obtained from the user study. Section 6 presents the conclusions and future work.

2   Activity-Aware Micro-displays Prototype

A micro-display in an activity-aware system provides activity-specific guidance to mobile workers according to the design guidelines proposed in [10]. A network of these micro-displays enables the presentation of contextual cues at critical places to aid human activities that are spatially dispersed. These contextual cues describe the necessity or possibility for action in a given location and involving a specific object. They also show the result or execution state of preceding actions, and present a possible next action. More specifically, the representations of these contextual cues have different properties according to generic activity patterns that define particular routines at structured workplaces. These properties are the following:

- *Colour*: Used to represent the relationship between a given entity (people or object) and the current activity.
- *Identity*: Represented by a number. We also use a circle to indicate that a given entity is present and active.
- *Textual description*: Provides an explanation about something; e.g. an instruction.

Accordingly, Fig. 1 shows examples of visual representations displayed in the micro-displays to the participants of our study. Fig. 1 (a) shows a representation that provides an overview of the activity that participants had to complete. Fig. 1 (b) shows information about an object related to such an activity.

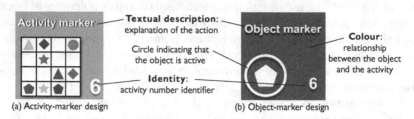

(a) Activity-marker design   (b) Object-marker design

Fig. 1. Design of the visual representations of activities

In our prototype activity-aware system, we have used shielded mobile devices of varying size as the placeholders (i.e., micro display) of these visual representations. In Fig. 2b, and Fig. 2c, two different form factors of micro-displays are shown, where the former is used to present object-specific information pertaining to a task at hand, and the latter is used to provide an overview of the activity in context. Each of these displays runs a tiny client application (*Ajax-Comet*) that shows this activity-related information, and all of the displays are connected to a central display server in a *RESTful* way following multitenancy principles. The activity information shown in the micro-displays is stored in the central display server, which pushes the appropriate information to a specific micro-display in a contextual fashion. Although we did not implement actual context recognition in our prototype, this pushing mechanism enabled us to dynamically display and update the information in the micro-displays appropriately. For instance, when a participant arrives to the main entrance of the room where the activity is taking place, a micro-display located at the entrance automatically provides him an overview of the whole activity.

The micro-displays network was implemented connecting several computing devices through Wi-Fi, using an Apple's Airport Express base station; particularly a MacBook laptop was used to run the server and allowed us to manage the control panel of the system (Fig. 2a); nine iPods touch that represent the regular micro-displays that provide object-related information and one Apple's iPad that emulates the main micro-display that shows the activity overview. We covered part of these devices screen with black acrylic plastic in order to create the effect of having displays with small size screens (see Fig. 2b and 2c). The iPad's micro-display had a screen size of 7 x 7 cm (i.e. the acrylic plastic window), whereas the iPods had a window of 3 x 3 cm.

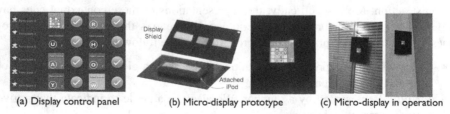

(a) Display control panel   (b) Micro-display prototype   (c) Micro-display in operation

Fig. 2. Micro-display network prototype

3   User Study

This section introduces the user study performed to explore the spatial distribution aspect of situated micro-displays and its impact in users' satisfaction, attention and performance. Particularly we want to understand whether and under what circumstances the use of situated micro-displays is useful to support human activities.

The user study involved mobile workers that had to complete a given activity using the information displayed in the micro-displays. We varied the distribution and density of micro-displays presented to the participants, generating thus different work conditions. The placement of situated micro-displays followed the guidelines given in [10], and the study involved three experimental scenarios. The first scenario considers that mobile workers only have one micro-display (activity-marker) located in an *activity-centric* fashion (i.e. the device is located at the main area where the activity is taking place) and it shows information about the activity as a whole. The second and third scenarios represent the *space-centric* and the *entity-centric* distribution respectively. The *space-centric* distribution considers micro-displays placed in a space shared by multiple entities (people or objects) and the *entity-centric* distribution involves a micro-display embedded in every entity.

For these last two scenarios, additionally to the activity-marker, we also had 3 and 9 extra micro-displays used as object-markers respectively. These object-markers show information about the objects involved in the main activity. In the second scenario, we placed 3 micro-displays at different locations of the physical space where the several objects involved in the activity had been placed. For the latter scenario, due to the study' activities entail interactions with 9 different objects, we placed the micro-displays very close to these objects location. We decided to use this number of micro-displays due to hardware restrictions –wireless connectivity– and also to make the study conveniently manageable and not tiring for the participants. Summarizing, the three experimentation scenarios involved 1, 4 and 10 micro-displays respectively.

Physical Setup. The space were the study took place was a conference room of 20.4 m2 approximately. Fig. 3 shows, on a blueprint of the area, the physical setup used in the third scenario. In this case the distance between micro-displays was about 1.5 m. It is important to notice that across the different study settings, the spatial distribution of the micro-displays in the room was maintained, independently of the number of devices. Particularly, the maximum distance (in metres) between the farthest pair of micro-displays was the same for all scenarios. Thus, we intend to assure that the different scenarios settings do not determine or affect the results of this study.

The activity took place mainly on a tall table placed at the main entrance of the room. There we placed the main micro-display with the activity overview (to represent the activity-centric placement of situated micro-displays). We also placed across the room the different objects involved in the study activities. Other objects and activities were intentionally introduced in the room to simulate a scenario where the same physical space can be shared between several activities and entities. The walls of the room were partially covered with Velcro material to be able to place and remove the micro-displays when needed, according to the study scenario.

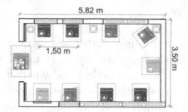

Fig. 3. Floor Plan showing the physical setup

Tasks. The activities that participants had to complete involved a number of simulated simple tasks. Little information processing was required to understand the information displayed and to carry out a single task. We decided to use simulated tasks instead of real-world work activities due to our research is a proof-of-concept focused on the use of micro-displays to build *situated information system* to support mobile workers, independently of the specific domain where it is applied. According to [7], these kinds of systems are based in the situational theory of action, which states that a goal-oriented activity can be done through the minimally reflective and fluid actions performed by skilled workers engaged in routine tasks. However, we have added some complexity to the activity as a whole due to the fact that the information about many operational tasks was displayed at the same time. Specifically, the activities were several puzzles that the participants had to solve using the information shown in the micro-displays. In order to do that, they had to pick up the correct objects –among the objects distributed around the room– and place them in the correct positions on a grid. The tasks selected for this study have the following properties:

1. *Physical:* The tasks involve physical movement and involve tangible interaction with objects.
2. *Spatially distributed:* Participants have to move from one place to another to complete the tasks.
3. *Goal oriented:* Tasks have a common final goal.
4. *Non-sequential:* The interdependency among tasks is minimal.

Accordingly, we selected this particular puzzle activity from the nine categories for manual tasks referenced in [11], however we normalized it to assess the quality of non-sequentially and spatial distribution of situated micro-displays. The *independent variable* of the study is the number of micro-displays. For this reason, each participant was always exposed to the same activity, but we varied the distribution granularity of the micro-displays between the different study scenarios. By doing so, we maintained the complexity level of the tasks that the participants have to perform, so that the activity itself does not influence the study results. In order to avoid learning effects that can lead to the improvement in the users' performance, for each study scenario we altered the pattern of the activity and the objects involved on it, as a way to make that the activity looked like a completely different one. Accordingly, each study scenario had a different activity pattern, as well as a specific number of micro-displays.

Participants. The participants in this study were 14 students from Lancaster University. We did not involve participants with a particular profile or groups with special characteristics, because the study was not intended for a specific domain. Prior to perform the study, we asked participants to provide demographic data. There were 9 male and 5 female, aged 21 to 27 (average of 24.3). The study took approximately one and a half hour per participant.

Method. Participants took part in the experiment individually. They began the study being told about the study purpose and with a brief training session. We used A/V equipment to record the experiments and the people interviews for later analysis. The study followed a *within-subjects design*, where each participant experienced the three study scenarios. In addition, we used a *Balanced Latin Square* for counterbalancing to mitigate potential learning effects. We ensured that two participants completed each row in the Latin Square. The scenarios entailed the completion of 3 different activity patterns composed by 9 tasks each, which corresponds to the number of objects the users had to interact with to complete the activity. Following the completion of each study scenario, we asked each participant to answer several subjective questions taken from the *IBM Computer Usability Satisfaction Questionnaires* [12] and the *NASA Task Load Index* [13]. We also asked them additional questions for further evaluation of divided attention and information overload issues. In addition, after the whole experimentation process, each participant answered the questions of a final *semi-structured interview* aimed at gathering additional feedback about the best distribution arrangement of micro-displays.

4   Study Result

In this section, we discuss the result of the study from four perspectives: Task performance, multitasking effect, context switch and participant' behaviour.

4.1   Completion Time and Errors

In [14] the author presents the use of the reaction time to measure the division of attention and also the accuracy and speed of an action as a measure of the spare cognitive capacity. Accordingly, we use completion time and errors to measure the appearance of divided attention and information overload respectively.

We computed the activity's *completion time* as the time elapsed from the moment the participants first looked at the main micro-display and the moment just after they placed the last piece of the puzzle in the right position. Results show that a higher number of micro-displays can help decrease the activities' completion time. We obtained an average difference of 8.67 seconds (7.9%) between the fastest and the slowest performance (considering the three scenarios). The difference in the maximum and minimum completion times was 11 and 28 seconds respectively.

Errors were classified into two types: *completion* and *location errors. Completion errors* are those occurred during the completion of the puzzle, e.g. placing a wrong object in the grid, having some missing, etc. The number of these errors was very small and we did not observe a direct correlation between the number of micro-displays and this kind of error. However, the completion errors for the scenario with the highest number of micro-displays were 50% smaller than those with the lowest number of micro-displays. *Location errors* were counted when the participant picked the wrong objects from the different room locations. Location errors are a good metric of performance and efficiency, especially when the tasks are physically dispersed.

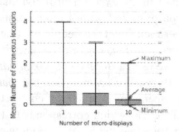

Fig. 4. Location errors

A high number of location errors imply that the individuals have to walk longer distances to complete the activity, and as a result, the effort and time required is higher. Fig 4 shows that the mean and maximum values of the location errors have a negative correlation with the number of micro-displays. The experiments in the first study scenario had a significantly higher average error rate (57.1%) than in the third one.

4.2   Simultaneous Tasks and Iteration Steps

The participants' performance shows a direct relationship between their overall satisfaction when completing the activity and the number of simultaneous physical tasks they engaged with. Participants' satisfaction also has a negative correlation with the number of iteration steps that they had to perform for completing the activity. For this reason, we have included this metric to try understanding the information overload on the mobile workers.

We computed the number of *simultaneous tasks* performed by participants, counting the maximum number of objects that they picked in the routes followed for completing the activity. We defined the *iteration steps* as the number of stages that participants needed for completing the activity, e.g., the number of rounds around the room.

Fig. 5 (a) shows the number of simultaneous tasks (minimum, maximum and average) performed by the participants. These results indicate a direct correlation between the average values of this variable and the micro-displays density. When we have nine object-related micro-displays, the number of simultaneous tasks is (in average) 43.3%, which is higher than when we only have the main micro-display (scenario 1).

Fig. 5 (b) shows the results of the iteration steps for the three study scenarios. The results show a negative correlation between the number of micro-displays and the number of iteration steps required for the activities completion. There is a difference of 33.3% between the average values obtained in first and the last study scenario respectively. The same tendency in followed by the maximum and minimum values.

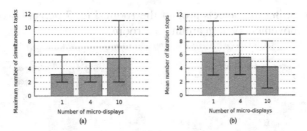

Fig. 5. (a) Simultaneous tasks and (b) iteration steps

4.3   Context Switches

A *context switch* happens when the users' view switches from the main activity mi-cro-display to any other point. Accordingly, we computed the number of eye move-ments of the participants. The results indicate that mobile workers in the study scena-rio with the smallest number of micro-displays required a higher number of switches to accomplish the tasks (Fig. 6). The average context switches in the first scenario were 32.5% higher than in the third scenario. The maximum and minimum values of context switches adhere to this tendency.

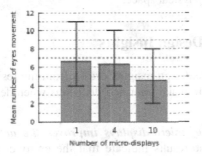

Fig. 6. Context switches

It seems reasonable to think that entity-centric micro-displays introduce maximum fragmentation of attention in comparison to activity-centric placement because the information is dispersed across a higher number of micro-displays, which could de-mand more context switches. However, these results confirm that a higher density of micro-displays actually reduces the context switching, because the information is presented in a more situated fashion. Therefore, we cannot claim that having a higher number of micro-displays increases the fragmentation of attention

4.4   Participants' Behaviour

Another interesting observation about the participants' behaviour while completing the activities is related to the physical path that they followed. We observed that there was an important difference in the number and shape of the routes that participants followed for collecting the objects around the room. Fig. 7 depicts two examples of the participants' movement pattern around the room.

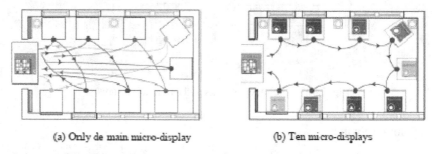

(a) Only de main micro-display   (b) Ten micro-displays

Fig. 7. Examples of the participants' physical movement pattern

Fig. 7 (a) shows a sample result for the scenario with only the main micro-display and Fig. 7 (b) shows the result when the participants also had 9 additional object-related micro-displays. Analysing these paths we can confirm the participants' impressions that a higher physical effort was needed when the number of micro-displays was small. We can also claim that increasing the number of micro-displays results in a more efficient use of the physical space.

5   Implications: Design Insights

Next we summarize some design insights drawn from the results of our study. These insights allow designers to make informed decisions when developing activity-aware systems.

Increasing the density of micro-displays improves the activity performance and information support. The results indicate that the entity-centric distribution of the micro-displays helps boost user experience and has a positive impact in the activity performance and the quality of the information support. Both, quantitative and qualitative data showed that activity performance increases with the number of micro-displays. Measurements of completion time, location errors, iteration steps and number of simultaneous activities confirmed that the best performance is achieved when we have as many micro-displays as objects has the activity. In addition, the participants' feedback reveals that most participants preferred to have a high density of micro-displays, because the information provided by them becomes clear and easy to find. This would indicate that the quality of the supporting information increases with the micro-displays granularity.

Situated micro-displays require focused attention. During the interviews, the participants mentioned that they looked at the micro-displays one at a time. Therefore, although we initially expected that situated micro-displays with an entity-centric placement would require divided attention, we found that instead they required focused attention. Previous researchers have found that the performance of a mobile worker correlates positively with the amount of information that he receives; however, if the information provided is too much, his performance rapidly decline [15]. For this reason, we hypothesized that increasing the number of situated micro-display would improve activity performance, but up to certain point due to the fragmentation of the users' attention. Nevertheless, our findings revealed that micro-displays require focused attention and a higher density of them help reduce the context switching, because the information is presented in a more situated fashion. The fastest completion times obtained during the experiments confirm this finding. We cannot unequivocally assert the claim due to the limited number of participants and micro-displays involved in the experiments. Therefore, it would be necessary to perform more longitudinal studies in order to confirm statistically these observations.

Spatial distribution does not affect the information capacity. According to the quantitative results and the participants' feedback, it seems that the spatial distribution of the information does not cause information overload. In contrast, the results confirmed that the quality of the provided information and the users' satisfaction increases with the density of micro-displays. Therefore, we can claim that an entity-centric placement of situated micro-displays, when the entities and task involved in the activity are spatially dispersed, does not affect the mobile workers' capacity to successfully process the information. In fact, we used some metrics and indicators of information overload, such as recall and emergent and implicit poles [16], by asking participants some specific questions after finishing the activity. These results did not show signs of information overload in any of the study scenarios.

Situated micro-displays can be used for structured activity route. As already expected and confirmed by the study, there are applications that could benefit of using situated micro-displays distributed in an entity-centric fashion; for instance, those involving a structured activity route. That is, we can deploy the micro-displays in the work area in a way that the user is led to follow a specific path to complete the activity. If the micro-displays are placed one after another in a structured fashion, there is a high possibility that people follow a controlled activity route. An additional benefit is that if the deployment of the micro-displays is carefully planned, we could use more efficiently the physical space.

6   Design Guidelines

The presented results allow us to provide several design guidelines, which can support the design of mobile and ubiquitous solutions to display activity-centric information into situated micro-displays. It is important to follow a user centric approach when deploying a situated micro-display network that supports mobile workers performing spatially distributed tasks. Thus, the designer improves the chances that the system implementation fits with the current practices at the specific workplace.

Entity-centric distribution. Entity-centric placement of situated micro-displays seems to be the best alternative to guide spatially distributed tasks. Therefore, micro-displays should be fully integrated in the work environment and linked to the physical entities that are relevant for the workplace activities.

Micro-display density. The scenario with highest density of micro-displays provided the most effective, enjoyable and effortless support for mobile workers. This finding was also perceived by the participants. Therefore, we recommend embedding as much micro-displays as possible in tools and entities used by mobile workers.

Trade-off between structured deployment of micro-displays and users' autonomy. We can use situated micro-displays to determine the physical movement patterns of the mobile worker at the workplace. Taking away part of the activity's control from the worker, it is possible to make a more effective use of the physical space and reduce the effort required for the activity completion. However, we cannot ensure that it would improve workers' efficiency. Therefore, the deployment of micro-displays should reach a delicate balance between regulating the work practices and preserving the autonomy and decision-making capacity of skilful workers.

Context-based customisation. It is important to consider the work context in the deployment of micro-displays. This work context should consider the current work activities and the environment in which they will be performed. Therefore, some factors such as screen size, visual design and the kind and amount of information to be provided by the micro-displays should be adapted accordingly.

7 Conclusions and Future Work

The use of situated micro-displays is an evident design alternative to present real-time in-situ information to support complex, dynamic and spatially distributed human activities. In this paper we provided a proof-of-concept towards this goal, by developing a prototype of a micro-display network and performing a user study that explores the users' experiences according to spatial distribution of situated micro-displays. We described the prototype solution, and also analysed the effect that the distribution granularity of micro-displays has on the users' performance. The results provide clear evidence of the advantages of having a high situated micro-displays density in the workplace. Some of these advantages are the improvement in activity completion time, the reduction of the errors, the improvement of the efficiency in the use of the physical space and a higher user satisfaction.

The results also indicate that the use of micro-displays to support spatially distributed fluid tasks, which are part of a complex and dynamic activity, can boost user experience and have a positive impact in the people performance. The results of the user study also helped us to gain further insights about the design implications of performing activities in environments with a high micro-displays density.

These results allowed us to provide some design guidelines that help designers of mobile and ubiquitous solutions to deal with the modelling of activity-centric information that will be deployed through situated micro-displays. The next steps consider performing a transversal study to determine the generalizability of the current findings. We also plan to perform a field study in real workplaces.

References

1. Feki, M.A., Kawsar, F., Boussard, M., Trappeniers, L.: The Internet of Things: The next technological revolution. IEEE Computer 46(2), 24–25 (2013)
2. Berkhoff, C., et al.: Clairvoyance: A framework to integrate shared displays and mobile computing devices. Future Generation Computer Systems (2013)
3. Hutchins, E.: Cognition in the Wild, vol. 262082314. MIT Press, Cambridge (1995)
4. Poslad, S.: Ubiquitous Computing: Smart Devices, Environments and Interactions (2009)
5. Heyer, C.: Investigations of ubicomp in the oil and gas industry. In: Ubicomp, pp. 61–64. ACM (2010)
6. Bardram, J.E.: A novel approach for creating activity-aware applications in a hospital environment. In: Gross, T., Gulliksen, J., Kotzé, P., Oestreicher, L., Palanque, P., Prates, R.O., Winckler, M. (eds.) INTERACT 2009. LNCS, vol. 5727, pp. 731–744. Springer, Heidelberg (2009)
7. Waller, V.: Information systems in the wild: Supporting activity in the world. Behaviour & Information Technology 28(6), 577–588 (2009)
8. Tentori, M., Favela, J.: Activity-aware computing in mobile collaborative working environments. In: Haake, J.M., Ochoa, S.F., Cechich, A. (eds.) CRIWG 2007. LNCS, vol. 4715, pp. 337–353. Springer, Heidelberg (2007)
9. Scott, S.D., Sasangohar, F., Cummings, M.: Investigating supervisory-level activity awareness displays for command and control operations. In: HSIS (2009)
10. Kawsar, F., Vermeulen, J., Smith, K., Luyten, K., Kortuem, G.: Exploring the design space for situated glyphs to support dynamic work environments. In: Lyons, K., Hightower, J., Huang, E.M. (eds.) Pervasive 2011. LNCS, vol. 6696, pp. 70–78. Springer, Heidelberg (2011)
11. Rosenthal, S., et al.: Augmenting on-screen instructions with micro-projected guides: When it works, and when it fails. In: Ubicomp, pp. 203–212. ACM (2010)
12. Lewis, J.R.: IBM computer usability satisfaction questionnaires: Psychometric evaluation and instructions for use. Int. J. of Human-Computer Interaction 7(1), 57–78 (1995)
13. Hart, S.G., et al.: Development of NASA-TLX: Results of empirical and theoretical research. In: Human Mental Workload. Advances in Psychology, vol. 52, pp. 139–183 (1988)
14. Kahneman, D.: Attention and Effort. Prentice-Hall Inc., Englewood Cliffs (1973)
15. Eppler, M.J., Mengis, J.: The concept of information overload: A review of literature from organization science, accounting, marketing, MIS, and related disciplines. The Information Society 20(5), 325–344 (2004)
16. Müller, J., Wilmsmann, D., Exeler, J., Buzeck, M., Schmidt, A., Jay, T., Krüger, A.: Display blindness: The effect of expectations on attention towards digital signage. In: Tokuda, H., Beigl, M., Friday, A., Brush, A.J.B., Tobe, Y. (eds.) Pervasive 2009. LNCS, vol. 5538, pp. 1–8. Springer, Heidelberg (2009)

From Annotated Objects to Distributed Planning in Heterogeneous and Dynamic Environments

Daniel Moos, Sebastian Bader, and Thomas Kirste

MMIS, Computer Science, University of Rostock
first.last@uni-rostock.de
https://mmis.informatik.uni-rostock.de

Abstract. Controlling a dynamic and distributed device ensemble is challenging. Such ensemble should support their users pro-actively, by taking useful actions automatically. Here, we propose an approach in which methods of deployed objects are annotated with preconditions and effects. From those annotations, we construct planning operators that are used in a distributed planning system. The resulting system is able to control a real laboratory infrastructure without any central control component such that goal-directed behavior emerges from the interplay of all deployed devices.

Keywords: distributed planning, goal-directed behavior, emergent behavior, smart environment, ambient intelligence.

1 Introduction and Motivation

Modern living or working environments offer a large number of services and options to their users. Pro-actively controlling such environments is a challenging task within the area of *Ambient Intelligence* and a yet open research problem. Given a goal the user wants to achieve, the ensemble of devices and services needs to compute a supporting sequence of actions that lead from the current state of the world into one satisfying the given goal. Our long-term aim is the realization of pro-active assistance in dynamic and heterogeneous device ensembles. As soon as new devices enter the ensemble, they integrate themselves seamlessly into it and support the user without the need for further setup or integration.

Recently an algorithm has been presented to compute and execute a supporting sequence of actions in smart environments in a completely decentralized manner [12,11]. This lack of a central planning component supports our long-term aim as goals are achieved via communication between all available devices and devices can join and leave this process at any time. In this paper, we describe our adaption of this approach, employ it in an existing environment, and evaluate its feasibility in a real-world setting. In addition, we rely on existing software components, which encapsulate the devices functionality, and present a way how they can be used for distributed planning without the need to change

N. Streitz and P. Markopoulos (Eds.): DAPI 2014, LNCS 8530, pp. 462–473, 2014.

them. To enable a goal-directed emergent behavior we annotate all methods with a formal specification of their preconditions and effects. These annotations allow an automatic planning of supporting actions. During the planning phase, we automatically construct planning operators and deploy those into the environment. The planning operators form a network and a spread of activation approach, which is described below, is taken to select actions for execution. Figure 1 contains an overview of this approach. For existing devices we deploy software components, which encapsulate the communication with them. We annotate these software components with a formal description of preconditions and effects of their actions to allow the generation of planning operators that are then used for decentralized action selection.

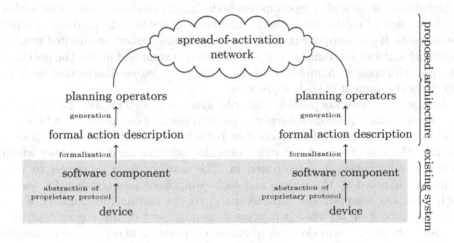

Fig. 1. Overall architecture of our system: From devices to spread-of-activation networks

As this is still ongoing research, we are here primarily interested in the feasibility of the approach within a real-world setting. Therefore, the system has been realized completely and is currently in use within our laboratory. The novelty of our approach presented here is the automatic construction of planning operators and the spread-of-activation network to enable decentralized planning in a smart environment. This extends the previous work, described below, which relies on a static ensemble and a pre-configured set of planning operators. The contribution of this paper is two-fold: (a) We show how to specify preconditions and effects of methods in a very modular manner, and how to derive formal planning operators from those annotations. As mentioned above, this does not require a modification of the underlying implementation - only an annotation of methods. (b) In addition we report on some initial experiments, showing the general applicability of the approach in non-trivial situations with a sufficient performance. The system is used on a daily basis to control a smart meeting room with various devices.

2   Related Work

Many researchers have developed techniques for the challenging task of a decentralized control of distributed systems. One aspect of this field is the emergence of complex functionality through interaction of components in the system. Below we give a brief overview of existing techniques that do not require a central component to achieve emergent functionality.

One technique is the tuple space [4] with extension to distributed tuple spaces [10]. In the field of autonomous robotics the PEIS system has been developed, which uses a distributed tuple space with an event mechanism to connect PEIS-Components [13]. Each component can consist of links to sensors and actuators, perception, modeling, and deliberation modules. The tuple space is used as an information storage and gives components the ability to store information, which can be accessed by other components, and thus allows links to modules of other components. If one component, e.g. a vacuum cleaning robot, has limited sensing capabilities, it can be connected to a monitoring system and access the provided location information. A middleware like PEIS provides an abstraction layer to ease the development of such applications.

Another technique are publish/subscribe systems [3,8]. The HELFERLEIN middleware contains a publish/subscribe system to connect components and emerge functionality from the information flow between them [2]. Here a component can take the role of a producer which provides information or subscriber which listens to information it is interested in. The transfer from producers to subscribers is handled by the system and each component just registers for one or both roles. On reception the subscriber can trigger certain functionality, e.g. a lamp can turn itself on when it receives a message sent by a presence detector.

Also Web services provide a way to enable cooperation of different components [9]. In form of a WSDL document a Web service can inform other Web services about its functionality and how to access it. This self-description is an interesting abstraction layer to build a system composed of distributed components, as components can access other components with minimal prior knowledge of their functionality.

Another example for a technique are the *spread-of-activation networks* as a mechanism for action selection for autonomous agents [6]. Based on the actions of an agent a network is constructed where actions that can (partly) enable or disable other actions are connected. The state of the world and the given goal are sources of *activation energy* which is distributed between actions. This flow of energy is controlled by a set of five parameters and leads to an accumulation of energy in actions, which are applicable in the current state and contribute towards the goal. If the energy of an action surpasses a threshold during this process it will be executed and thus a plan step-by-step constructed.

Based on the idea of spread-of-activation networks an algorithm for distributed planning in smart environments has been developed [12,11]. This algorithm requires a declarative description of the functionality of the devices in the environment. The activation network here is constructed between the devices, every device holds its own actions and connects to other actions via a local network, and the flow of activation energy is controlled by the same five parameters. This allows the creation of a plan without a central controller.

In this paper we will present an approach how components in a smart environment can provide information about the preconditions and effects of their actions. Then we utilize this to build a spread-of-action network on top of these descriptions and enable the components to find action sequences for given goals in a completely decentralized manner.

3   From Annotated Objects to Distributed Planning

Automatic planning is concerned with the following problem: Given a set of available actions (or operators), a starting state, and constraints on a goal state, a sequence of actions (plan) shall be computed such that the state reached after executing the plan satisfies the given constraints. In contrast to most other planning systems as for example evaluated within the international planning competition IPC[1], we follow an approach in which the full plan is not constructed in advance, but the plan is constructed and executed incrementally. As soon as a useful action is identified, it is executed and the planning process continues with the resulting state. Our approach is based on *activation networks* [6] and an adaptation thereof for distributed execution described in [11]. In addition it relies on our middleware that allows a dynamic construction of an ad-hoc ensemble [1].

Objects encapsulating services and devices are deployed with a given ID into a local network via our middleware. Those objects offer methods to modify their state or to interact with their environment. All methods are annotated with a formal specification of necessary preconditions to execute the method and the resulting effects as exemplified in Listing 1.1. Planning operator schemata as known from PDDL [5] can be derived from those annotations as described below. Listing 1.2 shows the resulting PDDL code. As soon as a new goal enters the system these schemata are used to instantiate all required planning operators.

Those operators connect themselves – again through our middleware – into a so called *activation network* in which activation energy is spread out. New energy enters the network as soon as a new goal is announced. All operators able to contribute to the goal receive some energy and forward some of it to all operators that might help to satisfy their preconditions. In addition, operators destroying already satisfied preconditions are inhibited by negative energy. After the energy is distributed through the network, the applicable operator with maximum energy is executed. The repetition of energy distribution and execution cycle leads to modification of the world towards a state satisfying the given goal constraints. The full details of the construction of operators [7], the formation of the network, and the distribution of energy can be found in [11,7].

---

[1] For further information we refer to `http://ipc.icaps-conference.org/`

The input to our system is a set of annotated objects, the present state of the world, and a characterization of the goal-state to be achieved. The result is the execution of an appropriate sequence of actions, leading from the current to the desired state of the world. The whole approach is divided into the following conceptual steps:

- For every object entering the ensemble, the planning operator schemata are synthesized.
- For every goal fed into the ensemble, a spread-of-activation network is constructed. This network contains all instantiated operators which influence the goal state together with the transitive closure of all operators effecting their preconditions.
- Once the network is constructed, it is executed as described in [11]. The execution of the network results in the execution of actions which lead to the goal state.

Here, we concentrate on the first step, namely the construction of planning operators for a given set of annotated objects. In our approach, we restrict ourselves to an object oriented setting in the following sense: The state of the world is described as a set of triples. Every triple contains an object-ID, a property name, and a corresponding value. Instead of allowing arbitrary first order predicates within goal and state specifications, as customary in the automatic planning, we restrict ourselves to such entity-property-value triples (EPVs).

Planning operator schemata are constructed for every annotated method as shown in Listing 1.1. An additional parameter ?this – referring to the object itself – is added. While synthesizing preconditions and effects, two cases need to be considered: a property can be either functional or relational in the following sense: Functional properties are properties which have exactly one value at any time, like the mute-property from the example. In our system all properties for which a nullary getter exists are assumed to be functional. In this case, effects can be added which ensure the removal of the previous state as shown in Listing 1.2. Non-functional properties define relations that hold in the current state of the world. For example, a PDF-viewer may have several files open simultaneously. In our system all properties with getter-functions accepting parameters are assumed to define a relation. For relational properties, we assume that all necessary effects are added to all methods manipulating this relation. An example of a relational property is the open-relation within the PDF-viewer shown in Listing 1.1. In our running implementation, the planning operators are not constructed explicitly, even though they form the theoretical foundation our planning is built on, but the underlying logic is implemented in our system. As for PDDL, we rely on add- and remove lists within the logical specification. That is the positive and negative effects are handled separately. Let E^+ and E^- be sets of positive and negative effect predicates. For a given state S of the world, the successor state

Listing 1.1. Annotations used in the definition of a projector (top) and a PDF-viewer (bottom)

```
public interface Projector {  ...
  @Getter(property="Mute")
  public String getMute();

  @PositivePreconditions(property="Power", value="on")
  @PositiveEffect(property="Mute", value="?ARG1")
  public void setMute(String mute);                    ... }

public interface PDFViewer {  ...
  @PositiveEffect(property="open", value="?ARG1")
  public String open(String filename);

  @PositivePreconditions(property="open", value="?ARG1")
  @NegativeEffect(property="open", value="?ARG1")
  public void close(String filename);

  @Getter(property="open")
  public boolean isOpen(String filename);              ... }
```

Listing 1.2. PDDL operator schemata for the setMute and close-actions from Listing 1.1

```
( :action Projector-setMute
  :parameters (?this - projector ?a1 - mute)
  :preconditions (holds ?this power on)
  :effect (and (not (holds ?this mute ?this.mute))
               (holds ?this mute ?a1) )                )
( :action PDFViewer-close
  :parameters (?this - pdfviewer ?a1 - filename)
  :preconditions (holds ?this open ?a1)
  :effect (not (holds ?this open ?a1))                 )
```

is defined as $S' = (S \setminus E^-) \cup E^+$. This add-over-delete semantic ensures that the combined definition of positive and negative effects leads to a well defined successor state.

4   Preliminary Experimental Evaluation

The spread of activation approach presented above is an interesting candidate for goal-based interaction for a decentralized control of dynamic and heterogeneous device ensembles, because it allows a modular specification and ad-hoc connection between all necessary components. Here we are not concerned with a formal treatment of the algorithm's properties, but rather with an evaluation in practice. A rigorous formal investigation will be subject to future work as discussed below. To evaluate our approach we used our laboratory, which is a prototype of a smart meeting room. It is equipped with 8 projectors, 8 projection screens, dimmable lamps, a video/audio matrix switcher, and several other sensors and actuators (shown in Figure 2). All available hardware components are encapsulated in Java classes and the resulting objects are deployed using our middleware. For the experiments wrt. our distributed planning approach, the implementation itself has not been modified, but only the above mentioned annotations were added to the class-files and later investigated via the Java reflection API. Instead of annotating the classes, it is also possible to specify preconditions and effects of methods in a separate file. This allows the direct use of third-party software components.

Fig. 2. The Smart Appliance Lab - a prototype of a future meeting room, equipped with various interconnected sensors and actuators

The tables 1, 2, 3, 4, and 5 contain an overview of five scenarios that have been used as test cases, describing setting, goal, and one possible action sequence. These scenarios where chosen with two aims in mind: (a) represent the daily usage of our laboratory in meeting situations and (b) show conflict resolution capabilities of spread-of-activation networks. They involve projectors and lamps, which can be turned on and off, projection screens, which can be lowered and raised, and a video/audio matrix switcher with 16 inputs and 16 outputs, which can route every input to every output.

The difference between the first and second scenario is the formulation of our goal: We want to give a presentation from our laptop, which is connected to table no. 1, on projection screen no. 3. We can express this goal on a device-level, which works without problems as every hardware component is represented by an annotated object. For the second scenario we provided the system with additional annotations about the preconditions of the effect "present table no. x on projection screen no. y". This concept enables the usage of goals on a

Table 1. scenario no. 1

setting	projector no. 3 off
	projection screen no. 3 up
	video/audio matrix switch output no. 3 unconnected
goal	projector no. 3 on
	projection screen no. 3 down
	video/audio matrix switch input no. 1 connected to output no. 3
actions	turn on projector no. 3
	move down projection screen no. 3
	connect input no. 1 to output no. 3 on video/audio matrix switch

Table 2. scenario no. 2

setting	projector no. 3 off
	projection screen no. 3 up
	video/audio matrix switch output no. 3 unconnected
goal	present table no. 1 on projection screen no. 3
actions	turn on projector no. 3
	move down projection screen no. 3
	connect input no. 1 to output no. 3 on video/audio matrix switch

Table 3. scenario no. 3 – the projection screen can only be lowered when lamp no. 1 and 2 are turned off

setting	lamp no. 1 on
	lamp no. 2 off
	lamp no. 3 off
	projection screen no. 4 up
goal	lamp no. 2 on
	lamp no. 3 on
	projection screen no. 4 down
actions	turn off lamp no. 1
	move down projection screen no. 4
	turn on lamp no. 2
	turn on lamp no. 3

higher level, but requires information about the setup of our laboratory and connections between the devices. Therefore we wrote a Java class to generate these annotations at runtime with the help of our middleware. To show the ability of spread-of-activation networks to handle conflicts we introduced in scenario no. 3 and 4 the restriction that projection screen no. 4 can only be lowered if lamp no. 1 and 2 are off. So in scenario no. 4 the system is required to undo an already satisfied condition and turn one lamp off and later back on to reach the goal. For scenario no. 5 the lecturer uses his own laptop and the stationary computer in the laboratory to give a presentation on two projection screens.

Table 4. scenario no. 4 – the projection screen can only be lowered when lamp no. 1 and 2 are turned off

setting	lamp no. 1 on
	lamp no. 2 on
	lamp no. 3 off
	projection screen no. 4 up
goal	lamp no. 2 on
	lamp no. 3 on
	projection screen no. 4 down
actions	turn off lamp no. 1
	turn off lamp no. 2
	move down projection screen no. 4
	turn on lamp no. 2
	turn on lamp no. 3

Table 5. scenario no. 5

setting	projector no. 1 off
	projector no. 3 off
	projection screen no. 1 up
	projection screen no. 3 up
	video/audio matrix switch output no. 1 unconnected
	video/audio matrix switch output no. 3 unconnected
goal	projector no. 1 on
	projector no. 3 on
	projection screen no. 1 down
	projection screen no. 3 down
	video/audio matrix switch input no. 10 connected to output no. 1
	video/audio matrix switch input no. 1 connected to output no. 3
actions	turn on projector no. 1
	turn on projector no. 3
	move down projection screen no. 1
	move down projection screen no. 3
	connect input no. 10 to output no. 1 on video/audio matrix switch
	connect input no. 1 to output no. 3 on video/audio matrix switch

To evaluate the runtime of the proposed system we measured the pure planning time, i.e., the time needed to find the action but without the time needed for executing them. The parameters to control the flow of activation energy were chosen by educated guessing and not changed between scenarios. Each scenario has been repeated 50 times, and the results are shown in Figure 3.

Our system found the next suitable action – between 3 and 6 are needed to satisfy a goal – in about 10 to 20 ms in average with the exception of scenario no. 2 with 20 to 30 ms. This outlier results probably from the structure of the scenario and the influence of the parameters. Overall an action sequence has

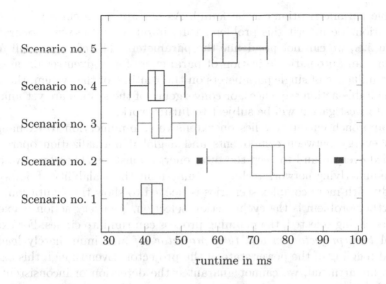

Fig. 3. box-and-whisker plot of the runtime in each scenarios

been found in less than 100 ms. These results indicate that distributed planning in smart environments is sufficient fast for scenarios with action sequences of length 6 or less. An evaluation of more complex scenarios is needed to show the limits of our system.

5 Open Problems and Future Work

The presented translation from annotations to planning operators enables the usage of distributed planning for deployed objects. Unfortunately, we are not yet able to provide any theoretical results about the behavior of the system. The flow of activation energy is controlled by the same five parameters introduced by Pattie Maes in [6]. During the spread of energy a normalization is applied to keep the overall energy in the network constant at value P_1 multiplied with the number of planning operators. P_2 defines the energy threshold for the execution of an operator. P_3 influences the amount of energy an operator receives for its effect needed in an open goal or unsatisfied precondition. P_4 controls how much energy an operator looses for its effect destroying a satisfied part of the goal or precondition. P_5 determines what energy an operator gets for its satisfied precondition from the current world state. Also an executable operator[2] will send a fraction of P_5 energy to propagate its influence on the world state.

It is yet unclear what an optimal set of parameters is, or whether it exists at all. In the work presented in [6] and [11] the set of available operators is assumed to be known and fixed. And it seems that for every set of operators

---

[2] All preconditions hold in the current world, but not all effects.

a suitable parametrization can be found. As our approach employs the spread of activation, we inherit this problem. But, in our case the set of operators is dynamic, i.e., we can not pre-define the parameters. Therefore, we will further investigate an automatic derivation of parameters for a given set of operators. Also the influence of single parameters on the runtime of the system, the ability to find suitable action sequences, or convergence of the system are yet unknown. A formal investigation will be subject to future work.

Our approach currently relies on extensive communication to exchange activation energy between components and a global normalization operation is performed every round to keep the total energy constant. Therefore, we expect that the underlying network technology may limit the scalability of our system. An study with more complex scenarios is needed to show this limitation.

A further problem is the cyclic action selection. As every action is executed right after being selected, the planning process can run into circles. For example the goal *turn projector on and turn projector off* will immediately lead to a repeated toggling of the power state of the projector. Even though this example seems a bit artificial, we cannot guarantee the detection of inconsistent goals and neither can we prevent the repeated execution of a loop. All those problems will be addressed by further research.

6   Conclusions

In this paper we addressed the problem of decentralized action selection in heterogeneous and dynamic software environments. We showed how to proceed from annotated objects towards a distributed planning system. Based on formal specification of the methods' preconditions and effects, we synthesize planning operators. By employing a spread of activation approach we were able to create a goal-directed behavior of a completely decentralized system within our laboratory. No modification of the available software components was necessary, but only a formal specification of the methods' preconditions and effects.

The preliminary experimental results are very encouraging. The system found a solution in all scenarios in a reasonable time. Nonetheless, much remains to be done. In particular, a thorough theoretical investigation of the employed spread of activation approach needs to be done. It is yet unclear under which conditions such a system terminates or converges to the desired solution. The underlying spread of activation approach is controlled by different parameters controlling the flow of energy within the network. For our work, different settings have been investigated until a sufficient solution has been found. But finding an optimal solution (if there is one) remains a challenge for the future. This is particularly interesting while scaling our approach to larger installation, as for example, beyond the setting of a single room.

We understand this work as a step towards automatically connecting ensembles of heterogeneous devices and services as already present in modern living and working environments, with their multitude of sensors and actuators. The proposed system enables a goal-directed behavior within such ensembles without any pre-configuration. Thus, it provides a necessary prerequisite for building truly intelligent ambient environments in which all available devices and services cooperate to support the users.

Acknowledgements. This work is supported by the german research foundation (DFG) within research training group 1424 MuSAMA.

References

1. Bader, S., Kirste, T.: An overview of the helferlein-system. Technical Report CS-03-12, Department of Computer Science, University of Rostock, Rostock, Germany (November 2012)
2. Bader, S., Nyolt, M.: A context-aware publish-subscribe middleware for distributed smart environments. In: Pfeifer, T., Stiller, B., O'Sulivan, D. (eds.) Proc. of MUCS 2012 (2012)
3. Eugster, P., Felber, P., Guerraoui, R., Kermarrec, A.: The many faces of publish/-subscribe. ACM Comput. Surv. 35, 114–131 (2003)
4. Gelernter, D.: Generative communication in linda. ACM Transactions on Programming Languages and Systems (TOPLAS) 7(1), 80–112 (1985)
5. Ghallab, M., Isi, C.K., Penberthy, S., Smith, D.E., Sun, Y., Weld, D.: PDDL - The Planning Domain Definition Language. Technical report, CVC TR-98-003/DCS TR-1165, Yale Center for Computational Vision and Control (1998)
6. Maes, P.: Situated agents can have goals. Robot. Auton. Syst. 6, 49–70 (1990)
7. Moos, D.: Umsetzung und Analyse eines dezentralen Planungssystems im Smart-Lab. Master's thesis, University of Rostock (2012)
8. Mühl, G., Fiege, L., Pietzuch, P.: Distributed Event-Based Systems. Springer (2006)
9. Papazoglou, M.: Web services: Principles and technology. Pearson Education (2008)
10. Patterson, L.I., Turner, R.S., Hyatt, R.M.: Construction of a fault-tolerant distributed tuple-space. In: Proceedings of the 1993 ACM/SIGAPP Symposium on Applied Computing: States of the Art and Practice, SAC 1993, pp. 279–285. ACM, New York (1993)
11. Plociennik, C.: Device cooperation in ad-hoc multimedia ensembles. PhD thesis, University of Rostock (October 2011)
12. Reisse, C., Kirste, T.: A distributed action selection mechanism for device cooperation in smart environments. In: Proceedings of the 4th International Conference on Intelligent Environments, Seattle, USA (2008)
13. Saffiotti, A., Broxvall, M.: Peis ecologies: Ambient intelligence meets autonomous robotics. In: Proceedings of the 2005 Joint Conference on Smart Objects and Ambient Intelligence: Innovative Context-Aware Services: Usages and Technologies, pp. 277–281. ACM (2005)

Taking Care of Elderly People with Chronic Conditions Using Ambient Assisted Living Technology: The ADVENT Perspective

Theodor Panagiotakopoulos[1], Christos Antonopoulos[2], Panayiotis Alefragkis[3], Achilles Kameas[1], and Stavros Koubias[2]

[1] e-CoMeT Lab, Hellenic Open University, Patras, Greece
(panagiotakopoulos,kameas)@eap.gr
[2] Electrical & Computer Engineering Dept, University of Patras, Patras, Greece
(cantonop,koubias)@ece.upatras.gr
[3] Computer & Informatics Engineering Dept, TEI of Western Greece, Antirio, Greece
alefrag@teimes.gr

Abstract. The population ageing trend has created an imperative need for ICT-based solutions that will support continuous care provision and help elders prolong the time they live independently in their own home environment. The ADVENT project aims at providing a comfortable, safe and secure environment to support the daily living of elders through a set of adaptive and demand-driven services. This paper presents the user and system requirements analysis results, based on which the high-level architecture of the core ADVENT system was drawn. This architecture highlights the home environment and the ambient intelligence platform, which are described in detail on a design level.

Keywords: Ambient Assisted Living, Home Monitoring, Sensor Networks.

1 Introduction

Due to advancements in medicine, average life expectancy is constantly growing in the last 50 years and the elderly population is expected to grow dramatically in the near future. Without receiving sufficient care and support, elderly are at risk of losing their independence and gradually being dispossessed from the ability to carry out everyday tasks and participate in social activity, thus becoming excluded from society. Consequently, the number of people requiring care will grow accordingly. On the other hand, elderly care around the globe is already suffering from skills shortage today [1]. Without new care models, this will lead to a large under-supply of care services in many regions.

The need for support of elderly people is highly individualized and often related to specific events, thus very variable over time. Care services, instead, are nowadays usually provided according to a fixed plan, which is not always effective. Matching service provision and need for support in a more sophisticated way could make care much more efficient, but has not been possible in the past due to the highly complex and dynamic nature of elderly care.

N. Streitz and P. Markopoulos (Eds.): DAPI 2014, LNCS 8530, pp. 474–485, 2014.

New technologies such as ambient home monitoring systems with automatic situation recognition together with mobile ICT solutions offer the possibility to completely change the way in which support for elderly people is being provided – from services provided according to fixed time-schedule to demand-driven assistance. This may improve a broad range of services from household services for independent living to highly specialized ambulatory palliative care. In this context, the ADVENT project aims at the development of an ICT system and associated service models for adaptive, demand-driven services for elderly care that provide enhanced in-house comfort, security and safety using advanced sensorial and wireless networking technologies.

The proposed system offers an intelligent platform for coordination and workflow management for care companies that create integrated care networks. Low priority events that can be automated will be supported through automatic detection by an integrated sensorial network that will be able to autonomously, accurately and immediately react to a variety of triggering events to enhance the living quality experience inside habitant area without outside intervention. High priority events, such as responding to an emergency call, unexpected bio-sensory data sequences or medication management will be provided through hybrid in-home / cloud care technology solutions alerting the caring company, which means help is always at hand. The ADVENT system targets at the remotely provisioning of high quality care services as well as autonomous operation aiming to maximize comfort and security and it complements in-home care services with around the clock monitoring so beneficiaries know that assistance is any time available.

2   User Requirements Analysis

A scenarios-based development process was selected for gathering requirements for the design and development of the ADVENT system and services. The conducted process aimed at identifying functional and non-functional requirements, including operational system parameters and constraints. In order to ensure the practical applicability of the ADVENT platform, a comprehensive analysis of care giving scenarios between potential beneficiaries was realized by Frontida Zois, a home care company that is partner of the project. The main concern was to decide the detailed directions that the added-value services should focus in order to primarily support the elders and healthcare professionals' needs. The analysis measured the importance of each feature in order to ensure system usability, reliability and responsiveness in a wide range of eventualities.

The requirements analysis revealed that there exist three main categories of elders that should be targeted. The first category are individuals that do not have a known chronic disease but prefer to live alone, have some minor kinetic problems due to age and would like to be supported sparsely both in their house and outside. The second category is persons which in addition to the requirements of the first category, have a known chronic disease, like cardiac problems and should be monitored by biosensors

476   T. Panagiotakopoulos et al.

around the clock. The third category is elders that have both health and kinetic problems, mainly stay at home and require full support for their daily living.

The above process helped us provide a detailed Use Case Diagram (Figure 1) and decide on a set of services that should be offered to the ADVENT system's end users. One non-functional requirement was that the system should be able to provide 24/7 support. This requirement was observed during extensive talks with elders and caregivers, as in the current operational state, where care givers stay with elders at home, the absence of support, even for short time periods, lead to extensive stress. Supportively, safety matters like unregulated temperature conditions for patient with breathing or heart problems can be automated and monitored systematically by sensorial systems. Temperature, lighting and humidity control as well as multi-parametric house monitoring that will enable accident preventions such as fire or gas leakage are required to create a holistic approach for assessing the overall condition of the elders. Finally, the analysis revealed that a baseline set of services, like timely usage of prescribed medication or an automated calendar that reminds elders of medical appointments can help both elders and caring companies optimize the support lifecycle.

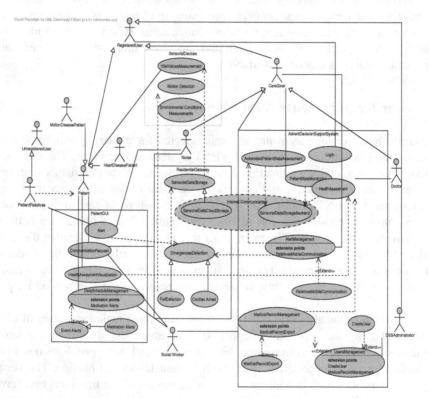

Fig. 1. ADVENT Requirements Use Case Diagram

3   System Architecture

The user and system requirement analysis paved the ground towards determining the core ADVENT system architecture that is shown in Figure 1 in a top-level view. Two major building blocks are distinguished: the home environment and the Ambient Intelligence Platform (AmIP). Each building block consists of several components that provide distinct functionalities for the provision of a coherent set of personalized services both to elders and their caregivers.

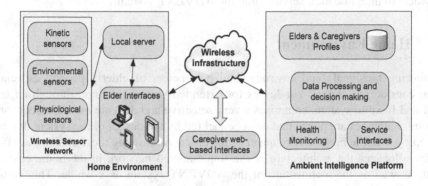

Fig. 2. ADVENT system architecture block diagram

The left building block of Figure 1 includes the Wireless Sensor Network, the local server and the elder interfaces. The wireless sensor network involves various heterogeneous sensing devices:

On-body sensors the that provide physiological signals, such as electrocardiograph (ECG), blood pressure and oxygen saturation, as well as kinetic parameters aiming to determine potential falls.

Environmental sensors providing ambient information, such as temperature, air-pressure and luminosity.

The local server is responsible of handling the sensor registration (type and number of sensors), initialization (e.g. specify sampling frequency), customization (e.g. run user specific calibration or user specific signal processing procedure upload), as well as the dynamical configuration of the sensor network according to the services needs. It collects all readings from sensing devices, pre-processes them (e.g. for removal of noise and deduction of redundant data) and transmits them to the AmIP for further processing and archiving. Furthermore, it has the responsibility to communicate the actions that must be performed by the system in the home environment. The local server also provides specially designed interfaces to the elders through which they interact with the system receiving service content and providing their feedback whenever this is required.

The AmIP hosts the elders and caregivers user profiles that contain various types of information, such as personal (e.g. preferences) and health-related (e.g. physiological thresholds indicating anomalies, health status history) data. Moreover, it processes the acquired information from the local server, in order to reason over the current overall status of the elder, performs decision making according to the identified status by determining the actions that should be performed based on predefined care plans, provides feedback to authorized persons for caregiving purposes and performs service personalization to tailor the offered services to the current needs and preferences of the users. It also includes the caregiver interfaces facilitating service content visualization, such as current health status and progress of the elders, as well as feedback provisioning and care plan administration. Finally, the AmIP provides service interfaces (APIs) that enable service delivery to the users and allow 3rd party service providers to integrate their services into the ADVENT system.

4   Home Environment

Monitoring biosignals and environmental parameters of elderly people, especially when considering chronic conditions for extended periods of time, through an efficient and flexible system, comprises a very sensitive and delicate task. Consequently, various challenges are posed that must be tackled by the design of the system that will be deployed in the home environment of the elder. Addressing these challenges effectively influences the architecture of the implemented network in the home environment, as well as the architecture of the ADVENT system as a whole. This section aims at exposing the main challenges concerning the home environment and respective choices made in the context of ADVENT.

Probably the most fundamental characteristic that the home environment network must have is non-instructiveness, in order to bring as less discomfort as possible to the elder. This is even more important to the scenarios ADVENT project focuses on, since elderly people tend to be more sensitive and less tolerant of sensors in the home environment. Size is of cornerstone importance in this matter and advancements in miniaturization of sensors and wireless network nodes are essential to this end. It is noted that size drastically affects the degree of obstruction when envisioning environmental parameters (e.g. temperature, air-pressure, open window-door detection sensors) that must be as "invisible" as possible in the surrounding environment, but it is of critical importance as well when considering sensors that must be constantly in direct contact with the user (e.g. biosensors, kinetic sensors). Number of sensors is also a quite significant parameter. Excessive number of sensors deployed in a small home environment may cause a feeling to the user of being watched all the time lacking of privacy. This diminishes the feeling of independence and self-reliance that are essential to the ADVENT objectives and, therefore, our focus is on implementing a small number of nodes able to acquire multiple signals. Wireless Sensor Networks (WSNs) represent one of the most active areas of networking during the last years able to meet these objectives. Indeed, miniaturization of sensors and very large scale circuits have led to a wide range of very small, smart and versatile nodes able to acquire a wide range of signals while being carried around or even been worn by the user for extended periods of time causing minimum discomfort [2-4].

Figure 2 depicts the main components of a WSN node effectively comprising its hardware architecture. Based on these components a series of design choices have been made with respect to the ADVENT's system objectives.

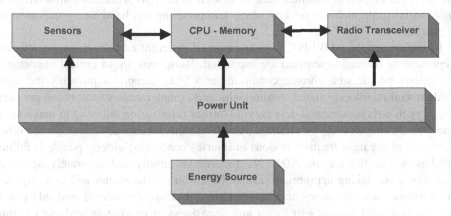

Fig. 3. Wireless Sensor Network Node's Components

Starting out the analysis from the right hand side of the figure, the "Transceiver" component is responsible for conveying data from and towards the node. To this end, the ADVENT system will rely on dominant wireless transmission technologies such as IEEE 802.15.4 and Bluetooth protocols, each offering respective advantages and key characteristics. They both operate on the 2.4GHz ISM frequency band, but while IEEE 802.15.4 main concern is very low complexity and energy consumption, Bluetooth provides a more complex communication protocol offering higher communication performance with higher energy consumption (although still lower that other well-known technologies such, as IEEE 802.11). A critical (especially when highly sensitive applications are considered) difference concerns the offered bandwidth. Regarding IEEE 802.15.4 this is 250Kbps, while Bluetooth based solutions vary significantly depending both on the version of the protocol supported and even more on the specific implementation's characteristics. Therefore, concerning data rates solutions covering a wide range from 300 Kbps up to 1.5 Mbps can be found. However, IEEE 802.15.4 being connectionless oriented offers higher flexibility when multi-hop communication is required.

Aiming to be as power conservative as possible, affordable and very small in size, WSN nodes processing capabilities rely on Micro Controller Units (MCUs) of significantly limited resources. Consequently, the ADVENT home environment will also be based on such MCUs widely used in typical WSN platforms. One such dominant solution is the Texas Instrument MSP430 MCU based on a 16bit RISC architecture offering very low power consumption performance since in active mode it draws 1.8mA while in sleep only 5.1μA. Of course such MCUs offer limited processing capabilities at frequencies of few tens of MHz and available program and RAM memory equal to 48KBytes and 10KBytes respectively [5,6]. ATMEL's AVR MCUs also comprise a frequently used solution of WSN networks. Relying on 8bit RISC architecture offer competitive operating frequencies and adequate memory to support WSN applications and software stacks [7]. Another critical characteristic of such MCUs is the support of adequate number as well as of appropriate resolution ADCs in order to integrate multiple sensors which comprise the left hand side component of Figure 2.

In the context of ADVENT, a wide range of different and diverse types of data (representing respective sensors) are supported. Biosignals are of critical importance for elderly people with chronic conditions and ECG comprises probably the most fundamental monitoring signal. Additionally and complementary to it, blood pressure and oxygen saturation related data provide further information allowing to make more fine grained and accurate monitoring, as well as emergencies detection. On the other hand, one of the most frequent reasons of injuries concerning elderly people is falling incidences. For this reason, ADVENT focuses on rapidly and accurately detecting such cases and taking appropriate actions based on accelerometer and gyro signals. Furthermore, several other characteristics of elders are considered and addressed, such as increased tendency to forget and uneasiness in moving around even within their home environment. Therefore, environmental sensors will be monitoring various parameters such as temperature, air-pressure, light, open window-door indicators, aiming to notify elders and caregivers of predefined abnormal situations.

Another critical component upon which the operation of all others depends, is the "power generation" which typical in WSN nodes is a small rechargeable battery. As seen in figure 1 each component is powered from a common energy source and thus, the aggregate power consumption of the sensors rather than the individual power consumption is the most important aspect. Indicatively, a WSN node can base its operation on small capacity batteries ranging from 450mAh up to 2AA batteries offering ~3300mAh. Extending the lifetime of a WSN node is very important with respect to the application requirements. Therefore, in the ADVENT project considerable effort is devoted upon methods and techniques minimizing the power wastage as well as selecting appropriate energy sources to meet the users' demands.

All the above concern hardware design characteristics of the nodes comprising the ADVENT home environment. However, being a research project ADVENT also led to important considerations as far as software design and development is concerned. In order to be able to study, evaluate and extended the performance and behavior of the home environment, it is crucial that home environment WSN nodes follow the open source paradigm. In that respect, all the software stack will be available enabling researchers and engineers to enhance, modify and extend its functionality as required. One the most well-known open source environment is the TinyOS operating system upon which numerous dominant WSN platforms are based [8]. TinyOS a flexible application specific operating system supporting concurrent execution of multiple programs though efficient scheduling while retaining a very small code footprint making ideal for low memory embedded systems such as WSN nodes. Figure 3 illustrates a high level architecture of a TinyOS based software stack.

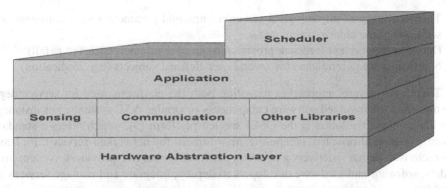

Fig. 4. A high level TinyOS based Software Stack Architecture

As indicated previously TinyOS is application specific, while an application comprises by a number of tasks and events. Events have higher priority and can preempt tasks or other events when enabled while tasks cannot preempt each other. Scheduler is a simple FIFO with limited number of tasks. When in "idle" state scheduler can shutdown contributing the power conservation. Through appropriate interfaces specific components related to acquiring monitored signals (i.e. Sensing component), transferring data through appropriate interfaces such as the wireless transceiver or a serial port (i.e. Communication component) and any other specific functionality, can be accessed. Another very powerful characteristic of TinyOS is the Hardware Abstraction Layer enabling to access a wide range of different hardware component though a unified interface thus increasing flexibility and limiting the needed for additional code for each specific device.

For ADVENT such an environment is adequate to enhance the efficiency of a node through various ways. On one hand, fall detection algorithms can be evaluated and a node will not have to steam continuous data of respective sensors (e.g. accelerometer), but only when an incident is identified. Such behavior could lead to drastic power conservations (assuming radio can be turned off when not used) as well as wireless channel bandwidth boost. On the other hand, data to be transmitted could be compressed on the sensor before actually transmitted also contributing significantly to performance enhancement. Finally, communication related evaluation concerning critical metrics such as throughput, delay and node lifetime can be carried with high accuracy. Such study is quite significant since the underlying communication channel must be able to convey the aggregated data workload without losses and in specific time constrained limits.

5   Ambient Intelligence Platform

The Ambient Intelligence Platform provides the core functionality of the ADVENT system for the delivery of differentiated types of Ambient Assisted Living (AAL) services. Driven by the user requirements analysis we concluded in three generic service packages aiming to provide an integrated solution to support the daily living of elders with chronic conditions:

1. Telemonitoring of physiological and environmental parameters and continuous assessment of the elder's overall status.
2. Decision support and feedback provisioning in case of emergencies (e.g. fall)
3. Notifications and reminders for several user-defined subjects (e.g. medication)

There exist several approaches regarding both the platforms used for service deployment and the involved software components in similar AAL systems. For instance, a widely adopted solution is the OSGi service platform [9], which offers a standardized, component-oriented, computing environment for networked services. Its main characteristic is that it delivers a common platform for service providers, content providers, software and hardware developers to deploy, integrate and manage services to a wide range of environments in a coordinated way. Another common practice is the use of web-based platforms [10]. ADVENT will adopt the later aiming to develop an open and standardized approach for communication and interaction of software components through web services, as well as to address heterogeneity and achieve interoperability between applications running in different devices and frameworks.

Regarding the software components an AAL middleware should have, these vary according to the developed system's requirements, limitations and objectives. In the context of ADVENT, we identified a primary group of components that will provide the required functionality for the effective realization of the aforementioned service packages. These span from the local server to the AmIP and are shown Figure 4, which illustrates the high level architecture of the ADVENT middleware.

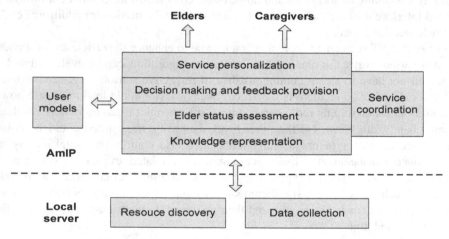

Fig. 5. ADVENT middleware high-level architecture

The resource discovery and data collection components are located at the local server and are responsible for managing sensing devices and provided data. Resource discovery is responsible of monitoring the entering/leaving of sensing devices in the local server's proximity. To achieve this a sensor registry is maintained that hosts information that describes each device, such as device communication protocol, information type it provides (e.g. location) and device address. This process offers the necessary scalability flexibility to the ADVENT middleware so that various sensing devices can be integrated during runtime in a seamless and transparent fashion. Furthermore, data collection deals with scheduling data acquisition allocating corresponding timers and pointers triggering data provision and includes the required APIs for data aggregation from sensors operating under different communication paradigms. It also administers data acquisition and their pre-processing and transmits them to the AmIP.

On the AmIP's side the main data processing is performed that involves the software components described below. The knowledge representation is crucial for systems that utilize diverse data from heterogeneous sources. It allows expressing acquired information in a semantic level and creates a unified vocabulary in a structured and organized form. There are several approaches to modeling contextual information acquired from various types of sensors, but especially in the healthcare domain the most widely used approach is ontologies. Ontologies offer many benefits against other solutions since they facilitate knowledge reuse and sharing among system components and count classes, inheritance, relationships between classes and instances as some of their major components. The ability to reason over relationships defined in an ontology and, therefore, relate instances to their abstracted types is the primary benefit of using ontologies.

In ADVENT we will develop a knowledge representation module based on ontologies, which will involve the systematic representation and processing of the elders' records, health condition and contextual information. Our aim is to develop the following ontologies: (a) Healthcare domain ontologies to encode health-related information, (b) Service ontologies to describe the services offered by the system; Youpi, a semantically-rich extension of UPnP service description will be used, (c) Ontology alignments to serve in matching heterogeneous domain and service ontologies; an attempt to use existing third party ontologies, such as WordNet [12] will be made and (d) Policies to encode decision making and privacy enforcement policies.

Elder status assessment realizes an inference process regarding the current overall status of the elder in a reactive manner. During this process low-level data directly acquired from sensors are transformed to high-level meaningful information that depicts the situation the elder is in. The term overall status is used due to the fact that in ADVENT we have three types of statuses concerning the elder: health, kinetic and environmental status. All are assessed by the same component either simultaneously or independently, but each of them has its own specific inference policies and action schemas. This reasoning process has been addressed by various approaches, such as rule-based and case-based reasoning, data mining techniques (e.g. bayesian networks) [13] and ontology-based reasoning [14]. In the context of ADVENT, several data mining algorithms and ontology-based reasoning will be examined to find the most suitable solution with regard to the project's scope and objectives.

Decision making and feedback provisioning utilizes information stemming from the elder status assessment component to define the actions that have to be performed according to the identified elder status. The action plan ranges from simple archiving when the elder's status is normal to alerting authorized caregivers to intervene and offer predefined types of treatment in case of worrying situations and emergencies.

For the purpose of this process, we plan to implement rule-based algorithms [15], while exploiting ontologies' reasoning potentials. The decision making process will be based on strict policies set by expertized medical staff following the medical protocol. These policies will define specific situation-dependent actions aiming to provide an integral care plan that will offer to the elders the feelings of safety and security throughout their daily lives.

Service personalization aims at a customized service delivery that will adapt to the current needs, requirements and preferences of the users. Service personalization has two dimensions. The first concerns the service content and the second the way the service will be presented to the user depending on time, location, surroundings and the access device. It is closely related with the user modeling process through which a user's information is represented electronically in a structured way. We consider several types of information the user models will host, such as health, personal, contextual, service-related and application specific data. Due to the fact static user models may fail to represent the actual user preferences in a temporal span, we are already focusing on developing dynamic user models which will be both implicitly evolving through processed context information and explicitly updating through user feedback.

Finally, service coordination is responsible of managing and orchestrating the interaction among the software components employed in the ADVENT middleware. Such interaction is essential for efficient service delivery, since each service is based on the smooth cooperation of various components. In addition, as the system evolves several new components may appear in its environment and through the service coordination these can be integrated to serve hybrid architectures for added value service provisioning. For this reason, this component includes specific APIs that allow third party service providers to use ADVENT as a bridge to offer their services.

6   Discussion and Future Directions

In this paper, we outlined the requirements analysis process that revealed different elder target groups, delineated a group of services that covers a range of their needs and pointed out critical design and development directions. Our focus was to collect the requirements employing a user-driven approach, in order to foster practical applicability and ensure a high level of efficiency and acceptance. The results of the requirements analysis served as the basis for creating the core ADVENT system architecture that consists of two major parts: the home environment and the ambient intelligence platform. We further analyzed the main design and implementation details of the key components of these parts, which are expected to undergo several modifications throughout the next phases of the ADVENT project that is currently in its design phase.

The next steps of the ADVENT project, concern the development of subsystems and components based on the described design principles, as well as the integration of a mobile subsystem to monitor the elders while being outdoors and facilitate mobile service provisioning. Subsequently, we will perform individual subsystem and interoperability tests and deploy the sensorial networks to pilot users, providing feedback for the potential of the installation to support the required services.

Acknowledgments. The research described in this paper has been funded by the project ADVENT (MIS 11ΣYN_10_1433), which is co-financed by the European Union (European Regional Development Fund) and Greek national founds through the Operational Program Competitiveness and entrepreneurship (OPC II). The authors would like to thank the fellow researchers in the ADVENT project.

References

1. Panagiotakopoulos, T., Theodosiou, A., Kameas, A.: Exploring Ambient Assisted Living Job Profiles. In: 6th International Conference on Pervasive Technologies Related to Assistive Environments, 17. ACM, Rhodes (2013)
2. Alemdar, H., Ersoy, C.: Wireless sensor networks for healthcare: A survey. Elsevier Computer Networks 54, 2688–2710 (2010)
3. Lecointre, A., Dragomirescu, D., Dubuc, D., Grenier, K., Pons, P., Aubert, A., Muller, A., Berthou, P., Gayraud, T., Plana, R.: Miniaturized Wireless Sensor Networks. In: International Semiconductor Conference, Sinaia, pp. 13–17 (2006)
4. Jin, M.-H., Lee, R.-G., Kao, C.-Y., Wu, Y.-R., Hsu, D.F., Dong, T.-P., Huang, K.-T.: Sensor Network Design and Implementation for Health Telecare and Diagnosis Assistance Applications. In: 11th International Conference on Parallel and Distributed Systems, pp. 407–411. IEEE, Fukuoka (2005)
5. WSN TelosB Platform, http://www.willow.co.uk/TelosB_Datasheet.pdf
6. WSN Shimmer Platform, http://www.shimmersensing.com/
7. WSN Platform for Medical Application, http://www.cooking-hacks.com/documentation/tutorials/ehealth-biometric-sensor-platform-arduino-raspberry-pi-medical
8. TinyOS WSN Operating System: http://www.tinyos.net/
9. Panagiotakopoulos, T., Lymberopoulos, D., Manolessos, G.: Monitoring of patients suffering from special phobias exploiting context and profile information. In: 8th International Conference on Bioinformatics and Bioengineering (BIBE 2008), pp. 1–6. IEEE, Athens (2008)
10. Katehakis, D.G., Sfakianakis, S.G., Kavlentakis, G., Anthoulakis, D.N., Tsiknakis, M.: Delivering a lifelong integrated electronic health record based on a service oriented architecture. IEEE Transactions on Information Technology in Biomedicine 11(6), 639–650 (2007)
11. Wordnet, http://www.w3.org/TR/2006/WD-wordnet-rdf-20060619/
12. van den Broek, G., Cavallo, F., Wehrmann, C.: AALIANCE Ambient Assisted Living Roadmap. In: Ambient Intelligence and Smart Environments. IOS Press (2010)
13. Banu, G., Erturkmen, L., Dogac, A., Olduz, M., Tasyurt, I., Yuksel, M., Okcan, A.: SAPHIRE: A Multi-Agent System for Remote Healthcare Monitoring through Computerized Clinical Guidelines. In: Annicchiarico, R., Cortes, U., Urdiales, C. (eds.) Agent Technology and e-Health. Whitestein Series in Software Agent Technologies and Autonomic Computing, vol. 41, pp. 25–44. Birkhäuser, Basel (2008)
14. Bikakis, A., Antoniou, G.: Rule-Based Contextual Reasoning in Ambient Intelligence. In: Dean, M., Hall, J., Rotolo, A., Tabet, S. (eds.) RuleML 2010. LNCS, vol. 6403, pp. 74–88. Springer, Heidelberg (2010)

User Indoor Location System with Passive Infrared Motion Sensors and Space Subdivision

Marios Sioutis and Yasuo Tan

School of Information Science
Japan Advanced Institute of Science and Technology, Ishikawa, Japan
{smarios,ytan}@jaist.ac.jp

Abstract. The use of indoor location information has the potential to enable ground-breaking smart services in a home environment. The objective of this research is to design a relatively inexpensive real time indoor location system which also poses no threat to user privacy. We propose an indoor location system that uses commodity parts such as infrared motion sensors and the idea of space subdivision. By evaluating the state of the sensors involved in a scene, it is further possible to evaluate each unique area and extract those that the user is most likely to be located at. In conclusion, despite a couple of flaws that should be addressed, the proposed system achieves its targets while maintaining an acceptable level of accuracy.

Keywords: indoor location system, infrared motion sensor, space subdivision, smart home.

1 Introduction

Compared to outdoor location systems where GPS is the de facto standard, there is no such standard for user indoor location systems. In the past many solutions have been proposed, based on technologies such as active RFID[5], cameras [4](survey), ultrasound[2], passive infrared sensors (most notably ThiLo[3]) as well as a number of solutions based on the Received Signal Strength Indication of different wireless systems (Wi-Fi[7], Bluetooth[1], ZigBee[6]). It is the authors conviction that such indoor location systems will be an indispensable part of a platform on which other smart services can be developed and assist the user in his everyday activities.

In this paper, a real time indoor location system for users utilizing passive infrared motion sensors that are readily available in the market and space subdivision is proposed. The rationale for such a system becomes quite clear when looking at the advantages of the system.

First, compared to indoor location systems that utilize cameras, the proposed system does not pose a threat to the user's privacy. For many users, the possibility of network enabled cameras being exploited and their streams subverted is enough of a deterrent for installing such systems, further hindering the adoption of smart technologies in the home environment.

N. Streitz and P. Markopoulos (Eds.): DAPI 2014, LNCS 8530, pp. 486–497, 2014.

Fig. 1. The sensor pod design and the final 3D printed prototype

Second, in contrast to systems that use active or passive transceivers the user is free from wearing or holding any such transceiver which is in turn one less hurdle towards the deployment of indoor location systems.

Third, due to the design of the sensor pods used in this system, it is unaffected by typical household furniture and the deployment cost is minimal. Furthermore, the cost of each sensor pod prototype can be roughly estimated at 200 USD, a cost that can further be suppressed.

Fourth, the proposed system is extendable and can be easily customized. Extending the coverage area is as simple as adding more sensor pods to the desired rooms. Furthermore, the position as well as the actual shape of the sensor pod can be customized to better fit the peculiarities of any room.

Finally, in contrast to ThiLo[3], no initialization step is necessary.

The proposed system has two significant downsides. First, compared to other solutions based on cameras and active/passive transceivers, the accuracy of the reported user location may be inferior. However, it can be argued that the accuracy of the predictions provided by this system is enough for developing location aware services in the home environment. Furthermore, the current system has no means of deducing the identity of a user.

The remaining sections of this paper discuss the technical aspects of the system and its design, the idea of subdividing space and how it is utilized in the proposed system, sensor behavior, the algorithm used for evaluating areas, the experimental setup and evaluation methodology, points of consideration and finally conclusion and future work.

2 Sensor Pod Design and Technical Considerations

The proposed system uses the AMN3111 passive motion sensor produced by Panasonic as the basic unit of collecting information. This sensor has a wide

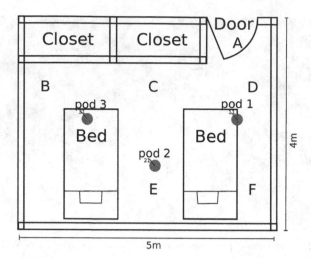

Fig. 2. Room details and sensor pod positioning

sensing angle of 90° degrees, a maximum detection distance of 5 meters as well as good response times. Our system utilizes these sensors as a cluster of 7 sensors, mounted on a sensor pod. Multiple such sensor pods can then be affixed to the ceiling of a room to provide user location information. The 7 sensors of a sensor pod are positioned as seen in Fig. 1. The first sensor faces downwards towards the floor, whereas the remaining six sensors are set so as to have an angle of 60° degrees with respect to ceiling plane and are spaced out evenly every 60° degrees on the half-spherical fixture of the sensor pod.

Three sensor pods where affixed to the ceiling of a room, as seen in Fig. 2. Excluding the first sensor of each sensor pod, the orientation of the second sensor is marked[1] as a short black line, along with the sensor's assigned ID tag. The remaining sensors are evenly spaced out by 60° degrees.

For controlling the sensors and transmitting data, one Arduino Fio board, an XBEE low power wireless module as well as a custom circuit board for multiplexing the output of the sensors were used. For collecting the data, one Arduino Fio equiped with an XBEE module was connected to a laptop. The raw data gathered for one of the experimental runs can be seen in Fig. 3. A green round mark shows that the given sensor is in a logical "HIGH" state, whereas a red triangle mark signifies a logical "LOW" state. These states are indicative of the presence or the absence of a user.

Finally, visualization of the coverage area and location results was achieved with custom software developed using Java and Open GL ES. The sensor pod design and video processing was done in Blender, a powerful open-source software mainly targeted at 3D modeling.

---

[1] Also marked with a small red arrow on the prototype unit.

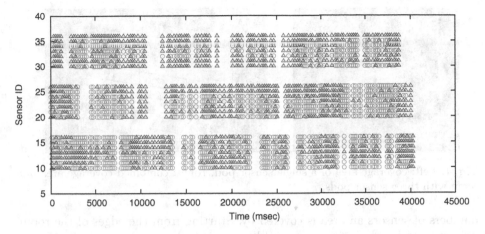

Fig. 3. The timeline of sensor events for the first run

3   Space Subdivision

The design of the sensor pod combined with the wide $90°$ degrees coverage angle of the sensors gives rise to some very interesting properties. Sensors 2 to 7 are spaced evenly in a circle pattern with their direction changing by $60°$ degrees with respect to the elevation axis, thus creating an overlapping area of $30°$ degrees between two consecutive sensors. Furthermore, the existence of the first sensor which is pointing downwards further subdivides space in areas that are "close" to the actual sensor pod and those that are further away. From the above, it is obvious that even with a single sensor pod useful deductions regarding the user's position in relation to the sensor pod can be made. The coverage area of a single sensor pod can be seen in Fig. 4 (left).

Further increase of the number of sensor pods in a scene leads to a rapid growth of the number of unique areas in which the scene space can be subdivided. During experimentation, the number of unique areas that were reported for the experiment scene used in the evaluation ranged from 700 to 850 unique areas. The number of unique areas varies depending on the coverage angle of the sensors, the location of the sensor pods as well as the furniture in the scene.

The octree used to model the scene and the coverage area of the sensors is 8 levels deep, with the nodes of the deepest level having a cube size of only 4 cm^3. By keeping track of which sensors cover which nodes, it is possible to extract the overlapping regions among sensors, thus creating unique detection areas for a given combination of active sensors.

One more topic worth mentioning is the number of sensors each unique area is covered by. Most areas are covered by anywhere between five and fourteen unique sensors, as shown in Fig. 4 (right). In this figure, areas that where covered by less than five sensors have been pruned from the scene, as such areas were marginal and very close to the ceiling, thus not corresponding to a realistic position for the user. The progression and change of the colors signifies the increase in the

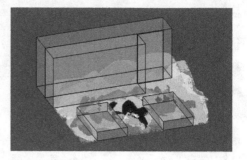

Fig. 4. Left: coverage area of a single sensor pod. Right: combined coverage area of a room with three sensor pods.

numbers of sensors an area is covered by. Starting from the edges of the room, light grey and gray areas are covered by five and six areas respectively. Moving progressively to the center of the room, areas colored black, green and white are covered by thirteen, fourteen and more than fourteen sensors respectively.

4   Sensor Behavior

4.1   Behavior Characteristics of an Ideal Digital Sensor

Before we look further into the specifics of how the infrared motion sensors that were deployed in this system work, the case for an ideal digital sensor must be made. Such an ideal sensor is able to report whether a user can be detected in its coverage area, even if the user is partially in this area. The absence of the user should also be reported as soon as the user leaves the area. Furthermore, such an ideal sensor must always report that a user is detected, even if the user stops moving entirely. The presence or absence of a user are communicated as a digital output of "HIGH" and "LOW" respectively.

As part of testing, sensor data from such an ideal sensor were generated by representing the user as a rectangular cuboid box that is 1.75 meters tall and 40 centimeters wide. This virtual user moved inside the modeled scene and the sensor data that was generated was fed back to the visualization system. As expected, the location prediction transitioned smoothly from one location to the next with great accuracy, verifying the core idea of the proposed location system.

Despite the arguably favorable results that such a sensor would produce, to our knowledge such a sensor has yet to be invented. The actual sensors used in this system have somewhat different behavior than the ideal sensor, which leads to certain complications. The characteristics of the sensors deployed will be discussed in the next section.

4.2   Behavior Characteristics of the AMN3111 Sensor

In stark comparison to the ideal sensor, the behavior of the AMN3111 sensor differs greatly in two aspects. First, the time this sensor needs to report the absence of a user exiting its coverage area varies from a couple hundred milliseconds to as many as a couple of seconds, depending on the distance from the sensor and the relative angle the user is exiting the region from.

The second aspect in which the AMN3111 sensor differs from the ideal digital sensor is the behavior regarding a user that remains relatively motionless inside the sensor coverage area. In such cases, the AMN3111 will stop reporting the presence of the user inside the area after a couple of seconds (or even longer, again depending on the relative position of the user to the sensor).

Both of these behavioral differences produce undesired side effects and interfere with the location prediction algorithm and should be accounted for. Their exact effects as well as the countermeasures that can be taken to avoid them are described in Sect. 7.

5   Algorithm Explanation

The proposed algorithm can be split into two parts, a sensor-independent area evaluation strategy and a sensor-dependent sensor state evaluation part. These are described in the next two sections.

5.1   Area Evaluation Strategy

The sensor-independent part of the proposed algorithm deals with the evaluation of each individual area. This part depends on the deduction of each sensor state and its assignment of a numerical value by the sensor-dependent part of this algorithm.

The sensor-independent part uses a set of key-pair values. Each entry in this set corresponds to a sensor (key) and the actual assigned numerical value for its given state (value). The sensor independent part then proceeds to compare this set of key-value pairs against each unique area in the scene.

At the start of the algorithm, the score for an area is zero. For each key-value pair, if the sensor is covering that unique area then the score for this area is increased by that sensor's current value, else that amount is subtracted. The top 2% of the areas with the highest scores is then visualized.

5.2   Sensor State Evaluation

The sensor-dependent part of this algorithm deals with the detection of the state the sensors in the current scene are in and the assignment of numerical values to these states.

The current implementation defines seven states, *RISING*, *UPTRIGGER*, *UP*, *FALLING*, *DOWNTRIGGER*, *DOWN* and *FLUX*. The first three states are associated with the presence of a user in its coverage area. In the *RISING* state, the sensor transitioned recently from a "LOW" state to a "HIGH" state in the past 300 msecs and has a numerical value of 30. In the *UPTRIGGER* state, the sensor transitioned to a "HIGH" state more than 300 msecs ago, thus it can be deduced with fair certainty that a user has indeed entered the area recently. Its numerical value is 100. The *UP* state shows that the sensor has been in the "HIGH" state for more than a second continuously. It has an associated value of 50.

The next three states are the logical equivalents of the first three states with the only difference being that the sensor transitions from a logical "HIGH" state to a logical "LOW" state, thus detecting the absence of a user. These states are assigned negative values equal to those of their equivalent positive states.

The *FLUX* state shows that in regards to this sensor, three (or more) discrete and logically alternating events have occurred in the past second, thus the sensor is in a state of flux, unable to deduce whether a user is in its coverage area or not. This state is associated with a numeric value of five, a slightly positive value, because the user is probably located at the edges of this sensor's detection area. It is not uncommon for a sensor to transition to a flux state first before it is possible to reliably determine its state.

This part of the algorithm also assigns a certain percentage bonus to the sensor score, depending on the time elapsed since the sensor entered its given state. The sensors are chronologically sorted and the sensors that most recently transitioned to logically "HIGH" states may get up to a hundred percent bonus to their base score, with the bonus assigned dropping linearly. Similar logic applies to the sensor states associated with user absence.

This part of the algorithm is sensor and circuit dependent in the sense that, other passive infrared motion sensors may exhibit different behaviors that can possibly be expressed better with a different time scale or a different set of states and transitions. Although our conviction is that the proposed states reflect the behavior of the AMN3111 sensor well, this may very well not be the case for other sensors.

6   Experiment Setup, Evaluation and Results

6.1   Experimental Setup

The experiments described later in this section where conducted in a single room as seen in Fig. 2. The room is 5 meters long and approximately 4 meters wide. The ceiling is 2.4 meters tall. The modeling of the room was based on exact floor plans and the space taken up by the wardrobe and beds is properly taken into consideration and removed from the scene's octree.

The positions of the sensor pods was chosen so that they would create an almost equilateral triangle, with one of the sensor pods slightly displaced to the right. The reasoning behind this formation is that it would create the most evenly distributed unique areas. Furthermore, the slight displacement of the rightmost sensor pod allows for better coverage of the door area.

In total, four recorded runs were performed, each one filmed by one camera view point. The paths taken for each of these runs can be seen in Table 1. A parenthesis around a letter means that the user passed through that given point

Table 1. Run paths

Run Name	Run Points
First run	E, (C), (D), A, (D), F, D , C, E
Second run	B, (C), D, (C), B
Third run	B, (C), D, A, D, (C), B
Fourth run	F, (D) , A, (D), F

without stopping, otherwise the user briefly stopped at that point for a brief amount of time (2 to 4 seconds).

In the first run, the user takes a more complicated path with more temporary stops compared to the other runs. Runs two and four were selected to test the accuracy of the system for straight paths; in run two the user walks along the length of the room, whereas in run four the user walks along the sort side of the room towards the door. Run three is a combination of run two and four, where the user walks along the length of the room, but makes a right turn towards the door. In all of the runs the user returns to its original position.

6.2 Evaluation

To evaluate the accuracy of the system, a qualitative comparison between the output of the visualization software and the actual footage is performed. For this purpose, virtual camera points were set up in the visualization software that matched the orientation, position and field of view of the original camera used to take the actual footage. Then, using the blue color as a channel key, transparency is added and the visualization output is superimposed on the original video.

For comparison purposes, the resulting video is also rendered as still pictures, which were used for evaluation. For the first run, ten frames per second were used. Eventually, this was deemed to not significantly increase the accuracy of the results, and for the second, third and fourth runs three frames per second of running video were considered adequate.

Each frame was assessed qualitatively in a five-rank scale, from excellent (five points) to bad (one point). The definition for each grade is as follows:

- excellent: the reported location matches and it is tightly focused around the user,
- good: the reported location matches, with a small percentage of it pointing out towards another direction
- fair: the reported location matches but it is relatively broad and/or visualized as floating, or the user is slightly outside the reported location (less than 50 cm) but the area still remains focused
- poor: the user is clearly outside of the reported location but less than a meter away
- bad: the user is clearly more than a meter away from the reported location, or the reported location is too wide and/or fragmented to be meaningful.

An example for each of the above categories can be seen in Fig. 5

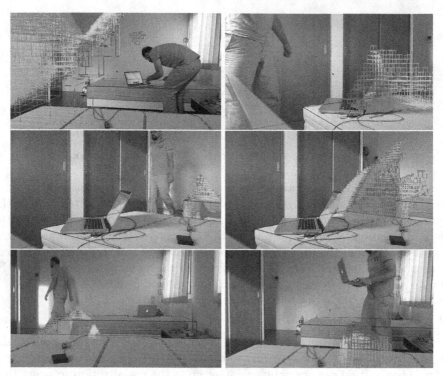

Fig. 5. Examples of evaluation frames.
Top left: a bad frame. Top right: a poor frame.
Middle left: a fair frame (near miss). Middle right: a fair frame (large area).
Bottom left: a good frame. Bottom right: an excellent frame.

Table 2. Experimental results

Run	Total Frames	Avg. Score	Bad	Poor	Fair	Good	Excellent
first	497	3.62	22	90	107	112	166
second	57	3.07	3	17	17	13	7
third	88	3.11	13	11	31	19	14
fourth	74	3.20	6	11	32	12	13

6.3   Run Results

The results of the four runs can be seen in Table 2.

The results are broken down to the total number of frames evaluated, an average score as well as the number of frames for each of the five categories. What is not readily apparent from Table 2 is the fact that most of the 'bad' states occur close to the start and end segments of each run. This can be seen clearly in Fig. 6, which represents the timeline for the state detection of the first run. 14 out of 22 bad states occur near the beginning of the run and another 4

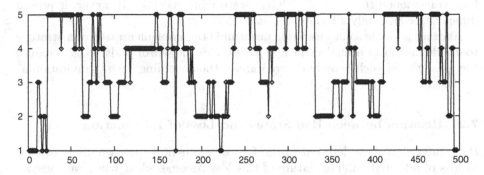

Fig. 6. State detection timeline for the first run

bad states occurring at the end of the run. Thus, only in 4 out of the 497 frames the actual reported user location was 'bad'.

On average, the system achieved a score more than 3 in all performed runs. This indicates that the average quality of the reported location should fit somewhere between the fair and good scales explained earlier. As a result, it is not a stretch to claim that the inaccuracy of the positions reported by the system is less than 50 centimeters.

7   Points of Consideration

There are two types of undesired side effects that manifest in this system, and the cause for both of them can be linked to the behavior the AMN3111 sensors exhibit. These side effects are explained in the next two subsections.

7.1   Strong "Gravitational" Field Effect

The first side effect is the presence of what can be casually described as a strong "gravitational" field directly below the installation point of each sensor pod. When the user walks away from such a gravitational field, the location projection the system reports has the tendency to lag behind the actual user location, seemingly unable to escape the "gravitational" field. This phenomenon is very pronounced in the second run as well as some parts of the forth run.

The reason for this phenomenon is the time delay observed between the user leaving a specific area and the actual sensor reporting this absence, as mentioned in sect. 4.2. When the user leaves such an area, some sensors linger longer to a "HIGH" state thus creating false positives. As a consequence, during the evaluation step of each area, the areas in the "gravitational" field that also happen to be covered by a larger number of sensors tend to be more favorably evaluated, earning higher scores. The bonus scoring strategy for the sensor does help alleviate this problem to a small extent, by assigning very small bonuses to areas that have been constantly on for a long time and awarding higher scores to sensors that transitioned to a logical "HIGH" state more recently. However, it proved difficult to completely alleviate this side effect.

Another possible solution to this problem is the implementation of a strategy to decide the most optimal shape and position for the sensor pods, so as to reduce the existence of such heavily covered areas, thus avoiding such "gravitational" fields.

7.2   Relation between Bad States and Loss of Information

Bad states that were detected in the four experimental runs are all associated to loss of information. The nature of this loss becomes clear when we consider the behavior of a sensor while the user remains motionless inside its coverage area: the sensor will eventually transition to a logical "LOW" state. This has the exact opposite effect from the previously described strong "gravitational" field: areas that are covered by multiple sensors now are heavily penalized as more and more sensors turn off, and the system favors marginal areas at the sides of the room. Such areas are covered by only a few sensors and are less heavily penalized when the number of sensors that go off increase.

As a counter measure, in the four runs presented earlier, a simple method was used: as soon as a sensor pod would report less than two active sensors, the state of the sensors for that sensor pod was frozen in time, representing a "last known good state". This technique served well to alleviate this problem when the user stands still during a run. Ultimately though, when a run comes at its end, all sensors transition to a logical "LOW" state. At this point it is not uncommon that less than six sensors are frozen in a logical "HIGH" state. In conjunction with the fact that most unique areas are covered by significantly more than six sensors, this loss of information prevents the system from making an accurate prediction when it comes to static users.

An algorithm that solves this end state problem can be implemented with relative ease. Such an algorithm would freeze the user location prediction as soon as the number of active sensors in a scene runs below a certain cut-off point. This cut-off point should take into consideration the distribution of the number of sensors the unique areas are covered by and adjust accordingly.

8   Conclusion and Future Work

In this paper, an indoor location system that utilizes the AMN3111 passive infrared motion sensors and subdivision of space was proposed. A qualitative evaluation of the system for four experimental runs showed that the system is fairly accurate and on average it reports a user location that reflects reality with possible small deviations.

The system compares favorably when compared against other location systems that do not use motion sensors in terms of user privacy, ease of use (no passive/active tags or badges are needed), extensibility, customization, deployment and cost. In comparison to ThiLo[3], there is no need for an initialization step. However, other solutions are capable of more accurate predictions and user identification.

As shortcomings of the system, two side effects were reported: strong "gravitational" fields and the relation between end states and loss of information. Both problems are closely related to the behavior of the sensors used in this system.

As future work, further research needs to be conducted in order to solve the two previously mentioned problems. Furthermore, alternative area evaluation methods such as particle filters should be evaluated and contrasted with the current implementation. Furthermore, a great challenge for this system would be to report the location of more than one user in a single room simultaneously. Lastly, an auxiliary user identification mechanism that would be used in conjunction with this system should be pursued.

References

1. Feldmann, S., Kyamakya, K., Zapater, A., Lue, Z.: An indoor bluetooth-based positioning system: Concept, implementation and experimental evaluation. In: Zhuang, W., Yeh, C.H., Droegehorn, O., Toh, C.T., Arabnia, H.R. (eds.) International Conference on Wireless Networks, pp. 109–113. CSREA Press (2003)
2. Harter, A., Hopper, A., Steggles, P., Ward, A., Webster, P.: The anatomy of a context-aware application. In: Proceedings of the 5th Annual ACM/IEEE International Conference on Mobile Computing and Networking, MobiCom 1999, pp. 59–68. ACM, New York (1999), http://doi.acm.org/10.1145/313451.313476
3. Hauschildt, D., Kirchhof, N.: Advances in thermal infrared localization: Challenges and solutions. In: 2010 International Conference on Indoor Positioning and Indoor Navigation (IPIN), pp. 1–8 (September 2010)
4. Mautz, R., Tilch, S.: Survey of optical indoor positioning systems. In: 2011 International Conference on Indoor Positioning and Indoor Navigation (IPIN), pp. 1–7 (September 2011)
5. Ni, L., Liu, Y., Lau, Y.C., Patil, A.: Landmarc: Indoor location sensing using active rfid. In: Proceedings of the First IEEE International Conference on Pervasive Computing and Communications, PerCom 2003, pp. 407–415 (March 2003)
6. Sugano, M., Kawazoe, T., Ohta, Y., Murata, M.: Indoor localization system using rssi measurement of wireless sensor network based on zigbee standard. In: Fapojuwo, A.O., Kaminska, B. (eds.) Wireless and Optical Communications. IASTED/ACTA Press (2006)
7. Xiao, J., Wu, K., Yi, Y., Ni, L.: Fifs: Fine-grained indoor fingerprinting system. In: 2012 21st International Conference on Computer Communications and Networks (ICCCN), pp. 1–7 (July 2012)

A Conceptual Framework for Augmented Smart Coach Based on Quantified Holistic Self

Hyoseok Yoon[1], Young Yim Doh[2], Mun Yong Yi[3], and Woontack Woo[1]

[1] KAIST UVR Lab., Daejeon, Korea
{hyoseok.yoon,wwoo}@kaist.ac.kr
[2] Graduate School of Culture Technology, KAIST, Daejeon, Korea
yydoh@kaist.ac.kr
[3] Department of Knowledge Service Engineering, KAIST, Daejeon, Korea
munyi@kaist.ac.kr

Abstract. Augmented human (AH) refers to a research direction of enhancing or augmenting human abilities by human-computer-integration. At its core, AH attempts to monitor and interpret domains of knowledge about human nature to actuate appropriate augmentation. We envision AH as a human-centered approach and a major milestone to be accomplished for ubiquitous virtual reality (i.e., combining the real human with assets of virtual environments). As a concrete example of augmenting human with intellectual abilities, we present a conceptual framework for augmented smart coach. In the proposed framework, multi-dimensional life experiences of human, are systematically captured, assessed, refined, encoded, and quantified into basis patterns of digital holistic self (D-Personality). By doing so, quantified holistic self serves a purpose of a dynamic user profile, which is exploited and explored by anthropomorphic and adaptive augmented interfaces for coaching the needs of individual. We highlight and identify foreseeable technical challenges for future research direction revolving around the presented framework.

1 Introduction

Ubiquitous virtual reality (UVR) [1] and several research projects enriched visual and intellectual capability of users by combining real and virtual environments over the last decade. In the early stages of UVR, visionary interaction technology was developed and simulated using built-in displays, devices, and sensors of smart spaces with smart phones. Now we are entering the next stages of UVR as smart wearable devices and sensors (e.g., smart watch, smart glass, and smart accessories) incrementally encroach on the saturating smart phone market to take supremacy in the coming era of wearable augmented reality. The compulsory adjustments to the next stages of UVR include dealing with increased computation power of smart wearables and personal cloud, and computational sensemaking of increased volume and velocity of personal big data generated in variety of forms. An explosion of personal big data through smart wearables, attracts end-users to keep track of personal activities for self-tracking

N. Streitz and P. Markopoulos (Eds.): DAPI 2014, LNCS 8530, pp. 498–508, 2014.

and self-awareness by numbers [2] known as quantified-self movement[1] and paves
the road to research and development of practical personalization through personal analytics[2] and personal informatics [3,4]. We believe that the next level of
interactions for ubiquitous virtual reality requires interdisciplinary and concen-
trated research on augmented human [5] by promptly monitoring user activity,
quantifying unique user patterns and delivering effective enhancements. In this
paper we present a concrete example of augmenting human in intellectual abilities through a conceptual framework for augmented smart coach. The presented
framework is consisted of components that systematically encode a disparate
sources of heterogeneous personal big data into quantified holistic self and interpret quantified holistic self to be exploited and explored by augmented smart
coach in wearable augmented reality. We review related works, present details of
the framework and scenarios, and discuss technical challenges and issues followed
by concluding remarks.

2   Related Work

In this section we briefly review relevant previous works on structural support
for augmented agents and frameworks in the context of personal big data and
quantified self.

Nagao and Rekimoto proposed agent augmented reality [6] where a special
kind of software agent called a real world agent, augments the real world with
information worlds via functions of situation awareness, user personalization,
situated conversation, learning, adaptation, and collaboration. Nagao and Katsuno further expanded the concept to agent augmented community [7] which
integrates cyberspace, the real world, and personal contexts for augmented communication via situation-aware and personalized agents. Rekimoto introduced
research direction of augmented human [5] and his research group is active in
augmented human research and applications [8,9].

Framework-level support for augmented agent is simulated mostly through
mobile devices. AR puppet is a hierarchical animation framework for context-
aware animated agents where the real world attributes can be used as input
modalities and affect animated agents in appearance and behavior patterns [10].
Ubiquitous AR agent [11] overcame limitations of AR puppet by adding supports
for migration of agents, ambient intelligence, multi-user interface adaptation,
proactive behavior, and belief-desire-intention (BDI) model for self-contained
reasoning engine. ARGarden is an augmented edutainment system where the
user sees augmented scenes to learn the gardening while interacting with an
augmented learning companion in a form of a bird [12]. The augmented bird
perceives information according to BDI model and carries out causal interpretation based on its domain knowledge [13]. Ubiquitous Mobile Augmented Reality
(UMAR) is a conceptual framework aiming to connect the digital and the real

---

[1] www.quantifiedself.com
[2] www.technologyreview.com/news/514356/
stephen-wolfram-on-personal-analytics/

domains with context-aware information [14]. UMAR retrieves and personalizes information from the Internet based on spatial relationship with GPS and cell ID of the real world. Lee et al. proposed a framework for context-aware visualization and interaction service with context-aware and adaptable service layer, interface layer and AR-based visualization and interaction layer [15]. This framework supports personalization using user preferences, device profiles, and security. AR-REHAB is an AR framework for patients in rehabilitation process to track and measure uses of tangible objects by patients [16]. In AR-REHAB framework, patient signs on to the patient subsystem and performs exercises where his hand movements are recorded. Afterwards patient's exercise records are reviewed and evaluated in therapist subsystem. Context-Aware Mobile Augmented Reality (CAMAR) integrated context-awareness and mobile augmented reality for personalized information augmentation, selective sharing and interaction of contents in smart spaces [17,18]. CAMAR 2.0 [19] and its unified application framework [20] further enriched the concept by including principles of ubiquitous augmentation, high-level of context-awareness and sustaining participatory ecosystem. Augmented Reality 2.0 (AR 2.0) is a hybrid of AR and Web 2.0 technologies for allowing AR applications to be deployed and used on a large scale [21]. AR 2.0 includes characteristics such as large-scale of users and working volume, no visual separation between local data and remote data, modular application modules, and user-generated AR content and mashups.

There are number of self-tracking tools and commercial devices for quantified-self including wearable arm band, activity trackers, fitness trackers and health trackers. Choe et al. studied extreme Quantified-Selfers' practices through video recordings of Quantified Self Meet Up talks and found that Quantified-Selfers (Q-Selfers) mainly self-track for the motivations of improving health, improving other aspects of life, and finding new life experiences [22]. Also the study found that Q-Selfers faced difficulties when tracking too many things, not tracking triggers and context, and current Q-Selfers' practices lack scientific rigor [22].

In comparison to related works, we attempt to polish current quantified-self practices to unobtrusive personal big data collection and analysis where an augmented smart coach with anthropomorphic appearance, better sympathizes, responses, and understands its user by forming, exploiting, and exploring an integrated multi-dimensions of self for interactive conversational coaching process.

3   Conceptual Framework for Augmented Smart Coach

Our goal is to build an augmented smart agent residing in UVR environment that invokes itself out on a need-to-know basis to guide, coach, and recommend its user by examining the individual's previous knowledge and experiences against the sensed context. The concept of augmented smart coach is depicted in Fig. 1. with three characteristics of personal big data as input, quantified holistic self as a dynamic user profile and augmented smart coach as an effective actuator.

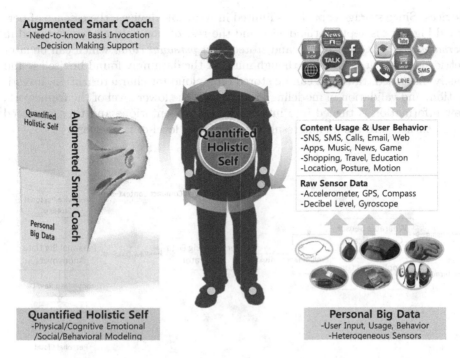

Fig. 1. Concept of augmented smart coach

3.1   Unobtrusive Life-Tracking of Personal Big Data

One of key elements to the framework is use of personal big data. Initiated from the mobile computing [23] and further accelerated by always-on wearable devices, an explosive volume of data is generated and consumed. By exploiting the increased volume of personal information known as personal big data, various episodic activities as well as continuous activities are tracked. Personal big data is generated from wearable sensors and devices such as smart glass and smart watch which include raw sensor data as well as application and content usages including user interaction. Specifically, personal big data contains various user-initiated and user-generated data from disparate and heterogeneous sources over the time for the user or by the user. Personal big data help predicting an individual's needs and store what one experiences computationally. There are many types of personal big data including photo, video, audio, calls, SMS, online/offline records, and activity records. These personal big data is used for numerous personalized applications and activity/trend prediction.

Various wearable sensors can track life activities where raw data are collected from *wearable sensor communicator* and application usages are tracked by recording logs in *application log aggregator*. Personal big data from disparate sources are integrated in a signal-level through seeking, filtering, reading, and extracting information in *personal big data integrator*. The result is stored in a schematic *compact context* which is stored on the internal storage of wearable devices. Since storage capacity is limited in wearable devices, the essence of personal big data is kept on the device and the rest of raw data are anonymized in *personal big data anonymizer* and stored on a *personal cloud* which can be later retrieved when needed. Even though much of the data may found be useless and easily discarded, raw data can be stored on a cloud for characterization, investigation, and validation in modeling processes. In the lower level of the framework, raw information is turned into intermediate representations and then prepared to be turned into reportable results in the upper level of framework.

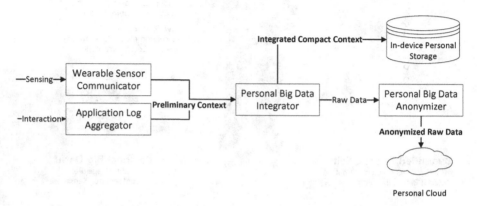

Fig. 2. Tracking of personal big data

3.2 Sensemaking of Quantified Holistic Self

Quantified self is known as using self-tracking tools and sensors to measure one's various activities of life for self-awareness [2]. Quantified self help the user to track activities with the technology and alter behavior to self-improve. A multitude of personal big data requires multiple perspectives to make sense. Therefore we propose quantified holistic self as a user model and sensemaking logic. We include multiple measurable paradigms related to time, frequency, activities, phenomenons and other variables that can be measured and uniquely characterized as personal yet salient patterns called Digital-Personality (D-Personality). Extending this concept further we define quantified holistic self as "a digital form of self that systematically integrates the reciprocal relationships across physical condition, cognitive emotional state, social relationship, and value-based Digital-consumer (D-consumer) behavior in a continuous time domain." Figure 3. and Figure 4. depicts how personal big data is first encoded into D-Personality, then combined to quantified holistic self.

QHS integrator and profiler find meanings in personal big data by analyzing compact context against various inter-related dimensions in *physical condition mapper* to quantify one's body, *cognitive emotional state mapper* to measure one's mind, *social relationship mapper* to track one's interacting targets, and *value-based consumer behavior mapper* to produce D-Personality and gauge one's culture in reference with specific domain knowledge base in *Knowledge Base*.

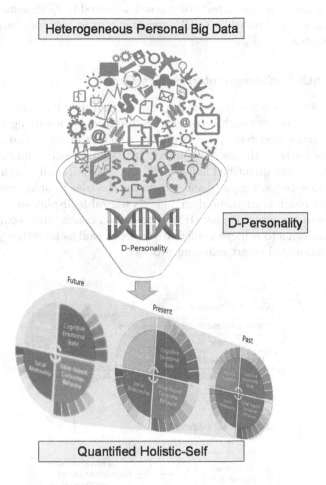

Fig. 3. Quantified holistic self generation concept

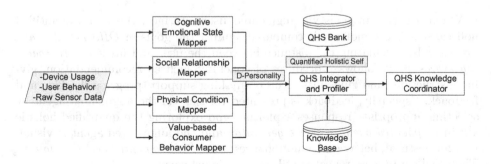

Fig. 4. Quantified holistic self generation procedures

The mapping result as quantified holistic self is stored in *QHS bank* with respect to time which is coordinated by *QHS knowledge coordinator* for continuous learnings and updates.

3.3 Invocation of Augmented Smart Coach

Augmented smart coach is transparent and natural user interface. More specifically, augmented smart coach is personalized and user-friendly agent residing in a wearable augmented reality environment which is enacted and invoked on a need-to-know basis by the sensed context. It is smart since it knows and understands the user from quantified holistic self. As a user-friendly augmented smart coach, it guides, helps, supports and motivates the user in achieving goals. Augmented smart coach is augmented on a user's wearable display such as glass-type display or head mounted display (HMD) to guide, coach, and recommend users in making decisions to achieve immediate tasks as well as long time goals. Figure 5. depicts augmented smart coaching process.

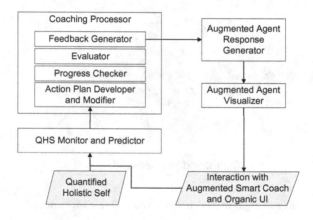

Fig. 5. Augmented smart coaching process

When a user sets goals via augmented user interface, the user's quantified holistic self at the moment is compared against the goals in *QHS monitor and predictor* by calculating the distance between the user and his goals. In *coaching processor*, it follows procedures of coaching such as recommendation, giving instructions and guidelines, decision-making support, progress checking and feedback. Especially, feedback is presented to user via the augmented agent by selecting appropriate responses exploiting and exploring the quantified holistic self in *augmented agent response generator* and the augmented agent is visualized for gestural, behavioral, emotional responses in *augmented agent visualizer*. The coaching process repeats until the goal is achieved.

3.4   Overall Procedures

Figure 6. shows the overall conceptual framework for augmented smart coach based on quantified holistic self.

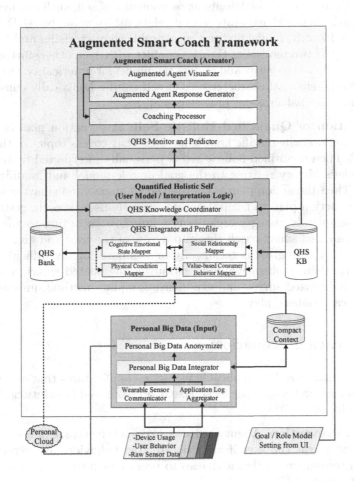

Fig. 6. Conceptual framework for augmented smart coach

3.5   Technical Challenges

Encoding Personal Big Data into Components of D-Personality: Heterogeneous wearable sensor data and wearable device usage (email, SMS, SNS, news, music, shopping, travel, game, education, etc.) are collected in real time. Personal big data is then represented with 5W1H (Who, When, Where, What, Why, How) according to many-to-many relations and encoded into corresponding D-Personality components. Modeling and analysis of personal big data are either processed in real-time on-device, offline batch processing, computation offloading to the cloud, or mixed/hybrid approach depending on the characteristics of personal big data (volume and frequency of data) and heuristics and rules determined by experiments.

Formation of Quantified Holistic Self from D-Personalities: By examining existing theories and models about components of self, such as physical conditions, cognitive emotional state, social relationship, value-based D-consumer behavior, we identify, model and test measurable characteristics and features as D-Personality. If two models or theories conflict with each other, further experiments are conducted to verify and update the model for practicality. On the other hand, multi-dimensional characteristics of self can be holistically considered to classify and make patterns out of D-Personalities.

Interpretation of Quantified Holistic Self: Basic action plan is prepared by referencing domain-specific knowledge base that covers topics of the goal or role-model. Then quantified holistic self is personally interpreted by referencing user's previous history relating to the goal or role-model and modifies the action plan. Then the action plan is transferred to augmented smart coach where it translates action plan to natural persuasive responses (speech, gesture, emotion) and adaptively changes organic user interface according to the required action. Augmented smart coach checks progress of the user and gives feedback. Also if the user's progress is technically or computationally difficult to check or indecisive, then unobtrusive intervention by augmented smart coach which incorporates digitized survey and experience sampling method questioning and answering, can come to play.

4   Application Scenarios

Augmented smart coach is applicable in various applications that needs personalized guidance and assistance. The coach presents viable solutions for many societal problems.

Addiction Prevention. Augmented smart coach keeps track of user's personal big data and warns the user if addiction-related behaviors are expected. The coach then recommends other activities to user or help the user to be aware of his current situation.

Role Model Follower/Virtual Life Coaching. Augmented smart coach helps the user to follow his role model or achieve certain goals. Quantified holistic self of user and role model is first compared to find difference between the two. Then the coach gives instructions to become like the model or necessary steps to achieve the goal.

Happiness Pursuer. Augmented smart coach measures user's activities and values to see when the user is happy and unhappy. With these characteristics captured in quantified holistic self, the coach can motivate users toward activities that yield to happiness.

5 Conclusions

In this paper, we presented a conceptual framework for smart augmented coach based on quantified holistic self. To assess a user as a whole, we used various sources for personal big data and defined D-Personality and quantified holistic self in terms of physical condition, cognitive emotional state, social relationship, value-based consumer behavior over the time domain. We presented detailed procedures in the conceptual framework and three revolving key ideas of personal big data, quantified holistic self, and augmented smart coach along with technical challenges and possible applications.

References

1. Kim, S., Lee, Y., Woo, W.: How to realize ubiquitous vr? In: Pervasive: TSI Workshop, pp. 493–504 (2006)
2. Swan, M.: The quantified self: Fundamental disruption in big data science and biological discovery. Big Data 1(2), 85–99 (2013)
3. Li, I., Dey, A., Forlizzi, J.: A stage-based model of personal informatics systems. In: Proceedings of the SIGCHI Conference on Human Factors in Computing Systems, CHI 2010, pp. 557–566. ACM, New York (2010)
4. Li, I., Dey, A.K., Forlizzi, J.: Understanding my data, myself: Supporting self-reflection with ubicomp technologies. In: Proceedings of the 13th International Conference on Ubiquitous Computing, UbiComp 2011, pp. 405–414. ACM, New York (2011)
5. Rekimoto, J.: From augmented reality to augmented human. In: 2013 IEEE International Symposium on Mixed and Augmented Reality (ISMAR), p. 1 (2013)
6. Nagao, K., Rekimoto, J.: Agent augmented reality: A software agent meets the real world. In: Proceedings of the Second International Conference on Multiagent Systems, pp. 228–235 (1996)
7. Nagao, K., Katsuno, Y.: Agent augmented community: Human-to-human and human-to-environment interactions enhanced by situation-aware personalized mobile agents. In: Ishida, T. (ed.) Community Computing and Support Systems. LNCS, vol. 1519, pp. 342–358. Springer, Heidelberg (1998)
8. Tsujita, H., Rekimoto, J.: Smile-encouraging digital appliances. IEEE Pervasive Computing 12, 5–7 (2013)
9. Higuchi, K., Fujii, K., Rekimoto, J.: Flying head: A head-synchronization mechanism for flying telepresence. In: 2013 23rd International Conference on Artificial Reality and Telexistence (ICAT), pp. 28–34 (December 2013)
10. Barakonyi, I., Psik, T., Schmalstieg, D.: Agents that talk and hit back: animated agents in augmented reality. In: Third IEEE and ACM International Symposium on Mixed and Augmented Reality, ISMAR 2004, pp. 141–150 (2004)
11. Barakonyi, I., Schmalstieg, D.: Ubiquitous animated agents for augmented reality. In: IEEE/ACM International Symposium on Mixed and Augmented Reality, ISMAR 2006, pp. 145–154 (2006)
12. Oh, S., Woo, W.: Argarden: Augmented edutainment system with a learning companion. In: Pan, Z., Cheok, D.A.D., Müller, W., El Rhalibi, A. (eds.) Transactions on Edutainment I. LNCS, vol. 5080, pp. 40–50. Springer, Heidelberg (2008)

13. Oh, S., Choi, A., Woo, W.: Sketch on lifelong ar agents in u-vr environments. In: International Symposium on Ubiquitous Virtual Reality, ISUVR 2009, pp. 47–50 (2009)
14. Henrysson, A., Ollila, M.: Umar: Ubiquitous mobile augmented reality. In: Proceedings of the 3rd International Conference on Mobile and Ubiquitous Multimedia, MUM 2004, pp. 41–45. ACM, New York (2004)
15. Lee, J.Y., Seo, D.W., Rhee, G.: Visualization and interaction of pervasive services using context-aware augmented reality. Expert Systems with Applications 35(4), 1873–1882 (2008)
16. Alamri, A., Cha, J., El-Saddik, A.: Ar-rehab: An augmented reality framework for poststroke-patient rehabilitation. IEEE Transactions on Instrumentation and Measurement 59, 2554–2563 (2010)
17. Suh, Y., Park, Y., Yoon, H., Woo, W.: Context-aware mobile ar system for personalization, selective sharing, and interaction of contents in ubiquitous computing environments. In: Pavlidis, I. (ed.) Human Computer Interaction. InTech (2008)
18. Oh, S., Woo, W.: Camar: Context-aware mobile augmented reality in smart space. In: International Workshop on Ubiquitous Virtual Reality 2009, pp. 48–51 (2009)
19. Shin, C., Lee, W., Suh, Y., Yoon, H., Lee, Y., Woo, W.: Camar 2.0: Future direction of context-aware mobile augmented reality. In: International Symposium on Ubiquitous Virtual Reality, ISUVR 2009, pp. 21–24 (2009)
20. Shin, C., Kim, H., Kang, C., Jang, Y., Choi, A., Woo, W.: Unified context-aware augmented reality application framework for user-driven tour guides. In: 2010 International Symposium on Ubiquitous Virtual Reality (ISUVR), pp. 52–55 (2010)
21. Schmalstieg, D., Langlotz, T., Billinghurst, M.: Augmented reality 2.0. In: Brunnett, G., Coquillart, S., Welch, G. (eds.) Virtual Realities, pp. 13–37. Springer, Vienna (2011)
22. Choe, E.K., Lee, N.B., Lee, B., Pratt, W., Kientz, J.A.: Understanding quantified-selfers' practices in collecting and exploring personal data. In: Proceedings of the SIGCHI Conference on Human Factors in Computing Systems, CHI 2014 (to appear, 2014)
23. Lane, N., Miluzzo, E., Lu, H., Peebles, D., Choudhury, T., Campbell, A.: A survey of mobile phone sensing. IEEE Communications Magazine 48, 140–150 (2010)

Crowd Target Positioning under Multiple Cameras Based on Block Correspondence

Qiuyu Zhu[1], Sai Yuan[1], Bo Chen[1], Guowei Wang[1], Jianzhong Xu[1], and Lijun Zhang[2]

[1] School of Communication & Information Engineering, Shanghai University, Shanghai, China
Zhuqiuyu@staff.shu.edu.cn, yuansai200888@qq.com
[2] Shanghai Advanced Research Institute, Chinese Academy of Sciences, China
zhanglj@sari.ac.cn

Abstract. In the research of crowd analysis in a multi-camera environment, the key problem is how to get target correspondence between cameras. Two main popular methods are epipolar geometric constraint and homography matrix constraint. For large view-angle and wide baseline, these two methods exist obvious disadvantages and have a low performance. The paper utilizes a new correspondence algorithm based-on the constraint of line-of-sight for the crowd positioning. Since the target area is discrete, the paper proposes to use blocking policy: dividing the target regions into blocks with certain size. The approach may provide appropriate redundancy information for each object and decrease the risk of objects missing which is caused by large view-angle and wide baseline between different perspective images. The experimental results show that the method has a high accuracy and a lower computational complexity.

Keywords: multiple cameras, constraint of line-of-sight, target positioning, blocks correspondence.

1 Introduction

With rapid development of economic, there are more and more skyscraper, underground constructions, and large commercial entertainment. The requirements for the function of intelligent video analysis platform are improving. For researchers, it is one of the principal subjects of concern about how to effectively detect crowd and to predict the crowd behavior. Current researches on intelligent video surveillance technology mainly focus on the fusion of multiple cameras, camera calibration, target detection, target positioning, target tracking, activity recognition etc.

The paper accomplishes crowd detection and positioning in the condition with multi-camera collaborative environments. It is a fundamental work for various advanced processing such as behavior analysis, behavior recognition, as well as advanced video processing and application. Under multi-camera setup, the key problem is how to realize targets correspondence between cameras. Two main popular methods are epipolar geometric constraint and homography matrix constraint. The former needs to segment foreground region and extract key-points of the targets firstly, and then, depending on epipolar geometric constraint, the correspondent object and

N. Streitz and P. Markopoulos (Eds.): DAPI 2014, LNCS 8530, pp. 509–518, 2014.

point in the other image can be found. But, in the actual dense crowd of video scene, it is too hard to segment single object from crowd accurately. Meanwhile, larger angle of view between cameras leads to larger difference between images and the matching task based on appearance would also be difficult to achieve. So, object matching method based on epipolar geometric constraint cannot be effectively applied to the crowd situation.

For the latter, it needs the matching points are projected from reality points belong to one plane which usually is ground plane and thus we ought to find feet in the image. Owing to high occlusion in crowds, it is impossible to find each foot. Afterwards, researchers utilize homography matrix constraint among multi-plane in different height [2]. This method needs accurately foreground segmentation and the familiar appearance of multi-view object in large baseline. These requirements are difficult to meet in dense crowd.

As Figure 3.1, there are many targets in the scene. It's hard to get a single individual in the crowd. Considering the cameras are generally set up higher than human, even in the crowded situation, the human head is still visible, so the paper regards head region as interesting region. The paper utilizes line-of-sight constraint between cameras to realize the positioning of objet. After detecting the interesting region, target area is discrete, the paper proposes to use of blocking policy: dividing the target region into blocks with certain size. The approach may provide appropriate redundancy information for each object and decrease the risk of objects missing which is caused from large view-angle and long baseline between different perspective images.

2   Related Work

In order to reduce the influence of occlusion in crowd, many researchers have analyzed the crowd under multi-camera. Eshel and Moses [1] associate several views data to detect head in crowd scene and obtain height information of targets from segmented head. The correspondence of head takes use of plane's homography. The paper [2] put forward to use homography existing among different height planes to detect and trace object. Based on their former work, W. Gee [3] et al proposed a statistics model of crowd structure which could manipulate the subordination in crowd and is not discrete for the space position of the object. Castle [4] et al proposed to utilize triangulation method that based on SIFT key-points extracted from key frame to recognize, reconstruct, and localize. They also extend to raise frame rate through FAST key-points and parallel tracking technology. Mazzonand Cavallaro [5] proposed to conduct re-recognize using SFM model for the object that are occluded in the process of trace. Huadong Ma [6] et al, proposed an algorithm that based on PMHL detector and multi-view fusion. This algorithm could detect static object rapidly and robustly. And authors make use of synergy between multiple cameras to improve the detection rate.

3   Target Positioning Based on Block Correspondence

Multi-camera positioning of crowd scene shows in Figure 3.1. If there are too many objects to be localized in the scene, occlusion would be worse. It is too hard to get complete single individual. As the cameras are generally set up higher than human, even in the crowded situation, the entire head contour is still visible. So we consider head as the whole body to detect as well as further vision processing.

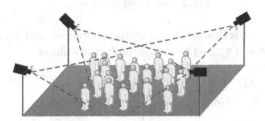

Fig. 1. Crowd scene under multi-camera

3.1   Moving Detection

Frame difference and background difference are two main methods suitable for motion detection in the static background scene. The former is simple and clear, and possess a stable robustness. However, there are holes in the moving object after detecting process. The latter could get entire object contour, but it is a hard work to do. Common methods are averaging method, Gaussian background modeling method, and so on. The paper also utilizes Gaussian background modeling method. In this step, the mathematical average of six images at different time is the background image. In the later step of processing, we join the morphology filter for binary image in order to get a full target area. Due to the influence of frame difference and noise, there may be non-moving region in foreground of the binary image. So we process this image with morphology filter to get better moving region.

After getting moving foreground, the paper detects head region by detecting skin color region and hair area. In the head region, the obvious and tractable regions are mainly skin color region and hair area. So, under the premise of no target missing, the paper put skin region and hair region as the target areas in order to improve the correct rate of head detection in dense crowd. Usually, target areas are some merged connected regions came from different individuals. Therefore, we need a target corresponding algorithm to separate each individual.

3.2   Object Matching Based On Line-Of-Sight Distance

Object matching based on line-of-sight distance is shown as Fig. 2. Here, the line-of-sight is the space line through camera optical center and object point in the world coordinate, for example L1, L2 in Figure 3.2. C1 and C2 stand for cameras, P1, stands for targets in the scene.

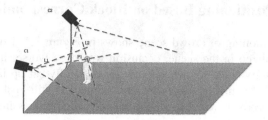

Fig. 2. Line-of-sight constraint

As we know, the pixel (u, v) in the image coordinate and its counterpart in the world coordinate (Xw, Yw, Zw) has a relationship as follows

$$Z\begin{bmatrix} u \\ v \\ 1 \end{bmatrix} = K\begin{bmatrix} R & T \end{bmatrix}\begin{bmatrix} X_w \\ Y_w \\ Z_w \\ 1 \end{bmatrix} = M\begin{bmatrix} X_w \\ Y_w \\ Z_w \\ 1 \end{bmatrix} = \begin{bmatrix} m_{11} & m_{12} & m_{13} & m_{14} \\ m_{21} & m_{22} & m_{23} & m_{24} \\ m_{31} & m_{32} & m_{33} & m_{34} \end{bmatrix}\begin{bmatrix} X_w \\ Y_w \\ Z_w \\ 1 \end{bmatrix} \tag{1}$$

where:

K-is a 3×3 Matrix of camera intrinsic parameters;

R-is a 3×3 unit rotation matrix;

T-is a3×1 translation vector, together with rotation matrix they are called external parameters;

M-is a 3×4 camera matrix.

In the case of the known camera matrix P, since the matrix P is a 3 × 4 matrix, then the linear algebraic theorems about linear equations can know right of formula (3.1), that is a known spatial points coordinates, the equation is well posed equations, then you can easily access a variety of corresponding points by solving linear equations method of pixel coordinates; But in the case knowing pixel coordinates, since P is not invertible matrix, the equations are underdetermined equations, then only get a simplified equations by solving the equations, the geometric concepts of equations at this time is represented a spatial line which through optical center of the camera, the image coordinates of a spatial point, linear spatial points. If the spatial point is visible to the two cameras, then two lines are certain. Two intersect lines determine the location of the target spatial position. So the method is able to obtain the spatial location of the target, to achieve the purpose of positioning.

If pixel p1 in image I1 and pixel p2 in image I2 are matched, L1 and L2 must intersect at point P.

$$\begin{cases} L1 : \dfrac{X - x2}{x1 - x2} = \dfrac{Y - y2}{y1 - y2} = \dfrac{Z - z2}{z1 - z2} = m \\ L2 : \dfrac{X - x4}{x3 - x4} = \dfrac{Y - y4}{y3 - y4} = \dfrac{Z - z4}{z3 - z4} = n \end{cases} \tag{2}$$

For correctly matched targets, we take the center point, and calculate the corresponding equation of the line-of-sight.

With common perpendicular line and pedals solution, we can get a series points of target P1 $\{P_{11} \quad P_{12} \quad ... \quad P_{1n} \quad , n = 2*camerasnum\}$. Due to the center of the corresponding blocks are not correspond to the same target, line-of-light equations do not always intersect. In most cases will be non-coplanar lines, but the common perpendicular of the line, which is the shortest distance between non-coplanar lines, will be included in the destination point for the sphere, spherical region within a certain distance radius.

3.3   Blocks Correspondence

Actual detected skin and hair region mostly is not completed, and broke, and discrete, thus the above positioning algorithm should do some modifications: first, each target area breaks into blocks, and in the process of line-of-sight correspondence we use the center of blocks take place of the whole block; addition, an image may contain several targets, the paper utilizes relaxation labeling algorithm to calculate the optimal solution corresponding multi-block problem.

An example of blocking is shown as Figure 3, where image size is 768*576 and the block size is 20*20. The object correspondence will be based on all blocks.

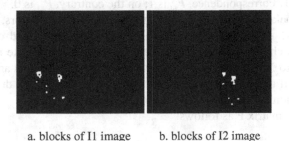

a. blocks of I1 image   b. blocks of I2 image

Fig. 3. Results of blocking

If the image I1 corresponding to the camera C1 has m1 blocks and image I2 corresponding to camera C2 has m2blocks. Thus, for the m1 blocks, we use following matrix:

$$X = \begin{bmatrix} x_{1,1} & ... & x_{1,N} \\ ... & & ... \\ x_{m1,1} & ... & x_{m1,N} \end{bmatrix} \tag{3}$$

Each row of the above matrix represents the characteristic of each correspondence block. In detail, $\begin{bmatrix} x_{i,1} & ... & x_{i,N-2} \end{bmatrix}$ represents the parameters of line equation of sight through the block, and $\begin{bmatrix} x_{i,N-1} & x_{i,N} \end{bmatrix}$ is the block color information. Similarly, for the m2 blocks of I2, there is corresponding matrix:

$$Y = \begin{bmatrix} y_{1,1} & \cdots & y_{1,N} \\ \cdots & & \cdots \\ y_{m2,1} & \cdots & y_{m2,N} \end{bmatrix} \tag{4}$$

Thus, the problem of multi-block correspondence is transformed into the corresponding problem between rows of X and rows of Y.

Under the previous definition, the paper expresses the correspondence problem as the model of constrained minimization problem:

$$P^* = \arg \min_{P} \quad J(X,Y,P) \tag{5}$$
$$s.t. \quad P \in \rho_p(m1+1, m2+1)$$

where J is the objective function, ρ_p is a permutation matrix.

Optimal solution P^* is a partial permutation matrix, and the arrangement of its internal element 0-1 is exactly the situation between the two correctly corresponding image block, the value of its elements are the relation of row of Y and the corresponding row of X: for each input, when the block X_i (i-th row of X) and block Y_j (j-th row of Y) are correctly correspondence, $P_{i,j}$ is 1; on the contrary, $P_{i,j}$ is 0.

In order to make the corresponding algorithm robust to outliers, P will be constructed as a (m1 +1) × (m2 +1) matrix, the additional rows and columns present target blocks which have not correspondence: there is no candidate row of Y which correspondence to X_i, the matrix P in the row i before m_2 elements are 0, $P_{i, m2 +1}$ is 1; on the contrary, if there is no block corresponding to the block Y_j, then the matrix P, before the first element m1 in the row j are 0, $P_{i, m1 +1}$ is 1.

The constraint matrix P as follows:

$$\begin{cases} P_{i,j} \in \{0,1\}, \forall i \leq m1+1, \forall j \leq m2+1 \\ \sum_{i=1}^{m1+1} P_{i,j} \leq 1, \forall j \leq m2+1 \\ \sum_{j=1}^{m2+1} P_{i,j} \leq 1, \forall i \leq m1+1 \end{cases} \tag{6}$$

Since each element of matrix P represents a correspondence between all the blocks, so that the model could not only achieve the correct correspondence between the blocks, but also eliminate false correspondence between the target block. Thus the correspondence problem between multi-target block is transformed into linear programming model to strike the global optimal solution of the problem, global optimal solution is to get all the possible correspondence between the actual correspondences with the most consistent situation.

In this paper, taking into account the characteristic of multi-objective corresponding process in solving the global optimal solution, the paper takes relaxation labeling (Relaxation Labeling) algorithm [7] [8] to optimize the correspondence to improve the accuracy and agility of the process. Relaxation labeling is a recognition method of using label to descript pattern. The whole process is similar to the human reasoning process, which uses a variety of constraints and gradually narrows the search scope, eventually obtaining correct results. In the application situation of this paper, the I1 image of each block corresponds to a straight line as the target space, each block in I2 image corresponding spatial line as a marker. When processing starts, correctly correspondence can't be achieved, since the attribute object is blurred. Relaxations marked the formal relationships between the target and the constraints of the system and gradually decrease ambiguity. First, an initial target correspondence condition is given. Then through constant iteration and gradually update the corresponding relationship, we can finally obtain an accurate representation of the target correspondence.

Once obtain the 3D position of each blocks, we project space points onto the ground plane. And use ISODATA clustering to categorize these spaces and to calculate a space region of the target. Thus target positioning is achieved.

4   Experimental Results

In our experiment, we captured two camera's images whose size are 768*576. After skin and hair region extraction and 20*20 blocking, there are 17 blocks in I1 image, and 18 blocks in I2 image, respectively. Through the calibration of internal and external camera parameters, 17 blocks in C1 correspond to 17 space straight lines, 18 blocks in C2 correspond to 18 space straight lines. After each calculation of lines, we got a 17×18 matrix of CC. In the matrix, each row represents spatial distance of a certain space line of C1 and each space line of C2. During the relaxation labeling iteration, the minimum value of each line is selected as the starting corresponding states.

In order to reduce the amount of calculation in the correspondence process, the paper sets a threshold distance Trb to do some preprocessing for matrix CC. In the case of exceeding the threshold Trb for each elements, the larger distance between two straight lines means larger space, this element's correspondence is deleted; If the number of elements which are less than Trb for each row or column is more than 15% of the total elements of a row or column(in the paper is 3), the minimum 15% elements are selected as candidate correspondences; otherwise, all these elements are used as an candidate elements, which are added to the process of relaxation iteration.

The paper sets Trb = 40 as the preprocessing threshold of matrix CC, the result of correspondence between each block of C1 and C2 and the obtained target three-dimensional information are shown as Table 1.

After projecting block spatial point onto the ground plane, we utilize ISODATA clustering algorithm to classify these spatial points and calculate the target region of space. As the result, these points are divided into two categories: G1{(2022.47 , 390.698), (2020.92 , 395.729), (2022.04 , 404.396)}, G2{(1729.82 , 825.062), (1741.47 , 826.806), (1735.62 , 832.622) , (1749.25 , 816.067)} as Fig. 4.

Table 1. Results of blocks positioning

I D	C1 blocks	C2 blocks	Distance mm	Spatial positioning mm
1	124, 346	430, 350	24.7812	2022.47 , 390.698 , 1715.35
2	124, 350	430, 254	21.6338	2020.92 , 395.729 , 1711.79
3	128, 368	435, 366	9.80092	2022.04 , 404.396 , 1706.48
4	238, 362	492, 372	14.1256	1729.82 , 825.062 , 1757.61
5	246, 368	494, 376	8.44677	1741.47 , 826.806 , 1770.3
6	274, 376	490, 384	8.4012	1735.62 , 832.622 , 1714.46
7	238, 394	492, 410	6.88672	1749.25 , 816.067 , 1733.53
8	206, 492	514, 498	19.4985	1741.98 , 675.042 , 795.833
9	260, 486	518, 498	10.3048	1702.55 , 978.119 , 853.541

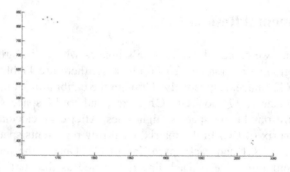

Fig. 4. Projected location

As each block includes the hands skin regions and the head skin regions, the horizontal plane of the spatial distance difference between hands and head should be taken into account in the classification of these regions. Finally, the target positioning in the scene shown in the figure 5.

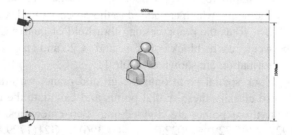

Fig. 5. Targets positioning in the scene

In the preprocessing step of matrix CC optimization, The corresponding results of C1 and C2 blocks are influenced greatly by the threshold value Trb, which is determined by experiment in this paper. With the reduction of the threshold the correspondence performance is reduced, this is because the restrictions are too stringent, resulting in the increasing of false matching, eventually leading to the decreasing of correct correspondence rate. Conversely, when the threshold value is increased, the result of correspondences will increase, including the false correspondence. Although the threshold value can be increased, due to the increasing of error correspondence rate, the overall correct correspondence rate didn't improve.

5   Conclusion

In the paper, we propose a new method for multi-camera target correspondence between different views. The method based on the idea of the line-of-sight constraints to obtain positioning of the target. The paper divides regions of interest into multiple blocks, providing appropriate redundancy information for each object and decreasing the risk of objects missing between different perspective images which are caused by large view-angle and wide baseline. When dealing with multi-objective correspondence problem, we constructed a multi-objective corresponding model; the target is transformed into the corresponding minimum objective function to solve a linear programming problem. The experimental results of the paper show that, the method has high accuracy corresponding based on multi-target line-of-sight constraints, the theory is more intuitive thinking, and algorithm is relatively simple. In order to further improve the measurement accuracy, in the next step, we plan to adopt more cameras and add more constraints in relaxation labeling processing, and then apply it in more crowded situation.

Acknowledgement. This work was supported by the Development Foundation of Shanghai Municipal Commission of Science and Technology (13dz1202404).

References

1. Eshel, R., Moses, Y.: Homography based multiple camera detection and tracking of people in a dense crowd. In: Proceedings of the IEEE Conference on Computer Vision and Pattern Recognition, June 24-26, pp. 1–8 (2008)
2. Eshel, R., Moses, Y.: Tracking in a Dense Crowd Using Multiple Cameras. International Journal of Computer Vision 88(1), 129–143 (2010)
3. Ge, W., Collins, R.T.: Crowd detection with a multi-view sampler. In: Daniilidis, K., Maragos, P., Paragios, N. (eds.) ECCV 2010, Part V. LNCS, vol. 6315, pp. 324–337. Springer, Heidelberg (2010)
4. Castle, R.O., Murray, D.W.: Key-frame-based recognition and localization during video-rate parallel tracking and mapping. Image and Vision Computing 29(8), 524–532 (2011)
5. Mazzon, R., Cavallaro, A.: Multi-camera tracking using a Multi-Goal Social Force Model. Neuro-Computing 100, 41–50 (2013)

6. Ma, H., Zeng, C., Ling, C.: A Reliable People Counting System via Multiple Cameras. ACM Transactions on Intelligent Systems and Technology 3(2), 1–22 (2012)
7. Lloyd, S.A.: An optimization approach to relaxation labelling algorithms. Image and Vision Computing 1(2), 85–92 (1983)
8. Kittlera, J., Illingworth, J.: Relaxation labelling algorithms — A review, Image and vision computing. Image and Vision Computing 3(4), 206–210 (1985)
9. Rosenfeld, A., Hummel, R.A., Zucker, S.W.: Scene labeling by relaxation operations. IEEE Trans. SMC. 6(6), 420–433 (1976)
10. Cui, L., Dongqing, F.: Improved image segmentation algorithm based on K-means clustering. Journal of Zhengzhou University (Natural Science) 43(1), 109–113 (2011)

Building a Sensory Infrastructure to Support Interaction and Monitoring in Ambient Intelligence Environments

Emmanouil Zidianakis[1], Nikolaos Partarakis[1],
Margherita Antona[1], and Constantine Stephanidis[1,2]

[1] Foundation for Research and Technology – Hellas (FORTH)
Institute of Computer Science Heraklion, GR-70013, Greece
{zidian,partarak,antona,cs}@ics.forth.gr
[2] University of Crete, Department of Computer Science

Abstract. In the context of Ambient Intelligence (AmI), the elaboration of new interaction techniques is becoming the most prominent key to a more natural and intuitive interaction with everyday things [2]. Natural interaction between people and technology can be defined in terms of experience: people naturally communicate through gestures, expressions, movements. To this end, people should be able to interact with technology as they are used to interact with the real world in everyday life [19]. Additionally, AmI systems must be sensitive, responsive, and adaptive to the presence of people [16]. This paper presents the design and implementation of an interaction framework for ambient intelligence targeting to the provision of novel interaction metaphors and techniques in the context of AmI scenarios. The aforementioned infrastructure has been deployed in vitro within the AmI classroom simulation space of the FORTH-ICS AmI research facility and used to extend existing applications offered by an augmented interactive table for young children (Beantable) to support also games that facilitate biometric information, rich interaction metaphors and speech input [20].

1 Introduction

Ambient Intelligence (AmI) presents a vision of a technological environment capable of reacting in an attentive, adaptive and active (sometimes proactive) way to the presence and activities of humans and objects in order to provide appropriate services to its inhabitants [17]. According to the Institute for the Future, "Emerging technologies are transforming everything that constitutes our notion of "reality" - our ability to sense our surroundings, our capacity to reason, and our perception of the world" [1]. In the context of Ambient Intelligence, several challenges emerge in the contributing domains of ubiquitous computing, mixed reality and HCI. This work presents the design and implementation of a technological framework to support the interaction requirements of AmI at large by offering a number of alternative natural interaction techniques such as gestures, face and skeleton tracking, head position estimation and speech recognition.

---

[1] Blended Reality report: http://www.iftf.org/uploads/media/SR-122~2.PDF, page 1.

N. Streitz and P. Markopoulos (Eds.): DAPI 2014, LNCS 8530, pp. 519–529, 2014.
© Springer International Publishing Switzerland 2014

2   Background and Related Work

2.1   Ambient Intelligence

The term "Ambient Intelligence" was coined from Philips Research' vision of "people living easily in digital environments in which the electronics are sensitive to people's needs, personalized to their requirements, anticipatory of their behavior and responsive to their presence" [15]. This concept was adopted by the Information Society Technologies Advisory Group (ISTAG) as one of their research focus. In their report [5], ISTAG show the concrete vision that humans will, in an Ambient Intelligent Environment, be surrounded by intelligent interfaces embedded in everyday objects (as furniture, clothes and the environment). Aarts and Marzano review the five key technology features that portray an AmI system [1]: (a) Embedded, (b) Context aware (c) Personalized, (d) Adaptive and (e) Anticipatory.

2.2   Interaction Techniques for Ambient Intelligence

Gestures are employed in the context of AmI for providing alternative ways of user input in a human like fashion. Gestures when used in the context of human to human communication are a quick and intuitive way of communication. On the contrary, identifying human gestures in a computerized environment is not an easy task. Research conducted in this field involves the usage of gestures for providing input to augmented desk interface systems using multiple fingertips recognition (identify fingertips and their trajectories and infer gestures based on these trajectories) [14], [9]. Computer vision is used for identifying hand gestures, facial expressions and body postures [12]. Furthermore, the usage of thimble-shaped fingertip markers made of white printing paper with a 'black light' source has been proposed for providing gesture recognition in the context of back projection walls [8].

Gaze recognition has recently got the attention of scientific community and is employed for facilitating alternative gesture based input [9, 10, 11]. Although this form of interaction is not generically applicable, it can be used in conjunction with face tracking and head position estimation to support various forms of natural implicit interaction with the environment.

Using speech as an input channel in ICT is not new. Research has been conducted in this field for years, and today thousands of commercial and research product have been developed.

This paper presents the design and implementation of a unified framework which supports a number of alternative natural interaction techniques through the integration of facilities to support: (a) gestures recording, parameterisation and recognition, (b) face tracking, (c) head position estimation, (d) skeleton tracking and (e) speech recognition. This novel interaction framework has been deployed in vitro in an augmented interactive table for young children (Beantable) [21]. Beantable, although supporting native means of interaction through the provision of a multi-touch surface (main features: blob tracking and objects recognition), also integrates the framework presented here in order to provide supplementary forms of interaction with children, thua extending the educational and learning experience into the surrounding environment.

3   Implementation

The sensory modules created in the context of this research work are embedded in a software platform called 'Nibbler'. This platform builds on the Microsoft Kinect sensor and was developed using the C# programming language, Microsoft Kinect software development kit (SDK) v1.8 and the .NET Framework. It is organized in various modules each of which is responsible for specific sensory requirements. The GUI of the proposed software platform is presented in Fig. 1. Each module is presented thoroughly in the following sections.

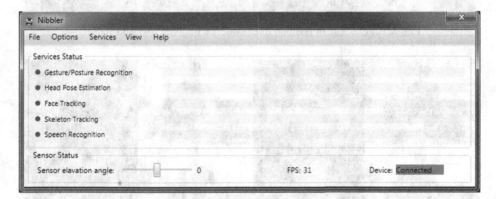

Fig. 1. Nibbler is the program implements the most of sensory services

3.1   Skeleton Tracking Module

The **skeleton tracking** module is responsible for reporting position information of each skeleton joint. This module performs geometric transformations on each skeleton joint position constituting every real time skeleton frame. This happens in order to get the same valid results regardless of the position of the user who may be located everywhere inside the sensor's field of view.

The skeleton tracking module transforms the user's skeleton to a local scope, i.e., expressed relatively to the 3-axis coordination system centered in the middle of the user's shoulders. The transformation is applied with respect to three distinct steps, translation, scaling and rotation as shown in Fig. 7②. Firstly, each joint's x-axis position is subtracted with the position dynamically calculated as the center of both shoulders: this way, skeleton tracking is performed regardless of the user's relative position to the sensor, as presented in Fig. 2. Secondly, the joints' positions are normalized in order to be scale-independent. Finally, the module rotates the skeleton so as to align the user's skeleton to the sensor. This is accomplished by multiplying each joint's position with a matrix calculated from the angle θ, where θ is equal to $-$yaw (yaw is the angle of line between the right and the left shoulder).

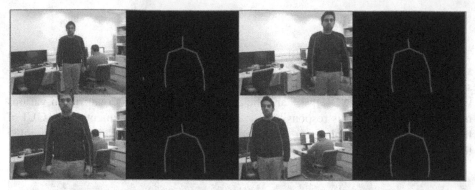

Fig. 2. An example of position independence between user and sensor

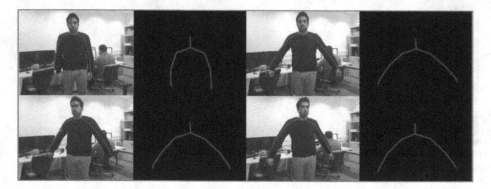

Fig. 3. An example of alignment independence between user and sensor

3.2 Gesture/Posture Recognition Module

Although much work has been done to date in the domain of Gesture/Posture recognition, no ready to use solutions are widely available to developers wishing to incorporate kinect based gesture recognition in their applications, with the exception of the Microsoft Kinect SDK samples (a sample is provided that implements two gestures: next, previous). The developed Gesture/Posture recognition module implements the dynamic time warping (DTW) algorithm [17] for measuring similarity between two skeleton sequences which may vary in time or speed. Additionally, it provides a training platform that allows developers to fine tune their gestures having access to a number of alternative biometric parameters. In general, the DTW algorithm can be applied to any data which can be turned into a linear sequence, i.e., a well-known application has been automatic speech recognition, to cope with different speaking speeds[2]. The **first skeleton sequence** is captured and fine-tuned only once during the training process while the **second** one is captured constantly in real time. During the training process, the author is able to record a skeleton sequence using his own body

---

[2] http://en.wikipedia.org/wiki/Dynamic_time_warping

as input data and store it in the database (Fig. 4). The number of the frames in a sequence may vary from 1 up to a maximum predefined variable, which is usually 30 considering that 30 is the maximum sensor's frame rate according to its specification details.

Fig. 4. The author starts recording of a skeleton sequence in seated mode

End users are provided with several functions to optimally adjust gesture/posture recognition. In particular, end users may (see Fig. 4): add a new gesture using button①, delete an existing one②, or start/stop skeleton sequence recording③. Once recording has been completed, the author is able to preview the recorded skeleton sequence, edit it and fine tune the captured skeleton sequence by pressing button ④ and using the pop up configuration window as shown in Fig. 5. This window offers functionality for: (a) renaming①, (b) adjusting the maximum distance with the real time skeleton sequence ② for successful recognition (see below for further details), (c) modifying the number of the minimum frames③ that have to be captured in real time before the recognition process is triggered, (d) trimming the corresponding skeleton sequence using⑤,⑥ and (e) adjusting some of the basic parameters used in the

DTW algorithm such as the slop constraint which determines the maximum slope in the optimal path⑦. Additionally, the author can select only the joints which mainly characterize a gesture⑧, i.e., when the goal is to recognize a gesture in which the user uses his right hand to select the next photo by slightly moving it from right to left, the remaining joints of the body do not need to be taken into account. Furthermore, if some axis doesn't play an important role for a gesture, such as the Z axis (the axis of depth) in the aforementioned example, the author is can disable it by unselecting the corresponding checkbox in④. Lastly, a gesture playback panel⑨ is available to allow the author to preview the recorded skeleton sequence in front and side realization.

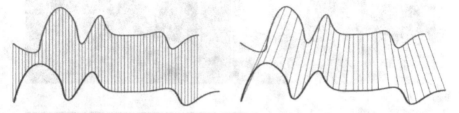

Fig. 5. Euclidean vs. Dynamic Time Warping Matching

When the recognition module is running, it captures constantly, in real time, skeleton frames, and when their total number reaches the number equivalent to one second then it starts the matching process. The latter calculates an optimal distance between the real time sequence and every sequence which is stored in the database. The sequences are "warped" non-linearly in the time dimension to determine a measure of their similarity independent of certain non-linear variations in the time dimension. It should be mentioned that Dynamic Time Warping (DTW) allows elastic shifting in the time domain and matches sequences that are similar but out of phase as shown in Fig. 6.

3.3   Head Pose Estimation/Face Tracking Module

The head pose estimation/face tracking module enables the creation of applications based on more natural and intuitive interaction styles. The implementation of this module builds on the Microsoft Kinect SDK and the provided facilities to track human faces in real time. The module reports measurements about the three axes of rotation of user's head pose (pitch, roll, and yaw) based on a right-handed coordinate system. Additionally, it reports the rectangle enclosing the head in the captured frame. For face tracking, six animation units (AUs) are tracked in real-time which are a subset of what is defined in the Candide3 model[3]. The results are expressed in terms of numeric weights which are deltas from the neutral shape varying between -1 and +1.

---

[3] http://www.icg.isy.liu.se/candide/

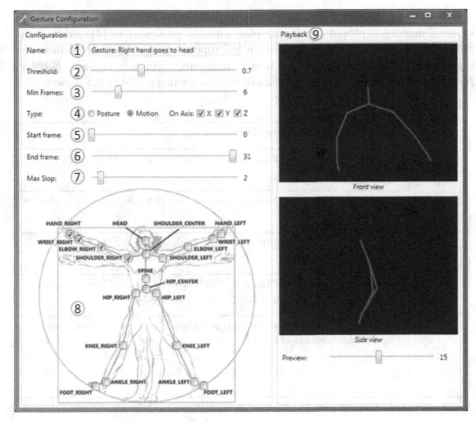

Fig. 6. Configure and fine tuning of a gesture

3.4 Speech Recognition Module

The speech recognition module is based on the Microsoft.Speech library found in the Microsoft Kinect SDK and the sensor's built-in microphone array as voice input device. This module takes a grammar as input and loads it to the recognition engine. At this time, speech recognition is supported only in a few languages. The module reports information about the spoken word or phrase which contains a unique tag, confidence as well as the speaking duration.

4 Using the Framework from a Developer's Perspective

The component modules of the Nibbler framework run simultaneously without any performance issues at almost 30fps on an ordinary pc (see Fig. 7). Fig. 7 illustrates the settings that are available for configuring Nibbler for the desired context of use. Nibbler communicates with clients and reports each module's measurements via a middleware network layer. The latter is designed to facilitate the communication of systems that are deployed on diverse platforms, as presented in [4]. Additionally, Nibbler can accept requests from clients in real time to change either the gesture training set or the grammar used for speech recognition. In this context, Nibbler's functionality is described in the interface definition language (IDL[4]) as follows:

Gesture recognition	`ami::StringSeq GetGestureNames ();`
	`boolean LoadGestures(in ami::OctetSeq gesturesConfigStream);`
	`void Event_GestureRecognized (in string gesture, in double distance);`
Head pose estimation	`void Event_HeadPoseChanged (in double pitch, in double yaw, in double roll);`
	`void Event_HeadRectChanged (in long left, in long bottom, in long top, in long width, in long height);`
Face tracking	`void Event_FaceAnimationUnitsChanged (in ami::FloatSeq faceAnimationUnits);`
Skeleton tracking	`void Event_HandRightPositionChanged (in Point3D position);`
	`void Event_HandLeftPositionChanged (in Point3D position);`
	`void Event_SkeletonChanged (in JointSeq joints);`
Speech Recognition	`SemanticResultValueSeq GetLoadedGrammar (out string culture);`
	`boolean LoadGrammar(in SemanticResultValueSeq grammar, in string culture);`
	`void Event_SpeechRecognized (in string value, in float confidence, in long long duration);`
	`void Event_SpeechRejected ();`

---

[4] http://en.wikipedia.org/wiki/Interface_description_language

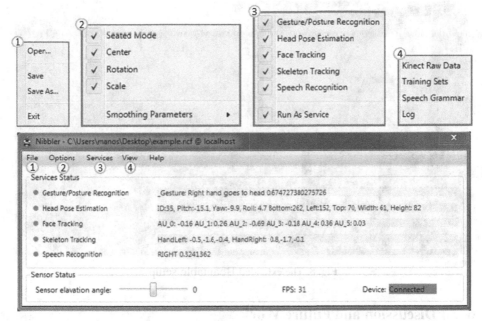

Fig. 7. Nibbler in a fully working mode

5   In Vitro Instantiation of the Framework

The interaction framework presented in this paper has been deployed and tested in vitro to extend the interaction capabilities of an augmented interactive table for young children (for ages 3 to 7) named Beantable [20]. Beantable has been developed in the context of the FORTH-ICS's AmI research program and is currently hosted within the AmI classroom simulation space of the FORTH-ICS AmI Research Facility. The purpose of Beantable is to support children's development through the monitored use of appropriate smart games in an unobtrusive manner. Beatable monitors the children's interactions and extracts indications of the achieved maturity level and skills by taking into account: (a) the way the child plays, (b) the selection of materials and game themes and (c) the way the child takes part into the activities. The addition of the interaction framework presented in this paper has expanded impressively the potential instantiations of Beantable by supporting also games facilitating biometric information and speech such the "Mimesis" game. The latter is an imitation game in which a virtual partner assumes various body postures and simultaneously invites the young child to imitate him as fast as he cans. The final setup of Beantable also includes a large wall mounted screen with an embedded Microsoft Kinect sensor collecting the data to be employed by the framework, as shown in Fig. 8.

Fig. 8. The extended Beantable setup

6   Discussion and Future Work

This paper has presented the implementation of a unified framework to support inter-action requirements in AmI environments at large, focusing on the architecture, driving technology and software infrastructure of the system. Regarding future improvements two are the main directions. First, a large scale user based evaluation is going to be conducted so as to evaluate the framework in different contexts and with alternative interaction scenarios, taking also into account biometric information of the target user population. Second, the framework itself is considered a living organism and is going to be enriched to take advantage of technology advancements both by creating new artefacts and enriching the supported interaction techniques. The first planned improvement is the integration of gaze tracking functionality so as to complete the suite of head tracking facilities.

Acknowledgments. This work is supported by the FORTH-ICS internal RTD Programme 'Ambient Intelligence and Smart Environments'.

References

1. Aarts, E.H., Marzano, S. (eds.): The new everyday: Views on ambient intelligence. 010 Publishers (2003)
2. Aarts, E., Encarnacao, J.L.: True Visions. The Emergence of Ambient Intelligence. Springer (2008) ISBN 978-3-540-28972-2
3. Alcañiz, M., Rey, B.: New technologies for ambient intelligence. The Evolution of Technology, Communication and Cognition Towards the Future of Human-Computer Interaction, 3–15 (2005)

4. Georgalis, Y., Grammenos, D., Stephanidis, C.: Middleware for Ambient Intelligence Environments: Reviewing Requirements and Communication Technologies. In: Stephanidis, C. (ed.) UAHCI 2009, Part II. LNCS, vol. 5615, pp. 168–177. Springer, Heidelberg (2009)
5. ISTAG, Ambient Intelligence: From Vision to Reality. In: Lakatta Riva, G., Vatalaro, F., Davide, F., Alcañiz, M. (eds.) Ambient Intelligence. IOS Press (2005)
6. Kaltenbrunner, M., Bencina, R.: reacTIVision: A computer-vision framework for table-based tangible interaction. In: Proceedings of the 1st International Conference on Tangible and Embedded Interaction. ACM (2007)
7. Kameas, A., Mavrommati, I., Markopoulos, P.: Computing in Tangible: Using Artifacts as Components of Ambient Intelligence Environments. IOS Press (2005), http://www.ambientintelligence.org
8. Kim, H., Fellner, D.W.: Interaction with hand gesture for a back-projection wall. In: Proceedings of the IEEE International Computer Graphics, pp. 395–402 (June 2004)
9. Nakanishi, Y., Oka, K., Kuramochi, M., Matsukawa, S., Sato, Y., Koike, H.: Narrative Hand: Applying a fast finger-tracking system for media art
10. Ohno, T., Mukawa, N., Kawato, S.: Just blink your eyes: A head-free gaze tracking system. In: CHI 2003 Extended Abstracts on Human Factors in Computing Systems, pp. 950–957. ACM (2003)
11. Ohno, T., Mukawa, N.: A Free-head, Simple Calibration, Gaze Tracking System That Enables Gaze-Based Interaction
12. Ohno, T., Mukawa, N., Yoshikawa, A.: FreeGaze: A gaze tracking system for everyday gaze interaction. In: Proceedings of the 2002 Symposium on Eye Tracking Research & Applications, pp. 125–132. ACM (March 2002)
13. Ohya, J.: Computer Vision Based Analysis of Non-verbal Information in HCI
14. Oka, K., Sato, Y., Koike, H.: Real-time tracking of multiple fingertips and gesture recognition for augmented desk interface systems. In: Proceedings of the Fifth IEEE International Conference on Automatic Face and Gesture Recognition, pp. 429–434. IEEE (May 2002)
15. Philips Research (2005), http://www.research.philips.com/technologies/syst_softw/ami/index.html
16. Phillips Research, Ambient intelligence: Changing lives for the better (2007), http://www.research.phillips.com/
17. Sakoe, H., Chiba, S.: Dynamic programming algorithm optimization for spoken word recognition. IEEE Trans. on Acoust., Speech, and Signal Process., ASSP 26, 43–49 (1978)
18. Stephanidis, C.: Human Factors in Ambient Intelligence Environments. In: Salvendy, G. (ed.) Handbook of Human Factors and Ergonomics, 4th edn., ch. 49, pp. 1354–1373. John Wiley and Sons, USA (2012)
19. Szeliski, R.: Image alignment and stitching: A tutorial. Foundations and Trends in Computer Graphics and Vision. Now Publishers Inc. (2006)
20. Valli, A.: The design of natural interaction. Multimedia Tools and Applications 38(3), 295–305 (2008)
21. Zidianakis, E., Antona, M., Paparoulis, G., Stephanidis, C.: An augmented interactive table supporting preschool children development through playing

Smart Cities

Applicability of Portable Health Clinic to Ageing Society

Ashir Ahmed[1], Andrew Rebeiro-Hargrave[1], Rafiqul Islam[2],
Sozo Inoue[3], and Naoki Nakashima[4]

[1] Faculty of Information Science and Electrical Engineering, Kyushu University
744, Moto'oka, Nishi-ku, Fukuoka, Japan
{ashir,andrew}@f.ait.kyushu-u.ac.jp
[2] Global Communicaiton Center, Grameen Communications
9F, Grameen Bank Bhaban, Mirpur-2, Dhaka-1216, Bangladesh
rimaruf@grameen.com
[3] Faculty of Engineering, Kyushu Institute of Technology
1-1 Sensui-cho, Tobata-ku, Kita kyushu, Japan
sozo@mns.kyutech.ac.jp
[4] Kyushu University Hospital, 3-1-1, Maidashi,
Higashi-ku Fukuoka, Japan
nnaoki@info.med.kyushu-u.ac.jp

Abstract. Portable Health Clinic is adapted to provide primary care to a super aged society. A super aged society occurs when, one third of the population is 65+ years and one fifth is 85+ years. The combination of aging society and incidence of non-communicable diseases increases the prevalence of elderly disability and places pressure on health care systems, health costs, and existing social norms. The goal is to reposition the Portable Health Clinic as a health information and affordable disability prevention system. In this paper, we show how the healthcare worker can supplement her competence on medical risk factors with sensor technology and share her knowledge with elderly patients within the community. We suggest that the remote telemedicine call center should be used to support distant screening and surveillance programs and provide early intervention to diseases. We investigate 18,278 Portable Health Clinic Electronic Health Records between 2012 and 2013 to see what are the most important risk factors for ill health in Bangladesh. The field data implies that elevated blood pressure and blood sugar and protein in the urine and the most important risk factors for the elderly population (>65 years) when compared to younger population (<65 years).

Keywords: Portable Health Clinic, Ageing Society, Personal Health Records (PHR), Remote Health Consultancy, BigData.

1 Introduction

The world is facing a situation without precedent: we soon will have more older people than children and more people at extreme old age than ever before. In Japan, it is expected that by 2030, one in every three people will be 65+ years and one in five

N. Streitz and P. Markopoulos (Eds.): DAPI 2014, LNCS 8530, pp. 533–544, 2014.

people 75+ years [1]. The transition from the current technological society to a super aged society will impact on long-term health care systems, local community support systems, and change the social structure with a large percent of elderly people living alone or with a spouse.

As aging populations grow there will be a corresponding increase of lifestyle related diseases. According to the World Health Organization over the next 10 to 15 years, people in every world region will suffer more death and disability from noncommunicable diseases (NCDs) such as heart diseases, cancers, and diabetes than from infectious and parasitic diseases [2]. Lifestyle related diseases are related to unhealthy diet and physical inactivity and manifest as raised blood pressure, blood glucose, raised blood lipids and overweight and obesity. Natural aging is also cause for disease and disability: for each decade after age 55, the chance of stroke roughly doubles; half of all new cases of type 2 diabetes occur over the age of 55; and the prevalence of Arrhythmia (irregular heartbeat) tends to increase with age.

To accommodate the social cost of aging society and lifestyle diseases, there is a strong need for affordable primary care. In particular, for healthcare delivery models that places less reliance on doctors and more on other health workers. Affordability is tightly coupled with information and communication technologies that integrate primary healthcare and the curative models and make healthcare environments more accessible for older and morbid people [2].

Information Communication and Technologies (ICT) remote healthcare consultancy systems have been deployed in the global market. Mobile health has increased access to healthcare and health-related information for many unreached communities. Health consultancy over mobile phone is popular in developing countries such as Bangladesh and provides an alternative solution for partial healthcare delivery [5]. To the extent that one such service holder receives 15000 calls per day for health consultancy [6]. However, these mobile health services do not test the patient against a diagnosis process or use Electronic Health Records and this reduces the primary care impact. In addition, there is little scope to empower the local healthcare worker with the mobile phone procedures.

2   Portable Health Clinic System

The Portable Health Clinic (PHC) system was designed by Kyushu University and Grameen Communication's GCC (Global Communication Center) to be an affordable e-health system solution for people in unreached communities [9]. It consists of back-end of data servers and a medical call center, and inexpensive front-end instances of portable briefcase consisting of medical sensors and measuring equipment. The front-end communicates with the back-end using mobile network coverage and Internet (see Figure 1).

The PHC back-end comprises GramHealth software applications, database, and medical call center. GramHealth software applications processes patient Electronic Health Records (EHR) and doctor's e prescriptions, and stores in a database. Doctors at the medical call center access GramHealth database through the Internet or have a copy in a local server. Upon receiving a multimedia call from a patient, the doctor can find patient's previous EHR, can create, and send an e-prescription [10]. This saves time and effort as the doctor does not need to questions about the patients' personal profile (basic attributes and medical history) but can focus on the immediate health inquiry.

The PHC front-end consists of a brief case containing medical sensor devices developed with international information standards, data transmission system with mobile network, data management application, telemedicine by Skype connection, and local Electronic health record preservation. The PHC briefcase is meant to be low cost and portable. It is envisaged to cost less than US$300 and can be carried by a female healthcare worker. The PHC briefcase will be owned and operated by a community health entrepreneur. This will be sustainable business model as the Health entrepreneur can build a professional relationship with her local cliental [11].

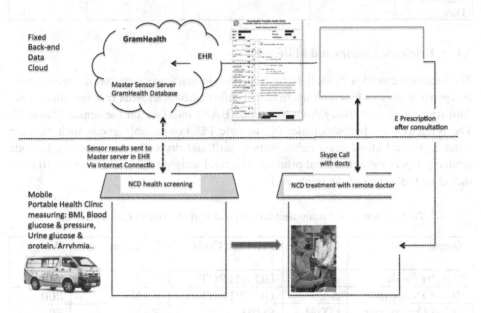

Fig. 1. Portable Health Clinic system architecture: back end data center and front ends health briefcases containing a comprehensive health measuring system that are be carried to a person house or community center.

3   Empowering the Healthcare Worker

The healthcare worker is the point of contact between the Portable Health Clinic service and the elderly patient health needs. The healthcare worker personally interacts with the elderly patient and can provide a social/community connection to socially isolated elderly persons (living alone). The Portable Health Clinic empowers the healthcare: she is responsible for large array of medical tests; she is in control of the sensors and devices; and she can explain the triage logic, and sets up the telemedicine call to the remote medical doctor (Table 1).

Table 1. Portable Heath Clinic tool kit

Personal Data	Personal Characteristics	Risk Factors	Medical Indicators	Intervention
Sex	Height (cm)	Body Temperature	Urine Sugar	Color Status
Age	Weight (kg)	Blood Sugar	Urine Protein	prescription_id
Address	BMI	PBS/FBS	Urine Urobilinogen	Site ID
Mobile No.	Waist	Blood Hemoglobin	SpO2	
Phase ID	Hip	Blood Pressure(sys)	Pulse Ratio	
Check-up ID	W/H Ratio	Blood Pressure(dia)	Arrythmia	
Check-up Date				

3.1   Briefcase Sensors and Materials

The healthcare worker 's toolkit is a light-weight briefcase consists of 'easy-to-use" inexpensive sensors based on international information standards that use either standard transmission or 'Body Area Network' (BAN) interface on the sensor (Table 2). The briefcase also includes tablet PC, or note PC, consumable goods such as urine tester tapes and blood sugar cubes, battery unit and dry cells, a measure, a barcode scanner, papers for writing and printing. The total weight of the case is about 10 kilos including the weight of the briefcase [12].

Table 2. Sensor and equipment for a typical Portable Health Clinic briefcase

Sensor	Maker	Product Code	Transmission	Weight (gms)
Weight Scale	A&D	UC-321PBT	BAN	2500
Blood Pressure	A&D	UC-321PBT	BAN	300
Pulse Oxymeter	OXiM	S-101	BAN	60
Blood Glucose	Terumo	MEDISAFEFIT	Felica	50
Body Temperature	Terumo	W520DZ	Felica	27
FeliCa Reader	Sony	PaSoRi	USB	35
Mobile Printer	Hewlett Packard	OfficeJet 100	Bluetooth	2500
Mobile Scanner	Fujitsu	FI-S1100	USB	350
Web Camera	Logicool	HD		

3.2   Sensor System Architecture

The healthcare worker samples the elderly patient's risk factors and medical indicators using sensors and devices during a 15-minute health checkup. A local sensor server (within the briefcase) receives and stores patient data via wireless-LAN and synchronizes its cache with the master sensor server when an Internet connection is available. The master sensor server in the back-end data cloud stores all sensor data and provides data to the Personal Health Record Server and doctors in the call center (see Figure 1). The interface of the local sensor server is the same of that of the master sensor server; therefore sensor boxes can directly connect to the master sensor server by changing the configuration address.

3.3   Morbidity Stratification Algorithm

The healthcare worker will inform the elderly patient that risk of morbidity (poor health) is identified using a triage stratification algorithm in the local sensor server. The elderly patient's risk factor measures of each health check-up item are compared against risk stratification matrix based on International diagnosis standards (WHO). The algorithm categorizes and grades the sensor results according to a triage: green (healthy), yellow (caution), orange (affected), and red (emergency). The current triage risk stratification is parameterized against a "B-logic" (Bangladesh logic) and an example of the categories is shown in Figure 2. The individual health condition can be enhanced by integrating results of a questionnaire into the 4 degrees by the worst color of all health check-up items.

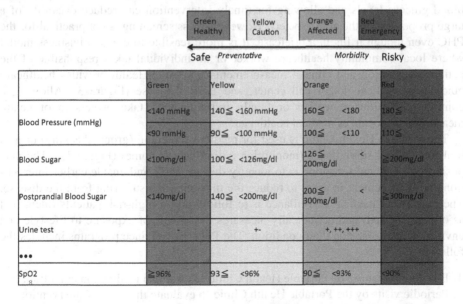

Fig. 2. Triage categories are based on medical recommendations

3.4   Booklet for Health Guidance

The healthcare worker gives the elderly patient a 11-page booklet that describes the advantages of a controlled diet and regular physical exercise and disadvantages of obesity, smoking, and chronic diseases such as hypertension, diabetes, and kidney disease.

3.5   Telemedicine and e-Prescription

The healthcare worker sets up a telemedicine session for orange (affected) and red (emergency) subjects using mobile network coverage to connect the patient to the medical call center at the back- end. In the call center, male and female doctors are available to provide telemedicine consultancy. Doctors access the electronic results of the patient's health check-up and provide advice for the disease or condition and can issue a e-prescription for the patient to access medicine via the network.

4   Healthcare Delivery Models

Portable Health Clinic is a healthcare delivery model that provides affordable primary care to the aging society. At it core, the Portable Health Clinic system is an ICT solution that informs the elderly person his or her health status. This is very important service, as most people are unsure of their own health status. For example, 35 to 44 per cent of people with diabetes do know they have it. Diabetes symptoms often do not show up until several years after the onset of the disease. PHC screening for high blood glucose levels and allowing for timely intervention can reduce disability of a large proportion of the aging society. However, mass screening is not practical for the PHC even though it fits in a briefcase. It is more feasible to create a business model where local community healthcare worker or an individual takes responsible of the patient registration and clinical measurements and GramHealth provides healthcare guidelines, medical doctor call center, and EHR database (Figure 3). Allowing a community healthcare worker or family individuals to take ownership of health measurements localizes medical health care.

The Portable Health Clinic is used for medical screening (group checking) or as a tool for medical surveillance (monitoring individuals at home) (Figure 3). The purpose of the medical screening is to identify disease early and enable earlier intervention and management in order to reduce the mortality and suffering from the disease. The purpose of medical surveillance is to follow-up on high-risk patients (identified as orange and red) and periodically measures the effects of exposure to lifestyle and environmental toxins on their condition. The PHC surveillance programs includes the following:

1. Baseline screening by Portable Health Clinic to establish medication condition;
2. Periodic visits by the Portable Health Clinic to evaluate the level of intervention;
3. Termination and handover to health system when the patient is chronically ill.

In each step, a doctor will available at the call center to evaluate the results, discuss the conditions with the patient, make recommendations, and send e prescriptions to the patient.

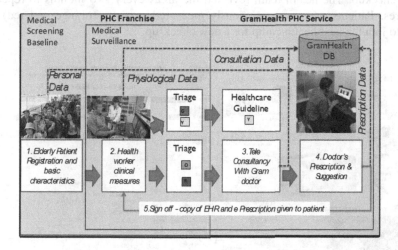

Fig. 3. Healthcare delivery models: group screening for early disease identification and home surveillance for elderly patient with a health risk

5   Identifying the Most Important Risk Factors in Aging Society

The Portable Health Clinic currently identifies 14 risk factors associated with heart attacks, strokes, diabetes and other conditions (Table 2).   For intervention policy, it is necessary to establish which are the most important risk factors in an aging society. This is achieved by analyzing the PHC data collected from Bangladesh.

Portable Health Clinic was tested against as random populations living in un-reached communities in Bangladesh. The test subjects were volunteers that responded to awareness campaigns conducted in urban, sub-urban and rural areas between September 2012 and November 2013. The experiment environment consists of the following facilities:

(a) Small call center in Dhaka (the capital city of Bangladesh) with two female and two male doctors, and one transcript writer;
(b) A portable health clinic briefcase with 12 diagnostic tools;
(c) Mobile health check-up team consisting two health assistants, 3 program assistants and one quality check officer. Patient data was captured from diagnostic tools wireless BAN and by manually inserted into our GramHealth database through a user-friendly web interface;
(d) Off-line version of GramHealth to store the patient's health profile and synchronize with the central server when the sufficient network bandwidth is available;
(e) On-line GramHealth software tools to process and store patient electronic health records.

The mobile health team visited rural villages and urban factories, and set up a PHC health camp service for one week (Figure 4). There was a marketing campaign 2 weeks in advance so that subjects could preregister to the event and book a time for a health checkup. The health team revisited the areas every two months to repeat the measures. Patients who were previously measured as risky (orange and red) were asked to join the next health camp for a new check-up.

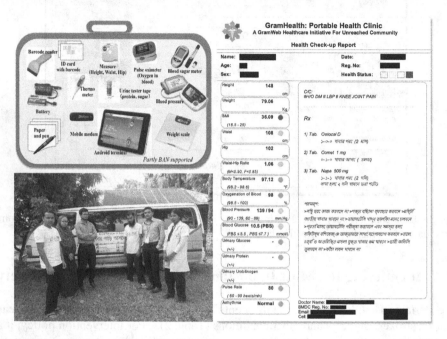

Fig. 4. Portable Health Clinic local team, the sensors used and Electronic Health Recorde generated during the experiment

During the experimental time frame, 18,278 patients received a health check and their EHRs are stored in the GramHealth database. The distribution between young and old is 17,252 less 65 years (younger cohort) and 1,026 greater then 65 years (elder cohort). The oldest patient was 106 years. The experiment was carried out in six rural regions and three urban areas including Dhaka. In one rural region, there is no mobile network coverage and the offline GramHealth(local sensor server) perfectly analyzed the data and classified patients into four groups. Telemedicine session with the remote doctor from this area point was not possible.

6   Comparing Elderly Cohort Data Against Young Cohort Data

The Portable Health Clinic identified morbidity for a large number of patients who were unaware of their illhealth. During the health checkup, 18,278 subjects were tested. PHC categorized 11,992 patients as low risk   (Green 1,976 and Yellow

10,016) and 6,276 patients as high risk (Orange (affected) 5,435 and Red (emergency) 841). There were 6,276 patient-doctor telemedicine consultations. The high-risk pa-tients were prescribed medicine and were informed to attend the next PHC health care camp for a follow-up health check-up, scheduled 2 months later. When comparing the young/old division, the elder cohort (greater than 65 years) was twice as likely to be categorized as high-risk patients than the younger cohort (less than 65 years). Of all the elderly tested, 60.1% had a telemedicine session and received treatment against 33% of the sample less than 65 years old (Table 3). In particular, the elder cohort was three times more likely to be categorized as an emergency case.

Table 3. Distribution of Triage results

Triage Categories	<65 younger	>65 Elder
Green (healthy)	11.3%	2.5%
Yellow (caution)	55.8%	37.9%
Orange (affected)	28.7%	47%
Red (emergency)	4.09%	13.1%

The general patient physical characteristic of the sampling frame reveals low BMI data for both younger cohort and the elder cohort. The experiment was conducted in rural Bangladesh villages and it appears that BMI is not currently an issue. Low BMI indicates that in this test, high blood glucose and blood pressure and are not related to overweight or obesity. There is a marked difference between patients suf-fering from Arrythmia (irregular heartbeat). The data shows that this is mainly a problem for the elder cohort (Table. 4.)

Table 4. Physical characteristics results

N=18,278	BMI		Arrythmia	
	<65	>65 Elderly	<65	>65 Elderly
Orange (affected)	0.4%	0.4%	0.23%	6.4%
Red (emergency)	0.05%	0.3%		
Total	0.45%	0.7%	0.23%	6.4%

The results of the blood tests of the sampling frame show significant differences between young cohort and elder cohort. Elderly patients were portrayed with high blood sugar levels inferring a greater propensity of developing diabetes II than the young cohort. Elderly patients were characterized with high blood pressure suggest-ing a significantly higher risk of stroke or heart attack compared to the younger cohort (Table 5). There are little differences in the SP02 measures between cohorts and this implies that blood oxygen is not an important risk factor in Bangladesh.

Table 5. Blood sample results showing increased risk for aging population

Blood Samples	High Blood Sugar		High Blood Pressure		SpO2	
	<65	>65 Elderly	<65	>65 Elderly	<65	>65 Elderly
Orange (affected)	0.4%	13.25%	0.017%	12.37%	0.15%	0.29%
Red (emergency)	0.15%	5.5%	0.008%	8.77%	0.08%	0.58%
Total	0.19%	18.75%	0.0026%	21.15%	0.23%	0.87%

The results of the urine tests of the sampling frame show noticeable differences between young cohort and elder cohort. High blood sugar in urine combined with high blood glucose indicates that 9% of the elders screened have developed diabetes II. High protein in urine is an indicator for heavy metal poisoning. The PHC data has captured the effects of arsenic contamination, and it appears the elder cohort have been exposed to groundwater arsenic for longer than the younger cohort. Urobilinogen is an indicator for liver disease and does not appear to be a high risk factor.

Table 6. Urine sample results shows increased risk for aging population

Urine Samples	Sugar		Protein		Urobilinogen	
Orange (affected)	<65	>65 Elderly	<65	>65 Elderly	<65	>65 Elderly
Low Risk +	2.08%	2.8%	5.65%	13.06%	0.25%	1.85%
Medium Risk ++	2.6%	2.14%	3.14%	4.77%	0.046%	0
High Risk +++	2.49%	3.5%	0.37%	0.9%	0.005%	0
Total	6.38%	8.47%	9.16%	18.85%	0.3%	1.85%

7   Discussion

The Portable Health Clinic is an affordable and efficient E health system that identifies morbidity in unreached communities. It's compact form, allows a healthcare worker to take the briefcase of sensors to any location or disaster area at short notice. The sensors and devices are easy-to-use, to the extent that that the healthcare worker can provide her local community a high-tech primary care. The back-end of servers, operated by Gramhealth can provide group medical screening and personal medical surveillance services to any community. The PHC system has been validated in Bangladesh. The system recognized diseases for 6,276 patients, of which 846 were emergencies (lives saved). Prior to their PHC measurements, the patients were apparently feeling in good health and were unaware of the their risk factor or they were feeling unwell but the disease was not diagnosed. The results show that elder cohort (>65) were at more risk than the younger sample. This is due to natural ageing process and longer exposure to life style disease. The most important risk factors were: blood pressure, blood glucose and protein in urine. These are followed by sugar in urine and Arryhmia.

These are good results, however there are constraints to the Portable Health Care system concerning scale, adaptability and interoperability. The portable health clinic is a mobile small-scale solution and cannot be compared to a large multifunctional health system such as a hospital. It can treat 1000s of patients and not millions of patients. The current PHC briefcase contains sensors that measure non-communicable morbidity and not infectious diseases or dementia. The Electronic Health Records are not interoperable with other E Health systems and the EHR stays within the Gram-Heath database until there is a standardized EHR format. Accepting these limitations, the Portable Health Clinic does provide 'on the ground' practical heath care for an aging society: low-income populations, and for short-term catastrophe coverage. It is based on a sustainable business model where the healthcare workers are localized (semi skilled entrepreneur and Health Assistant) and the experts consultants (doctors) do not travel or move to undesirable areas.

8   Conclusion and Future Works

In this work, we introduced the Portable Health Clinic system. We explained the system components, and operations. We created an experimental design and tested it against a large sample population in Bangladesh. Results showed that PHC could be used to identify morbidity and help reduce morbidity by providing health consultancy in unreached areas.

References

1. Muramatsu, N., Akiyama, H.: Japan: Super-Aging Society Preparing for the Future. The Gerontologist 51(4), 425–432
2. Global Health Issues, http://www.globalissues.org/issue/587/health-issues (accessed on March 1, 2013)
3. The Remote and Rural Steering Group.: Delivering for Remote and Rural Healthcare. The Scottish government, Edinburg (November 30, 2007)
4. Chaudhury, N., Hammer, J., Kremer, M., Muralidharan, K., Rogers, F.H.: Missing in Action: Teacher and Health Worker Absence in Developing Countries. The Journal of Economic Perspectives 20(1), 91–116 (2006)
5. Ahmed, A., Osugi, T.: ICT to change BOP: Case Study: Bangladesh. Shukosha, Fukuoka, 139–155 (November 2009)
6. Kai, E., Ahmed, A.: Technical Challenges in Providing Remote Health Consultancy Services for the Unreached Community. In: Proceeding of 27th IEEE International Conference (AINA), FINA-2013 Workshop, Barcelona, Spain (March 2013)
7. Chase, H.P., Pearson, J.A., Wightman, C., Roberts, M.D., Oderberg, A.D., Garg, S.K.: Modem Transmission of Glucose Values Reduces the Costs and Need for Clinic Visits. Diabetes Care 26(5), 1475–1479 (2003)
8. Bayliss, E., Steiner, J.F., Fernald, D.H., Crane, L.A., Main, D.S.: Descriptions of barriers to self-care by persons with comorbid chronic diseases. Ann. Fam. Med. 1(1), 15–21 (2003)

9. Cafazzo, J.A., Leonard, K., Easty, A.C., Rossos, P.G., Chan, C.T.: Bridging the self-care deficit gap: Remote patient monitoring and hospital at home. In: Electronic Healthcare First International Conference, eHealth (2008) (February 14, 2009)
10. Kato, S.: A Study on Implementing a Portable Clinic based on Social Needs. Undergraduate Thesis, Kyushu University (March 2012)
11. Nessa, A., Ameen, M., Ullah, S., Kwak, K.: Applicability of Telemedicine in Bangladesh: Current Status and Future Prospects. The International Arab Journal of Information Technology 7, 138–145 (2010)
12. Ahmed, A., Ishida, K., Okada, M., Yasuura, H.: Poor-Friendly Technology Initiative in Japan: Grameen Technology Lab. The Journal of Social Business 1(1) (January 2011)
13. Naoki, N., Nohara, Y., Ahmed, A., Kuroda, I.S., Ghosh, P., Islam, R., Hiramatsu, T., Kobayashi, K., Inoguchi, T., Kitsuregawa, M.: An Affordable, Usable and Sustainable Preventive Healthcare System for Unreached People in Bangladesh. Report (2013)
14. Kai, E., Ahmed, A.: Remote health consultancy service for unreached community: Amazing facts and technical challenges. In: Proceedings of the First MJIIT-JUC Joint Symposium, MJIIT, UTM, Kulalumpur, Malaysia, November 21-23 (2012)

The Vision of the Sociable Smart City

Eleni Christopoulou[1], Dimitrios Ringas[2], and John Garofalakis[1]

[1] Department of Computer Engineering & Informatics, University of Patras, Greece
hristope@gmail.com, garofala@ceid.upatras.gr
[2] Department of Informatics, Ionian University, 7 Tsirigoti square, Corfu, GR-49100, Greece
riggas@ionio.gr

Abstract. In this paper we define what is a Sociable Smart City and how this vision can be realised. This vision elaborates on recent developments in smart cities around the world where novel technologies and applications have been introduced in order to provide services and promote economic growth and sustainability. According to our approach a smart city has to also focus on social and cultural aspects, to allow people to interact with their cities in novel ways and to enable them to shape and decide the future of the city. This approach has originated from the large-scale deployment and evaluation of the CLIO urban computing system, which enables people to interact with the collective city memory. Our findings revealed that a system that exploits city infrastructure and both people's and artificial intelligence in order to empower and engage them in social activities may enhance citizen participation and sense of belonging as well as it may enable urban social interactions. Aiming to address the Sociable Smart City vision, we held a homonymous workshop in 2013 that brought together researchers of urban computing, smart cities, pervasive technologies and hci. Among its outcomes has been a definition of the Sociable Smart City, the identification of challenges in realising it, the proposition of applications that can accelerate its adoption and what their impact can be, as well as the identification of the major stakeholders involved.

Keywords: sociable smart city, urban computing, mobile computing, smart cities.

1   Introduction

A radical change in human evolution came when humans selected to live in permanent settlements and early forms of cities started to appear. From a demographic perspective a city is defined by four characteristics: permanence, large population size, high population density and social heterogeneity [1].

A city can be regarded as a permanent installation, large enough and structured in order to facilitate the collective and social life.

All cities offer certain functionalities; they may serve as political, religious and economical centres. A distinct characteristic of each city, though, is its relation with the physical landscape; the surrounding environment and the way a city is structured and has evolved affect the unique character of a city.

N. Streitz and P. Markopoulos (Eds.): DAPI 2014, LNCS 8530, pp. 545–554, 2014.

The diffusion of ubiquitous computing into modern cities and the massive use of mobile devices have shifted researchers vision to explore ideas about the cities of tomorrow; terms as "smarter cities", "iphone city", "sentient city", "digital cities", "intelligent cities" have emerged. A smart city invests in human and social capital, in transport and ICT communication infrastructure in order to fuel sustainable economic development and a high quality of life, as well as to achieve wise management of natural resources, through participatory action and engagement [2].

A smart city may touch upon all views of city life [3]: economy and the ability to transform, transport and ICT infrastructure, resource management and environmental protection, human capital and participation in public life, quality of life and socio-cultural progress, participation in public decision making. According to [4] an intelligent city combines three degrees of intelligence; the individuals' intelligence and creativity, the collective intelligence of the city population as well as the artificial intelligence embedded into the city.

There is a wealth of paradigms applying ubiquitous, pervasive and mobile computing to urban spaces focusing on providing new services to citizens and enhancing their daily routine; many attempts envision and gain inspiration from the *cities of the future*. Urban computing, a research field that lies on the intersection of architecture, social interaction and design of computer systems for use in urban areas [5], addresses not the city of the future; it rather allows people to interact with their cities in novel ways aiming to shape and decide the *future of their city*.

In this paper we define what is a Sociable Smart City and how this vision can be realised. We set off describing the experience we gained evaluating the effect of an urban computing system on the social and cultural life of a city. We then present our definition of the Sociable Smart City and we offer an account of a homonymous workshop that we organised inviting researchers to offer perspective on this vision. We discuss the approaches presented and the outcomes of group discussion on the identification of challenges in realising this vision, the proposition of applications that can accelerate its adoption and what their impact can be, as well as the identification of the major stakeholders involved. We conclude this paper with reflection on the role of technology and infrastructure, as well as of social and cultural processes in the realisation of this vision.

2   Evaluating Urban Computing Effect on a Smart City

In our study on the effect of urban computing on a smart city we utilised a system that allows people to interact with Collective City Memory. Collective city memory or urban memory [6] is a kind of collective memory that constitutes of individuals' experiences and the relations among them in shared contexts within a city. It is not located in sites but in individuals and their will to remember. Collective city memory is shared in a *Community* and is related to the *Place* as it is mentally anchored to the physical landscape [7]. In time it eludes as memories weaken and the landscape is altered.

Our system, CLIO [8], is a context-aware urban computing system that explores the possibilities that *Infrastructure* deployed in modern cities, ranging from smart personal devices to pervasive displays, offers in order to preserve collective city memory. It is a system that enables people to share personal memories and interact with the collective memory. It allows people to contribute pieces of memories using simple text or rich multimedia, to identify associations among memories, to rate them and to explore the city through them.

Deploying CLIO, our aim was to study how urban computing alters the city, the perception of people about the city, the communication and interaction among people and the social and cultural impact on the city and on city life. We employed a number of interfaces, exploiting available infrastructure, in two different settings in Corfu, Greece, and in Oulu, Finland. Following we shortly present our findings, which have motivated us to further pursue the definition of Sociable Smart City and to invite the research community in a dedicated workshop.

2.1   Impact on Social and Cultural Life

Regarding CLIO as a system empowering and engaging people in activities involving social interactions, we assessed its social and cultural impact on the city life. Field experience from the in-the-wild deployment of CLIO in two different cities, Corfu and Oulu, proves its benefits to a city community regarding participation, engagement, sense of belonging, social interactions and intergenerational dialogue, as well its contribution to cultural heritage preservation [8], [9].

We approached participation studying first whether people share their personal memories. Field experience shows that people who interact with CLIO start conversations and exchange similar personal memories; those who are fluent with mobile technology may share their comments and memories on the system. This exhibits the need for novel means of collecting memories, simulating the traditional human-to-human communication in society. Additionally, the pattern of interaction positively indicated community appeal and engagement.

Interviews and observations revealed that CLIO might enhance the sense of belonging in a community. People are initially hesitant to interact with CLIO, however, once they get familiar with it they rate, comment and share similar memories thus expressing their need to share their attachment to a memory, a location or an event.

Both the variety of user interfaces and the city infrastructure affected the social interactions we witnessed. Most people experienced strong emotions like laughing or arguing, as they often felt connected with the memories they viewed. The existence of public displays as anchors in the physical space attracted people and facilitated social interactions. Another positive outcome was the promotion of intergenerational dialogue, as groups of different ages often compared their memories and experiences. Finally, interviews recorded many positive comments about the idea of capturing personal memories and preserving this part of city culture.

3   Defining the Sociable Smart City

Sociable: willing to talk and engage in activities with other people; friendly
(Oxford dictionary)
Sociable is a place that is friendly and attracts people to spend time on it. It is a place that encourages communication among people and fosters a convivial mood. It is a place where people can be extrovert and engage in outgoing activities. It is open and welcome, approachable for all.

The sociable space concept [10] relates the physical structure, the functions and the activities in an urban environment. The structure and infrastructure of a city determine connectivity and accessibility; the design of structure makes it possible for functions to be established. The space functions in various forms; it provides communal, public and commercial services, it offers greenery and recreational facilities, it presents historical and aesthetical elements. Functions act as catalysts, attract people, encourage activity and movement and enhance quality of life and culture.

Activities that occur in a space reflect its sociable character. A public open space invites people to spend their leisure time: discuss the news, share a meal, linger and meet, play a game. Unexpected activities happen breaking the routine and providing variety; on a scheduled route one can meet unexpectedly a friend and chat for a minute or witness a street art performance. Occasional events, like personal or public celebrations, festivals and cultural events, markets and fairs, intervene the daily activities and the space is transformed to adapt. A responsive and creating environment can provide a fertile ground for learning and challenge experiences. A calm and harmonious space allows for spending some comfort and resting time.

Activities occurring in an urban setting are the catalysts for social interactions. Interactions among people and between people and the physical space in a modern city shape the unique character of each city. Cities are not just infrastructure and services; while all modern cities share the same infrastructure and offer similar functions, each and every one has evolved a unique character reflected in everyday life and culture. Cities are the people that inhabit them, their memories, stories, concerns and the culture that develops through social interaction.

A sociable smart city by definition should offer a wealth of novel infrastructure and services, however the focus should not be on technology, but on people. ICT infrastructure and digital technologies may empower people to participate and engage them to act on collectively shared issues. Such a city assists people to develop a shared sense of belonging and a feeling of ownership and responsibility to improve their city. Digital tools and new media can connect people and their experiences with the city. City infrastructure may enable game activities, learning processes and cultural events. A primary definition for the sociable smart city follows.

A *sociable smart city is one rich in infrastructure, which combines and exploits both people and artificial intelligence, empowering and engaging people in activities where urban social interactions thrive aiming to advance the quality of life and culture [11].*

4 Inviting the Research Community to Define Sociable Smart City

A number of workshops have been organised in conjunction with premium confe-rences under the general theme of smart cities. Most of them are technology-oriented, aiming to address key issues on infrastructure and services. We have put together a workshop to explore the societal dimension of the smart city and to introduce the term "sociable smart city" [12]. This workshop aimed to bring together researchers, practi-tioners and stakeholders from various domains to discuss and explore the sociable smart city.

The goal of this workshop has been to define what is a sociable smart city and how this vision can be realized, standing from the points of view of an urban informatics researcher, a city planner, and a citizen. Cities around the world integrate novel ICT infrastructure in the city fabric, we invited contributions that would attempt to answer how does it enhance participation, wellbeing and sustainability. We questioned whether digital technologies, ranging from telecommunication to social media, could affect citizens' ability and motivation to act on collectively shared issues or could assist citizens to develop a shared sense of belonging and responsibility. We encour-aged researchers to bring forward cases where local knowledge is transformed into collective one in an urban context, or urban applications enabled story-telling, game activities, learning processes, artistic installations, or even regeneration of urban areas. Finally, we welcomed contributions showcasing how big data, released by city authorities, transportation agencies, social media apis, can be opened up and exploited to reveal shared issues, processes and patterns and what digital tools and media can be designed to connect people and their experiences with the city.

Following we present how researchers approach the concept of sociable smart city as this is revealed from the presentations as well as the interesting insights and propo-sitions that emerged from the group discussion held during the workshop.

4.1 Approaches on Sociable Smart City

Contributions of our workshop revealed that researchers approach the concept of so-ciable smart city from diverse routes. The first course focused on methodologies that reveal and exploit city dynamics. Next tools, systems and applications that alter people's experience with the urban place were presented. Finally, all contributions exposed diverse aspects of a sociable smart city.

Methodologies on City Dynamics

A number of researchers work on the exploitation of data aiming to reveal city dy-namics. Sources of raw data can be public sector information released by city authori-ties, sensor readings relative to traffic, parking and environmental measurements as well as personal information from social media apis and crowdsourcing apps.

Citizens flows in cities is among the dominant issues on smart cities; [13] focused on pedestrian navigation aiming to expose the discontent that users often experience when machine intelligence proposes traversal paths based solely on GPS and map services. They identify the need to take into account subjective preferences affected by occasion and dynamically crowd-sourced data in order to generate paths tailored to the user's specific demands and safety.

Identifying interesting areas in a city assists both locals to explore their own city and tourists to better plan their activities. An approach proposed in [14] explores mining and appropriate visualisations of shared urban social context as this is manifested via tagging locations and check-ins on social networks. Their findings suggest that visualising social context as a background layer in maps, like heatmaps, does not hinder users cognitively and can lead to a useful service that can affect user choice.

Local knowledge, experiences and people become connected across a sociable smart city; [15] sees into connecting local memory web sites as a methodological tool to bring social benefits on a number of levels, the micro level were individual benefits are described, the meso level where effects for larger groups arise and the macro level on which local community strengthening effects appear. The proposed methodology researches how a sociably smart city can foster multilevel social empowerment leading to socially sustainable districts and neighborhoods.

Quick response to the ever-changing city dynamics is a theme that researchers and authorities seek to address. In [16] a system that assists tourists to explore places of art, architecture, culture and landscape through a personalised experience, also offers monitoring capabilities to local authorities thus enabling them to adapt public services to changing demand. In [17] exploitation of smart mobile devices for fast and accurate event reporting may also assist citizens in adapting their routines to avoid unforeseen disruptions.

Infrastructure, Tools and Applications

The keynote speech [18] revealed how vital is the city infrastructure for the exploitation of current technologies and the development and deployment of new tools and applications. The infrastructure available in Oulu, which includes an open municipal WiFi network as well as an array of large interactive public displays, essentially turns the urban space into a smart environment and provides unforeseen new opportunities and challenges for the interaction with the public. It thus allows research to advance from single user or small user group systems, which are dominated by prevalent mobile and personal devices, to complex sociotechnical systems for larger populations.

Public screens are widely used in modern cities, but their response to users' inputs is more often passive rather than spontaneously interactive. In [19] a tool that transforms a public screen into a public sociable medium connecting citizens and providing new opportunities for them to communicate with each other is presented. The transformed screen displays information according to user's context and allows citizens to easily and safely exchange resources through them. Ordinary places found in every city, like bus shelters, are thus reformed into sociable and intelligent public zones, capable of connecting citizens and enhancing social relationships.

People in smart environments often choose to mediate their experience of the place with a device or application. [16] presents a system that allows tourists to explore a place based on their interests and needs, accessing rich content while travelling via an augmented reality interface. Aiming to enhance the sociable character of visiting a place, it allows its users to interact by communicating with each other and sharing multimedia contents about their experience.

Participation is among the qualities that a sociable smart city seeks to promote. In [17] a crowd-source based sensing application is presented for emergency vent information gathering and dissemination through the use of smartphones. Data contributed by users and public services are combined and emergency or disruption situations are disseminated exploiting users' context.

Internet of Things technologies and embedded sensors find their way in smart cities. In [20] a smart city search service that allows citizens to exploit all these data is proposed. The conducted user survey reveals how citizens envisage an IoT search; user proposed scenarios cover most areas of life from daily to learning and leisure activities as well as social interactions. Important issues that emerged relate to privacy concern and the types of personal context that users are willing to share as well as the accuracy of results regarding their freshness and confidence.

Views on the Sociable Smart City
A number of contributions focused on highlighting the social and cultural impact of smart city systems and applications attempting to understand how the power of social technologies can be harnessed for social engagement in urban areas [21].

In [22] a new social form of play that involves a large number of participants as players engaged simultaneously in public areas is proposed. The presented platform allows the creation of interactive installations in public spaces. Observations revealed that large public displays enable sharing, informal interaction can be achieved shorty resulting to teaming up with strangers in the spur of the game.

Education is a shared priority in most smart cities. In [23] exploitation of smart city technologies to enhanced learning is explored. A methodology is proposed that promotes effective and meaningful learning experiences, expands learning beyond the classroom and fosters social interactions in the city. Students involved were engaged in an intergenerational dialogue, developed feelings of participation and an amplified sense of belonging.

Mobile, pervasive and locative media are systems of technologically mediated communication providing the opportunity to relate physical urban environments with digital information in order to create hybrid spatial experiences. Hybrid cities may function as the context for artistic installations and cultural activities and allow new kinds of collaborative activities and social interactions. In [24] the focus is on the concept of soundwalk, a subspecies of mobile sound art, and the relationships among sound art, mobile communication experience and artistic practices.

4.2   Discussion Outcomes

The main aim of this workshop was to bring together researchers, practitioners and stakeholders from various domains to discuss and explore the concept of the sociable smart city. Thus we invited the participants to work on two different groups and brainstorm on the following: define the sociable smart city, identify challenges in realising it, propose applications and case studies that can accelerate its adoption, imagine their impact and recognise the major stakeholders involved. The insights and propositions from the two groups as well as the final vibrant discussion came to interesting outcomes.

Commenting on the proposed definition of the sociable smart city [11], presented in section 3, both working groups emphasised on inclusiveness. This implies that everybody should be a beneficiary, without discrimination of any kind in a spirit of understanding, respect and acceptation. The smartness of the city regarding infrastructure and investment in technology was considered as a prerequisite. The term sociable suggests that smartness should be people-oriented.

Challenges in the adoption of the sociable smart city were identified on a number of levels. Technology challenges were considered easy to tackle as rapid developments soon solve difficulties of the present. Communicating the benefits of sociable smart city to key stakeholders, like politicians who can control the rate of adoption, is much more challenging, even more so when short term effects outrank long term ones in priority. Successful cases have been based on close collaboration among public authorities, researchers and community. Attracting a public audience to adopt such systems and applications requires overcoming privacy and security concerns, offering systems that prove themselves usable in the wild and allow users to self-organise.

The applications that were proposed covered most areas of life. Locality is important; users expect various location-based applications that ease their daily routine. Memory related applications were also favoured; local history, story telling, experience sharing develop a sense of belonging and participation. A number of applications move along the axis between learning and leisure; they might explore the urban environment as a playground for both education and recreational activities, as well as the setting for artistic installations and creative practices.

The impact of adopting sociable smart city is visible in social life on a number of levels; personal identify, common sense of belonging and community and citizenship. A strong impact on cultural life comes from the adoption of new communication channels among citizens. Community collaboration and participation leads to innovation via the exploitation of open data. Citizens are given the opportunity to redesign their future city or rejuvenate parts of it that have lost their ambience.

We are all stakeholders in this process with equal privileges and obligations, though we all have distinct roles. Research community, citizens, public authorities, learning communities, artists and participants of crowd-sourcing applications; all can contribute to the adoption and success of the sociable smart city.

5   Reflections on the Vision of the Sociable Smart City

Experience with our application and the systems and tools presented in our workshop has shown that a system that exploits city infrastructure and both people's and artificial intelligence in order to empower and engage them in social activities may advance the quality of life and culture. The city infrastructure has a vital role in empowering and engaging people in activities involving urban social interactions.

Modern cities should thus invest in deploying infrastructure, open communication systems should be offered ensuring people's right to access and cloud based solutions should be adopted providing a number of services and applications, Internet of Things technologies coupled with initiatives to open public data can offer real time access to the functions of cities and bring citizens are at the centre of the innovation process [25], and semantic web, linked and big data technologies can be exploited to process the expected vast amount of information.

Urban social interactions reflect the sociable qualities of a city; rich social interactions strengthen the community. A sociable smart city seeks to promote such interactions aiming to advance the quality of social and cultural life. The introduction of innovative applications in social life has the potential to promote citizen participation, develop a shared sense of belonging, assist decision-making and organise people into collective goals.

Acknowledgements. We would like to thank Iro Armeni, Carla Binucci, Dimitris Charitos, Huiliang Jin, Andreas Komninos, Mike de Kreek, Lambros Lambrinos, Irene Mavrommati, Richard Mietz, Timo Ojala and Katerina Talianni for their active participation at the workshop and their interesting insights and propositions towards the vision of the Sociable Smart City.

References

1. Wirth, L.: Urbanism as a Way of Life. American Journal of Sociology 44, 1–24 (1938)
2. Caragliu, A., Del Bo, C., Nijkamp, P.: Smart cities in Europe. Series Research Memoranda 0048 (VU University Amsterdam, Faculty of Economics, Business Administration and Econometrics) (2009)
3. Fertner, C., Kramar, H., Kalasek, R., Pichler-Milanović, N., Meijers, E.: Final Report on Smart cities – Ranking of European medium-sized cities. Centre of Regional Science, Vienna UT (2007)
4. Komninos, N.: Intelligent Cities and Globalization of Innovation Networks. Routledge, London (2008)
5. Hansen, F.A., Gronbaek, K.: Social web applications in the city: A lightweight infrastructure for urban computing. Hypertext 2008, 175–180 (2008)
6. Crinson, M. (ed.): Urban memory: History and amnesia in the modern city. Routledge, London (2005)
7. Halbwachs, M.: On Collective Memory. University of Chicago Press (1992)
8. Christopoulou, E., Ringas, D., Stefanidakis, M.: Experiences from the Urban Computing Impact on Urban Culture. In: Proc of the 16th Panhellenic Conference on Informatics, pp. 56–61 (2012)
9. Ringas, D., Christopoulou, E., Stefanidakis, M.: CLIO: Blending the collective memory with the urban landscape. Mobile and Ubiquitous Multimedia, 185–194 (2011)
10. Bäckman, M., Rundqvist, M.: Sociable Space in a City of Life - the Case of Hanoi. Master Thesis, Blekinge Tekniska Högskola/Sektionen för Teknokultur, Humaniora och Samhällsbyggnad, TKS (2005)
11. Christopoulou, E., Ringas, D.: Towards the Sociable Smart City. In: Workshop Proc. of the 9th Intelligent Environments, vol. 17, pp. 673–677. IOS Press (2013)

12. Christopoulou, E., Ringas, D., Garofalakis, J.: Introduction to the Proceedings of the Sociable Smart City 2013 Workshop. In: Workshop Proc. of the 9th Intelligent Environments, vol. 17, pp. 615–616. IOS Press (2013)

13. Armeni, I., Chorianopoulos, K.: Pedestrian Navigation and Shortest Path: Preference Versus Distance. In: Workshop Proc. of the 9th Intelligent Environments. AISE, vol. 17, pp. 647–652. IOS Press (2013)

14. Komninos, A., Barrie, P., Besharat, J.: Helping Tourists to Plan Activities with Shared Urban Social Context. In: Workshop Proc. of the 9th Intelligent Environments. AISE, vol. 17, pp. 663–672. IOS Press (2013)

15. de Kreek, M., Oosterbroek, M.: The Future of Local Memory Websites as Empowering Niches in Amsterdam. In: Workshop Proc. of the 9th Intelligent Environments. AISE, vol. 17, pp. 653–662. IOS Press (2013)

16. Binucci, C., Didimo, W., Liotta, G., Montecchiani, F., Sartore, M.: TRART: A System to Support Territorial Policies. In: Workshop Proc. of the 9th Intelligent Environments. AISE, vol. 17, pp. 629–634. IOS Press (2013)

17. Lambrinos, L., Bechara, K.: Integrating Modern Mobile Devices in Emergency Event Reporting and Notification. In: Workshop Proc. of the 9th Intelligent Environments. AISE, vol. 17, pp. 678–683. IOS Press (2013)

18. Ojala, T.: Keynote: Open UBI Oulu. In: Workshop Proc. of the 9th Intelligent Environments. AISE, vol. 17, pp. 693–694. IOS Press (2013)

19. Jin, H., David, B., Chalon, R.: A Proxemic Interactive Platform for Sociable Public Zones in the Smart City. In: Workshop Proc. of the 9th Intelligent Environments. AISE, vol. 17, pp. 617–628. IOS Press (2013)

20. Mietz, R., Römer, K.: Smart City Search: A User Survey. In: Workshop Proc. of the 9th Intelligent Environments. AISE, vol. 17, pp. 635–646. IOS Press (2013)

21. Foth, M.: From social butterfly to engaged citizen: Urban informatics, social media, ubiquitous computing, and mobile technology to support citizen engagement. MIT Press, USA (2011)

22. Mavrommati, I.: Keynote: Multiplayer Sensor-Based Games Used in Public Spaces. In: Workshop Proc. of the 9th Intelligent Environments. AISE, vol. 17, p. 695. IOS Press (2013)

23. Christopoulou, E., Ringas, D.: Learning Activities in a Sociable Smart City. Interaction Design and Architecture(s) Journal - IxD&A 17, 29–42 (2013)

24. Talianni, K., Charitos, D.: 'Soundwalk': An Embodied Auditory Experience in the Urban Environment. In: Workshop Proc. of the 9th Intelligent Environments. AISE, vol. 17, pp. 684–692. IOS Press (2013)

25. Mulder, I.: Opening Up: Towards a Sociable Smart City. In: Workshop Digital Cities 8 at the 6th Int. Conf. on Cummunities and Technologies (2013)

Communications in Emergency and Crisis Situations[*]

Andreas I. Miaoudakis[1], Nikolaos E. Petroulakis[1],
Diomedes Kastanis[2], and Ioannis G. Askoxylakis[1]

[1] Institute of Computer Science,
Foundation for Research and Technology - Hellas, Heraklion, Greece
[2] V.P PL Content Delivery BUSS, Ericsson A.B., Sweden
{miaoudak,npetro,asko}@ics.forth.gr, diomedes.kastanis@ericsson.com

Abstract. In emergency and crisis situations (ECS) like earthquakes, tsunamis, terrorist attacks, it is very important that communication facilities are operative to provide services both to rescue teams and civilians. In ECS it is very common that communication premises are often unable to provide services, either due to physical damages or traffic overload. In such a case there is the need for rapid reestablishment of communication services. In this paper the communication services that can be exploited for ECS mitigation are discussed. The usage scenarios of such services are studied. Following that and looking from a network perspective view an ECS communication network architecture is presented. This architecture aims to provide seamless interoperability of varies communication technologies often present in ECS to provide an ECS communication solution.

Keywords: Emergency, Crisis, Disaster, Critical Infrastructure, Heterogeneous Networks.

1 Introduction

A primary challenge in responding to Emergency and Crisis Situations (ECS) is communication which plays a crucial role. Emergency response is an open field for new innovative technologies due to the demanding nature of emergency operations. In the case of an ECS, communication infrastructure might be inoperative or have poor Quality of Service (QoS) to provide the required services. In ECS, different Emergency Response Authorities (ERA) are involved (civil protection, police, rescuers e.t.c.). This rises a major challenge regarding ECS communication infrastructures, the challenge of interoperability.

ECS management and mitigation is strongly related to the coordination of the authorized personnel. For example in the 9/11 terrorist attack at the World

---

[*] This work was performed in the framework of the PEFYKA project within the KRIPIS ction of the GSRT. The project is funded by Greece and the European Regional Development Fund of the European Union under the NSRF and the O.P. Competitiveness and Entrepreneurship.

N. Streitz and P. Markopoulos (Eds.): DAPI 2014, LNCS 8530, pp. 555–565, 2014.

Trade Center some of the police warnings were not heard by firefighters resulting in several casualties [1]. Thus communication infrastructure reliability is a key factor in such circumstances [2].

The primary technological challenge after a disaster is the adequate operation of the existing communication systems and/or the rapid deployment of emergency communication infrastructure for both first responders and civilians. The scope of studying communication scenarios in emergency and crisis situations is to acquire the necessary infrastructure specifications for emergency communications. In the case where fixed communication infrastructures have fail, the rapid deployment of an emergency communication platform could be the way to re-establish communication services [3, 4].

This paper studies the communication scenarios in emergency situations and presents a network architecture for emergency communication network. In section 2, the communication services utilized for disaster mitigation are analyzed. Emergency communication usage scenarios are described in section 3. In section 4, a network architecture to fulfill usage scenario requirements is presented. Finally in section 5 there are the conclusions.

2   Communication Services Utilized for Disaster Mitigation

Efficient ECS response can utilize various communication services that provide text, voice and video exchange. In this section ECS communication services in context to ECS mitigation are presented.

2.1   Push to Talk

Push-to-talk (PTT) is a technology that allows half-duplex communication between two users, where switching from voice reception mode to transmit mode takes place with the use of a dedicated momentary button. PTT works in a walkie-talkie fashion having several features and benefits [5]. PTT is a widely used service to ERAs and has to be taken into account in ECS communication infrastructures.

2.2   Audio/Voice Communications

In contrast to PTT, this service provides fullduplex voice channels. Public safety communication require novel full-duplex speech transmission services for emergency response [6].

2.3   Video Communication

Since first responders often need to share vital information, the transmission of real time video to a control center and vice versa could help disaster mitigation. For example in the case of a fire the transmission of live video footage from the disaster area to the Fire Department's command center and/or to the nearby-located fire fighters could be very useful.

2.4   Real Time Text Messaging (RTT)

Text messaging service is an effective and quick solution for sending alerts in case of emergencies. Typical examples can include: (i) individuals reporting suspicious actions to the police, (ii) people affected by a disaster communicating with their relatives, (iii) authorities informing the public about possible disasters. Types of text messaging can be SMS, email and instant messages.

2.5   Broadcasting and Multicasting

Broadcasting is the ability to transmit information to all users, while multicasting is the ability to send information to a group of users. Both functionalities, if supported by technology, can enhance public safety and rescue operations. For example, suspicious actions outside a bank can trigger the transmission of live video footage to the nearby police cars (multicasting).

2.6   Localization Services

Location information may be of great importance for disaster relief efforts. During emergency operations, the knowledge of the exact location of the victim can be used to guide first responders to provide immediate support. Location information can be obtained using several technologies [7], [8].

2.7   Transmission of Status Information

Status information refers to the status of several types of objects within a jurisdiction area. For example, in public safety operations, a sensor network can broadcast information related to the environmental measurements, the level of water or in the case of a terrorist nuclear attack a sensor network could sent Radiation levels of several locations.

3   Emergency Communications Usage Scenarios

Efficient ECS management is based on the efficient organization and cooperation of various ERAs in every country. To prepare the Civil Protection in dealing with ECS, the cooperation of ERAs at local, regional, national and European levels is tested in ECS scenarios [9]. The evaluation of the results of such drills increase ERAs readiness and give feedback about the usage of emergency communications. In this section emergency usage communication scenarios are presented.

3.1   Mobile Emergency Responder Usage

The emergency responder usage scenario involves access to services and applications by emergency responders. The key characteristic from the user point of view is to have seamless handovers without service interruptions or QoS degradation.

Mobile emergency responder usage refers either to the mobile or nomadic usage. In the mobile usage scenario the user is moving at a pedestrian / vehicular speed and has active service sessions. In the nomadic usage scenario the user suspend his applications and resume them in a later phase (for example when an ECS responder team move from one site to another).

To satisfy the above usage of the ECS network requirements are:

- **Interoperability.** Responders from different ERAs should be able to communicate with each other although they might have different type of equipment (Equipment that operates in different frequency bands for different authorities which seem to be a common case).
- **QoS support.** Efficient and scalable QoS support to support the needs for mobile responders including prioritization (for example a critical message to abandon the disaster area should be able to transmitted in higher priority), controlled jitter and latency and improved packet loss for voice and multimedia traffic [10].A Network traffic monitoring and tuning mechanism should introduced to provide the requested QoS.
- **Security and Privacy.** For example in the case of a terrorist attack responder communication should be available only to authorized personnel.To support interoperability, mechanisms for secure and fast hand-offs between heterogeneous networks and different operators supporting automatic reauthentication during handover should be incorporated.
- **Reliability availability.** The services should be available continuously and from all locations of the disaster areas as ECS responder are moving. The system should be able to adapt to varying network conditions as ECS mitigation is in progress.
- **Scalability.** As the number of active ECS responders changes (usually increases) the ECS network should be able to efficiently deal with network load variation. In addition the required coverage area usually grows as as ECS mitigation is carried out. The network should be able seamless extend its coverage area.
- **Location Services.** Knowing the location of the responders in the disaster site is very important for efficient coordination. Location services for the responders should collect responders location data that should be available to both fixed and mobile coordination centers.
- **Mobility.** In an disaster area, especially in the case of the mobile usage scenario where responders move into a large disaster site mobility support is a must.

3.2   Fixed Command/Coordination Center

This is the case of an emergency response command center in the premises of a civil protection authority, which is interconnected both to the wireless emergency response communication network, and to the national civil protection authorities.

The fixed command center coordinates the emergency response efforts and teams by delivering services such as VoIP, multimedia content sharing, peer to peer file sharing, tele-medicine services, and intergovernmental communications. The network requirements derived from this scenario are listed below:

- **Interoperability.** The different ECS network providers (different ERAs) should cooperate to provide services. A coordinator of one authority should be able to communicate with responder teams of other authorities.
- **QoS support.** Efficient and scalable QoS support. Prioritization of transmission should be offered. This is very important especially in the case where the network capacity is reached which might happen in the case of a emergency.
- **Security and Privacy.** This is very important especially in the case that sensitive personal data are being transferred (for example when tele-medicine applications are used to transfer vital data form a civilian under resque to a medical center).
- **Reliability/Availability.** Fixed coordination center relies on fixed network infrastructures. I case of an ECS fixed infrastructure load can be extremely high and can lead to network instability. In addition the fixed communication infrastructures may become inoperative due to physical damages. In such a case, alternative communication channels should be available (For example the deployment of an emergency wireless link).

3.3 Mobile Command/Coordination Center

This is the case of an emergency response command center on a vehicle, which is located in a strategic spot close or within the disaster scene and coordinates the emergency responders locally. It has to be interconnected to the wireless emergency response communication network, and to the national civil protection authorities (To the fixed coordination centers). The nomadic command center coordinates the emergency response efforts and teams by delivering services such as VoIP, multimedia content sharing, peer-to-peer file sharing, tele-medicine services, and intergovernmental communications.

The network requirements derived from this usage are listed below:

- **Interoperability.** The system should be able to operate with all available wireless access technologies as in the case of fixed coordinator centers. In addition the ECS network should be able to connect to the wired network infrastructure if available to improve the offered QoS.
- **QoS support.** Efficient and scalable QoS support should be available to provide classification to various responder teams. Again transmission prioritization is a must for such an application.
- **Security and Privacy.** Mechanisms for secure and fast hand-offs between heterogeneous networks and different operators supporting automatic re-authentication during handover to ensure user and application security.

- **Reliability/Availability.** The services should be available at all times and from all locations. The system should be able to adapt to varying network conditions as mobile command/coordination centers are deployed in the disaster areas.
- **Scalability.** As disaster mitigation takes place, the number of mobile coordination centers is growing as new ERAs are involved. The new coordinator centers should be able to join the ECS network. Doing so, the ECS network coverage increases as each ECS order to support load and area coverage growth as ECS mitigation is carried out.

3.4   Victim Communications

This usage scenario refers to communications capability between rescue workers and civilian victims. This communication can take place only with end user commercial devices such as cellular phones or Wi-Fi enabled mobile devices (Smart phones, Tablets, laptops etc.). This is a significant usage scenario, since current emergency response communications do not consider civilian victims communication. In this scenario, the victims are able to have direct communications with rescue workers to seek or guide assistance without the need of specialized communication equipment. The requirements derived from this scenario are listed below:

- **Ubiquitous Access.** The network should be easily accessible from everybody. No authorization should be required to use ECS network services (an example is the 112 emergency call.
- **Interoperability.** All end user devices such as cellular phones, internet enabled devices etc should be able to operate in the ECS network and no special devices should be needed.
- **QoS support.** The network should incorporate mechanisms for user prioritization to give priority to incidents requiring immediate response.
- **Security and Privacy.** The network should provide mechanisms for protecting victims privacy and should provide resilience to operational anomalies and security attacks.
- **Reliability/Availability.** The services should be available at all times and from all locations.
- **Location Service.** In the case of a disaster the civilian location is in most of the cases unknown especially in a large scale disaster. Locations services provided that ubiquitous network access is granted to transmit location data can be a useful tool for quick response. The system should autonomously detect and report civilians position in order to guide the rescue teams.

The requirements of the four above presented ECS communication usage scenarios are summarized in Table1.

Table 1. Requirements of Usage Scenarios

Requirements	Usage Scenarios			
	Mobile Responder	Fixed Coordination Center	Mobile Coordination Center	Victim Communications
Ubiquitous Access				•
Interoperability	•	•	•	•
QoS Support	•	•	•	•
Security and Privacy	•	•	•	
Reliability/ Availability	•	•	•	•
Scalability	•		•	
Location Services	•			•
Mobility	•			

3.5   Video Surveillance/Emergency Scene Video Monitoring

The ECS communication network can be applied for video surveillance applications by civil protection authorities. This type of usage differs from the previous four because video surveillance may be used not only in crisis situations but in a routine daily operation. The various ERAs can use this type of service to monitor places of interest as a precaution measure. In addition video surveillance can be used with specialized image recognition software to produce alarm services (for example to detect a fire and give an alarm to the fire department). In the case of a disaster, emergency scene monitoring can be very useful for disaster mitigation and responder teams coordination.

The preliminary requirements for the operators of the video surveillance application include the following:

- A large number of cameras are needed to provide enough coverage which leads to a high density network.
- Relatively high video quality that is high frame rate and high video resolution.
- High administration flexibility. Several authorities will be selected as administrators and they have to be able to access previous video captures or real-time events if special conditions occur. The members of the administrative groups might change during an event.
- High accessibility of the service. Civil protection authorities want to be able to access real time video from the command centers. In emergency conditions, the administrators of the system should be able to access the surveillance system through mobile computers.

4   Emergency Communication Network Architecture

In the ECS, emergency response does not take place all at once. In the beginning ECS responders arrive at the disaster site and operate independently. These teams gradually become part of coordinated action plan by a central disaster management entity, which requires more time to set up its infrastructure in place and become operational.

Traditionally ECS responders are using VHF/UHF PTT service for their communication and unfortunately the various ERA used communication technologies lacks interoperability. Approaching this scenario from a networking perspective, different responder teams form independent Mobile Ad-hoc NETworks [11] (MANETs). A MANET is a type of network, which is typically composed of peer nodes. When the nodes are located within the same radio range, they can communicate directly with each other using wireless links. This direct communication is employed in a distributed manner without hierarchical control. The absence of hierarchical structure introduces several problems, such as configuration advertising, discovery, maintenance, as well as ad hoc addressing, self-routing and security.

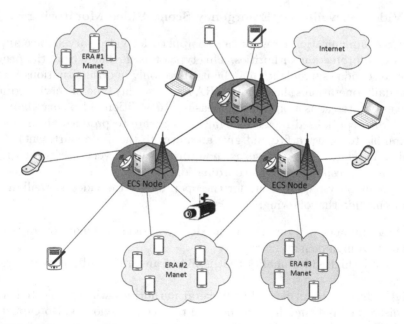

Fig. 1. Architecture of the emergency response network

A high-level emergency response network model is illustrated in Fig.1. According this approach, the network is based in the deployment of special ECS nodes in or near the disaster area. These nodes integrate various communication technologies such as Wi-Fi, GSM, VHF/UHF, TETRA, Satellite, and Radio

Broadcasting. Each node utilizes mesh networking capabilities to interconnect to each other. A mesh network consists of mesh routers that form a network with very similar networking attributes and characteristics of a static wireless ad hoc network. The mesh routers can function either as gateways to the Internet (either by using wireless infrastructure if available or satellite communications), and/or as wireless access points for mobile mesh clients.

The mesh network, which forms the wireless backbone of the emergency response communication system, provides various services to its clients such as Internet access, real-time communications, video streaming etc. In this approach, the mesh network is also designed to provide QoS applications with client mobility support. This way mobile mesh clients can perform seamless handovers between access points.

ECS nodes can use the installed communication technologies to provide all the types of services described in section 2. ECS nodes acts as routers-gateways for different technologies to provide seamless inter-networking. For example a coordinator located in a remote coordination center can establish voice communication with a responder that is part of an established MANET which is based in VHF/UHF PTT technology. A MANET node can be also considered as client to the mesh network and can perform seamless handovers between the ECS nodes.

GSM technology can be used from civilians to connect to the ECS network. This is very important as GSM terminals (mobile phones) are widely available from everyone and this way there is no need for purchase special equipment. In additional internet enabled devices such as smartphones or laptops can provide location services for the civilians rescue. Broadcasting techniques such as FM Radio Broadcasting can be utilized to transmit vital information to the public.

The proposed emergency response communication system can benefit applications and services such as:

- Multimedia exchange and sharing, of user-created content, such as pictures and videos taken by the first responders in the disaster scene. The main network requirements for multimedia sharing include high uplink throughput, and ubiquitous broadband access.
- Seamless service delivery across different network technologies: The presented emergency response architecture involves networking over heterogeneous access technologies and their integration with wired networks.
- Increased mobility: The proposed architecture aims to support seamless mobility through application-layer mechanisms, while guaranteeing the required QoS [12].
- Context-dependence: The support of ubiquitous broadband access service [13] for fixed, nomadic and mobile first responders and civil protection authorities can benefit other context-aware services, not necessarily designed for emergency response operations.

In addition to the above, all services and applications can benefit from the proposed emergency response system in terms of reduced cost, enhanced availability and coverage, and enhanced reliability.

Due to the fact that in disaster management, different emergency response authorities (police, first aid, fire departments etc.) are involved, the ECS nodes may belong to multiple operators (different emergency response authorities), and they cooperate to provide aggregate networking services to all of their mesh clients. Their networking cooperation model can be based on default agreements or, in case of multinational authorities, on agreed procedures technically similar to roaming of cellular networks. This way wireless clients can be associated with one or more operators.

5 Conclusions

The history has shown that in disaster and/or crisis situations communication plays a crucial role. In this paper the communication issues in disaster and/or crisis situation are addressed. First the communication services that can utilized for disaster mitigation are presented. Then usage scenario and need of both authorities and civilians of emergency communication infrastructures are discussed. Based on that and from the network perspective of view an emergency communication infrastructure architecture is presented.

The presented network architecture provide interoperability between different communication technologies. It utilises mesh networking capabilities to provide seamless handoffs between heterogeneous networks and different operators (This is the case when different authorities co-exist in the disaster scene). The presented architecture can be used either in the existing fixed and wireless infrastructure or to provide a rapid deployable communication platform to support emergencies and/or disasters.

References

1. Communications Broke Down on (September 2011) (2004),
   http://www.firehouse.com/news/10519316/
   report-communications-broke-down-on-9-11
2. International Federation of Red Cross and Red Crescent Societies. Report shows the benefit of two-way communication after a disaster (2013),
   http://www.ifrc.org/en/news-and-media/news-stories/americas/haiti/
   report-shows-the-benefit-of-two-way-communication-after-
   a-disaster-62291/
3. Sanderson, N.C., Skjelsvik, K.S., Drugan, O.V.: Developing mobile middleware: An analysis of rescue and emergency operations. Technical Report (June 2007)
4. REDCOMM: Rapid Emergency Deployment mobile Communication Infrastructure, http://www.redcomm-project.eu/
5. Push-To-Talk (PTT). InTechnology, White Paper (2011)
6. Public safety statement of requirements for communications and interoperability. Office for interoperability and compatibility, Department of Homeland Security, USA, vol. ii, v (2008)
7. D'Roza, T., Bilchev, G.: An overview of location-based services. BT Technology Journal (2003)

8. Naeem Akram, R., Markantonakis, K., Mayes, K.: Location Based Application Availability. In: Meersman, R., Herrero, P., Dillon, T. (eds.) OTM 2009 Workshops. LNCS, vol. 5872, pp. 128–138. Springer, Heidelberg (2009)
9. Earthquake followed by Tsunami in the Mediterranean Sea (2011), http://84.205.229.30/poseidon/
10. Kartsakli, E., Alonso-zárate, J., Alonso, L., Verikoukis, C.: QoS Guarantee over DQCA for Wireless LANs with Heterogeneous Traffic. ICT Summit 2009, 1–8 (2009)
11. Lu, W., Seah, W.K.G., Peh, E.W.C., Ge, Y.: Communications Support for Disaster Recovery Operations using Hybrid Mobile Ad-Hoc Networks. In: 32nd IEEE Conference on Local Computer Networks, LCN 2007 (2007)
12. Kartsakli, E., Cateura, A., Verikoukis, C., Alonso, L.: A Cross-Layer Scheduling Algorithm for DQCA-based WLAN Systems with Heterogeneous Voice-Data Traffic. In: 14th IEEE Workshop on Local & Metropolitan Area Networks (2005)
13. Fragkiadakis, A.G., Askoxylakis, I.G., Tragos, E.Z., Verikoukis, C.V.: Ubiquitous robust communications for emergency response using multi-operator heterogeneous networks. EURASIP Journal on Wireless Communications and Networking (1), 13 (2011)

Sociable Smart Cities: Rethinking Our Future through Co-creative Partnerships

Ingrid Mulder[1,2]

[1] Creating 010, Rotterdam University of Applied Sciences, Wijnhaven 99-107,
3011 WN Rotterdam, The Netherlands
[2] ID-Studiolab, Faculty of Industrial Design Engineering, Delft University of Technology,
Landbergstraat 15, 2628 CE Delft, The Netherlands
mulderi@acm.org

Abstract. The challenges of tomorrow's society demand new ways of innovation – a shift in thinking, doing and organising. It requires releasing existing paradigms, changing perspectives and doing things differently. In the current work, we envision a sociable smart city that enables transforming society into a more participative domain where participatory innovation takes place. A city that combines best a two worlds; on the one hand, a social city that is people-centred, values active citizenship and embraces community-driven innovation, and, on the other, a smart city that welcomes the possibility of Future Internet and related technology-driven innovations, such as Open Data, Internet of Things and Living Labs offer. The biggest challenges cities face is not the technology, but having an open mindset and a participatory attitude to rethink our future is far more challenging.

Keywords: Co-creative partnerships, empowerment, open mindset, participatory citizenship, social change, transformation design, transforming society.

1   Introduction

Cities are becoming more and more of a focal point for our economies and societies at large, particularly because of on-going urbanization, and the trend towards increasingly knowledge-intensive economies as well as their growing share of resource consumption and emissions. To meet public policy objectives under these circumstances, cities need to change and develop, but in times of tight budgets this change needs to be achieved in a smart way: our cities need to become 'smart cities' [14].

In November 2013, the European Innovation Partnership on Smart cities and communities has shared their "Strategic Implementation Plan" discussing how to put the outlined actions into practice. It is obvious that meeting our societal challenges asks for a deep socio-ecological transition of Europe. This implies changes on a city level, in urban development and our governmental structures, but also changes in our personal lifestyles, such as our consumption patterns, that directly impact our daily lives.

In order to drive such a social change, empowerment is crucial; without willingness and personal commitment of citizens, these challenges cannot be met.

N. Streitz and P. Markopoulos (Eds.): DAPI 2014, LNCS 8530, pp. 566–574, 2014.

Hence, citizens are at the heart of our cities, they therefore need to be at the heart of change as well.

1.1   Empowering People, Driving Change

In his New Year's speech Ahmed Aboutaleb, the Mayor of Rotterdam, said that the crisis made Rotterdam strong [4]. The city had faced substantial financial setbacks, though the international crisis has not discouraged city's initiatives, but rather made Rotterdam strong.

The Rotterdam. "While across the country the construction sector faces difficult times, in our city still structures of size arise. The Rotterdam, the building by architect Rem Koolhaas on the Wilhelmina Pier is national news sensation. The building is a city within a city, a motor for Rotterdam," said the mayor. He also referred to the Rotterdam Central Station, whose major renovation is almost finished.

Facelift. "The city centre has been given a facelift by numerous attractive projects, such as 'the Meent' and 'Nieuwe Binnenweg', two beautifully restored shopping streets, with the allure of the past and the facilities of the future." The port of Rotterdam shows, despite the crisis still growth. "The port grows to the epicentre of the world in the field of oil storage and oil trade."

Trust and Tolerance. However, not only the construction and port sector demonstrate the success of a city. It is the people that make the city, the Mayor argues. "Together we make the future of Rotterdam. And we do that with tools everyone has: with confidence and tolerance."

Air Singel. As an example he mentioned the Air Singel, a bridge realised by citizens through crowdfunding and awarded best city initiative in 2012. He also referred to those neighbourhoods where residents have made arrangements to make their living environment safer and cleaner. "Or look to those who help their new neighbours learning the Dutch language."

Peace in the City. These are the things that make life meaningful. These small things help. They lead to peace in the city, says the mayor. "Peace is not an abstract concept, it is a verb. Peace cannot be achieved with large conventions, but starts in dealing with people in the neighbourhood, at work or in the city. It starts with something small, something beautiful. It begins with trust."

The recent speech of the Mayor of Rotterdam nicely illustrates a social city open to empower its citizens in order to drive social change. Social innovation is crucial to every city, though driving social change is primary focus in Rotterdam, taken into account the extreme situation in the Southern part of Rotterdam. "On the South there is an accumulation of arrears in housing quality, work and income, training and education. Southern districts have a relatively young population, with many children who grow up in a deprived environment. Their parents are poorly educated, have little to spend and the environment gives little incentive to move forward. It can be said that the Southern part lacks a climate of learning and working" [8].

In a recent meeting the director of the National Program Rotterdam South clearly stated that doing the same in a better and more efficient way is not enough! The current situation in Rotterdam requires radical change and social innovation. It calls for "reshaping society in the direction of a more participative arena where people are empowered, learning is central which make policies more effective" [2].

1.2   Outline

In the current work, we envision a sociable smart city that enables transforming society into a more participative domain where participatory innovation takes place. A city that combines best a two worlds; on the one hand, a social city that is people-centred, values active citizenship and embraces community-driven innovation, and, on the other, a smart city that welcomes the possibility of Future Internet and related technology-driven innovations, such as Open Data, Internet of Things and Living Labs offer. This vision is illustrated with experiences from Rotterdam that demonstrate the power of a sociable smart city, and were helpful in co-designing futures that inform local policy. In keeping with Sangiorgi [11] we address the transformative role of design in order to reshape society while developing and applying methods for participatory innovation.

The challenges of tomorrow's society demand new ways of innovation – a shift in thinking, doing and organising. New strategies, ideas, concepts or ways of organisation are seen as to deal with societal challenges. It requires releasing existing paradigms, changing perspectives and doing things differently.

2   Towards a Participatory Domain

In his inaugural throne speech on September 17, 2013 the Dutch King stated that the traditional welfare state is slowly but surely turning into a participatory society. "When people shape their own future, they not only add value to their own lives, but also to society as a whole", was added as an explanation [16].

Since then, the Dutch government considers the so-called DIY-democracy referring to social initiative and social entrepreneurship, as a powerful development that should be embraced. Initiative is with the citizens; the government suites a modest role, although they must actively contribute to the DIY democracy. Differently put, the emphasis moves from citizen participation to the participation of government. It calls for a changing role of government. To facilitate it's own change, the government has drawn up an agenda with social partners.

Interestingly, the word 'participatory society' has been introduced in Dutch politics, years ago. Already in 1991, Wim Kok, a former leader of the Labour Party, addressed that "We are now in a state of transition from a welfare state to an active to a participatory society" [15].

2.1   Citizen Power

The previous policy anecdote nicely demonstrates that participation does not happen because it is on the political agenda. Citizen participation, user participation, and resident participation are all about participation; although different disciplines are involved dealing with different kinds of parlance, they also share a similar approach: participatory design. Whereas participatory design has its roots in the Scandinavian democratic movements, viewing participants as equal, as partner, current participatory practices still too often derive from an unequal relationship. Still too often, it is the designer that wants users to participate, the government that wants citizens to participate. In other words, a top-down approach towards citizen participation.

Having a look at Arnstein's ladder of citizen participation [1] that distinguish the level of participation, from non-participation to empowered citizens, it is clear that such an unequal relationship does not lead to empowered citizens (see Fig. 1). How can equal partnerships enable turning the public domain into a participatory domain?

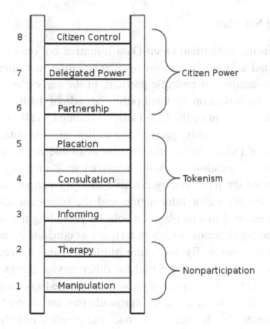

Fig. 1. Ladder of Citizen Participation [1]

2.2   Changing Role of Government

Local governments are increasingly using digital tools to inform and communicate with citizens, and are open for new ways to involve citizens in policymaking. At the same time the popularity of social media has spurred a demand for new forms of self-organising governance by citizens.

It can be said, that citizens' involvement in neighbourhood affairs and collective action are often below the potential given citizens' willingness to contribute. Although the Internet is a promising platform for e-Participation, existing websites, take for example, FixMyStreet emphasises the involvement of citizens, though they do not cultivate active citizenship [13]. Obviously, contemporary cities do not fully benefit from the opportunities a smart city offers.

The challenge is to embrace a new collaborative attitude, a participatory approach, and have a proper infrastructure that supports this social fabric.

3   Co-creative Partnerships Illustrating the Rotterdam Way

The current section briefly reports some initial participatory practices in order to have Rotterdam meet their ambitions of being an open government. These practices illustrate the value of the transformative role of design in order to reshape society.

3.1   Co-creating Services

Early prototyping in the Rotterdam Open Data initiative not only provided many insights, but it also had a larger impact on open innovation in Rotterdam. The active participation and co-creation of multiple partners in the early phases of idea generation managed to put open data on the local policy agenda of the Rotterdam municipality. The board of management of the City Council decided to allow the release of the City Development Service's Public Sector Information as open data, having currently significant amounts of Public Sector Information available in an open data store for experimentation and co-creation of public services in Rotterdam. In addition, the project also introduced the participating creative-industry partners to the potential of using and re-using Public Sector Information and the important role of the creative industry in that endeavor. Citizens played a role by providing the input for the creation of the prototype applications, which in turn act as concrete examples to illustrate the benefit of the cooperation. By animating public servants to free up more Public Sector Information for re-use, potential fuel for other service design applications was created. The final event where applications were presented also acted as a platform where partners with different strategic backgrounds met and discussed the developed applications. The partnership between academia, the creative industry, and the public sector was awarded with additional research funding for two projects to further ensure the release of Public Sector Information. By ensuring participation of the crucial partners, a sustainable infrastructure has been created to co-create public services and foster further innovation with Public Sector Information. The Rotterdam Open Data initiative demonstrates that co-creation can also lead to the development of better public services, with citizens and the private sector contributing data by means of crowdsourcing, and it paves the way for more co-creation through open service development (see [3] for details).

3.2   Open Mindset, Open Future

Release of Public Sector Information through co-creation not only resulted in a policy to opening up public data, it also demonstrated the value of experimentation and co-creation in order to inform social policy. Experiences with co-creative partnership show how to deal with and lower thresholds and being open to empowering, open to share, and open to change. This is in keeping with the open governance model promoted in DG CONNECT's vision on public services [5]. Pre-requisites for a sociable smart city are in place, a city as a true living lab enables co-creative practices and has citizens shaping their own surroundings; making and co-designing the city. The user-driven approach, do-it-yourself mindset, and the participatory character perfectly fit the down-to-earth Rotterdam attitude [7].

3.3   Citizen Power

In keeping with various trends, such as crowdsourcing, open innovation, open government, local municipality of Rotterdam is changing its role from top-down service provider towards a facilitator with their Rotterdammer-centered approach. The municipality of Rotterdam wants to strengthen collaboration with the citizens and organizations. For this purpose, local government launched for example the City Initiative aiming to facilitate active citizenship. Citizens are empowered and stimulated in building a beautiful and attractive city. The City Initiative supports people who are proud of our city and in realizing their ideas in making the city more beautiful and fun. This is in keeping with the participatory design principle that the user is expert of his or her own context [10]. In 2013 citizens proposed over 120 plans. The City Initiative board made a selection of these 120 plans. As a next step, citizens make their voices heard and vote on their preferred initiative. The municipality will provide up to € 2.5 million to realize the plan(s). The huge amounts of citizen initiatives address the existing social fabric, even though it cannot be expected that all citizens are becoming active citizens.

Although this is an example to encourage active citizenship, the Rotterdammer-centered approach implies that municipality has to participate as well. Several workshops and sessions are organised to discuss how participation can happen from all side leading to equal relationships. The mindset is there and it is clear that there is a passionate momentum, but even with motivated and committed civil agents, it is not easy to change an existing organisation. Changes are necessary, a focus on organising rather that the organisation, and a focus on empathy and collaboration rather than policies for the citizens, in order to make a transforming government happen.

3.4   Uncovering Hidden Talent

In the Ik ben STER(k) project [9], gaining trust and bonding with the local community, its gatekeepers and the culturally diverse array of residents has been a crucial strategy to build social capital throughout the whole process in a participatory, bottom-up approach. This approach allowed the design solution to come from within the community and not from outside, planting a seed for positive change in the local society.

The target community was a group of students from the neighborhood school, a school for drop-outs that gives them a last change to participate in society. The peer-to-peer learning by doing philosophy promoted at FabLab 010 has provided a strong drive in engaging the students in a workshop for talent empowerment facilitated by social media and Open Fabrication technologies. When appropriately facilitated, the skills and talents of these young adults started emerging, unlocking the potential envisioned at the beginning of this adventure and in many cases exceeding expectations by far.

3.5   Rotterdam City Lab: A Space for Co-creative Partnerships

Rotterdam has a FabLab, which started from educational needs [6]. It is designed as a FabLab+ with a strong emphasis on electronic and sensor devices, the Internet of Things, and Open Data (Applab). Although the lab is a prototyping workshop for students in the first place, it is also an interface to the city, a creative hotspot open to citizens enabling co-creation and participatory design. In other words, it is an active learning environment for practicing making, co-creation, and participatory design skills.

In the Applab, students, teachers and researchers, co-create with Rotterdam-based companies, civil agents and citizens in the design of meaningful applications making use of the Rotterdam Open Data, such as the ScoreZe App [12]. 'ScoreZe' (meaning: rate them) is an application for location-based quality of life measuring informing city maintenance. In this way, ScoreZe is different than other applications, such as Fix-MyStreet, which do provide citizens with the opportunity to log problems in public space. ScoreZe enables local municipality to re-use citizen-generated data for informing the budgeting of the Rotterdam Municipality maintenance budgeting. Budgeting can be determined based on the norm derived from data gathered by citizens. This participatory gathered data also makes execution of maintenance operations more accurate, since there is more data available about how citizens feel on certain locations at a certain moment in time [13].

3.6   Infrastructure as Social Fabric

Having a unique mobile and wireless infrastructure, enhanced with public screens and Open Data, the foundations for a smart city are there. Public sector information is released and available in the city's open data store. Currently, initiatives are launched to add crowd-sourced citizen-generated data as well. The city infrastructure has become much smarter aiming to facilitate the social fabric as well. However, to benefit from the opportunities offered by the smart city concept, citizens need to be able to participate fully in an internet-enabled society, through adequate skills and the ability to manage their rights online, such as their privacy.

4   Concluding Remarks

The challenges of tomorrow's society demand new ways of innovation – a shift in thinking, doing and organising. Not only are new strategies, ideas, and ways of organisation needed to cope with societal challenges, but also co-creative partnerships demonstrating a sustainable relationship to make a transforming society happen. It's not about who drives, but finding a mutual drive.

A future city needs to be a sociable smart city that enables transforming society into a more participative domain where participatory innovation takes place. A city that combines best a two worlds; on the one hand, a social city that is people-centred, values active citizenship and embraces community-driven innovation, and, on the other, a smart city that welcomes the possibility of Future Internet and related technology-driven innovations, such as Open Data, Internet of Things and Living Labs offer.

Even though, visions of the future give clear directions, and current achievements in citizen's engagement and empowerment provide a good fundament for establishing a social city, it appears not easy to apply best practises supporting a sociable smart city on a large scale. Differently put, contemporary cites do not fully benefit from smart infrastructures at hand. The biggest challenges are not the technology, the challenge is to embrace a new collaborative attitude, a participatory approach, and have a proper infrastructure that supports this social fabric.

Acknowledgements. Special thanks to my colleagues at Creating 010 for the many fruitful and co-creative discussions. Part of this work has been presented at Digital Cities 8 workshop in Munich, and shared among the workshop participants.

References

1. Arnstein, S.R.: A Ladder of Citizen Participation. JAIP 35(4), 216–224 (1969)
2. Bureau of European Policy Advisors, Empowering people, driving change: Social innovation in the European Union. Publications Office of the European Union, Luxembourg (2010)
3. Conradie, P., Mulder, I., Choenni, S.: Rotterdam Open Data: Exploring the release of public sector information through co-creation. In: Proc. of ICE 2012, Munich, Germany, pp. 187–196 (2012), http://dx.doi.org/10.1109/ICE.2012.6297651 (retrieved on February 7, 2014)
4. Crisis maakt Rotterdam sterk, In: Binnenlands Bestuur (2013) (January 8, 2013)
5. DG CONNECT. A vision for public services. European Commission (June 13, 2013)
6. Mostert-van der Sar, M., Mulder, I., Remijn, L., Troxler, P.: FabLabs in Design Education. In: Proc. of E&PDE 2013, International Conference on Engineering and Product Design Education, September 5-6, pp. 629–634. Dublin Institute of Technology (DIT), Dublin (2013)
7. Mulder, I.: Opening Up: Towards a Sociable Smart City. In: Proc. of Digital Cities 8, From Services to Partnerships, International Workshop Co-Located with the 6th Intl. Conf. on Communities and Technologies (C&T 2013), Munich, Germany, June 30 (2013)

8. National Program Rotterdam Zuid, Uitvoeringsplan 2012-2014 (National Program Rotterdam South, Executive Plan,
   http://www.rotterdam.nl/BSD/Document/Perskamer/
   RapportNPRZ%20dd%204%20juli%202012.pdf (retrieved on February 7, 2014)
9. Pucci, E.L.: IK BEN STER(K). A peer-to-peer talent development platform empowering young adults, video (2013), http://t.co/0u1vGyP7KE
10. Sanders, E.B.-N., Stappers, P.J.: Co-creation and the new landscapes of design. CoDesign 4(1), 5–18 (2008)
11. Sangiorgi, D.: Transformative Services and Transformation Design. International Journal of Design 5(2), 29–40 (2011)
12. ScoreZe: An App to rate your neighbourhood,
    https://itunes.apple.com/nl/app/
    score-ze-applicatie-om-je/id727141950?l=en&mt=8
13. Stembert, N., Conradie, P., Mulder, I., Choenni, S.: Participatory Data Gathering for Public Sector Reuse: Lessons Learned from Traditional Initiatives. In: Wimmer, M.A., Janssen, M., Scholl, H.J. (eds.) EGOV 2013. LNCS, vol. 8074, pp. 87–98. Springer, Heidelberg (2013)
14. Strategic Implementation Plan of the European Innovation Partnership on Smart cities and communities,
    http://ec.europa.eu/eip/smartcities/files/sip_final_en.pdf
    (retrieved on February 7, 2014)
15. Taalbank. Participatiesamenleving: het woord van de dag (Participatory Society: The word of the day) (September 17, 2013),
    http://www.taalbank.nl/index.php/woord-van-de-
    dag/item/participatiesamenleving (retrieved on February 5, 2014)
16. Throne Speech 2013. Elsevier,
    http://www.elsevier.nl/Nederland/nieuws/2013/9/Troonrede-
    2013-volledige-tekst-1365922W/ (retrieved on February 7, 2014)

The Design Process of an Urban Experience

Anne Nigten

Director of the Patching Zone, Leader of the PSI Research Group,
Centre of Applied Research and Innovation Art & Society,
Hanze University of Applied Sciences, Groningen, The Netherlands
anne@patchingzone.net

Abstract. In this paper we will be investigating the relevance of artistic practice-based research as a design method for interactive co-design works. Our
study is based on Are You for Real?, an urban co-creation project which was
developed by a cross-disciplinary project team with co-design contributions by
students and youngsters. Although this case study was initially developed with
and for youngsters and students of a technical vocational school, its design and
creation approach addressed assumptions that are expected to be valuable for
professionals as well as for educators in higher education. This study could contribute to people's understanding of 'real-life' research methods for 'real-life'
situations. For our reference framework we identified two issues that were
brought forward as impediments for new cross-disciplinary courses that dealt
with interactive works in a public space. Following that, the lessons learned
from our investigation are suggested as input for the next editions of these
courses.

Keywords: Design principles and guidelines for Distributed, Ambient and Pervasive Interactions, Social Interaction, Art, Design.

1   Introduction

First of all we would like to introduce you to The Patching Zone media laboratory and
the case study that was developed there. The Patching Zone is a trans-disciplinary
R&D media laboratory where young professionals and students work together with
experts and end-users. In their projects the participants cross over the boundaries of
their discipline. For the duration of the project the team members leave their usual
professional frameworks behind and venture into new territory. During the past seven
years, The Patching Zone has worked on a series of iterations of Nigten's flexible
Processpatching approach, where fitting methods and approaches are often loosely
combined [1]. Although Processpatching focused initially on the collaboration among
artists, technicians and computer scientists, over the years its focus has broadened.
Other creative and scientific branches, the humanities and the end-users were all taken
into account as collaborators who brought their domain-specific knowledge and
methodologies or ways of working.

N. Streitz and P. Markopoulos (Eds.): DAPI 2014, LNCS 8530, pp. 575–582, 2014.
© Springer International Publishing Switzerland 2014

(a)   (b)

Fig. 1. (a) Students as co-designers; (b) Are You For Real ? participant

The case study "Are You For Real?"(AYFR?) is a GPS driven, real-time, sound experience created for and by young people and played in their own local urban setting. As the players roam the familiar city streets, they are simultaneously experiencing and exploring a virtually sonified version of the urban space through modified smartphones/headphone sets. The sound experience is driven by the players' position, the position of other players and the influence of online users who virtually walk through the same streets and are able to broadcast messages to specific locations in the sonic cityscape. The project explores how sound and music influence the experience of moving through an urban environment while at the same time altering the possibilities for social interactions in the streets. The overall structure of the game-like experience follows the mechanics of a traditional treasure-hunt, with players collecting sonic elements located in physical space, but the result is an open-world game where the interaction between players (both online and in the streets) generates complex sets of rules and experiences. AYFR? was designed in a participatory way, in which all aspects of the project were subject of interactive workshops with students and / or local youth. After each workshop the team entered an iterative design cycle, in which output from the last workshop was integrated, together with newly gained knowledge, insight and ideas.

AYFR?'s projectteam included representatives from media art, game design, engineering, ethography, audio design and so on. Human Technology and ICT students from the Zadkine technical vocational school worked as collaborators, co-deisgners and later mingled with the end-users. The co-designing youngsters came from the Helderheid youth group in the neighborhood and brought in their interest in local rap and popular culture.

2   Reference Framework

Our reference framework for this study stems from a higher education environment: recently Academy Minerva (Hanze University of Applied Sciences) and the University of Groningen initiated a shared module 'Research & Development: New Media Art Practices' for their Master students Media Art Design and Scenography and students of the University's Art faculty. The students worked in cross-disciplinary teams on a media art experiment., Most experiments were situated in the urban public space. The two most striking issues that were brought forward in the evaluation of the first edition of this course were: the lack of knowledge about artistic research and the limited interest the students showed in the participant as a co-creator. It is worthwhile to note that both evaluative issues are related to the making process of interactive art and design works. In this paper therefore we will elaborate on the most eye-catching making methods that were used for the realisation process of AYFR? and how these relate to a theoretical framework. We'll complete this study with an extrapolation of the outcomes of the case study for our educational reference framework.

3   Design Methodology

The practice-based approach to AYFR? is inspired by the design and art practices. For this we draw especially from the explorative (hands-on) design process and the 'making' itself, the implementation aspect, as we know it in today's design and artistic practice. When we zoom in on its characteristics we'll notice that during and because of this creation process an important part of the research emerges. Following this there is an iterative cycle where the progress of the creative process brings about the necessity for background information and theory, and in its turn the theory feeds the practice. Furthermore the research and creation process usually has a holistic nature, as opposed to the conventional reductionist and solution-focused processes. From a classical engineering perspective this can sometimes be problematic, because it may lead to a myriad of different interpretations and viewpoints on one theme, or many possible solutions to a design problem [2]. However, it does link very well with the current interest in Human Computer Interaction (HCI) for multiple interpretations concerning emerging technical design areas, which are increasingly influenced by interaction of the end user with the technical system and with the designer. The space for multiple and personal interpretations, and holistic viewpoints is a counterpart or addition to the singular (reductionist) HCI interpretation. [3] This is closely connected to the recent shift from instrumental, work-related technology to technology for personal experience and the experience industry. Sengers and Gaver claim that the much-used traditional, objective utility and usability studies are not sufficient for personal, subjective experiences. They also refer to media art as an inspiration for the replacement of the singular interpretation, which is often still in the hands of the HCI designer.

"Systems that can be interpreted in multiple ways allow individual users to define their own meanings for them, rather than merely accepting those imposed by designers." [4]

The role of the designer in this situation, and in certain elements of the design process, is more appropriately described a facilitator of the process rather than *the* designer who always makes *all* design decisions. In AYFR? the work was often done according to a co-design approach, an approach derived from participatory design and user-centred design.[5] In co-design the emphasis is on the joint design process. During the various phases of the whole process (concept, pre-design, design and realisation,) the relationships of the participants towards each other shift. For example, The Patching Zone's team worked together as coaches with the students in the pre-design phase (co-design). At a later stage (development) the students partly represented the end users.

The responsibilities everyone had in AYFR? (student, designer and artist) kept shifting; a necessary role change, which was sometimes a bit confusing. After a largely democratic co-design trajectory, holding on to a democratic decision-making process can become an obstacle for the process, because it may lead to a design compromise. This gives a good idea of the dilemma between emancipatory work and artistic, or more general, creative work. What is the most important issue in each part of the whole process? From the huge collection of ideas gathered in the pre-design phase, it turned out to be quite difficult to arrive at a convincing design supported by everyone. Of course we considered several instrumental solutions to this situation, but it was preferred to study strategies from the professional practices, which surrounded us at the start of the R&D process.

3.1   New Design Paradigms

We see an extreme example of process-facilitated co-design in Conditional Design.[6] Based on a number of clear, logical rules a joint design (sketch) process is set up, to which various people contribute. The designers and artists have drawn up a manifesto, which reads:

"...Input engages logic and activates and influences the process.
Input should come from our external and complex environment: nature, society and its human interactions." [7]

A very interesting concept which, in their documentation and in their workbook, surprisingly often leads to more or less the same results. The drawings on the website of Conditional Design reminds one of machine-made drawings without a random function or any noise. In his afterword in the Conditional Design Workbook Koert van Mensvoort teleports this Conditional Design formula to the China of 2061 because, according to him, it offers perspectives for co-creation which remind him of a Lego system for urban development, which of course everyone is allowed to help build. Rather, Conditional Design reflects what is on the minds of many designers and artists these days. It was invented during the process of the search for the new role of the designer as a process facilitator. Quite a lot of literature is available about recent shifts in the design world; from the traditional designer who works on products, to designers who work on the designing of meaning (purpose). With this last one you can think of experience design, design for emotion and design for transformation. [8] The shift from problem or functionality based designing to designing 'for the sake of fun and pleasure' inspired Gaver and Dunn to the concept of 'ludic design' [9,10] Ludic design, a reference to Huizinga's Homo Ludens, a study of the play-element in culture [11] in many respects resembles a somewhat formalised art approach. Here designing no longer happens from a predetermined functionality or a specific use in order to become engaged with the world around us. We see that the old rules and laws of applied design discipline are shifting more and more towards the explorative way artists work. The dividing line between the design and the art practice is becoming ever more blurred. It is remarkable that a lot of literature is available from the design and technological perspective and much less from an art perspective. While it is precisely this media art practice to which Sengers et al look as inspiration for ambiguous interpretations and open scenarios for participation.[12] Media art and art & technology harbour a wealth of information. During the past decades the media artist has created a trail, which many people can learn from. For some time now the Creativity and Cognition Studios from Sydney, Australia, have been publishing about artistic experiments as forerunners and inspiration for interaction design and technology. Bilda, Edmonds and Candy [13] researched the interactive behaviour and the engagement of participants in different interactive media art installations over a longer period. This resulted in their 'Creative Engagement Model'. Bilda then 'translated' the sequential interaction phases and the different 'modes' of active audience behaviours into experience Design Principles for five different phases (from initial introduction to deep understanding) of the interaction process. [14]

3.2 Background

In personal, often informal, conversations with established media artists about the role they play in their projects, what often becomes clear is that they usually do many different kinds of jobs and switch roles very easily. It is worth mentioning that many media artists also have a professional practice as new style designers. Most media artists or media art collectives carry the final responsibility for the process, or for the final product (depending on how they look at it and what is developed). This brings us to an important point of what distinguishes media art from the co-creation processes of, for example, community art. The media artist is almost always the person who weighs the artistic deliberations and makes decisions in the design process, while in community art the emancipatory aspect often gets priority. Concerning the artistic quality of community art many interesting discussions have been held. [15]

It seems to us that the outcomes of community art, in which the emancipatory aspect is the central focus, should not be assessed for artistic quality but for the participation process, the realised empowerment and everything this entails. Although in media art public interaction is often essential and parts of the work are realised according to co-design principles, we do judge the final process or the media art experience according to (new) personal and subjective artistic criteria. Let's see what happens when we map the two approaches to different innovation layers in AYFR? The emancipatory (community art-like) approach was required during the first phase (pre-design), while the realisation would benefit from a media art-like approach. You may wonder whether this dichotomy did not complicate the process needlessly. Perhaps the ambition-bar had indeed been set a bit high here because we learned that this turnaround was complicated for both our team and for the students. Our team could, as far as we are concerned, relied even more on their discipline-specific expertise so team members could fall back on this at the change from process facilitator for empowerment to the designing of the final artistic and creative experience.

4   Lessons Learned

What can we learn from our case study regarding the articulation of artistic research; the iterative process of making and reflecting? This project, as well as earlier Patching Zone projects [16,17] confirms our findings that artists and designers often deal with a comprehensive and integral approach, which includes a constant dialogue between creating (making) and reflecting. This allows a reflective attitude to surface due to a continual exchange between practical knowledge, skills and theory (wisdom). It brings forward an integral practice, research and theory model that may provide fertile ground for the enhancement of practical knowledge through continuous feedback, from practice through to the context and the theory. Through this method the researcher and the co-creators become aware of the modelling powers of their own practice, during the work or learning processes. This interconnected approach will either succeed or fail with a balance between making and passing on of knowledge or the other way around, of generating new knowledge that is linked to the practical creation process. When summarizing the connection between practice and theory, we can state that in AYFR? the values and interpretations from academic research, design and art practices came together with the co-design interest from popular culture that was brought in by our young collaborators and young people in the online environment. In such a constellation, theory is a dynamic given; it is constantly renewed and questioned by the practice and vice versa. The theoretical background in this environment is always linked to the (new) practice. So we can speak of an 'integrated design where reflection informs practice and practice generates theory'. In a way this model reminds us of Schön's Reflective Practice theory. [18]

As we briefly mentioned earlier, the creation process of interactive media art doesn't stop after the artistic and technical development phase, it also embodies the shift from a final piece of art to the interactive process where the participants become co-creators of the experience. Here the participants all establish or create a highly personalised experience that could be described as an on-going co-creation process. An interactive artwork is therefore never finished. [19] In regard to understanding the co-creators' making process a working prototype as the interaction environment is of crucial importance.

These working prototypes make artistic research and development so interesting as a Real-Life design approach to technology for personal experiences and the experience industry. In other words: In our case study it would not have been easy to simulate AYFR? because of the personal involvement, which was essential for the experience. AYFR? therefore was a convincing example of a subjective and personal experience, which allowed space for multiple or ambiguous interpretations, with strong artistic, cultural and aesthetic aspects to boot. Our case study thus illustrates that artistic, practice based research could contribute to the establishment of real-life research methods for real-life situations. [20]

This brings forward valuable new knowledge for the academic discourse dealing with the making of media art, as this knowledge is only just at its initial stage today. This is an issue for academic researchers whose research practice will be positioned more and more in a so-called hyper reality. [21] where the interactive experience plays a role of crucial importance. Nor should we overlook the importance of a suitable discourse for contemporary artists and designers who plan to work with interactive experiences, in particular those who intend to collaborate with other disciplines in the research and development process.

5   Conclusion

What are the relevant lessons learned for the education as it was outlined in our reference framework? AYFR? and other interactive art pieces show a remarkable resemblance to the co-design process and could be characterised as never finished. The artistic research process represents an integrated practice, a creation and theory model that could lead the way to getting a grip on the never-ending making process, as this type of research is grounded in the creation process. The holistic nature of our case study links well with multiple or subjective interpretations that are brought forward by the end users' interaction process In this situation theory is a dynamic given that is thus by definition subjective. Finally, community art practice taught us about participants' engagement in a democratic co-design trajectory and media art taught us how to shift the design process to an artistic or design decision mode.

Author's Note. Some parts of this text are a slightly altered version of earlier writings by the author such as Real Projects for Real People Volume 3, 2013 and the epilogue in Research & Development: New Media Art Practice, 2014.

Acknowledgements. Are You For Real? Is developed by The Patching Zone team in 2012-13: Kati Bessenyei (HU), Waldek Rapior (PL), Ida Toft (DK), Victor Díaz (ES), Sebastien Seynaeve (BE) supervised by Kristina Andersen (NL/DK), David Jonas (NL/PT), Anne Nigten (NL) and staff. The Patching Zone is grateful to her project collaborators; the Zadkine students and Helderheid group, the projects' partners: Zadkine, Kosmopolis Rotterdam, Alares, CRISP IP-e and the DIVO partners Blast Theory (UK) and Translocal (FI). The CRISP project receives FES funding from the Dutch government and NWO (the Dutch organisation for scientific research). The Patching Zone is also grateful to the funding bodies for Are You For Real? DOEN, Cultural Participation Fund, SNS Reaal Fund, VSB Fund, The Prins Bernhard

Cultuurfonds, Stichting Bevordering van Volkskracht, and the Culture Programme of the European Union. This project has been funded with support from the European Commission. This publication reflects the views only of the authors, and the Commission cannot be held responsible for any use which may be made of the information contained therein. The Patching Zone also would like to thank their generous sponsors: Alcatel Onetouch and Gemeente Rotterdam Dienst Jeugd Onderwijs en Samenleving.

References

1. Nigten, A.: Processpatching, Defining new Methods in aRt&D, printed edition, p. 103 (2007); Nigten, A.: Leonardo The Journal of the International Society for the Arts, Sciences and Technology 42(5), 478–479 (2009); Nigten, A. (ed.) Real Projects for Real People, vol. 1 (2010); Nigten, A. (ed.) Real Projects for Real People, vol. 2 (2012); Nigten, A. (ed.) Real Projects for Real People, vol. 3 (2013)
2. Nigten, A.: Processpatching, Defining new Methods in aRt&D, printed edition, p. 103 (2007)
3. Sengers, P., Boehner, K., David, S., Kaye, J.: Reflective Design. Proceedings Critical Computing: Between Sense and Sensibility, 49–58 (2005)
4. Sengers, P., Gaver, B.: Staying Open to Interpretation: Engaging Multiple Meanings in Design and Evaluation. DIS / ACM 1 (2006)
5. Nigten, A. (ed.) Real Projects for Real People, vol. 1 (2010); Nigten, A. (ed.) Real Projects for Real People, vol. 2 (2012)
6. Maurer, L., Paulus, E., Puckey, J., Wouters, R.:
   http://conditionaldesign.org/ (assessed February 18, 2014)
7. Blauvelt, A., van Mensvoort, K. (eds.): Conditional Design: Workbook, van Mensvoort K., How Conditional Design Changed the World, p. vii (2013)
8. Sanders, E.B., Stappers, P.J.: Co-creation and the new landscapes of design (2008)
9. Gaffney, G.: Ludic Design: An interview with William Gaver, Information and Design (2007), http://infodesign.com.au/uxpod/ludicdesign/ (assessed January 27, 2014)
10. Gaver, B., et al.: The Drift Table: Designing for Ludic Engagement. In: CHI 2004 (2004)
11. Huizinga, J.: Homo Ludens, A study of the play-element in culture (1944)
12. Sengers, P., Gaver, B.: Staying Open to Interpretation: Engaging Multiple Meanings in Design and Evaluation. DIS / ACM 1 (2006)
13. Bilda, Z., Edmonds, E., Candy, L.: Designing for creative engagement. Design Studies 29(6), 525–540 (2008)
14. Bilda, Z.: Designing for Audience Engagement. In: Candy, L., Edmonds, E. (eds.) Interacting - Art, Research and the Creative Practitioner, pp. 163–181 (2012)
15. Bishop, C.: Is Everyone an Artist?, Van Abbemuseum, Eindhoven The Netherlands (2010), http://www.conferenceofconferences.com/is-everyone-an-artist (assessed January 27, 2014)
16. Nigten, A. (ed.): Real Projects for Real People, vol. 1 (2010)
17. Nigten, A. (ed.): Real Projects for Real People, vol. 2 (2012)
18. Schön, D.: The Reflective Practitioner: How professionals think in action (1983)
19. Nigten, A.: Epilogue in Research & Development: New Media Art Practice (2014)
20. Mulder, I.: Living Labbing the Rotterdam Way: Co-creation as an Enabeler for Urban. Technology Innovation Management Review, 39–43 (2012)
21. Eco, U.: Travels in Hyperreality. The Fortresses of Solitude (1990), http://public.callutheran.edu/~brint/American/Eco.pdf (accessed January 12, 2014)

Small Scale Collaborative Services: The Role of Design in the Development of the Human Smart City Paradigm[*]

Francesca Rizzo[1] and Alessandro Deserti[2]

[1] University of Bologna, Department of Architecture, Via Risorgimento 2, 40136 Bologna, Italy
[2] Politecnico di Milano, Design Department, Via Durando 38/a Milano, Italy
f.rizzo@unibo.it, alessandro.deserti@polimi.it

Abstract. Cities are facing disruptive challenges today. All these require smarter solutions and are creating pressure for the public and private sector to deliver innovative services and great expectations are put in the new Smart City paradigm. Most of these solutions keep technologies out of the urban environments, far from being considered components of the urban functioning and, furthermore, even farer from people and their urban spaces. In this framework design is today re-orienting its theories and practices to new kind of design contexts (neighborhoods, streets, squares, cities) where societal challenges are emerging that require different level of changes from everyday life to huge public institutions and complex organizations. This re-orientation is based on a different smart city paradigm that puts people at the center of the cities smartness and recognizes the need for developing micro and contextualized solutions to address larger cities problems in a sociable mode.

Keywords: Service Design, Complex Participatory Design, Human Smart City, Small Experiments, Collaborative Services.

1 Introduction

Complex problems are taking the stage in the current society. Meanwhile from Europe to US, austerity measures have been put in place, "wicked" societal challenges abound, spanning from youth unemployment, healthcare issues for elderly population, energy consumptions, mobility and transportation to mention some of them. All these require smarter solutions and are creating pressure for the public and private sectors to deliver innovative services [2] and great expectations are put in the new Smart City paradigm.

Many solutions, even integrating different perspectives in order to consider the complexity of the urban environments, are today proposed to cities mainly based on hard technological infrastructures: solutions that keep technologies far away from urban environments and, furthermore, even farer from people and their urban everyday life.

---

[*] This work comes from the joint effort of both authors. Nevertheless Francesca Rizzo directly edited sessions: 2, 2.1, 2.2, 2.2.1, 2.2.2, 3 and Alessandro Deserti directly edited sessions: 1 and 2.3.

N. Streitz and P. Markopoulos (Eds.): DAPI 2014, LNCS 8530, pp. 583–592, 2014.
© Springer International Publishing Switzerland 2014

Opposite to this mainstream there are visions of smart cities that are focusing on concepts like citizens needs, bottom-up initiatives, people centered solutions, communities centered solutions, grassroots smart solutions and social innovation. Common to these visions is the idea that smart city is a new paradigm for cities development that relies on the city system capability to boost, encourage, realize and scale up new intangible infrastructures for the cities based on new partnerships typologies for the development of smart services.

Through looking at My Neighborhood European project vision and experiments this paper explores complex participatory design processes [4] [9] [11] [15] as the most suitable design approach to the development of smart solutions for the so-called Human Smart City [6] [21] [17].

Human Smart City (HSC) paradigm as elaborated by the Peripheria European Project (Grant Agreement No.: 271015), moves from recognizing cities smartness in the capability of cities to include citizen driven developments and productions as concurrent city infrastructures together with physical, technical and technological layers. At the core of the HSC vision there is the human perspective, as elaborated by design culture [7] that considers that participatory design approaches to smart services development and production can bring contextual and cultural dimensions in the delivered solutions. Especially the knowledge elaborated in the domain of service design has focused the strength of collaborative services [1] as those collaborative solutions that may match the need for cities to balance the technical "smartness" of sensors, meters, and infrastructures with softer solutions based on public-citizens partnership. With the above trends in mind, the peculiar HSC approach developed in Periphèria project is mainly rooted on the idea that smart is a city where people, citizens, stakeholders are the main actors of ICT driven urban development. In such a human smart city new and innovative market opportunities for ICT and Future Internet based public services can be created, deeply rooted in the real problems of people, in their urban daily lives, in their commitment to respond proactively to their own problems and needs.

To peruse this vision Peripheria considered and applied complex participatory design processes, and the correspondent design culture, as the most suitable approach to create conditions to set up and generate innovation ecosystems where network of stakeholders can co-develop solutions in partnership with their administrations.

In line with Peripheria vision the My Neighborhood I My City Project (January 2013-June 2015, Grant agreement no.: 325227) is trying to further develop the HSC paradigm starting by amplifying and connecting existing grassroots social initiatives in 4 different European neighborhoods (in Lisbon, Milano, Aalborg and Birmingham) to show their potentials behind their connections and collaborations in designing smart cities through collaborative services to be experimented and eventually scaled-up. Here complex partnerships are involving the municipalities together with citizens, NGOs, public schools and private companies to develop micro solutions to be experimented and eventually networked and scaled.

In the rest of the paper the authors discuss the current experimentation in My Neighborhood project (especially the Milano pilot). Then the authors focus on the difficulties and lesson learnt when design takes the responsibility and the leadership of actively boosting collaborative partnerships as basis for implementing new collaborative services. In the final section the authors propose a preliminary route for micro solutions scalability to affect larger smart city vision.

2   Complex Participatory Design Processes: The My Neighborhood Project Experience

In the tradition of co-design many researchers [18] [8] [20] have focused on the potentiality of end users collaborations and prototyping to engage stakeholders in the exploration of innovation. In this tradition it is possible to consider two basic modes.

The first one is the dialogue mode, and deals with the processes of collaborative design and tools for engaging users and other stakeholders in collective creative envisioning together and eventually in rethinking the current state. This mode grows from practices that have their roots in close connection with participatory design tradition but also 'beyond usability' research dealing with experience design and empathy. The second one is the prototyping mode that addresses in particular the ways in which designers tend to reflect and make sense of complicated and often yet non-existing things by giving shape, sketching, visualizing and prototyping in various ways. These two modes conceptual are most of the time overlapping in practice and they are today converging to the foundations of those design labs (living labs, urban living labs, ecosystem of innovations) that are blooming in a variety of initiatives [16]. These labs are similar to new urban context where envisioning solutions for territorial end urban transformation by establishing strong connections with the network of stakeholders that belongs to a place; establishing long term engagement with local communities that leads to the emergence of new everyday practices that point to new opportunities for design [3] [5] [13] [14] [10] [11] [12] [19].

Contrary to those living labs that emphasize technology evaluation or adaptation My Neighborhood project applies a situated and human centered approach for local communities to develop innovation. My Neighborhood works directly from the particular conditions and resources of the local communities engaged in each of the project pilot in order to employ relevant service systems that may facilitate social innovation. Scalability in this approach comes about not through the similarity between communities but through the robustness and generic qualities of the service design concepts.

In a world of heterogeneity of use and users and entanglement of infrastructures and practices My Neighborhood provides a platform for engagement that transcends traditional models of research and development. The challenge for My Neighborhood is to provide evidence for what can be accomplished beyond the co-design with a twofold aim: (i) addressing problems of the contexts; (ii) establish a long last strategy of innovation for that context. To achieve these objectives the project is operating within the pilots by:

— Modeling and releasing to the municipalities methodologies of complex participatory process that put together citizens private and public stakeholders in new partnership typologies;

— pushing the need to focus on collaborative services: i.e. those services where citizens have a role in maintaining and delivering them;
— supporting the scaling up of the envisioned solutions.

2.1 The Service Design Phases

My Neighborhood project started in January 2013 with the clear goal in mind of applying service design to help grassroots and community based initiatives in the 4 involved neighborhoods to emerge, network and scale up them. The project is operating in a typical ICT research area bringing with it the idea that advanced participatory design methods could make the difference in the level of innovation of the developed solutions since the development process starts from people and not form the available technological paradigm. The work carried out by the pilots in the first months has been than organized in 4 typical design steps or phases: exploration, sense making, idea generation and service design.

Exploration. Exploration deals with understanding the contexts where design is acting. The context analysis in My Neighborhood started with explorative activities aimed at entering the context trying to identify context resources like: entry points, active people and associations, gatekeepers, infrastructures, projects and initiatives, socio-economic context characteristics and everything that could help designers to set the starting conditions for My Neighborhoods small projects and the already existing points of strength and weaknesses in each of the pilots.

Sense Making. Exploration slowly was transformed into a sense making work where the rich amount of information collected in the exploration phase has been analyzed and interpreted, in order to work out facts that could be usable in the design phase. In this phases pilots formalized all the semi-worked elements that would support the following design phases (maps of the stakeholders, resources maps, personas, video and pictures from the contexts, people and stakeholders WIN (wishes, interests, needs). This is also the work during which a first hierarchy of priorities was pointed out: issues and challenges to be addressed have been extracted and prioritized with respect to the stakeholders' feelings and opinions.

Idea Generation. This phase was the first design activity that was conducted in collaboration between designers, citizens and stakeholders and municipalities. It mainly devoted to working together and sharing provisional ideas – new activities, processes, systems or touch-points – that could be of relevance in terms of find an effective solutions to the challenges listed during the sense making activity. In each of the pilot this phase ended with a set of ideas that were further analyzed and selected applying different criteria. Among the others idea selection has been conducted on the following elements: idea feasibility with respect to the context available resources and to the My Neighborhood larger objectives; first group of stakeholders interested in entering the phase of service design and in experimenting with the envisioned solutions; idea potentially to be scaled and to have a market; a robust digital dimension with which to experiment FI solutions.

Service Design. This phase moved forward in the design process from the concept selected to what they could be really become in reality. This phase than included typical design activity conducted in strong collaboration with non-professional designers from the context and from the municipality. The design team so composed developed for each services the detailed design of the services users experience, the new service blue print for the service front end and back front; the map of stakeholders that would support the service implementation and delivery, the service business models. With these elements in hands the pilots entered the services implementation phase.

The following sub-sections describe the design process applied in Milano.

2.2   The Envisioned Solutions: The Milano Pilot Case

The Milano pilot takes place in the neighborhood of Quarto Oggiaro, located in the north west of Milan, not far away from the area where the 2015 Expo – Universal Exposition – will take place. Here the entire service design process has been conducted thanks to a strong collaboration between the Politecnico di Milano (that hold a long tradition in design research and in urban planning) and the Milano Municipality. This mixed team of designers performed all the activities in the contexts and managed the interactions with the local communities and stakeholders to engage them in the co-design process and in the service experimentation.

First months in quarto Oggiaro have been spent to explore and approach the neighborhood. The design team started to understand the neighborhood physical characteristics, the populations, the main actors in the contexts, the relation between the neighborhood and the rest of the city, the socio-economic dimensions, the characteristics of the services offered in the neighborhood.

After that an intensive period of co-design meeting started. The design teams in this phase established 4 different design tables (with designers, urban planners, people from the municipality of Milano, people and representatives from the neighborhood). Each table started from a complex discussion on the main neighborhood issues that ended with a list of main challenges:

— to regenerate disused and derelict public areas;
— to improve social life and inclusion of elderly people in Quarto Oggiaro;
— to prevent school drop outs and create job opportunities for young people;
— to test new potential business models for start-up and spin off.

Related to these challenges the design tables then worked to elaborate possible service ideas as smart solutions for the framed problems.

Service ideas developed for Quarto Oggiaro were: ICT bread, Quarto gardening, Quarto Food and Integrated communication. Out of these service ideas, My Neighborhood focused on two of them: Quarto Food and Quarto Gardening.

The Quarto Food Service. Quarto Food Club is a service that combines the need to improve social life for a vulnerable group of single elderly citizens that would enjoy a meal prepared with special care and consumed in a sociable and enjoyable condition so that to have an impact on their sense of loneliness (the elderly community in Quarto Oggiaro is large and it is expressing many important needs). At the same time the service seems to respond to a second neighborhood issue: that of the young people unemployment. The opportunity for young people from the Hoteling School of the neighborhood to be recognized in the practical training, having the possibility also to test new business model hypotheses.

Specifically the service involves two high schools in Quarto Oggiaro where students prepare every week some meals as part of their training for catering and food preparation. Starting from this resource the service ideas is to deliver these meals to a group of elders living in the Neighborhood. By preparing for the occasion a kind of social space in the "school" where elderly can come and enjoy the meal together the service idea is that of connecting the school and the students with the elderly from the neighborhood. The students will benefit interaction too, as their work becomes visible and recognized by users. They will also receive academic credits for it.

To be implemented the service required also the development of a formal partnership and it will be really delivered thanks to the agreement between the Professional Schools of Hotel Management (providing food) and some local Associations that will provide the contact with elderly people, and a van for transportation (from private place to the school and vice versa).

Through ordinary activities of food processing, students will prepare -from 1 to 3 days per week- meals for the target group. An IT Platform will support the process of the booking of the meal and the trip, and a personal rechargeable Lunch Card would be provided to the users to partially cover the costs of the meal and the service.

The Quarto Gardening Service. Quarto Gardening is a co-designed service that provides the possibility for the Municipality to access the competences of the students of the Quarto Oggiaro Agricultural School to take care of some the green areas in the neighborhood.

The service is made possible thanks to the agreements between the Property Management of Green Areas (Municipality of Milano and the public institute for Social Housing in Milano) and the technical high school for agriculture. Through practical training activities – formative credits are acknowledged – students will take care of some green spaces in the neighborhood. A focal point could be Piazza Capuana, one of the crucial physical place in Quarto Oggiaro. The square will be one of the first place from which the service will start. This decision was made in order to make visible the impact of the service in the neighborhood and the active action of My Neighborhood project. The service goal is to contribute to reduce expenditure for green space conservation and maintenance, to regenerate public spaces and to discover new job opportunities for young people (by testing a new business model hypothesis). The users would be both public (Municipality) and private (building supervisors, resident citizens).

2.3   Further Steps towards Scaling-Up

In the perspective of up-scaling, the design actions that has been adopted in the development of new solutions in My Neighborhood project (and here presented in details for the Milano pilot) can be seen as a process of building up and enabling infrastructures that would work (from the project beginning) in order to make the service ideas robust to be scaled after their experimentations. To realize these enabling infrastructures a variety of artifacts have been used in the pilots: from co-design methods, to specific toolkits, from digital platforms to dedicated products and services. The process adopted in designing new collaborative services in Milano aimed to support their up-scaling by suggesting the adoption of a methodological frame (processes and tools) in their design phase rather than the replication or adaptation of the solutions.

On the first point, we observe that – even if we cannot recognize specific elements of the Quarto Gardening and Quarto Food that can guarantee their success – deepening some aspects helps to build a sound base for the implantation and the future development of both services. In particular, the issues related to the business modeling, the main network of actors that contribute to the service and to the economic underpinning of the envisioned solutions are quite relevant in facilitating or in braking their up-scaling process and they will be explored in deep for both services during their experimentations.

On the second point, we observe that some features of Quarto Gardening and Quarto Food are intrinsically connected to the development process (as results of the process), and that the issues raised and the problems faced within the development process might be more relevant than its sheer results. E.g., the configuration of a network of actors and stakeholders and the management of their relationships can be a fundamental step in their development.

In the following, the authors describe the development process of the solutions, introducing a larger set of phases and actions (with respect to the 4 phases of the service design process described above) representing a methodological reference that can be adopted in the perspective of up-scaling and that has been applied in My Neighborhood project and specifically in the Milano pilot.

The adoption of this strategic conceptual frame in the development of a solution cannot automatically guarantee its scalability, but it may ensure the quality of the solution itself, and can facilitate its adoption and its adaptation to the specific conditions and necessities of different sites.

The frame, already adopted in previous research projects (PERL: *The Partnership for Education and Research about Responsible Living*, November 2009- November 2012, Project no.: 155927-LLP-1- 2009-1-NO-ERASMUS-ENWA), is based on 7 phases/areas of work:

1. **ANALYSING.** The exploration and mapping of existing solutions and initiatives oriented toward the inspiration of new solutions or systems of solutions. It includes the identification of a consistent design opportunity for a competitive and innovative solution.

2. **ENVISIONING.** The development of scenarios, visions and proposals, used both to define the overall directions to take and to stimulate and align the actors and stakeholders in the development process.
3. **DESIGNING.** The development of the solution through the adoption of participatory design tools supporting interaction and convergence among the involved parties.
4. **ENABLING.** The development of digital platforms, toolkits and other supporting tools and actions (such as knowledge-transfer initiatives), to enable the new network of actors in carrying on the development process by themselves.
5. **PROTOTYPING.** The solution experimentation in a local and small scale; including the assessment and the testing of the network of the involved actors, to give feedbacks for the assessment of the new idea.
6. **COMMUNICATING.** The development of presentations, visualisations, and communication tools and actions to inform about the solution before, during and after its development, with different aims such as convincing potential actors to join or sponsor the initiative, create consensus, foster the adoption of the solution etc.
7. **SYSTEMATISING.** The activities oriented towards organising synergies and multiplication effects among different single projects and different elements of the same project.

3   Conclusions

The co-design processes implemented in My Neighborhood have been a good laboratory to experiment some key issues related to co-design of public services and to the development of co-design approach in complex neighborhood communities. In the following the most important lessons learnt are reported:

- transferring the new service design approach to the public sector can change the way in which municipalities design services. There are many experiments that are going on in Europe and that are demonstrating that larger governmental programs are looking at service design with interest. Here it is important to underline as My Neighborhood is experimenting with service design not as a method to redesign users experience but as set of competence that may trigger profound and unexpected change in public organizations, if transferred and interiorized by the employees from the municipality;
- Small experiments and initiatives are crucial for gluing citizens around "the same story" and to make them active with respect to larger urban transformation;
- Volunteers and associations can work as good entry points but also there is the risk that they introduce element of resistance due to their roles as leaders in the contexts where they operate that may negatively impact on new ideas, processes and solutions;
- My Neighborhood started from people wishes, interests and needs and tried to transform them in new collaborative services also against a larger context. As example, in Milano the design tables had also the role of being the place where the

Municipality discusses its vision for the neighborhood together with the people from Quarto Oggiaro (the vision for urban transformation should govern and drive the flourishing of small initiatives to synergize them towards the larger change);
- Services can be interpreted as tools for triggering the development of the cities intangible infrastructures. New partnerships involving service design, ICT application, services management and governance, are needed for re-thinking the smartness of cities;
- current national regulation and policies can be constraints for the design of new services (My Neighborhood is suggesting new practices for developing policies and regulation much more opened to experimentations from the cities bottom side);
- opposite interests may lead different stakeholders. Complex participatory processes can be applied to find short terms convergence among stakeholders that can both peruse their larger objective but find convenient to be partners in some small experiment. For example, in Milano the Schools involved in QuartoFood and Quarto Gardening have no interest in developing new businesses but My Neighborhood can give them the possibility to involve their students in real meal and gardening services experiences;
- collaborative services developed in My Neighborhood need to find an owner that will maintain them after the end of the project. For this purpose My Neighborhood is developing strategies for service scaling-up.

References

1. Baek, J., Manzini, E., Rizzo, F.: Sustainable Collaborative Services on the digital Platform. In: Proceedings of Design Research Society, DRS 2010, Montreal 7-9 Luglio (2010)
2. Bason, C.: Leading public sector innovation: Co-creating for a better society. Policy Press, Bristol (2010)
3. Binder, T., Brandt, E., Halse, J., Foverskov, M., Olander, S., Yndigegn, S.: Living the (codesign) Lab. In: Proceedings of the Nordic Design Research Conference, Helsinki (2011)
4. Bjorgvinsson, E., Ehn, P., Hillgren, P-A.: Participatory design and democratizing innovation. In: Proceedings of the Participatory Design Conference, Sydney, Australia (2010)
5. Brandt, E., Binder, T.: Design Research: Six Views in a Box: Dialogues on everyday life with Alzheimer's. The Danish Design School Press (2011)
6. Concilio, G., Deserti, A., Rizzo, F.: The Human approach to Smart Cities: The Perphèria Project as a Case of Complex Participatory Design. In: Proceedings of IV International Forum of Design, Belo Horizonte, MG, Brazil, September 19-22 (2012)
7. Deserti, A., Rizzo, F.: Design and the cultures of the enterprises. Design Issues 30(1), 36–56 (2014)
8. Deserti, A., Rizzo, F.: Cocreating with companies. A design led process of Learning. In: Proceedings of Design research Sociaty Conference, Bangkok, July 1-4 (2012)
9. Ehn, P.: Participation in design things. In: Proceedings of the 10th Anniversary Conference on Participatory Design. ACM, New York (2008)
10. Halse, J., Brandt, E., Clark, B., Binder, T. (eds.): Rehearsing the future. Danish Design School Press, Copenhagen (2010)

11. Hillgren, P.-A., Seravalli, A., Emilson, A.: Prototyping and infrastructuring in design for social innovation. The CoDesign Journal 7, 3–4 (2011)
12. Yanki, L., Ho, K.L.D.: New roles of designers in democratic innovation: A case study in the ingenuity of ageing. In: Proceedings of the Participatory Design Conference, vol. 2. ACM, New York (2012)
13. Light, A.: Democratising Technology: Making Transformation using Designing, Performance and Props. In: Proceedings of CHI 2011, BC, Canada, Vancouver (2012)
14. Malmborg, L., Yndigegn, S.L.: Sustainable Infrastructure for Ad Hoc Social Interaction. In: Brandt, E., Ehn, P., Johansson, T.D., Reimer, M.H., Markussen, T., Vallgårda, A. (eds.) Experiments in Design Research. Proceedings of Nordic Design Research Conference 2013, Copenhagen-Malmö, June 9-12 (2013)
15. Manzini, E., Rizzo, F.: Small projects/large changes: Participatory design as an open participated process. CoDesign 7(3-4), 199–215 (2011)
16. Manzini, E., Rizzo, F.: The SEE project: a cases based study to investigate the role of design in social innovation initiatives for smart cities. In: Planning Support Tools: Policy Analysis, Implementation and Evaluation Proceedings of the Seventh International Conference on Informatics and Urban and Regional Planning INPUT, Italy, Cagliari (2012)
17. Marsh, et al.: The Peripheria Cookbook, Peripheria project (2013)
18. Mattelmäki, T., Vaajakallio, K., Ylirisku, S.: Active@work - Design dealing with social change. In: Online Proceedings of the Include Conference (2007)
19. Messeter, J.: Disruptive Interactions Based On Social Media as a Design Strategy for Empowering Socially Challenged Communities. In: 8th Swiss Design Network Symposium, November 9 (2012)
20. Rizzo, F.: Co-design versus User Centred Design: Framing the differences. In: (a cura di) Guerrini, L. (ed.) Notes on Design Doctoral Research, Franco Angeli, Milano (2010)
21. Rizzo, F., Concilio, G., Marsh, J., Molinari, F.: The living lab approach to codesign solutions for human smart cities: Lessons learnt from Perihèria Project. In: Proceedings of Co-create Conference, June 16-19, Aalto University, Espoo (2013)

A Methodology for Gamifying Smart Cities: Navigating Human Behavior and Attitude

Mizuki Sakamoto[1], Tatsuo Nakajima[1], and Sayaka Akioka[2]

[1] Department of Computer Science and Engineering
Waseda University
{mizuki,tatsuo}@dcl.cs.waseda.ac.jp
[2] Department of Network Design
Meiji University
akioka@meiji.ac.jp

Abstract. We are now living in smart cities, where information technologies enhance our everyday life. For example, our energy management and traffic management have become smarter, making our daily lives more convenient and efficient. However, from a citizen's point of view, a person's happiness needs to be more important than achieving efficient and convenient smart city infrastructures. This is, in particular, an essential issue for achieving human-centered smart city design. In this paper, we present our methodology to gamify smart city services. Our methodology consists of three tools, one model and two infrastructures. The tools contain the *value-based design framework*, the *personality-based analysis framework*, and the *reality-based analysis framework*. The model is named the *GamiMedia* model, and the infrastructures include the *Virtual Form* infrastructure and the *Digital-Physical Hybrid Role-Playing* infrastructure. The methodology to gamify smart city services is extracted from our long experiences with building applications services and middleware infrastructures for ubiquitous computing environments.

Keywords: Human behavior and attitude, Agency, Immersion, Procedural rhetoric, Transmedia.

1 Introduction

When designing future smart cities, maintaining a desirable lifestyle from a citizen's point of view is an important research topic. There have been many previous studies focusing on efficient physical resource management in underlying smart city infrastructures, such as traffic management systems and energy management systems [3]. However, in a future aging society, a person's happiness is more crucial than achieving efficient smart city infrastructures, and this is an essential issue for human-centered smart city design.

Information technologies have made our daily lives safer and more reliable. For example, the progress of bioinformatics makes it possible to develop better medicine and to make our life healthier. The progress of low-power technologies has reduced

N. Streitz and P. Markopoulos (Eds.): DAPI 2014, LNCS 8530, pp. 593–604, 2014.
© Springer International Publishing Switzerland 2014

the consumption of natural resources. However, only considering the recent progress in information technologies limits our ability to address critical social, health, and environmental issues. The limitation can be overcome by taking our ordinary daily life activities into account when navigating human attitude and behavior.

The design of past information technologies typically assumes that human decisions are always rational. For example, studies on usability or ergonomics are based on human rationality in terms of physiology and psychology. However, recent discoveries on cognitive biases in behavioral economics and self-efficacy and positivity in social psychology have shown that information design based on rational thinking is not sufficient to navigate human attitude and behavior [9].

There are two issues in developing gameful smart city services. The first issue is a lack of tools to design the services [4]. The second issue is a lack of software infrastructures to simplify the design of smart city services. These two issues are very critical to make our daily environment smarter [25]. The goal of our project is to solve the issues by offering a set of tools and software infrastructures. Additionally, we provide a model to integrate these tools and infrastructures within one unified methodology.

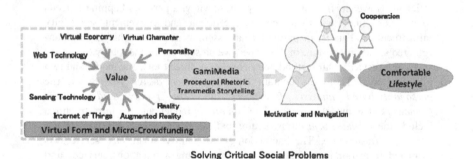

Fig. 1. An Overview of Gamifying Smart Cities

As shown in Fig. 1, our approach proposes a set of design tools, a model, and infrastructures to navigate human attitudes and behavior to tackle critical social problems. In our approach, the central idea is the value-based design framework, which is a tool to design gamified smart city services based on the perceived human values of the services. The value can be translated into the real world by using various information technologies. The GamiMedia model allows people to develop gameful services that are fragmented into multiple pieces of visual expression distributed in multiple virtual forms. A virtual form is an abstraction to show dynamically changing visual information in daily artifacts. Additionally, our approach focuses on modifying the attitudes and behaviors of a community, rather than an individual, by using a micro-crowdfunding concept. Each community can select desirable activities that solve targeted social problems in their communities and help members lead a comfortable lifestyle.

The paper is organized as follows. In Section 2, we present and define the properties of agency and immersion to exploit the procedural rhetoric concept. Section 3 presents three design frameworks as tools to gamify smart cities. Specifically, the value-based design framework is explained in detail, and we show how to use the framework to design smart city services. In Section 4, we propose a model and two infrastructures for gamifying smart city services. Section 5 presents several related studies; finally, we conclude the paper in Section 6.

2   Agency and Immersion in Procedural Rhetoric

Future smart cities will include a large amount of embedded computing power, and the real world will be enhanced through efficient physical resource control and information generated from the embedded computers. In particular, such ubiquitous computing technologies as public networked displays and augmented reality technologies make it possible to physically represent virtual information generated from the embedded computers. In [14], we present that a gaming concept is a useful tool for maintaining a desirable lifestyle; thus, we believe that the concept is also useful for designing future smart cities. As presented in [1], procedural rhetoric allows us to develop a new type of media and services based on a game concept, and the procedural rhetoric effectively navigates human attitudes and behaviors via its persuasive nature. The combination of the procedural rhetoric and ubiquitous computing technologies allow us to develop a strong tool to enhance our daily lives by immersively integrating virtuality into the real world.

In this paper, we first define agency and immersion, essential properties for defining video games, and characterize the concept of procedural rhetoric based on the two properties. In the original definition, agency means the player is able to participate in computer simulations or video games, and immersion is understood as suspension of disbelief [5]. Ubiquitous computing technologies allow these properties to be enhanced as follows: the agency property is enhanced such that each person plays a fictional role augmented through a fictional story in which the role enhances the player's actual abilities in the real world. The story is embodied in our real world through a transmedia storytelling technique [20]: the story is fragmented into several different pieces and presented through different various media, such as networked public displays or projectors. When each person adopts a virtual role that enhances his or her actual abilities, he or she may increase self-efficacy, increase positive thinking, or modify his or her behavior toward a desirable lifestyle. The immersion property is also enhanced; virtual goods are represented in the real world through networked public displays and projectors. When virtual objects offer a simulation property, whereby people can manipulate them similar to real objects, the feeling of immersion is further enhanced. Additionally, the current environmental situation and people's behavior can be reflected in the visual expression presented on ubiquitous displays as procedural rhetoric by extracting the information about the real world with sensors. As shown in [14], the ambient information presentation can be used to shape people's attitude and behavior towards more desirable lifestyle.

3   Design Tools for Gamifying Smart City Services

The above vision promises to realize gameful smart cities by navigating people's attitudes and behaviors toward their desirable lifestyle, but one of the current problems is a lack of good design tools for gamifying smart city services. To successfully engage people, they need to feel some values of the agency and immersion properties offered by procedural rhetoric embodied in the visual expressions on ubiquitous display or projector technologies. If they do not value the services, their attitude and behavior cannot be changed. To solve the problem, we have developed three design frameworks as tools to gamify smart city services, as shown in Fig. 2. The first framework is named the value-based design framework [16, 17, 25], the second is the personality-based analysis framework [19] and the final one is the reality analysis framework [21, 24]. These frameworks enable us to design an effective procedural rhetoric that a variety of people value by designing services offering persuasive visual expressions through the participatory design technique. The frameworks have been extracted from our experiences with building several case studies [6, 14, 18, 20, 28], and organizing workshops and field studies [21, 22, 24].

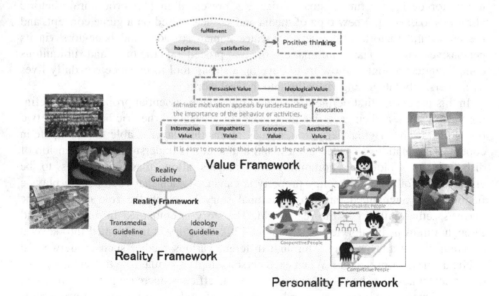

Fig. 2. Design Frameworks

Fig. 3 illustrates the value-based design framework to use the proposed six values to increase people's intrinsic motivation and to make them think positively when incorporating a fictional story into persuasive transmedia storytelling[1].

---

[1] The values are originally proposed in [16, 17]. The current definition of the values is enhanced from the experiences with *Augmented TCG* and presented in [20, 25].

The empathetic, economic, and aesthetic values offer people extrinsic incentives, and the informative value provides the reason to change a person's attitude or tips and tactics for making a better decision. The four values are used as tools in the model to change people's current behavior by emphasizing the importance of changing their behavior and encouraging this change at an early stage. In contrast, the ideological value makes people's dreams and expectations explicit and demonstrates how changing people's attitude helps to realize their dreams. Additionally, the persuasive value delivers the importance of the ideological value to people through stories or procedural rhetoric embodying the ideological value. The values are used to increase the intrinsic motivation to change their attitude in the latter stage of the transtheoretical model [15]. In our approach, we assume that each person already knows the story; thus, the persuasion in the latter phase becomes faster than using traditional methods [25].

Fig. 3. Value-based Design Framework

In our project, the value-based design framework is used with the participatory design. We assume that participants with different personalities cooperate to design services based on the GamiMedia model described in the next section. They usually choose different values because each person prefers a different value. The personality-based analysis framework helps to choose participants who have different personalities. Thus, if they cooperate to design a service together, various values will be embodied into the service, and the service will satisfy a large number of people. The values defined in the value-based design framework also become a good tool for participatory design. When using the value-based design framework in participatory design, the ideological value is an essential value to increase people's intrinsic motivation related to a service. When intrinsic motivation is increased, people's activities are encouraged regardless of their personalities; thus, it is easy to develop attractive services that do not depend on their personalities. If they understand the importance of the ideological message embodied in the service, their increased intrinsic motivation encourages them to perform activities that satisfy the ideological message [23]. When procedural rhetoric is embedded into the ideological message or a story to explain the ideological message is offered, the persuasive value is increased, persuading people that the ideological message is important to them by increasing their self-efficacy or positive thinking. However, people who are not interested in performing the activities can be activated by values that increase their extrinsic motivation. For example, some people like to collect rare objects that offer the economic value, or other people may like to see a beautiful landscape that offers the aesthetic value. When cooperatively designing a smart city service, different people will incorporate the values they prefer.

The services based on the GamiMedia model are represented on multiple virtual forms. By presenting the visual expressions of virtual forms on various daily artifacts, virtuality can be embedded into our real world [24]. The reality analysis framework ensures the reality when using virtual forms. In [21], design patterns that increase extrinsic motivation without losing the reality are proposed; in [24], design patterns that increase intrinsic motivation without losing the reality are proposed. The frameworks also propose design patterns protect the reality when multiple stories are composed. These design patterns are very important when developing services based on the GamiMedia model. Each person may prefer different stories, but many people usually simultaneously watch virtual forms shown on public ubiquitous displays. Thus, the respective person's stories should be combined into one story and be shown on virtual forms embedded into our real world without losing the consistency among the respective stories.

4   Experiences from Case Studies and Extracting Insights to Develop a Model and Infrastructures for Gamifying Smart City Services

In this section, we present our ongoing work on developing a model and two software infrastructures to gamify smart city services. The GamiMedia model is a model for developing multimedia digital content based on transmedia storytelling [22]. The Virtual Form infrastructure coordinates various public displays and projectors; it is implemented on various distributed software infrastructures for ubiquitous computing [21, 24]. The Digital-Physical Hybrid Role-Playing infrastructure offers a way to navigate human attitudes and behaviors [18, 23].

In our current project, as shown in Fig. 4, the GamiMedia model, the Virtual Form infrastructure, and the Digital-Physical Hybrid Role-Playing infrastructure have been developed based on the previous infrastructures from our project. The proposed model and infrastructures have been designed based on insights extracted from experiences with these case studies.

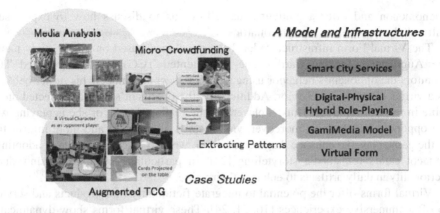

Fig. 4. Extracting Common Patters to Design a Model and Infrastructures

From our experiences with the case studies, we found that one visual expression offered by a smart city service should be easily distributed on multiple displays and projectors. The software infrastructure needs to locate them in a spontaneous way. Additionally, a service programmer using the infrastructure should hide network programming to make it easy to develop distributed visual expressions containing procedural rhetoric. Furthermore, navigating human attitudes and behaviors is difficult to implement as an application program. We need a model to develop distributed visual expressions based on a transmedia storytelling concept, which is executed on virtual forms. In this section, we explain an overview of the model and software infrastructures.

Because we believe that procedural rhetoric is one of desirable tools in persuasive technology, we propose the GamiMedia model to navigate human attitudes and behaviors based on procedural rhetoric. The model has been developed by experiences with analyzing various media contents in workshops and field projects, as shown in one of our case studies [20]. The GamiMedia model allows us to develop services presenting visual expressions based on a transmedia storytelling concept by incorporating a game concept. The model is useful to develop gameful services for advertisements and news that have the purpose in the real world. The value-based design framework and the personality-based analysis framework enable us to develop visual expressions to increase both intrinsic and extrinsic motivation based on the GamiMedia model systematically. The model also enables us to design cultural digital multimedia contents that can be accepted in other cultures. In the model, each GamiMedia object contains at least one element from the following three elements: Dynamics, Visual and Story, where Aesthetic in the MDA Model [8] is divided into Visual and Story in our model. Additionally, a GamiMedia object has a link to another GamiMedia object, with the meaning of a GamiMedia object being explained in another GamiMedia object that is connected with a link. The purpose of the GamiMedia model is to define the semantics of digital multimedia contents, such as Krippendorff's product semantics [11], a methodology to define the meanings of products. The approach can well explain various Japanese fanfic and gamified phenomenon and offer a guideline that allows us to discuss how to export such cultural phenomenon to foreign countries.

The Virtual Form infrastructure has been developed based on a case study named the Augmented Trading Card Game (Augmented TCG) [20]. Augmented TCG monitors the opponent's behavior using an MS Kinect and models his or her behavior as a virtual character's behavior. Additionally, the opponent's card is projected on the table in front of a player. Thus, a player has the feeling that he or she is playing with the opponent face-to-face; moreover, virtual cards allow us to add more information to the game play. To enhance Augmented TCG, we also discuss the idea of adopting a concept called transmedia storytelling [20]. In particular, our approach introduces fictionality in daily artifacts to enhance their value.

Virtual forms offer the potential to integrate fictionality into products and services to offer immersive experiences [16, 21, 24]. These virtual forms show dynamical-ly generated visual expressions containing information that both encourages a person to feel that the artifacts have some additional value and enables him or her to consider the activities that use the artifacts as more attractive. For example, incorporating visual expressions into a display or projecting some information onto an artifact adds computational visual forms to existing daily artifacts. A virtual form can be used as an abstraction to incorporate procedural rhetoric in the real world to gamify smart city services. As described above, the procedural rhetoric incorporated through the GamiMedia model is effective to incorporate virtuality in the real world by exploiting the agency and immersion property.

To present distributed visual expressions for smart city services, which is based on the GamiMedia model, we need a software infrastructure to fragment the visual expressions in distributed virtual forms. There are several software infrastructures in previous studies that satisfy these requirements, such as Personal Home Server [13], FedNet [10], or Mirage [26], which federate a large number of Internet of Things. We have also developed persuasive ambient mirrors [14] and playful training systems [28] to offer infrastructures to use ubiquitous displays and projectors. The Virtual Form infrastructure reuses these software infrastructures, offers a virtual form abstraction and represents distributed visual expressions based on the GamiMedia model. The Virtual Form infrastructure also adopts the ambient feedback techniques proposed in [14] to offer people a psychological incentive. To increase the persuasiveness of the ambient feedback, we also consider adopting an approach used in documentary games [5] to incorporate ideological messages represented as procedural rhetoric [1].

The Digital-Physical Hybrid Role Playing infrastructure is a direct enhancement of a case study named micro-crowdfunding [18]. In micro-crowdfunding, each community manages the sustainability of its shared resources by using a micro-level crowdfunding method. One of a community's members proposes a small mission to improve the sustainability of shared community resources. Usually, the mission is trivial and easy to accomplish, such as clearing a shared garbage box. In our approach, a crowdfunding concept is adopted to increase each community member's awareness, learning which activities are effective for increasing the social sustainability. He or she owns some amount of virtual money, and the money is used to invest to support the proposed mission. Through the investment, he or she can know why the mission is important. The above basic approach to offer a social and economic incentive is encourages people to support missions that are more related to the sustainability of their communities.

Micro-crowdfunding focuses only on social sustainability, but the Digital-Physical Hybrid Role Playing infrastructure can be easily enhanced for other activities for tackling critical social problems. The infrastructure is a higher-layer infrastructure top on the Virtual Form infrastructure to navigate human daily activities. This makes it easy to gamify smart city services by navigating human attitudes and behaviors. In the infrastructure, we assume that many daily artifacts in various locations are made as an Internet of Things. A user can use his or her NFC-capable mobile phone to register a new mission by touching on any artifacts related to the missions with his or her phone. Additionally, a community member invests in the missions from his or her mobile phone. The approach is radically different from traditional crowdfunding systems, such as Kickstarter, Indiegogo, RocketHub, Fundable, and Crowdfunder, because a crowdfunding concept is used to encourage a community to act to solve critical social problems. In the infrastructure, we also need to consider how the payment transaction is light-weighted to lower the threshold to accept ubiquitous payment [27].

In the near future, we believe that we need another infrastructure to analyze the data extracted from human behavior to design better ambient feedback. Currently, we use information extracted from the Digital-Physical Hybrid Role Playing infrastructure. The information includes how and by whom missions are performed and funded. However, to monitor human behavior we need more information from social media [29] and physical sensors [7]. The monitoring infrastructure gathers information about each person's activities, and the information can be used to reflect their current attitude and behavior on virtual forms. Specifically, sensing information from each person's mobile phone is promising to extract accurate human behavior. Because the infrastructure requires a large amount of computational power, the infrastructure will be developed in a cloud computing environment.

5   Related Work

MINDSPACE, proposed in the UK, is a framework that adopts some concepts from behavioral economics to affect human attitudes and behaviors [9]. However, using public policy to modify behavior has a significant disadvantage; it takes a long time to formulate the policies. Therefore, it is effective to use technologies that have strong effects on our mind to navigate human attitude and behavior. In fact, information technologies can be used to solve health problems by increasing people's self-efficacy. For example, Re-mission[2] is a game in which a player finds cancer cells and destroys them in an accurately modeled virtual body. A cancer patient who plays the game believes that he can overcome the cancer in the real world and tackles the

---

[2] http://www.re-mission.net/

treatment positively. This is evidence that information technologies can encourage people to make their behavior more desirable.

Maslow claims that human motivation is based on a hierarchy of needs [12]. In Maslow's hierarchy, the basic needs include such needs as physiological needs and food. Other needs are safety, attachment, esteem, cognitive needs and aesthetic needs. At the highest level, when all other needs are satisfied, we can start to satisfy self-actualization needs. Because people value products when they satisfy their needs, satisfying needs is closely related to defining values. Boztepe proposes four values: utility value, social significance value, emotional value and spiritual value [2].

There are several distributed infrastructures to integrate multiple appliances or smart daily artifacts. For example, a Personal home server makes it possible to coordinate a variety of home appliances spontaneously, such as televisions and video recorders [13]. Because each person has a different personal home server, it allows him or her to personalize how to use the appliances according to his or her preferences. FedNet is a distributed infrastructure for building distributed pervasive computing applications [10]. FedNet adopted a document-centric design using a RESTful approach to modularize system components and to support seamlessly building end-user interaction tools. Mirage [26] is a software infrastructure to build distributed augmented reality applications. Mirage offers a high level abstraction to control distributed continuous media data.

Playful training systems superimpose necessary information on the real world [28]. The basic technology behind playful training systems is augmented reality. The systems make hidden information visible to the user to make a decision more rationally. In particular, less skillful users do not have enough abilities to find useful information embedded in our environment. If information technologies can make more useful information explicitly visible to users, they can make more desirable decisions. The approach is useful to project information support our decision making on daily artifacts. The approach offers a possibility to make every surface of a daily artifact a virtual form. Additionally, a persuasive ambient mirror monitors people's current attitude and behavior by using sensors and presents visual expressions reflecting their current attitude and behavior [14]. For example, in Virtual Aquarium the condition of the Virtual Aquarium reflects people's daily toothbrushing behavior. Additionally, in Mona Lisa Bookshelf, people's housekeeping of their public bookshelf is reflected in a Mona Lisa picture.

6   Conclusion and Future Direction

Our daily lives have becomes increasingly complex. The current progress to develop smart cities helps us to make our lifestyle more comfortable because a variety of automation in smart cities reduce the complexities in our world. However, as describe in the paper, simply reducing the complexities does not create a truly desirable lifestyle. We believe that directing human attitudes and behaviors towards more desirable lifestyle is more important. The paper proposes three design frameworks for gamifying smart city services: the value-based design framework, the personality-based analysis framework and the reality-based analysis framework, the GamiMedia model, the Virtual Form infrastructure, and the Digital-Physical Hybrid Role Playing infrastructure.

In the future, we also need to discuss the ethical issues of modifying human attitudes and behaviors because, if misused, the approach makes it possible to control humans unintentionally or maliciously. We will investigate the issue by introducing a concept called the magic circle, which is widely used in game studies.

References

1. Bogost, I.: Persuasive Games: The Expressive Power of Video Games. MIT Press (2007)
2. Boztepe, S.: User value: Competing Theories and Models. International Journal of Design 1(2), 55–63 (2007)
3. Dohler, M., Ratti, C., Paraszczak, J., Falconer, G.: Smart Cities: Guest Editorial. IEEE Communications Magazine (June 2013)
4. Edwards, W.K., Newman, M.W., Poole, E.S.: The Infrastructure Problem in HCI. In: Proceedings of the 28th International Conference on Human Factors in Computing Systems (2010)
5. Frasca, G.: Rethinking Agency and Immersion: Videogames as a Means of Consciousness-raising. In: SIGGRAPH (2001)
6. Fujinami, K., Nakajima, T.: Sentient Artefacts: Acquiring User's Context through Daily Objects. In: Proceedings of the 2005 International Conference on Embedded and Ubiquitous Computing, pp. 335–344 (2005)
7. Hanaoka, K., Takagi, A., Nakajima, T.: A Software Infrastructure for Wearable Sensor Networks. In: Proceedings of the 12th IEEE Conference on Embedded and Real-Time Computing Systems and Applications (2006)
8. Hunicke, R., LeBlanc, M., Zubek, R.: MDA: A Formal Approach to Game Design and Game Research. In: Proceedings of the Challenges in Game AI Workshop, Nineteenth National Conference on Artificial Intelligence (2004)
9. Institute of Government, MINDSPACE: Influencing Behaviour through Public Policy, CabinetOffice (2010)
10. Kawsar, F., Nakajima, T., Fujinami, K.: Deploy Spontaneously: Supporting End-Users in Building and Enhancing a Smart Home. In: Proceedings of the 10th International Conference on Ubiquitous Computing (2008)
11. Krippendorff, K.: The Semantic Turn: A New Foundation for Design. CRC Press (2005)
12. Maslow, A.H.: Motivation and Personality. Harper and Row, New York (1970)
13. Nakajima, T., Satoh, I.: A Software Infrastructure for Supporting Spontaneous and Personalized Interaction in Home Computing Environments. Personal and Ubiquitous Computing 10(6), 379–391 (2006)
14. Nakajima, T., Lehdonvirta, V.: Designing Motivation using Persuasive Ambient Mirrors. Personal and Ubiquitous Computing 17(1), 107–126 (2013)
15. Prochaska, J.O., Velicer, W.F.: The Transtheoretical Model of Health Behavior Change. American Journal of Health Promotion 12(1), 38–48 (1997)
16. Sakamoto, M., Nakajima, T., Alexandrova, T.: Digital-Physical Hybrid Design: Harmonizing the Real World and the Virtual World. In: Proceedings of the 7th International Conference on the Design & Semantics of Form & Movement (2012)
17. Sakamoto, M., Nakajima, T., Alexandrova, T.: Incorporating Virtual Forms into Traditional Things to Increase Their Values. In: Proceedings of the 5th International Conference on Human-Centric Computing (2012)

18. Sakamoto, M., Nakajima, T.: Micro-Crowdfunding: Achieving a Sustainable Society through Economic and Social Incentives in Micro-Level Crowdfunding. In: Proceedings of International Conference on Mobile and Ubiquitous Multimedia (2013)

19. Sakamoto, M., Alexandrova, T., Nakajima, T.: Analyzing the Effects of Virtualizing and Augmenting Trading Card Game based on the Player's Personality. In: Proceedings of the Sixth International Conference on Advances in Computer-Human Interactions (2013)

20. Sakamoto, M., Alexandrova, T., Nakajima, T.: Augmenting Remote Trading Card Play with Virtual Characters used in Animation and Game Stories - Towards Persuasive and Ambient Transmedia Storytelling. In: Proceedings of the 6th International Conference on Advances in Computer-Human Interactions (2013)

21. Sakamoto, M., Nakajima, T., Akioka, S.: Designing enhanced daily digital artifacts based on the analysis of product promotions using fictional animation stories. In: Yoshida, T., Kou, G., Skowron, A., Cao, J., Hacid, H., Zhong, N. (eds.) AMT 2013. LNCS, vol. 8210, pp. 266–277. Springer, Heidelberg (2013)

22. Sakamoto, M., Nakajima, T.: The gamiMedia model: Gamifying content culture. In: Rau, P.L.P. (ed.) CCD/HCII 2014. LNCS, vol. 8528, pp. 786–797. Springer, Heidelberg (2014)

23. Sakamoto, M., Nakajima, T.: Gamifying social media to encourage social activities with digital-physical hybrid role-playing. In: Meiselwitz, G. (ed.) SCSM/HCII 2014. LNCS, vol. 8531, pp. 581–591. Springer, Heidelberg (2014)

24. Sakamoto, M., Nakajima, T.: A Better Integration of Fictional Stories into the Real World for Gamifying Intelligent Daily Life. In: Proceedings of the First International Symposium on Simulation and Serious Games (2014)

25. Sakamoto, M., Alexandrova, T., Nakajima, T.: Designing Values for Digital-Physical Hybrid Gameful Artifacts, Waseda University Distributed Computing Laboratory Research Report 2014-2 (2014)

26. Tokunaga, E., van der Zee, A., Kurahashi, M., Nemoto, M., Nakajima, T.: A Middleware Infrastracture for Building Mixed Reality Applications in Ubiquitous Computing Environments. In: Proceedings of the 1st Annual International Conference on Mobile and Ubiquitous Systems, Networking and Services (2004)

27. Yamabe, T., Lehdonvirta, V., Ito, H., Soma, H., Kimura, H.: Applying Pervasive Technologies to Create Economic Incentives that Alter Consumer Behavior. In: Proceedings of the 11th International Conference on Ubiquitous Computing, pp. 175–184. ACM, New York (2009)

28. Yamabe, T., Nakaima, T.: Playful Training with Augmented Reality Games: Case Studies towards Reality-Oriented System Design. Multimedia Tools and Applications 62(1), 259–286 (2013)

29. Zhu, Z., Blanke, U., Calatroni, A., Tröster, G.: Human Activity Recognition Using Social Media Data. In: Proceedings of International Conference on Mobile and Ubiquitous Multimedia (2013)

U.App: An Urban Application Design Environment Based on Citizen Workshops

Tomoyo Sasao[1] and Shin'ichi Konomi[2]

[1] Department of Socio-Cultural Environmental Studies, The University of Tokyo
Kashiwa, Chiba, 277-8563, Japan
[2] Center for Spatial Information Science, The University of Tokyo
Kashiwa, Chiba, 277-8568, Japan
{sasaotomoyo,konomi}@csis.u-tokyo.ac.jp

Abstract. Designing usable applications for coping with civic challenges can be extremely difficult without an appropriate design environment. We explore a novel application design process based on the analysis of real citizen workshops, and propose U.App, a design environment that allows citizens to create urban applications based on the process. We expect that the proposed environment will facilitate citizens' daily activities for addressing urban issues and extend the possibility of citizen-centered mobile applications.

Keywords: urban application, citizen workshop, application design platform.

1 Introduction

Mobile computing is not merely a technology for passive consumption of information. It can enhance community-wide programs and activities, potentially converting bystanders into activists of city issues as well. Location-based technologies and sensing technologies can support various civic programs to improve their neighborhoods. For example such technologies are used in participatory sensing, citizen science, community health activities and so on.

A key limitation is the difficulty of developing mobile tools that support apt civic issues. When designing them, system engineers need to understand the problems, sometimes interviewing citizens or observing the field. These processes take much time and need help from various experts (e.g., urban planners) and users. Oftentimes, these design processes can be useful for creating tools for dealing with major civic issues, but not smaller yet important local issues that only citizens are aware of.

U.App, which we propose in this paper, is an urban application design environment that respects the creative insight of citizens to create solutions and tools for coping with local issues in daily life. To develop an optimal citizen-centered design platform of urban applications, we focus on a traditional citizen workshop in the urban design field, which has a systematic process to share and discuss social/local problems in detail with citizens.

N. Streitz and P. Markopoulos (Eds.): DAPI 2014, LNCS 8530, pp. 605–616, 2014.

First, we review citizens' actions/activities in antecedent urban design processes and existing citizen-centered approach in mobile application design, we thoroughly observe a real citizen workshop, from which we distill five action/activity patterns for improving neighborhood. Based on these patterns, we create paper prototypes of U.App and sample urban applications that can be generated by it. Finally, we interview citizen workshop experts to obtain initial feedback about our prototypes, and uncover some important issues of urban application design based on their comments.

2   Citizens and Urban Applications

In this section, we discuss an optimal environment for creating urban applications. We first review both citizen-centered approach in urban design field and mobile urban application design field. Then, we discuss a novel workshop-based process for co-designing urban applications.

2.1   Citizens Actions/Activities in Urban Design Processes

In urban planning field, citizen-centered approaches for urban design, originated in 1960s, have encouraged many urban designers to consider inherent virtue and potential in a given site, and thus have made an impact on recent region-specific design movements such as New Urbanism [1]. Above all, citizens' actions/activities play key roles in these approaches.

William H. Whyte and Jane Jacobs are prominent pioneers of these approaches. Whyte's famous work "Street Life Project" is a study based on careful observations of human behaviors in urban settings, looking at, listening to, and asking questions of the people in a community to discover their needs and aspirations. His field survey techniques that emphasize citizen insights laid the foundations of on-site design in a lot of recent projects and approaches such as Placemaking [2], an approach to creating good public spaces that are capitalized on local community resources. While Jane Jacobs is a seminal urban activist who advocated for recovering citizen ownership of urban spaces from car-centered planning, she offered groundbreaking ideas about supporting citizens to self-improve lively neighborhoods in everyday life [3]. For example "Natural Surveillance," the strategy she formulated, limits the opportunities for crime by increasing the perception that people can be seen. Based on this strategy, she also discussed designs of entrances, streets and nighttime lighting that increase visibility of people.

2.2   Existing Urban Applications and Their Design Platforms

An *issue-centric urban application* (see Fig.1a) is a tool for urging citizens to take actions on specific city/neighborhood issues that designers have identified, and it is often created and released by urban planning experts and/or technical experts. There is no need for citizens to have advanced skills because they can simply participate in the activities defined by experts. For example, Pirika[4] and FixMyStreet[5] are issue-centric mobile applications that citizens report specific field contents (e.g., garbage and things that are broken). Also, in many existing projects of citizen science or participatory sensing, experts define data gathering activities.

A *citizen-centric urban application* (see Fig.1b) is a tool that users can customize or select some of its functions so that users will be able to define the purposes, goals and suitable actions/activities. While some platforms require users to have basic programming skills when customizing applications and ordinary citizens cannot use for themselves [6], a few platforms provide more citizen-friendly interfaces. Sensr, which is a design platform of mobile data-collection tools for citizen science, allows non-technical data collectors to create original input forms combining various widgets flexibly [7]. In this platform, citizens can be urban application creators. However, a key challenge in designing urban applications is the difficulty to clearly understand "what activities contribute to neighborhoods" and "what tools can support citizens' activities effectively." ActivityDesigner [8] is a prototyping environment that considers this challenge. It supports the pre-design phase for exploring application concepts so that non-experts can design and use personalized applications easily.

2.3   Workshop-Based Process

U.App is also designed to support the pre-design phase, from which citizens could derive urban application concepts. Moreover, it needs a novel feature that supports citizens to co-prototype urban applications by themselves, because these applications will be used by many citizens other than their developers. Citizens should be able to enhance their urban applications to broaden their horizons.

A workshop-based design platform (see Fig.1c) can be expected to suit urban application design environment such as U.App, because a workshop can include a fieldwork phase that helps gain knowledge of city/neighborhood issues and solutions, and also include a discussion phase that promotes citizen collaboration. In addition, it is easy to involve experts in a workshop to encourage citizens.

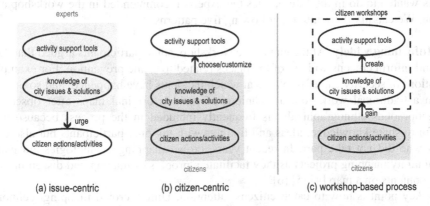

Fig. 1. Three types of relations between citizens and urban applications. They are characterized by activity support tools, knowledge of city issues & solutions and citizen actions/activities.

3   Case Study

We participated in a real citizen workshop and gathered qualitative data to analyze the patterns of activities for improving their neighborhood. Here we describe the overview of the workshop and the five common patterns of citizen actions/activities. These patterns lead to effective urban application types.

3.1   Overview

We participated in a one-day citizen workshop at a district in Tokyo called "My City Walking Tour for Crime Prevention," which is a typical example of participatory crime prevention programs. About 15 people aged 30-70, who belong to the district's neighborhood association, participated in the workshop. Former police officers, administrative officers, researchers and a facilitator were workshop support staffs. First, researchers gave lectures on crime prevention and a facilitator organized civic activities into three types: (1) recommended activities for crime prevention, (2) existing activities that citizens have already tried, and (3) novel activities that they have not tried yet. Second, participants walked around in their neighborhood with expert guides (e.g., a former police officer). Participants learned and found dangerous/good spots receiving advice from the guides on site. They took photographs, jotted down their findings and ideas, and marked relevant locations on a paper map. After the fieldwork, they made a large crime-prevention map of their town cooperatively using their collected information as material. Finally, they presented it to all. Participants discussed their next personal and cooperative actions/activities for improving their neighborhoods.

3.2   Patterns of Actions/Activities for Neighborhood Improvement

There are various activities for improving a neighborhood such as ones which participants wanted to do in the future, ones the experts recommended in the workshop and so on. We classify them into the following five patterns.

(a) **Informing widely.** At the end of the workshop, some participants argued that they should inform citizens widely, of the places related to crime prevention. For example, locations of security cameras, places at which incidents have happened, and so on.

In a traditional workshop, a technique of making original maps after observing neighborhoods ethnographically is frequently included in the process because it is useful to share knowledge, ideas and findings with not only participants but also citizens who did not take part. In recent years, crowd mapping technologies aid many community mapping projects as they facilitate a process of making and disseminating user contents on a map [4] [5] [6].

A key point is how to catch citizens' attention. Unlike crowd mapping technologies, mobile urban applications are aware of their context, i.e., they can provide information in relevant context. As research on mobile learning (e.g., [9]) suggests, citizens would be able to absorb richer local knowledge when information is pushed or embedded in the suitable contexts than in irrelevant places or at irrelevant timing.

(b) Investigating in detail. In the fieldwork, many of the participants found some dangerous spots in the neighborhood, and they pointed out the necessity to make maps of them, such as illuminance at night, vacant houses and insufficiently managed places. In this way, findings from citizen workshops can lead to citizens' needs of detailed investigations.

Considering such requests from citizens is in line with Whyte's urban design approach, and it can be supported by applying participatory sensing [10] or VGI [11] technologies, which facilitates collection of detailed data opportunistically in everyday life.

A key point is the support of regular observations to collect detailed data incrementally at same or different spots.

(c) Asking citizens' experience. Some participants focused on their concerns about a broken signboard in their surrounding park. Leaving neglected features like the signboard can be dangerous, but they do not know how to treat it. In such a case, comments from neighbors or passers-by might be helpful for them.

To get comments from people in specific place based on Whyte's approach, there are many traditional techniques such as questionnaires and interviews on streets. Also, digital technologies, such as interactive public displays [12] can catch citizens' attentions and urge them to contribute ideas. Experience sampling tools on mobile phones [13][14] can gather citizens' comments in relevant places or at relevant timing.

A key point is targeting right respondents who understand the civic issues well, stay at a relevant place, or be at a specific place at the best timing.

(d) Urging citizens into sustained actions/activities. One of the crime-prevention experts told that a local safety network can be created from citizens' small, sustained activities, for example, people walking their dogs or keeping their gardens can keep an eye on children on their way home from school. Such activities can increase the situations of *natural surveillance*.

One of the ways for urging citizens into such activities is visualization and social awareness. In case of "citizens' dog patrol," dog owners may use uniform armbands, caps, or dog leads for sharing individual activities as a major social contribution. Recently, many kinds of visualizations of user's workout status to encourage physical activities on digital devices can be built by users easily [15][16].

A key point is again support for sustained activities based on social awareness and visualization.

(e) Fostering a community of public spaces management. In the workshop, a ward office staff showed us two flowerbeds: one of them is managed by the ward and the other one by active citizens. The latter has many planted flowers and is maintained better than the former. He said that cities are full of public and common spaces like parks, sidewalks, vacant lots and so on, then those places will possibly be better if citizens are given the opportunity to manage them cooperatively.

In general, when carrying out a particular work with multiple members, sharing tasks and schedules are important. Many kinds of shared task management systems already exist, such as KanbanFlow[17] for sharing checklists of members' tasks.

A key point is that taking care of public spaces is not mandatory for citizens. Urban applications should support voluntary participation and privacy protection (e.g., via anonymous schedule sharing).

4   Prototype

We developed a paper prototype of U.App based on a workshop-based design process and frameworks to support different activities. In the following, we present show the details of each.

4.1   Workshop Based Design Process

In our case study, we realized that a collaborative citizen workshop process includes an essential element for designing urban applications. It is not until citizens get together and think collaboratively that they find the issues of their city and next actions/activities come to mind. Therefore, we suggest an urban application design process that integrates application design in an urban design workshop environment (see Fig.2). The roles and effects of each step is as follows:

(1) Field observations. Participants walk around in their neighborhood and capture their findings using any tools; a camera, jots, voice recorder, twitter and so on. In particular, information about where, when, by whom the data is captured often helps understand other participants' findings and also turns captured data into useful resources for designing urban applications.

(2) Discussion/finding issues. The gathered data in step 1 can be of considerable quantity and variety. The participants present their own data on a large map and share the details of what they found. After that, they seek and discuss several urban issues based on the data. Some issues will be the seed of an urban application theme.

(3) Creating/improving urban application prototypes. After finding various issues, participants start thinking what actions/activities for improving their city citizens can start and decide urban application themes. At this point, participants can fetch relevant data into U.App and start creating prototypes of urban applications.

(4) Testing in field. Participants can test the created prototypes on their smartphones easily. The prototypes keep operation logs and inputted data. Participants can verify and analyze the data on a PC to improve the prototypes.

(5) Release. After iterative improvements, anyone can release and use the applications in daily lives. Widespread uses of the applications can lead to improvement of their neighborhoods.

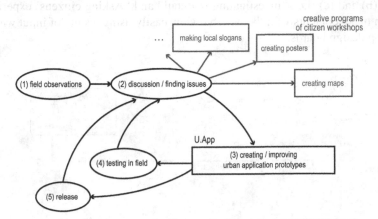

Fig. 2. A workshop-based urban application design process, contrasted with traditional ones

4.2   Frameworks to Support Different Regional Activities

As shown in Table 1, the five action/activity patterns discussed in section 3.2 correspond to the two simple application frameworks, and we designed the four modules to support the frameworks. By combining these modules, users can create various kinds of urban applications.

Table 1. Five action/activity patterns correspond to two frameworks and four modules

Action/Activity Patterns	Application Frameworks	Modules
(a) Informing widely	Contextual Alert (Fig.3)	Activity Trigger (Fig.3-1)
(b) Investigating in detail		
(c) Asking citizens' experience		Alert Contents (Fig.3-2)
(d) Urging citizens into sustained actions/activities	Sharing User States (Fig.4)	Activity Tracker (Fig.4-1)
(e) Fostering a community of public spaces management		Activity Visualizer (Fig.4-2)

Framework of Contextual Alert. This framework is used when the participants want to communicate specific contents (e.g., local knowledge, requests to participate in investigations) to citizens (see Fig.3). The following two modules support it.

Activity Trigger. This module controls the timing to trigger alerts by exploiting various sensors on user devices. U.App creators can employ area-based, timespan-based or weather-based triggering mechanisms.

Alert Contents. This module stores contents of alerts, and users access them through *views.* U.App creators can choose from two view templates: (1) the read-only view that suits pattern (a) (i.e., "Informing widely") and (2) the "writable" view that suits patterns (b) and (c) (i.e., "Investigating in detail" and "Asking citizens' experience"). They can make contents with the writable view easily using a suite of input widgets in the U.App design boards.

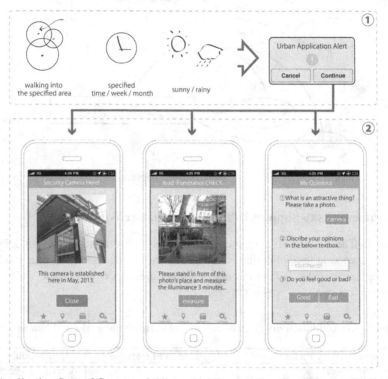

Fig. 3. Application flow of Contextual Alert, which has two functions, (1) Activity Trigger and (2) Alert Contents, to support U.App creators to communicate with their application users

Framework of Sharing User States. This framework helps U.App creators to manage/promote activities in a local community (Fig.4). The following two modules support this framework.

Activity Tracker. This module tracks the progress of an activity and shares it with the whole community, which suits pattern (d) ("Urging citizens into sustained actions/activities"), or with specific community members, which suits pattern (e) "Fostering a community of public spaces management"). U.App creators set an application theme, which corresponds to a local issue, and make a list of several civic routines contributing to its solution. They can also choose checking methods of their daily routines: automatic (e.g., using GPS or a timer) or manual (e.g., tapping a calendar).

Activity Visualizer. The progresses of their activities are interpreted as the nutrition of the digital garden on their smartphones everyday (see Fig.4). It has a simple logic: the more they perform the activities, the more the garden flowers increase.

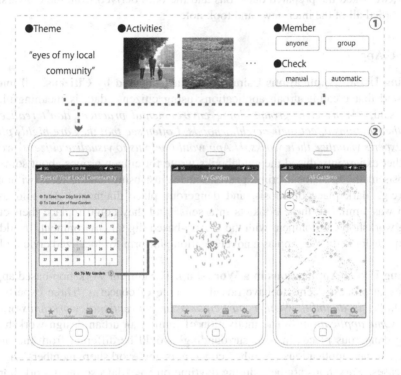

Fig. 4. Sharing User States has two functions, (1) Activity Tracker and (2) Activity Visualizer, to support managing/promoting activities in a local community

5   Expert Interviews

To reveal strengths and weaknesses of the proposed approach, we interviewed four workshop experts (two researchers, one organizer, and one facilitator)[1].

We asked them to discuss the following 5 topics in the semi-structured interviews:

1. Significance and feasibility of creating urban applications in a workshop
2. Processes for creating urban applications in a workshop
3. Range of urban applications that can be created with U.App modules
4. Roles/effects of urban applications for citizens
5. Features of U.App

---

[1] Interview comments were originally given in Japanese. They were translated into English by the authors.

Each interview session lasted about 1 hour. First, we explained the background and the purpose of U.App. Then, we presented five urban application patterns and these functions. Then, we explained how to operate U.App, showing the paper prototype. Finally, we asked the prepared questions and the ones derived from the conversation. We recorded all of the interviews and took notes.

5.1   U.App

Creating Urban Applications Using the Data Collected by Citizens. All interviewees said that creating urban applications using citizens' data is meaningful. One expert said, *"Many civic groups doing environmental practices don't realize how much their actions affect their neighborhoods. I often see that they are highly pleased when experts visualize their works. U.App would help us to visualize citizens' works."* The other expert introduced the guidebooks wrote for citizen groups about some self-diagnosis methods of local crime prevention by just using analog tools without experts (e.g., dark place diagnosis, and dangerous place diagnosis). He told us that U.App was similar to these booklets in a sense and they could replace their current analog workshop environment with the U.App-based digital environment. In addition, two experts looked on U.App as a novel creation platform for localized civic tools.

Creating Urban Applications in a Workshop. The current workshop-based application design process seems to have raised a couple of concerns. Three experts commented, *"It is doubtful whether participants in conventional workshops want to create some applications."* The motivation of joining an urban design workshop for finding dangerous places in their surroundings would be different from the ones of creating urban applications. Another concern is the workshop members' ages. In many cases, workshops are held during daytime on weekdays so most workshop participants are elderly people. Most of them don't have smartphones; thus they wouldn't be motivated to create smartphone applications. Despite these concerns, there still is a significant value in exploiting workshops in urban application design as two experts emphasized the importance of workshops, *"citizens and experts get together."* One expert said, *"A workshop is a special environment for people to consider what they don't think in daily lives, discuss local problems deeper with neighbors, and build new communities."* We believe it is worthwhile to go forward with opening up even wider opportunities to co-create urban applications by considering a right mix of different people (e.g., an urban planning specialist who has the minimum IT literacy, kids, college students), or using alternative workshop formats (e.g., a more collaborative program with non-experts and experts creating urban applications together).

5.2   Urban Applications

Urban Applications Variation. All experts said that the range of applications that can be created with U.App modules (see section 4.2) is almost enough in that they cover a sufficiently wide spectrum of citizens actions/activities. They also said that the proposed modules can support other workshop themes such as cooperative management of a forest and some sightseeing projects. Especially, three experts emphasize that the most versatile function is an information notification. One of the experts desired more flexible control of alert conditions to accommodate application designers' creativity, while another expert desired that application designers should be able to use more pictures/animations in the activity visualizer for localizing urban applications.

Accessibility. The current version of urban application platform is designed only for smartphones; the user interface will have to provide higher-accessibility. Two experts pointed out that smartphone-based applications cannot be widely used among senior citizens who have never touched smartphones. In addition, they also said that the urban applications are highly public tools, so their user interfaces should be improved to be more universal. For elderly people in Japan, a fax machine would be a familiar technology for sending information, and large public displays in their surrounding would be better than small smartphones for accessing visual information. One expert said, if urban applications can be used on these devices, many eldery people would be willing to join civic actions/activities for improving neighborhoods. All experts recommend holding workshops to provide opportunities for smartphone beginners to learn how to use urban applications. One of them argued that "urban application-use workshops" could grow in popularity than "urban application-design workshops."

6   Conclusion and Future Work

This paper proposed U.App, which allows citizens to easily create applications for addressing local issues with their actions/activities. We presented our field observation, paper prototype, and expert interviews Based on these results, we discussed strengths and weaknesses of U.App as well as general issues related to the design of mobile urban applications. In our future work, we will consider the following approaches to address some of the issues highlighted in our expert interviews:

1. *Alternative workshop scenarios*. To integrate application design and workshops seamlessly, we will examine three alternative workshop scenarios: (1) *complementary workshops*. Citizens and professionals create urban applications together. Citizens can propose concepts of urban applications and professionals can help implement them. (2) *learning-and-homework style workshops*. Citizens learn how to use U.App in a workshop, and then as their homework, they create original applications. (3) *test/use workshops*. Citizens can just acquire skills of using urban applications in a workshop so that they can use the applications in daily lives.
2. *Universal urban application interfaces*. To encourage participation by various people, we should consider devices other than smartphones so that citizens can input and output information more easily. We would like to consider digital signboards in the city, vacant store walls, and other stocks of urban infrastructures, as well as fax, letters, and other technologies that are familiar to elderly people.
3. *Design environment of localized urban applications*. To improve urban applications make them truly helpful in solving issues that citizens are aware of, we

should study urban applications' customization method, especially for localizing. We plan to implement a data import function to enhance the value of field data.

4. *Generalizability of U.App/urban applications.* So far, U.App is largely based on the case study of "a crime prevention workshop." We intend to make the platform as generic as possible, acknowledging the need to look into various kinds of workshops besides crime-prevention workshops.

If our urban application design approach succeeds in future, we can expect that U.App will become fertile ground for participatory urban design efforts, enhancing citizen engagement and increasing civic actions/activities to improve neighborhood.

References

1. Bohl, C.C.: New urbanism and the city: Potential applications and implications for distressed inner-city neighborhoods. Housing Policy Debate 11, 761–801 (2000)
2. Project for Public Spaces | Placemaking for Communities, http://www.pps.org/
3. Jacobs, J.: The death and life of great American cities. Random House LLC (1961)
4. Pirika, http://www.pirika.org/
5. FixMyStreet, http://www.fixmystreet.com/
6. Ushahidi, http://www.ushahidi.com/
7. Kim, S., Mankoff, J.: Sensr: Evaluating A Flexible Framework for Authoring Mobile Data - Collection Tools for Citizen Science. In: Proc. CSCW 2013, pp. 1453–1462 (2013)
8. Li, Y., Landay, J.A.: Activity-Based Prototyping of Ubicomp Applications for Long-Lived, Everyday Human Activities. In: Proc. CHI 2008, pp. 1303–1312 (2008)
9. Sharples, M., Taylor, J., Vavoula, G.: A Theory of Learning for the Mobile Age. Medien-bildung in Neuen Kulturräumen SE - 6, 87–99 (2010)
10. Willett, W., Aoki, P., Kumar, N., Subramanian, S., Woodruff, A.: Common Sense Community: Scaffolding Mobile Sensing and Analysis for Novice Users. In: Proc. Pervasive, pp. 301–318 (2010)
11. Seeger, C.: The role of facilitated volunteered geographic information in the landscape planning and site design process. GeoJournal, 199–213 (2008)
12. Kukka, H., Oja, H., Kostakos, V., Gonçalves, J., Ojala, T.: What Makes You Click: Exploring Visual Signals to Entice Interaction on Public Displays. In: Proc. CHI 2013, pp. 1699–1708 (2013)
13. Mappiness, http://www.mappiness.org.uk/
14. Konomi, S., Sasao, T., Ohno, W., Shoji, K.: Crowd-Powered Mechanisms for Viewing and Imaging Public Spaces. In: Proceedings of the 2013 International Conferences on Computer Graphics, Visualization, Computer Vision, and Game Technology (VisioGame 2013), Jakarta, Indonesia, pp. 67–72 (December 2013)
15. Consolvo, S., Libby, R., Smith, I., Landay, J.A., McDonald, D.W., Toscos, T., Chen, M.Y., Froehlich, J., Harrison, B., Klasnja, P., LaMarca, A., LeGrand, L.: Activity sensing in the wild. In: Proc. CHI 2008, pp. 1797–1806 (2008)
16. Lin, J.J., Mamykina, L., Lindtner, S., Delajoux, G., Strub, H.B.: Fish' n' Steps: Encouraging Physical Activity with an Interactive Computer Game. In: Dourish, P., Friday, A. (eds.) UbiComp 2006. LNCS, vol. 4206, pp. 261–278. Springer, Heidelberg (2006)
17. KanbanFlow, https://kanbanflow.com/

Meaningful Interactions in a Smart City

Peter van Waart[1,2] and Ingrid Mulder[1,2]

[1] Creating 010, Rotterdam University of Applied Sciences,
Wijnhaven 99-107, 3011 WN, Rotterdam, The Netherlands
[2] ID-Studiolab, Faculty of Industrial Design Engineering, Delft University of Technology,
Landbergstraat 15, 2628 CE Delft, The Netherlands
p.van.waart@hr.nl

Abstract. A city is a public space where people find meaning by living together. Although cities are governed by city councils, it is mainly the citizens that make their own city. The contemporary cityscape is increasingly pervaded with emerging media. Recent invasions of interactive media in the cityscape, however, are to a large extent commercial broadcasting systems that do not encourage interaction and communication among citizens. This is not trivial; the public space is the city's medium for communication with its citizens. The current work derives from the notion that interactive media can be used to enrich people's lives in a meaningful way. In three design cases is illustrated how the symbolic level of interactions is of major importance for designing meaningful interactions in cities.

Keywords: Smart city, interaction design, meaning, human values.

1 Introduction

In the Meaningful Design in the City programme of research centre Creating010 we investigate how to design for smart cities in a human-centred way. Originally, research on Internet of Things and Big Data generally focus on connecting a variety of information systems and data sets, including physical objects such as bus stops, billboards, waste containers and devices like smart watches and other wearables, in order to optimise processes in the field of traffic management, mobility, energy, security, or shopping. In doing so, the position of the individual might be ignored by the organisational goals of governments and companies. In contrast, research centre Creating010 studies how the design process on an urban interaction level can be people-led. The accompanying values-based approach starts from out the needs, goals and values of individuals and groups of people in the city. That is what we call meaningful design. In doing that, not so much an Internet of Things is the objective here, as well as an Internet of People [1]. The central question in the Meaningful Design programme is: how to provide meaningful experiences by exploiting omnipresent technologies. Technology that is accessible for people to influence their local living environment and society at city level. We enable people to invent alternative ways of value creation or product trade systems (economics), to organise themselves to influence local

N. Streitz and P. Markopoulos (Eds.): DAPI 2014, LNCS 8530, pp. 617–628, 2014.

policy (participation, democracy), and to support and take care for each other (health and well-being). When aligned with organisational goals, this also is an opportunity for governments and companies to improve their proposition and customer experiences.The current contribution describes the challenges for designing hybrid interactive environments that mix pervasive technologies (such as sensors and public displays) in physical spaces with virtual (social media and individual) content (data), to create the experience of meaning over time and space in cities. We introduce three design cases to illustrate how accounting for human values improves the symbolic features in the design for meaningful interactions throughout time and space in the city.

1.1   Human Values and the Experience of Meaning in Interactions

Early work on human values [2, 3, 4] explains how human values drive people's attitude and behaviour. The insight that addressing people's values result in stronger product and brand preferences of consumers, is widely used since then in the marketing and market research industry for product development, communication, and advertising purposes [5, 6, 7].One characteristic of human values according to Schwartz [4] is that they refer to desirable goals that motivate action. According to Csikszentmihalyi [8] one element of the experience of meaning is an 'ultimate goal' (or reason of living). Human values probably are the most important goals in life of people, according to the definition of Rokeach [2]: "an enduring belief that a specific mode of conduct or end state of existence is personally or socially preferable to an opposite or converse mode of conduct or end state of its existence".Another characteristic mentioned by Schwartz [4] is that values are beliefs that are linked inextricably to affect. Once values are 'activated' they become infused with feelings. In the field of emotional design, Desmet's [9] model of product emotion reflects this process: emotions emerge from an appraisal process in which (external) stimuli are weighted against one's (internal) concerns such as human values. In summary, from out their human values people envision an ideal world to pursue that gives meaning to life. Based on that we define 'meaningful design' as 'design that accounts for human values and empower people in pursuing life goals'.In order to explore how designers can evoke meaningful experiences with their artefacts we found that in user experience (UX) research instrumental, task-oriented, (pragmatic) goals are distinguished from noninstrumental (hedonistic) goals such as beauty [10, 11, 12, 13]. Few researchers describe instrumentality, aesthetics and symbolism as integrated aspects in one design [14, 15]. Based on earlier work from UX research, we made a generalisation of three levels of experiences as results from specific features of design disciplines. Table 1 shows these three levels, which are: aesthetic experiences based on sensory perceivable properties of artefacts, experiential experiences based on the behaviour of artefacts, and symbolic experiences based on the extent to which artefacts comply to our values [16].

Table 1. Three levels of experience of design. Information processing in design models [16].

Generalisa-tion	Aesthetic: How it *feels*	Experiential: How it *works*	Symbolic: What it *means*
Design features	Inherent qualities, formal properties, appearance, physical properties, first impressions	Interaction, performance, instrumental benefits of use	What it says about ourselves and others, memories, appraisals of motive compliance against concerns (goals and values)
Experience duration	Immediate	Short-term, mid-term	Long-term
Design discipline	Visual design, sensorial design	Interaction design, information architects, network engineering, software engineering	Brand experience designers, artists, story-tellers

While specific disciplines focus on specific features of design resulting in certain types of experiences, we conclude that the most rich user experience result from designs for which the designer achieved to integrate all features as a whole. When it comes to designing single artefacts such as a website or a smartphone app, designing for aesthetic, experiential, as well as symbolic experiences is already a challenge. Without doubt, the challenge to design in a meaningful way for smart cities, which are complicated large-scale urban technological ecosystems that are present always and everywhere, becomes even bigger.

1.2 Time and Space

Now pervasive technology is present everywhere and all the time, it has is impact on the way people experience the city. We argue that space and time deserve more attention as factors in the design of meaningful experiences in a smart city. In recent years, among UX researchers attention has grown to the temporal and spatial factors of pervasive technology [17, 18, 19]. With regard to the experience of meaning, efforts are made to measure and explain how user experience evolves over time from orientation through incorporation to identification [20, 21, 22]. Longitudinal and retrospective approaches appear to result in a proper insight in aspects and changes in user experience over time [23, 24]. Where Karapanos et al. [22] indicate meaningfulness to appear in the phase of incorporation with the realisation of usability and usefulness, our definition of meaningfulness would position meaningfulness in the last phase of identification when a product relates to personal experiences, daily rituals and self-expression. Nonetheless, time appears to be an influential factor in the experience of meaning of technology design. Also the aspects of space and place have been thoroughly investigated. Since designing pervasive technology is designing 'new context' in which people live, much emphasis has been given already to the embodied interaction in space and place [25, 26, 27, 28]. An interesting perspective is that of the multiverse presented by Pine and Korn [35] with which they challenge companies to explore the 'infinite possibilities' of hybrid realms in the spectrum of time and no-time, space and no-space and matter and no-matter. Harrison et al. [29] stress the importance to focus on embodied interaction, because our location in the physical and social world is crucial in understanding ourselves, the world around us, as well as our interactions. In what they call the third paradigm of HCI, Harrison et al. [29] argue that the question how context gives meaning to the design of technological systems, should be replaced by the question how design of technology accommodate the context.So, much research already has been done on temporal and spatial factors of pervasive technology and also more attention has been given to hedonistic goals next to pragmatic goals in Human-Computer Interaction (HCI). The interplay between these trends reveals new possibilities for the design of meaningful interactions in the real world. In the remainder of this work, we focus on the symbolic aspect of the design for smart cities. Hence, the current aim is to design a 'meaningful' experience of the user. In keeping with the third paradigm, we focus on the diversity of human values as ground for making meaning as well [29, 30, 31, 32].

2   Moodly, Cosy and Nosey: Three Cases of Meaningful Design

In the Meaningful Design in the City programme, we work in close collaboration with the City of Rotterdam. Public servants of the local government are connected to certain groups of citizens that aim for improvement of their neighbourhood or societal issues at city level. Rotterdam politicians support alternative ways of influencing city's policy by citizens. Many governmental services are eager to learn about how to consult citizens and how to involve citizens in crowd-sourced data collection. That demand is a ground for projects that go one step further towards people-led projects. We especially focus on how to design the interactions in-between citizens and between citizens and local government at one hand, and between citizens and the designed technology at the other hand, in order to evoke a meaningful experience for citizens. The cases are used to illustrate the symbolic features of the design, which we have marked with [M] in the following paragraphs.

2.1   Moodly: Art Installation for City Emotion Insights

Moodly is an interactive art installation that allows people to value their mood, and communicates these values through public screens using a mobile app enabling people's awareness of each other's emotions. Several physical interactive installations are placed at different semi-public spaces and connected via the (mobile) web application. After gathering real-time data we analyze the mood assessed in different locations in the city of Rotterdam, taking into account the difference among different locations and moments, and compare these Moodly assessments with a wellbeing index based upon public sector information derived from the Rotterdam Open Data Store. In the design project for the interactive cityscape the central question was how meaningful design can enhance interaction among citizens, cultivate citizens' happiness, and contribute to a city's wellbeing. In this design, private emotions are aggregated into emotional-state-of-the-city maps. Individuals gain insight in how personal emotional states relates to the city crowd emotional state [M]. Personal emotional data is combined with geo-data for mapping to create maps. Other city stakeholders, e.g., the police, can use the categorisation of mood states as indications of emergency situations. The aim is that people experience connectedness by expressing emotions and sharing them with others in the public domain [M]. Multiple physical installations on different locations offer an input device and a display of digital maps of emotions in the city. The input devices can be used over a longer period of time. The installation make visible that an individual is part of a larger city community [M]. All together people make the mood of the city [M].

2.2   Cosy: Hybrid Smart Cafe

In the city of Rotterdam, certain districts were initially built just for the purpose of housing workers for nearby industries. In those areas, public spaces for people to gather are rare, even today. The physical infrastructure of these neighbourhoods supports social contacts insufficiently leading to a low social cohesive environment. For social meet-ups, people are making appointments to meet outside their own neighbourhood.Rotterdam New West is such an area for which we are designing a 'smart neighbourhood community cafe'. The design goal was to create a hybrid, 'permanent pop-up' cafe where people can meet and feel at home. This cafe adapts to the goal and preferences of its visitors. By means of social media data (e.g., Facebook, Instagram, Twitter, Spotify, Flickr, Pinterest), sensors, identification technologies, projections and displays, an ecology has been created that transforms its interior and ambiance each time another group of people is present at place. The cafe detects who is inside and projects those persons social media images to the wall, it plays their combined music play-lists, and it communicates publicly in social media who is inside. The ecosystem also offers possibilities to collect preferences from people with regard to drinks and food beforehand that will be served at the moment visitors attend. Distributed individual personal data is merged together with those of others into one physical location. Individual's personal digital information and preferences are blended in a physical social meeting place. Individuals are invited to participate in group meetings with common interests [M]. An important aim is that people experience connectedness and recognition [M]. More social connectedness (cohesion) improves public safety and tidiness, and increase feelings of well-being as well as increase of property value in the long run [M]. Visitors can prepare personal information before meetings and can retrieve information of their activity during meetings afterwards. The strengthened relations give opportunities for easier exchange of knowledge and services. Stronger connections between people improve the experience of safety, tidiness, and connectedness [M].

2.3   Nosey: Mobile Device for Real-Time Climate Sensing

Air quality in the urban area of Rotterdam is poor. The City of Rotterdam is strug-
gling in meeting European standards of air quality and seeks for extra measures to
improve air quality in the city. Several citizen groups organised themselves to deploy
private sensor networks to collect climate data independently form local government
as evidence in defending their interests in city policy and politics. Governmental as
well as private sensing systems consists of locative sensors that measure only few
parameters for air quality over certain periods of time. With Nosey, a mobile device
for real-time climate sensing, we aim for a large number of mobile sensor devices that
measure air quality in real-time all around the city.The challenge is to design a prod-
uct-service system in which citizens benefit form carrying the Nosey device throughout the city while the generated data can also be offered as an open dataset in the
Rotterdam Open Data Store (and to be combined with other datasets). One of city's
stakeholders, the environmental protection agency of local and regional authorities in
the Rotterdam area (DCMR), is looking forward to this additional stream of climate
data in order to intervene in inconvenient situations and to enforce local, national and
European policies.The mobile device is sensing the city's climate state in real-time.
Locally sensed air quality measurements are aggregated into high-density real-time
maps. Digital sensor data is aggregated and send back to individuals as digital layer
on present location. Individual's data contributes to open/public collective mappings
of clean and polluted areas in the city. Real-time sensor data is combined with periodically measured data and geo-data. Prediction of critical future climate states based
on historical data becomes possible. The aim is that through collecting the data, people experiencing control, independence and achievement [M]. In such way we empower individual citizens to have insights in clean areas for living, commuting, etc. as
well as providing local authorities with data for interventions and policy making [M].
The collection of air quality and people insight into it, improves the debate and
decision making on air quality policy [M].

3   Aspects of Designing Meaningful Interactions in Smart Cities

To get better insight in designing meaningful interactions, we look in more detail at
the three design cases to explore the different features that the cases have in common.
Based on experiences in student design projects, various challenges are identified and
written down on statement cards. Subsequently, these are clustered by two experts.
Table 2 shows the corresponding findings, how the designs aim to contribute to
meaningful experiences.

Table 2. Results of the analysis of three design cases and their common design aspects

Moodly: Interactive art installation allowing people to value and express their mood	Cosy: Smart neighbourhood community cafe	Nosey: Mobile device sensing the city's climate state in real-time	Common aspect
Private emotions are aggregated into emotional-state-of-the-city maps	Merging distributed individual personal data together with those of others into one physical location	Aggregate locally sensed air quality measurements into high density real-time maps	*Connect the local/small with the global/big*
Insight in how personal emotional states relates to the city crowd emotional state.	Individual's personal digital information and preferences are blended in a physical social meeting place.	Individual data contrib.-utes to open/public collective mappings of clean and polluted areas in the city.	*Create reciprocal connections in-between the personal and the collective*
Combination of personal emotion data with geo-data for mapping.	Combination of individual's identification and location data with data stored in social media	Combining real-time sensor data with periodically measured data and geo-data	*Combine dynamic sensor data and user generated data with static data*
Possibility: Categorising mood states as indications of emergency situations for police	Adaptation to preferences of identified person present at location. Notifying individuals to participate in group meetings with common interests.	Prediction of critical future climate states based on historical data	*Bring about intelligence through prediction and/or anticipation*
Experiencing connectedness	Experiencing connectedness, recognition	Experiencing control, independence and achievement	*Make people experience meaning by empowering them to strive for what they value in life (human values)*
Expressing emotions and sharing them with others	Social connectedness (cohesion) improves public safety and tidiness, and increase feelings of well-being as well as increase of property value in the long run	Empowering individual citizens to have insights in clean areas for living, commuting, etc. as well as providing local authorities with data for interventions and policy making.	*Balance one's individual meaningful experience with the (organisational) concerns of other stakeholders*
Physical installation as input device displaying digital maps of emotions in the city The input devices are installed at several places in the city, to be used over a longer period of time	Digital social media information of visitors is made visible in a physical meeting place. Visitors can prepare personal information before meetings and can retrieve information of their activity during meetings afterwards	Digital sensor data is aggregated and send back to individuals as digital layer on present location The device is carried around throughout the city and collects data real-time. The stored historical data can be reviewed later on.	*Enrich people's environment to blend physical and digital elements into hybrid places* *Expand the experience over time and space*
The installations is a means of expression in the public domain for people	Stronger relationships give opportunities for easier exchange of knowledge and services	Collaborative generation of air quality data improves opportunities for a cleaner thus healthier environment	*Encourage value creation by people for people in the city*
The installation make visible that an individual is part of a larger city community. All together people make the mood of the city.	Stronger connections between people improve the experience of safety, tidiness and connectedness. The presence of Cosy also improves meaningful placemaking.	The collection of air quality and people insight into it, improves the debate and decision making on air quality policy.	*Make the city as a whole attractive for living and working*

4 Discussion

Although the three cases were different in scope, several common aspects were found in the design cases. In the remainder of this section, we elaborate on these commonalities and discuss what lessons can be learnt in order to design meaningful interactions in a smart city.

4.1 Make It Smart

Connect the local/small with the global/big. By aggregating information of individual situations and locations into a collective dataset, new insights in the state of the city as a whole become possible. Connecting virtual as well as physical things (Internet of Things) at personal level with technology in the home and in the neighbourhood makes it possible to create ubiquitous city networks. Data that seem less relevant on a local and individual level might yield added value at city level, and might even provide insights on a global scale. **Create reciprocal connections in-between the personal and the collective.** In a reciprocal service, an individual benefits from providing personal information to the group if the aggregated group information returns a surplus value for his personal use and goal. In such kinds of crowd intelligence, one can feel connected with a group of others. **Combine dynamic sensor data and user generated data with static data (statistics, geo data, open data, etc.).** By connecting different kinds of data sources, it becomes feasible to combine static data, gathered through traditional research methods (e.g., periodical questionnaires), with continuous streams of user generated and sensor data. Data generated by citizens can result in high-density grids of city information that would not haven been possible with traditional methods only. Citizens as well as public servants can profit from these additional information sources. **Bring about intelligence through prediction and/or anticipation.** When vast amounts of data on city phenomena are gathered, historical analysis of this data makes it possible to predict what phenomena may be expected in the future. Algorithms can be built to predict and signal these situations so people can act upon these signals. On top of that, when people have open access to the data that are collected as a crowd, people may even act upon what to be expected before systems algorithms warnings.

4.2 Make It Social

Make people experience meaning by empowering them to strive for what they value in life (human values). Many smart city applications help people out with guiding them to the fastest routes, the most efficient ways to buy products, or to monitor energy usage in the home. However, those are typically not end goals in people's lives. People might experience meaningful relevance from applications if those account for their human values, for instance feeling connected to a family, enjoying achievements, or by contributing to a cleaner planet. **Balance one's individual meaningful experience with the (organisational) concerns of other stakeholders.** Although organisational services (either provided by governments or companies) try to target people's needs, organisational goals and constrains may not be exactly inline with people's concerns. Not always do both the organisation and the individual user experience the service as relevant. The application of pervasive technology in the city currently demands and enforces a change in the relationship between governments and citizens. Interestingly, the transformation society along with budgetary pressures pose challenges for governments that are already affecting this relation between government and citizens, and actually enabling citizens to inform city government with issues in the city, contrarily to the classic situations in which the government serve citizens by informing them on city issues. **Enrich people's environment to blend physical and digital elements into hybrid places**. City planners have mainly focussed on physical features of areas in the city, where now digital elements are becoming an integrated part of the citizen's experience of the city. Modern ways of city planning make room for an approach in which the city is envisioned as a hybrid place. What's interesting here is that the control over the digital layer in the city is not solely at the locus of public servants, but that it offers opportunities to have citizens decide themselves, even on individual level, what digital information they like to include in their view on the city, or even 'make their city'. **Expand the experience over time and space.** The pervasiveness of internet access throughout the city makes it possible to let data flow continuously from different locations at different times of the day, resulting in vast amounts of data that can be used to monitor the city in real-time, to use it for retrospective insights and to inform and guide future actions and interactions. People will be able to inform themselves on what's happening in the city at any time and any place. Also, the breadth and duration of city interactions that take place at a certain time at a certain place, can be strengthened: the connectedness of people and the data that results from interactions can be used to endure the experience later on and at other locations.

4.3   Make It for City Life

Encourage value creation by people for people in the city. The more people get connected to each other and generate data together to gain insights in their concerns, the more people can empower themselves by exchanging information, knowledge, time, products or anything else without interference of governments or companies. The opportunity for alternative ways of value creation is growing. People then become less dependent from institutions or companies to consume services that fulfil their needs. **Make the city as a whole attractive for living and working.** Although urbanisation makes cities grow, feelings of well-being do not necessarily grow accordingly. For the city of Rotterdam, the 'flight' of higher educated young professionals to other cities is a threat for the cultural diversity and for the economic prosperity of the city. By improving the city experience with the use of pervasive technologies, the city can become more meaningful to every sort of citizen.

5   Conclusion and Reflection

When designing for a smart city, many challenges occur in order to integrate the aesthetic, experiential, and symbolic features into a meaningful design, which empowers people in pursuing their goals in life. We argued that space and time are important factors in the design for meaningful interactions. By describing and analysing three design cases in the city of Rotterdam, we have gained a better understanding of what aspects contribute to the design of meaningful interactions in the city.With regard to the factor space, we conclude that city space can exist out of connections between different systems from individual level (body area) to a city level (local area, wide area). These connections make it possible to let people's individual data flow from a large number of locations to one aggregated set of data that reveals new insights in city phenomena. An important issue here is reciprocity, which implies that the contributing individual immediately gets a benefit from providing his personal data. Another conclusion is that for making place out of space, it seems that not only physical presence of people and their (inter)actions are needed, but that placemaking is also changing by means of the individual use of digital information. Once people can individually control what kind of digital information of their preference is bound to certain locations, the meaningfulness of a place can become more directed to its individual visitors. We also conclude that with the increase of technology and thus 'virtual spaces', physical spaces become blended with virtual space and becomes less bound to the physical location of itself and of its visitors. With regard to the factor time, the experience people have had at a certain location at a certain time is more easily expanded over time. On the one hand, because data (photos, texts, sensor data, metadata) that is generated by the people during the event itself can be used later on in, for example, social media platforms, on the other hand, because people with one had interaction with, can easily be made an online connection to be followed in other activities. Next to that, the storage of historical data makes it possible to review what has happened in the city resulting in insights that can be used to guide future decisions and actions. From the analysis of the design cases, we learned that the locus of control of both data and applications is important. Our focus has been on the human values in the design process. Once one has control of and access to the data that are self-generated, the more one use that information for personal benefit and concerns. The reciprocity between individual contribution and the use of citizens' information at city level balances the concerns between individuals and organisations. Apart from that, people are able to interact in-between using pervasive technologies without interference of organisations, to create value for each other. Here, the symbolic features of the design are crucial: do those depend on the intentions of governments and companies or can the design be open enough for citizens to load it with their values?In our future work we will aim to deepen our understanding of the role of time and space as factors in the design process of meaningful interactions in which designers have focus on human values of people that want to become social and smart citizens of their own city.

Acknowledgements. Special thanks to our colleagues and students, who were involved in the design of Moodly, Cosy, and Nosey.

References

1. Hernández-Muñoz, J.M., Vercher, J.B., Muñoz, L., Galache, J.A., Presser, M., Gómez, L.A.H., Pettersson, J.: Smart cities at the forefront of the future internet. In: Domingue, J., et al. (eds.) Future Internet Assembly. LNCS, vol. 6656, pp. 447–462. Springer, Heidelberg (2011)
2. Rokeach, M.: The Nature of Human Values. Free Press, New York (1973)
3. Fishbein, M., Ajzen, I.: Belief, attitude, intention and behavior: An introduction to theory and research (1975)
4. Schwartz, S.H.: Universals in the content and structure of values: Theoretical advances and empirical tests in 20 countries. In: Zanna, M. (ed.) Advances in Experimental Social Psychology. Academic Press, San Diego (1992)
5. Ascheberg, C., Uelzhoffer, J.: Transnational Consumer Cultures and Social Milieus. International Journal of Market Research 41(1) (1991)
6. Gutman, J.: A Means-End Chain Model Based on Consumer Categorization Processes. Journal of Marketing 46(2), 60–72 (1982)
7. Reynolds, T.J., Gutman, J.: Laddering theory, method, analysis, and interpretation. Journal of Advertising Research 28(1), 11–31 (1988)
8. Csikszentmihalyi, M., Rochberg-Halton, E.: The Meaning of Things: Domestic Symbols and the Self. Cambridge University Press, Cambridge (1981)
9. Desmet, P.: Designing Emotions. TU Delft, Delft (2002)
10. Jordan, P.: Designing pleasurable products: An introduction to the new human factors. CRC Press (2000)
11. Sheldon, K.M., Elliot, A.J., Kim, Y., Kasser, T.: What is satisfying about satisfying events? Testing 10 candidate psychological needs. Journal of Personality and Social Psychology 80, 325–339 (2001)
12. Wiklund-Engblom, A., Hassenzahl, M., Bengs, A., Sperring, S.: What needs tell us about user experience. In: Gross, T., Gulliksen, J., Kotzé, P., Oestreicher, L., Palanque, P., Prates, R.O., Winckler, M. (eds.) INTERACT 2009. LNCS, vol. 5727, pp. 666–669. Springer, Heidelberg (2009)
13. Hassenzahl, M., Ullrich, D.: To do or not to do: Differences in user experience and retrospective judgments depending on the presence or absence of instrumental goals. Interacting with Computers 19(4), 429–437 (2007)
14. Mahlke, S.: Aesthetic and Symbolic Qualities as Antecedents of Overall Judgements of Interactive Products, People and Computers XX - Engage. In: Proceedings of HCI 2006. Springer, London (2006)
15. Karapanos, E., Zimmerman, J., Forlizzi, J., Martens, J.B.: User experience over time: an initial framework. In: Proceedings of the SIGCHI Conference on Human Factors in Computing Systems, pp. 729–738. ACM (2009)
16. van Waart, P., Mulder, I., de Bont, C.: Meaningful Advertising. In: Pervasive Advertising, pp. 57–81. Springer, London (2011)
17. Hassenzahl, M., Tractinsky, N.: User experience-a research agenda. Behaviour & Information Technology 25(2), 91–97 (2006)
18. Kranz, M., Holleis, P., Schmidt, A.: Embedded Interaction: Interacting with the Internet of Things. IEEE Internet Computing 14(2), 46–53 (2010)

19. Schmidt, A., Pfleging, B., Alt, F., Sahami, A., Fitzpatrick, G.: Interacting with 21st-Century Computers. IEEE Pervasive Computing 11(1), 22–31 (2012)
20. Karapanos, E., Hassenzahl, M., Martens, J.-B.: User experience over time. In: CHI 2008 Extended Abstracts on Human Factors in Computing Systems, pp. 3561–3566. ACM, Florence (2008)
21. Karapanos, E., Martens, J.B., Hassenzahl, M.: On the retrospective assessment of users' experiences over time: memory or actuality? In: CHI 2010 Extended Abstracts on Human Factors in Computing Systems, pp. 4075–4080. ACM (2010)
22. Karapanos, E., Zimmerman, J., Forlizzi, J., Martens, J.B.: User experience over time: An initial framework. In: CHI 2009: Proceedings of the 27th International Conference on Human Factors in Computing Systems, pp. 729–738. ACM (2009)
23. Kahneman, D., Krueger, A.B., Schkade, D.A., Schwarz, N., Stone, A.A.: A survey method for characterizing daily life experience: The day reconstruction method. Science 306(5702), 1776–1780 (2004)
24. Kujala, S., Roto, V., Väänänen-Vainio-Mattila, K., Karapanos, E., Sinnelä, A.: UX Curve: A method for evaluating long-term user experience. Interacting with Computers 23(5), 473–483 (2011)
25. Dourish, P.: Where the action is: The foundations of embodied interaction. Cambridge, Massachusetts Institute of Technology (2001)
26. Dourish, P., Bell, G.: Divining a digital future: Mess and mythology in ubiquitous computing. MIT Press (2011)
27. Lakoff, G., Johnson, M.: Why cognitive linguistics requires embodied realism. Cognitive Linguistics 13(3), 245–263 (2002)
28. McCullough, M.: Digital ground: Architecture, pervasive computing, and environmental knowing. The MIT Press (2005)
29. Harrison, S., Sengers, P., Tatar, D.: The Three Paradigms of HCI. In: Proceeding of Alt. Chi. Session at the SIGCHI Conference on Human Factors in Computing Systems, San Jose, California, USA (2007)
30. Gaver, W.W., Beaver, J., Benford, S.: Ambiguity as a resource for design. In: Proceedings of the SIGCHI Conference on Human Factors in Computing Systems, pp. 233–240. ACM (2003)
31. Boehner, K., Hancock, J.T.: Advancing ambiguity. In: Proceedings of the SIGCHI Conference on Human Factors in Computing Systems, pp. 103–106. ACM (2006)
32. Karapanos, E., Martens, J.-B.: Characterizing the diversity in users' perceptions. In: Baranauskas, C., Abascal, J., Barbosa, S.D.J. (eds.) INTERACT 2007. LNCS, vol. 4662, pp. 515–518. Springer, Heidelberg (2007)

A Smart City Case Study: Dynamic Management of Road Lanes

Chen Wang, Bertrand David, and René Chalon

Université de Lyon, CNRS, Ecole Centrale de Lyon, LIRIS, UMR5205,
36 avenue Guy de Collongue, F-69134 Ecully Cedex, France
{Chen.Wang,Bertrand.David,Rene.Chalon}@ec-lyon.fr

Abstract. The SMART CITY is an important field for ubiquitous computing (UC), ambient intelligence (AmI), connected vehicles (CV), and new styles of User Interfaces, mainly mobile. Data vitalization related to in-city data collection and their appropriate diffusion to city actors (private and professional) and their services (applications) is one issue. In a more precise and specific context of dynamic lane allocation system, which is presented in this paper, we describe the use of Location-Based services and Internet of Things, as well as the User Interfaces proposed. A simulation environment allows us to conduct a first validation of the system and to study acceptability of User Interfaces before in-the-field deployment.

Keywords: smart city, ambient intelligence, ubiquitous computing, data vitalization, location-based services, mobile internet, internet of things, dynamic lane allocation.

1   Introduction – Smart City Issue

In recent years, the concept of "smart cities" has emerged to describe how investments in human and social capital and modern Information and Communication Technologies (ICT) infrastructure and e-services fuel sustainable growth and quality of life, enabled by wise management of natural resources and via participative government.

In Smart City systems there are two extreme approaches: 1/ Opportunistic systems allowing access to collected information and its "vitalization" by integration – interaction – aggregation in a non-predetermined way; 2/ Well-defined systems able to solve identified problems. While in our international China-France academic research project we study these two approaches, in this paper we focus on explaining one typical Smart City system, the goal of which is to solve a precise problem:

- More appropriate traffic management, avoiding congestion by better allocation of traffic lanes

Before providing a detailed description of our system, the next section gives an overview of related works. We then present and discuss two main techniques used in our system: Location-Based Services (LBS) and Internet of Things (IoT).

N. Streitz and P. Markopoulos (Eds.): DAPI 2014, LNCS 8530, pp. 629–640, 2014.
© Springer International Publishing Switzerland 2014

According to Z. Xiong [1], the "Smart City" principle in opportunistic perception is based on the concept of "Data Vitalization". The idea is to give data life, to combine separated data by avoiding information islands, to build a combination between each type of data, and to increase utilization of data. The main issue concerns the sharing and integration of data that are separated due to their type or different collection methods. Contextual access and use of these data are fundamental, as well as location-based services, the goal of which is to increase data and services utility and contextual and location-based usability.

In another extreme perception, based on precise demands to be solved, the system architecture is the same [1], but diversity and "vitalization" are not the main goals. In this case, direct usability, reliability and performance are more important. In our case, we studied a precise situation characterized by appropriate communication and collaboration between several categories of users (private and professional), their vehicles and corresponding services.

2   ICT Techniques to Be Used: Internet of Things and Location-Based Services

2.1   Internet of Things

The Internet of things allows static and dynamic environmental objects to communicate and update real situations. The basic idea behind the Internet of Things (IoT) concept is the pervasive presence around us of a variety of things or objects - such as Radio-Frequency IDentification (RFID) tags, sensors, actuators, mobile phones, etc. which, through unique addressing schemes, are able to interact with each other and cooperate with their neighbors to reach common goals [2].

At first glance, the concept of IoT recalls the idea of Ambient Intelligence (AmI) and Ubiquitous Computing (UC). The former refers to electronic environments that are sensitive and responsive to the presence of people. In an AmI world, devices work together to support people in carrying out their everyday life activities, tasks and rituals in an easy and natural way using information and intelligence that is hidden in the network connecting these devices; when the devices are smaller and more integrated into our environment, only the user interface remains perceivable by users [3]. The UC focuses on the omnipresence of processing devices, which are small, inexpensive, robust, networked, and distributed at all scales [4]. The concept of IoT is closely linked to AmI and UC, but its central issues are to make a full interoperability of interconnected devices possible, providing them with an ever higher degree of smartness by enabling their adaptation and autonomous behavior, while guaranteeing trust, privacy and security [5].

Although IoT has not been fully deployed, industrial, standardization and research bodies believe that it could have a huge impact on the behavior and social life of potential users. Possible application domains could be domestic and working fields such as domotics and healthcare, and could also include industrial manufacturing, intelligent transportation and business management. The US National Intelligence Council has placed the IoT in the list of six "Disruptive Civil Technologies" that will have potential impacts on US national power [6]. According to the NIC, "by 2005, Internet nodes may reside in everyday things - food packages, furniture, paper documents, and more", "popular demand combined with technology advances could drive wide-spread diffusion of an internet of things that could, like the present Internet, contribute invaluably to economic development".

2.2   Location-Based Services

Location-Based Services (LBS) provide personalized services to mobile users according to their locations. In actual fact, LBS has evolved from online map services and other internet Geographical Information Systems (GIS) applications to the current form where more lightweight mobile devices (smart-phones, wearable computers, etc.) are used to deliver services, thanks to the development of Global Positioning Systems (GPS) and other location sensing technologies [7]. The authors of [8] view the evolution of LBS in other perspectives, (a) from reactive to proactive, (b) from self- to cross-referencing and (c) from single- to multi-target: reactive LBS are explicitly invoked by the user, while proactive LBS are automatically initiated when a predefined event occurs; user and target coincide in self-referencing LBS, while cross-referencing LBS make use of one target location for service-provisioning of another user; the major focus is on tracking one target's position in single-target LBS, while in multi-target LBS, focus is rather on interrelating the positions of several targets. We will see, later, in the following sections, how proactive and cross-referencing LBS contribute to our system design when integrating IoT that allows static and dynamic environmental objects to communicate and collaborate with each other.

Just as in other interactive systems, user modeling is a basic consideration in LBS as the services finally delivered must correspond to user needs. We have to make sure right from the start who the users are and what kind of services they need. One description of user modeling could be "the acquisition or exploitation of explicit, consultable models of either human users of systems or the computational agents which constitute the system" [9]. We are pleased to extend these "computational agents" to the objects in the IoT, since an object could either provide or consume LBS in the form of a "Web Service".

Location modeling is also a central part of LBS. One static location can be represented either as a geometric coordinate such as "48°51′29.6″N, 2°17′40.2″E", in the World Geodetic System (WGS) [10], or as a symbolic expression such as "Champ de Mars, 5 Avenue Anatole France, 75007 Paris". The difference comes from the two distinctive models for representing space [7]: geometric models that "treat location and objects as points, areas and volumes within a reference coordinate system" and symbolic models that consider locations as sets and located objects as members of sets, so that "interrelationships are established among a set of locations and a set of located objects". Geometric models are largely adopted by GIS applications, while symbolic models are more easily accepted by the general public. Depending on the scenarios of applications or the degrees of accuracy, it would be helpful to carry out some combinations or merges of these two models. For example, a semantic location model was developed by the authors of [11], able to create location hierarchy (belonging to one location and being a boundary point from and into which an entity can leave and enter) and exit hierarchy automatically without manual intervention. Dynamic location data, in other words spatio-temporal data, could provide more information (especially in real time management systems), making modeling and processing of spatio-temporal data hot topics in LBS.

3   Using These Techniques in the Case of Dynamic Management of Road Lanes

Our study concerns dynamic management of road traffic, which is regularly increasing both in towns and outside agglomerations. A first approach to allow increase in traffic leads to solutions such as increasing the number of lanes, while a second aims to segment traffic according to categories (private vehicles, heavy vehicles, public transport, priority vehicles) by proposing specific development and traffic rules, with, in particular, the creation of specialized lanes for high-occupancy vehicles (bus, tram, trolley). This second choice can lead to satisfying solutions provided that there is enough space.

When space is lacking and the frequency of this type of specialized traffic is not sufficient, there is a sense of waste and poor management. A third solution is the dynamic allocation of lanes to different types of transport. A significant work of data gathering, analysis and classification was carried out by J. Nouvier of CERTU (Centre for studies on networks, transports, urbanism and public construction) [12]. He provides a large amount of varied solutions, from the more physical (ad hoc movement of low walls with trucks) to the more informational (signposts with variable displays), enabling a greater or lesser speed of dynamicity.

Today it is true that telematic or embedded and/or mobile ICT can provide solutions leading to a very high dynamicity (clear a lane for a bus or an ambulance in real time) provided that users are sufficiently informed and that regulations are complied with in terms of transport (or suggestions to modify it) and, in particular, of user safety. Hereafter we give a brief description of our ICT vision, in a system-perspective.

"Dynamic circulation lane allocation" aims at providing a system designed to share circulation lanes dynamically between public and rescue service transportation (buses, fire-fighters and ambulances) and personal vehicle transportation in order to share traffic lanes appropriately in the context of traffic jams and lack of space (impossibility or inadequacy of static allocation of circulation lanes). When there are no buses, all lanes are allocated to the general public. When a bus approaches and on the bus driver's request, the right-hand lane is reserved for it. Once the bus has passed, the reserved lane is returned to the general public (Fig. 1).

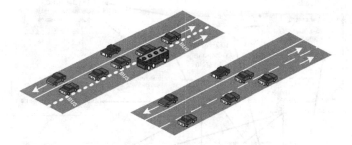

Fig. 1. Dynamic circulation lane allocation

3.1   System Vision

An overview of our application is shown in figure 2. Its goal is to collect in-environment information, communicate with active and passive users (and their vehicles), and take into account authorities' decisions. In the street, sensors collecting traffic evaluation and specific demands from authorized drivers (buses, emergency vehicles, etc.) are able to communicate observed situations to the system. The system decides on the appropriate action, commands dynamically the position of vertical and horizontal signaling, and propagates the new system state to all users by appropriate media (radio, GSM, Wi-Fi, etc.) to inform them as to expected behavior (use of reserved lanes for a bus by non-priority drivers if no bus is expected, leaving a lane which is now reserved for priority drivers when a bus is approaching, etc.).

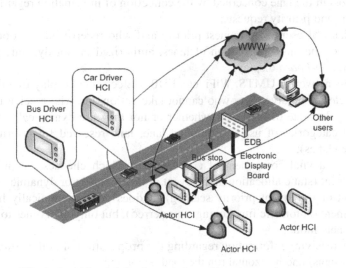

Fig. 2. Overview of the dynamic lane allocation environment

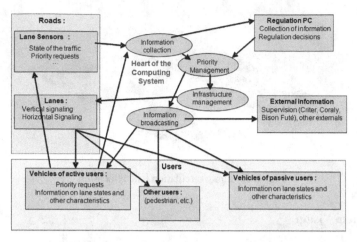

Fig. 3. Diagram of the system architecture

The corresponding dynamic management system for lanes is based on a set of sensors, displayers and activators located in strategic places: on the lane (sensors as well as displayers and activators), with the active users (requestors such as bus drivers, ambulances, firemen, possibly trucks) involved, passive users received the imposed modifications (displayers only) and external traffic regulators, as shown in figure 2. All the elements must be integrated in the global system, collecting, aggregating, processing and diffusing the appropriate information to all users. This system vision (Fig. 3) brings into play the main elements, namely:

- the sensors in the lane concerned by the collection of information regarding state of the traffic and priority requests;
- the vehicles of users who request priority and who receive information regarding the state of the lanes (allocation of lanes, authorized or not dynamic priority requests) for *on-board* display;
- 2 wireless networks: UMTS, WiFi, etc. EDB – Electronic Display Boards;
- the vehicles of passive users who cannot take action, but who receive information regarding the state of the lanes (whether or not they are dynamically allocated to different categories of users: prohibited lane, lane reserved for priority vehicles, unmarked lanes);
- regulation, a vital component of coordination, which chooses the mode of lane management (static allocation in the event of heavy traffic or dynamic allocation in the event of infrequent priority seeking). It does not systematically intervene in management (automatic functioning is preferred), but only intervenes to change the management mode;
- the lanes receiving information regarding the propagation of both vertical (variable message signs) and horizontal (on the road) signaling;
- the system of dynamic management of so-called priority roads; management includes the following main components: collection of information, management of priorities, management of lanes, and diffusion of information;
- the information transmission system (the information network).

3.2   HCI Vision

With respect to the users identified in the system vision, it is important to deal with the user aspect as soon as possible, by designing and implementing appropriate human-computer interfaces: as observed, active users (requestors – beneficiaries of the system), passive users (subjected to the system), deciders (regulation command center) and all users via vertical and horizontal signaling must receive useful information to act appropriately. It is essential that this information and these actions comply with the work context and the corresponding requirements:

- in the vehicle, compatibility with the dual task – driving and managing; in a regulation work station for example, it is efficiency which dominates;
- when information is displayed outside, it has to be compatible with meteorological constraints of visibility – legibility.

Design of these HCIs therefore also forms an important part of the system and conditions its acceptability. Simulator-based ergonomic studies of acceptability for this kind of interface as a complementary task to driving will be presented in the next section.

General Description of the Simulator. We first simulate the system, with the appropriate simplifications that need to be chosen. This lays down the base for implementation of the digital simulator. The main elements presented in the diagram in figure 3 are included in the simulation. There are two types of view in the simulation: vertical views and horizontal views. In the vertical point of view (overlook), as in figure 4, the road is represented as a rectangular area and is made up of several lanes (3 for the

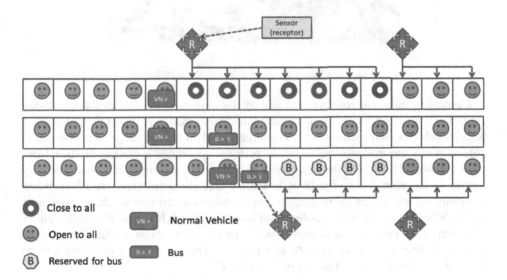

Fig. 4. Simulation scenario view and graphic editor tool

actual version), with each lane in straight line form. Each lane is divided into a series of squares for relative location modeling, so that the positions of vehicles and signaling facilities as well as sensors could be found easily. The squares can also receive horizontal signaling to inform users about the current status of lane allocation, for example "open to all", "reserved for bus" or "closed to all", with the number of squares showing the length of the allocation area.

The horizontal view is from the interior of the vehicle, as in figure 5; a driving scene is presented in real time with the corresponding simulated elements. The driver can see the vertical signaling on the roadside as well as the horizontal signaling on the ground from the front window of the vehicle. Moreover, the surrounding circumstances are also reflected in the rearview mirrors of the vehicle. An embedded interface is designed for passive users and active users to receive information and/or request priority.

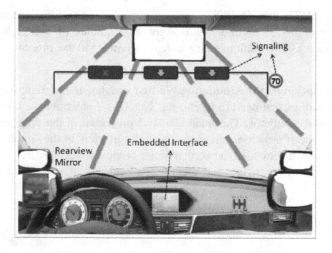

Fig. 5. Interior view of a vehicle in the simulation

Communication and collaboration among the objects in the IoT in the simulation could be: a set of sensors is located on the lane to automatically detect the presence of priority vehicles, and each sensor is in charge of only a certain range of region and is able to notify the management center to perform operations according to their locations (proactive LBS). On the other hand, vehicles with priority could send a priority request to the nearest sensor in front, to initiate lane allocation (reactive LBS). When a priority vehicle leaves the region, the sensor detects it and notifies the management center, which gradually sets the allocation back to normal. It is also the responsibility of a sensor to deliver information about current traffic status within its range of region via displayers such as vertical signaling. The information collected can be disseminated to vehicles via an "on board display".

Simulator Functionalities. The goal of the simulation is to validate principles and provide support for implementation of the system. Functionalities are described in figure 6.

A scenario editing tool is a complementary tool to the simulator. Its goal is to specify simulation parameters such as lane length, number of lanes, duration of simulation, number of sensors and initial status of lane allocation. This graphic editing tool (Fig. 4) also includes a sensor editor toolkit able to set sensors at appropriate locations in order to adjust the sensor parameters such as range of region in charge, or to test the influence of different placements.

Vehicles, with or without priority, are planned to travel through the area from left to right, with distinctive parameters (speed, initial time, etc.), respecting strictly the signaling of lane allocation throughout the process. A traffic generator tool is able to generate traffic flow, in which there are vehicles with or without priority, and different parameters can be specified, as well as possible itinerary preferences. Moreover, this generator tool helps choose how to launch the traffic flow, with different time intervals and densities.

Simulation visualization can provide opportunities for conducting a usability and acceptability test, which is presented in the following paragraphs.

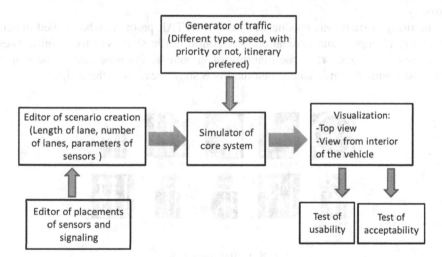

Fig. 6. Simulator functionalities

UI Testing. The simulator goal is to allow ergonomic studies of acceptability of this kind of approach to dynamic lane management. Several levels of tests can be produced, using different views. A map view, as shown in Fig. 4, is used for a global bird's eye view of system functioning. A subjective view, a view from the interior of the vehicle, is used to test users' behaviors.

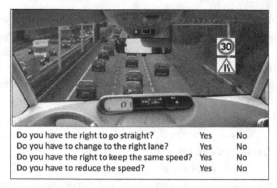

Do you have the right to go straight?	Yes	No
Do you have to change to the right lane?	Yes	No
Do you have the right to keep the same speed?	Yes	No
Do you have to reduce the speed?	Yes	No

Fig. 7. A scenario of the acceptability study

A scenario screen shot of the acceptability study is shown in Fig. 7. In the test, a set of photos was produced to simulate a static environment. These photos show a multiple lane configuration with insertion of appropriate vertical and horizontal signaling. The pictures are shown to a driver, letting him/ her observe the situation, and then questions are asked, requesting him/ her to choose the appropriate behavior. If the signaling is not easy to remark or understand, the driver may not choose to behave correctly.

The first test study was conducted by our IFSTTAR partners, who studied understandability of appropriate vertical and horizontal traffic signs and road signs. These signs are either static or, in the majority of situations, dynamic (electronic display signs), following dynamic lane evolution. Fig.8 shows several of these signs.

Fig. 8. Traffic signs tested

To increase understanding of acceptability, it is important to study the temporal behavior of drivers. It is not enough to observe appropriate interpretation of driving situations, if the user can take all the time he/ she needs to think about the situation. Rather than creating driving situations by using static photos, our simulation goal is to support dynamic behavior in which the subjective view during simulation is related to driving speed. The situation shown at Fig. 5 can be used to conduct dynamic tests. Speed is not the only dynamic property; external vehicle traffic can also be taken into account, for instance, to what degree a user adapts him/ herself to a more complex situation with the changing of surrounding circumstances such as a car appearing in the rearview mirror and the changing of the message on the panel or signaling as well as use of the embedded interface. Examples of the usability test for embedded interfaces are shown in Fig. 9. The GPS, LANE INFOS and the REPORT ACCIDENT one are open to all users, while the PRIORITY page is reserved for active users.

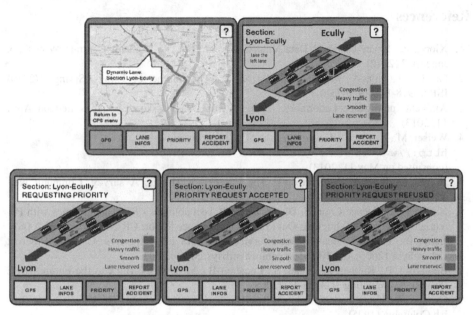

Fig. 9. Usability study of embedded interfaces

4 Conclusion

In this paper we briefly explained our view of the Smart City in the context of transportation and citizens' everyday life on which we are currently working [13, 14, 15]. We gave the main principles and techniques used, and presented a precise application based on IoT and LBS. Before in-the-field deployment of this kind of system, it is important to validate it theoretically from technological and human acceptability points of view. For this reason we created a simulator allowing us to design and simulate different scenarios of infrastructure behaviors. We can also connect this simulator to UI testing studies, the goal of which is to validate (or invalidate) acceptability of new driving situations based on the driver's behavior in relation with new vertical and horizontal road signs (Fig. 7). The goal of future work is to increase the realism of our simulator to take into account temporal aspects of driving, allowing us to study the relationship between traffic density and acceptability of dynamicity of lane management.

Acknowledgements. We extend our thanks to the French Department of Ecology who partially supported this project, and to our colleagues from IFSTTAR, LIRIS, CEA-LETI, EGIS and VOLVO.

References

1. Xiong, Z.: Smart City and Data Vitalisation. In: The 5th Beihang Centrale Workshop, January 7 (2012)
2. Giusto, D., Iera, A., Morabito, G., Atzori, L.: The Internet of Things. Springer (2010) ISBN: 978-1-4419-1673-0
3. Ambient Intelligence Laboratory, http://www.ami-lab.org, (consulted on April 11, 2013)
4. Weiser, M., Brown, J.: The coming age of calm technology, http://www.johnseelybrown.com/calmtech.pdf (consulted on May 11, 2013)
5. Atzori, L., Iera, A., Morabito, G.: The Internet of Things: A survey. Computer Networks 54, 2787–2805 (2010)
6. National Intelligence Council. Disruptive Civil Technologies - Six Technologies with Potential Impacts on US Interests Out to 2025. Conference Report CR 2008-07 (April 2008)
7. Jiang, B., Yao, B.: Location-based services and GIS in perspective. Comput. Environ. Urban Syst. (2006), doi:10.1016/j.compenvurbsys.2006.02.003
8. Bellavista, P., Kupper, A., Helal, S.: Location-Based Services: Back to the Future. IEEE Pervasive Computing 7(2), 85–89 (2008)
9. Csinger, A.: Users models for intent-based authoring. Dessertation. The University of British Columbia (1995)
10. World Geodetic System, http://en.wikipedia.org/wiki/World_Geodetic_System (consulted on October 12, 2013)
11. Hu, H., Lee, D.: Semantic location modeling for location navigation in mobile environment. In: Proceedings of the 2004 IEEE International Conference on Mobile Data Management, pp. 52–61 (2004)
12. Nouvier, J.: Entrez dans le monde des ITS = Enter the world of ITS, Lyon: CERTU, célérom TU CE12 10450 disponible auprès du département Systèmes du CERTU (2007)
13. David, B., Chalon, R., Favre, B.: ICT and new human-machine interactions for trucks and buses in the future: e-Truck and e-Bus perspectives. In: Kolski, C. (ed.) Human-Computer Interactions in Transport, pp. 157–201. ISTE Ltd and John Wiley & Sons, Inc. (2011) ISBN: 978-1-84821-279-4
14. David, B., Yin, C., Zhou, Y., Xu, T., Zhang, B., Jin, H., Chalon, R.: SMART-CITY: Problematics, techniques and case studies. In: ICCM 2012, 8th International Conference on Computing Technology and Information Management, Seoul, Korea, pp. 168–174. IEEE Conference Publications (2012) ISBN 978-1-4673-0893-9
15. David, B., Xu, T., Jin, H., Zhou, Y., Chalon, R., Zhang, B., Yin, C., Wang, C.: User-oriented System for Smart City approaches. In: 12th IFAC/IFIP/IFORS/IEA Symposium on Analysis, Design, and Evaluation of Human-Machine Systems, Las Vegas, Nevada, USA, August 11-15, pp. 333–340. IFAC/Elsevier (2013) ISSN 1474-6670. 2013

Author Index